Visit us at

www.syngress.com

Syngress is committed to publishing high-quality books for IT Professionals and delivering those books in media and formats that fit the demands of our customers. We are also committed to extending the utility of the book you purchase via additional materials available from our Web site.

SOLUTIONS WEB SITE

To register your book, visit www.syngress.com/solutions. Once registered, you can access our solutions@syngress.com Web pages. There you may find an assortment of valueadded features such as free e-books related to the topic of this book, URLs of related Web sites, FAQs from the book, corrections, and any updates from the author(s).

ULTIMATE CDs

Our Ultimate CD product line offers our readers budget-conscious compilations of some of our best-selling backlist titles in Adobe PDF form. These CDs are the perfect way to extend your reference library on key topics pertaining to your area of expertise, including Cisco Engineering, Microsoft Windows System Administration, CyberCrime Investigation, Open Source Security, and Firewall Configuration, to name a few.

DOWNLOADABLE E-BOOKS

For readers who can't wait for hard copy, we offer most of our titles in downloadable Adobe PDF form. These e-books are often available weeks before hard copies, and are priced affordably.

SYNGRESS OUTLET

Our outlet store at syngress.com features overstocked, out-of-print, or slightly hurt books at significant savings.

SITE LICENSING

Syngress has a well-established program for site licensing our e-books onto servers in corporations, educational institutions, and large organizations. Contact us at sales@syngress.com for more information.

CUSTOM PUBLISHING

Many organizations welcome the ability to combine parts of multiple Syngress books, as well as their own content, into a single volume for their own internal use. Contact us at sales@syngress.com for more information.

SYNGRESS®

The Best Damn Windows Server 2008 Book Period

Tony Piltzecker

KEY	SERIAL NUMBER
001	HJIRTCV764
002	PO9873D5FG
003	829KM8NJH2
004	BAL923457U
005	CVPLQ6WQ23
006	VBP965T5T5
007	HJJJ863WD3E
008	2987GVTWMK
009	629MP5SDJT
010	IMWQ295T6T

PUBLISHED BY
Syngress Publishing, Inc.
Elsevier, Inc.
30 Corporate Drive
Burlington, MA 01803

The Best Damn Windows Server 2008 Book Period

Printed and bound in the United Kingdom
Transferred to Digital Printing, 2010

ISBN 13: 978-1-59749-273-7

Publisher: Andrew Williams
Technical Editors: Tony Piltzecker, Brien Posey
Cover Designer: Michael Kavish

Acquisitions Editor: David George
Project Manager: Andre Cuello

For information on rights, translations, and bulk sales, contact Matt Pedersen, Commercial Sales Director and Rights, at Syngress Publishing; email m.pedersen@elsevier.com.

Technical Editors

Tony Piltzecker (CISSP, MCSE, CCNA, CCVP, Check Point CCSA, Citrix CCA), author and technical editor of Syngress Publishing's *MCSE Exam 70-296 Study Guide and DVD Training System* and *How to Cheat at Managing Microsoft Operations Manager 2005*, is an independent consultant based in Boston, MA. Tony's specialties include network security design, Microsoft operating system and applications architecture, and Cisco IP Telephony implementations. Tony's background includes positions as Systems Practice Manager for Presidio Networked Solutions, IT Manager for SynQor Inc, Network Architect for Planning Systems, Inc, and Senior Networking Consultant with Integrated Information Systems. Along with his various certifications, Tony holds a bachelor's degree in business administration. Tony currently resides in Leominster, MA, with his wife, Melanie, and his daughters, Kaitlyn and Noelle.

Brien Posey is a freelance technical writer who has received Microsoft's MVP award four times. Over the last twelve years, Brien has published over 4,000 articles and whitepapers, and has written or contributed to over 30 books. In addition to his technical writing, Brien is the co-founder of Relevant Technologies and also serves the IT community through his own Web site.

Prior to becoming a freelance author, Brien served as CIO for a nationwide chain of hospitals and healthcare facilities, and as a network administrator for the Department of Defense at Fort Knox. He has also worked as a network administrator for some of the nation's largest insurance companies.

Brien wishes to thank his wife Taz for her love and support throughout his writing career.

Contributing Authors

Tariq Bin Azad is the Principal Consultant and founder of NetSoft Communications Inc., a consulting company located in Toronto, Canada. He is considered a top IT professional by his peers, co-workers, colleagues, and customers. He obtained this status by continuously learning and improving his knowledge and information in the field of Information Technology. Currently, he holds more than 100 certifications including MCSA, MCSE, MCTS, MCITP (Vista, Mobile 5.0, Microsoft Communications Server 2007, Windows 2008, and Microsoft Exchange Server 2007), MCT, CIW-CI, CCA, CCSP, CCEA, CCI, VCP, CCNA, CCDA, CCNP, CCDP, CSE, and many more. Most recently, Tariq has been concentrating on Microsoft Windows 2000/2003/2008, Exchange 2000/2003/2007, Active Directory, and Citrix implementations. He is a professional speaker and has trained architects, consultants, and engineers on topics such as Windows 2008 Active Directory, Citrix Presentation Server and Microsoft Exchange 2007. In addition to owning and operating an independent consulting company, Tariq works as a senior consultant, and has utilized his training skills in numerous workshops, corporate trainings, and presentations. Tariq holds a Bachelor of Science in Information Technology from Capella University, USA, a Bachelor Degree in Commerce from University of Karachi, Pakistan, and is working on his ALMIT (Masters of Liberal Arts in Information Technology) from Harvard University, MA, USA. Tariq has been a coauthor on multiple books, including the best selling *MCITP: Microsoft Exchange Server 2007 Messaging Design and Deployment Study Guide: Exams 70-237 and 70-238* - (ISBN: 047018146X) and *The Real MCTS/ MCITP Exam 640 Preparation Kit* (ISBN: 978-1-59749-235-5). Tariq has worked on projects or trained for major companies and organizations including Rogers Communications Inc. Flynn Canada, Capgemini, HP, Direct Energy, Toyota Motors, Comaq, IBM, Citrix Systems Inc., Unicom Technologies, Amica Insurance Company, and many others. He lives in Toronto, Canada, and would like to thank his father, Azad Bin Haider, and his mother, Sitara Begum, for his lifetime of guidance for their understanding and support to give him the skills that have allowed him to excel in work and life.

Colin Bowern is the Vice President of Technology at officialCOMMUNITY in Toronto, Canada. Through his work with the clients, Colin and the team help recording artists build and manage an online community to connect with their fans. Colin came to officialCOMMUNITY from Microsoft where he was a Senior Consultant with the Microsoft Consulting Services unit working with enterprise customers on their adoption of Microsoft technology. During his time at Microsoft, Colin worked with several product groups to incorporate customer feedback into future product releases, as well as the MCSE certification exam development. Colin holds two Microsoft DeliverIt! awards for work done within the financial industry in Canada to drive the adoption of .NET as a development platform and developing an SMBIOS inventory tool that was incorporated into the Windows Pre-installation Environment. Colin has delivered a number of in-person and Microsoft Developer Network (MSDN) webcast sessions since the early part of the decade on topics ranging from .NET Development to infrastructure deployment with the Microsoft platform. In addition to technical talks, Colin participates in the community through active contributions on the MSDN and ASP.NET Forums, publishing code examples, sharing experiences through his blog, and attending local user group events. Colin has been a technical reviewer for Addison-Wesley's .NET development series, the Windows Server 2003 series from Microsoft Press, and has co-authored a Windows Server 2003 MCSE study guide for Syngress Publishing. In addition, he holds a Masters of Science degree from the University of Liverpool.

Dustin Hannifin (Microsoft MVP – Office SharePoint Server) is a Systems Administrator with Crowe Chizek and Company LLC. Crowe (www.crowechizek.com), is one of the nation's leading public accounting and consulting firms. Under its core purpose of "Building Value with Values®," Crowe assists both public and private companies in reaching their goals through services ranging from assurance and financial advisory to performance, risk and tax consulting. Dustin currently works in Crowe's

Information Services delivery unit, where he plays a key role in maintaining and supporting Crowe's internal information technology (IT) infrastructure. His expertise resides in various Microsoft products including Office Share-Point Server, System Center Operations Manager, Active Directory, IIS and Office Communications Server. Dustin holds a bachelor's degree from Tennessee Technological University and is a founding member of the Michiana IT Professionals Users Group. He regularly contributes to technology communities including his blog (www.technotesblog.com) and Microsoft newsgroups. Dustin, a Tennessee native, currently resides in South Bend, Indiana.

Ira Herman (MCSE, CCAI, CCNA, CNA, A+, Network+, i-Net+, CIW Associate) is Co-Chief Executive Officer and Co-Founder of Logic IT Consulting (www.logicitc.com), a consulting firm specializing in Business Information Technology solutions with an emphasis on Work-Life Balance, Stress-Free Productivity, and Efficiency training and coaching. Prior to founding Logic IT Consulting, Ira held various technical and executive positions with companies including Microsoft, Keane, The University of Arizona, Xynetik, and Brand X LLC. Ira has written and delivered technical training for Logic IT Consulting and its clients as well as various organizations including Pima Community College, JobPath, and SeniorNet. Ira holds Microsoft Certified Systems Engineer (MCSE and MCSE+I), Cisco Certified Academy Instructor (CCAI), Cisco Certified Network Associate (CCNA), Certified Novell Administrator (CNA), CompTIA A+ Certified Computer Service Technician (A+), CompTIA Network+, CompTIA Internetworking (i-Net+), and Prosoft Training Certified Internet Webmaster Associate (CIW Associate) certifications as well as Microsoft internal endorsements in Windows NT 4 Fundamentals (Workstation), Windows NT 4 Advanced (Server), Microsoft TCP/IP on Windows NT 4, Windows 2000 Foundational Topics, and Windows 2000 Setup Specialty.

Laura E. Hunter (CISSP, MCSE, MCT, MCDBA, MCP, MCP+I, CCNA, A+, Network+, iNet+, Security+, CNE-4, CNE-5) is a Senior IT Specialist with the University of Pennsylvania, where she provides network planning, implementation, and troubleshooting services for various business units and schools within the University. Her specialties include

Microsoft Windows 2000/2003 design and implementation, troubleshooting, and security topics. As an "MCSE Early Achiever" on Windows 2000, Laura was one of the first in the country to renew her Microsoft credentials under the Windows 2000 certification structure. Laura's previous experience includes a position as the Director of Computer Services for the Salvation Army and as the LAN administrator for a medical supply firm. She also operates as an independent consultant for small businesses in the Philadelphia metropolitan area and is a regular contributor to the TechTarget family of websites.

Laura has previously contributed to the Syngress Publishing's *Configuring Symantec Antivirus, Corporate Edition* (ISBN 1-931836-81-7). She has also contributed to several other exam guides in the Syngress Windows Server 2003 MCSE/MCSA DVD Guide and Training System series as a DVD presenter, contributing author, and technical reviewer.

Laura holds a bachelor's degree from the University of Pennsylvania and is a member of the Network of Women in Computer Technology, the Information Systems Security Association, and InfraGard, a cooperative undertaking between the U.S. Government other participants dedicated to increasing the security of United States critical infrastructures.

John Karnay is a freelance writer, editor, and book author living in Queens, NY. John specializes in Windows server and desktop deployments utilizing Microsoft and Apple products and technology. John has been working with Microsoft products since Windows 95 and NT 4.0 and consults for many clients in New York City and Long Island, helping them plan migrations to XP/Vista and Windows Server 2003/2008. When not working and writing, John enjoys recording and writing music as well as spending quality time with his wife Gloria and daughter Aurora. You can contact/visit John at: www.johnkarnay.com.

Jeffery A. Martin, MS/IT, MS/M (MCSE, MCSE:Security, MCSE: Messaging, MCDBA, MCT, MCSA, MCSA:Security, MCSE:Messaging, MCP+I, MCNE, CNE, CNA, CCA, CTT, A+, Network+, I-Net+, Project+, Linux+, CIW, ADPM) has been working with computer networks for over 20 years. He is an editor, co-editor, author, or co-author of over

15 books and enjoys training others in the use of technology. He can be contacted at jeffery@jefferymartin.com.

Shawn Tooley owns a consulting firm, Tooley Consulting Group, LLC, that specializes in Microsoft and Citrix technologies, for which he is the Principle Consultant and Trainer. Shawn also works as Network Administrator for a hospital in North Eastern Ohio. Shawn's certifications include Microsoft Certified Trainer (MCT), Microsoft Certified System Engineer (MCSE), Citrix Certified Enterprise Administrator, Citrix Certified Sales Professional, HP Accredited System Engineer, IBM XSeries Server Specialist, Comptia A+, and Comptia Certified Trainer. In his free time he enjoys playing golf.

Contents

Chapter 1 Configuring Network Services 1

Introduction 2

Configuring Domain Name System (DNS) 3

    Identifying DNS Record Requirements 8

    Installing and Configuring DNS 12

    Using Server Core and DNS 17

    Configuring Zones 19

        Zone Transfer 22

        Active Directory Records 26

        Reverse Lookup Zones 27

            Configuring Reverse Lookup Zones 28

    Configuring Zone Resolution 31

Configuring Dynamic Host Configuration Protocol (DHCP) 34

    DHCP Design Principles 35

        DHCP Servers and Placement 37

    Installing and Configuring DHCP 37

    Using Server Core and DHCP 40

    Configuring DHCP for DNS 42

Configuring Windows Internet Naming Service (WINS) 43

    Understanding WINS Replication 45

        Automatic Partner Configuration 45

        Push Partnerships 46

        Pull Partnerships 47

        Push/Pull Partnerships 48

    Replication Models 48

        Ring Models 49

        Hub-and-Spoke Models 49

        Hybrid Replication Models 50

    Static WINS Entries 50

    Installing and Configuring 51

    Using Server Core for WINS 52

    Configuring WINS for DNS 53

Summary 54

Solutions Fast Track 55

Frequently Asked Questions 57

Chapter 2 Configuring the Active Directory Infrastructure 59

Introduction 60
Working with Forests and Domains 61
  Understanding Forests 62
  Understanding Domains 62
  Forest and Domain Functional Levels 64
    Using Domain Functional Levels 66
      Using the Windows 2000 Domain Functional Level 66
      Windows Server 2003 Domain Functional Level 67
      Windows Server 2008 Domain Functional Level 68
    Configuring Forest Functional Levels 68
      Windows 2000 Forest Functional Level (default) 69
      Windows Server 2003 Forest Functional Level 69
      Windows Server 2008 Forest Functional Level 70
    Raising Forest and Domain Functional Levels 71
      Raising the Domain Functional Level 71
  Understanding the Global Catalog 73
    UPN Authentication 75
    Directory Information Search 75
    Universal Group Membership Information 76
  Understanding GC Replication 77
    Universal Group Membership 77
    Attributes in the Global Catalog 78
  Placing GC Servers within Sites 79
    Bandwidth and Network Traffic Considerations 80
    Universal Group Membership Caching 81
  Working with Flexible Single Master Operation (FSMO) Roles 82
    Placing, Transferring, and Seizing FSMO Role Holders 86
      Locating and Transferring the Schema Master Role 86
      Locating and Transferring the Domain Naming Master Role 89
      Locating and Transferring the Infrastructure, RID,
        and PDC Operations Master Roles 91
      Placing the FSMO Roles within an Active
        Directory Environment 94
Working with Sites 95
  Understanding Sites 96
    Subnets 98
  Site Planning 99
    Criteria for Establishing Separate Sites 100

Creating a Site 100
Renaming a Site 104
Creating Subnets 106
Associating Subnets with Sites 109
Creating Site Links 111
Configuring Site Link Cost 114
Understanding Replication 116
Intrasite Replication 118
Intersite Replication 119
Bridgehead Servers 120
Site Link Bridges 121
Scheduling 121
Forcing Replication 122
Replication Protocols 122
Planning, Creating, and Managing the
    Replication Topology 123
Planning Replication Topology 123
Creating Replication Topology 123
Configuring Replication between Sites 124
Troubleshooting Replication Failure 125
Troubleshooting Replication 125
Using Event Viewer 126
Working with Trusts 128
Default Trusts 133
Forest Trusts 133
External Trusts 134
Shortcut Trusts 135
SID Filtering 136
Summary 137
Solutions Fast Track 139
Frequently Asked Questions 141

Chapter 3 Configuring Certificate Services and PKI **145**
Introduction 146
What Is PKI? 147
The Function of the PKI 149
Components of PKI 150
How PKI Works 152
PKCS Standards 154

How Certificates Work 158
Public Key Functionality. 161
    Digital Signatures. 162
    Authentication. 163
    Secret Key Agreement via Public Key. 164
    Bulk Data Encryption without Prior Shared Secrets 164
    User Certificates 175
    Machine Certificates 176
    Application Certificates 176
Analyzing Certificate Needs within the Organization 176
Working with Certificate Services. 177
    Configuring a Certificate Authority 177
        Certificate Authorities 177
            Standard vs. Enterprise 178
            Root vs. Subordinate Certificate Authorities 179
            Certificate Requests. 180
            Certificate Practice Statement. 184
    Key Recovery 185
        Backup and Restore. 185
        Assigning Roles. 191
        Enrollments 192
        Revocation 192
Working with Templates. 196
    General Properties 198
    Request Handling 200
    Cryptography. 201
    Subject Name 202
    Issuance Requirements 203
    Security. 206
    Types of Templates 207
        User Certificate Types 207
        Computer Certificate Types 209
        Other Certificate Types 210
        Custom Certificate Templates. 211
    Securing Permissions 214
    Versioning 215
    Key Recovery Agent. 215
Summary. 217
Solutions Fast Track 218
Frequently Asked Questions 220

Chapter 4 Windows Server 2008 Core 223

Introduction 224
Using Server Core and Active Directory 227
Using Server Core and DNS 233
Configuring Dynamic Host Configuration Protocol (DHCP)
    Using Server Core 235
    Installing DHCP Using Server Core 237
Installing Internet Information Services. 239
Installing the FTP Publishing Service 244
Installing and Managing Hyper-V on Windows
    Server Core Installations 247
Summary. 248
Solutions Fast Track 248
Frequently Asked Questions 249

Chapter 5 Configuring DNS 251

Introduction 252
An Introduction to Domain Name System (DNS). 252
    Understanding Public Name Resolution 255
    Understanding Private Name Resolution. 256
    Understanding Microsoft's DNS Terminology 257
Configuring a DNS Server. 258
    Installing the DNS Server Role. 258
    Understanding Cache-Only DNS Servers 259
    Configuring Root Hints. 259
        Adding Root Hint Records 260
        Editing Root Hints Records 261
        Removing Root Hints Records 263
        Copying Root Hints from Another Server 263
    Configuring Server-Level Forwarders 263
    Configuring Conditional Forwarding 266
        Creating Conditional Forwarders 266
        Managing Conditional Forwarders 268
    Server Core 270
Creating DNS Zones 271
    Creating a Standard Primary Forward Lookup Zone 274
    Creating a Secondary Forward Lookup Zone. 278
    Creating an Active Directory Integrated Forward Lookup Zone 279
    Creating a Standard Primary Reverse Lookup Zone 283
    Creating a Standard Secondary Reverse Lookup Zone. 286

Creating a Zone Delegation 287
Creating a Stub Zone. 290
Using the New GlobalNames Zone Feature 290
    Enabling a Domain Controller to Support GlobalNames Zones. 291
    Creating the GlobalNames Zone 292
Configuring and Managing DNS Replication. 294
Manually Initiating Replication Using DNS Manager 294
Configuring DNS Servers to Allow Zone Transfers 294
    Configuring a Standard Primary Zone for Transfers. 295
    Configuring an AD Integrated or Secondary Zone for Transfers. 296
Configuring the SOA Record. 297
Creating an Application Directory Partition. 299
Creating and Managing DNS Records 300
Managing Record Types 300
    Creating Host Records. 300
        Creating A Records 301
        Creating AAAA Records 302
    Creating Pointer Records. 304
    Creating MX Records 305
    Creating SRV Records. 307
    Creating CNAME Records 310
    Creating NS Records. 311
Configuring Windows Internet Name Service (WINS) and
    DNS Integration. 312
    Creating a WINS Lookup Record 313
    Creating a WINS Reverse Lookup Record. 315
Understanding the Dynamic Domain Name System (DDNS). 318
    Configuring DDNS Aging and Scavenging. 319
    Enabling Automatic Scavenging 321
    Initiating Manual Scavenging 322
Configuring Name Resolution for Client Computers 323
How Name Resolution Works in Windows XP and Later 325
Configuring the DNS Server List 326
Configuring the Suffix Search Order. 328
Configuring the HOSTS File 329
Configuring the NetBIOS Node Type. 330
Configuring the WINS Server List 332
Configuring the LMHOSTS File 334

Understanding Link-Local Multicast Name Resolution (LLMNR) 336
Managing Client Settings by Using Group Policy 336
Summary. 340
Solutions Fast Track 342
Frequently Asked Questions 345

Chapter 6 Configuring Network Access. 349
Introduction 350
Windows Server 2008 and Routing 351
Windows Server 2008 and Remote Access 352
Windows Server 2008 and Wireless Access. 352
Configuring Routing. 353
Routing Fundamentals 353
Static Routing 355
Routing Internet Protocol (RIP) 356
Open Shortest Path First (OSPF) 357
Configuring Remote Access. 358
Routing and Remote Access Services (RRAS) 359
Network Policy Server and Network Access Protection. 361
Dial-Up. 364
Remote Access Policy. 365
Network Address Translation (NAT) 368
Internet Connection Sharing (ICS) 370
Remote Access Protocols 373
Virtual Private Networks 378
Installing and Configuring a SSL VPN Server 379
Inbound/Outbound Filters 383
Configuring Remote Authentication Dial-In User Service
(RADIUS) Server. 384
Configuring Wireless Access 388
Set Service Identifier (SSID) 392
Wi-Fi Protected Access (WPA) 393
Wi-Fi Protected Access 2 (WPA2). 393
Ad Hoc vs. Infrastructure Mode 394
Wireless Group Policy 396
Summary. 397
Solutions Fast Track 397
Frequently Asked Questions 401

Chapter 7 Configuring File and Print Services. 403

Introduction 404
Configuring a File Server. 404
   File Share Publishing 405
      Additional Role Services 408
      File Screening 410
      Sharing a Folder 411
   Share Permissions. 413
   NTFS Permissions 414
   Offline Files 416
   Encrypting File System (EFS) 423
      Working with EFS. 424
Configuring Distributed File System (DFS). 429
   DFS Namespaces 429
   DFS Configuration and Application 430
   Creating and Configuring Targets 433
   DFS Replication 434
Configuring Shadow Copy Services 435
   Recovering Previous Versions 437
   Setting the Schedule. 439
   Setting Storage Locations 440
Configuring Backup and Restore 440
   Backup Types 441
   Backup Schedules. 441
   Managing Remotely. 444
   Restoring Data. 446
Managing Disk Quotas. 447
   Quota by Volume or Quota by User 447
   Quota Entries. 449
      Configuring Quotas Using FSRM 450
   Quota Templates. 452
Configuring and Monitoring Print Services 452
   Printer Share 452
   Publishing Printers to Active Directory 454
   Printer Permissions. 454
   Deploying Printer Connections. 456
   Installing Printer Drivers. 457
   Exporting and Importing Print Queues and Printer Settings. 459
   Adding Counters to Reliability and Performance
      Monitor to Monitor Print Servers 461

    Printer Pooling. 463
    Print Priority 464
  Summary. 466
  Solutions Fast Track 468
  Frequently Asked Questions 471

Chapter 8 Monitoring and Managing a Network Infrastructure. 477
  Introduction 478
  Configuring Windows Server Update Services Server Settings 478
    Installing Windows Server Update Services 479
    Update Type Selection 491
    Client Settings 493
      Configuring WSUS Computer Group Assignment Settings 495
    Group Policy Objects (GPOs). 497
    Client Targeting 501
    Software Updates 501
    Test and Approval 503
    Disconnected Networks 507
  Capturing Performance Data 509
    Data Collector Sets. 509
    Performance Monitor 522
    Reliability Monitor 526
    Monitoring the System Stability Index 528
  Monitoring Event Logs 529
    Custom Views 529
    Application and Services Logs. 533
      Admin Logs. 533
      Operational Logs 533
      Analytic Logs 534
      Debug Logs 534
    Subscriptions 534
    DNS Event Log 537
  Gathering Network Data 538
    Simple Network Management Protocol (SNMP). 538
    Baseline Security Analyzer 542
    Network Monitor. 545
  Summary. 549
  Solutions Fast Track 549
  Frequently Asked Questions 551

Chapter 9 Network Access Protection 553

Introduction 554
Working with NAP 555
   Network Layer Protection. 555
      NAP Clients 556
      NAP Enforcement Points. 557
      Active Directory Domain Services 557
      NAP Health Policy Server 558
      Health Requirement Server 558
      Restricted Network. 558
      Software Policy Validation. 559
   DHCP Enforcement. 559
   VPN Enforcement 565
      Communication Process with VPN Client and NAP 565
   Configuring NAP Health Policies. 569
      Connection Request Policies 570
      Network Policies 571
      Health Policies. 572
      Network Access Protection Settings 574
   IPsec Enforcement 576
      Secure Network. 577
      Boundary Network 577
      Restricted Network. 578
      Flexible Host Isolation 578
   802.1x Enforcement 581
Summary. 584
Solutions Fast Track 585
Frequently Asked Questions 587

Chapter 10 Configuring Windows Server Hyper-V and Virtual Machines 589

Introduction 590
   Advancing Microsoft's Strategy for Virtualization 590
   Understanding Virtualization. 592
   Understanding the Components of Hyper-V 596
Configuring Virtual Machines. 599
   Installing Hyper-V 599
   Installing and Managing Hyper-V on Windows Server
      Core Installations 602
   Virtual Networking 603
   Virtualization Hardware Requirements 606

Virtual Hard Disks 607
Adding Virtual Machines. 609
Migrating from Physical to Virtual Machines 614
Backing Up Virtual Machines 619
Virtual Server Optimization 623
Summary. 626
Solutions Fast Track 627
Frequently Asked Questions 630

Chapter 11 Configuring Web Application Services. 633
Introduction 634
Installing and Configuring Internet Information Services. 634
Differences in Windows Editions 639
Typical Deployment Scenarios 640
Simple Web Server 640
Small Web Farms 640
Large Web Farms 641
Installing Internet Information Services 642
Provisioning Web Sites 649
Adding a Virtual Directory 653
Configuring the Default Document 653
Enabling Directory Browsing 654
Customizing Error Pages 656
Redirecting Requests. 659
Adding Custom Response Headers. 660
Adding MIME Types 661
Configuring Web Applications. 662
Application Pool Settings 668
Application Development Settings 670
Enabling Third-Party Runtime Environments 671
Migrating from Previous Releases 673
Securing Your Web Sites and Applications 674
Transport Security 675
Authentication 684
Considerations When Using Client Certificates 687
Authorization. 689
URL Authorization 689
IP Authorization 693
Request Filtering. 694
.NET Trust Levels 696

Managing Internet Information Services 697
    Configuration and Delegation 697
        Remote Administration 701
    Health and Diagnostics 702
        Failed Request Tracing 703
        Logging 706
    Scaling Your Web Farm 707
        Output Caching 707
        Compression 710
        Network Load Balancing 713
            Shared Configuration 714
            TCP and HTTP Service Unavailable Responses 714
    Backing Up and Restoring Server Configuration 715
Summary 717
Solutions Fast Track 719
Frequently Asked Questions 722

Chapter 12 Configuring Web Infrastructure Services 725
Introduction 726
Installing and Configuring FTP Publishing Services 726
    Installing the FTP Publishing Service 727
    Provisioning FTP Sites 734
        Directory Browsing 737
        Firewall Support 739
        Messages 740
        Virtual Directories 741
        Application Pools 742
    Securing Your FTP Site 744
        Transport Security 744
        Authentication 751
        Authorization 751
            URL Authorization 752
            IP Authorization 753
        User Isolation 754
Installing and Configuring SMTP Services 756
    Installing Simple Mail Transfer (SMTP) Services 757
    Provisioning Virtual Servers 760
        Configuring a Virtual Server 762
            Server Bindings 763
            Logging 764

Message Limits. 765
Delivery Options 766
LDAP Routing 769
Securing Your SMTP Virtual Server. 770
Transport Security 770
Authentication. 771
Connection Control 772
Relay Restrictions 773
Summary. 775
Solutions Fast Track 776
Frequently Asked Questions 778

Index. 781

## Chapter 1

Configuring
Network Services

Solutions in this chapter:

- Configuring Domain Name System (DNS)

- Configuring Dynamic Host Configuration
  Protocol (DHCP)

- Configuring Windows Internet Naming
  Service (WINS)

☑ Summary

☑ Solutions Fast Track

☑ Frequently Asked Questions

Introduction

When internetworking was first conceived and implemented in the 1960s and 1970s, the Internet Protocol (IP) addressing scheme was also devised. It uses four sets of 8 bits (octets) to identify a unique address, which is comprised of a network address and a unique host address. This provided enormous flexibility because the scheme allowed for millions of addresses. The original inventors of this system probably didn't envision the networking world as it is today—with millions of computers spanning the globe, many connected to one worldwide network, the Internet.

Network Services are to Active Directory what gasoline is to a combustion engine—without them, Active Directory would simply be a shiny piece of metal that sat there and looked pretty. As a matter of fact, network services are not only crucial to Active Directory, but are equally important to networking on a much larger scale. Imagine watching television at home and hearing the voice-over for a Microsoft commercial say "Come visit us today at 207.46.19.190!" instead of "Come visit us today at www.microsoft.com!" Networking services make networking much easier to understand for the end user, but they also go well beyond that in terms of what they provide for a networking architecture.

In this chapter, we will explore the *Domain Name System (DNS)*, a method of creating hierarchical names that can be resolved to IP addresses (which, in turn, are resolved to MAC addresses). We explain the basis of DNS and compare it to alternative naming systems. We also explain how the DNS namespace is created and resolved to an IP address throughout the Internet or within a single organization. Once you have a solid understanding of DNS, you will learn about Windows Server 2008 DNS servers, including the different roles DNS servers can play, the ways DNS Servers resolve names and replicate data, and how Windows Server 2008 Active Directory integrates with DNS. By the end of this chapter, you'll have a detailed understanding of DNS on the Internet, as well as how DNS works within a Windows Server 2008 network.

We will also discuss two additional services: Windows Internet Naming Service (WINS) and Dynamic Host Configuration Protocol (DHCP), two common services used on Transmission Control Protocol/Internet Protocol (TCP/IP) networks. Each of these services plays an important role in your environment, ultimately assisting IT professionals in their quest to automate much of the mundane tasks that would otherwise need to be managed manually.

Configuring Domain Name System (DNS)

Microsoft defines the Domain Name System (DNS) as a hierarchical distributed database that contains mappings of fully qualified domain names (FQDNs) to IP addresses. DNS enables finding the locations of computers and services through user-friendly names and also enables the discovery of other types of records used for additional resources (which we will discuss later) in the DNS database.

A much broader definition comes from the original Request For Comment (RFC), which was first released way back in November of 1983. RFC 882 (http:// tools.ietf.org/html/rfc882) describes DNS conceptually, explaining how various components (domain name space, name servers, resolvers) come together to provide a domain name system.

As you can imagine, a number of changes have been made to the original RFC. In fact, there have been three major RFC releases since the original debuted 25 years ago: RFC 883, RFC 1034, and RFC 1035.

As you probably came to realize by looking at the date of the original DNS RFC, Microsoft was certainly not the first company to develop DNS services. In fact, the first Unix-based DNS service was written by four college students way back in 1984. Later, the code was rewritten by an engineer at Digital Equipment Corporation (DEC) and renamed Berkeley Internet Name Domain, or BIND, as it is more commonly known. Since the original DNS code was written, it has been rewritten by several companies, including Microsoft, Novell, Red Hat, and many others.

Now that you've had a little history lesson on DNS, let's discuss some of the various record types that can be held inside a DNS database. The record type will determine what information is provided to a DNS client requesting data. For instance, if the DNS server is configured to use an "A" record (a naming resource record), it converts an IP address to a hostname. As an example, consider using 207.46.19.190 as the IP address, and www.microsoft.com as the hostname. This would be a good example of how DNS resolution works.

Another example of a record in use is the MX record. This record type is used when an e-mail server is trying to determine the IP address of another e-mail server. Table 1.1 outlines the types of records that can exist in a Windows Server 2008 DNS.

Table 1.1 Common DNS Record Types

Type	Description
Host (A)	Maps a domain name (such as.www.microsoft.com) to an IP address
Canonical Name (CNAME)	Maps an alias domain name to another server name
Mail exchanger (MX)	Maps a domain name to a system that controls mail flow
Pointer (PTR)	Reverses the mapping process; used to convert domain names to IP addresses
Service location (SRV)	Used to map domain names to a specific service

Regardless of the type of DNS you're using—Microsoft, Linux, or another vendor—the DNS database holds a nearly identical format. Several components make up a DNS database. Figure 1.1 provides an example of a primary zone database (we will discuss the various types of zones later in this chapter).

Figure 1.1 A DNS Database File

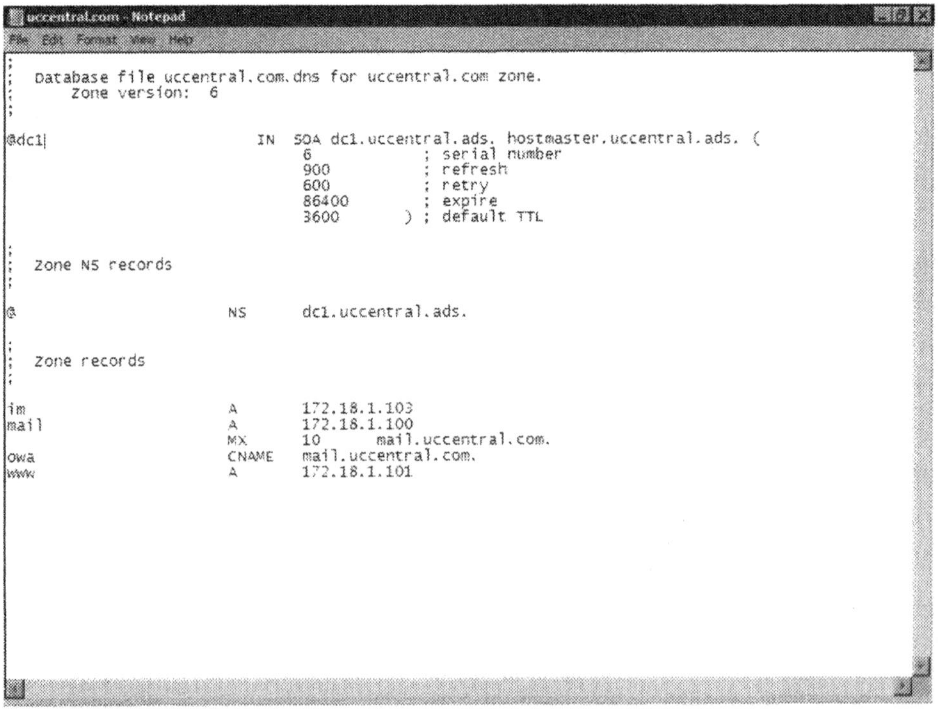

Let's take a moment to discuss some of the other information held in the database file.

- **IN – Internet Name** This calls out that the information *preceding* the IN is the common name of the server. In the first line of the preceding database file, it indicates that the name at the top-left is the domain name this server supports. The names shown *after* the IN are the actual names of the server.

- **SOA – Start of Authority** This indicates that the server shown in Figure 1.1 is authoritative over this particular domain. Thus, it has rights to add, remove, and change records for the domain.

- **1 – Serial number** Each time a change is made to a DNS database, a new serial number is assigned. Other servers—known as secondary servers—can copy DNS databases for local storage. If this serial number changes, the secondary servers know they need to update their copy.

- **900 – Refresh Rate** How often—in seconds—the secondary computer checks to see if it needs to update its database.

- **600 – Retry** How long a secondary DNS server should wait before requesting another update, should an update fail.

- **86400 – Expire** How long a secondary server can hold a database—without update—before it must purge its records.

- **3600 – Time to Live (TTL)** How long a client machine can store a requested record before it must request a refreshed record.

Thus far, we've been focusing on how an individual DNS server is configured. However, we must also look at DNS structures on a much higher level as well. The first thing to understand is that the worldwide DNS structure is just incredibly massive—and continues to grow on a daily basis as new domains are brought online. As large as it is, the general structure behind it is relatively simple. DNS is based on a "tree" format—and an upside-down tree, at that. At the top of the tree is the root—the root is the beginning of all DNS naming conventions and has total authority over all naming conventions beneath it. *DNS Root* is essentially a period—yes, a period. Technically speaking, if you decide to shop online at Elsevier's Web site, you are shopping at "www.elsevier.com." If that doesn't make sense, let's break it down. Basically, domains (and domain server names) are really read from right-to-left in the computer world. The "." is assumed in any DNS resolution, but is still the highest level.

Com would be the second-highest level, followed by another period for separation, and then *Elsevier*. So, in regards to DNS hierarchy, the top level domain would be ".", followed by the second-highest level domain, which would be *com*, followed by the third-highest level domain, *Elsevier*. When combined to form an FQDN, the result would be "Elsevier.com."

WWW represents nothing more than the name of a server that exists in the Elsevier.com domain. WWW has become commonplace for World Wide Web services, but it could just as easily be supercalafragalisticexpialidotious.elsevier.com—though I doubt it would get as many hits. If you are still confused by how DNS naming structures work, take a look at Figure 1.2, which shows a sample of how a DNS tree looks.

Figure 1.2 A Sample DNS Tree

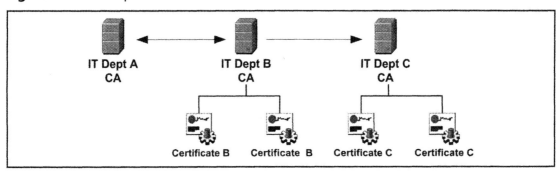

The summit of the DNS namespace hierarchy is the root, which has several servers managed by the Internet Name Registration Authority (INRA). Immediately below the root are the COM, NET, EDU, and other top-level domains listed in Table 1.2. Each of these domains is further divided into namespaces that are managed by the organizations that register them. For example, syngress.com is managed by a different organization than umich.edu.

Table 1.2 Domain Suffixes Used on the Internet

Domain Suffix	Typical Usage
.mil	United States military
.edu	Educational facilities
.com	Commercial organizations

Continued

Table 1.2 Continued. Domain Suffixes Used on the Internet

Domain Suffix	Typical Usage
.net	Networks
.org	Nonprofit organizations
.gov	United States government—nonmilitary
.us	United States
.uk	United Kingdom
.au	Australia
.de	Germany
Other two-letter abbreviations (.xx)	Other countries

NOTE

In addition to the domain suffixes shown in Table 1.2, you will also find the occasional privately used domain suffix .local. The .local suffix is not managed by a DNS root server, so the namespace cannot be published on the Internet when you design the namespace for an Active Directory network, you can choose to use the .local suffix for domains that will not have any hosts on the Internet. Keep in mind that using the .local namespace internally will not prevent an organization from using Internet resources, such as browsing the Web.

Organizations often split the ownership of their DNS namespace. One team might be responsible for everything inside the firewall, while another team may be responsible for the namespace that faces the public. Since Active Directory often replaces Windows NT as an upgrade, the team responsible for Windows NT will often take over the DNS namespace management for Active Directory domains. Since Active Directory DNS design and implementation does differ somewhat from the standard DNS design and implementation, you can often find the two types of tasks split between two different groups in the same organization.

Those are the basics on how Domain Name Services function on a much grander scale. In the coming sections of this chapter, we will discuss how to use DNS within a Windows Server 2008 environment. First, though, let's discuss how to install and perform the initial configuration of a DNS on Windows Server 2008.

Identifying DNS Record Requirements

A Resource Record (RR) is to DNS what a table is to a database.

A *Resource Record* is part of DNS's database structure that contains the name information for a particular host or zone. Table 1.3 contains an aggregation of the most popular RR types that have been collected from the various RFCs that define their usage:

Table 1.3 RR Types

Record Type	Common Name	Function
RFC		
A	Address record	Maps FQDN to 32-bit IPv4 addresses.
RFC1035		
AAAA	IPv6 address record	Maps FQDN to 128-bit IPv6 addresses.
RFC1886		
AFSDB	Andrews file system	Maps a DNS domain name to a server subtype that is either an AFS Version 3 volume or an authenticated name server using DCE or NCA.
RFC1183		
ATMA	Asynchronous Transfer Mode address	Maps a DNS domain name in the owner field to an ATM address referenced in the atm_ address field.
CNAME	Canonical name or alias name	Maps a virtual domain name (alias) to a real domain name.
RFC1035		
HINFO	Host info record	Specifies the CPU and operating system type for the host.
RFC1700		
ISDN	ISDN info record	Maps an FQDN to an ISDN telephone number.

Continued

Table 1.3 Continued. RR Types

Record Type	Common Name	Function
RFC1183		
KEY	Public key resource record	Contains a public key that is associated with a zone. In full DNSSEC (defined later in this chapter) implementation, resolvers and servers use KEY resource records to authenticate SIG resource records received from signed zones. KEY resource records are signed by the parent zone, allowing a server that knows a parent zone's public key to discover and verify the child zone's key. Name servers or resolvers receiving resource records from a signed zone obtain the corresponding SIG record, and then retrieve the zone's KEY record.
MB	Mailbox name record	Maps a domain mail server name to the host name of the mail server.
RFC1035		
MG	Mail group record	Maps a domain mailing group to the mailbox resource records.
RFC1035		
MINFO	Mailbox info record	Specifies a mailbox for the person who maintains the mailbox.
RFC1035		
MR	Mailbox renamed record	Maps an old mailbox name to a new mailbox name for forwarding purposes.
RFC1035		
MX	Mail exchange record	Provides routing info to reach a given mailbox.

Continued

Table 1.3 Continued. RR Types

Record Type	Common Name	Function
RFC974		
NS	Name server record	Specifies that the listed name server has a zone starting with the owner name. Identify servers other than SOA servers that contain zone information files.
RFC1035		
NXT	Next resource record	Indicates the nonexistence of a name in a zone by creating a chain of all of the literal owner names in that zone. It also indicates which resource record types are present for an existing name.
OPT	Option resource record	One OPT resource record can be added to the additional data section of either a DNS request or response. An OPT resource record belongs to a particular transport level message, such as UDP, and not to actual DNS data. Only one OPT resource record is allowed, but not required, per message.
PTR	Pointer resource record	Points to another DNS resource record. Used for reverse lookup to point to A records.
RFC1035		
RP	Responsible person info record	Provides info about the server admin.
RFC1183		
RT	Route-through record	Provides routing info for hosts lacking a direct WAN address.

Continued

Table 1.3 Continued. RR Types

Record Type	Common Name	Function
RFC1183		
SIG	Signature resource record	Encrypts an RRset to a signer's (the RRset's zone owner) domain name and a validity interval.
SOA	Start of Authority resource record	Indicates the name of origin for the zone and contains the name of the server that is the primary source for information about the zone. It also indicates other basic properties of the zone. The SOA resource record is always first in any standard zone. It indicates the DNS server that either originally created it or is now the primary server for the zone. It is also used to store other properties such as version information and timings that affect zone renewal or expiration. These properties affect how often transfers of the zone are done between servers that are authoritative for the zone.
RFC1537		
SRV	Service locator record	Provides a way of locating multiple servers that provide similar TCP/IP services.
RFC2052		
TXT	Text record	Maps a DNS name to a string of descriptive text.
RFC1035		
WKS	Well-known services record	Describes the most popular TCP/IP services supported by a protocol on a specific IP address.

Continued

Table 1.3 Continued. RR Types

Record Type	Common Name	Function
RFC1035		
X25	X.25 info record	Maps a DNS address to a public switched data network (PSDN) address number.
RFC1183		

The official IANA (Internet Assigned Numbers Authority) list of DNS parameters can be found at www.iana.org/assignments/dns-parameters, and a really good DNS glossary is available at www.menandmice.com/online_docs_and_faq/glossary/glossarytoc.htm.

Installing and Configuring DNS

DNS can be installed and configured on any version of Windows Server 2008—Web Edition, Standard Edition, Enterprise Edition, or Datacenter Edition. It is a network service that can be integrated with Active Directory (for security and replication purposes), or as a stand-alone service. A Windows Server 2008 DNS can manage not only internal namespaces, but external (Internet-facing) namespaces as well.

In the following examples, we will be installing DNS on a Windows Server 2008 Standard Server.

1. Choose **Start | Administrative Tools | Server Manager**.

2. Scroll down to **Role Summary** and click **Add Roles**.

3. When the **Before You Begin** page opens, click **Next**.

4. On the **Select Server Roles** page, select **DNS Server** (see Figure 1.3), and then click **Next**.

Figure 1.3 Selecting the DNS Server Role

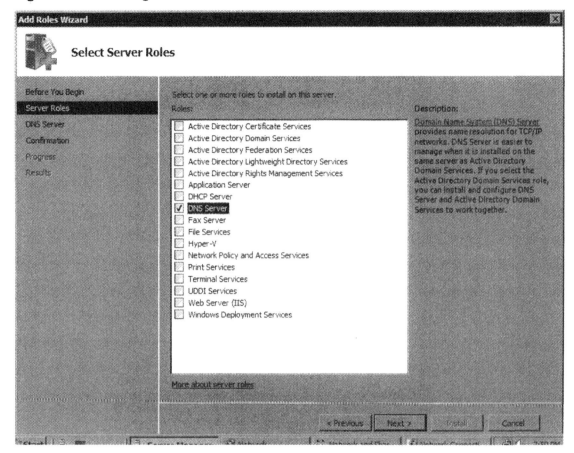

5. At the **DNS Server** window, read the overview, and then click **Next**.

6. Confirm your selections, and then click **Install**.

7. When installation is complete, click **Close**.

Next, we will configure some basic server settings:

1. Choose Start | **Administrative Tools** | **DNS**.

2. Find your server name in the left pane and double-click it. This will open the DNS configuration for this server (see Figure 1.4).

Figure 1.4 The Opening DNS Configuration Data

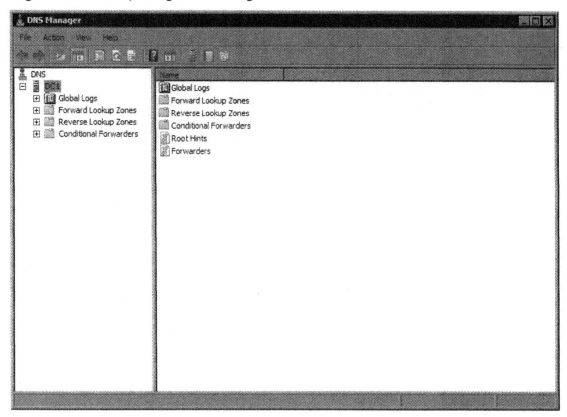

3. Look at the DNS properties of this server. Right-click the server name and select **Properties** from the drop-down menu.

4. The first tab that opens is the **Interfaces** tab. This tab can be adjusted *if* you have additional NICs in your server. This is particularly useful if you only want DNS queries to be answered by systems on a particular subnet. In general, you will likely leave it at the default of **All IP Addresses**.

5. Click the **Root Hints** tab. Notice there are multiple name servers with different IP addresses (Figure 1.5). With root hints, any queries that cannot be answered locally are forwarded to one of these root servers. Optionally, we can clear our root hints by selecting them and clicking **Remove**. Remove all of the servers, and click **Forwarders**.

Figure 1.5 DNS Root Hints

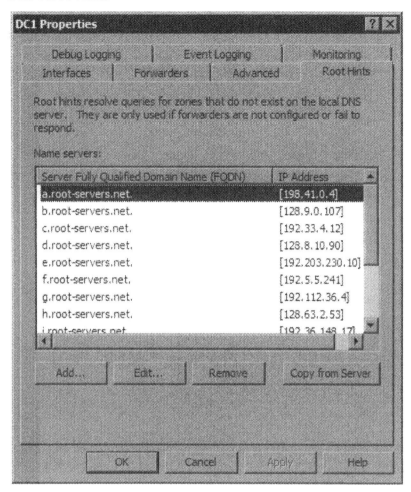

6. On the **Forwarders** tab, we can specify where DNS queries that are not resolved locally will be resolved. As opposed to Root Hints, this gives us much more control over where our queries are sent. For example, we can click **Edit...** and enter **4.2.2.1**—a well-known DNS server. After you enter the IP address, click **OK**.

7. Look through the other tabs in the Properties dialog box. In particular, take a look at the **Advanced** tab (Figure 1.6). Notice the check box for **BIND Secondaries**—this makes it possible for BIND servers to make local copies of DNS databases. Also, look at the **Enable Automatic Scavenging Of Stale Records** option. With this option, you can specify the period before which DNS will perform a cleanup of old records.

Figure 1.6 Advanced DNS Settings

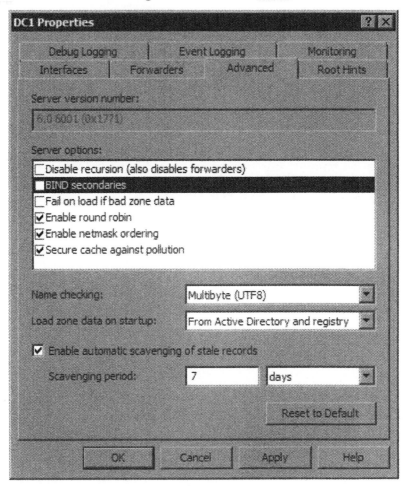

8. Click **Apply** to save the changes we made, and then click **OK** to close the window.

We still have a lot to do with configuring a DNS server, but before we move on to configuring zones, let's walk through the process of installing DNS on a Windows Server 2008 Core Installation.

Using Server Core and DNS

As we discussed in Chapter 1, a Windows Server 2008 Core Server Installation can be used for multiple purposes. One of the ways Server Core can be used is to provide a minimal installation for DNS. In the coming sections, we will discuss the various ways you can manipulate, manage, and configure DNS servers through the various Windows Server 2008 DNS Graphical User Interfaces (GUIs): DNS Manager and the Server Manager tool.

However, as you will recall, no GUIs are provided with Windows Server 2008 Core Server. A number of advantages to running DNS within Server Core include:

- **Smaller Footprint:** Reduces the amount of CPU, memory, and hard disk needed.

- **More Secure:** Fewer components and services running unnecessarily.

- **No GUI:** No GUI means that users cannot make modifications to the DNS databases (or any other system functions) using common/user-friendly tools.

If you are planning to run DNS within a Server Core install, several steps must be performed prior to installation. The first step is to set the IP information of the server. To configure the IP addressing information of the server, do the following:

1. Identify the network adapter. To do this, in the console window, type **netsh interface ipv4 show interfaces** and record the number shown under the **Idx** column.

2. Set the IP address, Subnet Mask, and Default Gateway for the server. To do so, type **netsh interface ipv4 set address name="<ID>" source=static address=<StaticIP> mask=<SubnetMask> gateway=<DefaultGateway>**. ID represents the interface number from step 1, <StaticIP> represents the IP address we will assign, <SubnetMask> represents the subnet mask, and <Default Gateway> represents the IP address of the server's default gateway. See Figure 1.7 for our sample configuration.

Figure 1.7 Setting an IP Address in Server Core

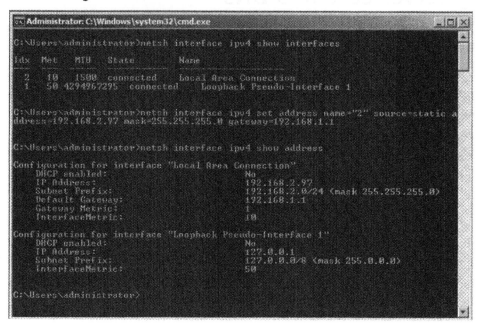

3. Assign the IP address of the DNS server. If this server is part of an Active Directory domain and is replicating Active Directory–integrated zones (we will discuss those next), we would likely point this server to another AD-integrated DNS server. If it is not, we would point it to another external DNS server—usually the Internet provider of your company. From the console, type **netsh interface ipv4 add dnsserver name="<ID>" address=<DNSIP> index=1. >**. ID represents the number from step 1, while <StaticIP> represents the IP address of the DNS server.

   Once the IP address settings are completed—you can verify this by typing **ipconfig /all**—we can install the DNS role onto the Core Server installation:

4. To do this, from the command line, type **start /w ocsetup DNS-Server-Core-Role**.

5. To verify that the DNS Server service is installed and started, type **NET START**. This will return a list of running services.

6. Use the *dnscmd* command-line utility to manipulate the DNS settings. For example, you can type **dnscmd /enumzones** to list the zones hosted on this DNS server.

7. We can also change all of the configuration options we modified in the GUI section earlier by using the **dnscmd /config** option. For example, we can enable BIND secondaries by typing **dnscmd <servername> /config /bindsecondaries 1**.You can see the results in Figure 1.8.

Figure 1.8 Using the *dnscmd* Utility

There are many, many more things you can do with the dnscmd utility. For more information on the dnscmd syntax, visit http://technet2.microsoft.com/WindowsServer/ en/library/d652a163-279f-4047-b3e0-0c468a4d69f31033.mspx. So far, you have learned how to install and configure the DNS server, now we will discuss how to configure DNS zones.

Configuring Zones

We've mentioned "zones" several times already in this chapter. Simply put, a zone is the namespace allocated for a particular server. Each "level" of the DNS hierarchy represents a particular zone within DNS. For the actual DNS database, a *zone* is a contiguous portion of the domain tree that is administered as a single separate entity by a DNS server. The zone contains resource records for all of the names within the zone. If Active Directory–integrated zones are not being used, some zone files will contain the DNS database resource records required to define the zone. If DNS data is Active Directory–integrated, the data is stored in Active Directory, not in zone files.

- **Primary Zone** With a primary zone, the server hosting this zone is authoritative for the domain name. It stores the master copy of the domain information locally. When the zone is created, a file with the suffix .dns is created in the %windir%\System32\dns subdirectory of the DNS server.

- **Secondary Zone** This is a secondary source—essentially a copy—of the primary DNS zone, with read-only capabilities.

- **Stub Zone** Only stores information about the authoritative name servers for a particular zone.

Primary and secondary zones are standard (that is, non–Active Directory–integrated) forward lookup zones. The principal difference between the two is the ability to add records. A standard primary zone is hosted on the master servers in a zone replication scheme. Primary zones are the only zones that can be edited, whereas secondary zones are read-only and are updated only through zone transfer. DNS master servers replicate a copy of their zones to one or more servers that host secondary zones, thereby providing fault tolerance for your DNS servers. DNS standard zones are the types of zones you should use if you do not plan on integrating Active Directory with your DNS servers.

An Active Directory–integrated zone is basically an enhanced primary DNS zone stored in Active Directory and thus can, unlike all other zone types, use multimaster replication and Active Directory security features. It is an authoritative primary zone in which all of the zone data is stored in Active Directory. As mentioned previously, zone files are not used nor necessary. Integrating DNS with Active Directory produces the following additional benefits:

- **Speed** Directory replication is much faster when DNS and Active Directory are integrated. This is because Active Directory replication is performed on a *per-property* basis, meaning that only changes that apply to particular zones are replicated. Because only the relevant information is to be replicated, the time required to transfer data between zones is greatly reduced. On top of this, a separate DNS replication topology is eliminated because Active Directory replication topology is used for both ADI zones and AD itself.

- **Reduced Administrative Overhead** Any time you can reduce the number of management consoles you have to work with, you can reduce the amount of time needed to manage information. Without the advantage of consolidating the management of DNS and Active Directory in the same console, you would have to manage your Active Directory domains and

DNS namespaces separately. Moreover, your DNS domain structure mirrors your Active Directory domains. Any deviation between Active Directory and DNS makes management more time-consuming and creates more opportunity for mistakes. As your network continues to grow and become more complex, managing two separate entities becomes more involved. Integrating Active Directory and DNS provides you with the ability to view and manage them as a single entity.

- **Automatic Synchronization** When a new domain controller is brought online, networks that have integrated DNS and Active Directory have the advantage of automatic synchronization. Even if a domain controller will not be used to host the DNS service, the ADI zones will still be replicated, synchronized, and stored on the new domain controllers.

- **Secure Dynamic DNS** Additional features have been added that enhance the security of secure dynamic updates. These features will be discussed in the "DNS Security Guidelines" section later in this chapter.

A *reverse lookup* zone is an authoritative DNS zone that is used primarily to resolve IP addresses to network resource names. This zone type can be primary, secondary or Active Directory–integrated. Reverse lookups traverse the DNS hierarchy in exactly the same way as the more common forward lookups.

Stub zones are a new feature introduced in Windows Server 2008. They contain a partial copy of a zone that can be hosted by a DNS server and used to resolve recursive or iterative queries. A *recursive* query is a request from a host to a resolver to find data on other name servers. An *s* query is a request, usually made by a resolver, for any information a server already has in memory for a certain domain name. Stub zones contain the Start of Authority (SOA) resource records of the zone, the DNS resource records that list the zone's authoritative servers, and the glue address (A) resource records that are required for contacting the zone's authoritative servers. Stub zones are useful for reducing the number of DNS queries on a network, and consequently the resource consumption on the primary DNS servers for that particular namespace. Basically, stub zones are used to find other zones and can be created in the middle of a large DNS hierarchy to prevent a query for a distant zone within the same namespace from having to ascend, traverse, and return over a multitude of zones.

Windows Server 2008 also allows for a special type of Primary Zone—known as an *AD-integrated zone*—which basically means that the data is stored within Active

Directory Domain Services, and is replicated to other DNS servers during normal AD replication periods. AD-integrated zones offer a number of benefits, including:

- **Secure Dynamic Updates** Systems that are authenticated by Active Directory can update their DNS records. This allows name resolution for clients and servers while eliminating DNS poisoning by rogue systems that create DNS records.

- **Automatic Synchronization** Zones are created and synchronized to new domain controllers (with DNS installed) automatically.

- **Efficient Replication** Less data is replicated since only relevant changes are propagated.

Zone Transfer

Zone transfer is the process of copying the contents of the zone file on a primary DNS server to a secondary DNS server. Using zone transfer provides fault tolerance by synchronizing the zone file in a primary DNS server with the zone file in a secondary DNS server. The secondary DNS server can continue performing name resolution if the primary DNS server fails. Furthermore, secondary DNS servers can transfer to other secondary DNS servers in the same hierarchical fashion, which makes the higher-level secondary DNS server a master to other secondary servers. Three transfer modes are used in a Windows Server 2008 DNS configuration:

- **Full Transfer** When you bring a new DNS server online and configure it to be a secondary server for an existing zone in your environment, it will perform a *full transfer* of all the zone information in order to replicate all the existing resource records for that zone. Older implementations of the DNS service also used full transfers whenever updates to a DNS database needed to be propagated. Full zone transfers can be very time-consuming and resource-intensive, especially in situations where there isn't sufficient bandwidth between primary and secondary DNS servers. For this reason, incremental DNS transfers were developed.

- **Incremental Transfer** When using *incremental zone transfers*, the secondary server retrieves only resource records that have changed within a zone, so that it remains synchronized with the primary DNS server. When incremental transfers are used, the databases on the primary server and the secondary server are compared to see if any differences exist. If the zones are identified as the same (based on the serial number of the *Start of Authority* resource record), no zone transfer is performed. If, however, the serial number on the primary server database is higher than the serial number on the secondary server, a transfer of the delta resource records commences. Because of this configuration, incremental zone transfers require much less bandwidth and create less network traffic, allowing them to finish faster. Incremental zone transfers are often ideal for DNS servers that must communicate over low-bandwidth connections.

■ **DNS Notify** The third method for transferring DNS zone records isn't actually a transfer method at all. To avoid the constant polling of primary DNS servers from secondary DNS servers, *DNS Notify* was developed as a networking standard (RFC 1996) and has since been implemented into the Windows operating system. DNS Notify allows a primary DNS server to utilize a "push" mechanism for notifying secondary servers that it has been updated with records that need to be replicated. Servers that are notified can then initiate a zone transfer (either full or incremental) to "pull" zone changes from their primary servers as they normally would. In a DNS Notify configuration, the IP addresses for all secondary DNS servers in a DNS configuration must be entered into the notify list of the primary DNS server to pull, or request, zone updates.

Each of the three methods has its own purpose and functionality. How you handle zone transfers between your DNS servers depends on your individual circumstances.

TIP

Remember that full and incremental transfers actually transfer the data between the DNS servers, and that DNS Notify is not a mechanism for transferring zone data. It is used in conjunction with AXFR (Full Transfer) and IXFR (Incremental Transfer) to notify a secondary server that new records are available for transfer.

Let's take a look at how to create a new DNS zone:

1. Choose **Start | Administrative Tools | DNS**.

2. In the console tree, double-click your server, and then click **Forward Lookup Zones**.

3. Right-click **Forward Lookup Zones**, and then select **New Zone**.

4. The **New Zone Wizard** appears. Click **Next** (see Figure 1.9).

Figure 1.9 The New Zone Wizard

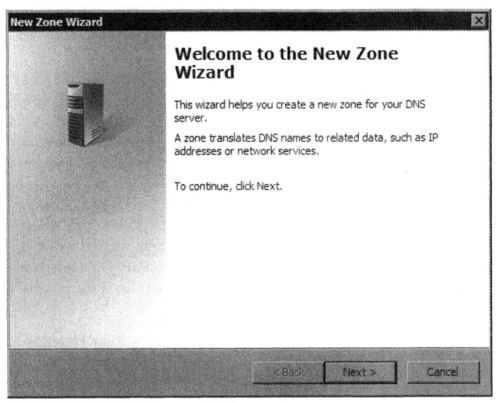

5. On the **Zone Type** page, click **Primary zone** and then click **Next**.

6. On the **Active Directory Zone Replication Scope** page, click **Next**.

7. On the **Zone Name** page, in the **Name** field, type a name for a test zone (Figure 1.10), and then click **Next**.

Figure 1.10 The Zone Name Page

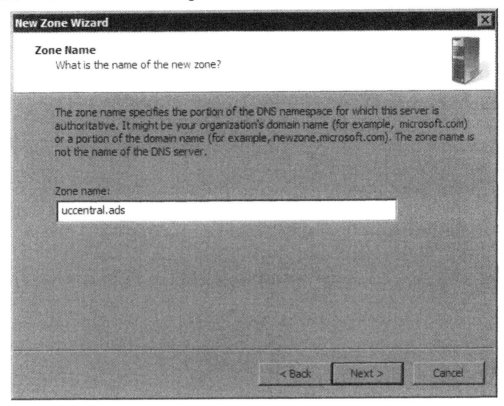

8. On the **Zone File** page, click **Next**.

9. On the **Dynamic Update** page, choose **Allow Both Nonsecure And Secure Dynamic Updates** and click **Next**.

NOTE

Normally, when configuring Dynamic Updates, you should choose the **Secure Only** option. For lab purposes in this book, however, you can choose **Allow Both Nonsecure And Secure Dynamic Updates**.

---

10. On the **Completing The New Zone Wizard** page, click **Finish**.

Active Directory Records

If you turned on dynamic updates in the previous sidebar, and you have Active Directory loaded on your server, reboot your system.

After your system reboots, notice the following new records in your zone.

- **_ldap._tcp.<DNSDomainName>** Enables a client to locate a domain controller in the domain named by *<DNSDomainName>*. A client searching for a domain controller in the domain uccentral.ads would query the DNS server for _ldap._uccentral.ads.

- **_ldap._tcp.<SiteName>._sites.<DNSDomainName>** Enables a client to find a domain controller in the domain and site specified (such as _ldap._tcp.lab._sites.uccentral.ads for a domain controller in the Lab site of uccentral.ads).

- **_ldap._tcp.pdc._msdcs.<DNSDomainName>** Enables a client to find the PDC Emulator flexible single master operations (FSMO) role holder of a mixed- or native-mode domain. Only the PDC of the domain registers this record.

- **_ldap._tcp.gc._msdcs.<DNSForestName>** Found in the zone associated with the root domain of the forest, this enables a client to find a Global Catalog (GC) server. Only domain controllers serving as GC servers for the forest will register this name. If a server ceases to be a GC server, the server will deregister the record.

- **_ldap._tcp. ._sites.gc._msdcs.<DNSForestName>** Enables a client to find a GC server in the specified site (such as _ldap._tcp.lab._sites.gc._msdcs. uccentral.ads).

- **_ldap._tcp.<DomainGuid>.domains._msdcs.<DNSForestName>** Enables a client to find a domain controller in a domain based on the domain controller's globally unique ID (GUID). A *GUID* is a 128-bit (8 byte) number that is generated automatically for the purpose of referencing Active Directory objects. This mechanism and these records are used by domain controllers to locate other domain controllers when they need to replicate, for example.

- **<DNSDomainName>** Enables a client to find a domain controller via a normal Host (A) record.

Special records specifically associated with Active Directory allow servers and clients to interact with Active Directory services in a meaningful way.

Reverse Lookup Zones

As mentioned earlier, a *reverse lookup* zone is an authoritative DNS zone that is used primarily to resolve IP addresses to network resource names. This zone type can be primary, secondary, or Active Directory–integrated. Reverse lookups traverse the DNS hierarchy in exactly the same way as the more common forward lookups.

To handle reverse lookups, a special root domain called in-addr.arpa was created. Subdomains within the in-addr.arpa domain are created using the reverse ordering of the octets that form an IP address. For example, the reverse lookup domain for the 192.168.100.0/24 network would be 100.168.192.in-addr.arpa. The reason the IP addresses are inverted is that IP addresses, when read from left to right, get more specific; the IP address starts with the more general information first. FQDNs, in contrast, get more general when read from left to right; the FQDN starts with a specific host name.

In order for reverse lookup zones to work properly, they use a special RR called a PTR record that provides the mapping of the IP address in the zone to the FQDN.

Reverse lookup zones are used by certain applications, such as NSLookup (an important diagnostic tool that should be part of every DNS administrator's arsenal). If a reverse lookup zone is not configured on the server to which NSLookup is pointing, you will get an error message when you invoke the *nslookup* command.

Configuring & Implementing...

Security Considerations for the Presence of a Reverse Lookup Zone

Being able to make NSLookup work against your DNS servers is not the only, or most important, reason why you should configure reverse lookup zones. Applications on your internal network, such as DNS clients that are trying to register PTR records in a reverse lookup zone, can "leak" information about your internal network out to the Internet if they cannot find a reverse lookup zone on the intranet. To prevent this information from leaking from your network, you should configure reverse lookup zones for the addresses in use on your network.

Configuring Reverse Lookup Zones

Now, we need to create a matching reverse lookup zone. This will handle reverse resolution for our subnet. In this case, it is 192.168.1.x.

1. Choose **Start | Administrative Tools | DNS**.

2. In the console tree, click **Reverse Lookup Zones**.

3. Right-click **Reverse Lookup Zones**, and then click **New Zone**.

4. When the **New Zone Wizard** appears, click **Next**.

5. On the **Zone Type** page, select **Primary Zone**, and then click **Next**.

6. On the **Reverse Lookup Zone Name** page, make sure **IPv4** is selected, and then click **Next**.

7. On the **Reverse Lookup Zone Name** page (Figure 1.11), in the **Network ID** field, type the start of the subnet range of your network (in this case, 192.168.1.x), and then click **Next**.

Figure 1.11 The Reverse Lookup Zone Name Page

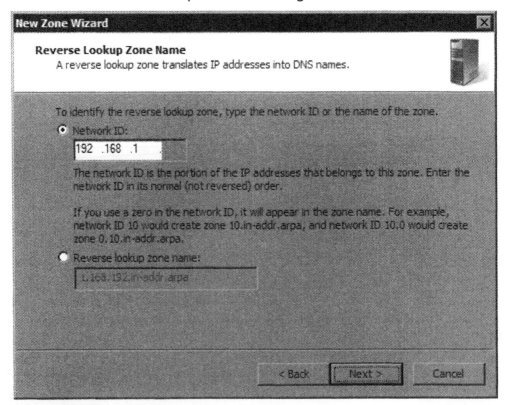

8. On the **Zone File** page, click **Next**.

9. On the **Dynamic Update** page, click **Next**.

10. On the **Completing The New Zone Wizard** page, click **Finish**.

Now we need to enable IPv6 so we can offer domain name resolution for clients who may use IPv6 as opposed to IPv4. We're also going to need it if we want to enable IPv6 DHCP addressing later in this chapter.

First, we need to set an IPv6 address for our server. To do so, perform the following steps:

1. Choose **Start** and right-click **Network**.

2. Select **Properties** from the drop-down menu.

3. Click **Manage Network Connections**.

4. Right-click the **Network** connection and choose **Properties**.

5. Double-click Internet Protocol Version 6 (TCP/IPv6).

6. Click the radio button for **Use The Following IPv6 Address**. If you are not familiar with IP addressing, you can use 2001:0db8:29cd:1a0f:857b:455b: b4ec:7403.

7. Enter a Subnet prefix length of **64**.

8. Your preferred DNS server would be the same as that mentioned earlier (your IPv6 address).

9. Close the Network Connections window and re-open the DNS administrator console.

10. In the console tree, click **Reverse Lookup Zones**.

11. Right-click **Reverse Lookup Zones**, and then click **New Zone**.

12. When the **New Zone Wizard** appears, click **Next**.

13. On the **Zone Type** page, select **Primary Zone**, and then click **Next**.

14. On the **Reverse Lookup Zone Name** page, make sure **IPv6** is selected, and then click **Next**.

15. In the **Reverse Lookup Zone Name** field, type in the prefix **2001:0db8: 29cd:1a0f::/64**, and then click **Next**.

16. On the **Dynamic Update** page, choose **Allow Both Nonsecure And Secure Dynamic Updates** (for testing purposes in this book only—normally, you should use Secure Only), and click **Next**.

17. Click **Finish** to create the New Zone.

18. To create an IPv6 record, right-click the Primary Lookup Zone for your domain (in our lab, it is uccentral.ads), and then click **New Host**.

19. In the **Name** field, enter the name of your server. Our server name is **dc1**.

20. In the **IP address** field, enter the IPv6 address we set for the server.

21. Verify that **Create Associated Pointer (PTR) Record** is checked, and click **Add Host**.

You should now see a new AAAA record for the server, as well as a new PTR record in the Reverse Lookup Zone we created.

Configuring & Implementing...

Developing the DNS Design for Your Network

There are few limitations to developing DNS designs and deploying the service thereafter. You should consider the following points during your design process:

- Each domain contains a set of resource records. Resource records map names to IP addresses or vice versa depending on which type of record it is. Special resource records exist to identify types of servers on the networks. For example, an MX resource record identifies a mail server.

- If the organization has a large number of hosts, use subdomains to speed up the DNS response.

- The only limitation to using subdomains on a single DNS server is the server's own memory and disk capacity.

- A zone contains one or more domains and their resource records. Zones can contain multiple domains if they have a parent and child relationship.

Continued

- A DNS server with a primary zone is authoritative for the zone, and updates can be made on that server. There can only be one primary zone for each zone defined.

- A DNS server with a secondary zone contains a read-only copy of the zone. Secondary zones provide redundancy and speed up query responses by being placed near the computers that place DNS queries.

- DNS servers can use primary and secondary zones whether they are running Windows Server 2008 or are a third-party DNS server.

Now you can double-click the **Forward Lookup Zones** and **Reverse Lookup Zones** and view the zones you have created. The zones will be displayed in the console pane under the appropriate zone type. From here, you can add records by right-clicking the zone and selecting the type of record you want to create. Likewise, you can right-click the zone and select **Properties** to modify the properties of the zone. Some of the properties you can modify include:

- **Dynamic Updates:** The ability for clients to automatically update DNS records.

- **Zone Type:** You can change a zone type from Primary, to Secondary, or to Stub Zone. If Active Directory is installed, you can also make the zone Active Directory–integrated.

- **WINS integration:** We will discuss this later in the chapter, but this is where you can involve WINS resolution with DNS resolution.

- **Name Servers:** You can add the names and IP addresses of servers that have the rights to create copies of the DNS zone.

- **Zone Transfer:** Here, you can specify whether the zone can be transferred to another DNS server. You can also specify whether it can be transferred to any server, only the servers in the Name Servers tab (discussed earlier), or to only specific DNS servers by IP address or FQDN.

Configuring Zone Resolution

There is a new name resolution available with the release of Windows Server 2008: GlobalNames Zones. The GlobalNames zone was introduced to help phase out the Windows Internet Naming Service (WINS), which we will discuss later. However, it is important to note that the GlobalNames zone is not intended to support the same type of name resolution provided in WINS, records which typically are not managed by IT administrators. After the configuration of the GlobalNames zone, you are responsible for management of all records in the zone, as there are no dynamic updates.

So, where this is really relevant is within organizations that have multiple domain names. Without single-label names (also known as NetBIOS names), Windows-based computers will append DNS suffixes based on the order provided, either via the individual TCP/IP settings of the client, DHCP settings, or Group Policy settings. Again, the key here is that if there are MULTIPLE domain names an organization must manage, they may find it easier to use the GlobalNames zone since the GlobalNames zone records can be configured globally for the single-label names. Records that are contained within the GlobalNames zone are known as *global names*.

Several prerequisites must be met before using the GlobalNames zone:

- No existing DNS zone can be named GlobalNames.

- All authoritative DNS servers must be running Windows Server 2008.

- All DNS servers running on Windows Server 2008 must store a local copy of the GlobalNames zone or must be able to remotely communicate with a server that does.

- The GlobalNames Zone Registry setting must be enabled on the server. This can be done by typing *dnscmd <hostname>/config /enableglobalnamessupport 1*.

Let's walk through the steps in configuring a GlobalNames zone:

1. Choose **Start**.

2. Right-click **Command Prompt** and select **Run As Administrator**.

3. At the command prompt, type **dnscmd <hostname>/config /enable-globalnamessupport 1**.

4. Close the command-line prompt.

5. Select **Start | Administrative Tools | DNS**.

6. Right-click your DNS server, and then click **New Zone** to open the New Zone Wizard.

7. Create a new zone and give it the name **GlobalNames** (see Figure 1.12).

Figure 1.12 Creating a GlobalNames Zone

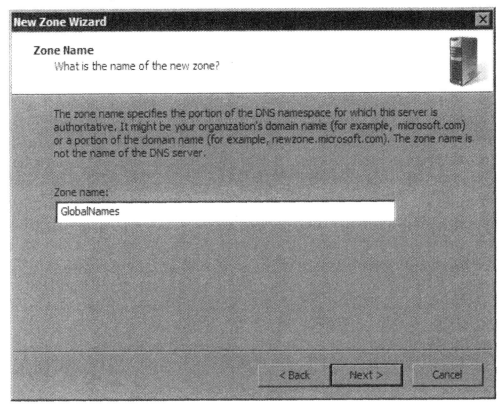

8. Complete the remaining configuration options as we have done previously, and then click **Finish** to complete the process.

Next, we will create a CNAME record for use with the GlobalNames zone:

1. Right-click the **GlobalNames** zone now available under the **Forward Lookup Zones**.

2. Select **New Alias (CNAME)**.

3. Enter the alias of the server. For example, we can name it **widgetserver**.

4. Enter the FQDN of the target host. In this case, it will be our DNS server for testing purposes: **dc1.uccentral.ads**. If you do not have a record for your server, you may need to stop the CNAME process, and create an A record in the primary zone for your domain.

5. Click **OK**.

To test the GlobalNames zone record, simply go to the command prompt of a client PC and type **ping gnztest**. This will return the IP address as expected.

Configuring Dynamic Host Configuration Protocol (DHCP)

The Dynamic Host Configuration Protocol (DHCP) is a protocol that allows administrators to manage and automate the assignment of IP addresses in a centralized console. Without DHCP, the IP address must be "statically" configured on each computer. This isn't such a big deal in a small (ten client-or-less) environment, but when you get into significantly larger environments, static IP address management can become a nightmare. Factor in the mobility of using laptops, and the need to be able to connect to other networks dynamically, and you'll find it's almost impossible in today's world not to use DHCP.

The way DHCP works is fairly simple. Using a client/server model, a DHCP server maintains a pool of IP addresses. DHCP clients request and obtain leases for IP addresses during the boot process. DHCP was derived from the Bootstrap Protocol (BOOTP), which was a protocol typically used to allow clients to boot from the network rather than from a hard drive. Through this boot process, BOOTP assigned an IP address dynamically to the client computer.

Some benefits of using a Windows Server 2008 DHCP server include:

- **DNS integration** Windows Server 2008 DHCP integrates directly with DDNS. When a computer obtains a lease for an IP address, the DHCP server can then register or update the computer's Address (A) records and pointer (PTR) records in the DNS database via Dynamic DNS on behalf of the client computer. The result of the two—DHCP used with DDNS—is true dynamic IP address management. Any computer can start up on the network and receive an IP address that is further registered in the DNS name server.

- **Multicast address allocation** The Windows Server 2008 DHCP can assign IP addresses to multicast groups in addition to the standard individual hosts. Multicast addresses are used to communicate with groups such as server clusters using network load balancing.

- **Detection of unauthorized DHCP servers** By restricting DHCP servers to those that are authorized, you can prevent conflicts and problems on the network. An administrator must configure Active Directory to recognize the DHCP server before it begins functioning on the network. The Windows Server 2008 DHCP service contacts Active Directory to determine whether it is an authorized DHCP server. Active Directory also enables you to configure which clients a DHCP server can service.

■ **Enhanced monitoring** With the Windows Server 2008 DHCP service, you have the ability to monitor the pool of IP addresses and receive notification when the address pool is utilized at a threshold level. For example, you might monitor for a threshold of 90 percent or above.

■ **Vendor and user classes** Vendor and user classes enable you to distinguish the types of machines that are obtaining DHCP leases. For example, you can use a predefined class to determine which users are remote access clients.

■ **Clustering** Windows Server 2008 DHCP services support clustering. Through a cluster, you can ensure a higher reliability and availability of DHCP services to clients.

The negotiation process consists of only four messages, two from the client and two from the server. The first message is the DHCP Discover message from the client to the server. This message looks to a DHCP server and asks for an IP address lease. The second message is the DHCP Offer message responding from the server to the client. A DHCP Offer tells the client that the server has an IP address available. The third message is a DHCP Request message from the client to the server. In this message, the client accepts the offer and requests the IP address for lease. The fourth and final message is the DHCP Acknowledge message from the server to the client. With the DHCP Acknowledge message, the server officially assigns the IP address lease to the client. Each DHCP server requires a statically applied IP address.

DHCP was originally introduced in RFC 2131 back in March of 1997 (http://www.rfc-editor.org/rfc/rfc2131.txt). Since the inception of DHCP, a number of add-on DHCP options have made it possible to disburse even more IP-related information to clients, making IP management much more flexible for IT administrators.

DHCP Design Principles

DHCP is heavily reliant on network topology, and is heavily relied upon by the hosts within a network. For DHCP to function at an optimal level, client computers must be able to access at least one DHCP server at all times.

When developing a DHCP approach for your network, you must consider several things first:

- How many clients will be using DHCP for IP addresses?

- Where are these clients located and what roles do they have?

- What does the network topology look like?

- Are there any unstable WAN links that might cause a network outage if DHCP clients cannot contact a DHCP server for an IP address lease?

- Are there any clients that cannot use DHCP?

- Are there any clients that will be using BOOTP?

- Which IP addresses are dedicated and must be held outside the IP address pool?

- Will you be using Dynamic DNS?

DHCP clients do not wait for the DHCP lease to be over before beginning renewal. Instead, they begin the renewal at the point when 50 percent of the lease is up. For example, when a client has a ten-day lease, then after five days, the client sends the DHCP Request message to the DHCP server. If the server agrees to renew the lease, it responds with a DHCP Acknowledge message. If the client does not receive the DHCP Acknowledge response, the client waits for 50 percent of the remaining time (7.5 days after the original lease was made) before sending another DHCP Request message. This is repeated at 50 percent that remaining time (8.75 days after the original IP address lease). If the client cannot renew the address, or if the DHCP server sends a DHCP Not Acknowledged response, the client must begin a new lease process.

DHCP has only a couple of design requirements:

- You should have at least two DHCP servers to ensure redundancy. You can use clustering to ensure availability, but also keep in mind that two separate DHCP servers at different locations in the network can prevent DHCP problems resulting from a network link failure.

- You must either provide a DHCP server on each network segment or configure routers in between those segments to forward the DHCP messages.

When planning the DHCP servers, the network topology comes into play. It is critical you place DHCP servers at locations most available to the computers that need IP addresses.

DHCP Servers and Placement

The number of DHCP servers you need on a network is driven by the number of clients, availability requirements for the DHCP server, and the network topology. The number of clients a DHCP server can serve varies based on the hardware of the server and whether it provides multiple roles or is strictly a DHCP server. Most can provide IP addresses to thousands of hosts. Server hardware that will have the greatest impact on DHCP performance includes the network interface and hard disk. The faster the network interface card (NIC) and disk access, the better. In addition, multiple NICs will greatly improve performance, since NIC speed in no way compares to the speed of the internal PC hardware, and adding NICs literally relieves a bottleneck.

The availability of the DHCP services to the network drives multiple DHCP servers. You must have at least two DHCP servers. You might want to cluster the server if you have a large scope of addresses that are provided to a network segment.

The network topology will drive additional servers as well. This is something that must be reviewed and then planned. Ideally, a network should have a DHCP server on each segment, although this becomes impractical. Because you can configure routers to forward DHCP requests using a DHCP Relay Agent, you can place DHCP servers at any location on the network. Therefore, you should probably look at the unstable WAN links as the deciding factors for additional DHCP servers. A network that has a highly unstable satellite link to a location that has thousands of clients will require its own DHCP server. However, a network with a highly unstable satellite link to a location that has only a few clients will probably be better served by a statically applied IP address or alternate IP configuration used with DHCP from across the link.

Installing and Configuring DHCP

Installing DHCP in Windows Server 2008 is as simple as adding another role to a server. Some additional steps must be taken, however, to authorize the DHCP server. Back in Windows 2000 Server, Microsoft introduced the concept of authorizing a DHCP server. Microsoft did this because of the problem of "rogue" DHCP servers—servers that users would install on the network, and configure to hand out IP addresses, thus causing problems with production DNS servers. The problem with rogue DHCP servers was that IP addresses that were handed out would either:

- Overlap with existing IP addresses in the network, causing a conflict

- Hand out correct IP addresses, but possibly hand out other incorrect information, such as DNS, WINS, Subnet Mask, and Gateway information

- Hand out a completely incorrect range of IP addresses

- Create unnecessary traffic on the network

During the installation process, we will walk through installing the DHCP role, configuring DHCP settings, and authorizing the DHCP server. Let's begin.

1. Choose **Start | Administrative Tools | Server Manager**.

2. Scroll down to **Role Summary** and click **Add Roles**.

3. When the **Before You Begin** page opens, click **Next**.

4. On the **Select Server Roles** page, select DHCP Server, and then click **Next**.

5. Click **Next** to get through the DNS Server settings. This screen is verifying the IP address of our DNS server, which will be passed to clients.

6. Click **Next** again to skip the WINS settings. If WINS was running (we will discuss WINS later), we could select the WINS server here.

Next, we need to configure a DHCP scope. A DHCP scope is a range of IP addresses (as well as additional IP options, such as gateway, DNS servers, and WINS servers) that can be handed out by a DHCP server. In the first example, we are going to configure both an IPv4 and IPv6 scope.

Now, let's configure our scope:

1. Click **Add...** to add a new DHCP Scope.

2. In the **Scope Name** field, type **Internal Scope**.

3. In the **Starting IP Address** field, type **192.168.1.200**, or any IP range you have available on your network.

4. In the **Ending IP Address** field, type the end of your scope. We will use **192.168.1.220**.

5. In the **Subnet Mask** field, enter the subnet mask of your network. Our subnet mask is **255.255.255.0**.

6. Skip the default gateway for now, we will add this later.

7. Choose **Wired** as the Subnet type, but click the down arrow to see the Wireless option.

8. Verify that **Activate This Scope** is checked (see Figure 1.13), and then click **OK**.

Figure 1.13 Scope Settings for DHCP

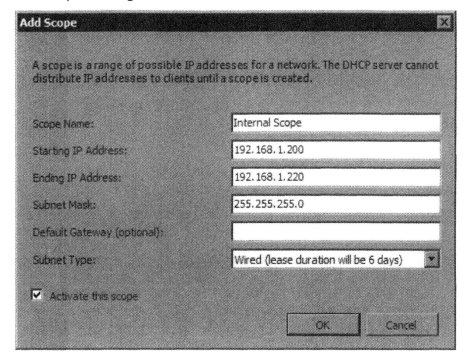

9. Click **Next** once your scope is added.

10. Determine what to do with IPv6 clients. We want to manage IPv6 clients through DHCP when necessary. To do this, select **Disable DHCPv6 Stateless Mode For This Server** and click **Next**.

11. Specify the IP address of an IPv6-enabled DNS server. To do this, enter the IP address of this server. If you recall, we set IPv6 options in the DNS section. Verify that our server's IPv6 settings appear in the **Preferred DNS Server IPv6 Address**, validate it, and then click **Next**.

12. On the **Authorize DHCP Server**, you can specify the credentials of an authorized user, or just click **Next**.

13. Click **Install** to begin the installation.

14. When installation is complete, click **Close**.

Using Server Core and DHCP

DHCP is also a role that is supported in a Windows Server 2008 Core installation. DHCP installation is handled via the command line of the Server Core installation. However, management of the DHCP server (as well as the DHCP scopes) can be controlled from a remote Windows Server 2008 system. In this section, we will install the DHCP role and configure a DHCP scope using the Server Core command line. Let's begin by installing the role:

1. Sign in to your Windows Server 2008 Core Server system.

2. Install the DHCP bits. To do this, type in **start /w ocsetup DHCPServerCore** (Figure 1.14).

Figure 1.14 Installing the DHCP Role

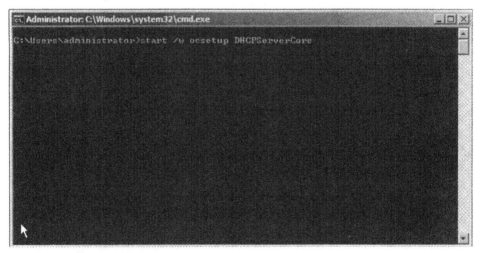

3. Start the DHCP service and set it to start automatically. To do this, type in **sc config dhcpserver start= auto**.

4. Type **sc query dhcpserver**. If the service is not running, start it by typing **sc start dhcpserver**. You can see the command syntax in Figure 1.15.

Figure 1.15 Starting the DHCP Role

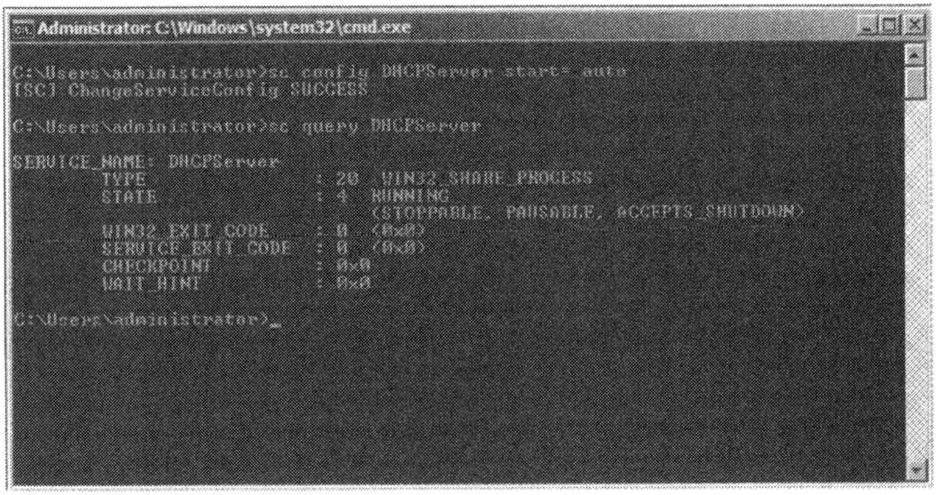

5. Next, we need to configure our DHCP server by adding the DHCP scope. To do this, we must first start the **netsh** application. At the command prompt, type **netsh**.

6. At the **netsh>** prompt, type **dhcp server**.

7. Add the DHCP Scope at the **dhcp server>** prompt by typing in **initiate auth**.

8. Add the scope by typing in **add scope 10.0.0.0 255.0.0.0 BackupScope**. 10.0.0.0 indicates the network leased by the DHCP server, while 255.0.0.0 represents the subnet mask. BackupScope is the name we've given to the scope.

9. Type in **scope 10.0.0.0**. This allows us to begin adjusting the scope options.

10. Configure the start and end of the lease range. To set the start of the range, type **set optionvalue 003 IPAddress 10.0.0.1**.

11. To set the end of the range, type **set optionvalue 006 IPAddress 10.0.0.50**.

12. Enable the scope by typing in **set state 1**.

13. Type **exit** to close the netsh application. The preceding syntax can be seen in Figure 1.16.

Figure 1.16 The *netsh* Syntax for DHCP

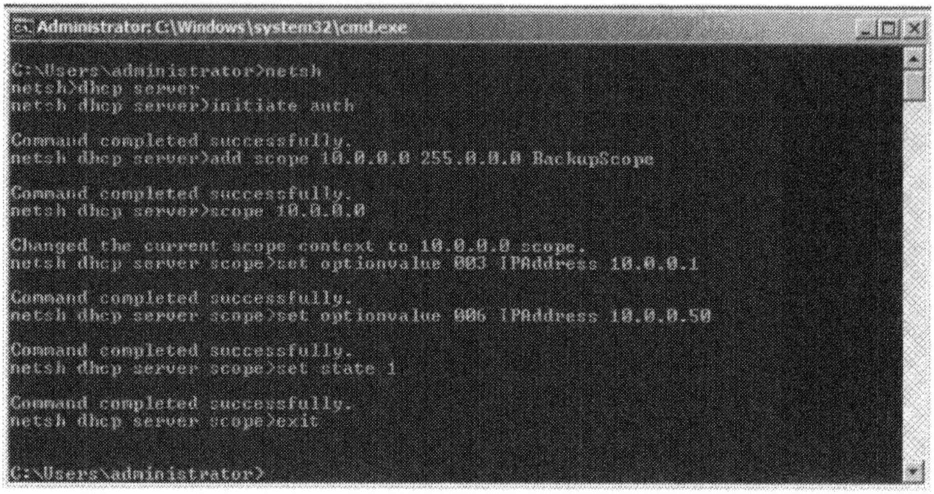

Configuring DHCP for DNS

We discussed dynamic updates earlier in this chapter, but it is important to note that, by default, DHCP does not automatically update DNS servers. Instead, DHCP can update DNS in two different ways—it can either pass fully qualified domain name (FQDN) information to client computers running Windows Server or Workstation 2000 (or later), which can in turn update DNS themselves, *or* DHCP can be configured to update DNS for legacy (or non-Windows) clients. Non-legacy Windows clients can update DNS when:

- Static IP address information is updated

- An IP address lease period ends and a new address is given to a client

- When the *ipconfig /registerdns* command is entered at a command prompt. This re-registers a client within DNS.

In order for clients to update automatically, we must adjust the properties of our DHCP scope appropriately by performing the following steps:

1. Choose **Start | Administrative Tools | DHCP**.

2. Right-click your IPv4 scope.

3. Click the **DNS** tab.

4. Notice that, by default, dynamic updates are set for DHCP to control updates only when requested by the client.

5. We need to set DHCP to also dynamically update clients (such as Windows NT 4.0) that cannot update automatically. Place a checkmark next to the **Dynamically Update DNS A And PTR Records For DHCP Clients That Do Not Request Updates** option.

6. Click **Apply** and then **OK**.

This is not required for IPv6 scopes since IPv6 was not available in these older operating systems.

Configuring Windows Internet Naming Service (WINS)

Windows Internet Naming Service (WINS) was originally developed by Microsoft as a part of Windows NT. Similar to DNS, WINS adds an IP address-to-system name mapping in a server-side database. Unlike DNS, WINS focused solely on the hostname and does not offer a complete naming structure. WINS is a service that has been "going away" since Windows 2000 Server, and yet it remains part of Windows even today.

Many problems existed with WINS, particularly in terms of scalability. Over the years, the need for WINS and NetBIOS name resolution has been greatly reduced. However, some applications (legacy versions of Outlook, for example) still require NetBIOS resolution. In certain situations, *LMHOST* files can be used in the absence of a WINS server. LMHOST files have their own problems and limitations as well—most specifically, the fact that LMHOST files can become outdated and contain incorrect data. They require constant updating and maintenance. Similar to DHCP, once the need for NetBIOS name resolution goes beyond a handful of systems, using WINS is a much more reasonable solution since it allows for dynamic updates. Interestingly enough, WINS has become such an afterthought that the TechNet site for WINS under Windows Server 2008 simply refers you to the documents for Windows Server 2003.

Your first task in developing a WINS design is to determine whether you need WINS at all. One thing you need to test for is whether NetBIOS over TCP/IP is being used to communicate across the network. You can do this through the Performance. Once you determine whether NetBIOS naming is currently needed, your next task is to determine whether the network can function without NetBIOS naming at all. This will require you to test applications and services on a test network in a lab without using NetBIOS, LMHOSTS, or WINS.

The design of a WINS topology should take into account how WINS servers replicate. Each WINS server pushes or pulls the database from its replication partners. If you configure the replication partners so they replicate in a domino fashion, it will take several steps for any change to be updated across the network. The time for replication to fully synchronize across all WINS servers is called *convergence time*. The longer convergence takes, the higher the likelihood of errors. To reduce convergence time, you can create a hub and spoke topology in which all WINS servers replicate with a central WINS server. In this topology, you will have the result of a two-step replication process at any point in time when an update is made on any WINS server in the network. Windows Server 2008 DNS is compatible with WINS. You can use both in a network environment that has WINS clients and DNS clients. We will discuss this a little later in the chapter.

Keep in mind that WINS is a flat file database. All names are considered equal, and as such, must be unique. This means you can only have one computer named Ned and one computer named Joe. When there are two computers configured with the same NetBIOS name, only the first will be able to access the network.

Older Microsoft networks not only used WINS, but also transmitted data across NetBEUI, a protocol that does not incorporate a network layer. Without a network layer, NetBEUI is not routable. However, NetBIOS can be routed over TCP/IP or even over IPX. In the Windows Server 2003 and Windows Server 2008 operating systems, NetBIOS is only routed over TCP/IP, if it is used at all.

If you determine that you will install or upgrade an existing WINS network, you must first determine whether the hardware of your server will be sufficient for WINS. WINS servers use their hard disks quite heavily, so you should make certain you have sufficient hard disk performance.

You should also determine how many WINS servers you should deploy. A single WINS server with sufficient hardware and network performance can provide services to 10,000 clients. You should always plan for at least two WINS servers for redundancy.

WINS has the ability to integrate with DNS so DNS clients can use DNS to look up records in the WINS database. This helps in case a network has client computers running non-Microsoft operating systems, such as Unix or Linux. To use the WINS Lookup Integration feature, you must add a special WINS resource record for the WINS servers on the network.

From the client perspective, you should be aware of how the node types will affect the communication preferences of the client computer. Node types affect the type of WINS traffic that traverses the network. For example, if you want to avoid all broadcast traffic, you would configure WINS clients to be p-nodes because they do not invoke broadcasts to resolve NetBIOS names. You can then configure DHCP to tell a computer what type of WINS node it will be. The options you have are:

- **b-node** A b-node depends on broadcasts to register and resolve names. If there are no WINS servers configured, this is the default node type used.

- **h-node** An h-node will search the configured WINS server first, and then resort to broadcasts, followed by LMHOSTS, and then DNS to register and resolve names.

- **m-node** The m-node is the opposite of an h-node. It will broadcast first, and then search the configured WINS server.

- **p-node** A p-node only uses point-to-point connections with a configured WINS server.

Understanding WINS Replication

If WINS is a network service that you will require in your organization, it will be important to understand how WINS handles redundancy and partnerships. In order for WINS servers to replicate WINS records with each other, a replication partnership must be configured between them. Three possible kinds of replication partnerships can be configured between WINS servers: *push/pull* (also known as *full*), *push-only*, and *pull-only* (also known as *limited*). You can set up a replication partnership manually or implement it automatically.

Automatic Partner Configuration

Automatic partner configuration is an option that can be implemented on small networks to eliminate the administrative effort of configuring replication partnerships between WINS servers. When the automatic partner configuration is enabled, the WINS server will send announcements using the multicast Internet Group Messaging Protocol (IGMP) address at 224.0.1.24, which is the well-known multicast address for WINS servers. When the WINS server discovers other WINS servers that are announcing themselves, the WINS server will automatically configure a partnership agreement between itself and the discovered WINS server. (Both must be enabled for automatic partner configuration.) When the WINS server discovers another WINS server, it will add the server to its list of replication partners, configure push/pull replication between the servers, and set the pull replication interval for every two hours.

Normally, routers do not forward IGMP traffic, so this configuration is best used on small unsegmented LANs. However, it is possible to configure routers to forward this traffic, allowing automatic partner configuration to be used in a routed environment. If the environment has only a few routers, the amount of multicast broadcast traffic should be minimal.

Push Partnerships

As the name implies, when a push partnership is configured, changes in the WINS database are *pushed* to the remote WINS server. More accurately, a WINS server with records to replicate sends a push notification to target servers (those configured to use it as a pull partner), alerting them that it has records to update on the target WINS servers. The push notification includes an owner table that lists the owner IDs and the highest version ID for each owner. The target servers compare this information with their own owner tables to determine which records to replicate. The target servers reply to the push notification with a pull request, and the transfer of records takes place. Accordingly, since a transfer of records will not take place until a pull request has been received by the server that sent the push notification, pull replication is the single mechanism for replication. The process for push replication occurs as follows:

1. The source WINS server receives updates to its database and, based on a configurable threshold, sends a push notification to the destination WINS server (its push partner), indicating it has updates to replicate.

2. The destination WINS server for the notification (the push partner) responds by initiating a pull request to its pull partner (the WINS server that sent the notification), and the replication is initiated between the replication partners.

Push replication is not schedulable according to an interval of time. Rather, the WINS administrator configures an update threshold that will trigger a push notification. For example, the WINS server could be configured to send a notification to its push partner after it has received 100 updates.

It is also possible to manually initiate the push notification. When you manually initiate the push notification, you can choose to push the notification to the replication partner or trigger the replication to send a notification to all its partners as well. As an example, consider a replication topology where three WINS servers are configured as push replication partners. WINS-A replicates to WINS-B, which replicates to WINS-C. So, if you manually sent a push notification from WINS-A to its replication partner, WINS-B, you could force WINS-B to also send a push notification to its other replication partner, WINS-C.

In certain rare situations, it might be desirable to use a *push-only* replication partnership for one-way replication—for instance, from a head office to a branch office. As an example, suppose WINS-A in the head office configures WINS-B in the branch office as its push-only partner. (WINS-B should also configure WINS-A as its pull-only partner.) When WINS-A receives updates to its records, it notifies WINS-B, which sends an update (pull) request to WINS-A for the changed records since the last replication cycle. In this scenario, WINS-B never sends its updated records to WINS-A.

Push partnerships are generally configured in LAN environments where bandwidth is not an issue, and it is not necessary to schedule replication to occur during off-peak hours. In general, you should use push replication partnerships in the following situations:

- There is ample bandwidth over LAN or WAN connections.

- There is a need to ensure that updates are replicated as soon as possible and the frequency of replication traffic is not a consideration.

Pull Partnerships

Pull replication differs from push replication in that the replication frequency is defined as an interval of time. At regularly scheduled intervals, a pull partner requests updates from other WINS servers (those configured to use it as a push partner) for updated records that have a higher version ID than the ones it currently has in its database.

Pull replication is configured similarly to push replication. The primary difference is that the WINS administrator schedules the times that the pull replication will take place.

In some situations, it might be desirable to configure *pull-only* replication between replication partners. Usually, this configuration is implemented where WAN links are operating close to capacity and there is a need to schedule WINS replication during off-peak hours. Pull-only replication has an advantage over push-only replication in that the replication schedule can be known in advance. With push-only replication, replication is triggered by reaching a configured threshold of updates, and you can only estimate when this would occur based on experience with the network. However, a disadvantage of pull-only replication is that the WINS server could potentially have acquired a large number of updates to replicate between cycles.

In general, you should use pull replication partnerships in the following situations:

■   There is limited bandwidth between WINS servers that requires replication to be scheduled during off hours.

■   There is a need to consolidate updates and reduce the frequency and amount of replication traffic.

■   There is a need to exercise finer control over the timing and frequency of replication traffic.

Push/Pull Partnerships

A push/pull partnership is the default when you configure replication between WINS servers. In fact, Microsoft recommends a push/pull partnership as a best practice and it further recommends that all WINS partnerships be set up this way, unless there is an overriding need to implement a limited partnership. The only need that Microsoft cites for a limited partnership is the presence of a large network connected by relatively slow WAN links. Microsoft often stresses the need for simplicity in a WINS environment.

With a push/pull partnership, a WINS server will be configured both to send push notifications and to make pull requests to its replication partner. The replication partner will also be configured in a similar way. Such a configuration helps ensure that synchronization among WINS servers is optimal, depending on the pull schedule and the configured threshold for push notifications, among other factors. For example, suppose a WINS server suddenly experiences a large number of updates and immediately sends a push notification to its push partner. The push partner would immediately request these updates, without waiting for the request to be triggered by its pull schedule. Conversely, a WINS server always pulls up-to-date records from its pull partner according to the replication schedule, regardless of how few records have been updated on the pull partner WIN server.

You should always try to deploy a push/pull partnership, unless there is an over-riding concern that requires the implementation of a limited partnership.

Replication Models

As we mentioned earlier, the replication model you design will have an effect on the convergence time for replicated WINS records and fault tolerance for replicated records.

A replication model that is appropriate for your network topology will ensure the shortest convergence time for replicated WINS records. Where possible, it is recommended your replication model mirror your network topology and that you keep this model as simple as possible.

In WINS environments where there are three or more WINS servers, you can employ either a *ring* replication model or a *hub-and-spoke* replication model. In more complex environments, these models can be combined to ensure optimal convergence time and fault tolerance for a given network topology. In the following sections, we will discuss each of these models in more detail.

Ring Models

In a ring model, three or more WINS servers are configured to replicate with one another in a circular fashion. The ring model provides for good convergence times for all replication partners when there are no more than four WINS servers.

In this model, fault tolerance for replication of WINS records is given priority. Imagine that a record is updated on WINS-A. The record must travel through either WINS-A or WINS-B before it is replicated to WINS-C. However, suppose that the WAN link connecting WINS-A and WINS-D fails. The updated record can still arrive at WINS-C and WINS-D (via WINS-C). Conversely, a record created on WINS-D can still be replicated to WINS-A via WINS-C and WINS-B.

Hub-and-Spoke Models

In a hub-and-spoke model, all WINS servers replicate with a centrally located hub WIN server. The hub-and-spoke model provides for the shortest convergence time in a replication environment that comprises five or more WINS servers, because it provides for the shortest replication paths between any two WINS servers. Furthermore, by implementing a hub-and-spoke model, you reduce the number of replication partnership agreements that you need to maintain.

Even though there are five WINS servers that replicate information, there are only four replication agreements to maintain. Furthermore, no server is more than two hops from any other server, regardless of the number of servers added to the topology.

A disadvantage of this model is that it is not as fault tolerant as the ring model. If WINS-A fails, no WINS server will be able to replicate its records to other WINS servers. Furthermore, depending on the average number of records the spoke WINS servers need to replicate and the settings for the push and pull triggers, WINS-A can be continuously replicating with other servers and processing updates. It should be well connected to the other WINS servers and have the capacity to handle the load.

To enhance fault tolerance in this situation, you could set up a backup WINS server in the same location as WINS-A and configure a replication partnership agreement between them. This solution, however, increases administrative complexity for the maintenance of replication partnerships. An alternative solution that still provides a high degree of availability is to use Windows clustering for the hub WINS server.

A Windows cluster gives you the ability to set up separate WINS servers, known as *cluster nodes*, that use the same database located in a shared SCSI or Fibre Channel device. When the WINS server that is the active node in the cluster fails, the services will *failover* to another node. Failover is the process of taking resources offline in one node and bringing them online in a new node. The primary advantage of using a Windows cluster is that in the event of a failure of a WINS server, no subsequent replication needs to occur to synchronize records when the failed server is brought online, because only a single database is used.

Hybrid Replication Models

In many situations, it is desirable to combine replication models. As an example, consider a large organization that has three divisions in different geographic locations. Each of these divisions has a number of branch offices that are connected to their respective divisional offices. It might be advantageous to use a ring model of WINS replication among the divisional offices and use hub-and-spoke replication for replication between the divisional offices and their respective branch offices. Many other variations are possible. A hybrid replication model can employ any mixture of full and limited replication partnerships, driven by the contingencies of the network topology.

Static WINS Entries

One of the advantages of using WINS is that it provides a way to dynamically register NetBIOS names, eliminating the need for static entries in LMHOSTS files. However, certain situations require the use of static mappings in the WINS server database. For example, if you have non-WINS clients that are running NetBIOS applications, you might find it desirable to have entries for these clients in the WINS database so you can allow WINS clients to resolve the NetBIOS names of those clients. Static mappings are superior to entries in an LMHOSTS file because they can be replicated throughout the WINS infrastructure.

The use of static mappings can create problems on your network. Unlike dynamic mappings, static mappings stay in the WINS database until they are manually removed. (The expiration date for the static mapping entry in the WINS database is labeled as *infinite*.) Furthermore, unless the migrate on setting is enabled, static mappings are not overwritten by dynamic mappings. For example, a client computer might be given a static mapping in the WINS database, or an LMHOSTS file might be imported to the WINS database, creating a number of static WINS entries. If the clients associated with the static mappings are later configured as WINS clients, they would not be able to perform dynamic registration of their NetBIOS names, unless the migrate on setting was enabled.

NOTE

Even though the migrate on setting can prevent a number of problems associated with the ability to overwrite static entries, this setting does not affect all NetBIOS record types. For example, the domain [1Ch] record type is never overwritten, regardless of this setting.

In general, static entries should never be created for WINS-capable client computers. However, it is sometimes desirable for security purposes to use static entries for mission-critical servers to prevent redirection.

Now that you understand the purpose of WINS design fundamentals, as well as some of the history behind it, let's take a look at how to configure WINS in Windows Server 2008.

Installing and Configuring

Unlike DNS and DHCP, WINS is a *feature* of Windows Server 2008, not a *role*. Features in Windows Server 2008 simply augment the functionality of roles. In this scenario, WINS is a feature used to add functionality to name resolution as a whole. That said, we will discuss how to integrate WINS with DNS later in this section. Let's install our WINS feature:

1. Choose **Start | Administrative Tools | Server Manager**.

2. Scroll down to the **Features Summary** section and click **Add Features**.

3. At the **Select Features** window, scroll down and click **WINS Server** and then click **Next**.

4. Click **Install** to begin the installation process.

5. Click **Close** once the installation is complete.

Using Server Core for WINS

Installing a feature in Windows Server 2008 Server Core is basically the same as adding a role. In this section, we are going to walk though the setup of the feature, as well as set the role to start automatically.

As you know from Chapter 1 of this book, very few roles can be installed as part of Windows Server 2008 Server Core. However, many *features* can be installed, including:

■ Failover Cluster

■ Network Load Balancing

■ Subsystem for Unix-based applications

■ Multipath IO

■ Removable Storage Management

■ BitLocker Drive Encryption

■ Backup

■ Simple Network Management Protocol (SNMP)

■ WINS

Obviously, at this point in this book, we are only focusing on WINS. So, let's take a look at how to install the WINS feature and start the service:

1. At the command line, type **start /w ocsetup WINS-SC**.

2. When installation completes, type **sc query WINS** or **NET START** to verify that the WINS service is running.

3. If the service is not running, type **sc start WINS**.

4. We can also verify that the service will start automatically by typing **sc config WINS start= auto**.

Generally speaking, management of WINS will occur via the GUI from another Windows Server. However, a number of command-line management options exist for WINS. Essentially, most of the management will be through the *netsh* tool, which we used earlier for setting IP information. To learn more about these commands, visit http://technet2.microsoft.com/WindowsServer/en/library/430701f0-743a-4af5-9dd6-95c5c2f956531033.mspx.

Configuring WINS for DNS

As mentioned, WINS has become less relevant in organizations that are running the latest operating systems and applications. However, there *are* situations where WINS is still necessary. One way we can improve name resolution is to tie WINS to DNS so the two are aware of one another, thereby increasing response time to name requests and reducing complexity in name resolution scenarios. Let's look at how we configure DNS to use WINS as a secondary resource for naming:

1. Choose **Start | Administrative Tools | DNS**.

2. Find your server name in the left pane and double-click it. This will open the DNS configuration for this server.

3. Right-click your domain name and select **Properties**.

4. Select the **WINS** tab.

5. Place a checkmark next to the **Use WINS Forward Lookup** option.

6. Enter the IP address of the WINS server and click **Add**.

7. Click **Apply** and **OK** to save your changes.

DNS will now be able to forward requests to WINS to resolve names not found within its own namespace.

Summary

Having the proper network services installed on your server can make the difference between a functional Active Directory environment, and one that is infested with various errors and latency. Microsoft focused on the Core Infrastructure Optimization model—taking IT organizations from a "basic" approach to infrastructure design to a more dynamic one. DNS, DHCP, and even WINS are steps that move IT professionals from the basic model. Imagine the time (and pain) involved in updating spreadsheets with client IP addresses, HOSTS, and LMHOSTS files on client machines for a 500-PC organization!

DNS truly is the backbone of the Windows network. Without DNS, Active Directory would cease to function. When it comes to Active Directory, DNS does much more than simple name resolution. It stores information about our LDAP resources, Global Catalog resources, as well as other resources (such as SIP servers) within our environment. If a client or server is unable to find these resource records, having Active Directory in place does us very little good. As an IT professional, you will also be required to understand the different types of Resource Records (RRs) that can be used as part of DNS. There are traditional—or more common—Resource Records such as A and PTR records, but you should also familiarize yourself with special records such as SIP records, since the demand for these types of records is becoming more and more common.

DHCP is another crucial piece of the network services puzzle. Again, trying to maintain static addresses for hundreds of systems is not only impractical, it is quite foolish. Trying to maintain IP ranges for IPv4 systems is cumbersome enough, but trying to do it with the extended IPv6 addresses will likely become impossible! Add in the additional information we can push out to our DHCP clients (such as gateways, Trivial File Transfer Protocol [TFTP] servers, time clock servers, and domain suffixes, for example) and it makes this a crucial tool in the IT professional's toolbox. Anyone who is familiar with the Microsoft management consoles can probably create and authorize a DHCP scope, but it takes a skilled professional to correctly design and implement a DHCP strategy. In order to do this, you need to understand not only fundamental IP principles, but also network topologies and common requirements, such as the 80/20 rule.

Lastly, we have WINS. Although it is going away, there are still places in certain organizations where it is necessary. Older Microsoft networks not only used WINS, but also transmitted data across NetBEUI, a protocol that does not incorporate a network layer. Without a network layer, NetBEUI is not routable. However, NetBIOS can be routed over TCP/IP or even over IPX. In the Windows Server 2003 and Windows Server 2008 operating systems, NetBIOS is only routed over TCP/IP, if it is used at all. The replication model you design will have an effect on the convergence time for replicated WINS records and fault tolerance for replicated records. A replication model that is appropriate for your network topology will ensure the shortest convergence time for replicated WINS records. Where possible, it is recommended that your replication model mirror your network topology and that you keep this model as simple as possible. If NetBIOS resolution is only necessary for a few systems, you should consider using GlobalNames zone as an alternative.

Will we still see WINS in the next version of Windows? Only time will tell.

Solutions Fast Track

Configuring Domain Name System (DNS)

- ☑ DNS in Windows Server 2008 supports primary zones (including Active Directory–integrated zones), secondary zones, and stub zones.

- ☑ Active Directory–integrated zones provide additional functionality, including secure dynamic updates and Active Directory–integrated replication.

- ☑ The GlobalNames zone was introduced to help phase out the Windows Internet Naming Service. The GlobalNames zone requires the creation of a zone named GlobalNames.

Configuring Dynamic Host Configuration Protocol (DHCP)

- ☑ Since the inception of DHCP, there have been a number of add-on DHCP options that make it possible to disburse even more IP-related information to clients, which makes IP management much more flexible for IT administrators.

- ☑ DHCP works by "leasing" IP addresses for a period of time to a specific computer. The lease time can be adjusted based on the need for a client to maintain the address for a period of time.

- ☑ DHCP can also be used to "reserve" addresses for systems that would otherwise need a static address, such as departmental servers and some client machines where it is required by third-party applications.

☑ The 80/20 rule means that IP scopes should be split between DHCP servers, and that server A can distribute 80 percent of IP addresses, while server B can hand out the remaining 20 percent of IP addresses.

Configuring Windows Internet Naming Service (WINS)

☑ WINS was originally introduced by Microsoft as part of Windows NT Server and was intended to be the de facto name resolution solution.

☑ WINS is still required for the NetBIOS name resolution of legacy operating systems and applications.

☑ WINS can be incorporated into DNS to provide seamless name resolution.

Frequently Asked Questions

Q: Is the GlobalNames zone intended to replace WINS?

A: No. In fact, Microsoft has gone out of its way to stress the fact that the GlobalNames Zone is not a replacement for WINS. The GlobalNames zone is simply intended to assist in the retirement of WINS. As companies upgrade their legacy operations systems and legacy applications, the need for both GlobalNames zones and WINS will eventually go away.

Q: I have seen several examples where non-Internet standard DNS names are used. Is it better to use a standard DNS name (such as .com, .net, or .edu) or to use a private nonstandard name (for example, .ads or .internal)?

A: This really is a matter of preference—and in some cases, a bit of a "religious war." Separation of name spaces is common in organizations that do not want their external namespace (for example, uccentral.com) to match their internal namespace. This can be beneficial when you want to use similar server names both internally and externally. Separating namespaces can, however, create confusion at times when you try to tell someone to go to a server. For example, you may have a server called "mail," which could be an internal or external server, and if someone doesn't specify "mail.uccentral.ads," you may end up on the wrong server!

Q: Why did Microsoft make WINS a feature and not a role?

A: Simply put, WINS is a solution that is end-of-life. WINS alone cannot provide an enterprisewide solution for name resolution. In today's environment, we need DNS in order for Active Directory to function properly—we don't need WINS.

Q: I have a mixed Unix/Windows environment. Some of my DNS zones are hosted on BIND, and some on Windows Server 2008. Is there any way to integrate the two?

A: Yes, there are a few ways. First, you can create "secondary zones" on each of the DNS servers that stores a local copy of the other's zones. Second, you create "DNS Forwarders" on the Windows Servers, which will forward any requests for these zones to the BIND servers. Lastly, you can delegate DNS zones to the BIND or Windows servers for control over a particular zone.

Q: I like the idea of being able to implement DNS, WINS, and DHCP on a Windows Server 2008 Core Server installation. However, I'm not much of a command-line person. Is there any way I can manage these roles and features from a GUI?

A: Yes, however you must use the MMC from another Windows Server 2008 (full installation) server to manage these roles and features. If you recall, no GUIs are provided with Windows Server 2008 Core Server, even after a role has been installed.

Q: In the past when I've installed DNS with Active Directory onto a Windows Server, a domain called "." was created. Because of this, I couldn't get to external servers. Why does this happen?

A: Depending on how DNS was installed, it is possible for the "." (root) domain to be installed within your DNS. Because "." is the top-level DNS zone, if installed, it assumes that there are no other domains except those listed on the server itself. To fix this, you simply need to remove the "." from DNS.

Q: I see there are numerous options that I can push out via DHCP to client machines. What is the bare minimum I need in order to offer networking services?

A: The absolute bare minimum would be the IP address and subnet mask to communicate with a directly connected host on the same subnet. However, this will severely limit the resources that a client can contact outside of that subnet. Realistically, you need the IP address, subnet mask, gateway (called the router in the DHCP options), and at least one DNS server to at least be able to connect to and use the Internet through your Internet service provider (ISP) or to communicate with other hosts on remote subnetworks.

Q: I want to use Active Directory–integrated zones for my DNS servers, but I need to be able to create secondary copies of the zones to non-Microsoft servers. Is this possible?

A: Yes, but it couldn't be a live/replicated copy of the zone. In this scenario, you can only create a secondary copy of the DNS zone. This means that DNS clients of this non-Microsoft server will have the ability to resolve records, but the zone cannot be updated (either manually or via dynamic update).

## Chapter 2

Configuring the Active Directory Infrastructure

Solutions in this chapter:

- Working with Forests and Domains
- Working with Sites
- Working with Trusts

☑ Summary

☑ Solutions Fast Track

☑ Frequently Asked Questions

Introduction

A Microsoft Active Directory network has both a physical and a logical structure. Forests and domains define the logical structure of the network, with domains organized into domain trees in which subdomains (called child domains) can be created under parent domains in a branching structure. Domains are logical units that hold users, groups, computers, and organizational units (OUs, which in turn can contain users, groups, computers, and other OUs). Forests are collections of domain trees that have trust relationships with one another, but each domain tree has its own separate namespace.

In order to allow Active Directory to support the physical structure of your network, we will also discuss the configuration of Active Directory sites, site links, and subnet objects. Active Directory sites and subnets define the physical structure of an Active Directory network. Sites are important in an enterprise-level multiple location network, for creating a topology that optimizes the process of replicating Active Directory information between domain controllers (DCs). Sites are used for replication and for optimizing the authentication process by reducing authentication traffic across slow, high-cost WAN links. Site and subnet information is also used by Active Directory-enabled services to help clients find the nearest service providers.

In this chapter, you will learn all about the functions of forests and domains in the Windows Server 2008 Active Directory infrastructure, and we will walk you through the steps of creating a forest and domain structure for a network. You'll learn to create the forest root domain and a child domain, as well as the importance of Flexible Single Manager Operation (FSMO) roles within an Active Directory domain and forest. We will also discuss the role of sites in the Active Directory infrastructure, and how replication, authentication, and distribution of services information work within and across sites. We will explain the relationship of sites with domains and subnets, and how to create sites and site links. You'll also learn about site replication and how to plan, create, and manage a replication topology. We'll walk you through the steps of configuring replication between sites, and discuss how to troubleshoot replication failures.

In addition to these concepts, we will also discuss Active Directory trust relationships. Trust relationships define the ways in which users can access network resources across domains and forests. Without a trust between the domain to which a user belongs and the domain in which a resource resides, the user won't be able to access that file, folder, printer, or other resource. Hence, it is important for network administrators to understand how the built-in (implicit) trusts in the Active Directory network function, and how to create explicit trusts to provide access (or faster access) between domains.

Working with Forests and Domains

Active Directory is composed of a number of components, each associated with a different type of Active Directory functionality; you should understand each component before making any changes to the network. Active Directory Domain Services is a distributed database, which means it can be spread across multiple computers within a domain or a forest. Among the major logical components that you need to be familiar with are:

- Forests
- Trees
- Domains
- The domain namespace

Administrative boundaries, network and directory performance, security, resource management, and basic functionality are all dependent on the proper design and placement of these elements.

Figure 2.1 shows the logical view of a Windows Server 2008 Active Directory. Note that the differentiation between forests and trees is most obvious in the namespace. By its nature, a tree is one or more domains with a contiguous namespace. Each tree consists of one or more domains, and each forest consists of one or more trees. Because a forest can be composed of discrete multiple trees, a forest's namespace can be discontiguous. By discontiguous, we mean that the namespaces anchor to different forest-root domain name system (DNS) domains, such as cats.com and dogs.com. Both are top-level domains and are considered two trees in a forest when combined into a single directory, as shown in Figure 2.1.

Figure 2.1 The Logical View of a Windows Server 2008 Active Directory

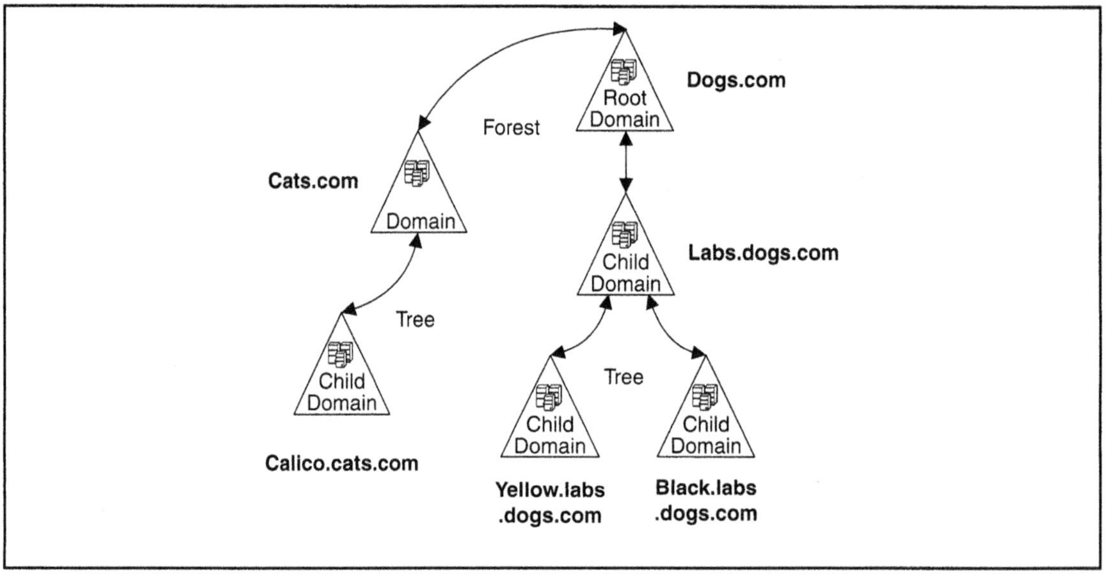

Understanding Forests

An Active Directory always begins with a *forest root domain*, which is automatically the first domain you install. This root domain becomes the foundation for additional directory components. As the cornerstone of your enterprise-computing environment, you should protect it well. Fault tolerance and good backups are not optional—they are essential. If an administrative error or hardware failure results in the unrecoverable loss of this root structure, the entire forest becomes inoperable. Certain forest objects and services are present only at the root (e.g., the Enterprise Administrators and Schema Administrators groups, and the Schema Master and Domain Naming Master FSMO roles which we will discuss later in this chapter).

Understanding Domains

The *domain* serves as the administrative boundary of Active Directory. It is the most basic component that can functionally host the directory. Simply put, Active Directory uses the domain as a container of computers, users, groups, and other object containers. Objects within the domain share a common directory database partition, replication boundaries and characteristics, security policies, and security relationships with other domains.

Typically, administrative rights granted in one domain are valid only within that domain. This also applies to Group Policy Objects (GPOs), but not necessarily to trust relationships, which you will learn more about later in the book. Security policies such as the password policy, account lockout policy, and Kerberos ticket policy are defined on a per-domain basis. The domain is also the primary boundary defining your DNS and NetBIOS namespaces. The DNS infrastructure is a requirement for an Active Directory domain, and should be defined before you create the domain.

There are several good reasons for a multiple-domain model, although a significant number of Active Directory implementations rely on a single-domain forest model. In the early days of Windows 2000, the most common recommendation was for a so-called "empty forest root" model, in which the forest root domain contains only built-in objects, and all manually created objects reside in one or more child domains. Whatever the design decision reached by your organization, it is a good practice to avoid installing additional domains unless you have a specific reason for them, as each additional domain in a forest incurs additional administrative overhead in the form of managing additional DCs and replication traffic. Some of the more common reasons to create additional domains include:

- Groups of users with different security policy requirements, such as strong authentication and strict access controls.

- Groups of users requiring additional autonomy, or administrative separation for security reasons.

- A requirement for decentralized administration due to political, budgetary, time zone, or policy pressures.

- A requirement for unique namespaces.

- Controlling excessive directory replication traffic by breaking the domain into smaller, more manageable pieces. This often occurs in an extremely large domain, or due to a combination of geographical separation and unreliable WAN links.

- Maintaining a preexisting NT domain structure.

You can think of a domain tree as a DNS namespace composed of one or more domains. If you plan to create a forest with discontiguous namespaces, you must create more than one tree. Referring back to Figure 2.1, you see two trees in that forest, Cats.com and Dogs.com. Each has a *contiguous namespace* because each domain in the hierarchy is directly related to the domains above and below it in each tree. The forest has a *discontiguous namespace* because it contains two unrelated top-level domains.

The primary Active Directory partitions, also called *naming contexts*, are replicated among all DCs within a domain. These three partitions are the schema partition, the configuration partition, and the domain partition.

- The **schema partition** contains the *classSchema* and the *attributeSchema* objects that make up the directory schema. These classes and attributes define all possible types of objects and object properties within the forest. Every DC in the entire forest has a replica of the schema partition.

- The **configuration partition**, replicated identically on all DCs throughout the forest, contains Active Directory's replication topology and other configuration data.

- The **domain partition** contains the local domain objects, such as computers, users, and groups, which all share the same security policies and security relationships with other domains. If multiple DCs exist within a domain, they contain a replica of the same domain partition. If multiple domains exist within a forest, each domain contains a unique domain partition.

Because each domain contains unique principles and resources, there must be some way for other domains to locate them. Active Directory contains objects that adhere to a naming convention called the DN, or *distinguished name*. The DN contains enough detail to locate a replica of the partition that holds the object in question. Unfortunately, most users and applications do not know the DN, or what partition might contain it. To fulfill that role, Active Directory uses the *Global Catalog (GC)*, which can locate DNs based on one or more specific attributes of the needed object. (We will discuss the GC later in this chapter.)

Forest and Domain Functional Levels

Forest functional levels and *domain functional levels* are a mechanism that Microsoft uses to support backward compatibility with previous versions of Active Directory, and to expose more advanced functionality as functional levels are raised. Functional levels are a feature that helps improve performance and security. In Windows 2000, each domain had two functional levels (which were called "modes"), native mode and mixed mode, and the forest had only one functional level. Windows Server 2003 introduced two more functional levels to consider in both domains and forests. Windows Server 2008 drops support for two legacy functional levels that were designed to support Windows NT Backup Domain Controllers, and adds another forest and domain functional level to support pure Windows Server 2008 environments. To enable the Windows Server 2008 forest and domain-wide features, all DCs must be running Windows Server 2008 and the functional levels must be set to Windows Server 2008. Table 2.1 summarizes the levels, DCs supported in each level, and each level's primary purpose.

Table 2.1 Domain and Forest Functional Levels

Type	Functional Level	Supported DCs	Purpose
Domain Default	Windows 2000	2000, 2003, 2008	Supports upgrades from 2000 to 2008; no support for NT backup domain controllers (BDCs).
Domain	Windows Server 2003	2003, 2008	Supports upgrades from 2003 to 2008; all Windows Server 2003 domain-wide Active Directory features are enabled.
Domain	Windows Server 2008	2008	Provides support for all features of Windows Server 2008 Active Directory
Forest Default	Windows 2000	2000, 2003, 2008	Supports mixed environments during upgrade; lower security, high compatibility
Forest	Windows Server 2003	2003, 2008	Supports upgrades from 2003 to 2008; all Windows Server 2008 Active Directory features are enabled.
Forest	Windows Server 2008	2008	Provides support for all features of Windows Server 2008 Active Directory

Using Domain Functional Levels

Active Directory technology debuted with Windows 2000. Now, with Windows Server 2008, it has been refined and enhanced. Active Directory is now easier to deploy, is more efficient at replication, has improved administration, and poses a better end-user experience. Some features are enabled right away, whereas others require a complete migration of DCs to the new release before they become available. There are countless new features, the most significant of which we will discuss next.

Using the Windows 2000 Domain Functional Level

The Windows 2000 domain functional level is the default domain functional level in Windows Server 2008, and is primarily intended to support an upgrade from Windows 2000 to Windows Server 2008. This domain functional level offers full compatibility with all down-level operating systems for Active Directory DCs, and is characterized by the following features:

- Microsoft Windows NT 4.0 DCs are not supported.

The following Active Directory features are supported in this mode:

- Universal Security Groups
- Group nesting
- Converting groups between distribution and security groups
- SIDHistory

The following Active Directory features are *not* supported in this mode:

- DC rename
- Logon timestamp attribute updated and replicated
- User password support on the *InetOrgPerson objectClass*
- Constrained delegation
- Users and Computers container redirection
- Can be raised to the Windows Server 2003 or Windows Server 2008 domain functional level

Windows Server 2003 Domain Functional Level

The Windows Server 2003 domain functional level supports both Windows Server 2003 and Windows Server 2008 DCs. This level does not allow for the presence of Windows NT or Windows 2000 DCs, and is designed to support an upgrade from 2003 to 2008. All 2003 Active Directory domain features are enabled at this level, providing a good balance between security and backward compatibility.

DCs *not* supported at this level:

- Windows NT 4.0 DCs
- Windows 2000 DCs

The following Active Directory domain-wide functions are supported at both this level and the Windows 2000 domain functional level:

- Universal Security Groups
- Group nesting
- Converting groups between distribution and security groups
- SIDHistory

The following upgraded Active Directory domain-wide functionality is supported at this domain functional level:

- DC rename
- Logon timestamp attribute updated and replicated
- User password support on the *InetOrgPerson objectClass*
- Constrained delegation
- Users and Computers container redirection
- Can be raised to the Windows Server 2008 domain functional level
- Can never be lowered to the Windows 2000 domain functional level

In the Windows Server 2003 domain functional level, only Windows Server 2003 and Windows Server 2008 DCs can exist.

Windows Server 2008 Domain Functional Level

The Windows Server 2008 domain functional level supports only Windows Server 2008 DCs. This level does not allow for the presence of Windows NT, Windows 2000, or Windows Server 2003, and is designed to support the most advanced Active Directory feature set possible. All 2008 Active Directory domain features are enabled at this level, providing the highest level of security and functionality and the lowest level of backward compatibility.

The following Windows Server 2008 domain-wide functions are supported only at this level:

- Distributed File System (DFS) replication support for the Windows Server 2008 System Volume (SYSVOL) share, providing more robust and fault-tolerant replication of SYSVOL and its contents

- Advanced Encryption Standard (AES 128 and AES 256) encryption support for the Kerberos protocol

Logging of Last Interactive Logon Information, including:

- The time of the last successful interactive logon for a user

- The name of the workstation from which the used logged on

- The number of failed logon attempts since the last logon

- Fine-grained password policies, which allow you to specify password and account lockout policies for individual users and groups within an Active Directory domain

- Cannot be raised to any higher domain functional level, because no higher level exists at this time

- Can never be lowered to the Windows 2000 or Windows Server 2003 domain functional level

In the Windows Server 2008 domain functional level, only Windows Server 2008 DCs can exist.

Configuring Forest Functional Levels

The Windows Server 2008 forest functional levels are named similarly to the domain functional levels, and serve a similar purpose. Table 2.1 summarizes the levels, the DCs supported in each level, and each level's primary purpose.

As with domain functional levels, each forest functional level carries over the features from lower levels, and activates new features as well. These new features apply across every domain in your forest. After you raise the forest functional level, earlier OSs cannot be promoted to DCs. For example, Windows NT 4.0 BDCs are not supported by any forest functional level, and Windows 2000 DCs cannot be part of the forest except through external or forest trusts once the forest level has been raised to Windows Server 2003.

Windows 2000 Forest Functional Level (default)

The Windows 2000 forest functional level is primarily designed to support mixed environments during the course of an upgrade. Typically, this applies to a transition from Windows 2000 to Windows Server 2003 or Windows Server 2008. It is also the default mode for a newly created Windows Server 2008 domain. It is characterized by relatively lower-security features and reduced efficiency, but maintains the highest compatibility level possible for Active Directory. In the Windows 2000 forest functional level:

- Windows 2000, Windows Server 2003, and Windows Server 2008 DCs are supported
- Windows NT 4.0 BDCs are *not* supported

A Windows Server 2008 forest at the Windows 2000 forest functional level can be raised to either the Windows 2003 or the Windows Server 2008 forest functional level.

Windows Server 2003 Forest Functional Level

The Windows Server 2003 forest functional level enables a number of forest-wide features that were not available at the Windows 2000 forest functional level, and is designed to allow for a 2003 to 2008 upgrade process. This level does not allow for the presence of Windows NT or Windows 2000 DCs anywhere in the forest. All Windows Server 2003 Active Directory forest features are enabled at this level, as follows:

- DCs *not* supported at this level:
  - Windows NT 4.0 DCs
  - Windows 2000 DCs
- All new Active Directory forest features are supported at this level.

The following forest-wide improvements are available at this forest functional level:

- Efficient group member replication using linked value replication

- Improved Knowledge Consistency Checker (KCC) intersite replication topology generator algorithms

- ISTG aliveness no longer replicated

- Attributes added to the GC, such as ms-DS-Entry-Time-To-Die, Message Queuing-Secured-Source, Message Queuing-Multicast-Address, Print-Memory, Print-Rate, and Print-Rate-Unit

- Defunct schema objects

- Cross-forest trust

- Domain rename

- Dynamic auxiliary classes

- InetOrgPerson objectClass change

- Application groups

- Reduced NTDS.DIT size

- Improvements in intersite replication topology management

- Can be raised to the Windows Server 2008 forest functional level

- Cannot be downgraded to the Windows 2000 forest functional level without performing a full forest recovery

In the Windows Server 2003 forest functional level, both Windows Server 2003 and Windows Server 2008 DCs can exist.

Windows Server 2008 Forest Functional Level

The Windows Server 2008 forest functional level is the highest forest functional level available in Windows Server 2008, and supports only Windows Server 2008 DCs in each domain within a forest. At present, this forest functional level does not expose any new functionality over and above the 2003 forest functional level. The primary advantage of the 2008 forest functional level at present is that, once you have raised the functional level to 2008, any domains that are subsequently added to the forest will be automatically created at the Windows Server 2008 domain functional level.

Raising Forest and Domain Functional Levels

Before increasing a functional level, you should prepare for it by performing the following steps:

1. Inventory your domain or forest for DCs that are running any earlier versions of the Windows Server operating system.

2. *Physically* locate any down-level DCs in the domain or forest as needed, and either upgrade or remove them.

3. Verify that end-to-end replication is working in the forest using repadmin. exe and/or dcdiag.exe.

4. Verify the compatibility of your applications and services with the version of Windows that your DCs will be running, and specifically their compatibility with the target functional level. Use a lab environment to test for compatibility issues, and contact the appropriate vendors for compatibility information.

When you are considering raising the domain functionality level, remember that the new features will directly affect only the domain being raised. The two domain functional levels available to raise are:

- Windows Server 2003
- Windows Server 2008

Once the functional level of a particular domain has been raised, no prior version DCs can be added to the domain. In the case of the Windows Server 2003 domain functional level, no Windows 2000 servers can be promoted to DC status after the functionality has been raised. In the case of the Windows Server 2008 domain functional level, no Windows Server 2003 DCs can be added to the domain after the functional level has been raised to Windows Server 2008.

Raising the Domain Functional Level

Before raising the functional level of a domain, all DCs must be upgraded to the minimum OS level as shown in Table 2.1. Remember that when you raise the domain functional level to Windows Server 2003 or Windows Server 2008, it can never be changed back to a previous domain functional level. The following Sidebar takes you systematically through the process of verifying the current domain functional level. The following Sidebar takes you through the process of raising the domain functional level. To raise the domain functional level, you must be a Domain Admin in the domain in question.

Configuring & Implementing...

Verifying the Domain Functional Level

1. Log on as a Domain Admin of the domain you are checking.

2. Click on **Start | Control Panel | Performance and Maintenance | Administrative Tools | Active Directory Users and Computers**, or use the Microsoft Management Console (MMC) preconfigured with the Active Directory Users and Computers snap-in.

3. Locate the domain in the console tree that you are going to raise in functional level. Right-click the domain and select **Raise Domain Functional Level**.

4. In the Raise Domain Functional Level dialog box, the current domain functional level appears under **Current domain functional level**.

Configuring & Implementing...

Raising the Domain Functional Level

1. Log on locally as a Domain Admin to the PDC or the PDC Emulator FSMO of the domain you are raising.

2. Click on **Start | Administrative Tools | Active Directory Domains and Trusts**, or use the MMC preconfigured with the Active Directory Domain and Trusts snap-in.

3. Locate the domain in the console tree that you are going to raise in functional level. Right-click the domain and select **Raise Domain Functional Level**.

4. A dialog box will appear titled **Select an available domain functional level**. There are only two possible choices, although both might not be available:

Continued

5. Select **Windows Server 2003**, and then click the **Raise** button to raise the domain functional level to Windows Server 2003.

6. Select **Windows Server 2008**, and then click the **Raise** button to raise the domain functional level to Windows Server 2008.

Understanding the Global Catalog

Active Directory uses the Global Catalog (GC), which is a copy of all the Active Directory objects in the forest, to let users search for directory information across all the domains in the forest. The GC is also used to resolve user principal names (UPNs) when the DC that is authenticating logon isn't aware of the account (because that account resides in a different domain). When the DC can't find the user's account in its own domain database, it then looks in the GC. The GC also stores information about membership in Universal Groups.

The GC contains a portion of every naming context in the directory, including the schema and configuration partitions. To be able to find everything, the GC must contain a replica of every object in the Active Directory. Fortunately, it maintains only a small number of attributes for each object. These attributes are those most commonly used to search for objects, such as a user's first, last, and logon names. The GC extends an umbrella of awareness throughout the discontiguous namespace of the enterprise.

Although the GC can be modified and optimized, it typically requires infrequent attention. The Active Directory replication system automatically builds and maintains the GC, generates its replication topology, and determines which attributes to include in its index.

The GC is a vital part of Active Directory functionality. Given the size of enterprise-level organizations, on many networks, there will be multiple domains and, at times, multiple forests. The GC helps in keeping a list of every object without holding all the details of those objects; this optimizes network traffic while still providing maximum accessibility.

NOTE

The first DC in a domain becomes the GC server by default.

Whenever a user is searching for an object in the directory, the GC server is used in the querying process for multiple reasons. The GC server holds partial replicas of all the domains in a forest, other than its own (for which it holds a full replica). Thus, the GC server stores the following:

- Copies of all the objects in the domain in which it resides
- Partial copies of objects from other domains in the forest

NOTE

When we say that the GC server holds a partial copy of an object, we mean that it includes only some of the object's attributes in its database. Attributes are object properties, and each object has a number of attributes. For example, one attribute of a *User Account* object would be the username. You can customize the attributes of a particular object type by editing the *schema*, which we will discuss later in this chapter.

The key point is that the GC is designed to have the details that are most commonly used for searching for information. This allows for efficient response from a GC server. There is no need to try to find one item out of millions of attributes, because the GC has the important search-related items only. This makes for quick turnaround on queries.

The scope of Directory Services has changed from the days of Windows NT 4.0 Directory Services. With Active Directory, a user record holds more than just a user-name for an individual. The person's telephone number, e-mail address, office location, and so forth can be stored in Active Directory. With this type of information available, users will search the directory on a regular basis. This is especially true when Microsoft Exchange is in the environment.

Whether a person is looking for details on another user, looking for a printer, or simply trying to locate another resource, the GC will be involved in the final resolution of the object. As mentioned previously, the GC server holds a copy of every object in its own domain and a partial copy of objects in other domains in the forest. Therefore, users can search outside their own domains as well as within, something that could not be done with the old Windows NT Directory Services model.

UPN Authentication

The UPN is meant to make logon and e-mail usage easier, because the two (your user account and your e-mail address) are the same. An example of a UPN is Brian@syngress.com. The GC provides assistance when a user from a domain logs on and the DC doesn't know about the account. When the DC doesn't know the account, it generally means that the account exists in another domain. The GC will help in finding the user's account in Active Directory. The GC server will help to resolve the user account so that the authenticating DC can finalize logon for the user.

WARNING

With Windows Server 2008 and beyond, you will see more and more references to UPN use in single or multiple domain environments. Be sure to understand how the UPN works in relation to logon, and how the GC keeps this information available efficiently.

Directory Information Search

With Active Directory, users have the ability to search for objects such as other users or printers. To help a user who is searching the database for an object, the GC answers requests for the entire forest. Because the complete copy of every object available is listed in the GC, searches can be completed quickly and with little use of network bandwidth.

When you search the entire directory, the request is directed to the default GC port 3268. The GC server is also known to other computers on the network because of SRV records in the DNS. That is how a node on the network can query for a GC server. There are SRV records specifically for GC services. These records are created when you create the domain.

When users search for information in Active Directory, their queries can cross WAN links, depending on the network layout. Each organization is different. Figure 2.2 shows an example layout with GC servers in the corporate office in Chicago and a branch office in Seattle. The other two sites do not have GC servers. When queries are initiated at the Chicago branch office, the queries use the corporate office GC server. With a high-speed fiber connection, bandwidth isn't an issue.

Figure 2.2 Example GC Search Query

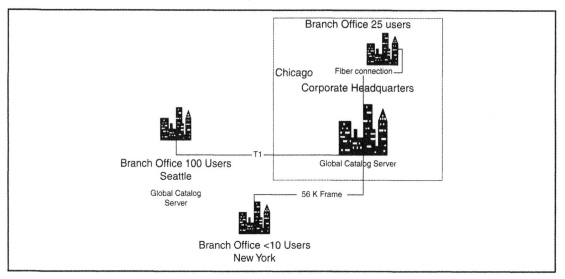

The branch office in New York has a slow link but less than 10 users. These users will use the GC in Chicago as well. Even though the pipe between these locations is only 56 K, the minimal number of users doesn't warrant having a GC server in New York. The Seattle office has a T1, which is decent connectivity, but there are more than 100 users in this location. Considering that, searches will be more efficient with a GC server locally. We will look at sites later in the chapter, but Figure 2.2 will help you get a basic understanding of how the query process works.

Universal Group Membership Information

When setting up your network, certain features will be available based on the forest functional level and domain functional level. Universal Groups is one of these features that will or will not be available depending on your functional level. If your domain functional level is set to at least Windows 2000 Native or later, you will have Universal Groups available on your network. Universal Groups can have members belonging to various domains in the forest. Without a GC server, Universal Groups could not exist. That is because Universal Group membership is stored in the GC only. This means that every DC will not have a copy of Universal Group membership; only the DCs serving as GC servers have this information. When a user logs on, his Universal Group membership is checked. The GC provides this information to the authenticating DC.

Universal Group membership information is stored in all GC servers, so you need to consider the design of your GC server layout when adding to or changing the

GC server configuration. The number of users at a location will help to determine when you need a GC server. A large number of queries of the GC information over slow links aren't recommended; placing a GC at each site is a better design. With sites with a small number of users, you can get away with not having a GC server at each site. We discuss this in more detail later in this chapter, in the section "Placing GC Servers within Sites."

Understanding GC Replication

You know now that GC servers hold information for all of the objects in their own domains and a partial copy of the objects from other domains in the forest. For this to be possible, some type of replication has to happen between the GC servers. The default attributes included in the GC make up the most commonly searched for items. These items are part of normal Active Directory replication.

The Knowledge Consistency Checker (KCC) generates the GC replication topology. The GC is only replicated between DCs that are GC servers; the information is not replicated to other DCs. A few things can affect replication; for example, Universal Group membership, and the number of attributes included in the GC.

Universal Group Membership

The GC holds the sole responsibility of maintaining Universal Group membership. The names of the Global Groups and Domain Local Groups are also in the GC, but their membership lists are not. This helps to keep the size of the database small enough to efficiently answer queries.

For replication purposes, it is best to keep Universal Group membership relatively static. Every change made to a Universal Group is replicated to every GC server. Keeping these changes to a minimum will keep the GC replication traffic to a minimum.

TIP

Universal Groups can exist only if the functional level of your network is Windows 2000 native or later. Universal Group information is replicated between GC servers. Replication traffic can consume bandwidth, which is why site topology is important; putting a GC at each site keeps replication traffic to a minimum.

Attributes in the Global Catalog

When you first set up Active Directory, a series of default attributes from Active Directory are in the GC. Sometimes the default set of attributes is missing an item you would like to see. For example, perhaps you want to have a coworker's department number as part of his user record; you can accomplish this by adding an attribute. You can use the Active Directory Schema snap-in to include additional attributes in the GC by placing a checkmark next to the **Index this attribute** checkbox, as shown in Figure 2.3. To get to this option, open the **Schema** snap-in, and expand the **Attributes** section. Right-click any attribute, and select **Properties**.

Figure 2.3 Adding Attributes to the GC

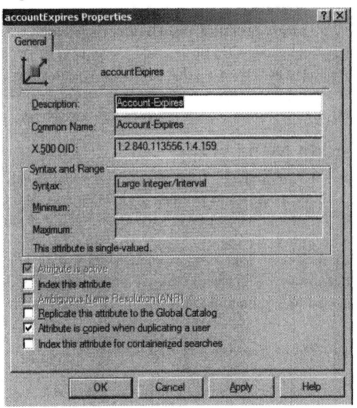

Prior to Windows Server 2003, each time the GC attribute set was extended, a full synchronization of all attributes stored in the GC was completed. In a large network, this often caused a serious amount of network traffic. With Windows Server 2003 and Windows Server 2008, only the additional attribute or attributes are replicated to other GC servers. This makes for more efficient use of network bandwidth.

Placing GC Servers within Sites

Another consideration when it comes to replication is placement of your GC servers. In a small network with one physical location, GC server placement is easy. Your first DC that is configured will hold the GC role. If you have one site, but more than one DC, you can move the role to another DC if you want to or configure additional DCs as GCs. Most networks today consist of multiple physical locations, whether in the same city or across the country. If you have high-speed links connecting your branch offices you might be okay, but many branch office links use limited bandwidth connections. If the connection between locations is less than a T1, you might have limited bandwidth depending on what traffic is crossing the wire. As a network administrator, you will have to work with your provider to gauge how much utilization there is across your WAN links.

Another factor is reliability. If your WAN links are unreliable, replication traffic and synchronization traffic might not successfully cross the link. The less reliable the link, the more the need for setting up sites and site links between the locations.

Without proper planning, replication traffic can cause problems in a large network. Sites help to control replication traffic. Making the most of available bandwidth is an important factor in having a network that allows your users to be productive. Logon and searching Active Directory are both affected by GC server placement. If users cannot find the information they need from Active Directory, they might not be able to log on or find the information or data they need.

Configuring & Implementing...

GC in an Exchange Server Environment

Now that Active Directory is the single directory used in Windows 2000, Windows Server 2003, and Windows Server 2008 networks, there is very tight integration with Microsoft Exchange. Prior to Exchange 2000, Exchange had its own directory and the domain had its own directory service. There were links between the two, but they were still technically separate directories.

Continued

> Because all user information (first name, last name, and contact information) is kept in Active Directory, users will be searching more and more throughout the directory. In previous versions of Exchange, there was a Global Address List that you could search to locate people within your organization. Information such as telephone numbers, fax numbers, and office locations can be part of your GC strategy with Windows Server 2003. It is important for administrators to ensure that users can reach the data for which they are searching as quickly and easily as possible. Proper planning and location of your GC information is important to successful queries of your directory information.

Bandwidth and Network Traffic Considerations

Active Directory replication works differently depending on whether it is *intersite* or *intrasite* replication. DCs that are part of the same site (intrasite) replicate with one another more often than DCs in different sites (intersite). If you have sites that are geographically dispersed, you need to be careful how you handle your GC server placement. The bandwidth between geographically dispersed offices is often minimal. The rule of thumb is to have GC servers in selected sites. In most cases, you do not want to have a GC server in every site because of the vast amount of replication that would occur. The following examples describe situations in which you should have a GC server within a site:

- If you have a slow WAN link between geographic locations. If you have a DC at each location, a good rule is to also have a GC server at each location. If the WAN link supports traffic for normal DC traffic, it should also handle GC traffic.

- If you have an application that relies heavily on GC queries across port 3268, you'll want to have a GC server in the site in which the application runs. An example of this is Exchange 2000, which relies heavily on GC information.

- You'll want to have GCs in as many sites as possible to support Universal Group membership authentication. We look at caching of Universal Groups, which can reduce traffic related to this, in the next section.

TIP

Microsoft's documentation recommends that if you have 50 or more users at a given location, you should give that location a DC serving as a GC server. This will help to reduce the number of queries crossing the WAN for Active Directory object searches.

Data replicated between sites is compressed, which makes better use of available bandwidth. Because the data is compressed, more can be sent over a limited amount of bandwidth. This is how site placement and design can be critical to efficient network operation.

Universal Group Membership Caching

The Windows Server 2003 Active Directory introduced *Universal Group caching* as a new feature, and this feature is also available in Windows Server 2008. When a user logs on to the network, his membership in Universal Groups is verified. For this to happen, the authenticating DC has to query the GC. If the GC is across a WAN link, the logon process will be slow every time. To alleviate this, the DC that queries the GC can cache this information, which cuts down on the amount of data traveling across the WAN link for Universal Group information.

The cache is loaded at the first user logon. Every eight hours by default, the DC will refresh the cache from the nearest GC server. Caching functionality is administered in Active Directory Sites and Services as shown in Figure 2.4, and can be turned off if desired. You can also designate the GC server from which you want the cache to refresh, giving you more control over traffic distribution on the network.

NOTE

The NTDS Site Settings Properties box is not the same NTDS Settings Properties box you accessed to make a DC act as a GC. Instead of accessing the properties of NTDS settings under the DC node in the Servers container, you must access the properties of NTDS Site Settings in the right console pane when you select a site name (e.g., Default-First-Site-Name). The similarity of these two settings can be confusing if you haven't worked with the console much.

Figure 2.4 Configuring Universal Group Caching

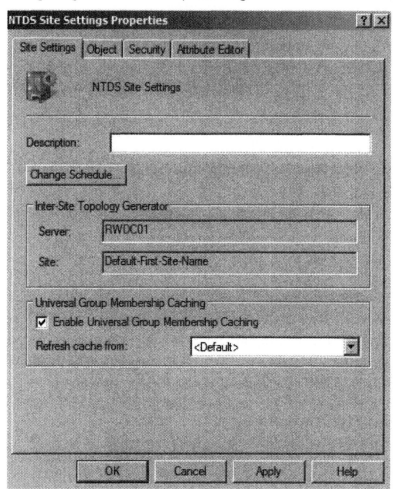

Prior to Windows Server 2003, Active Directory logon would immediately fail if a GC could not be located to check Universal Group membership. With Universal Group caching in Windows Server 2003 and Windows Server 2008, DCs cache complete group membership information, so even if a GC server cannot be reached, logon will still happen based on cached Universal Group information.

Working with Flexible Single Master Operation (FSMO) Roles

In Windows NT 4.0, the domain had only one authoritative source for domain-related information, the primary domain controller or PDC. With the implementation of

Active Directory came the multimaster replication model, where objects and their properties can be modified on any DC and become authoritative through replication conflict resolution measures. This scalability effort came with a price in complexity, however, and Active Directory FSMO roles were introduced to control certain domain and forest-wide operations that are not well suited for a multimaster environment. Some operations such as modifying the Active Directory schema or adding or removing a domain or domain tree are sufficiently critical or sensitive that their functions need to reside on a single DC within the domain or forest.

The advantage of using FSMOs is that conflicts cannot be introduced while a particular Operations Master is offline; the alternative would involve resolving conflicts later, possibly to significantly negative result. The disadvantage is that all Operations Masters must be available at all times to support all dependent activities within the domain or forest. Windows Server 2008 Active Directory requires five operational master roles:

- **Schema Master** To update the schema of a forest, you must have access to the Schema Master DC, which controls all schema updates and modifications. There can be only one Schema Master in the forest.

- **Domain Naming Master** The Domain Naming Master DC controls the addition or removal of domains in the forest as well as adding and removing any cross-references to domains in external Lightweight Directory Access Protocol (LDAP) directories. There can be only one Domain Naming Master in the forest.

- **Infrastructure Master** The Infrastructure Master is responsible for updating references from objects in the local domain to objects in other domains. There can be only one Infrastructure Master DC in each domain.

- **Relative ID (RID) Master** The RID Master processes RID pool requests from all DCs in the local domain. These relative identifiers are the unique part of the SID, which is a Security Identifier used to uniquely identify objects and group memberships. There can be only one RID Master DC in each domain.

- **PDC Emulator** The PDC Emulator is a DC that advertises itself as the PDC to workstations, member servers, and BDCs running Windows NT. It is also the Domain Master Browser, and handles Active Directory password changes, maintenance of trust relationships, as well as time synchronization for servers and clients within a domain. There can be only one PDC Emulator in each domain.

Two of these operate at the forest level only, you will have a single Schema Master and Domain Naming Master within each Active Directory forest regardless of how many domains exist within the forest. Conversely, the RID Master, PDC Emulator, and Infrastructure Master operate at the domain level. To examine this role relationship between master roles and the required authorization for administering them in the forest and domains, refer to Table 2.2.

Table 2.2 Valid Authorization Levels for Viewing, Transferring, and Seizing Operations Master Roles

Role	Task	Domain Administrator on the Local Domain	Domain Administrator on the Forest-Root Domain	Enterprise Administrator
Schema Master	Viewing, transferring, or seizing		X (Plus *Schema Admins* membership)	X
Domain Naming Master Viewing, transferring, or seizing	X		X	
Infrastructure Master	Viewing, transferring, or seizing	X		X
RID Master	Viewing, transferring, or seizing	X		X
PDC Emulator	Viewing, transferring, or seizing	X		X

To illustrate, if you have a single Active Directory forest containing a parent domain and a child domain, you will have one each of the Schema Master and Domain Naming Master FSMO roles, and two each of the Infrastructure Master, RID Master, and PDC Emulator, with one of each domain-wide FSMO configured in each of the two domains. A single-domain forest, therefore, has five roles—one of each.

Each domain added after the forest root domain has three additional masters. With that information, we can determine the number of operations master servers required in a given forest with the following formula:

((*Number of domains * 3) + 2*)

Given the formula, we can determine that the forest depicted in Figure 2.5, with three domains, needs a maximum of 11 server platforms to support the 11 FSMO roles (3 * 3 = 9, and 9 + 2 = 11), unless you assign multiple roles to a single DC. Often, small domains, empty root domains, or best practices will make combining several of these roles onto a single DC desirable. In the example shown in Figure 2.5, the following roles exist:

- One Schema Master in Dogs.com

- One Domain Naming Master in Dogs.com

- Three PDC Emulators (one each in Dogs.com, Fish.com, and Cat.fish.com)

- Three RID Masters (one each in Dogs.com, Fish.com, and Cat.fish.com)

- Three Infrastructure Masters (one each in Dogs.com, Fish.com, and Cat.fish.com)

Figure 2.5 Creating a New Child Domain in an Existing Domain

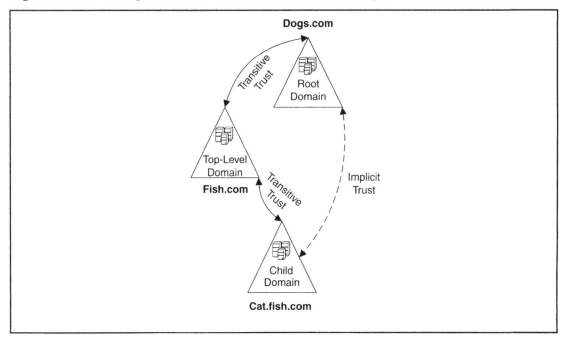

Placing, Transferring, and Seizing FSMO Role Holders

The first DC that you install in the forest root will automatically host all five roles. The first DC that you install in any additional domains will automatically host the three roles of PDC Emulator, RID Master, and Infrastructure Master.

You can use the ntdsutil.exe command-line utility to transfer FSMO roles, or you can use an MMC snap-in tool. Depending on which role you want to transfer, you can use one of the following three MMC snap-in tools:

- Active Directory Schema snap-in (Schema Master role)

- Active Directory Domains and Trusts snap-in (Domain Naming Master role)

- Active Directory Users and Computers snap-in (RID Master, Infrastructure Master, and PDC Emulator roles)

To forcibly seize a role, you must use the ntdsutil utility. If a computer cannot be contacted due to a hardware malfunction or long-term network failure, the role must be seized. If the PDC Emulator role holder fails, you can seize the PDC Emulator FSMO role to another DC and then return the role to the original role holder when it comes back online. In the case of other FSMO role holders, particularly the RID Master and Schema Master FSMO role holders, you must take significantly greater care if you need to seize the FSMO role due to a hardware or network failure. If you seize the Schema Master or RID Master FSMO role holder to another DC, the original role holder must never be returned to Active Directory; the original role holder must be reformatted before being returned to your production environment.

Locating and Transferring the Schema Master Role

The DC that hosts the Schema Master role controls each update or modification to the schema. You must have access to the Schema Master to update the schema of a forest.

NOTE

You must be a member of the Schema Admins group to perform this operation. The built-in Administrator account in the forest root domain is automatically configured as a member of this group when the Active Directory forest is created.

Temporary loss of the Schema Master is not noticeable to domain users. Enterprise and domain administrators will not notice the loss either, unless they are trying to install an application that modifies the schema during installation or trying to modify the schema themselves. You should seize the schema FSMO role to the standby operations master only if your old Schema master will be permanently offline.

Configuring & Implementing...

Locating the Schema Operations Master

1. Log on as an Enterprise Administrator in the forest you are checking.

2. Click **Start | Run**.

3. Type **regsvr32 schmmgmt.dll** in the **Open** box, and click **OK**. This registers the Schmmgmt.dll.

4. Click OK in the dialog box showing that the operation succeeded.

5. Click **Start | Run**, type **mmc**, and then click **OK**.

6. On the menu bar, click **File | Add/Remove Snap-in**, click **Add**, double-click **Active Directory Schema**, click **Close**, and then click **OK**.

7. Expand and then right-click **Active Directory Schema** in the top-left pane, and then select **Operations Masters** to view the server holding the Schema Master role, as shown in Figure 2.6.

Figure 2.6 The Server Holding the Schema Master Role

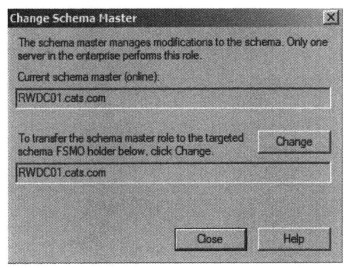

Configuring & Implementing...

Transferring the Schema Operations Master Role

1. Log on as an Enterprise Administrator in the forest where you want to transfer the Schema Master role.

2. Click **Start | Run**.

3. Type **regsvr32 schmmgmt.dll** in the **Open** box, and then click **OK**. This registers the Schmmgmt.dll.

4. Click **OK** in the dialog box showing that the operation succeeded.

5. Click **Start | Run**, type **mmc**, and then click **OK**.

6. On the menu bar, click **File | Add/Remove Snap-in**, click **Add**, double-click **Active Directory Schema**, click **Close**, and then click **OK**.

7. Right-click **Active Directory Schema** in the top-left pane, and then click **Change Active Directory Domain Controller**.

8. As shown in Figure 2.7, select the **This Domain Controller or AD LDS instance**, enter the name of the DC that will be the new role holder, and then click **OK**.

Continued

9. Right-click **Active Directory Schema** again, and then click **Operations Master**.

10. Click **Change**.

11. Click **OK** to confirm that you want to transfer the role, and then click **Close**.

Figure 2.7 Changing an Active Directory Domain Controller

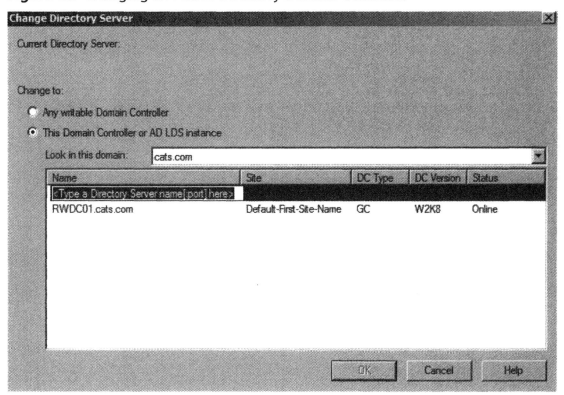

Locating and Transferring the Domain Naming Master Role

The Domain Naming Master DC controls the addition or removal of domains in the forest, *and* adding and removing any cross-references to domains in external LDAP directories. There can be only one Domain Naming Master in the forest.

Configuring & Implementing...

Locating the Domain Naming Operations Master

1. Log on as an Enterprise Administrator in the forest you are checking.

2. Click **Start | Run**, type **mmc**, and then click **OK**.

3. On the menu bar, click **File | Add/Remove Snap-in**, click **Add**, double-click **Active Directory Domains and Trusts**, click **Close**, and then click **OK**.

4. Right-click **Active Directory Domains and Trusts** in the top-left pane, and then click **Operations Masters** to view the server holding the Domain Naming Master role.

Configuring & Implementing...

Transferring the Domain Naming Master Role

1. Click Start | Administrative Tools | Active Directory Domains and Trusts.

2. Right-click Active Directory Domains and Trusts, and click Change Active Directory Domain Controller, *unless you are already on the DC to which you are transferring the role*. Select the This Domain Controller or AD LDS instance, enter the name of the DC that will be the new role holder, and then click OK.

3. In the console tree, right-click Active Directory Domains and Trusts, and then select Operations Master. Click Change.

4. Click OK for confirmation, and click Close.

Locating and Transferring the Infrastructure, RID, and PDC Operations Master Roles

The Infrastructure Master is responsible for updating references from objects in the local domain to objects in other domains. There can be only one Infrastructure Master DC in each domain. The RID Master processes RID pool requests from all DCs in the local domain. There can be only one RID Master DC in each domain. The PDC Emulator is a DC that advertises itself as the PDC to workstations, member servers, and BDCs running Windows NT. It is also the Domain Master Browser, and handles Active Directory password collisions, or discrepancies. There can be only one PDC Emulator in each domain.

Configuring & Implementing...

Locating the Infrastructure, RID, and PDC Operations Masters

1. Log on as an Enterprise Administrator in the forest you are checking.

2. Click **Start | Run**, type **dsa.msc**, and click **OK**. This is an alternative method for opening the **Active Directory Users and Computers** administrative tool.

3. Right-click the selected Domain Object in the top-left pane, and then click **Operations Masters**.

4. Click the **Infrastructure** tab to view the server holding the Infrastructure Master role.

5. Click the **RID** tab to view the server holding the RID Master role.

6. Click the **PDC** tab to view the server holding the PDC Master role.

Configuring & Implementing…

Transferring the Infrastructure, RID, and PDC Master Roles

1. Click Start | Administrative Tools | Active Directory Users and Computers.

2. Right-click **Active Directory Users and Computers,** and click **Connect to Domain Controller** *unless you are already on the DC you are transferring to.* Select the **This Domain Controller or AD LDS instance,** enter the name of the DC that will be the new role holder, and then click **OK.**

3. In the console tree, right-click Active Directory Users and Computers, and click All Tasks | Operations Master.

4. Take the appropriate action for the role you want to transfer:

   Click the **Infrastructure** tab, and click **Change.**

   Click the **RID** tab, and click **Change.**

   Click the **PDC** tab, and click **Change.**

5. Click **OK** for confirmation, and click **Close.**

Configuring & Implementing…

Seizing the FSMO Master Roles

1. Log on to any working DC.

2. Click **Start | Run,** type **ntdsutil** in the Open box, and then click **OK.**

3. Type activate instance ntds and press Enter.

4. Type **roles,** and press **Enter.**

5. In ntdsutil, type **?** at any prompt to see a list of available commands, and press **Enter.**

Continued

6. Type **connections**, and press **Enter**.

7. Type **connect to server** *servername*, where *servername* is the name of the server that will receive the role, and press **Enter**.

8. At the **Server connections:** prompt, type **q**, and press **Enter**.

9. Type the appropriate seizing command, as shown next. See the example in Figure 2.8. If the FSMO role is available, ntdsutil.exe will perform a transfer instead. Respond to the Role Seizure Confirmation Dialog box, as shown in Figure 2.9.

```
seize Schema master

seize domain naming master

seize Infrastructure master

seize RID master

seize PDC
```

Figure 2.8 Seizing the PDC Master Role

```
D:\WINDOWS\system32\ntdsutil.exe: activate instance ntds
Active instance set to "ntds".
ntdsutil: roles
fsmo maintenance: connections
server connections: connect to server DC4
Binding to DC4 ...
Connected to DC4 using credentials of locally logged on user.
server connections: q
fsmo maintenance: seize PDC
Attempting safe transfer of PDC FSMO before seizure.
FSMO transferred successfully - seizure not required.
Server "DC4" knows about 5 roles
Schema - CN=NTDS Settings,CN=DC3,CN=Servers,CN=Default-First-Site-
    Name,CN=Sites,
CN=Configuration,DC=Dogs,DC=com
Domain - CN=NTDS Settings,CN=DC3,CN=Servers,CN=Default-First-Site-
    Name,CN=Sites,
CN=Configuration,DC=Dogs,DC=com
PDC - CN=NTDS Settings,CN=DC4,CN=Servers,CN=Default-First-Site-
    Name,CN=Sites,CN=
Configuration,DC=Dogs,DC=com
RID - CN=NTDS Settings,CN=DC4,CN=Servers,CN=Default-First-
    Name,CN=Sites,CN=
Configuration,DC=Dogs,DC=com
Infrastructure - CN=NTDS Settings,CN=DC4,CN=Servers,CN=Default-First-Site-
    Name,CN=Sites,CN=Configuration,DC=Dogs,DC=com fsmo maintenance:q
```

Continued

Figure 2.9 Seizing the Schema Operations Master Role

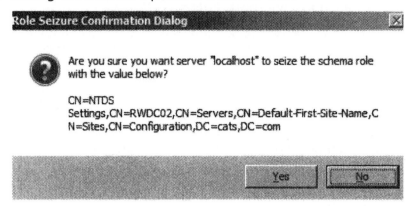

9. After you seize the role, type **q**, and then press **Enter** repeatedly until you quit the Ntdsutil tool.

Placing the FSMO Roles within an Active Directory Environment

It is a good idea to place the RID and PDC Emulator roles on the same DC. Down-level clients and applications target the PDC, making it a large consumer of RIDs. Good communication between these two roles is important. If performance demands it, place the RID and PDC Emulator roles on separate DCs, but make sure they stay in the same site and that they are direct replication partners with each other.

As a general rule, you should place the Infrastructure Master on a DC that is not a GC server to maintain proper replication. There are two exceptions to this rule:

- **Single domain forest** If your forest contains only one Active Directory domain, there can be no phantoms. The Infrastructure Master has no functionality in a single domain forest. In that case, you can place the Infrastructure Master on any DC.

- **Multidomain forest where every DC holds the GC** Again, there can be no phantoms if every DC in the domain hosts a GC. There is no work for the Infrastructure Master to perform. In that case, you can place the Infrastructure Master on any DC.

Additionally, ensure that the Infrastructure Master has a direct connection object to a GC server somewhere in the forest, preferably in the same site.

Considering the forest-wide FSMOs, the Schema Master and Domain Naming Master roles are rarely used and should be tightly controlled. For that reason, you can place them on the same DC. Another Microsoft-recommended practice is to place the Domain Naming Master FSMO on a GC server. Taking all of these practices together, a Microsoft-recommended best-practice empty root domain design might consist of two DCs with the following FSMO/GC placement:

- DC 1:
    - Schema Master
    - Domain Naming Master
    - GC
- DC 2:
    - RID Master
    - PDC Emulator
    - Infrastructure Master

Working with Sites

In today's distributed network environment, the communication must always be rapid and reliable. Geographical and other restrictions resulted in the need to create smaller networks, known as *subnets*. These subnets provide rapid and reliable communication between locations, which can also be attained in larger networks by using Microsoft Windows Server 2008 Active Directory Sites. They ensure rapid and reliable communication by using the methods offered by Microsoft Windows Server 2008 Active Directory Sites to regulate inter-subnet traffic.

A *site* defines the network structure of a Windows Server 2008 Active Directory. A site consists of multiple Internet Protocol (IP) subnets linked together by rapid and reliable connections. The primary role of sites is to increase the performance of a network by economic and rapid transmission of data. The other roles of sites are replication and authentication. The Active Directory physical structure manages when and how the authentication and replication must take place. The Active Directory physical structure allows the management of Active Directory replication scheduling between sites. The performance of a network is also based on the location of objects and *logon authentication* as users log on to the network.

Understanding Sites

A site is as a collection of interconnected computers that operate over IP subnets. A site is also a place on a network having high-bandwidth connectivity. The relationship of sites to Active Directory components is based on the following network operations performed by sites:

- Control of replication occurrences
- Changes made with the sites
- How efficiently DCs within a domain can communicate

A site can contain one or more domains, and a domain can be part of one or more sites. Sites and domains do not have to maintain the same *namespace*. Sites and domains are interrelated because sites control replication of the domain information.

Configuring & Implementing...

The Relationship between Sites and Domains

Domains are also defined as *units of replication*. All the DCs present in a particular domain can receive changes and replicate those changes to all other DCs present in the domain of a network. A DNS server recognizes each domain that is present in a particular site. If your network requires more than one domain, you can easily create multiple domains. Figure 2.10 illustrates the relationship between sites and domains in a network, and helps us to understand that a site can have one or more domains, and a domain can have one or more sites.

Continued

Figure 2.10 The Relationship between the Sites and Domains
Present in a Network

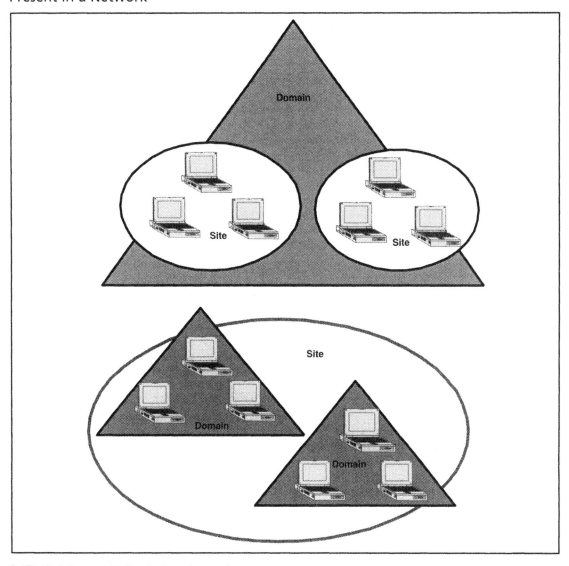

In Figure 2.10, we see how multiple sites reside in a single domain, and how a single site can consist of multiple domains. A domain provides the following benefits:

- It organizes domain objects.
- It publishes resources and information about domain objects.
- It applies GPOs to the domain to perform resource and security management.

Continued

> - It delegates authority to eliminate the need for administrators with broad administrative authority.
> - Security policies and settings such as user rights and password policies do not change from one domain to another.
> - Each domain stores only the information about the objects located in that domain.

The sites present in an Active Directory denote the *physical structure* of a network. The physical structure information is available as site and site link objects in the directory. This information is used to build the most efficient replication topology. Generally, Active Directory Sites and Services are used to define sites and site links.

Whereas sites represent the physical structure of the network, domains represent the *logical structure* of the organization. This partitioning of physical and logical structures offers the following advantages:

- You can develop and manage the logical and physical structures of your network independently.

- You do not have to base domain namespaces on your physical network.

- You can deploy DCs for multiple domains within the same site.

- You can deploy DCs for the same domain in multiple sites.

Subnets

In Active Directory, a site consists of a set of computers that are interconnected in a LAN. Computers within the same site typically exist in the same building, or on the same campus network. A single site consists of one or more IP subnets. These subnets are a section of an IP network, with each subnet having a unique network address.

A subnet address consists of a cluster of neighboring computers in much the same way as the postal codes group neighboring postal addresses. Figure 2.11 shows one or more clients residing within a subnet that defines an Active Directory site.

Figure 2.11 The Active Directory Site with One or More
Client Computers within a Subnet

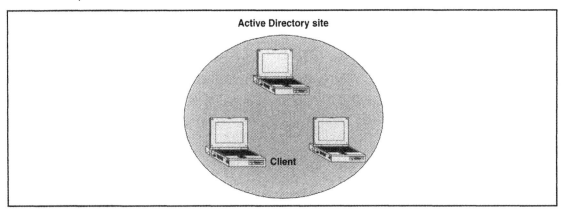

The subnet created through Active Directory Sites and Services are sections of an
IP network, with each subnet having a unique network address. In Figure 2.11,
231.01.01.0/19 is a unique network address of the Active Directory site.

Sites and subnets are represented in Active Directory by site and subnet objects,
which we create through the Active Directory Sites and Services administrative tool.
Each site object is associated with one or more subnet objects.

Site Planning

You should plan thoroughly before creating and deploying an Active Directory. Site
planning enables you to optimize the efficiency of the network and reduce administrative overhead. High-performance sites are developed based on the proper planning of
the physical design of your network. Site planning enables you to determine exactly
which sites you should create and how they can be linked using *site links* and *site link
bridges*. Site information is stored in the *configuration partition*, which enables you to
create sites and related information at any point in your deployment of Active Directory.

> **NOTE**
>
> A configuration partition is a portion of a basic disk that can contain logi-
> cal drives. A configuration partition is used if you want to have more than
> four volumes on your basic disk. A DC always stores the partitions for the
> schema and configuration. The schema and configuration are replicated to
> every DC in the domain tree or forest.

Site planning enables you to publish site information in the directory for use by applications and services. Generally, the Active Directory consumes the site information. You'll see how replication impacts site planning later in this chapter.

Criteria for Establishing Separate Sites

When you initially create a domain, a single default Active Directory site called *Default-Site-First-Name* is created. This site represents your entire network. A domain or forest consisting of a separate site can be highly efficient for a LAN connected by high-speed bandwidth.

NOTE

A forest is defined as multiple Active Directory domains that share the same class, site, attribute definitions, and replication information (but not necessarily the same namespace). The domains present in the same forest are linked with two-way transitive trust relationships.

If a single LAN consists of a separate subnet or if a network consists of multiple subnets connected by a high-speed connection, establishing a separate site topology offers the following advantages:

- Simplified replication management
- Regular directory updates between all DCs

Establishing separate site topology enables all replication to occur as intrasite replication, which requires no manual replication configuration. A separate site design enables DCs to receive updates with respect to directory changes.

NOTE

Intrasite replication refers to replication among DCs within the same site. *Intersite* replication refers to replication among DCs located at different sites.

Creating a Site

Sites are created using the Active Directory Sites and Services tool of Windows Server 2008. The following Sidebar walks you through the steps involved in creating a site.

Active Directory Sites and Services is an MMC that you can use to administer the replication of directory data. You can also use this tool to create new sites, site links, subnets, and so forth.

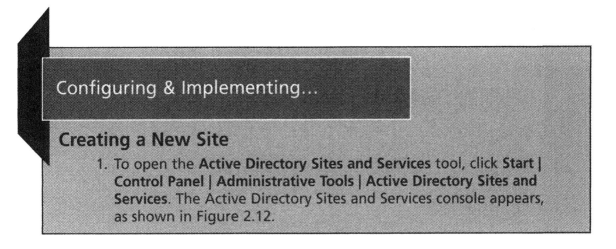

Configuring & Implementing...

Creating a New Site

1. To open the **Active Directory Sites and Services** tool, click **Start | Control Panel | Administrative Tools | Active Directory Sites and Services**. The Active Directory Sites and Services console appears, as shown in Figure 2.12.

Figure 2.12 The Active Directory Sites and Services Tool

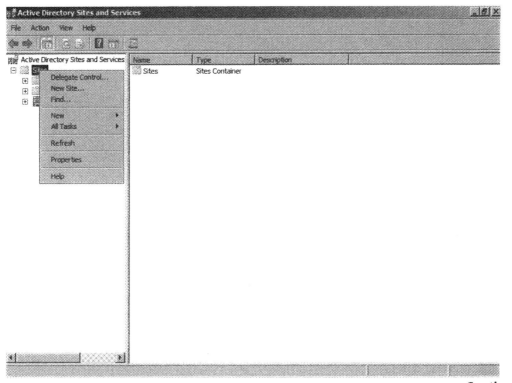

Continued

2. Highlight the **Sites** folder in the left-hand tree pane of the **Active Directory Sites and Services** console. Right-click and select the **Sites** folder's **New Site** option from the context menu, as shown in Figure 2.13.

Figure 2.13 The New Site Option

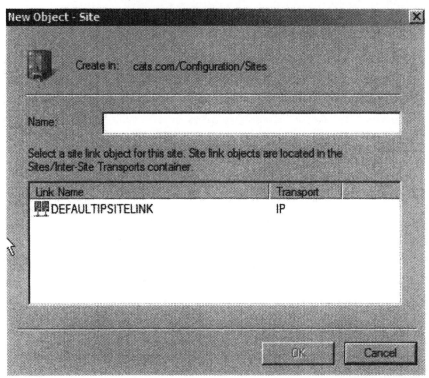

3. Selecting the **New Site** option opens a **New Object – Site** dialog box, as shown in Figure 2.14.

Continued

Figure 2.14 The New Object – Site Dialog Box

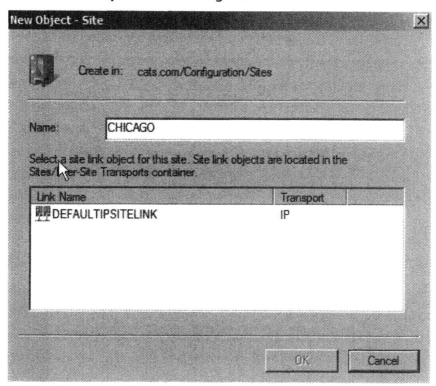

4. Type the name of the site in the **Name** box present in the **New Object – Site** dialog box, as shown in Figure 2.15.

Continued

Figure 2.15 The Name of the Site

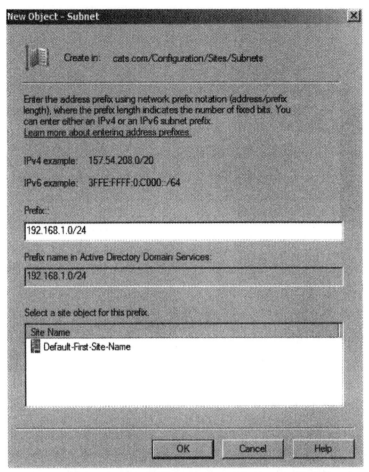

5. Select an initial site link object for the site from the **New Object – Site** dialog box.

6. Click **OK**. You will be presented with a pop-up box indicating the next steps that you should follow once the new site is created. Read this informational message and then click **OK**. This completes the process of creating a site using the **Active Directory Sites and Services** tool.

Renaming a Site

Renaming a site is one of the first tasks you should perform when administering a site structure. When you create a site initially, it is created with the default name

Default-First-Site-Name. You can change this name based on the purpose of the site, such as the name of the physical location.

A site is also renamed when a network of an organization is expanded by one or more sites. Even if an organization is located in a single location, it makes sense to rename the Default-First-Site-Name, because you never know when the network will expand. Renaming a site enables administrators to differentiate sites present in a network easily and perform administration tasks efficiently.

When a DC becomes aware that its site has been renamed, it will update its DNS records appropriately. Because of issues with cached DNS lookups and client caching of site names that will lead to temporary delays in connectivity directly after a rename, it's best to name and rename sites as early as possible in the deployment. After renaming a site, it's advisable to manually force replication with other DCs in the same site.

You rename a site using the Active Directory Sites and Services tool of Windows Server 2008. The following Sidebar walks you through the steps involved in renaming a new site.

Configuring & Implementing...

Renaming a New Site

1. To open the Active Directory Sites and Services tool, click Start | Control Panel | Administrative Tools. Double-click Active Directory Sites and Services. The Active Directory Sites and Services dialog box appears.

2. Expand the **Sites** folder in the left-hand tree pane of the **Active Directory Sites and Services** console.

3. Right-click the site you want to rename and select the **Rename** option from the context menu.

4. Type the new name of the site in the **Name** box in the left console pane.

5. Click **OK**. This completes the process of renaming a site using the Active Directory Sites and Services tool.

NOTE

The Windows Server 2008 Active Directory consists of the default site link, named DEFAULTIPSITELINK, which is created automatically when the first domain in the network is created. This link is assigned to the Default-First-Site-Name site. These are the names assigned automatically when you create the first site. You should change the default names to something more descriptive.

Creating Subnets

Subnets are associated with the Active Directory sites to match client computers. The subnets are denoted by a range of IP addresses. The Active Directory Sites and Services user interface prevents you from having to provide the subnet names manually; instead, you are prompted for a network address. An example of a subnet name for an IP Version 4 network is 10.14.208.0/20. This IP address consists of two portions: The network address appears before the slash, and a representation of the subnet mask appears after the slash. Table 2.3 shows some common subnet masks and the corresponding slash notations. The number following the slash indicates the number of binary digits (bits) that make up the network partition of the IP address. The number 255 in decimal translates to 11111111 in binary (8 bits); thus, you can see how the subnet masks in Table 2.3 translate to the corresponding slash notations.

Table 2.3 Subnet Masks and Slash Notation

Subnet Mask	Slash Notation
255.0.0.0	/8
255.255.0.0	/16
255.255.255.0	/24
255.255.255.128	/25
255.255.255.192	/26
255.255.255.224	/27
255.255.255.240	/28
255.255.255.248	/29
255.255.255.252	/30
255.255.255.254	/31

IP Version 6 (IPv6) is a new implementation of the Transmission Control Protocol/Internet Protocol (TCP/IP) that is increasing in prevalence, as it addresses a number of shortcomings that have appeared in IPv4 over time. Windows Server 2008 is the first version of the Windows operating system that has included support for IPv6 out of the box; IPv6 is one of the default protocols included in a fresh installation of the Windows Server 2008 operating system. IPv6 was developed to address a number of limitations of IPv4, the most notable being the limitations of the IPv4 address space, that is, the list of usable TCP/IP addresses provided by IPv4. When TCP/IP was developed in the 1960s, no one foresaw the Internet explosion of the 1990s that would threaten to exhaust the 4-billion-plus IP addresses available through IPv4. The useful lifespan of IPv4 has been extended through the use of private IP networks and the network address translator (NAT), but a long-term solution is still required. To this end, IPv6, the next generation of TCP/IP, was developed to provide a significantly larger address space for current and future implementations of TCP/IP networks.

IPv6 uses 128 bits, or 16 bytes, for its addressing scheme, which provides 2^{128} (about 340 billion) IP addresses. IPv6 address notation is noticeably different from the dotted-decimal of IPv4, using eight groups of four hexadecimal digits, separated by colons. For example, 192.168.1.243 is an example of an IPv4 IP address, and 5ab1:0c12:63d7:0237:9175:bade:0370:7334 is an example of an IPv6 IP address. If an IPv6 address contains a series of sequential zeros, the address can be shortened to use a single zero in each group, or else the entire grouping can be represented using a double colon (::). So, the following three strings all represent the same IPv6 address:

- 5925:0000:0000:0000:0000:0000:0000:2742

- 5925:0:0:0:0:0:0:2742

- 5925::2742

NOTE

The loopback address in IPv6 is expressed as ::1.

IPv6 includes a few other enhancements for performance and security. Notably, IP security through the use of IPSec is an integral part of IPv6, whereas it was an optional feature under IPv4.

You create subnets using the Active Directory Sites and Services tool of Windows Server 2008. The following Sidebar shows the steps involved in creating subnets.

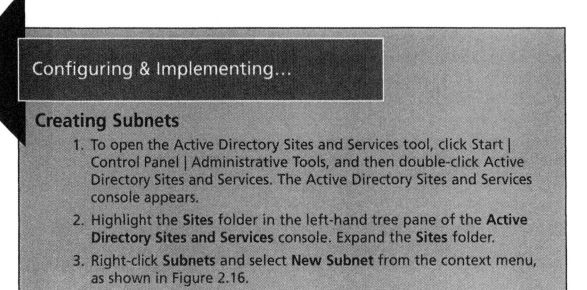

Configuring & Implementing...

Creating Subnets

1. To open the Active Directory Sites and Services tool, click Start | Control Panel | Administrative Tools, and then double-click Active Directory Sites and Services. The Active Directory Sites and Services console appears.

2. Highlight the **Sites** folder in the left-hand tree pane of the **Active Directory Sites and Services** console. Expand the **Sites** folder.

3. Right-click **Subnets** and select **New Subnet** from the context menu, as shown in Figure 2.16.

Figure 2.16 The New Subnet Option

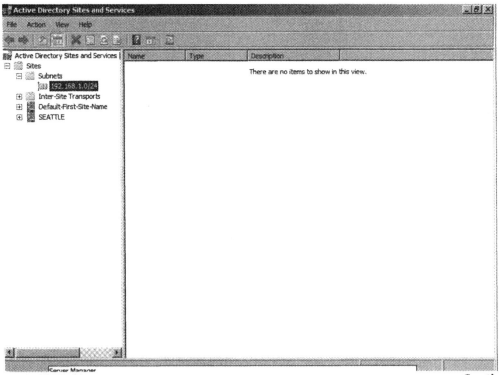

Continued

4. Selecting the New Subnet option opens a **New Object – Subnet** dialog box. Type the network address and subnet mask in the form of dotted-decimal notation in the text boxes present in the **New Object – Subnet** dialog box.

6. Select a site object for this subnet from the list provided in the **New Object – Subnet** dialog box.

7. Click **OK**. This completes the process of creating a subnet using the Active Directory Sites and Services tool.

Associating Subnets with Sites

After creating sites and subnets, the next step is to associate your subnets with sites. Computers on Active Directory networks communicate with each other using the TCP/IP assigned to sites based on their locations in a subnet. Remember that a site consists of one or more IP subnets. You specify the subnets associated with each site on your network by creating subnet objects in the Active Directory Sites and Services console. The association of subnets with sites enables the computers on the Active Directory network to use the subnet information to find a DC in the same site so that authentication traffic will not cross over WAN links. Active Directory also uses subnets during the replication process to determine the best routes between DCs.

You associate subnets with sites using the Active Directory Sites and Services tool of Windows Server 2008. The following Sidebar walks you through the steps involved in associating subnets with sites.

Configuring & Implementing...

Associating Subnets with Sites

1. To open the Active Directory Sites and Services tool, click Start | Administrative Tools, and then click Active Directory Sites and Services.

2. Highlight the **Subnet** folder present in the left-hand tree pane of the **Active Directory Sites and Services** console (see Figure 2.17).

Continued

Figure 2.17 The Subnet Folder

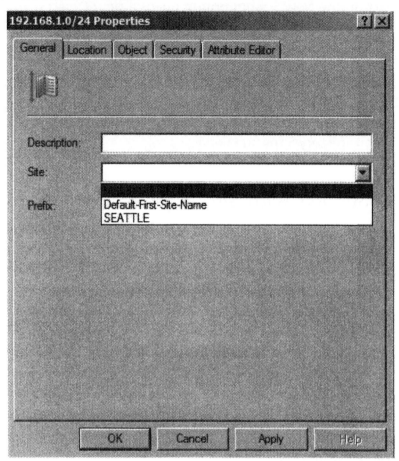

3. Right-click the newly created subnet and select the **Properties** option; this will open a Properties dialog box, as shown in Figure 2.18.

Continued

Figure 2.18 Subnet Dialog Box for Associating/Changing the Site

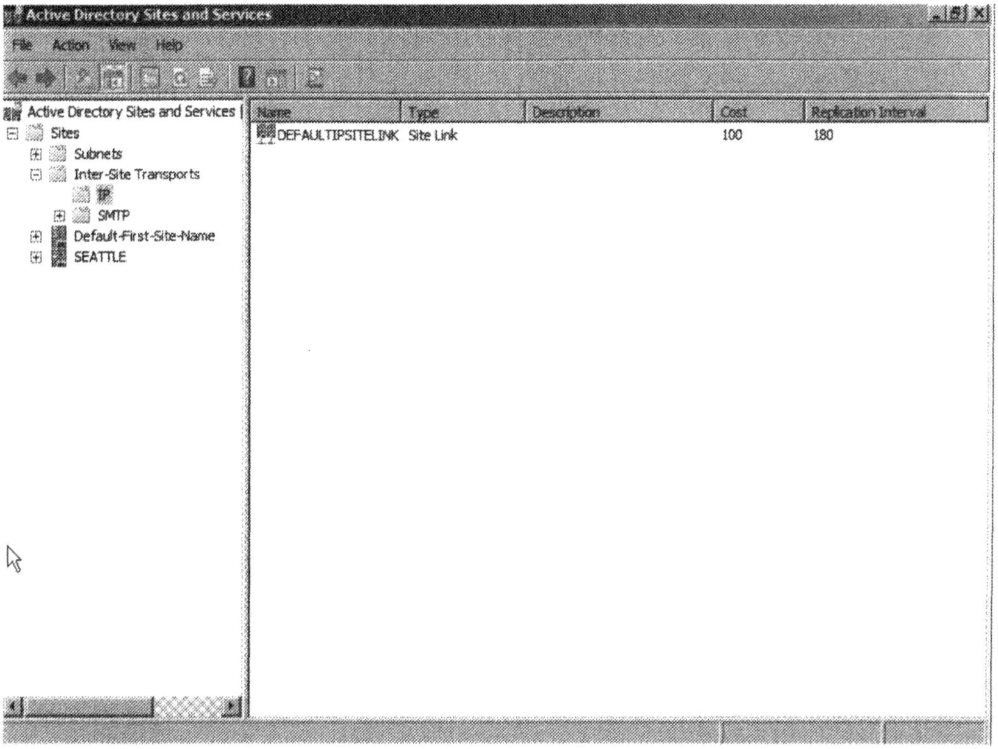

4. Associate any site with this subnet by selecting the available site from the site drop-down menu, and click **OK**. This completes the process of associating a subnet with a site using the Active Directory Sites and Services tool.

Creating Site Links

After creating and defining the scope of each site, the next step in the site configuration process is to establish connections between the sites. The physical connectivity between the sites is established between the Active Directory databases by site link objects. A *site link object* is an Active Directory object that embodies a set of sites that can communicate at uniform cost. A *site link* connects only two sites and corresponds to a WAN link for an IP transport. A site link connecting more than two sites corresponds to Asynchronous Transfer Mode (ATM) and metropolitan area network (MAN) through leased lines and IP routers. Each site link is based these four components:

- **Transport** The networking technology to move the replication traffic

- **Sites** The sites that the site link connects

- **Cost** The value to calculate the site links by comparing to others, in terms of speed and reliability charges

- **Schedule** The times and frequency at which the replication will occur

You create site links using the **Active Directory Sites and Services** tool of Windows Server 2008. The following Sidebar walks you through the steps involved in creating sitae links.

Configuring & Implementing...

Creating Site Links

1. To open the Active Directory Sites and Services tool, click Start | Administrative Tools, and then click Active Directory Sites and Services.

2. Highlight the **Inter-Site Transports** folder in the left-hand tree pane of the **Active Directory Sites and Services** console. Expand the **Inter-Site Transports** folder, as shown in Figure 2.19.

Continued

Figure 2.19 The Inter-Site Transports Folder

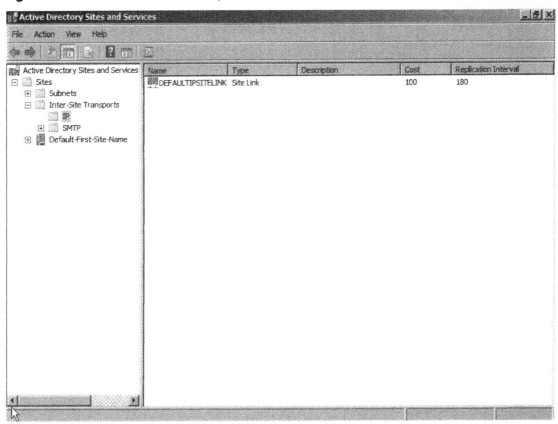

3. Right-click either the **IP** or the **SMTP** folder (depending on what protocol the network is based on) in the left-hand tree pane of the **Active Directory Sites and Services** console. Select **New Site Link** from the context menu, as shown in Figure 2.20.

Continued

Figure 2.20 The New Site Link Option

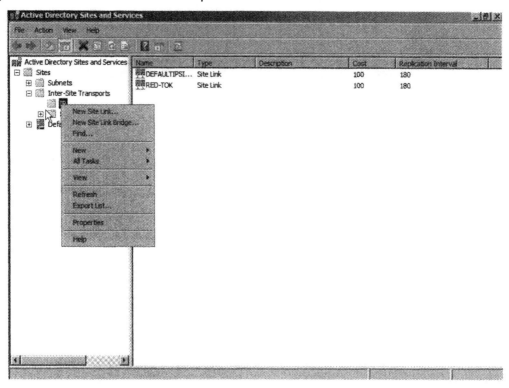

4. Selecting the **New Site Link** option opens a **New Object – Site Link** dialog box.

5. Type the name of the new site link object in the **Name** box in the **New Object – Site Link** dialog box.

6. Select two or more sites for establishing connection from the **Sites not in this site link** box, and click **Add**.

7. Click **OK**. This completes the process of creating a new site link object using the Active Directory Sites and Services tool.

Configuring Site Link Cost

Site link costs are calculated to determine how expensive an organization considers the network connection between two sites that the site link is connecting.

Higher costs represent more expensive connections. If two site links are available between two sites, the lowest-cost site link will be chosen. Each site link is assigned an IP or Simple Mail Transfer Protocol (SMTP) transport protocol, a cost, a replication frequency, and an availability schedule. All these parameters reflect the characteristics of the physical network connection.

The cost assigned to a site link is a number on an arbitrary scale that should reflect, in some sense, the expense of transmitting traffic using that link. Cost can be in the range of 1 to 32,767, and lower costs are preferred. The cost of a link should be inversely proportional to the effective bandwidth of a network connection between sites. For example, if you assign a cost of 32,000 to a 64 kbps line, you should assign 16,000 to a 128 kbps line and 1,000 to a 2 Mbps line. It makes sense to use a high number for the slowest link in your organization. As technology improves and communication becomes cheaper, it's likely that future WAN lines will be faster than today's, so there's little sense in assigning a cost of 2 for your current 128 kbps line and a cost of 1 for your 256 kbps line, because quicker links can't be priced more cheaply.

You configure site link costs using the Active Directory Sites and Services tool of Windows Server 2008. The following Sidebar illustrates the steps involved in creating site link costs.

Configuring & Implementing...

Configuring Site Link Costs

1. To open the Active Directory Sites and Services tool, click Start | Administrative Tools, and then click Active Directory Sites and Services.

2. Highlight the **Sites** folder in the left-hand tree pane of the **Active Directory Sites and Services** console and expand the **Sites** folder.

3. Highlight the **Inter-Site Transports** folder in the left-hand tree pane of the **Active Directory Sites and Services** console and expand the **Inter-Site Transports** folder.

4. Right-click the site link whose cost you want to configure in the left-hand tree pane of the **Active Directory Sites and Services** console, and select **Properties**. Selecting **Properties** opens a dialog box, as shown in Figure 2.21.

Continued

Figure 2.21 The Properties Option

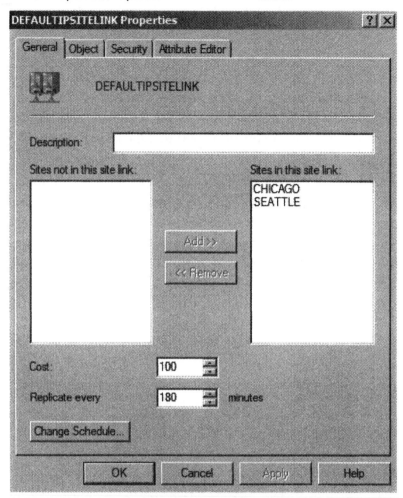

5. Type the value for the cost of replication of the site link object in the **Cost** box in the dialog box.

6. Click **OK**. This completes the process of configuring site link costs using the Active Directory Sites and Services tool.

Understanding Replication

Replication is defined as the practice of transferring data from a data store present on a source computer to an identical data store present on a destination computer to *synchronize* the data. In a network, the directory data must live in one or more places on the network to be equally available to all users. The Active Directory directory service manages a replica of directory data on one or more DCs, ensuring the availability of directory data to all users. The Active Directory works on the concept of sites to perform replication efficiently, and it uses the KCC to choose the best replication topology for the network automatically.

> **NOTE**
>
> The KCC is a process that runs on a DC, and identifies the most efficient replication topology for the network automatically, based on the data provided by the network in Active Directory Sites and Services.

Replication is an essential process for any domain that has multiple DCs. Replication ensures that each copy of the domain data is up-to-date, and is done by sending information regarding changes from one DC to another. Earlier versions of NT were configured in a single-master environment where the PDC was used to maintain and manage the master copy of the domain database, and was also in charge of replicating changes to the BDCs. In a *single-master environment*, if for some reason the PDC is unavailable, no changes can be made to the database.

In Windows Server 2008 domains, every writable DC has a complete copy of the Active Directory of its own domain. This is similar to the NT model, but the difference is that each Windows Server 2008 DC first accepts and makes changes to the database and then replicates those changes to other DCs. An environment in which multiple computers are used for managing changes is known as a *multimaster environment*.

A multimaster environment has many advantages over the single-master configuration, including the following:

- There are no single points of failure, as every DC can accept changes to the database.

- DCs that accept changes to the database are distributed throughout the network. This allows administrators to make changes on local DCs and let the replication ensure that these changes are updated to all other DCs in an efficient manner.

Replication in a Windows Server 2008 environment is one of two types:

- **Intrasite replication** Replication that occurs between DCs within a site
- **Intersite replication** Replication that occurs between DCs in different sites

It is important to understand the differences between these methods when planning the site structure and replication.

Intrasite Replication

Intrasite replication occurs between DCs within a site. The system implementing such replication uses high-speed, synchronous Remote Procedure Calls (RPCs).

Within a site, a ring topology is created by the KCC between the DCs for replication (see Figure 2.22). The KCC is a built-in process that runs on all DCs and helps in creating replication topology. It runs every 15 minute by default and delegates the replication path between DCs based on the connection available. The KCC automatically creates replication connections between DCs within the site. The ring topology created by the KCC defines the path through which changes flow within the site. All the changes follow the ring until every DC receives them.

Figure 2.22 Ring Topology for Replication

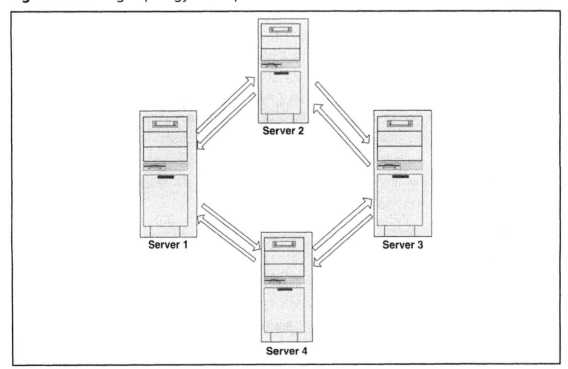

The KCC analyzes the replication topology within a site to ensure efficiency. If a DC is added or removed, it reconfigures the ring for maximum efficiency. It also configures the ring so that there will be no more than three hops between any two DCs within the site, which sometimes results in the creation of multiple rings (see Figure 2.23).

Figure 2.23 The Three-Hop Rule of Intrasite Replication

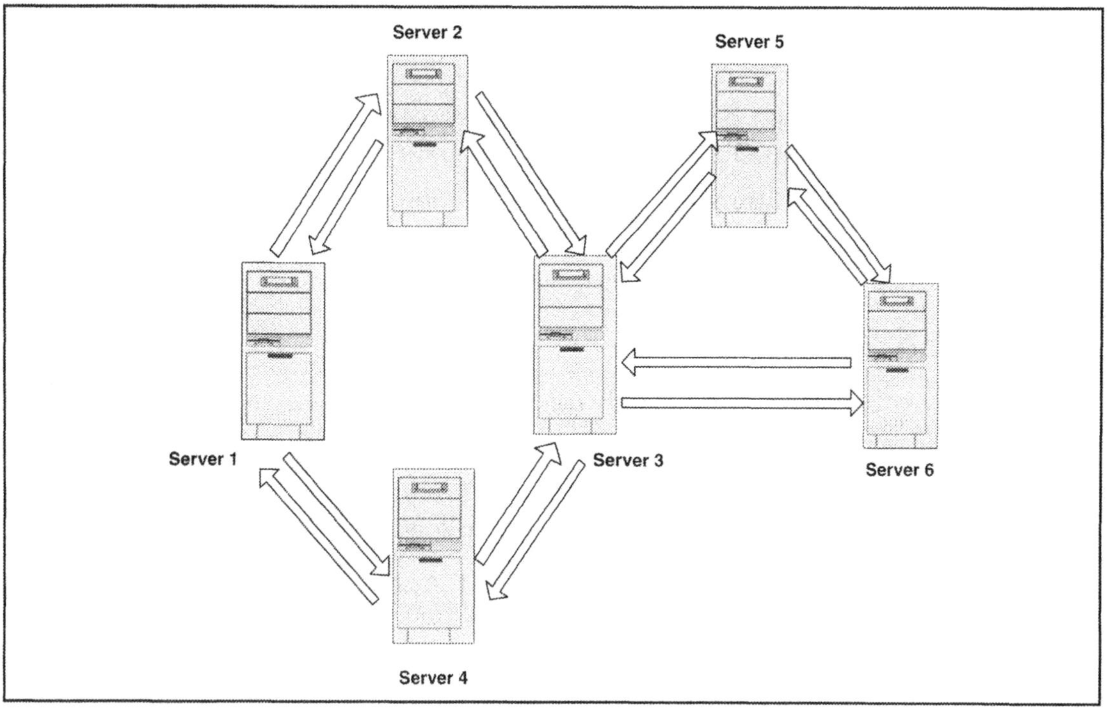

Intersite Replication

Intersite replication takes place between DCs in different sites. The drawback of intersite communication is that you have to configure it manually. Active Directory builds an efficient intersite replication topology with the information provided by the user. The directory saves this information as site link objects. A DC running the ISTG service is used to build the topology. An Inter-site Topology Generator is an Active Directory process that runs on one DC in a site and considers the cost of intersite connections. It ensures that the previous DCs are no longer available, and checks to determine whether new DCs have been added. The KCC process updates the intersite replication topology. A least-cost spanning-tree algorithm is used to eliminate superfluous replication paths between sites. An intersite replication topology is updated regularly to respond to any changes that occur in the network. It would be useful if the traffic needs to cross a slower Internet link.

Intersite replication across site links occurs every 180 minutes; you can change this if necessary. In addition, you can schedule the availability of the site links for use. By default, a site link is accessible to carry replication 24 hours a day, seven days a week, and you can also change this if necessary. You also can configure a site link to use low-speed synchronous RPCs over TCP/IP or asynchronous SMTP transport. That is, replication within a site always uses RPC over IP, whereas replication between sites can use either RPC over IP or SMTP over IP. Replication between sites over SMTP is supported for only DCs of different domains. DCs of the same domain must replicate by using the RPC over IP transport. Hence, you can configure a site link to point-to-point, low-speed synchronous RPC over IP between sites, and low-speed asynchronous SMTP between sites.

Bridgehead Servers

A *bridgehead server* is a server that is mainly used for intersite replication. You can configure a bridgehead server for every site that is created for each intersite replication protocol. This helps to control the server that is used to replicate information to other servers.

To configure a server as a bridgehead server, follow these steps:

1. Choose **Start | Administrative Tools | Active Directory Sites and Services**.

2. Expand the **Sites** folder.

3. Expand the site in which a bridgehead server has to be created, and then expand the **Servers** folder.

4. Right-click on the server and choose **Properties**.

5. In the **Transports available for inter-site transfer** area, select the protocol for which this server should be a bridgehead and click **Add**.

6. Click **OK** to set the properties, and then close **Active Directory Sites and Services**.

The ability to configure a server as a bridgehead server gives you greater control over the resources used for replication between intersites.

Site Link Bridges

Often, there is no need to deal with site link bridges separately, as all the links are automatically bridged by a property known as a *transitive site link*. Sometimes when you need to control through which sites the data can flow, you need to create site link bridges. By default, all the site links created are bridged together.

The bridging enables the sites to communicate with each other. If this is not enabled by the automatic bridging due to the network structure, disable the same and create an appropriate site link bridge. In some cases, it is necessary to control the data flow through the sites. In these cases, it is necessary to create site link bridges. To disable transitive site links (automatic bridging), follow these steps:

1. Choose **Start | Administrative Tools | Active Directory Sites and Services**.

2. Expand the **Sites** folder and then expand the **Inter-Site Transports** folder.

3. Right-click on the transport for which the automatic bridging should be turned off, and choose **Properties**.

4. On the **General** tab, clear the **Bridge all site links** checkbox and click **OK**.

To create a site link bridge, follow these steps:

1. Choose **Start | Administrative Tools | Active Directory Sites and Services**.

2. Expand the **Sites** folder and then the **Inter–Site Transports** folder.

3. Right-click on the transport that needs to be used, and choose **New Site Link Bridge**.

4. In the **Name** box, enter a name for the site link bridge.

5. From the list of **Site links not in this bridge**, select the site link to be added.

6. Remove any extra site links in the **Site links in this bridge** box and click **OK**.

Scheduling

You can configure replication frequency by providing an integer value that informs the Active Directory as to how many minutes it should wait before it can use a connection to check replication updates. The interval of time must be not less than 15 minutes and not more than 10,080 minutes. For any replication to happen, a site link is essential. Follow these steps to configure site link replication frequency:

1. Choose **Start | Administrative Tools | Active Directory Sites and Services**.

2. Expand the **Inter-Site Transports** folder; select either the **IP** or the **SMTP** folder and right-click the site link for which the site replication frequency is to be set.

3. Click **Properties**, and in the Properties dialog box for the site link, enter in the **Replicate Every** box the number of minutes between replications. The default value is 180.

4. Click **OK**.

Forcing Replication

Data is usually replicated based on a change notification within sites. It's up to the administrator to force immediate replication. To do so for all data on a given connection in a single direction, perform the following steps:

1. Choose **Start | Administrative Tools | Active Directory Sites and Services**. Expand **Sites** in the left-hand tree pane.

2. Expand the name of the site that has to replicate to.

3. Expand the name of the server for replicating.

4. Select the server's **NTDS Settings** object. The right console pane will be populated with the server's inbound connection objects.

5. In the right pane, right-click the name of the server from which you want to replicate, and select **Replicate Now**.

You also can force replication from the command line by using the repadmin.exe utility from the Support Tools.

Replication Protocols

When creating site links, you have the option of using either IP or SMTP as the transport protocol:

■ **SMTP replication** You can use SMTP only for replication over site links. It is asynchronous; that is, the destination DC does not wait for the reply, so the reply is not received in a short amount of time. SMTP replication also neglects Replication Available and Replication Not Available settings on the site link schedule, and uses the replication interval to indicate how often the server requests changes When choosing SMTP, you must install and configure an enterprise certificate authority (CA), as it signs the SMTP messages that are exchanged between DCs. SMTP replication is designed for use over slow or unreliable WAN links, in situations where IP connectivity between sites is too unreliable to be used for Active Directory replication.

- **IP replication** All replication within a site occurs over synchronous RPC over IP transport. The replication within a site is fast and has uncompressed delivery of updates. Replication events occur more frequently within a site than between sites, and the overhead of compression would be inefficient over fast connections.

Planning, Creating, and Managing the Replication Topology

An important job when implementing replication topology is planning, creating, and managing the replication topology, as discussed next.

Planning Replication Topology

Let's now discuss how to plan a replication topology:

- Before starting a replication planning process, we need to first finish the forest, domain, and DNS.

- It is essential to have an understanding of Active Directory replication, the File Replication Service (FRS), and SYSVOL replication used to replicate group policy changes.

- For Active Directory replication, a rule of thumb is that a given DC that acts as a bridgehead server should not have more than 50 active simultaneous replication connections at any given time.

Creating Replication Topology

The next step is to create the replication topology. Let's discuss how to create a replication topology:

- Active Directory replication is a one-way *pull* replication whereby the DC that needs updates (the target DC) gets in touch with the replication partner (the source DC). Then, the source DC selects the updates that the target DC needs, and copies them to the target DC. Because Active Directory uses a multimaster replication model, each DC functions as both source and target for its replication partners. From the view of a DC, it has both inbound and outbound replication traffic, depending on whether it is the source or the destination of a replication sequence.

- Inbound replication is the incoming data transfer from a replication partner to a DC, and outbound replication is the data transfer from a DC to its replication partner.

- System policies and logon scripts that are stored in SYSVOL use FRS to replicate. Each DC keeps a copy of SYSVOL for network clients to access. FRS is also used for DFS.

- Components of the replication topology such as the KCC, connection objects, site links, and site link bridges are to be checked by the administrator.

- There are two methods for creating a replication topology:

- Use the KCC to create connection objects. This method is recommended if there are 100 or fewer sites.

- Use a scripted or third-party tool for the creation of connection objects. This method is recommended if there are more than 100 sites.

Configuring Replication between Sites

To ensure that users can log on within a given span of time, it is necessary to locate DCs near them, which sometimes involves moving the DCs between sites. The purpose of a site is to help manage the replication between DCs and across slow network links. In addition to creating the site and adding subnets to that site, we also need to move DCs into the site, as replication happens between DCs. The DC has to be added to a site to which it belongs so that clients within a site can look for the DCs in the site and can log on to it.

To move DCs, follow these steps:

1. Select **Click Active Directory Sites and Services**.

2. Choose the **Sites** folder and then select the site where the server is located.

3. In the site, expand the **Servers** folder.

4. Right-click on the DC you want to move, and choose **Move**.

5. Select the destination subnet from the dialog box and click **OK**.

Troubleshooting Replication Failure

DCs usually handle the process involved with replication automatically. Unsuccessful network links and wrong configurations prevent the synchronization of information between DCs.

There are many ways to monitor the behavior of Active Directory replication and correct problems if they occur.

Troubleshooting Replication

A common symptom of replication problems is that the information is not updated on some or all DCs. There are several steps that you can take to troubleshoot Active Directory replication, including:

- **Check the network connectivity** The basic requirement for any type of replication to work properly in a distributed environment is network connectivity. The ideal situation is that all the DCs are connected by high-speed LAN links. In the real world, either a dial-up connection or a slow connection is common. Check to see whether the replication topology is set up properly. In addition, confirm whether the servers are communicating. Failed dial-up connection attempts can prevent important Active Directory information from being replicated.

- **Examine the replication topology** The Active Directory Sites and Services tool helps to verify whether a replication topology is logically consistent. You do this by right-clicking the **NTDS Settings** within a Server object and selecting **All Tasks | Check Replication Topology**. If there are any errors, a dialog box will alert you to the problem.

- **Validate the event logs** Whenever an error in the replication configuration occurs, events are written to the Directory Service event log. The Event Viewer administrative tool can provide the details associated with any problems in replication.

- **Verify whether the information is synchronized** Many administrators forget to execute manual checks regarding the replication of Active Directory information. One of the reasons for this is that Active Directory DCs have their own read/write copies of the Active Directory database. Therefore, no failures are encountered while creating new objects if connectivity does not exist. It is important to regularly check whether the objects have been synchronized between DCs. The manual check, although tedious, can prevent inconsistencies in the information stored on DCs.

- **Check router and firewall configurations** Firewalls are used to restrict the types of traffic transferred between networks. They increase security by preventing unauthorized users from transferring information. In some cases, company firewalls might block the types of network access that should be available for Active Directory replication to occur.

- **Verify site links** Before any DCs in different sites can communicate, the sites must be connected by site links. If replication between sites doesn't occur properly, verify whether the site links are in the proper positions.

Using Event Viewer

You use the Event Viewer for configuring Active Directory event logging. To configure Active Directory event logging, follow these steps:

1. Select **Start** | **Run**. In the **Open** box, type **regedit**, and click **OK**.

2. Locate and click the following Registry key: **HKEY_LOCAL_MACHINE\ SYSTEM\CurrentControlSet\Services\NTDS\Diagnostics**.

3. Each entry in the right-hand pane of the Registry Editor window represents a type of event that Active Directory can log. All entries are set to the default value of 0 (None).

To configure event logging for the appropriate component, follow these steps:

1. In the right-hand pane of the Registry Editor, double-click the entry that represents the type of event that is to be logged; for example, **Security Events**.

2. Type the logging level that's needed in the **Value data** box, and click **OK**.

3. Repeat step 2 for each component that you want to be logged. Then, on the **Registry** menu, click **Exit** to quit the Registry Editor.

Some of the events that you can write to the event log include:

- KCC

- MAPI events

- Security events

- Replication events

- Directory access

- Internal configuration

- Internal processing

- Intersite messaging

- Service control setup

Each entry is assigned a value of 0 through 5, which determines the level of details of the events that are logged:

- **0** (None) Only critical events and error events are logged at this level. This is the default setting for all entries.

- **1** (Minimal) Very high-level events are recorded in the event log at this setting. Events can include one message for each major task that the service performs. You can use this when the location to start an investigation is not known.

- **2** (Basic) This level adds additional information beyond what is logged at the minimal level, without significantly impacting the system resources required to capture these log events

- **3** (Extensive) This level records more detailed information than the lower levels, such as steps that are performed to complete a task.

- **4** (Verbose) This level records significant details, but excludes the debug strings that are recorded at the highest logging level.

- **5** (Internal) This level logs all events, including debug strings and configuration changes. A complete log of the service is recorded.

NOTE

Logging levels should always be set to the default value of 0 (None) unless there is an investigation at issue. If the Registry Editor is used incorrectly, it can cause serious problems that will require reinstalling the operating system.

Working with Trusts

One of the many issues that need to be dealt with in any computer organization is how to protect resources. The main difficulty that administrators face is the dilemma of how to ensure that the company's resources are not accessible by those who do not need access. The other side of that coin, and something that is equally important, is how to ensure that people who do need access are granted access with the least amount of hassle. In small companies, the issues are simpler, because multiple domains rarely exist. In today's larger corporations and conglomerates, the issues of security are compounded. What administrators need is an easy tool to manage access across multiple domains and, often, across forests.

The tool is Active Directory Domains and Trusts. With Active Directory Domains and Trusts, an administrator can establish relationships between domains that will allow users in one domain to access the resources in another. This way, the administrator can ensure that all users who need access can have it without the hassles involved in having user accounts in multiple domains.

As the name implies, trusts are all about sharing information. For security purposes, you should carefully consider your reasons before creating a new trust relationship, as well as knowing which type of trust to implement. In Active Directory, a *shortcut* trust doesn't add more trust; rather, it can make the trusts you already have more efficient. *External* trusts are a concept left over from Windows NT, but are still necessary for sharing resources with a Windows NT domain or any other Windows domain outside your forest. Finally, you should consider the Windows Server 2008 *forest trust* to provide a transitive trust relationship between two Active Directory forests that are running Windows Server 2003 or Windows Server 2008 on all installed DCs. As you can see, trusts are varied in properties and purposes. The most important concepts to understand about trusts before you create them are *direction* and *transitivity*. Always be aware of the extent of any internal access that you grant to external users.

Trusts are predetermined avenues of access to forest resources. It is like giving someone a key to your house and hoping that he or she won't misuse your trust. DCs do the authenticating, but not all DCs necessarily trust each other. That's where you come in, setting the relationships between domains that govern the flow of information.

Two primary attributes of trusts are direction and transitivity. The *direction of trust* flows from the trusting domain to the trusted domain, as shown by the arrow in Figure 2.24. Cats.com *trusts* Dogs.com. The *direction of access* is always in the opposite direction; Dogs.com *accesses* resources in Cats.com. This is a one-way trust. Likewise, Dogs.com trusts Fish.com, but does not trust Cats.com. Two one-way trusts can combine to simulate a single two-way trust.

Figure 2.24 The Nontransitive Trust

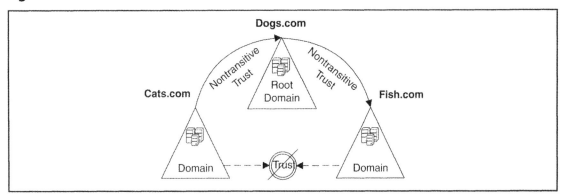

The second attribute of the trust is *transitivity*, or a measure of how far the trust extends. A nontransitive trust has limits. The trusted domain, *and only the trusted domain*, can access resources through the trust to the trusting domain. As shown in Figure 2.24, if the Dogs.com domain has trusts to other domains such as Fish.com, those other domains are barred from access to Cats.com unless they have a nontransitive trust of their own. The absence of the third leg of the trust breaks the circle of access. This is the behavior of all trusts in Windows NT.

Conversely, transitive trusts, such as the ones shown in Figure 2.25, are the skeleton keys of access. Anyone on the trusted side of the trust relationship can enter, including anyone trusted by the trusted domain. When a user or process requests access to a resource in another domain, a series of hand-offs occurs within the authentication process down the *trust path*, as shown in Figure 2.25. When Cats.com trusts Dogs.com, they must trust all Dogs.com child domains equally at the level of the trust. There are two types of trusts in Figure 2.25, *parent and child* and *tree-root*. All trusts shown are bidirectional and transitive, as they are by default in Windows Server 2008. Calico.cats.com has a trust relationship with Yellow.labs.dogs.com because of the trust path that extends through all three intervening domains. If Calico.cats.com has no reason to trust Yellow.labs.dogs.com, the cats must apply permissions to limit or block the access.

Figure 2.25 The Transitive Trust

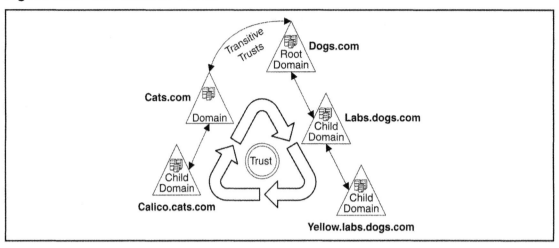

A *trust* is a logical authentication path between two domains. A *trust path* is the number of trusts that must be traversed between the source and destination of a resource request. Two trusts, *tree-root* and *parent and child*, are created by default when running the Active Directory Installation Wizard. You can create the other four trusts—*shortcut*, *external*, *realm*, and *forest*—as needed with the New Trust Wizard or the Netdom.exe command-line tool.

When creating those four trusts, you have the option of creating two one-way relationships, simulating bidirectional capabilities. As with any use of passwords, it is a security best practice to use long, random, and complex passwords in the establishment of trusts. The best option is to use the New Trust Wizard to create both sides simultaneously, in which case the wizard generates a strong password for you. Naturally, you must have the appropriate administrative credentials in both domains for this to work.

We've been talking about two-way (bidirectional) trusts; but a trust can also be one-way (unidirectional). One-way trusts are created to allow more restrictive control over which users are allowed access to resources. For example, in Figure 2.26, a one-way trust is created between Domain X and Domain Y. Users in Domain X have access to resources in Domain Y. However, users in Domain Y do not have access to resources in Domain X. In this definition, Domain X is referred to as the trusted domain, and Domain Y is the trusting domain. A two-way trust allows users in either domain to have access to resources in the other domain.

One-way trusts must specify the *direction* of the trust. One-way trusts can be either *incoming* or *outgoing,* depending on whether the trust is created from the trusting or the trusted domain. Incoming trusts permit the users in the domain where the trust is created (the *trusted* domain) to access resources in the specified domain (the *trusting* domain). Users in the trusting domain do not have access, through this trust, to the resources in the trusted domain. (You can, however, create a second trust that goes the other way, to accomplish the same effect as a two-way trust.)

Outgoing trusts allow the users in the specified domain (the trusted domain) to have access to resources in the originating domain (the trusting domain). Users in the originating domain do not have access to resources in the specified domain.

Figure 2.26 One-Way Trust

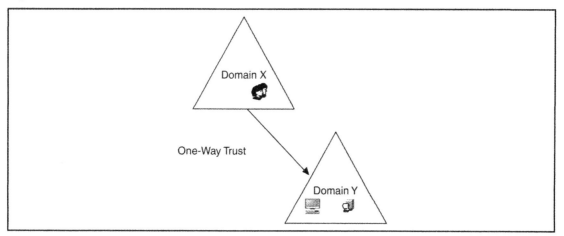

Another concept and set of terms to understand in regard to trusts is:

- Implicit
- Explicit

Implicit trusts are trusts that are created automatically by the nature of the built-in relationships between domains within a forest. These implicit trusts are two-way and transitive. Implicit trusts automatically exist between each domain that is created and its child domain(s). An implicit trust also exists between the root domain of each domain tree and the root domains of every other domain tree in the forest.

An *explicit* trust is one that is created by an administrator; it does not exist automatically, but has to be explicitly created. For example, an administrator can create an explicit trust (in this case, called a *shortcut trust*) between any two child domains in different domain trees to provide for a direct trust (and faster authentication) between them.

Explicit trusts are also used to enable authentication across forests. When a forest trust is created, a transitive trust is created between the forest root domains in both forests. This allows all the members in the forest to exchange authentication information with the other forest. The forest trust is also called an explicit trust between the two forests. If an additional forest trust is created between one of the original forests and a third forest, an implicit trust with the other original forest is not established to the third forest. For the third forest to have a trust relationship with the other forest, an explicit forest trust must be created between the two (see Figure 2.27).

Figure 2.27 Implicit Trust

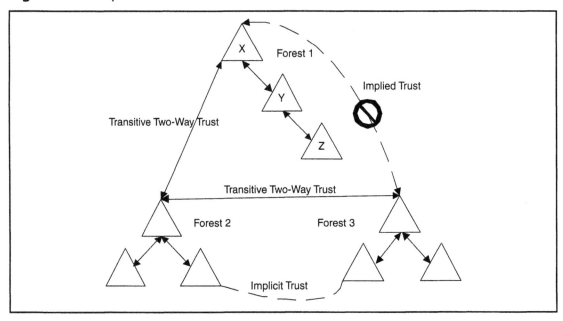

The primary advantage of Active Directory trust relationships is that administrators no longer need to create multiple user accounts for each user who needs access to resources within each domain. Administrators can now add the users of the other domains to their access control lists (ACLs) to control access to a resource. To take full advantage of these relationships, the administrator must know about the various types of trust that exist, and when to use them.

Default Trusts

When the Active Directory Installation Wizard is used to create a new domain within an existing forest, two default trusts are created: a parent and child trust, and the tree-root trust. Four additional types of trusts can be created using the New Trust Wizard or the command-line utility netdom. The default trust relationships inside a Windows 2000, Windows Server 2003, and Windows Server 2008 forest are transitive, two-way trusts.

A parent and child trust is a transitive, two-way trust relationship. It allows authentication requests made in the child domain to be validated in the parent domain. Because the trusts are transitive, these requests pass upward from child to parent until they reach the root of the domain namespace. This relationship will allow any user in the domain to have access to any resource in the domain if the user has the proper permissions granted.

An additional transitive, two-way trust is created to simplify the navigation: the tree-root trust. This is especially needed in large organizations that might have multiple levels of child domains. The tree-root trust is a trust that is created between any child domain and the root domain. This provides a shortcut to the root. This trust relationship is also automatically created when a new domain is created.

Forest Trusts

A forest trust can only be created between the root domains in two forests. Both forests must be Windows Server 2003 or Windows Server 2008 forests. These trusts can be one- or two-way trusts. They are considered transitive trusts because the child domains inside the forest can authenticate themselves across the forest to access resources in the other forest.

WARNING

Although the trust relationship is considered transitive, this applies only to the child domains within forests. The transitive nature of the trust exists only within the two forests explicitly joined by a forest trust. The transitivity does not extend to a third forest unless you create another explicit trust (see Figure 2.27).

Forest trusts help to manage the Active Directory infrastructure. They do this by simplifying the management of resources between two forests by reducing the required number of external trusts. Instead of needing multiple external trusts, a two-way forest trust between the two root domains will allow full access between all the affected domains. Additionally, the administrator can take advantage of both the Kerberos and NTLM authentication protocols to transfer authorization data between forests.

Forest trusts can provide complete two-way trusts with every domain within the two forests. This is useful if you have created multiple forests to secure data within the forest or to help isolate directory replication within each forest.

External Trusts

You use an external trust when you need to create a trust between domains outside of your forest. These trusts can be one- or two-way trusts. They are always nontransitive in nature. This means you have created an explicit trust between the two domains, and domains outside this trust are not affected. You can create an external trust to access resources in a domain in a different forest that is not already covered by a forest trust (see Figure 2.28).

Figure 2.28 External Trust

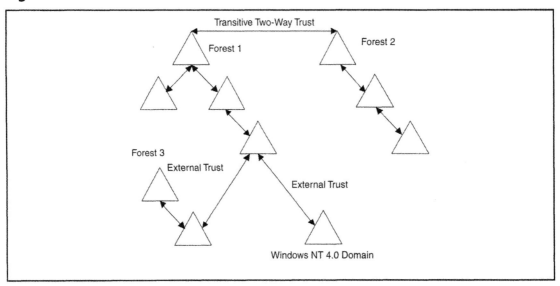

After the trust has been established between a domain in a forest and a domain outside the forest, the security principals from the domain outside the forests will be able to access the resources in the domain inside the forest. Security principals can be the users, groups, computers, or services from the external domain. They are account holders that are each assigned a SID automatically to control access to the resources in the domain.

The Active Directory in the domain inside the forest will then create foreign security principal objects representing each security principal from the trusted external domain. You can use these foreign security principals in the domain local groups. This means that the domain local groups can have members from the trusted external domain. You use these groups to control access to the resources of the domain.

The foreign security principals are seen in Active Directory Users and Computers. Because the Active Directory automatically creates them, you should not attempt to modify them.

Shortcut Trusts

Shortcut trusts are transitive in nature and can be either one-way or two-way. These are explicit trusts that you create when the need exists to optimize ("shortcut") the authentication process. Without shortcut trusts in place, authentication travels up and down the domain tree using the default parent and child trusts, or by using the tree-root trusts. In large, complex organizations that use multiple trees, this path can become a bottleneck when authenticating users. To optimize access, the network administrator can create an explicit shortcut trust directly to the target domain (see Figure 2.29).

Figure 2.29 Shortcut Trust

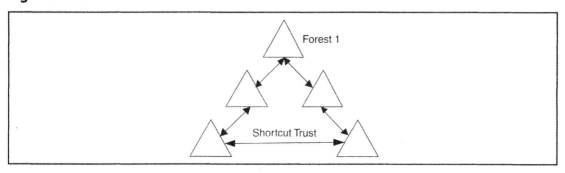

You use these trusts when user accounts in one domain need regular access to the resources in another domain. Shortcut trusts can be either one- or two-way. You should establish one-way shortcut trusts when the users in one domain need access to resources in the other domain, but those in the second domain do not need access to resources in the first domain. You should create two-way trusts when the users in both domains need access to the resources in the other domain. The shortcut trust will effectively shorten the authentication path, especially if the domains belong to two separate trees in the forest.

SID Filtering

One security concern when using trusts is a malicious user who has administrative credentials in the trusted domain sniffing the trusting domain to obtain the credentials of an administrator account. With the credentials of the trusting domain administrator, the malicious user could add his SID to allow full access to the trusting domain's resources. This type of threat is called an *elevation of privilege attack*.

The security mechanism used by Windows Server 2003 and Windows Server 2008 to counter an elevation of privilege attack is *SID filtering*. SID filtering is used to verify that an authentication request coming in from the trusted domain only contains the domain SIDs of the trusted domain. It does this by using the *SIDHistory* attribute on a security principal.

NOTE

Security principal is a term used to describe any account that has a SID automatically assigned. Examples of security principals are users, groups, services, and computers. Part of each security principal is the domain SID to identify the domain in which the account was created.

SID filtering uses the domain SID to verify each security principal. If a security principal includes a domain SID other than one from trusted domains, the SID filtering process removes the SID in question. This is done to protect the integrity of the trusting domain. This will prevent the malicious user from being able to elevate his or her privileges or those of other users.

There are some potential problems associated with SID filtering. It is possible for a user whose SID contains SID information from a domain that is not trusted to be denied access to the resources in the trusting domain. This is can be a problem when universal groups are used. Universal groups should be verified to contain only users that belong to the trusted domain.

You can disable SID filtering if there is a high level of trust for all administrators in the affected domains, there are strict requirements to verify all universal group memberships, and any migrated users have their *SIDHistories* preserved. To disable SID filtering, use the *netdom* command.

Summary

The logical structure of the network is defined by forests and domains, with domains organized into domain trees in which subdomains (called child domains) can be created under parent domains in a branching structure. Domains are logical units that hold users, groups, computers, and OUs (which in turn can contain users, groups, computers, and other OUs). Forests are collections of domain trees that have trust relationships with one another, but each domain tree has its own separate namespace. Aspects of the physical structure include sites, servers, roles, and links.

An Active Directory always begins with a forest root domain, which is automatically the first domain that you install. This root domain becomes the foundation for additional directory components. The domain is the starting point of Active Directory. It is the most basic component that can functionally host the directory. Simply put, Active Directory uses the domain as a container of computers, users, groups, and other object containers. Objects within the domain share a common directory database partition, replication boundaries and characteristics, security policies, and security relationships with other domains. The process of creating the forest and domain structure is centered on the use of the Active Directory Installation Wizard, which is also known as the dcpromo utility.

In Windows NT 4.0, the domain had only one authoritative source for domain-related information: the primary DC, or PDC. The implementation of Active Directory brought the multimaster model, where objects and their properties could be modified on any DC and become authoritative through replication conflict resolution measures. The problem with the multimaster architecture is that some domain and enterprise-wide operations are not well suited for it. The best design placed those functions on a single DC within the domain or forest, and Microsoft created the Active Directory FSMO roles. The Active Directory supports five operational master roles: the Schema Master, Domain Master, RID Master, PDC Emulator, and Infrastructure Master. Two of these operate at the forest level only: the Schema Master and the Domain Naming Master. Conversely, the RID Master, PDC Emulator, and Infrastructure Master operate at the domain level. You can use the ntdsutil.exe command-line utility to transfer FSMO roles, or you can use an MMC snap-in tool. Depending on which role you want to transfer, you need to use one of the following three MMC snap-in tools: Active Directory Schema, Active Directory Domains and Trusts, or Active Directory Users and Computers. To seize a role, you must use the ntdsutil utility. If a computer cannot be contacted due to a hardware malfunction or long-term network failure, the role must be seized. After you seize a Master role, the old DC that hosted it should never be brought back online. This is especially true of the Schema Master, Domain Naming Master, and RID Master roles.

The GC server is one of the most important roles played by one or more DCs in your network. It might not appear to do much on the surface, but the GC is responsible for helping to resolve names for objects throughout your forest. The GC server holds a copy of all the objects in the domain in which the server is located. That same GC server holds a partial replica of other domains in the forest. The information that the GC holds from other domains includes common search items. This limited but frequently accessed information makes queries very efficient.

GC servers are responsible for UPN authentication. When a user logs on using the UPN, the GC is queried to locate the user account and a DC in the appropriate domain. GC servers are also responsible for answering queries against Active Directory. If a user wants to locate another person within the organization, that user could use his workstation to search Active Directory. The queries are sent to IP port 3268, which is used for GC communication.

You must consider placement of GC servers early in the design process for your network. If you don't determine where you do and do not need a GC server and plan accordingly, you could have communication problems and users could be adversely affected. A good rule of thumb is to remember that if a location has more than 50 users, a DC is needed at that location. Dividing the network into *sites* makes a difference in how replication traffic is handled in regard to GC information. Replication within a site (intrasite replication) is handled differently than replication between different sites (intersite replication). Placement of GC servers within every site might not be necessary, but you should keep track of how much bandwidth computers are using. GC queries in large quantities can tie up significant bandwidth.

Active Directory trust relationships come in many flavors to meet the needs of the situation where users in one domain need access to the resources in another domain. First, there are the default trusts created between parent and child domains. These trusts are automatically created to simplify usage of resources in a tree. The network administrator can create additional types of trusts, such as external, shortcut, realm, and forest trusts. External trusts link two external domains. Shortcut trusts simplify the authentication paths needed to authenticate users. Realm trusts are created to connect a non-Windows network to a Windows Server 2003 or Windows Server 2008 domain. Forest trusts link forests together in the enterprise.

As you create these additional trust types, you can determine whether the trust will work in one direction only, or in both directions. When the trust works in both directions, it is called a two-way or bidirectional trust, and users in both domains have access to resources in both domains.

Another issue is whether the trust is transitive. A transitive trust "passes" through one trusted domain to another. A transitive trust implies a trust relationship when more than two domains are involved. If Domain A trusts Domain B and Domain B trusts Domain C, Domain A trusts Domain C. This is sometimes not the effect you want when creating trusts. The administrator has control over the transitive nature of the trust. As a further protection, SID filtering prevents users from an untrusted domain from being able to access resources in your domain.

Finally, this chapter also explained the role of sites, and discussed the relationship of sites to other Active Directory components. We showed you how to create sites and site links, and explained site replication.

Solutions Fast Track

Working with Forests and Domains

- ☑ You should know what type of domain you want to install before you begin, and the namespace it will use.

- ☑ To improve a domain's reliability, you should always create at least two DCs in each domain.

- ☑ The first DC that you install in the forest is the root DC. It is responsible for the GC and for all five FSMO roles. Some roles can later be transferred to other DCs for performance and diversification.

Working with Sites

- ☑ Sites are used for optimizing the authentication process, by reducing authentication traffic across slow, high-cost WAN links.

- ☑ Subnets provide rapid and reliable communication between locations.

- ☑ The primary role of sites is to increase the performance of a network, which is achieved by economic and rapid transmission of data.

☑ Replication enables transferring data from a data store present on a source computer to an identical data store present on a destination computer.

☑ The KCC is a process that runs on a DC.

☑ The process of associating a subnet with a site notifies Active Directory sites about the physical networks that are represented by the site.

☑ Cost is the value used to calculate site links by comparing one to others, in terms of speed and reliability charges.

Working with Trusts

☑ Active Directory trust relationships allow users in one domain to access resources in another domain without having to create additional accounts in the domain with the resources.

☑ Whenever a child domain is created, two-way transitive trusts are automatically created between the parent and the child.

☑ Forest trusts are created between the root domains of two forests to allow users in one forest to access resources in the other forest.

☑ SID filtering is a security device that uses the domain SID to verify each security principal.

Frequently Asked Questions

Q: What is the big deal about raising the functional levels of my domains and forests? Shouldn't I raise the levels as soon as they meet the prerequisites?

A: No. Remember that functional levels, once raised, cannot be lowered again. In addition, some situations are better suited to skipping a level, rather than raising to one level and then the other. In this case, known future restructuring and upgrade activities should be considered before raising functional levels.

Q: How much of the Active Directory design stage should be complete before I install my first DC?

A: Primarily, the DNS design should be complete, and the decision should be made about how the forest-root domain will be used. Additional DCs and domains can be added later. FSMO roles and GCs can be shifted as needed, and trusts with other forests and external domains can be added later. Essentially, the first DC that you install should be in a lab environment. From that perspective, you should install your first DC for testing and training purposes as soon as possible.

Q: What are the differences between external, realm, and shortcut trusts?

A: An external trust is created to establish a relationship with a domain outside your tree or forest. A realm trust is created to establish a relationship with a non-Microsoft network using Kerberos authentication. A shortcut trust is used to optimize the authentication process.

Q: What type of trust needs to be created between the root domain and a domain that is several layers deep inside the same tree?

A: None. Transitive two-way trusts are automatically created between the layers of the tree structure. A root trust is also created automatically so that any child domain has a shortcut to the root domain.

Q: What is the difference between implied, implicit, and explicit trusts?

A: An implicit trust is one that is automatically created by the system. An example is the trusts created between parent and child domains. An explicit trust is one that is manually created. An example is a forest trust between two trees. An implied trust is one that is implied because of the transitive nature of trusts. An example is the trust between two child domains that are in different trees, and a forest trust was created between the roots of the tress.

Q: What exactly does SID filtering accomplish?

A: SID filtering is used to secure a trust relationship where the possibility exists that someone in the trusted domain might try to elevate his or her own or someone else's privileges.

Q: How do you change the time the KCC runs?

A: The KCC, which manages connection objects for inter- and intrasite replication, runs every 15 minutes by default. To change this, start **regedit** and go to the **HKEY_LOCAL_MACHINE\SYSTEM\CurrentControlSet\Services\ NTDS\Parameters** Registry entry. Then, from the **Edit** menu, select **New**, **DWORD Value**.

Q: How do I move a server to a different site?

A: If the sites and subnets are configured, new servers are automatically added to the site that owns the subnet. However, a server can be manually moved to a different site. To perform this task, start the **Active Directory Sites and Services**. Expand the site that currently contains the server, and expand the **Servers** container. Right-click the server and select **Move** from the context menu. There will be a list of all the sites. Select the new target site, and click **OK**.

Q: How can a server belong to more than one site?

A: By default, a server belongs to only one site. However, you can configure a server to belong to multiple sites. Because sites are necessary for replication, for clients to find resources, and to decrease traffic on intersite connections, simply modifying a site's membership might cause performance problems. To configure a server for multiple site membership, log on to the server you want to join multiple sites. Start **regedit** or **regedt32**. Go to the **HKEY_LOCAL_MACHINE\SYSTEM\CurrentControlSet\ServicesNetlogon\Parameters** Registry entry, select **Add Value** from the **Edit** menu, enter the name **Site Coverage** and a **REG_MULTI_SZ** value, and click **OK**. Next, enter the names of the sites to join, each on a new line. (Press **Shift + Enter** to move to the next line.) Click **OK**. Close the Registry Editor.

Q: How do I disable site link transitivity?

A: Site links are bridged together to make them transitive so that the KCC can create connection objects between DCs. We can disable site link transitivity manually by bridging specific site links. Start the **Active Directory Sites and Services** snap-in. (Select **Administrative Tools | Active Directory Sites and Services** from the **Start menu**.) Expand the **Sites** folder and expand the **Inter-Site Transports** folder. Right-click the protocol for which you want to disable transitivity (IP or SMTP), and select **Properties**. Clear the **Bridge all site links** checkbox, and click **Apply**.

Q: How do you rename a site?

A: When you install your first DC, the DC creates the default site, Default-First-Site-Name. This name isn't very descriptive, so you might want to rename it. Start the **Active Directory Sites and Services** snap-in. (Select **Administrative Tools | Active Directory Sites and Services** from the **Start** menu.) Expand the **Sites** folder. Right-click the site that is to be renamed (e.g., Default-First-Site-Name), and select **Rename**. Enter the new name, and press **Enter**.

Q: I want to enable GC functionality on a DC. Where do I do that?

A: In the **NTDS Settings Properties** window on the **General** tab. You simply check the box next to **Global Catalog** and click **OK**.

Q: I have an office with only 10 users. Should I put a GC server at this location?

A: Probably not; Microsoft recommends that 50 or more users at a location constitutes the necessity for a local DC at that office.

Q: I am noticing a large amount of traffic between my corporate office and branch office. I recently added a GC server/DC at my branch office. Why all the extra traffic?

A: More than likely, you didn't set up a site for each location. Having GC servers located in sites helps to control replication and should cut down on bandwidth usage. Data is compressed before being sent between sites, which keeps bandwidth usage down.

## Chapter 3

Configuring Certificate Services and PKI

Solutions in this chapter:

- **What Is PKI?**

- **Analyzing Certificate Needs within the Organization**

- **Working with Certificate Services**

- **Working with Templates**

☑ Summary

☑ Solutions Fast Track

☑ Frequently Asked Questions

Introduction

Computer networks have evolved in recent years to allow an unprecedented sharing of information between individuals, corporations, and even national governments. The need to protect this information has also evolved, and network security has consequently be-come an essential concern of most system administrators. Even in smaller organizations, the basic goal of preventing unauthorized access while still allowing legitimate information to flow smoothly requires the use of more and more advanced technology.

That being stated, all organizations today rely on networks to access information. These sources of information can range from internal networks to the Internet. Access to information is needed, and this access must be configured to provide information to other organizations that may request it. When we need to make a purchase, for example, we can quickly check out vendors' prices through their Web pages. In order not to allow the competition to get ahead of our organization, we must establish our own Web page for the advertising and ordering of our products. Within any organization, many sites may exist across the country or around the globe. If corporate data is available immediately to employees, much time is saved. In the corporate world, any time saved is also money saved.

In the mid 1990s, Microsoft began developing what was to become a comprehensive security system of authentication protocols and technology based on already developed cryptography standards known as public key infrastructure (PKI). In Windows 2000, Microsoft used various standards to create the first Windows-proprietary PKI—one that could be implemented completely without using third-party companies. Windows Server 2008 expands and improves on that original design in several significant ways, which we'll discuss later in this chapter.

PKI is the method of choice for handling authentication issues in large enterprise-level organizations today. Windows Server 2008 includes the tools you need to create a PKI for your company and issue digital certificates to users, computers, and applications. This chapter addresses the complex issues involved in planning a certificate-based PKI. We'll provide an overview of the basic terminology and concepts relating to the public key infrastructure, and you'll learn about public key cryptography and how it is used to authenticate the identity of users, computers, and applications/services. We'll discuss different components of PKI, including private key, public key, and a trusted third party (TTP) along with PKI enhancements in Windows Server 2008. We'll discuss the role of digital certificates and the different types of certificates (user, machine, and application certificates).

You'll learn about certification authorities (CAs), the servers that issue certificates, including both public CAs and private CAs, such as the ones you can implement on your own network using Server 2008's certificate services. Next, we'll discuss the CA hierarchy and how root CAs and subordinate CAs act together to provide for your organization's certificate needs. You'll find out how the Microsoft certificate services work, and we'll walk you through the steps involved in implementing one or more certification authorities based on the needs of the organization. You'll learn to determine the appropriate CA type—enterprise or stand-alone CA—for a given situation and how to plan the CA hierarchy and provide for security of your CAs. We'll show you how to plan for enrollment and distribution of certificates, including the use of certificate requests, role-based administration, and autoenrollment deployment.

Next, we'll discuss how to implement certificate templates, different types of templates that you can use in your environment. Finally, we'll discuss the role of key recovery agent and how it works in a Windows Server 2008 environment.

What Is PKI?

The rapid growth of Internet use has given rise to new security concerns. Any company that does not configure a strong security infrastructure is literally putting the company at risk. An unscrupulous person could, if security were lax, steal information or modify business information in a way that could result in major financial disaster. To protect the organization's information, the middleman must be eliminated. Cryptographic technologies such as public key infrastructure (PKI) provide a way to identify both users and servers during network use.

PKI is the underlying cryptography system that enables users or computers that have never been in trusted communication before to validate themselves by referencing an association to a trusted third party (TTP). Once this verification is complete, the users and computers can now securely send messages, receive messages, and engage in transactions that include the interchange of data.

PKI is used in both private networks (intranets) and on the World Wide Web (the Internet). It is actually the latter, the Internet, that has driven the need for better methods for verifying credentials and authenticating users. Consider the vast number of transactions that take place every day over the internet—from banking to shopping to accessing databases and sending messages or files. Each of these transactions involves at least two parties. The problem lies in the verification of who those parties are and the choice of whether to trust them with your credentials and information.

The PKI verification process is based on the use of *keys*, unique bits of data that serve one purpose: identifying the owner of the key. Every user of PKI actually generates or receives two types of keys: a *public key* and a *private key*. The two are actually connected and are referred to as a *key pair*. As the name suggests, the public key is made openly available to the public while the private key is limited to the actual owner of the key pair. Through the use of these keys, messages can be *encrypted* and *decrypted*, allowing data to be exchanged securely (this process will be covered in a few sections later in this chapter).

The use of PKI on the World Wide Web is so pervasive that it is likely that every Internet user has used it without even being aware of it. However, PKI is not simply limited to the Web; applications such as Pretty Good Privacy (PGP) also leverage the basis of PKI technology for e-mail protection; FTP over SSL/TLS uses PKI, and many other protocols have the ability to manage the verification of identities through the use of key-based technology. Companies such as VeriSign and Entrust exist as trusted third-party vendors, enabling a world of online users who are strangers to find a common point of reference for establishing confidentiality, message integrity, and user authentication. Literally millions of secured online transactions take place every day leveraging their services within a public key infrastructure.

Technology uses aside, PKI fundamentally addresses relational matters within communications. Specifically, PKI seeks to provide solutions for the following:

- Proper authentication
- Trust
- Confidentiality
- Integrity
- Nonrepudiation

By using the core PKI elements of public key cryptography, digital signatures, and certificates, all these equally important goals can be met successfully. The good news is that the majority of the work involved in implementing these elements under Windows Server 2008 is taken care of automatically by the operating system and is done behind the scenes.

The first goal, proper *authentication*, means that you can be highly certain that an entity such as a user or a computer is indeed the entity he, she, or it is claiming to be. Think of a bank. If you wanted to cash a large check, the teller will more than likely ask for some identification. If you present the teller with a driver's license and the picture on it matches your face, the teller can then be highly certain that you are that person—that is, if the teller trusts the validity of the license itself. Because the driver's license is issued by a government agency—a trusted third party—the teller is more likely to accept it as valid proof of your identity than if you presented an employee ID card issued by a small company that the teller has never heard of. As you can see, trust and authentication work hand in hand.

When transferring data across a network, *confidentiality* ensures that the data cannot be viewed and understood by any third party. The data might be anything from an e-mail message to a database of social security numbers. In the last 20 years, more effort has been spent trying to achieve this goal (data confidentiality) than perhaps all the others combined. In fact, the entire scientific field of cryptology is devoted to ensuring confidentiality (as well as all the other PKI goals).

> **NOTE**
>
> *Cryptography* refers to the process of encrypting data; *cryptanalysis* is the process of decrypting, or "cracking" cryptographic code. Together, the two make up the science of *cryptology.*

As important as confidentiality is, however, the importance of network data *integrity* should not be underestimated. Consider the extreme implications of a patient's medical records being intercepted during transmission and then maliciously or accidentally altered before being sent on to their destination. Integrity gives confidence to a recipient that data has arrived in its original form and hasn't been changed or edited.

Finally we come to *nonrepudiation*. A bit more obscure than the other goals, nonrepudiation allows you to prove that a particular entity sent a particular piece of data. It is impossible for the entity to deny having sent it. It then becomes extremely difficult for an attacker to masquerade as a legitimate user and then send malevolent data across the network. Nonrepudiation is related to, but separate from authentication.

The Function of the PKI

The primary function of the PKI is to address the need for privacy throughout a network. For the administrator, there are many areas that need to be secured. Internal and external authentication, encryption of stored and transmitted files, and e-mail privacy are just a few examples. The infrastructure that Windows Server 2008 provides links many different public key technologies in order to give the IT administrator the power necessary to maintain a secure network.

Most of the functionality of a Windows Server 2008-based PKI comes from a few crucial components, which are described in this chapter. Although there are several third-party vendors such as VeriSign (www.verisign.com) that offer similar technologies and components, using Windows Server 2008 can be a less costly and easier to implement option—especially for small and medium-sized companies.

Components of PKI

In today's network environments, key pairs are used in a variety of different functions. This series will likely cover topics such as virtual private networks (VPNs), digital signatures, access control (SSH), secure e-mail (PGP—mentioned already—and S/MIME), and secure Web access (Secure Sockets Layer, or SSL). Although these technologies are varied in purpose and use, each includes an implementation of PKI for managing trusted communications between a host and a client.

While PKI exists at some level within the innards of several types of communications technologies, its form can change from implementation to implementation. As such, the components necessary for a successful implementation can vary depending on the requirements, but in public key cryptography there is always:

- A private key
- A public key
- A trusted third party (TTP)

Since a public key must be associated with the name of its owner, a data structure known as a public key certificate is used. The certificate typically contains the owner's name, their public key and e-mail address, validity dates for the certificate, the location of revocation information, the location of the issuer's policies, and possibly other affiliate information that identifies the certificate issuer with an organization such as an employer or other institution.

In most cases, the private and public keys are simply referred to as the private and public key certificates, and the trusted third party is commonly known as the certificate authority (CA). The certificate authority is the resource that must be available to both the holder of the private key and the holder of the public key. Entire hierarchies can exist within a public key infrastructure to support the use of multiple certificate authorities.

In addition to certificate authorities and the public and private key certificates they publish, there are a collection of components and functions associated with the management of the infrastructure. As such, a list of typical components required for a functional public key infrastructure would include but not be limited to the following:

- Digital certificates

- Certification authorities

- Certificate enrollment

- Certificate revocation

- Encryption/cryptography services

Although we have already covered digital certificates and certificate authorities at a high level, it will be well worth our time to revisit these topics. In the sections to follow, we will explore each of the aforementioned topics in greater detail.

New & Noteworthy...

PKI Enhancements in Windows Server 2008

Windows Server 2008 introduces many new enhancements that allow for a more easily implemented PKI solution and, believe it or not, the development of such solutions. Some of these improvements extend to the clients, such as the Windows Vista operating system. Overall, these improvements have increased the manageability throughout Windows PKI. For example, the revocations services have been redesigned, and the attack surface for enrollment has decreased. The following list items include the major highlights:

- **Enterprise PKI (PKIView)** PKIView is a Microsoft Management Console (MMC) snap-in for Windows Server 2008. It can be used to monitor and analyze the health of the certificate authorities and to view details for each certificate authority certificate published in Active Directory Certificate Servers.

- **Web Enrollment** Introduced in Windows Server 2000, the new Web enrollment control is more secure and makes the use of scripts much easier. It is also easier to update than previous versions.

- **Network Device Enrollment Service (NDES)** In Windows Server 2008, this service represents Microsoft's implementation of the Simple Certificate Enrollment Protocol (SCEP), a communication protocol that makes it possible for software running on network devices,

Continued

such as routers and switches that cannot otherwise be authenticated on the network, to enroll for x.509 certificates from a certificate authority.

- **Online Certificate Status Protocol (OCSP)** In cases where conventional CRLs (Certificate Revocation Lists) are not an optimal solution, Online Responders can be configured on a single computer or in an Online Responder Array to manage and distribute revocation status information.

- **Group Policy and PKI** New certificate settings in Group Policy now enable administrators to manage certificate settings from a central location for all the computers in the domain.

- **Cryptography Next Generation** Leveraging the U.S. government's Suite B cryptographic algorithms, which include algorithms for encryption, digital signatures, key exchange, and hashing, Cryptography Next Generation (CNG) offers a flexible development platform that allows IT professionals to create, update, and use custom cryptography algorithms in cryptography-related applications such as Active Directory Certificate Services (AD CS), Secure Sockets Layer (SSL), and Internet Protocol Security (IPSec).

How PKI Works

Before we discuss how PKI works today, it is perhaps helpful to understand the term encryption and how PKI has evolved. The history of general cryptography almost certainly dates back to almost 2000 B.C. when Roman and Greek statesmen used simple alphabet-shifting algorithms to keep government communication private. Through time and civilizations, ciphering text played an important role in wars and politics. As modern times provided new communication methods, scrambling information became increasingly more important. World War II brought about the first use of the computer in the cracking of Germany's Enigma code. In 1952, President Truman created the National Security Agency at Fort Meade, Maryland. This agency, which is the center of U.S. cryptographic activity, fulfills two important national functions: It protects all military and executive communication from being intercepted, and it intercepts and unscrambles messages sent by other countries.

Although complexity increased, not much changed until the 1970s, when the National Security Agency (NSA) worked with Dr. Horst Feistel to establish the Data Encryption Standard (DES) and Whitfield Diffie and Martin Hellman introduced the first public key cryptography standard. Windows Server 2008 still uses Diffie-Hellman (DH) algorithms for SSL, Transport Layer Security (TLS), and IPSec. Another major force in modern cryptography came about in the late 1970s. RSA Labs, founded by Ronald Rivest, Adi Shamir, and Leonard Adleman, furthered the concept of key cryptography by developing a technology of key pairs, where plaintext that is encrypted by one key can be decrypted only by the other matching key.

There are three types of cryptographic functions. The hash function does not involve the use of a key at all, but it uses a mathematical algorithm on the data in order to scramble it. The secret key method of encryption, which involves the use of a single key, is used to encrypt and decrypt the information and is sometimes referred to as symmetric key cryptography. An excellent example of secret key encryption is the decoder ring you may have had as a child. Any person who obtained your decoder ring could read your "secret" information.

There are basically two types of symmetric algorithms. Block symmetric algorithms work by taking a given length of bits known as blocks. Stream symmetric algorithms operate on a single bit at a time. One well-known block algorithm is DES. Windows 2000 uses a modified DES and performs that operation on 64-bit blocks using every eighth bit for parity. The resulting ciphertext is the same length as the original cleartext. For export purposes the DES is also available with a 40-bit key.

One advantage of secret key encryption is the efficiency with which it takes a large amount of data and encrypts it quite rapidly. Symmetric algorithms can also be easily implemented at the hardware level. The major disadvantage of secret key encryption is that a single key is used for both encryption and decryption. There must be a secure way for the two parties to exchange the one secret key.

In the 1970s this disadvantage of secret key encryption was eliminated through the mathematical implementation of public key encryption. Public key encryption, also referred to as asymmetric cryptography, replaced the one shared key with each user's own pair of keys. One key is a public key, which is made available to everyone and is used for the encryption process only. The other key in the pair, the private key, is available only to the owner. The private key cannot be created as a result of the public key's being available. Any data that is encrypted by a public key can be decrypted only by using the private key of the pair. It is also possible for the owner to use a private key to encrypt sensitive information. If the data is encrypted by using the private key, then the public key in the pair of keys is needed to decrypt the data.

DH algorithms are known collectively as *shared secret key* cryptographies, also known as symmetric key encryption. Let's say we have two users, Greg and Matt, who want to communicate privately. With DH, Greg and Matt each generate a random number. Each of these numbers is known only to the person who generated it. Part one of the DH function changes each secret number into a nonsecret, or public, number. Greg and Matt now exchange the public numbers and then enter them into part two of the DH function. This results in a private key—one that is identical to both users. Using advanced mathematics, this shared secret key can be decrypted only by someone with access to one of the original random numbers. As long as Greg and Matt keep the original numbers hidden, the shared secret key cannot be reversed.

It should be apparent from the many and varied contributing sources to PKI technology that the need for management of this invaluable set of tools would become paramount. If PKI, like any other technology set, continued to develop without standards of any kind, then differing forms and evolutions of the technology would be implemented ad hoc throughout the world. Eventually, the theory holds that some iteration would render communication or operability between different forms impossible. At that point, the cost of standardization would be significant, and the amount of time lost in productivity and reconstruction of PKI systems would be immeasurable.

Thus, a set of standards was developed for PKI. The Public-Key Cryptography Standards (PKCS) are a set of standard protocols sued for securing the exchange of information through PKI. The list of these standards was actually established by RSA laboratories—the same organization that developed the original RSA encryption standard—along with a group of participating technology leaders that included Microsoft, Sun, and Apple.

PKCS Standards

Here is a list of active PKCS standards. You will notice that there are gaps in the numbered sequence of these standards, and that is due to the retiring of standards over time since they were first introduced.

- **PKCS #1: RSA Cryptography Standard** Outlines the encryption of data using the RSA algorithm. The purpose of the RSA Cryptography Standard is in the development of digital signatures and digital envelopes. PKCS#1 also describes a syntax for RSA public keys and private keys. The public-key syntax is used for certificates, while the private-key syntax is used for encrypting private keys.

- **PKCS #3: Diffie-Hellman Key Agreement Standard** Outlines the use of the Diffie-Hellman Key Agreement, a method of sharing a secret key between two parties. The secret key used to encrypt ongoing data transfer between the two parties. Whitefield Diffie and Martin Hellman developed the Diffie-Hellman algorithm in the 1970s as the first public asymmetric cryptographic system (asymmetric cryptography was invented in the United Kingdom earlier in the same decade, but was classified as a military secret). Diffie-Hellman overcomes the issue of symmetric key system, because management of the keys is less difficult.

- **PKCS #5: Password-based Cryptography Standard** A method for encrypting a string with a secret key that is derived from a password. The result of the method is an octet string (a sequence of 8-bit values). PKCS #8 is primarily used for encrypting private keys when they are being transmitted between computers.

- **PKCS #6: Extended-certificate Syntax Standard** Deals with extended certificates. Extended certificates are made up of the X.509 certificate plus additional attributes. The additional attributes and the X.509 certificate can be verified using a single public-key operation. The issuer that signs the extended certificate is the same as the one that signs the X.509 certificate.

- **PKCS #7: Cryptographic Message Syntax Standard** The foundation for Secure/Multipurpose Internet Mail Extensions (S/MIME) standard. It is also compatible with Privacy-Enhanced Mail (PEM) and can be used in several different architectures of key management.

- **PKCS #8: Private-key Information Syntax Standard** Describes a method of communication for private-key information that includes the use of public-key algorithm and additional attributes (similar to PKCS #6). In this case, the attributes can be a DN or a root CA's public key.

- **PKCS #9: Selected Attribute Types** Defines the types of attributes for use in extended certificates (PKCS #6), digitally signed messages (PKCS #7), and private-key information (PKCS #8).

- **PKCS #10: Certification Request Syntax Standard** Describes a syntax for certification request. A certification request consists of a DN, a public key, and additional attributes. Certification requests are sent to a CA, which then issues the certificate.

- **PKCS #11: Cryptographic Token Interface Standard** Specifies an application program interface (API) for token devices that hold encrypted information and perform cryptographic functions, such as smart cards and Universal Serial Bus (USB) pigtails.

- **PKCS #12: Personal Information Exchange Syntax Standard** Specifies a portable format for storing or transporting a user's private keys and certificates. Ties into both PKCS #8 (communication of private-key information) and PKCS #11 (Cryptographic Token Interface Standard). Portable formats include diskettes, smart cards, and Personal Computer Memory Card International Association (PCMCIA) cards. On Microsoft Windows platforms, PKCS #12 format files are generally given the extension *.pfx*. PKCS #12 is the best standard format to use when exchanging private keys and certificates between systems.

RSA-derived technology in its various forms is used extensively by Windows Server 2008 for such things as Kerberos authentication and S/MIME. In practice, the use of the PKI technology goes something like this: Two users, Dave and Dixine, wish to communicate privately. Dave and Dixine each own a key pair consisting of a public key and a private key. If Dave wants Dixine to send him an encrypted message, he first transmits his public key to Dixine. She then uses Dave's public key to encrypt the message. Fundamentally, since Dave's public key was used to encrypt, only Dave's private key can be used to decrypt. When he receives the message, only he is able to read it. Security is maintained because only public keys are transmitted—the private keys are kept secret and are known only to their owners. Figure 3.1 illustrates the process.

Figure 3.1 Public/Private Key Data Exchange

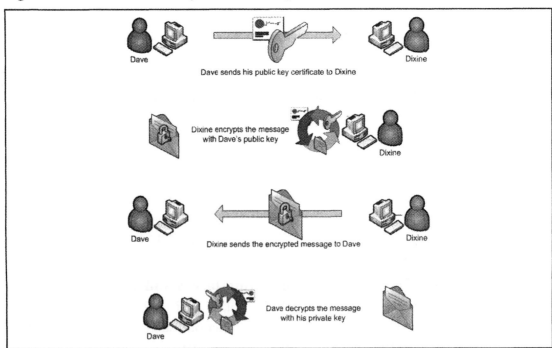

WARNING

In a Windows Server 2008 PKI, a user's public and private keys are stored under the user's profile. For the administrator, the public keys would be under *Documents and Settings\Administrator\System Certificates\My\Certificates* and the private keys would be under *Documents and Settings\Administrator\Crypto\ RSA* (where they are double encrypted by Microsoft's Data Protection API, or DPAPI). Although a copy of the public keys is kept in the registry, and can even be kept in Active Directory, the private keys are vulnerable to deletion. If you delete a user profile, the private keys will be lost!

RSA can also be used to create "digital signatures" (see Figure 3.2). In the communication illustrated in Figure 3.1, a public key was used to encrypt a message and the corresponding private key was used to decrypt. If we invert the process, a private key can be used to encrypt and the matching public key to decrypt. This is useful, for example, if you want people to know that a document you wrote is really yours. If you encrypt the document using your private key, then only your public key can decrypt it. If people use your public key to read the document and they are successful, they can be certain that it was "signed" by your private key and is therefore authentic.

Figure 3.2 Digital Signatures

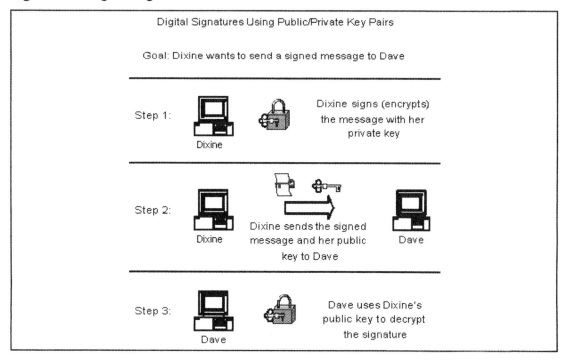

How Certificates Work

Before we delve into the inner workings of a certificate, let's discuss what a certificate actually is in layman's terms. In PKI, a digital certificate is a tool used for binding a public key with a particular owner. A great comparison is a driver's license. Consider the information listed on a driver's license:

- Name
- Address
- Date of birth
- Photograph
- Signature
- Social security number (or another unique number such as a state issued license number)
- Expiration date
- Signature/certification by an authority (typically from within the issuing state's government body)

The information on a state license photo is significant because it provides crucial information about the owner of that particular item. The signature from the state official serves as a trusted authority for the state, certifying that the owner has been verified and is legitimate to be behind the wheel of a car. Anyone, like an officer, who wishes to verify a driver's identity and right to commute from one place to another by way of automobile need only ask for and review the driver's license. In some cases, the officer might even call or reference that license number just to ensure it is still valid and has not been revoked.

A digital certificate in PKI serves the same function as a driver's license. Various systems and checkpoints may require verification of the owner's identity and status and will reference the trusted third party for validation. It is the certificate that enables this quick hand-off of key information between the parties involved.

The information contained in the certificate is actually part or the X.509 certificate standard. X.509 is actually an evolution of the X.500 directory standard. Initially intended to provide a means of developing easy-to-use electronic directories of people that would be available to all Internet users, it became a directory and mail standard for a very commonly known mail application: Microsoft Exchange 5.5. The X.500

directory standard specifies a common root of a hierarchical tree although the "tree" is inverted: the root of the tree is depicted at the "top" level while the other branches—called "containers"—are below it. Several of these types of containers exist with a specific naming convention. In this naming convention, each portion of a name is specified by the abbreviation of the object type or a container it represents. For example, a *CN=* before a username represents it is a "*common name*", a *C=* precedes a "*country*,", and an *O=* precedes "*organization*". These elements are worth remembering as they will appear not only in discussions about X.500 and X.509, but they are ultimately the basis for the scheme of Microsoft's premier directory service, Active Directory.

X.509 is the standard used to define what makes up a digital certificate. Within this standard, a description is given for a certificate as allowing an association between a user's *distinguished name* (*DN*) and the user's public key. The DN is specified by a *naming authority* (*NA*) and used as a unique name by the *certificate authority* (*CA*) who will create the certificate. A common X.509 certificate includes the following information (see Table 3.1 and Figures 3.3 and 3.4):

Table 3.1 X.509 Certificate Data

Item	Definition
Serial Number	A unique identifier.
Subject	The name of the person or company that is being identified, sometimes listed as "Issued To".
Signature Algorithm	The algorithm used to create the signature.
Issuer	The trusted authority that verified the information and generated the certificate, sometimes listed as "Issued By".
Valid From	The date the certificate was activated.
Valid To	The last day the certificate can be used.
Public Key	The public key that corresponds to the private key.
Thumbprint Algorithm	The algorithm used to create the unique value of a certificate.
Thumbprint	The unique value of every certificate, which positively identifies the certificate. If there is ever a question about the authenticity of a certificate, check this value with the issuer.

Figure 3.3 A Windows Server 2008 Certificate Field and Values

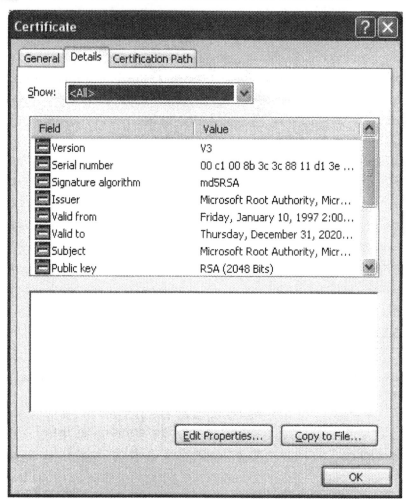

Figure 3.4 A Windows Server 2008 Certificate Field and Values

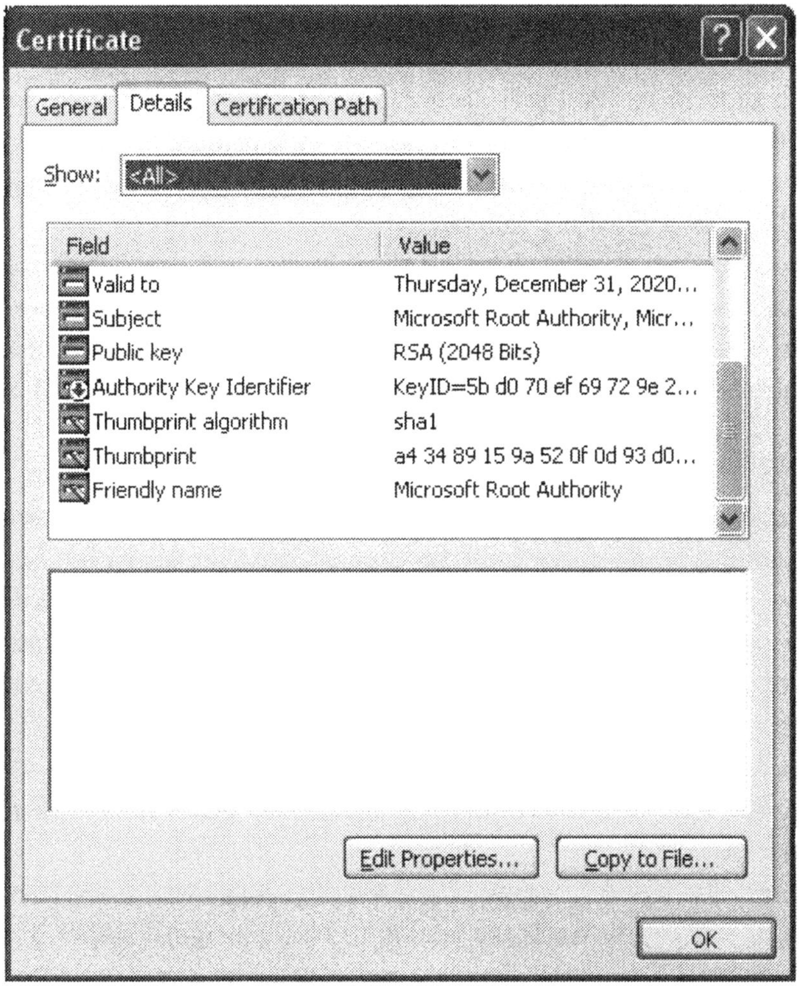

Public Key Functionality

Public key cryptography brings major security technologies to the desktop in the Windows 2000 environment. The network now is provided with the ability to allow users to safely:

- Transmit over insecure channels

- Store sensitive information on any commonly used media

- Verify a person's identity for authentication

- Prove that a message was generated by a particular person

- Prove that the received message was not tampered with in transit

Algorithms based on public keys can be used for all these purposes. The most popular public key algorithm is the standard RSA, which is named after its three inventors: Rivest, Shamir, and Adleman. The RSA algorithm is based on two prime numbers with more than 200 digits each. A hacker would have to take the ciphertext and the public key and factor the product of the two primes. As computer processing time increases, the RSA remains secure by increasing the key length, unlike the DES algorithm, which has a fixed key length.

Public key algorithms provide privacy, authentication, and easy key management, but they encrypt and decrypt data slowly because of the intensive computation required. RSA has been evaluated to be from 10 to 10,000 times slower than DES in some environments, which is a good reason not to use public key algorithms for bulk encryption.

Digital Signatures

Document letterhead can be easily created on a computer, so forgery is a security issue. When information is sent electronically, no human contact is involved. The receiver wants to know that the person listed as the sender is really the sender and that the information received has not been modified in any way during transit. A hash algorithm is implemented to guarantee the Windows 2000 user that the data is authentic. A hash value encrypted with a private key is called a digital signature. Anyone with access to the corresponding public key can verify the authenticity of a digital signature. Only a person having a private key can generate digital signatures. Any modification makes a digital signature invalid.

The purpose of a digital signature is to prevent changes within a document from going unnoticed and also to claim the person to be the original author. The document itself is not encrypted. The digital signature is just data sent along with the data guaranteed to be untampered with. A change of any size invalidates the digital signature.

When King Henry II had to send a message to his troops in a remote location, the letter would be sealed with wax, and while the wax was still soft the king would use his ring to make an impression in it. No modification occurred to the original message if the seal was never broken during transit. There was no doubt that King Henry II had initiated the message, because he was the only person possessing a ring that matched the waxed imprint. Digital signatures work in a similar fashion in that only the sender's public key can authenticate both the original sender and the content of the document.

The digital signature is generated by a message digest, which is a number generated by taking the message and using a hash algorithm. A message digest is regarded as a fingerprint and can range from a 128-bit number to a 256-bit number. A hash function takes variable-length input and produces a fixed-length output. The message is first processed with a hash function to produce a message digest. This value is then signed by the sender's private key, which produces the actual digital signature. The digital signature is then added to the end of the document and sent to the receiver along with the document.

Since the mere presence of a digital signature proves nothing, verification must be mathematically proven. In the verification process, the first step is to use the corresponding public key to decrypt the digital signature. The result will produce a 128-bit number. The original message will be processed with the same hash function used earlier and will result in a message digest. The two resulting 128-bit numbers will then be compared, and if they are equal, you will receive notification of a good signature. If a single character has been altered, the two 128-bit numbers will be different, indicating that a change has been made to the document, which was never scrambled.

Authentication

Public key cryptography can provide authentication instead of privacy. In Windows 2000, a challenge is sent by the receiver of the information. The challenge can be implemented one of two ways. The information is authenticated because only the corresponding private key could have encrypted the information that the public key is successfully decrypting.

In the first authentication method, a challenge to authenticate involves sending an encrypted challenge to the sender. The challenge is encrypted by the receiver, using the sender's public key. Only the corresponding private key can successfully decode the challenge. When the challenge is decoded, the sender sends the plaintext back to the receiver. This is the proof for the receiver that the sender is truly the sender.

For example, when Alice receives a document from Bob, she wants to authenticate that the sender is really Bob. She sends an encrypted challenge to Bob, using his public key. When he receives the challenge, Bob uses his private key to decrypt the information. The decrypted challenge is then sent back to Alice. When Alice receives the decrypted challenge, she is convinced that the document she received is truly from Bob.

The second authentication method uses a challenge that is sent in plaintext. The receiver, after receiving the document, sends a challenge in plaintext to the sender. The sender receives the plaintext challenge and adds some information before adding a digital signature.

The challenge and digital signature now head back to the sender. The digital signature is generated by using a hash function and then encrypting the result with a private key, so the receiver must use the sender's public key to verify the digital signature. If the signature is good, the original document and sender have at this point been verified mathematically.

Secret Key Agreement via Public Key

The PKI of Windows 2000 permits two parties to agreed on a secret key while they use nonsecure communication channels. Each party generates half the shared secret key by generating a random number, which is sent to the other party after being encrypted with the other party's public key. Each receiving side then decrypts the ciphertext using a private key, which will result in the missing half of the secret key.

By adding both random numbers together, each party will have an agreed-upon shared secret key, which can then be used for secure communication even though the secret key was first obtained through a nonsecure communication channel.

Bulk Data Encryption without Prior Shared Secrets

The final major feature of public key technology is that it can encrypt bulk data without generating a shared secret key first. The biggest disadvantage of using asymmetric algorithms for encryption is the slowness of the overall process, which results from the necessary intense computations; the largest disadvantage of using symmetric algorithms for encryption of bulk data is the need for a secure communication channel for exchanging the secret key. The Windows 2000 operating system combines symmetric and asymmetric algorithms to get the best of both worlds at just the right moment.

For a large document that must be kept secret, because secret key encryption is the quickest method to use for bulk data, a session key is used to scramble the document. To protect the session key, which is the secret key needed to decrypt the protected data; the sender encrypts this small item quickly by using the receiver's public key. This encryption of the session key is handled by asymmetric algorithms, which use intense computation but do not require much time, due to the small size of the session key. The document, along with the encrypted session key, is then sent to the receiver. Only the intended receiver will possess the correct private key to decode the session key, which is needed to decode the actual document. When the session key is in plaintext, it can be applied to the ciphertext of the bulk data and then transform the bulk data back to plaintext.

The Windows Server 2008 PKI does many things behind the scenes. Thanks in part to auto enrollment (discussed later in this chapter) and certificate stores (places where certificates are kept after their creation), some PKI-enabled features such as EFS work with no user intervention at all. Others, such as IPSec, require significantly less work than would be required without an advanced operating system.

Even though a majority of the PKI is handled by Server, it is still instructive to have an overview of how certificate services work.

1. First, a system or user generates a public/private key pair and then a certificate request.

2. The certificate request, which contains the public key and other identifying information such as user name, is forwarded on to a CA.

3. The CA verifies the validity of the public key. If it is verified, the CA issues the certificate.

4. Once issued, the certificate is ready for use and is kept in the certificate store, which can reside in Active Directory. Applications that require a certificate use this central repository when necessary.

In practice, it isn't terribly difficult to implement certificate services, as the following sidebar shows. Configuring the CA requires a bit more effort, as does planning the structure and hierarchy of the PKI—especially if you are designing an enterprise-wide solution. We'll cover these topics later in this chapter.

Configuring & Implementing...

Installing Certificate Services

1. After logging on with administrative privileges, click **Start**, click **All Programs**, click **Administrative Tools**, and then click **Server Manager**.

2. In the **Roles Summary** section, clic k **Add Roles**.

3. On the **Before You Begin** page, click **Next** (see Figure 3.5).

Continued

Figure 3.5 Before You Begin Page

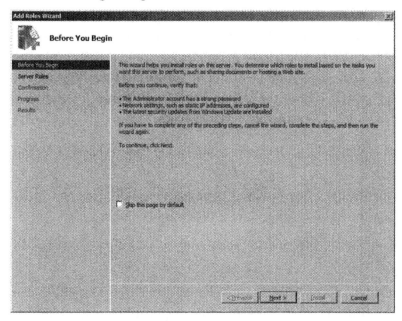

4. On the Select Server Roles page, click the Active Directory Certificate Services (see Figure 3.6). Click Next.

Figure 3.6 Select Server Roles Page

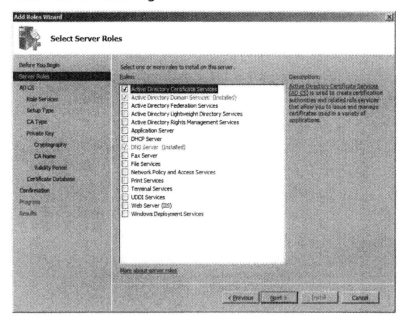

Continued

Configuring Certificate Services and PKI • Chapter 3   167

5. On the Introduction to Active Directory Certificate Services page, click Next.

6. On the **Select Role Services** page, click the **Certification Authority** check box, as shown in Figure 3.7. Click **Next**.

Figure 3.7 Select Role Services Page

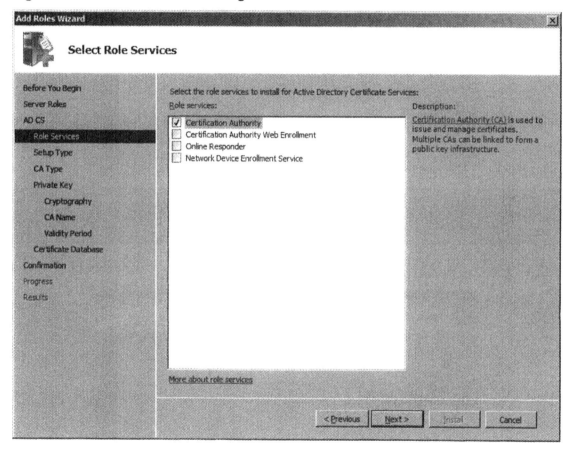

7. On the **Specify Setup Type** page, click **Enterprise**, as shown in Figure 3.8. Click **Next**.

Continued

Figure 3.8 Specify Setup Type Page

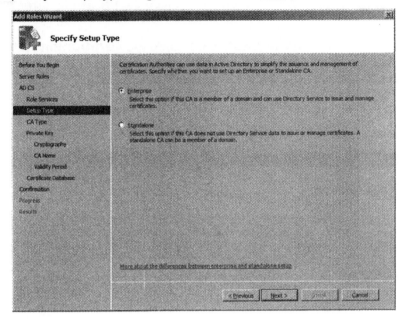

8. On the **Specify CA Type** page, click **Root CA**, as shown in Figure 3.9. Click **Next**.

Figure 3.9 Specify CA Type Page

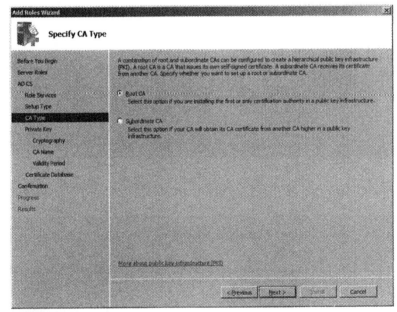

Continued

9. On the **Set Up Private Key** page, either accept the default value or configure optional configuration settings. For this exercise, choose the default settings as shown in Figure 3.10. Click **Next**.

Figure 3.10 Set Up Private Key Page

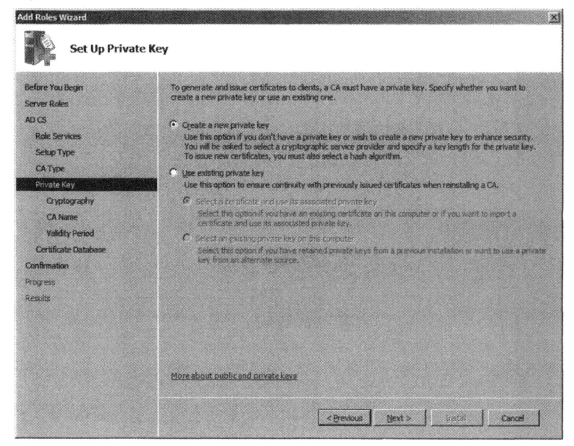

10. On the **Configure Cryptography for CA** page, either accept the default value or configure optional configuration settings as per project requirements. For this exercise, choose the default settings as shown in Figure 3.11. Click **Next**.

Continued

Figure 3.11 Configure Cryptography for CA Page

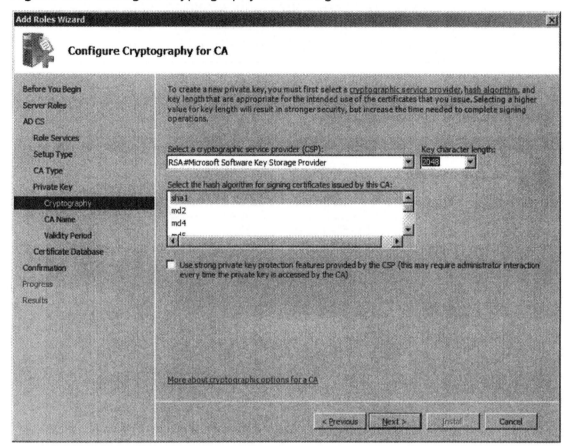

11. In the **Common name for this CA** box, type the common name of the CA. For this exercise, type **MyRootCA** as shown in Figure 3.12. Click **Next**.

Continued

Figure 3.12 Configure CA Name Page

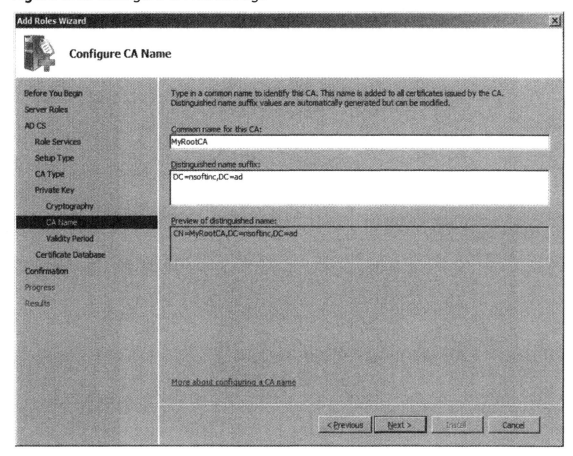

12. On the **Set the Certificate Validity Period** page, you can change the default five-year validity period of the CA. You can set the validity period as a number of days, weeks, months or years. Accept the default validity duration for the root CA as shown in Figure 3.13, and then click **Next**.

Continued

Figure 3.13 Set Validity Period Page

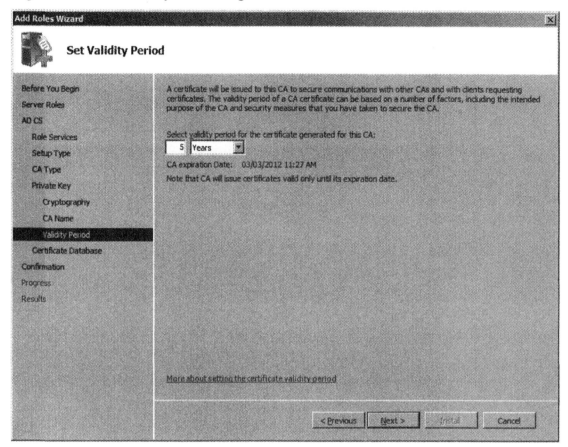

13. On the **Configure Certificate Database** page, for this exercise, accept the default values or specify other storage locations for the certificate database and the certificate database log (see Figure 3.14). Click **Next**.

Continued

Figure 3.14 Configure Certificate Database Page

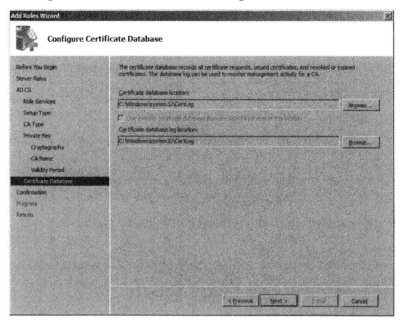

14. On the **Confirm Installation Selections** page, click **Install** (see Figure 3.15).

Figure 3.15 Confirm Installation Selections Page

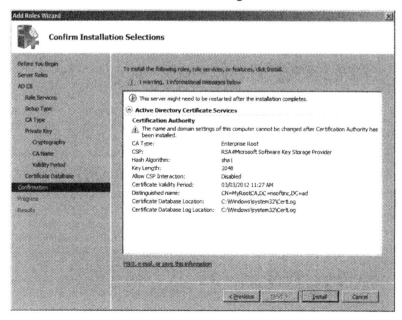

Continued

15. On the Installation Results page, review the information and make sure it read **Installation succeeded**
16. Click **Close** to close the **Add Roles Wizard**.

In our previous discussion of public and private key pairs, two users wanted to exchange confidential information and did so by having one user encrypt the data with the other user's public key. We then discussed digital signatures, where the sending user "signs" the data by using his or her private key. Did you notice the security vulnerability in these methods?

In this type of scenario, there is nothing to prevent an attacker from intercepting the data mid-stream, and replacing the original signature with his or her own, using of course his or her own private key. The attacker would then forward the replacement public key to the unsuspecting party. In other words, even though the data is signed, how can you be sure of who signed it? The answer in the Windows PKI is the certificate.

Think of a certificate as a small and portable combination safe. The primary purpose of the safe is to hold a public key (although quite a bit of other information is also held there). The combination to the safe must be held by someone you trust—that trust is the basis for the entire PKI system. If I am a user and want to send you my public key so that you can encrypt some data to send back to me, I can just sign the data myself, but I am then vulnerable to the attack mentioned above. However if I allow a trusted third party entity to take my public key (which I don't mind because they're trustworthy), lock it away in the safe and then send the safe to you, you can ask the trusted party for the combination. When you open the safe, you can be certain that the public key and all other information inside really belongs to me, because the safe came from a trustworthy source. The "safe" is really nothing more than a digital signature, except that the signature comes from a universally trusted third party and not from me. The main purpose of certificates, then, is to facilitate the secure transfer of keys across an insecure network. Figure 3.16 shows the properties of a Windows certificate—notice that the highlighted public key is only part of the certificate.

Figure 3.16 A Windows Server 2008 Certificate

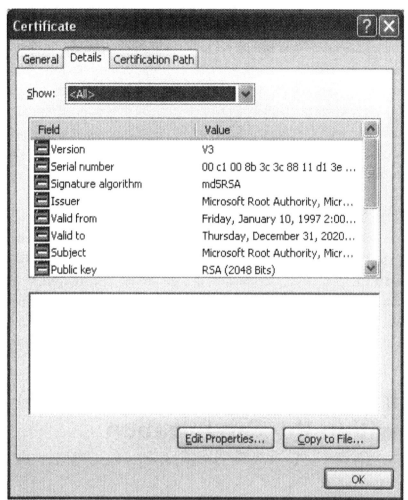

User Certificates

Of the three general types of certificates found in a Windows PKI, the *user certificate* is perhaps the most common. User certificates are certificates that enable the user to do something that would not be otherwise allowed. The Enrollment Agent certificate is one example. Without it, even an administrator is not able to enroll smart cards and configure them properly at an enrollment station. Under Windows Server 2008, required user certificates can be requested automatically by the client and subsequently issued by a certification authority (discussed below) with no user intervention necessary.

Machine Certificates

Also known as computer certificates, *machine certificates* (as the name implies) give the system—instead of the user—the ability to do something out of the ordinary. The main purpose for machine certificates is authentication, both client-side and server-side. As stated earlier, certificates are the main vehicle by which public keys are exchanged in a PKI. Machine certificates are mainly involved with these behind-the-scenes exchanges, and are normally overseen by the operating system. Machine certificates have been able to take advantage of Windows' autoenrollment feature since 2000 Server was introduced. We will discuss auto-enrollment later in this chapter.

Application Certificates

The term *application certificate* refers to any certificate that is used with a specific PKI-enabled application. Examples include IPSec and S/MIME encryption for e-mail. Applications that need certificates are generally configured to automatically request them, and are then placed in a waiting status until the required certificate arrives. Depending upon the application, the network administrator or even the user might have the ability to change or even delete certificate requests issued by the application.

Analyzing Certificate Needs within the Organization

We've just concluded a tour of most of the properties associated with a CA, but knowing what you *can* do does not mean that we know what you *should* do. To find out more about what you should do, you need to analyze the certificate needs of your organization, and then move on to create an appropriate CA structure.

According to Microsoft's TechNet, the analysis of certificate needs springs primarily from "the analysis of business requirements and the analysis of applications that benefit from PKI-based security". In other words, when designing a PKI/CA structure, you will need to understand the different uses for certificates and whether your organization needs to use certificates for each of these purposes. Examples include SSL for a secure Web server, EFS for encryption of files, and S/MIME for encryption of e-mail messages. The use of S/MIME might dictate that your CA hierarchy have a trust relationship with external CAs, and the use of SSL might lead you to implement a stand-alone CA instead of an enterprise CA. Thus, analyzing these needs *before* you implement your PKI can save you a lot of time and trouble.

Working with Certificate Services

Certificate Services in Windows Server 2008 is an easier venture than ever before. As we look at what is entailed in the components involved in establishing and supporting a PKI in Windows Server 2008 we need to quickly discuss what Certificate Services do for us.

In Active Directory and Windows Server 2008, Certificate Services allow administrators to establish and manage the PKI environment. More generally, they allow for a trust model to be established within a given organization. The trust model is the framework that will hold all the pieces and components of the PKI in place. Typically, there are two options for a trust model within PKI: a *single CA model* and a *hierarchical model*. The certificate services within Windows Server 2008 provide the interfaces and underlying technology to setup and manage both of these type of deployments.

Configuring a Certificate Authority

By definition, a certificate authority is an entity (computer or system) that issues digital certificates of authenticity for use by other parties. With the ever increasing demand for effective and efficient methods to verify and secure communications, our technology market has seen the rise of many trusted third parties into the market. If you have been in the technology field for any length of time, you are likely familiar with many such vendors by name: VeriSign, Entrust, Thawte, GeoTrust, DigiCert and GoDaddy are just a few.

While these companies provide an excellent and useful resource for both the IT administrator and the consumer, companies and organizations desired a way to establish their own certificate authorities. In a third-party, or external PKI, it is up to the third-party CA to positively verify the identity of anyone requesting a certificate from it. Beginning with Windows 2000, Microsoft has allowed the creation of a trusted *internal* CA—possibly eliminating the need for an external third party. With a Windows Server 2008 CA, the CA verifies the identity of the user requesting a certificate by checking that user's authentication credentials (using Kerberos or NTLM). If the credentials of the requesting user check out, a certificate is issued to the user. When the user needs to transmit his or her public key to another user or application, the certificate is then used to prove to the receiver that the public key inside can be used safely.

Certificate Authorities

Certificates are a way to transfer keys securely across an insecure network. If any arbitrary user were allowed to issue certificates, it would be no different than that user simply signing the data. In order for a certificate to be of any use, it must be issued by a trusted entity—an entity that both the sender and receiver trust. Such a trusted entity is known as a *Certification Authority* (CA). Third-party CAs such as VeriSign or Entrust can be trusted because they are highly visible, and their public keys are well known to the IT community. When you are confident that you hold a true public key for a CA, and that public key properly decrypts a certificate, you are then certain that the certificate was digitally signed by the CA and no one else. Only then can you be positive that the public key contained inside the certificate is valid and safe.

In the analogy we used earlier, the state driver's licensing agency is trusted because it is known that the agency requires proof of identity before issuing a driver's license. In the same way, users can trust the certification authority because they know it verifies the authentication credentials before issuing a certificate. Within an organization leveraging Windows Server 2008, several options exist for building this trust relationship. Each of these begins with the decisions made around selecting and implementing certificate authorities. With regard to the Microsoft implementation of PKI, there are at least four major roles or types of certificate authorities to be aware of:

- Enterprise CA
- Standard CA
- Root CA
- Subordinate CA

Believe it or not, beyond this list at least two variations exist: intermediate CAs and leaf CAs, each of which is a type of subordinate CA implementation.

Standard vs. Enterprise

An enterprise CA is tied into Active Directory and is required to use it. In fact, a copy of its own CA certificate is stored in Active Directory. Perhaps the biggest difference between an enterprise CA and a stand-alone CA is that enterprise CAs use Kerberos or NTLM authentication to validate users and computers before certificates are issued. This provides additional security to the PKI because the validation process relies on the strength of the Kerberos protocol, and not a human administrator. Enterprise CAs also use templates, which are described later in this chapter, and they can issue every type of certificate.

There are also several downsides to an enterprise CA. In comparison to a stand-alone CA, enterprise CAs are more difficult to maintain and require a much more in-depth knowledge about Active Directory and authentication. Also, because an enterprise CA requires Active Directory, it is nearly impossible to remove it from the network. If you were to do so, the Directory itself would quickly become outdated—making it difficult to resynchronize with the rest of the network when brought back online. Such a situation would force an enterprise CA to remain attached to the network, leaving it vulnerable to attackers.

Root vs. Subordinate Certificate Authorities

As discussed earlier, there are two ways to view PKI trust models: single CA and hierarchical. In a single CA model PKIs are very simplistic; only one CA is used within the infrastructure. Anyone who needs to trust parties vouched for by the CA is given the public key for the CA. That single CA is responsible for the interactions that ensue when parties request and seek to verify the information for a given certificate.

In a hierarchical model, a root CA functions as a top-level authority over one or more levels of CAs beneath it. The CAs below the root CA are called subordinate CAs. Root CAs serve as a *trust anchor* to all the CA's beneath it and to the users who trust the root CA. A trust anchor is an entity known to be trusted without requiring that it be trusted by going to another party, and therefore can be used as a base for trusting other parties. Since there is nothing above the root CA, no one can vouch for its identity; it must create a *self-signed* certificate to vouch for itself. With a self-signed certificate, both the certificate issuer and the certificate subject are exactly the same. Being the trust anchor, the root CA must make its own certificate available to all of the users (including subordinate CAs) that will ultimately be using that particular root CA.

Hierarchical models work well in larger hierarchical environments, such as large government organizations or corporate environments. Often, a large organization also deploys a Registration Authority (RA, covered later in this chapter), Directory Services and optionally Timestamping Services in an organization leveraging a hierarchical approach to PKI. In situations where different organization are trying to develop a hierarchical model together (such as post acquisition or merger companies or those that are partnered for collaboration), a hierarchical model can be very difficult to establish as both parties must ultimately agree upon a single trust anchor.

When you first set up an internal PKI, no CA exists. The first CA created is known as the root CA, and it can be used to issue certificates to users or to other CAs. As mentioned above, in a large organization there usually is a hierarchy where the root CA is not the only certification authority. In this case, the sole purpose of the root CA is to issue certificates to other CAs in order to establish their authority.

Any certification authority that is established after the root CA is a subordinate CA. Subordinate CAs gain their authority by requesting a certificate from either the root CA or a higher level subordinate CA. Once the subordinate CA receives the certificate, it can control CA policies and/or issue certificates itself, depending on your PKI structure and policies.

Sometimes, subordinate CAs also issue certificates to other CAs below them on the tree. These CAs are called *intermediate CAs*. Is most hierarchies, there is more than one intermediate CA. Subordinate CAs that issue certificates to end users, server, and other entities but do not issue certificates to other CAs are called *leaf CAs*.

Certificate Requests

In order to receive a certificate from a valid issuing CA, a client—computer or user—must request a certificate from a CA.

There are three ways that this request can be made:

- Autoenrollment
- Use of the Certificates snap-in
- Via a web browser

It is very likely that the most common method for requesting a certificate is autoenrollment, and we'll discuss its deployment shortly. A client can also request a certificate by use of the **Certificates** snap-in. The snap-in, shown in Figure 3.17, can be launched by clicking **Start | Run**, and then typing in **certmgr.msc** and pressing **Enter**. Note that the **Certificates** snap-in does *not* appear in the **Administrative Tools** folder as the **Certification Authority** snap-in does after installing certificate services. Once you open the Certificate Snap-in, expand the **Personal** container, and then right-clicking the **Certificates** container beneath it. You can start the **Certificate Request Wizard** by choosing **All Tasks | Request New Certificate…**, as shown in the following figure:

Figure 3.17 Certificates Snap-in

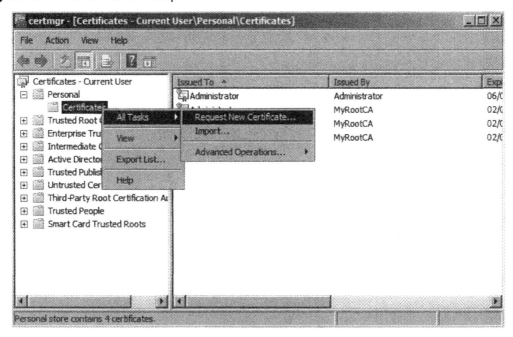

Next, you will receive the **Before You Begin** welcome screen, as shown in Figure 3.18. Click **Next**.

Figure 3.18 Before You Begin

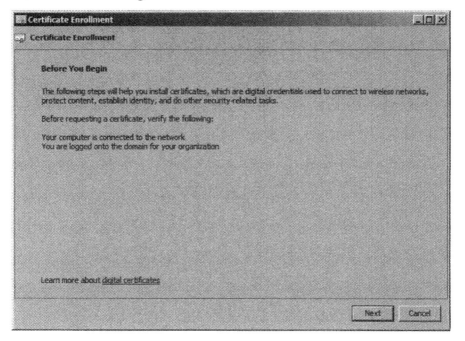

Next to Welcome screen, the wizard prompts you to choose the certificate enrollment type. Figure 3.19 shows you the available options. You can choose only a type for which the receiving CA has a template. Once you choose an appropriate template, click **Enroll**.

Figure 3.19 Request Certificates

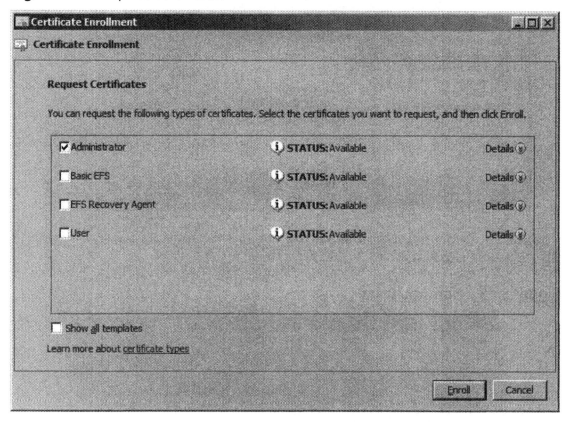

Next to Certificate Enrollment screen, verify it reads, STATUS: Succeeded, as shown in Figure 3.20. Click **Finish** to complete the request.

Figure 3.20 Certificate Installation Results

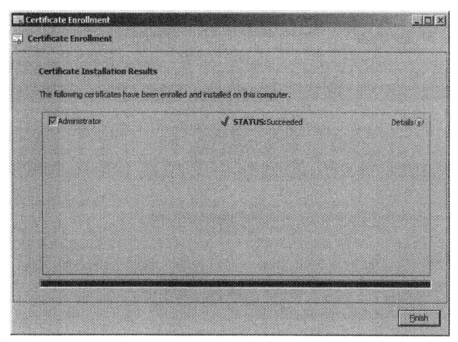

The last method for requesting a certificate is to use a Web browser on the client machine. Note that if you use this option, IIS must be installed on the CA. The following sidebar shows the steps for requesting a certificate using a client machine in this manner.

Configuring & Implementing...

Request a certificate from a web server

1. On any computer for which you want to request a certificate, launch Internet Explorer (version 5.0 or later) by clicking **Start | Programs** or **All Programs | Internet Explorer**.

2. In the address bar, type **http://servername/certsrv**, where servername is the name of the issuing CA.

3. When the welcome screen appears, as shown in Figure 3.21, click **Request a Certificate**.

Continued

Figure 3.21 Welcome Screen of the CA's Web Site

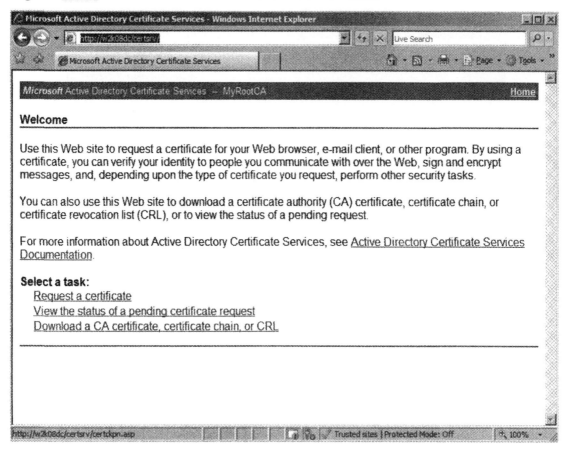

4. Click **User Certificate**, then **Submit** when the next screen appears.
5. When the **Certificate Issued** page appears, click **Install This Certificate**. Close the browser.

Certificate Practice Statement

As the use of X.509-based certificates continues to grow it becomes increasingly important that the management an organization of certificates be as diligent as possible. We know what a digital certificate is and what its critical components are, but a CA can issue a certificate for a number of different reasons. The certificate, then, must indicate exactly what the certificate will be used for. The set of rules that indicates exactly how a certificate may be used (what purpose it can e trusted for, or perhaps the community for which it can be trusted) is called a certificate policy. The X.509 standard defines certificate policies as "a named set of rules that indicates the applicability of a certificate to a particular community and/or class of application with common security requirements."

Different entities have different security requirements. For example, users want a digital certificate for securing e-mail (either encrypting the incoming messages signing outgoing mail), Syngress (as other Web vendors do) wants a digital certificate for their online store, etc. Every user will want to secure their information, and a certificate owner will use the policy information to determine if they want to accept a certificate.

It is important to have a policy in place to state what the appropriate protocol is for use of certificates—how they are requested, how and when they may be used, etc.—but it is equally as important to explain exactly how to implement those policies. This is where the Certificate Practice Statement (CPS) comes in. A CPS describes how the CA plans to manage the certificates it issues.

Key Recovery

Key recovery is compatible with the CryptoAPI architecture of Windows 2008, but it is not a necessary requirement. For key recovery, an entity's private key must be stored permanently. The storage of private keys guarantees that critical information will always be accessible, even if the information should get corrupted or deleted. On the other hand, there is a security issue in the backup of the private keys. The archived private key should be used to impersonate the private key owner only if corruption occurs on your system.

Backup and Restore

Microsoft recommends that you back up your entire CA server. By backing up the system state data on your CA, you will automatically get a backup of the certificate store, the registry, system files, and Active Directory (if your CA is a domain controller). Sometimes, you may want to just back up the certificate services portion of your computer without doing a full backup of everything else.

The following sidebar walks you through backing up Certificate Services. Your backups are only useful if you can restore them.

Configuring & Implementing...

Backing up Certificate Services

1. On any computer for which you want to take a backup, Log on with administrative privileges.

2. Click Start, click All Programs, click Administrative Tools, and then click Certification Authority.

3. Right-click the name of your CA, and choose **All Tasks | Back up CA...** from the pop-up menu, as shown in Figure 3.22.

Figure 3.22 Certificate Authority Page

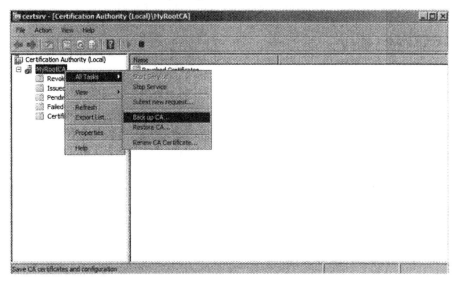

4. On the Welcome to the Certification Authority Backup Wizard page, click Next to continue.

5. On Items to Back Up page, click Private key and CA certificate and Certificate database and certificate database log. Type in the path of back up location, and then click Next (see Figure 3.23).

Continued

Figure 3.23 Items to Back Up

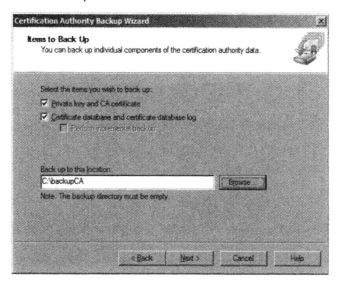

6. Type in the backup password twice and click **Next**.
7. On **Completing the Certification Authority Backup Wizard** page, verify it reads as follows: You have successfully completed the **Certification Authority Backup Wizard**, as shown in Figure 3.24.

Figure 3.24 Completing the CA Backup Wizard

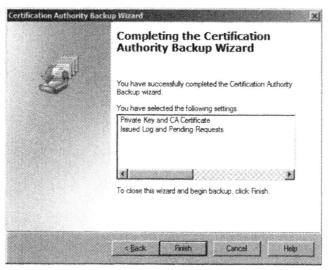

8. Click **Finish** to close the wizard.

Configuring & Implementing...

Restoring Certificate Services

1. On any computer for which you want to take a restore, Log on with administrative privileges.

2. Click Start, click All Programs, click Administrative Tools, and then click Certification Authority.

3. Right-click the name of your CA, and choose **All Tasks | Restore CA...** from the pop-up menu, as shown in Figure 3.25.

Figure 3.25 Certificate Authority page

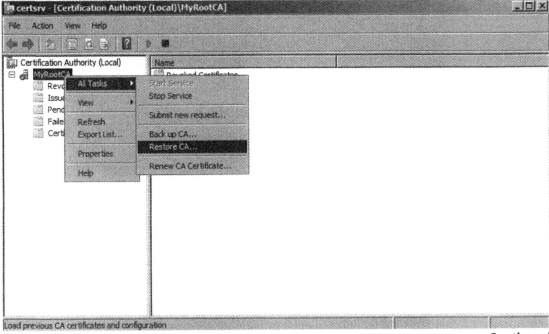

Continued

4. Click **OK** to stop Certificate Services from running and start the wizard.

5. On the Welcome to the Certification Authority Restore Wizard page, click Next to continue.

6. On Items to Restore page, click Private key and CA certificate and Certificate database and certificate database log to restore the backup of Private key, CA certificate, Certificate database and database log file (see Figure 3.26). Alternatively, you can choose only few components as per your requirements. Type in the path of back up location, and then click Next.

Figure 3.26 Items to Restore

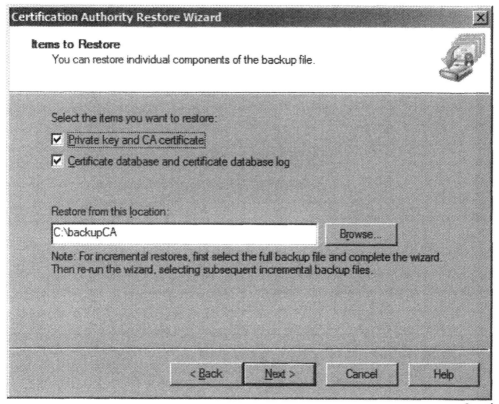

Continued

7. On the **Provide Password** page, type in the restore password, and then click **Next**.

8. On **Completing the Certification Authority Restore Wizard** page, verify it reads as You have successfully completed the **Certification Authority Restore Wizard**, as shown in Figure 3.27.

Figure 3.27 Completing the CA Restore Wizard

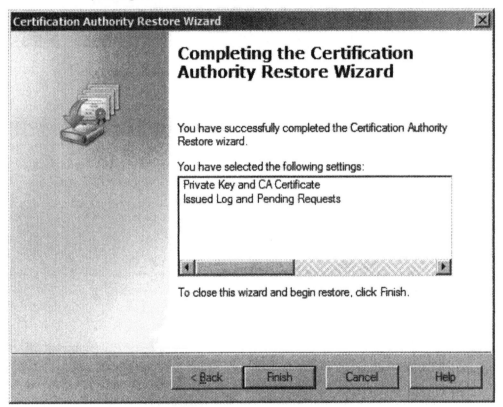

9. Click **Finish** to complete the wizard.

10. You will now be prompted to restart the certificate services, as shown in Figure 3.28. Click **Yes** to restart the services.

Figure 3.28 Certification Authority Restore Wizard

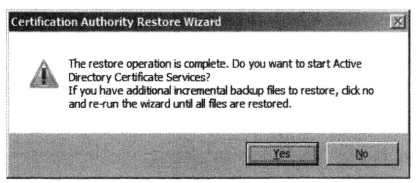

Assigning Roles

In a small network of one or two servers and just a handful of clients, administration is generally not a difficult task. When the size of the network increases, however, the complexity of administration seems to increase exponentially. Microsoft's recommendations for a large network include dividing administrative tasks among the different administrative personnel. One administrator may be in charge of backups and restores, whereas another administrator may have complete control over a certain domain and so on. The role of each administrator is defined by the tasks that he or she is assigned to, and individual permissions are granted based on those tasks. PKI administration, which can be as daunting as general network administration, can be similarly divided. Microsoft defines five different roles that can be used within a PKI to facilitate administration:

- CA Administrator
- Certificate Manager
- Backup Operator
- Auditor
- Enrollee

At the top of the hierarchy is the CA administrator. The role is defined by the *Manage CA* permission and has the authority to assign other CA roles and to renew the CA's certificate. Underneath the CA administrator is the certificate manager.

The certificate manager role is defined by the *Issue and Manage Certificates* permission and has the authority to approve enrollment and revocation requests.

The Backup Operator and the Auditor roles are actually operating system roles, and not CA specific. The Backup Operator has the authority to backup the CA and the Auditor has the authority to configure and view audit logs of the CA. The final role is that of the Enrollees. All authenticated users are placed in this role, and are able to request certificates from the CA.

Enrollments

In order for a PKI client to use a certificate, two basic things must happen. First, a CA has to make the certificate available and second, the client has to request the certificate. Only after these first steps can the CA issue the certificate or deny the request. Making the certificate available is done through the use of certificate templates and is a topic that we discuss in detail below.

Like Windows Server 2003, Windows Server 2008 PKI also supports autoenrollment for user certificates as well as for computer certificates. The request and issuance of these certificates may proceed without user intervention. Group policies are used in Active Directory to configure autoenrollment. In **Computer Configuration | Windows Settings | Security Settings | Public Key Policies**, there is a group policy entitled **Automatic Certificate Request Settings**. The Property sheet for this policy allows you to choose to either **Enroll certificates automatically** or not. Also, you will need to ensure that **Enroll subject without requiring any user input** option is selected on the **Request Handling** tab of the certificate template Property sheet. Finally, be aware that doing either of the following will cause autoenrollment to fail:

- Setting the **This number of authorized signatures** option on the **Issuance Requirements** tab to higher than one.

- Selecting the **Supply in the request** option on the **Subject Name** tab.

Revocation

A CA's primary duty is to issue certificates, either to subordinate CAs, or to PKI clients. However, each CA also has the ability to revoke those certificates when necessary. Certificates are revoked when the information contained in the certificate is no longer considered valid or trusted. This can happen when a company changes

ISPs (Internet Service Providers), moves to a new physical address or when the contact listed on the certificate has changed. Essentially, a certificate should be revoked whenever there is a change that makes the certificate's information "stale" and no longer reliable from that point forward.

> **NOTE**
>
> Information that has already been encrypted using the public key in a certificate that is later revoked is not necessarily invalid. Maintaining the example of a driver's license, checks that are written and authenticated by a cashier using your driver's license one week are not automatically voided if you lose your license or move states the next.

In addition to the changes in circumstance that can cause a certification revocation, certain owners may have their certificate revoked upon terminating employment. The most important reason to revoke a certificate is if the private key as been compromised in any way. If a key has been compromised, it should be revoked immediately.

Along with notifying the CA of the need to revoke a certificate, it is equally important to notify all certificate users of the date that the certificate will no longer be valid. After notifying users and the CA, the CA is responsible for changing the status of the certificate and notifying users that it has been revoked.

When a certificate revocation request is sent to a CA, the CA must be able to authenticate the request with the certificate owner. Once the CA has authenticated the request, the certificate is revoked and notification is sent out. CAs are not the only ones who can revoke a certificate. A PKI administrator can revoke a certificate, but without authenticating the request with the certificate owner. This allows for the revocation of certificates in cases where the owner is no longer accessible or available as in the case of termination.

The X.509 standard requires that CA's publish certificate revocation lists (CRLs). In their simplest form, a CRL is a published form listing the revocation status of certification that the CA manages. There are several forms that revocation lists may take, but the two most noteworthy are *simple CRLs* and *delta CRLs*.

A simple CRL is a container that holds a list of revoked certificates with the name of the CA, the time the CRL was published, and when the next CRL will be published. It is a single file that continues to grow over time. The fact that only information about the certificates is included and not the certificate itself helps to manage the size of a simple CRL.

Delta CRLs can handle the issues that simple CRLs cannot- size and distribution. While simple CRLs contain only certain information about a revoked certificate, it can still become a large file. How, then, do you continually distribute a large file to all parties that need to see the CRL? The solution is in Delta CRLs. In an environment leveraging delta CRLs, a base CRL is sent to all end parties to initialize their copies of the CRL. Afterwards, updates know as deltas are sent out on a periodic basis to inform the end parties of any changes.

In practice within Windows Server 2008, the tool that the CA uses for revocation is the *certificate revocation list*, or CRL. The act of revoking a certificate is simple: from the **Certification Authority** console, simply highlight the **Issued Certificates** container, right-click the certificate and choose **All | Revoke Certificate.** The certificate will then be located in the **Revoked Certificates** container.

When a PKI entity verifies a certificate's validity, that entity checks the CRL before giving approval. The question is: how does a client know where to check for the list? The answer is the CDPs, or CRL Distribution Points. CDPs are locations on the network to which a CA publishes the CRL; in the case of an enterprise CA under Windows Server 2008, Active Directory holds the CRL, and for a stand-alone, the CRL is located in the *certsrv\certenroll* directory. Each certificate has a location listed for the CDP, and when the client views the certificate, it then understands where to go for the latest CRL. Figure 3.29 shows the Extensions tab of the CA property sheet, where you can modify the location of the CDP.

Figure 3.29 Extensions Tab of the CA Property Sheet

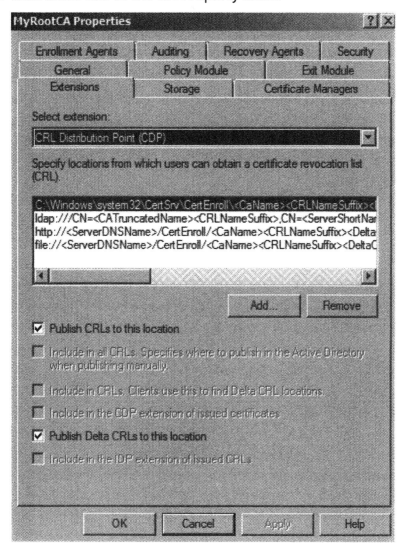

In order for a CA to publish a CRL, use the **Certificate Authority** console to right-click the **Revoked Certificates** container and choose **All Tasks | Publish**. From there, you can choose to publish either a complete CRL, or a Delta CRL.

Whether you select a New CRL or a Delta CRL, you are next prompted to enter a publication interval (the most frequent intervals chosen are one week for full CRLs and one day for Delta CRLs). Clients cache the CRL for this period of time, and then check the CDP again when the period expires. If an updated CDP does not exist or cannot be located, the client automatically assumes that all certificates are invalid.

Working with Templates

A *certificate template* defines the policies and rules that a CA uses when a request for a certificate is received. Often when someone refers to building and managing a PKI for their enterprise, they are usually only thinking of the Certificate Authority and the associated infrastructure needed to support the authentication and authorization required to support the function of the CA. While this is certainly important for the proper function of the PKI, it is only half of the picture—the certificates themselves must be carefully planned to support the business goals that are driving the need to install and configure the PKI.

When you consider that certificates are flexible and can be used in scores of different scenarios, the true power of the certificate becomes apparent. While these different uses can all coexist within a single PKI, the types and functions of the certificates can be very different. Certificates that are used to support two-factor authentication on smart cards can be very different than those used to establish SSL connections to web servers, sign IPSec traffic between servers, support 802.1x wireless access through NAP, or even certificates used to sign e-mail communication.

In all of these cases, the CA and the PKI it supports are the same, but it is the certificate itself that is changing. For each of these different uses, it is important for the certificate to contain appropriate data to facilitate in the function that the designer of the PKI has intended and no more. While additional data could be provided in the certificate, the fact that these are intended to mediate security exchanges makes it inappropriate to include any more information than is necessary to complete the certificate's objective. It is the Certificate Template that specifies the data that must be included in a certificate for it to function as well as to ensure that all of the needed data are provided to ensure the certificate's validity.

For an individual certificate, there are a number of properties and settings that go into the certificate template specification. Each of these combine to build the final template that will determine the settings for the resulting Certificate.

There are many built-in templates that can be viewed using the **Certificate Templates** snap-in (see Figure 3.30). The snap-in can be run by right-clicking the **Certificate Templates** container located in the **Certification Authority** console and clicking **Manage**. You can use one of the built-in templates or create your own.

Figure 3.30 Certificate Templates Snap-in

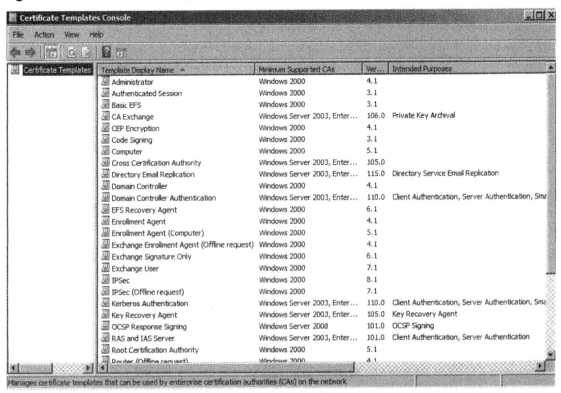

When creating your own template, you have multiple options that will guide the CA in how to handle incoming requests. The first step in the creation process is to duplicate an existing template. You do this by using the **Certificate Templates** snap-in, then right-clicking the template you wish to copy and selecting *Duplicate Template*. On the **General** tab that appears by default (seen in Figure 3.31), there are time-sensitive options such as validity period and renewal period. Note the default validity period of one year, and the default renewal period of six weeks. There are also general options such as the template display name and a checkbox for publishing the certificate in Active Directory.

Figure 3.31 General Tab of the New Template Property Sheet

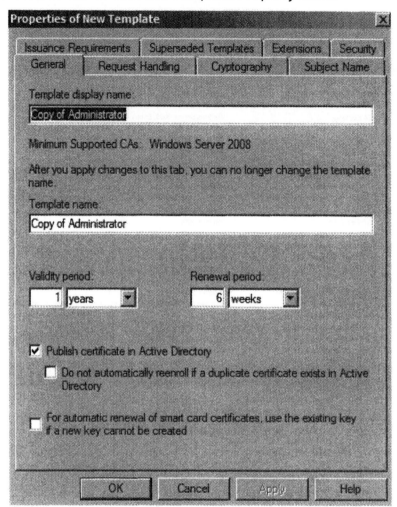

General Properties

Now we'll describe the following settings under the General tab of the new certificate template:

- **Template Display Name** It is important that the certificate that you are creating has a descriptive name accurately describes the function of the certificate. This name cannot be changed once it is assigned, but you can always recreate the certificate from another template later.

- **Validity Period** This is the period for which the derived certificates are valid. This time should be long enough so as not to create a burden on the end user, but not so long as to create a security problem.

- **Renewal Period** This is the period in which the certificate is notified of its expiration and that it will attempt to renew if this is an option for the certificate.

- **Publish in Active Directory** Some certificates can be stored in the active directory tied to security principals there. This generally applies to User certificates that are not ties to specific hardware.

The **Request Handling** tab, shown in Figure 3.32, has options to enroll without user interaction.

Figure 3.32 Request Handling Tab of the New Template Property Sheet

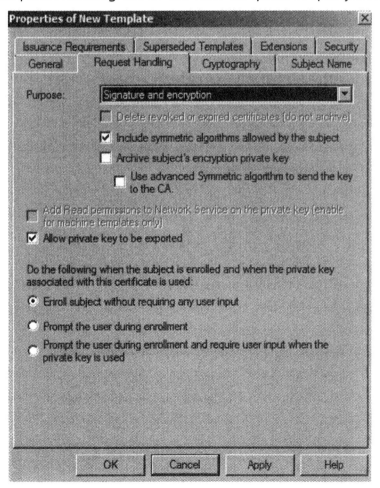

Request Handling

The Request Handling tab includes the following settings:

- **Purpose** It is important to consider the activities for which this new certificate will be responsible. Some keys can be used just to validate identity while others can also provide signing for encryption.

  - The private key can also be archived or shared with the CA so that it may be recovered in the event of loss. Otherwise, the certificate must be recreated.

- **Enrollment Actions** Different notification actions can be specified when the private key for this certificate is used. This can range from transparent usage of the key to full notification prompting the certificate owner for permission.

The **Cryptography** tab seen in Figure 3.33, gives you the choice of algorithms that can be used.

Figure 3.33 Cryptography Tab

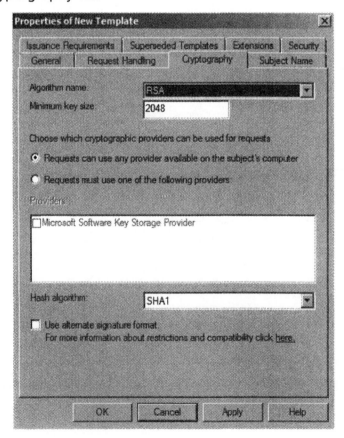

Cryptography

The Cryptography tab includes the following settings:

- **Algorithm Name** There are a number of cryptographic Algorithms that can be used to provide encryption for the keys. Valid methods under server 2008 are RSA, ECDH_P256, ECDH_P384, ECDH_P521.

  - Note: If the Purpose is changed to Signature, additional algorithms become available: ECDSA_P256, ECDSA_P384, ECDSA_P521

- **Hash Algorithm** To provide one-way hashes for key exchanges, a number of algorithms are available. These include: MD2, MD4, MD5, SHA1, SHA256, SHA384, SHA512.

The **Subject Name** tab seen in Figure 3.34, gives you the choice of obtaining subject name information from Active Directory or from the certificate request itself. In the latter case, autoenrollment (which we'll discuss later in the chapter) is not available.

Figure 3.34 Subject Name Tab of the New Template Property Sheet

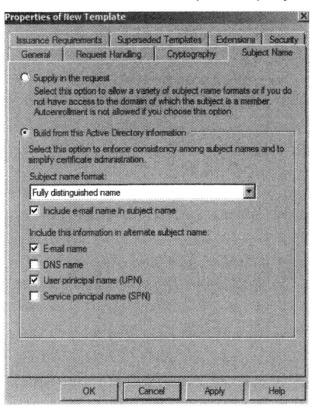

Subject Name

The Subject Name tab includes the following settings:

- **Supply in the Request** Under this option, the CA will expect to get additional subject information in the certificate request. As noted, this will not permit autoenrollment, requiring intervention to issue the certificate.

- **Build from this AD Information** Under this option, the Active Directory will be queried and the certificate will be built based on the AD files you specify.

Usually the default of the Distinguished Name is adequate for most purposes, but the common name will sometime be preferable.

The **Issuance Requirements** tab seen in Figure 3.35 allows you to suspend automatic certificate issuance by selecting the CA certificate manager approval checkbox.

Figure 3.35 Issuance Requirements Tab of the New Template Property Sheet

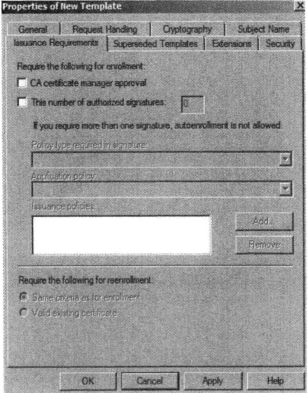

Issuance Requirements

These settings can be used to manage the approval requirements in order for a certificate to be issued. These settings allow for a workflow or approval chain to be applied to the certificate type.

- **CA Certificate Manager Approval** Using this setting will require that the CA Manager assigned in the CA approve of the certificate before it is released to the end-user of the certificate.

- **Number of Authorized Signatures** Under these settings, additional approvals steps may be required to release the certificate. In these scenarios, two or more approval authorities will have to consent before the certificate is generated.

- **Require the Following for Reenrollment** These settings specify the approval and prerequisites that are in place for renewal of the certificate. This gives the network administrator to allow subjects with valid certificates to renew without having to go through the approval chain.

The **Superseded Templates** tab, as shown in Figure 3.36, is used to define which certificates are superseded by the current template. Usually, this tab is used to configure a template that serves several functions, e.g. IPSec and EFS. In this case, a template used *only* for IPSec or a template used *only* for EFS would be placed on the superseded templates list. This section allows the network administrator to specify other templates that are superseded by the new template type. This allows control of both versioning and wholesale template replacement.

As templates evolve, it may be useful to replace templates that are already deployed in the wild with a new template.

Figure 3.36 Superseded Templates Tab of the New Template Property Sheet

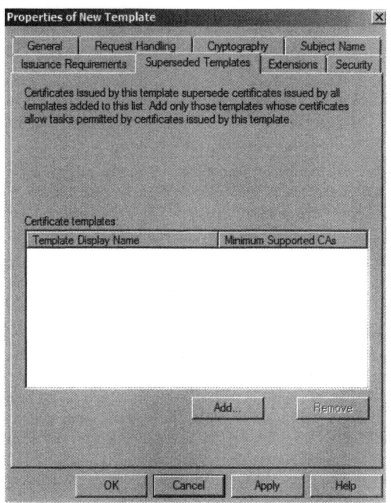

In addition to the standard usage patterns that are inherited from the parent certificate, it is sometimes important to specify new circumstances and roles that a certificate will fill. In this case, additional extensions to the certificate will be applied to provide this new functionality.

Under these settings, a new ability such as code signing can be applied to all derivative certificates to allow these new subjects the ability to complete multiple tasks.

The **Extensions** tab as seen in Figure 3.37 can be used to add such things as the Application Policies extension, which defines the purposes for which a generated certificate can be used. The Issuance Policies extension is also worth mentioning, because it defines when a certificate may be issued.

Figure 3.37 Extensions Tab of the New Template Property Sheet

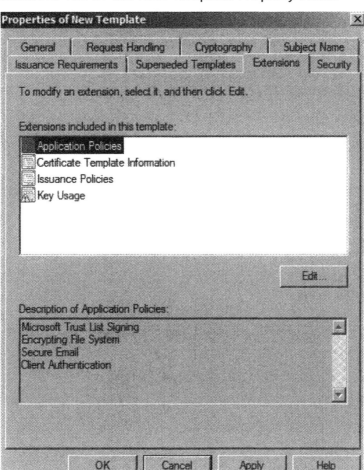

The **Security** tab is similar to the **Security** tab that we saw in Figure 3.38, except that this tab is used to control who may edit the template and who may request certificates using the template. Figure 3.38 shows the default permission level for the **Authenticated Users** group. In order for a user to request a certificate, however, the user must have at least the **Enroll** permission assigned to them for manual requests, and the **Autoenroll** permission for automatic requests.

Figure 3.38 Security Tab of the New Template Property Sheet

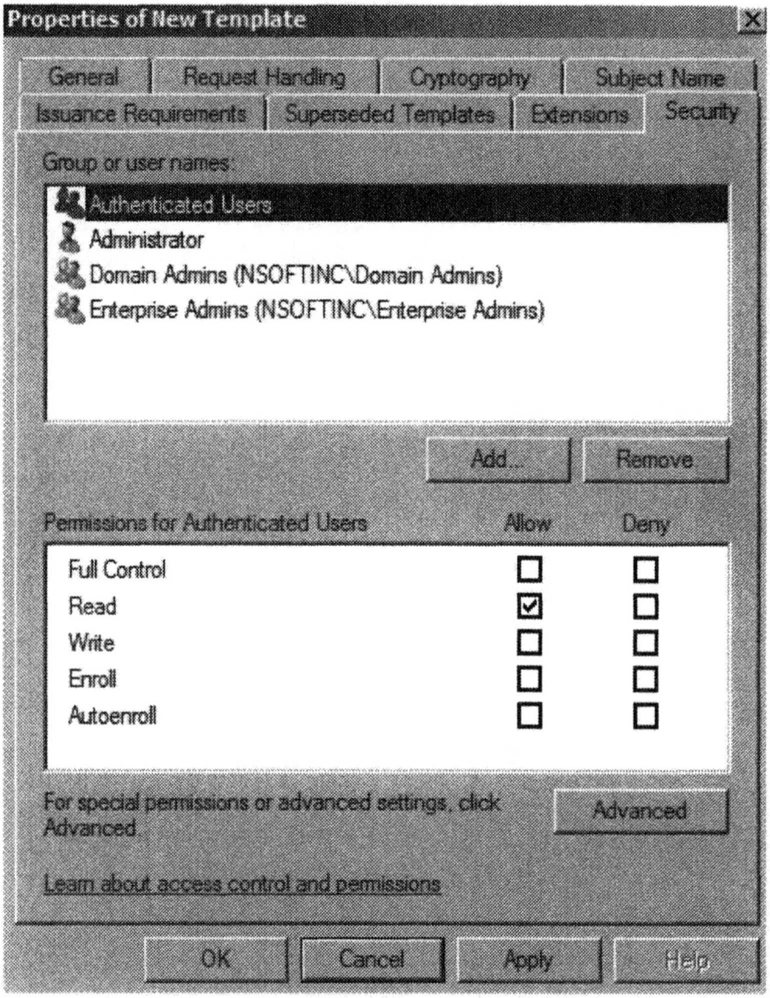

Security

The security settings control the actions that different types of users are able to perfume on a certificate template.

- **Enroll** These subjects are able to request that a certificate be created from this template and assigned to them. This enrollment process will abide by the constraints listed under the Issuance Requirements tab.

- **Autoenroll** These subjects are able to make a request to the CA and will be automatically issued the certificate if the subject meets the Issuance Requirements. In this case, the certificate will be applied without administrator intervention or assistance.

After you have configured a particular template, it still cannot be used by the CA to issue certificates until it is made *available*. To enable a template, you use the **Certification Authority** console and right-click the **Certificate Templates** container. Selecting **New | Certificate Template to Issue** completes the process.

Types of Templates

There are a number of different templates that are included with Windows Server 2008 that provide basic signing and encryption services in the Enterprise Windows PKI role. In addition to these pre-built templates, the network administrator also has the option to build custom templates to address needs that might not be covered by the standard templates or to provide interoperation with other systems.

The Subject Field of the Certificate templates determines the scope of action and the types of objects to which the resulting certificates can be bound.

User Certificate Types

User Certificate Templates are intended to be bound to a single user to provide identity and/or encryption services for that single entity.

- **Administrator** This certificate template provides signature and encryption services for administrator accounts providing account identification and trust list (CTL) management within the domain. Certificates based on the Administrator Template are stored in the Active Directory.

- **Authenticated Session** This certificate template allows users to authenticate to a web server to provide user credentials for site logon. This is often deployed for remote users as a way to validate identity without storing formation insecurely in a cookie while avoiding the need for a user to log on to the site each time.

- **Basic EFS** Certificates derived from this template are stored in Active Directory with the associated user account and are used to encrypt data using the Encrypting File System (EFS).

- **Code Signing** These certificate templates allow developers to create certificates that can be used to sign application code. This provides a check on the origin of software so that code management systems and end-users can be sure that the origin of the software is trusted.

- **EFS Recovery Agent** Certificates of this type allow files that have been encrypted with the EFS to be decrypted so that the files can be used again. EFS Recovery Agent certificates should be a part of any disaster recovery plan when designing an EFS implementation.

- **Enrollment Agent** Certificates derived from this template are used to request and issue other certificates from the enterprise CA on behalf of another entity. For example, the web enrollment application uses these certificates to manage the certificate requests with the CA.

- **Exchange Enrollment Agent** These certificates are used to manage enrollment services form within exchange to provide certificates to other entities within the exchange infrastructure.

- **Exchange Signature** Certificates derived from the Exchange Signature template are user certificates used to sign e-mail messages sent from within the Exchange system.

- **Exchange User** Certificates based on the Exchange User template are user certificates that are stored in the Active Directory used to encrypt e-mail messages sent from within the Exchange system.

- **Smartcard Logon** These certificates allow the holder of the smart card to authenticate to the active directory and provides identity and encryption abilities. This is usually deployed as a part of a two-factor security schema using smart cards as the physical token.

- **Smartcard User** Unlike the Smartcard Logon certificate template, these types of certificates are stored in the Active Directory and limit the scope of identity and encryption to e-mail systems.

- **Trust List Signing** These certificates allow the signing of a trust list to help manage certificate security and to provide affirmative identity to the signer.

- **User** This template is used to create general User Certificates—the kind that are usually thought of when talking about user certificates. These are stored in the Active Directory and are responsible for user activities in the AD such as authentication, EFS encryption, and interaction with Exchange.

- **User Signature Only** These certificates allow users to sign data and provide identification of the origin of the signed data.

Computer Certificate Types

Computer Certificate Templates are intended to be bound to a single computer entity to provide identity and/ or encryption services for that computer. These are often the cornerstone of workstation authentication systems like NAP and 802.1x which might require computer certificates for EAP authentication.

- **CA Exchange** These certificates are bound to Certificate Authorities to mediate key exchange between CAs allowing for PK sharing and archival.

- **CEP Encryption** Certificates of this type are bound to servers that are able to respond to key requests through the Simple Certificate Enrollment Protocol (SCEP).

- **Computer** This template is used to generate standard Computer certificates that allow a physical machine to assert its identity on the network. These certificates are extensively used in EAP authentication in identifying end-points in secured communication tunnels.

- **Domain Controller Authentication** Certificates of this type are used to authenticate users and computers in the active directory. This allows a Domain Controller to access the directory itself and provide authentication services to other entities.

- **Enrollment Agent (Computer)** These certificates allow a computer to act as an enrollment agent against the PKI so that they can offer computer certificates to physical machines.

- **IPSec** Certificates based on this template allow a computer to participate in IPSec communications. These computers are able to assert their identity as well as encrypt traffic on the network. This is used in IPSec VPN tunnels as well as in Domain and Server Isolation strategies.

- **Kerberos Authentication** These certificates are used by local computers to authenticate with the Active Directory using the Kerberos v5 protocol.

- **OCSP Response Signing** This is a unique certificate type to Windows Server 2008 allowing a workstation to act as an Online Responder in the validation of certificate request queries.

- **RAS and IAS Server** These certificates are used to identify and provide encryption for Routing and Remote Access Server (RRAS) as well as Internet Authorization Servers (IAS) to identify themselves in VPN and RADIUS communications with RADIUS Clients.

- **Router** This is also a new role to Windows Server 2008 providing services to provide credentials to routers making requests through SCEP to a CA.

- **Web Server** These certificates are commonly used by servers acting as web servers to provide end=point identification and traffic encryption to their customers. These kinds of certificates are used to provide Secure Socket Layer (SSL) encryption enabling clients to connect to the web server using the HTTPS protocol.

- **Workstation Authentication** Like general computer certificates, the workstation certificate allows computers that are domain members the ability to assert their identity on the network and encrypt traffic that they send across the network.

Other Certificate Types

There are a number of other certificate types that are not directly tied to either user or computer entities. These are usually infrastructure-based certificate types that are used to manage the domain or the Certificate Authorities themselves.

- **Cross-Certification Authority** These certificates are used within the Certificate Authority Infrastructure to cross -certify CAs to validate the hierarchy that makes up the PKI.

- **Directory E-mail Replication** Certificates that are derived from this type are used within the larger Exchange infrastructure to allow for the replication of e-mail across the directory service.

- **Domain Controller** This kind of certificate is only held by the Domain Controllers in the domain. These differentiate from the Domain Controller Authentication certificates as they identify the individual DC rather than facilitate authorization of inbound authentication requests.

- **Root CA** These certificates are only issued to Root Certificate Authorities to assert its identity in the Public Key Infrastructure.

- **Subordinate CA** This certificate type is used to assert the identity of Subordinate Certificate Authorities in the PKI. This type of certificate can only be issued by a computer holding the Root CA certificate or another Subordinate CA that is the direct parent of the on to which the new certificate is being issued.

Custom Certificate Templates

In some circumstances, it might be necessary to create a custom certification type that can be used to support a specific business need. If you are using a version of Windows Server 2008 that is not either the WEB or Standard edition, you can create your own templates.

Configuring & Implementing...

Creating a Custom Template

In this exercise, we will create a new User Template based on the existing default user template. This new template will be valid for 10 years rather than the default 1-year expiration date.

1. Log in to your domain with an account that is a member of the Domain Admins group.
2. Navigate to Start | Administrative Tools | Certificate Authority.
3. Right-click the **Certificate Templates** folder on the left pane. Choose **Manage** to open the Certificate Templates Console (see Figure 3.39).

Continued

Figure 3.39 Creating a Custom Template

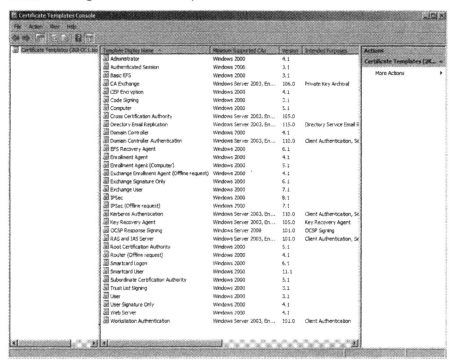

4. Right-click the User Template. Choose Duplicate Template.
5. On the Duplicate Template page, choose **Server 2008** versioning as all of our CAs are running Server 2008 (see Figure 3.40). Click **OK**.

Figure 3.40 Creating a Custom Template

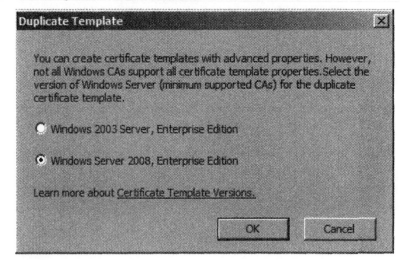

Continued

6. In the Template display name, enter Long-term User.

7. Change the **Validity Period** to 10 Years (see Figure 3.41).

Figure 3.41 Creating a Custom Template

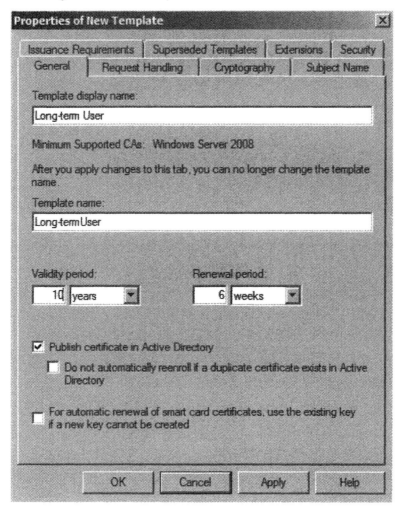

8. Click **OK**.

The new Long-term User certificate template has now been created on this CA and is ready to be used to create new derivative certificates.

Securing Permissions

With the wide set of configuration options that are available when creating a new Certificate Template, it might come as a surprise that the permissions model is relatively simple. All of the more complicated security controlling the approval process and revocation is already built into the Certificate Template itself, so there is little left to control through the more traditional Access Control Entries on the template's Access Control List.

- **Full Control** Users with this permission have access to do anything with the Certificate Template. Users with this right should be confined to the Domain Administrators and CA Managers who will be maintaining the CA and the associated Templates.

- **Read** These users will be able to read the template and view its contents. It is important for users to be able to Read the template if they are to apply it and continue to use the associated certificates issued from the template.

- **Write** Users who are able to modify and manage the template will need to have write permissions on the template. Again, this should be confined to Domain Administrators and CA Managers who will be responsible for maintaining the Templates.

- **Enroll** Users who will request certificates of this type or who already have these certs will need to have Enroll privileges.

- **AutoEnroll** Subjects that will request new certificates through the auto-enrollment process will need to have autoenrollment privileges in addition to the enroll and read permissions.

NOTE

In order to keep the Certificate Authority communicating with the Active Directory, it is important that the Cert Publishers group be protected. Make sure that this group is not inadvertently destroyed or changed.

Versioning

Certificates are all tagged with version information allowing them to evolve over time. Without this feature, when a Certificate Template would get updated, all of the certificates based on the old template would have to be revoked forcing the end-users to apply for new certificates again. This is disruptive to business and introduces a large amount of risk to business continuity as the certificates are brought into compliance again.

With versioning, a new version of the Certificate Template can be issued into the production environment. Then using the autoenrollment process, these certificates can be superseded bring all of the certificate holding subjects into compliance quickly and with a minimum of both disruption to the business and administrative intervention.

Key Recovery Agent

Sometimes it is necessary to recover a key from storage. One of the problems that often arise regarding PKI is the fear that documents will become lost forever—irrecoverable because someone loses or forget their private key. Let's say that employees use Smart Cards to hold their private keys. If a user were to leave his smart card in his wallet which was left in the pants that he accidentally threw into the washing machine, then that user might be without his private key and therefore incapable of accessing any documents or e-mails that used his existing private key.

Many corporate environments implement a key recovery server solely for the purpose of backing up and recovering keys. Within an organization, there is at least one *key recovery agent*. A key recovery agent is an employee who has the authority to retrieve a user's private key. Some key recover servers require that two key recovery agents retrieve private user keys together for added security. Some key recovery servers also have the ability to function as a key escrow server, thereby adding the ability to split the keys onto two separate recovery servers, further increasing security.

Luckily, Windows Server 2008 provides a locksmith of sorts (called a Registration Authority, or RA) that earlier versions of Windows did not have. A key recovery solution, however, is not easy to implement and requires several steps. The basic method follows:

1. Create an account to be used for key recovery.

2. Create a new template to issue to that account.

3. Request a key recovery certificate from the CA.

4. Have the CA issue the certificate.

5. Configure the CA to archive certificates by using the **Recovery Agents** tab of the CA property sheet (shown in Figure 3.42).

6. Create an archive template for the CA.

Figure 3.42 Recovery Agents Tab of the CA Property Sheet

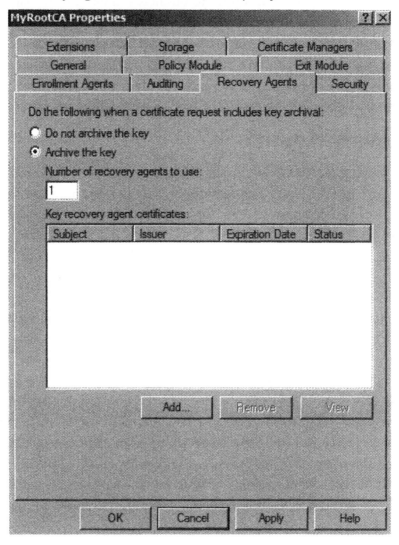

Each of these steps requires many substeps, but can be well worth the time and effort. It is worth noting again that key recovery is not possible on a stand-alone CA, because a stand-alone cannot use templates. It is also worth noting that only encryption keys can be recovered—private keys used for digital signatures cannot.

Summary

The purpose of a PKI is to facilitate the sharing of sensitive information such as authentication traffic across an insecure network. This is done with public and private key cryptography. In public key cryptography, keys are generated in pairs so that every public key is matched to a private key and vice versa. If data is encrypted with a particular public key, then only the corresponding private key can decrypt it. A digital signature means that an already encrypted piece of data is further encrypted by someone's private key. When the recipient wants to decrypt the data, he or she must first "unlock" the digital signature by using the signer's public key, remembering that only the *signer's* public key will work. This might seem secure, but because anyone at all can sign the data, how does the recipient know for certain the identity of the person who actually signed it?

The answer is that digital signatures need to be issued by an authoritative entity, one whom everyone trusts. This entity is known as a certification authority. An administrator can use Windows Server 2008, a third-party company such as VeriSign, or a combination of the two to create a structure of CAs. Certification authorities, as the name implies, issue certificates. In a nutshell, certificates are digitally signed public keys. Certificates work something like this: party A wants to send a private message to party B, and wants to use party B's public key to do it. Party A realizes that if B's public key is used to encrypt the message, then only B's private key can be used to decrypt it and since B and no one else has B's private key, everything works out well. However, A needs to be sure that he's really using B's public key and not an imposter's, so instead of just asking B for B's public key, he asks B for a certificate. B has previously asked the CA for a certificate for just such an occasion (B will present the certificate to anyone who wants to verify B's identity). The CA has independently verified B's identity, and has then taken B's public key and signed it with its own private key, creating a certificate. A trusts the CA, and is comfortable using the CA's well-known public key. When A uses the CA's public key to unlock the digital signature, he can be sure that the public key inside really belongs to B, and he can take that public key and encrypt the message.

The "I" in PKI refers to the infrastructure, which is a system of public key cryptography, certificates, and certification authorities. CAs are usually set up in a hierarchy, with one system acting as a root and all the others as subordinates at one or more levels deep. By analyzing the certificate requirements for your company, you can design your CA structure to fit your needs. Most organizations use a three-tier model, with a root CA at the top, an intermediate level of subordinates who control CA policy, and a bottom level of subordinates who actually issue certificates to users, computers, and applications. In addition to choosing root and subordinate structure for the CA hierarchy, each CA during installation needs to be designated as either an enterprise or a stand-alone. Each of these choices has distinct advantages and disadvantages. Most CA configuration after installation is done through the Certification Authority snap-in. In addition to issuing certificates, CAs are also responsible for revoking them when necessary. Revoked certificates are published to a CRL that clients can download before accepting a certificate as valid.

Enterprise CAs use templates to know what to do when a certificate request is received and how to issue a certificate if approved. There are several built-in templates included in Server 2008, or you can configure new ones. Once a CA is ready to issue certificates, clients need to request them. Autoenrollment, Web enrollment, or manual enrollment through the Certificates snap-in are the three ways by which a client can request a certificate. Autoenrollment is available for computer certificates, and in Windows Server 2008, for user certificates as well.

Solutions Fast Track

Planning a Windows Server 2008 Certificate-Based PKI

- ☑ A PKI combines public key cryptography with digital certificates to create a secure environment where network traffic such as authentication packets can travel safely.

- ☑ Public keys and private keys always come in pairs. If the public key is used to encrypt data, only the matching private key can decrypt it.

- ☑ When public key-encrypted data is encrypted again by a private key, that private key encryption is called a digital signature.

- ☑ Digital signatures provided by ordinary users aren't very trustworthy, so a trusted authority is needed to provide them. The authority (which can be Windows-based) issues certificates, which are basically digitally signed containers for public keys and other information.

- ☑ Certificates are used to safely exchange public keys, and provide the basis for applications such as IPSec, EFS, and smart card authentication.

Implementing Certification Authorities

☑ Certificate needs are based on which applications and communications an organization uses and how secure they need to be. Based on these needs, CAs are created by installing certificate services and are managed using the Certification Authority snap-in.

☑ A CA hierarchy is structured with a root and one or more level of subordinates—three levels are common. The bottom level of subordinates issues certificates. The intermediate level controls policies.

☑ Enterprise CAs require and use Active Directory to issue certificates, often automatically. Stand-alone CAs can be more secure, and need an administrator to manually issue or deny certificate requests.

☑ CAs need to be backed up consistently and protected against attacks. Keys can be archived and later retrieved if they are lost. This is a new feature for Windows Server 2008.

☑ CAs can revoke as well as issue certificates. Once a certificate is revoked, it needs to be published to a CRL distribution point. Clients check the CRL periodically before they can trust a certificate.

Planning Enrollment and Distribution of Certificates

☑ Templates control how a CA acts when handed a request, and how to issue certificates. There are a quite a few built-in templates, or you can create your own using the Certificate Template snap-in. Templates must be enabled before a CA can use them.

☑ Certificates can be requested with the Certificates snap-in or by using Internet Explorer and pointing to *http://servername/certsrv* on the CA.

☑ Machine and user certificates can be requested with no user intervention requirement by using autoenrollment. Autoenrollment for user certificates is new to Windows Server 2008.

☑ Role-based administration is recommended for larger organizations. Different users can be assigned permissions relative to their positions, such as certificate manager.

Frequently Asked Questions

Q: In what format do CAs issue certificates?

A: Microsoft certificate services use the standard X.509 specifications for issued certificates and the Public Key Cryptography Standard (PKCS) #10 standard for certificate requests. The PKCS #7 certificate renewal standard is also supported. Windows Server 2003 also supports other formats, such as PKCS #12, DER encoded binary X.509, and Base64 Encoded X.509, for exporting certificates to computers running non-Windows operating systems.

Q: If certificates are so important in a PKI, why don't I see more of them?

A: Many portions of a Windows PKI are hidden to the end user. Thanks to features such as autoenrollment, some PKI transactions can be completely done by the operating system. Most of the work in implementing a PKI comes in the planning and design phase. Operations such as encrypting data via EFS use certificates, but the user does not "see" or manually handle the certificates.

Q: I've heard that I can't take my laptop overseas because it uses EFS. Is this true?

A: Maybe. The backbone of any PKI-enabled application such as EFS is encryption. Although the U.S. government now permits the exporting of "high encryption" standards, some countries still do not allow their import. The Windows Server 2008 PKI can use high encryption, and so the actual answer depends on the country in question. For information on the cryptographic import and export policies of a number of countries, see http://www.rsasecurity.com/rsalabs/faq/6-5-1.html.

Q: Can I create my own personal digital signature and use it instead of a CA?

A: Not if you need security. The purposes behind digital signatures are privacy and security, and a digital signature at first glance seems to fit the bill. The problem, however, is not the signature itself, but the lack of trust in a recipient. Impersonations become a looming security risk if you can't guarantee that the digital signatures you receive came from the people with whom they were supposed to have originated. For this reason, a certificate issued by a trusted third party provides the most secure authentication.

Q: Can I have a CA hierarchy that is five levels deep?

A: Yes, but that's probably overkill for most networks. Microsoft's three-tier model of root, intermediate, and issuing CAs will more than likely meet your requirements. Remember that your hierarchy can be wide instead of deep.

Q: Do I have to have more than one CA?

A: No. Root CAs have the ability to issue all types of certificates and can assume responsibility for your entire network. In a small organization, a single CA might be sufficient for your purposes. For a larger organization, however, this structure would not be suitable.

Q: How can I change the publishing interval of a CRL?

A: From the **Certification Authority** console, right-click the **Revoked Certificates** container and choose **Properties**. The **CRL Publishing Parameters** tab allows you to change the default interval for full and Delta CRLs.

Q: Why can't I seem to get autoenrollment for user certificates to work?

A: Remember that autoenrollment for machines is a feature that has been around since Windows 2000, but autoenrollment for user certificates is new to Windows Server 2003. In order to use this feature, you need to be running either a Windows Server 2003 or XP client and you must log on to a Windows Server 2003 domain. Finally, autoenrollment must be enabled through Active Directory's group policy. Also, you won't be able to autoenroll a user unless the user account has been assigned an e-mail address.

Q: What is the default validity period for a new certificate?

A: The default, which can be changed on the **General** tab of a new template's **Property** sheet, is one year. Other important settings, such as minimum key size and purpose of the certificate, can be found on the sheet's other tabs.

Q: If my smart card is lost or stolen, can I be reissued one?

A: Yes. The enrollment agent can enroll a new card for you at the enrollment station. Although most smart card providers allow cards to be reused (such as when they are found), a highly secure company may require old cards to be destroyed. For similar security reasons, PINs should not be reused on a newly issued card although it is possible. Remember that a card is only good to a thief if the corresponding PIN is obtained as well.

Q: When setting up smart cards for my company, can I use the MS-CHAP or MS-CHAP v2 protocols for authentication?

A: No. EAP is the only authentication method you can use with smart cards. It is considered the pinnacle of the authentication protocols under Windows Server 2003. MS-CHAP v2 is probably the most secure of the password-based protocols, but still does not provide the level of protection that smart cards using EAP do. This is because EAP is not really an authentication protocol by itself. It interfaces with other protocols such as MD5-CHAP, and is therefore extremely flexible. As a result it has been widely implemented by many different vendors. MS-CHAP and MS-CHAP v2 are Microsoft proprietary, and do not enjoy the same popularity or scrutiny applied to EAP. It is this scrutiny over the last several years that gives EAP the reputation of a highly secure protocol.

Q: How can I determine the length of time for which a certificate should be valid?

A: It is important to plan out your PKI implementation before it goes into production. In the case of certificate validity, you'll want to choose a time period that will cover the majority of your needs without being so long as to open your environment up to compromise.

If you are planning a certificate to support a traveling workforce that only connects to the corporate infrastructure once a quarter, it would be detrimental to expire certificates once a month. At the same time, specifying a certificate to be valid for 20 years might open your business up to compromise by an ex-employee long after his employment has been terminated.

Finally, you will want to ensure that your certificate lifetime is less than the lifetime for the lifetime of the CA's own cert. If the issuing CA will only be valid for a year, having a subordinate cert that is good for 5 years will lead to problems when the parent authority is revoked.

Q: My domain has been active for some time, but I have only recently implemented a Certificate Authority in my domain. I am now getting messages that my Domain Controllers do not have appropriate certificates. What should I do?

A: Make sure that you have enabled auto enrollment on your Domain Controller certificate templates. This step is often missed and can lead to a number of secondary problems, the least of which is annoying messages in the Event Logs.

Chapter 4

Windows Server 2008 Core

Solutions in this chapter:

- Using Server Core and Active Directory

- Using Server Core and Domain Naming System

- Configuring Dynamic Host Configuration Protocol Using Server Core

- Installing Internet Information Services

- Installing the FTP Publishing Service

- Installing and Managing Hyper-V on Windows Server Core Installations

☑ Summary

☑ Solutions Fast Track

☑ Frequently Asked Questions

Introduction

For years, Microsoft engineers have been told that Windows would never stand up to Linux in terms of security simply because it was too darn "heavy" (too much) code, loaded too many modules (services, startup applications, and so on), and was generally too GUI heavy. With Windows Server 2008, Microsoft engineers can stand tall, thanks to the introduction of Server Core. The concept behind the design Server Core is to truly provide a minimal server installation. The belief is that rather than installing all the application, components, services, and features by default, it is up to the implementer to determine what will be turned on or off.

Table 4.1 is an overview of features available across Windows Server 2008, both Full and Server Core installations, and the various editions of Windows Vista.

Table 4.1 Features Available for Windows Server 2008

Feature	Windows Server 2008		Windows Vista		
	Full Install	Server Core Install	Ultimate, Business, Enterprise	Home Premium	Home Basic, Starter
Common HTTP Features					
Static Content	•	•	•	•	○
Default Document	•	•	•	•	○
Directory Browsing	•	•	•	•	○
HTTP Errors	•	•	•	•	•
HTTP Redirection	•	•	•	•	•
Application Development Features					
ASP.NET	•	○	•	•	○
.NET Extensibility	•	○	•	•	•
Active Server Pages (ASP)	•	•	•	•	○
Common Gateway Interface (CGI)	•	•	•	•	○
ISAPI Extensions	•	•	•	•	○

Continued

Table 4.1 Continued. Features Available for Windows Server 2008

Feature	Windows Server 2008		Windows Vista		
	Full Install	Server Core Install	Ultimate, Business, Enterprise	Home Premium	Home Basic, Starter
ISAPI Filters	●	●	●	●	○
Server-Side Includes	●	●	●	●	○
Health and Diagnostics Features					
HTTP Logging	●	●	●	●	●
Logging Tools	●	●	●	●	●
Request Monitor	●	●	●	●	●
HTTP Tracing	●	●	●	●	●
Custom Logging	●	●	●	●	○
ODBC Logging	●	●	●	○	○
Security Features					
Basic Authentication	●	●	●	●	○
Windows Authentication	●	●	●	○	○
Digest Authentication	●	●	●	○	○
Client Certificate Mapping Authentication	●	●	●	○	○
IIS Client Certificate Mapping Authentication	●	●	●	○	○
Uniform Resource Location (URL) Authorization	●	●	●	●	●

Continued

Table 4.1 Continued. Features Available for Windows Server 2008

Feature	Windows Server 2008		Windows Vista		
	Full Install	Server Core Install	Ultimate, Business, Enterprise	Home Premium	Home Basic, Starter
Request Filtering	•	•	•	•	•
IP Address and Domain Name Restrictions	•	•	•	•	•
Performance Features					
Static Content Compression	•	•	•	•	•
Dynamic Content Compression	•	•	•	•	•
Management Features					
Management Console	•	○	•	•	○
Management Scripts and Tools	•	•	•	•	•
Management Service	•	○	•	•	○
IIS 6.0 Management Compatibility	•	•	•	•	•
IIS 6.0 Metabase Compatibility	•	•	•	•	•
IIS 6.0 Windows Management Instrumentation (WMI) Compatibility	•	•	•	•	○

Continued

Table 4.1 Continued. Features Available for Windows Server 2008

Feature	Windows Server 2008		Windows Vista		
	Full Install	Server Core Install	Ultimate, Business, Enterprise	Home Premium	Home Basic, Starter
IIS 6.0 Management Console	●	○	●	●	○
IIS 6.0 Management Scripts and Tools	●	●	●	●	○
Windows Process Activation Services (WAS) Features					
Process Model	●	●	●	●	●
.NET Environment	●	○	●	●	●
Configuration Programming Interface	●	○	●	●	●
File Transfer Protocol (FTP) Publishing Service Features					
FTP Publishing Service	●	●	●	○	○
Management Console	●	○	●	○	○
Connection Limits					
Simultaneous Connections	Unlimited	Unlimited	10	3	3

Using Server Core and Active Directory

What is Server Core, you ask? It's the "just the facts, ma'am" version of Windows 2008. Microsoft defines Server Core as "a minimal server installation option for Windows Server 2008 that contains a subset of executable files, and five server roles." Essentially, Server Core provides only the binaries needed to support the role and the base operating systems. By default, fewer processes are generally running.

Server Core is so drastically different from what we have come to know from Windows Server NT, Windows Server 2000, or even Windows Server 2003 over the past decade-plus, that it looks more like MS-DOS than anything else (Figure 4.1). With Server Core, you won't find Windows Explorer, Internet Explorer, a Start menu, or even a clock! Becoming familiar with Server Core will take some time. In fact, most administrators will likely need a cheat sheet for a while. To help with it all, you can find some very useful tools on Microsoft TechNet at http://technet2.microsoft.com/ windowsserver2008/en/library/e7e522ac-b32f-42e1-b914-53ccc78d18161033. mspx?mfr=true. This provides command and syntax lists that can be used with Server Core. The good news is, for those of you who want the security and features of Server Core with the ease-of-use of a GUI, you have the ability to manage a Server Core installation using remote administration tools.

Figure 4.1 The Server Core Console

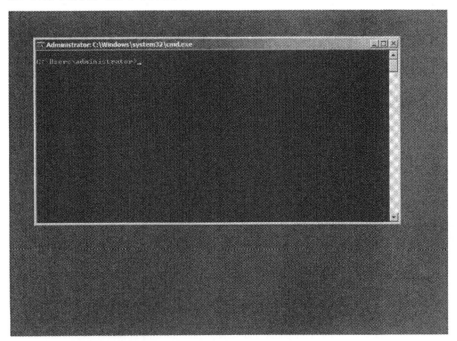

Before going any further, we should discuss exactly what will run on a Server Core installation. Server Core is capable of running the following server roles:

- Active Directory Domain Services Role
- Active Directory Lightweight Directory Services Role

- Dynamic Host Configuration Protocol (DHCP)

- Domain Name System (DNS) Services Role

- File Services Role

- Hyper-V (Virtualization) Role

- Print Services Role

- Streaming Media Services Role

- Web Services (IIS) Role

NOTE

Internet Information Server is Microsoft's brand of Web server software, utilizing Hypertext Transfer Protocol to deliver World Wide Web documents. It incorporates various functions for security, allows for CGI programs, and also provides for Gopher and FTP servers.

Although these are the roles Server Core supports, it can also support additional features, such as:

- Backup

- BitLocker

- Failover Clustering

- Multipath I/O

- Network Time Protocol (NTP)

- Removable Storage Management

- Simple Network Management Protocol (SNMP)

- Subsystem for Unix-based applications

- Telnet Client

- Windows Internet Naming Service (WINS)

NOTE

BitLocker Drive Encryption is an integral new security feature in Windows Server 2008 that protects servers at locations, such as branch offices, as well as mobile computers for all those roaming users out there. BitLocker provides offline data and operating system protection by ensuring that data stored on the computer is not revealed if the machine is tampered with when the installed operating system is offline.

Installation of Windows 2008 Server Core is fairly simple. During the installation process, you have the option of performing a Standard Installation or a Server Core installation. Once you have selected the hard drive configuration, license key activation, and End User License Agreement (EULA), you simply let the automatic installation continue to take place. When installation is done and the system has rebooted, you will be prompted with the traditional Windows challenge/response screen, and the Server Core console will appear.

Configuring & Implementing...

Configuring the Directory Services role in Server core

So let's put Server Core into action and use it to install Active Directory Domain Services. To install the Active Directory Domain Services Role, perform the following steps:

1. The first thing we need to do is set the IP information for the server. To do this, we first need to identify the network adapter. In the console window, type **netsh interface ipv4 show interfaces** and record the number shown under the **Idx** column.

2. Set the IP address, Subnet Mask, and Default Gateway for the server. To do this, type **netsh interface ipv4 set address name="<ID>" source=static address=<StaticIP> mask=<SubnetMask> gateway=**

Continued

<DefaultGateway>. ID represents the number from step 1, <StaticIP> represents the IP address we will assign, <SubnetMask> represents the subnet mask, and <Default Gateway> represents the IP address

Figure 4.2 Setting an IP Address in Server Core

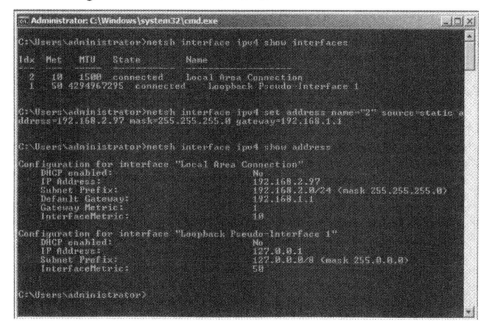

of the server's default gateway. See Figure 4.2 for our sample configuration.

3. Assign the IP address of the DNS server. Since this will be an Active Directory Domain Controller, we will set the DNS settings to point to itself. From the console, type **netsh interface ipv4 add dnsserver name="<ID>" address=<DNSIP> index=1. >**. ID represents the number from step 1, and <StaticIP> represents the IP address of the DNS server (in this case, the same IP address from step 2).

So, here is where things get a little tricky. When installing the Directory Services role in a full server installation, we would simply open up a **Run** window (or a command line) and type in **DCPromo**. Then, we would follow the prompts for configuration (domain name, file location, level of forest/domain security),

Continued

and then restart the system. Installing the role in Server Core isn't so simple, yet it's not exactly rocket science. In order to make this installation happen, we are going to need to configure an *unattended installation file*. An unattended installation file (see Figure 4.3) is nothing more than a text file that answers the questions that would have been answered during the DCPromo installation. So, let's assume you have created the unattended file and placed it on a floppy disk, CD, or other medium, and then inserted it into the Server Core server. Let's go ahead and install Directory Services:

1. Sign in to the server.
2. In the console, change drives to the removable media. In our example, we will be using drive E:, our DVD drive.

Figure 4.3 Installing Directory Services in Server Core

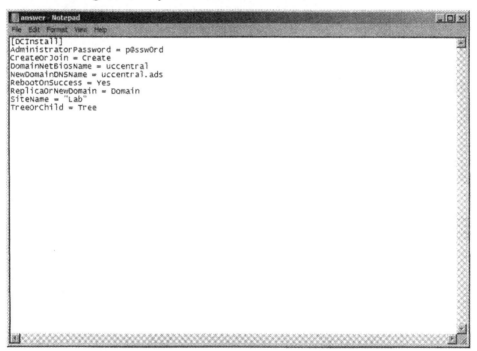

3. Once you have changed drives, type **dcpromo answer:\answer.txt**. Answer.txt is the name of our unattended file (see Figure 4.3).
4. Follow the installation process as it configures directory services. Once the server has completed the installation process, it will reboot automatically.

Using Server Core and DNS

A Windows Server 2008 Core Server Installation can be used for multiple purposes. One of the ways Server Core can be used is to provide a minimal installation for DNS. As you will recall, no GUIs are provided with Windows Server 2008 Core Server. A number of advantages to running DNS within Server Core include:

- **Smaller Footprint:** Reduces the amount of CPU, memory, and hard disk needed.

- **More Secure:** Fewer components and services running unnecessarily.

- **No GUI:** No GUI means that users cannot make modifications to the DNS databases (or any other system functions) using common/ user-friendly tools.

If you are planning to run DNS within a Server Core install, several steps must be performed prior to installation. The first step is to set the IP information of the server. To configure the IP addressing information of the server, do the following:

1. Identify the network adapter. To do this, in the console window, type **netsh interface ipv4 show interfaces** and record the number shown under the **Idx** column.

2. Set the IP address, Subnet Mask, and Default Gateway for the server. To do so, type **netsh interface ipv4 set address name="<ID>" source=static address=<StaticIP> mask=<SubnetMask> gateway= <DefaultGateway>**. ID represents the interface number from step 1, <StaticIP> represents the IP address we will assign, <SubnetMask> represents the subnet mask, and <Default Gateway> represents the IP address of the server's default gateway. See Figure 4.4 for our sample configuration.

When the server reboots, you will have a fully functional Active Directory implementation!

Figure 4.4 Setting an IP Address in Server Core

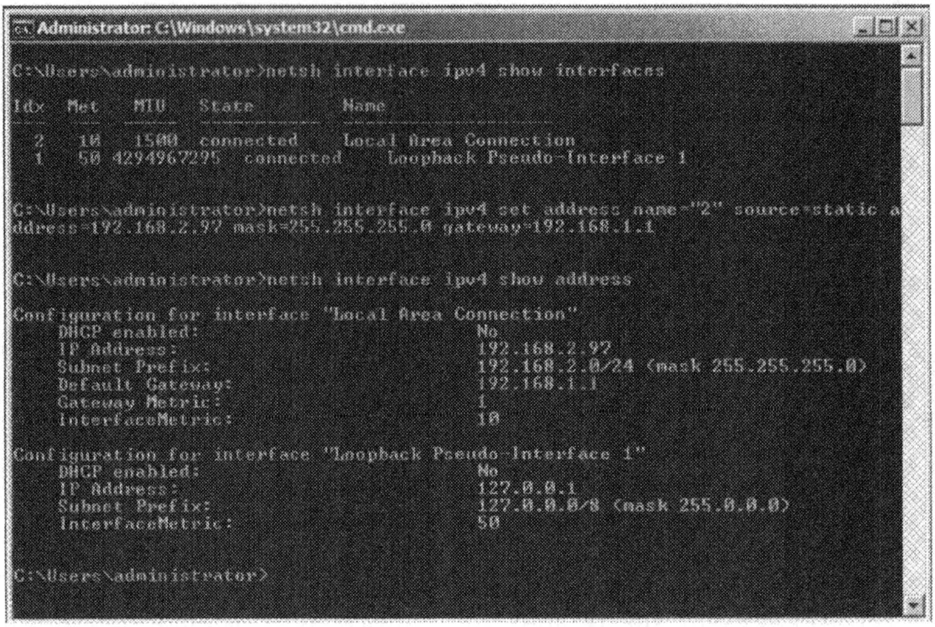

3. Assign the IP address of the DNS server. If this server is part of an Active Directory domain and is replicating Active Directory–integrated zones (we will discuss those next), we would likely point this server to another AD-integrated DNS server. If it is not, we would point it to another external DNS server—usually the Internet provider of your company. From the console, type **netsh interface ipv4 add dnsserver name="<ID>" address=<DNSIP> index=1. >**. ID represents the number from step 1, while <StaticIP> represents the IP address of the DNS server.

   Once the IP address settings are completed—you can verify this by typing **ipconfig /all**—we can install the DNS role onto the Core Server installation:

4. To do this, from the command line, type **start /w ocsetup DNS-Server-Core-Role**.

5. To verify that the DNS Server service is installed and started, type **NET START**. This will return a list of running services.

6. Use the *dnscmd* command-line utility to manipulate the DNS settings. For example, you can type **dnscmd /enumzones** to list the zones hosted on this DNS server.

7. We can also change all of the configuration options we modified in the GUI section earlier by using the **dnscmd /config** option. For example, we can enable BIND secondaries by typing **dnscmd <servername> /config /bindsecondaries 1**. You can see the results in Figure 4.5.

Figure 4.5 Using the *dnscmd* Utility

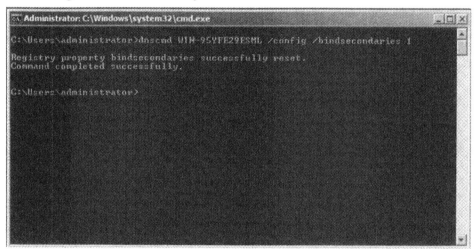

There are many, many more things you can do with the dnscmd utility. For more information on the dnscmd syntax, visit http://technet2.microsoft.com/WindowsServer/ en/library/d652a163-279f-4047-b3e0-0c468a4d69f31033.mspx.

Configuring Dynamic Host Configuration Protocol (DHCP) Using Server Core

You can enable and manage DHCP through the Server Core command-line interface. This can be helpful when remotely managing a DHCP server across a slower WAN link or when creating batch files to perform repetitive DHCP tasks. We'll include some of the commands you can use in Windows Server 2008 Core, but a more extensive listing of command line commands can be found in the Windows Server 2008 Help file or online at the Microsoft Windows Server 2008 Web site.

The **netsh** command can be implemented via the command line. Open a command window and type:

`netsh dhcp` (then press **Enter**)

to begin command line management of DHCP. Once you've done this, the command prompt line will show **dhcp>**. Commands include:

Add Server (Adds a DHCP server to the domain)

Syntax = **add server** DNSname IPaddress

Example = **add server dhcpsrv1.example.microsoft.com 10.2.2.2**

Change Command Line focus to different DHCP Server

Syntax = **server** IPaddress (**or server** \\path)

Example = **server 10.0.0.1**

Add Scope

Syntax = **add scope** ScopeAddress SubnetMask ScopeName [ScopeComment]
Example = **add scope** 10.2.2.0 255.255.255.0 MainOfficeScope

You can manage the server scope from the netsh command as well. In the command line window, type:

`netsh dhcp server scope` (then press **Enter**)

This will result in a **dhcp server scope>** prompt. From there, you can utilize the following commands. You can get syntax assistance by using the ? variable.

- add excluderange
- add iprange
- add reservedip
- delete excluderange
- delete iprange
- delete lease
- delete optionvalue
- delete reservedip
- delete reservedoptionvalue
- dump
- initiate reconcile

- set comment
- set name
- set optionvalue
- set reservedoptionvalue
- set scope
- set state
- set superscope
- show clients
- show clientsv5
- show excluderange
- show iprange
- show optionvalue
- show reservedip
- show reservedoptionvalue
- show scope
- show state

Installing DHCP Using Server Core

DHCP is also a role that is supported in a Windows Server 2008 Core installation. DHCP installation is handled via the command line of the Server Core installation. However, management of the DHCP server (as well as the DHCP scopes) can be controlled from a remote Windows Server 2008 system. In this section, we will install the DHCP role and configure a DHCP scope using the Server Core command line. Let's begin by installing the role:

1. Sign in to your Windows Server 2008 Core Server system.
2. Install the DHCP bits. To do this, type in **start /w ocsetup DHCPServerCore** (Figure 4.6).

Figure 4.6 Installing the DHCP Role

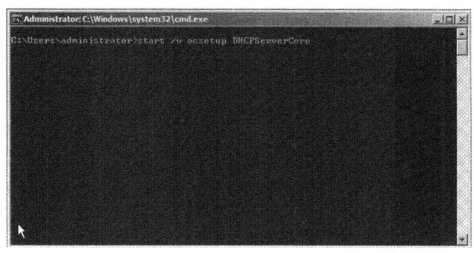

3. Start the DHCP service and set it to start automatically. To do this, type in **sc config dhcpserver start= auto**.

4. Type **sc query dhcpserver**. If the service is not running, start it by typing **sc start dhcpserver**. You can see the command syntax in Figure 4.7.

Figure 4.7 Starting the DHCP Role

C:\Users\administrator>sc config DHCPServer start= auto
[SC] ChangeServiceConfig SUCCESS

C:\Users\administrator>sc query DHCPServer

SERVICE_NAME: DHCPServer
        TYPE   : 20 WIN32_SHARE_PROCESS
        STATE   : 4   RUNNING
                            (STOPPABLE, PAUSABLE, ACCEPTS_SHUTDOWN)
        WIN32_EXIT_CODE   : 0   (0x0)
        SERVICE_EXIT_CODE : 0   (0x0)
        CHECKPOINT   : 0x0
        WAIT_HINT   : 0x0

C:\Users\administrator>_

5. Next, we need to configure our DHCP server by adding the DHCP scope. To do this, we must first start the **netsh** application. At the command prompt, type **netsh**.

6. At the **netsh>** prompt, type **dhcp server**.

7. Add the DHCP Scope at the **dhcp server>** prompt by typing in **initiate auth**.

8. Add the scope by typing in **add scope 10.0.0.0 255.0.0.0 BackupScope**. 10.0.0.0 indicates the network leased by the DHCP server, while 255.0.0.0 represents the subnet mask. BackupScope is the name we've given to the scope.

9. Type in **scope 10.0.0.0**. This allows us to begin adjusting the scope options.

10. Configure the start and end of the lease range. To set the start of the range, type **set optionvalue 003 IPAddress 10.0.0.1**.

11. To set the end of the range, type **set optionvalue 006 IPAddress 10.0.0.50**.

12. Enable the scope by typing in **set state 1**.

13. Type **exit** to close the netsh application. The preceding syntax can be seen in Figure 4.8.

Figure 4.8 The *netsh* Syntax for DHCP

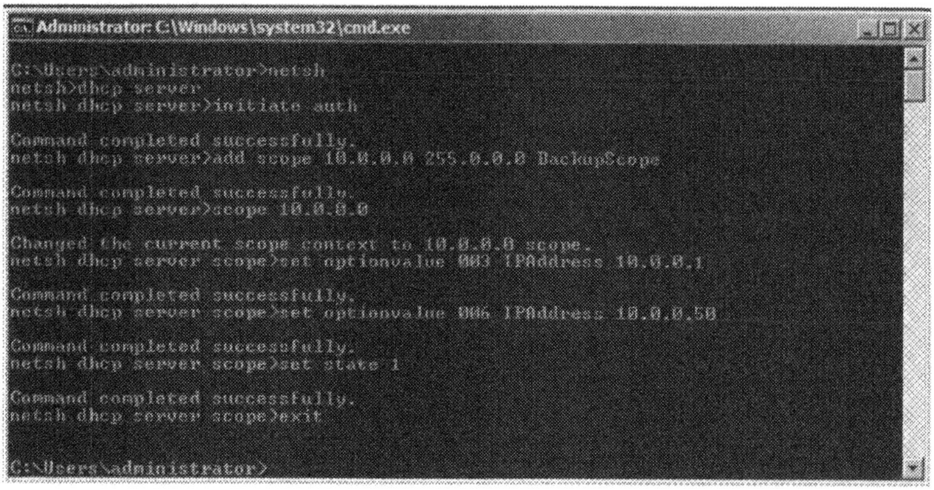

Installing Internet Information Services

The installation process for IIS follows the same process as most other Windows roles. The IIS features are found under the Web Server role alongside file transfer services. In this chapter we are focused on the Web functionality.

Configuring & Implementing...

Installing the Web Server Role on Server Core

1. Execute the following command to install the Web Server (IIS) role and all the role services available on a Server Core installation:

```
Start /W PkgMgr /IU:IIS-WebServerRole;IIS-WebServer;
IIS-CommonHttpFeatures;IIS-StaticContent;IIS-DefaultDocument;
IIS-DirectoryBrowsing;IIS-HttpErrors;IIS-HttpRedirect;
IIS-ApplicationDevelopment;IIS-ASP;IIS-CGI;IIS-ISAPIExtensions;
IIS-ISAPIFilter;IIS-ServerSideIncludes;IIS-HealthAndDiagnostics;
IIS-HttpLogging;IIS-LoggingLibraries;IIS-RequestMonitor;
IIS-HttpTracing;
IIS-CustomLogging;IIS-ODBCLogging;IIS-Security;
IIS-BasicAuthentication;
IIS-WindowsAuthentication;IIS-DigestAuthentication;
IIS-ClientCertificateMappingAuthentication;
IIS-IISCertificateMappingAuthentication;IIS-URLAuthorization;
IIS-RequestFiltering;IIS-IPSecurity;IIS-Performance;
IIS-HttpCompressionStatic;
IIS-HttpCompressionDynamic;IIS-WebServerManagementTools;
IIS-ManagementScriptingTools;IIS-IIS6ManagementCompatibility;
IIS-Metabase;IIS-WMICompatibility;IIS-LegacyScripts;WAS-
WindowsActivationService;
WAS-ProcessModel
```

Role Service Dependencies on Server Core

When you are installing any role and the corresponding set of features on Server Core you will need to be aware of dependencies. In the full installation you are notified of dependencies when you are selecting roles and role services. In Server Core the dependencies are not quite as clear. For example, classic ASP depends on the ISAPI Extensions and Request Filtering role services along with the Windows Activation Service role and its Process Model role service to be installed.

One of the easiest ways to identify the dependencies is through the OCLIST command, which is available on Server Core installations. Simply executing the command without parameters will show you the list dependencies underneath a particular role or role service as well as their current installation status.

Continued

For example, Listing 4.1 shows you that the IIS-ISAPIExtensions role service is required to use IIS-ASP by listing it as a child of the IIS-ISAPIExtensions entry.

Listing 4.1 Role Service Dependencies Example

```
Not Installed:IIS-WebServerRole
    |--- Not Installed:IIS-WebServer
    |        |--- Not Installed:IIS-ApplicationDevelopment
    |        |        |--- Not Installed:IIS-ASP
    |        |        |--- Not Installed:IIS-ISAPIExtensions
    |        |        |        |--- Not Installed:IIS-ASP
```

2. If you have enabled Windows Firewall on your server you will need to add the following exceptions:

■ Remote Administration Service Exception:

```
NetSh Firewall Set Service Type=RemoteAdmin Mode=Enable
```

■ Windows Management Instrumentation Exception:

```
NetSh AdvFirewall Firewall Set Rule Group="Windows Management
Instrumentation (WMI)" New Enable=Yes
```

■ Lockdown the AHAdmin DCOM Endpoint to Port 49494:

```
Reg Add "HKCR\AppId\{9FA5C497-F46D-447F-8011-05D03D7D7DDC}"
/v Endpoints /t REG_MULTI_SZ /d "ncacn_ip_tcp,0,49494"
```

■ Remote Web Server Management Exception:

```
NetSh AdvFirewall Firewall Add Rule Name="Remote Web Server
Management (RPC)" Dir=In Action=Allow Program="C:\WINDOWS\
SYSTEM32\dllhost.exe" Protocol=TCP LocalPort=49494

NetSh AdvFirewall Firewall Add Rule Name="Remote Web Server
Management (RPC-EPMap)" Dir=In Action=Allow Program="C:\Windows
\system32\svchost.exe" Service=RPCSS Protocol=TCP LocalPort=RPC-EPMap
```

■ If your security policy requires a more strict security setting you can use port exceptions on all or specific interfaces.

3. If you want to use Windows Remote Shell you will need to enable it:

```
WinRM QuickConfig
```

Depending on your environment, you may not be able to directly administer your servers via the console. To aid in the management of our servers, especially Server Core installations that lack an administrative interface and command line tools, the product group has delivered a package of Remote Server Administration Tools. On Windows Vista the IIS Remote Server Administration Tool supplements the IIS Management Console to enable it to communicate with remote servers and sites.

Configuring & Implementing...

Installing the Remote Server Administration Tools

If you are running Windows Vista or Windows Server 2008 follow these steps:

1. From the Control Panel choose Programs and click the Turn Windows Features On or Off link.

2. In the Windows Features dialog expand Internet Information Services, Web Management Tools, and choose **IIS Management Console**.

If you are running Windows XP or Windows Server 2003 follow the next steps. For Windows Vista you will also need to follow these steps to allow you to remotely administer an IIS server since the out-of-the-box tools provide support for only the local IIS installation.

1. Double-click the **IIS Manager installation** package, follow the prompts for the update process to acknowledge the package, and accept the license agreement.

2. On the **Destination Folder** page accept the default value and click **Next**.

3. On the **Ready to Install** page click **Install**.

4. On the final page click **Finish.**

To access the administration tools you can find them in the Control Panel under System and Maintenance, Administration Tools, Internet Information Services Manager. Figure 4.9 shows the start page for Internet Information Services Manager.

Figure 4.9 Internet Information Services Manager

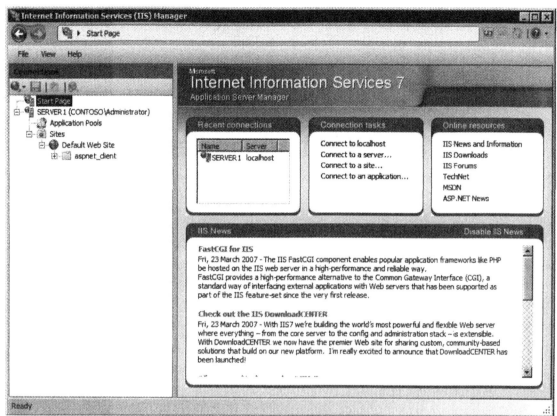

A word of warning—the graphical tools cannot connect to a Server Core installation. There are a few ways to remotely administer IIS on Server Core:

- **Command-line Tools** Using WinRS you can make calls to AppCmd.exe. Note that WinRM does not allow for interact sessions, instead outputting the results of your command.

```
WinRS.exe -Remote:WEBSERVER %SYSTEMROOT%\SYSTEM32\INETSRV\AppCmd.exe
LIST SITE
```

- **Windows Management Instrumentation** Scripting, programming languages, Windows PowerShell, WMIC, WinRM, and WinRS can all administer IIS on Server Core through WMI.

```
WMIC.exe /Output:Sites.txt /Node:WEBSERVER
/Namespace:\\root\WebAdministration Path Site Get
```

- **COM and .NET Programming Interfaces** In addition to WMI you can use the Microsoft.ApplicationHost.AdminManager DCOM object in

VBScript/JScript or the Microsoft.Web.Administration assembly through Windows PowerShell scripts and .NET applications.

```
[Reflection.Assembly]::LoadFrom("C:\WINDOWS\SYSTEM32\inetsrv\Microsoft.
Web.Administration.dll");

$WebServer = [Microsoft.Web.Administration.ServerManager]::
OpenRemote("WEBSERVER");

$WebServer.Sites Ð Format-Table Id, Name;
```

Installing the FTP Publishing Service

With the amount of work undertaken by the IIS product group, the major enhancements to the FTP Publishing Service did not make it into this release. Microsoft shipped the IIS 6 FTP Publishing Service with some compatibility fixes in its place. To gain access to all of the new FTP Publishing Service features you will need to download the out-of-band release from the IIS Download Center (www.iis.net/downloads).

The Web release is a full installation; however it does require that the Web Server (IIS) role be installed, as it integrates in with the IIS Management functionality. If you have previously installed the Web Server role with the FTP Publishing Service you will need to uninstall it before using the Web release.

Server Core installations of Windows Server 2008 allow you to install FTP Services in its entirety. The only functionality that will not be available is the graphical administrative interface and managed authentication modules.

Configuring & Implementing...

Installing the FTP Server on Server Core

1. Execute the following command to install the Web Server (IIS) role and the basic set of the role on a Server Core installation:

```
Start /W PkgMgr /IU:IIS-WebServerRole;IIS-WebServer;
IIS-CommonHttpFeatures;IIS-StaticContent;IIS-DefaultDocument;
IIS-DirectoryBrowsing;IIS-HttpErrors;IIS-HealthAndDiagnostics;
IIS-HttpLogging;IIS-RequestMonitor;IIS-Security;IIS-RequestFiltering;
IIS-Performance;IIS-HttpCompressionStatic;IIS-WebServerManagementTools;
IIS-IIS6ManagementCompatibility;IIS-Metabase;WAS-WindowsActivationSe
rvice;WAS-ProcessModel
```

Continued

2. Execute the following command to start installation of the FTP Server, follow the prompts for the update process to acknowledge the package, and read and accept the license agreement:

```
MSIEXEC /I FTP7_X86.msi
```

3. On the Custom Setup page, accept the defaults and click **Next.**

4. On the Ready to Install page click **Install.**

5. On the Completed page click **Finish.**

6. If you have enabled Windows Firewall and intend on using only non-secure FTP connections you will need to enable communication using the following commands:

```
NetSh AdvFirewall Set Global StatefulFTP Enable

NetSh AdvFirewall Firewall Add Rule Name="File Transfer Protocol
(In)" Dir=In Action=Allow Program="C:\WINDOWS\SYSTEM32\SvcHost.exe"
Protocol=TCP Service=ftpsvc
```

7. If you have enabled Windows Firewall and intend on using secure FTP (FTPS) connections you will need to disable stateful FTP inspection:

```
NetSh AdvFirewall Set Global StatefulFTP Disable
```

8. If you have enabled Windows Firewall and intend on using passive FTP connections, enable the FTP Publishing Service to communicate outwards as well:

```
NetSh AdvFirewall Firewall Add Rule Name="File Transfer Protocol
(Out)" Dir=Out Action=Allow Program="C:\WINDOWS\SYSTEM32\SvcHost.
exe" Protocol=TCP Service=ftpsvc
```

9. If you have enabled Windows Firewall on your server you will need to add the following exceptions:

■ Remote Administration Service Exception

```
NetSh Firewall Set Service Type=RemoteAdmin Mode=Enable
```

■ Windows Management Instrumentation Exception

```
NetSh AdvFirewall Firewall Set Rule Group="Windows Management
Instrumentation (WMI)" New Enable=Yes
```

■ Lockdown the AHAdmin DCOM Endpoint to Port 49494

```
Reg Add "HKCR\AppId\{9FA5C497-F46D-447F-8011-05D03D7D7DDC}" /v
Endpoints /t REG_MULTI_SZ /d "ncacn_ip_tcp,0,49494"
```

Continued

> ■ Remote Web Server Management Exception
>
> NetSh AdvFirewall Firewall Add Rule Name="Remote Web Server
> Management (RPC)" Dir=In Action=Allow Program="C:\WINDOWS\
> SYSTEM32\dllhost.exe" Protocol=TCP LocalPort=49494
>
> NetSh AdvFirewall Firewall Add Rule Name="Remote Web Server
> Management (RPC-EPMap)" Dir=In Action=Allow Program="C:\Windows
> \system32\svchost.exe" Service=RPCSS Protocol=TCP LocalPort=RPC-EPMap
>
> ■ If your security policy requires a more strict security setting you
> can use port exceptions on all or specific interfaces.
>
> 10. If you want to use Windows Remote Shell you will need to
> enable it:
>
> WinRM QuickConfig

A word of warning—the graphical tools cannot connect to a Server Core installation. This is because the graphical tools have a dependency on the IIS Management Service which is built on the .NET Framework and cannot be run on Server Core because of that. There are a few ways to remotely administer IIS on Server Core:

■ **Command-line Tools** Using WinRS you can make calls to AppCmd.exe. Note that WinRM does not allow for interact sessions, instead outputting the results of your command.

```
WinRS.exe -Remote:FTPSERVER %SYSTEMROOT%\SYSTEM32\INETSRV\AppCmd.exe
LIST SITE
```

■ **Windows Management Instrumentation** Scripting, programming languages, Windows PowerShell, WMIC, WinRM, and WinRS can all administer IIS on Server Core through WMI.

```
WMIC.exe /Output:Sites.txt /Node:FTPSERVER /Namespace:\\root
\WebAdministration Path Site Get
```

■ **COM and .NET Programming Interfaces** In addition to WMI you can use the Microsoft.ApplicationHost.AdminManager DCOM object in VBScript/JScript or the Microsoft.Web.Administration assembly through Windows PowerShell scripts and .NET applications.

```
[Reflection.Assembly]::LoadFrom("C:\WINDOWS\SYSTEM32\inetsrv\Microsoft.
Web.Administration.dll");

$WebServer = [Microsoft.Web.Administration.ServerManager]::
OpenRemote("FTPSERVER");

$WebServer.Sites Đ Format-Table Id, Name;
```

Installing and Managing Hyper-V on Windows Server Core Installations

The Windows server core installation option of Windows Server 2008 and Windows Server virtualization are two new features of Windows Server 2008 that work together to a mutually beneficial end. Windows server core installation option is a new shell-less and GUI-free installation option for Window Server 2008 Standard, Enterprise, and Datacenter Editions. It will lower the level of management and maintenance required by an administrator. The Windows server core installation option provides several advantages over a full installation of Windows Server 2008. It is intended to act as a complement to Windows Server virtualization. Hyper-V is compatible with Server Core installations but requires certain preparation to install. In order to take advantage of this installation process you must be aware of certain procedures before installing. If you wish to install Hyper-V on to a Server Core, run the following command: **Start /w ocsetup Microsoft-Hyper-V**. Once installed you can manage Hyper-V on a Server Core installation, by doing the following:

1. Use Hyper-V Manager to connect to the Server Core installation remotely from a full installation of Windows Server2008 on which the Hyper-V role is installed.

2. Use the Windows Management Instrumentation (WMI) interface to manage the installation process.

NOTE

WMI is used to define a nonproprietary set of environment-independent specifications. By doing this it allows management information to be shared between management applications that run in both similar and dissimilar operating system environments.

Summary

The new FTP Publishing Service supports both full and Server Core installations. When you are ready to create your first FTP site you can create a standalone or bound FTP site. The standalone version works much like a typical FTP site where you point it to a folder that may or may not contain content for users to download and upload. In the bound FTP site the functionality is tied into an existing Web site setup in IIS.

Solutions Fast Track

☑ Server Core is a minimal server installation option for Windows Server 2008 that contains a subset of executable files, as well as five server roles.

☑ DHCP can be configured using command line commands. This is helpful for managing DHCP servers remotely across the network.

☑ On Server Core you will not be able to install role services that rely on the .NET Framework.

Frequently Asked Questions

Q: I like the idea of being able to implement DNS, WINS, and DHCP on a Windows Server 2008 Core Server installation. However, I'm not much of a command-line person. Is there any way I can manage these roles and features from a GUI?

A: Yes, however you must use the MMC from another Windows Server 2008 (full installation) server to manage these roles and features. If you recall, no GUIs are provided with Windows Server 2008 Core Server, even after a role has been installed.

Q: I've heard that Server Core is only supported in 64-bit edition. Is that true?

A: No. Server Core works in both 32-bit and 64-bit editions, Hyper-V (virtualization) only runs on 64-bit. It should be noted that as of the writing of this book, Windows Server 2008 is expected to be the final 32-bit server operating system released by Microsoft.

Q: How do I administer IIS on Server Core?

A: You can administer the server through AppCmd, Windows Management Instrumentation, and the COM/.NET programmatic interfaces. You cannot use IIS Manager, even to connect to the server remotely.

Frequently Asked Questions

## Chapter 5

Configuring DNS

Solutions in this chapter:

- **An Introduction to Domain Name System (DNS)**

- **Configuring a DNS Server**

- **Creating DNS Zones**

- **Configuring and Managing DNS Replication**

- **Creating and Managing DNS Records**

- **Configuring Name Resolution for Client Computers**

☑ **Summary**

☑ **Solutions Fast Track**

☑ **Frequently Asked Questions**

Introduction

Today, most of the computers in the world are identified by IP address. Although computers are great at working with numbers, humans generally have an easier time remembering names than long strings of numbers. This is where Domain Name Servers (DNS) comes into play. DNS is responsible for resolving host names to IP addresses, so that we do not have to remember each individual host's IP address.

DNS is by far one of the most important parts of most networks. There are several reasons why DNS is so important. For starters, there are countless computers on the Internet, and new ones are being added all the time. There is no way that a single database could possibly maintain a list of all these machines, and keep the list up to date. DNS takes a hierarchical approach to name resolution, making it ideal for keeping up with vast numbers of hosts. When you enter an Internet domain into your Web browser, it is the DNS server that figures out the IP address that's associated with Web site you have requested.

DNS is also important on Windows networks, because the Active Directory is completely dependent on DNS. You cannot even create an Active Directory forest without having a DNS server on your network.

In this chapter, we will start with the basics, by talking more in depth about what DNS is and what it does. As the chapter progresses, we will cover fundamental concepts such as forward and reverse lookup zones, forwarders, root hints, and dynamic DNS updates. The chapter will also discuss some of the more common types of DNS records, and explain how DNS fits in with legacy host name resolution mechanisms.

An Introduction to Domain Name System (DNS)

The domain name system allows the use of user-friendly names to locate hosts on IP networks. Since Windows Server 2003 and Windows XP DNS has been the primary method used to resolve names into IP addresses on Windows networks. In addition to hostname resolution, DNS also facilitates reverse lookup of IP addresses into hostnames, as well as the location of network services such as domain controllers. Windows Server 2008 includes major updates to DNS that allow it to fully support IPv6 addresses.

Name resolution on IP networks originally took place using *hosts* files that were originally stored centrally and later locally on every host. Most hosts, including all Windows computers, still contain these files and can use them for name resolution. The files were nothing more than long lists consisting of every hostname on the network and its corresponding IP address. Over time the ability of these single, flat files began to hinder performance and became far too difficult to manage.

The domain name system solved these problems by allowing for a partitioning of the global hostname space. This partitioning occurs on two levels, the logical and the physical. The logical portion is covered in this section. The physical portion is covered in the section entitled *Creating DNS Zones*. Logically, DNS is divided into tiers of domains and subdomains. Technically, there is no name for the domain at the very top, but often it is represented as the "." domain. Every fully qualified domain name (FQDN) has a period (.) at the end of it, though most users never see it because it is entered for them automatically in the background. When a user types *www.syngress.com* into a web browser, the actual name resolution request that goes out onto the network is *www.syngress.com.*, with the period being added by either the browser or name resolution (DNS) client software.

A FQDN tells you everything you need to know about what a host is called and where it is located within DNS. The previous example, *www.syngress.com*, means that the user is looking for the *www* host in the *syngress.com* domain. Typically the leftmost portion of a FQDN is a hostname. Sometimes, however, you will see a domain name without the host and it will look just like a FQDN. For example, a FQDN might be *host1.authors.syngress.com*, but you might see only *authors.syngress.com* referred to. It's easy to think that *authors* is a hostname in circumstances like this, and really there is no way to differentiate it. You just have to be on your guard as to whether a domain name is being referred to or a FQDN (which includes the hostname).

The domain portion of the FQDN lets you know the location of the host on the network. *Host1.authors.syngress.com* tells you that the host is located in the *authors* subdomain, of the *syngress* subdomain, of the *com* domain. Often you will see portions of the name space being referred to differently. For example, you might see the *com*, *net*, *org*, and other upper level namespace domains being referred to as top-level domains (TLDs). The major TLDs are listed in Table 5.1. Countries also typically have their own TLDs; a sample of these can be found in Table 5.2. It is appropriate to refer to them as TLDs or domains; we will use domain in this book because Microsoft's software uses only the terms domain and subdomain.

Table 5.1 Internet Top-Level Domain Names

TLD	Designated Use
.aero	Air-transport industry related
.asia	Asia-Pacific region
.biz	Business related
.cat	Catalan language or culture related
.com	Originally designated for commercial purposes, but now in wide use for any purpose; this is the most commonly used TLD
.coop	Cooperatives as defined by the Rochdale Principles
.edu	Educational, generally limited to institutions of learning, such as 2- and 4-year colleges and universities
.gov	U.S. government entities and agencies
.info	Information
.int	International organizations, offices, and programs that are endorsed by a treaty between two or more nations
.jobs	Used by companies with jobs to advertise
.mil	United States Military
.mobi	Mobile-compatible sites
.museum	Museums
.name	Individuals, by name; registrations may be challenged if they are not by individuals, or the owners of fictional characters, in accordance with the domain's charter
.net	Originally designated for use by a network, but now in wide use for any purpose
.org	Originally designated for use by nonprofit organizations, but now in wide use for any purpose
.pro	Professions, currently reserved for licensed doctors, attorneys, and certified public accountants
.tel	Internet communication services
.travel	Travel and tourism industry related sites

Table 5.2 Country Top-Level Domain Names

TLD	Country
.au	Australia
.cn	Mainland China
.ca	Canada
.de	Germany
.es	Spain
.eu	European Union
.uk	United Kingdom
.us	United States

Understanding Public Name Resolution

Different servers are often responsible for the various logical domain partitions seen in a FQDN. When a user takes an action that requires name resolution, such as typing a FQDN into a web browser, a flurry of activity is set in motion on the network. Each host is configured to communicate with one or more DNS server(s). If the first DNS server is contacted successfully, any additional DNS servers are not used. This is true even if the first DNS server contacted isn't able to successfully resolve the FQDN to an IP address.

The first server contacted may physically contain the record being requested. For example, your host (host1.syngress.com) may be attempting to locate a second host (host2.syngress.com) that is part of the same logical portion of the domain namespace. It's likely that the DNS server your host is configured to use is *authoritative* for the domain your computer belongs to (syngress.com). This means that it physically contains the information that maps host, service, and other names to IP addresses within the domain. If this is the case, your DNS server will return the requested information and the name resolution process ends.

If, however, your server doesn't contain the needed information, a longer process is initiated. Let's say that your host (host1.syngress.com) is attempting to contact *www. elsevier.com*. Because the *elsevier* domain is different than your *syngress* domain, it is unlikely that your DNS server contains the needed information for it. Remember that all FQDNs have a period (.) appended to them. When a DNS server cannot directly answer a request, it next contacts a name server for this "." domain. By default,

DNS servers contain *root hints* that tell the server who these "." name servers are, and where they can be found. The "." domain name server examines the request and attempts to determine if there is any part of it that it can answer. In this case, it is likely to be configured for high-level domain name servers such as *com, net, org, edu*, and so forth; and will return a list of the name servers for the *com* domain to your DNS server.

Your DNS server will next send a request to one or more of the name servers for the *com* domain. These name servers will examine the request and attempt to determine if they have information relating to any portion of the requested FQDN. Assuming the *elsevier* domain is registered properly through an Internet name registrar, and not simply made up by someone, the *com* DNS servers will know where to find the *elsevier* domain name servers. The addresses for these DNS servers will be returned to your DNS server.

Finally, your DNS server will contact one or more *elsevier* DNS server(s). Because these name servers should contain the information for the *www* host, your DNS server finally receives the IP address that your computer needs to contact. It caches the information locally for a period of time so it can answer other potential requests for the same resource more rapidly, and returns the requested information to your computer. Your computer also caches it for a period of time so that it doesn't have to continue to ask the DNS server for the information each time you type the FQDN into your web browser. With the IP address now in hand, your computer can contact the host.

Understanding Private Name Resolution

The previous example used a host with Internet access attempting to resolve the name of a publicly accessible web server with a publicly registered domain name. Not all name resolution involves publicly resolvable names, however. It is also possible for a DNS namespace to be private, and not connected to the Internet. For example, a highly sensitive network may not allow external connections for security reasons. These may include governmental, research and development, and similar types of networks. When this is the case, it is not necessary to use publicly registered names.

Private DNS networks are configured with the equivalent of their own "." name servers. These are private DNS servers that sit at the top of the organization's network. DNS servers in the organization typically are configured to query them when they don't have the information a client is requesting. Accordingly, the DNS administrators for the organization configure these servers to know where at least one other level of the logical domain name space resides. Although more flexibility can be accommodated, essentially, these administrators build a structure of DNS servers that mirrors the publicly resolvable namespace. Very small organizations might have everything required on just one or two DNS servers. Large multinational organizations may have layers of DNS servers that rival the complexity of the public name servers. Regardless of which is the case, clients and DNS servers follow the same resolution process as the one covered in the previous section.

Understanding Microsoft's DNS Terminology

Much of the terminology Microsoft uses for DNS is standard across the industry, but some of it isn't. Now that you have a good idea of how DNS works, in this section you'll get an overview of the official terminology that accompanies the preceding process as well as a bit more detail for some of them. The local DNS software on a Windows host is referred to as the *resolver*. When a user makes a request, such as for a Web page, the resolver first checks the local cache to see if it contains the needed information. Next, the local hosts file is checked. Finally, a query is sent to the first DNS server that the resolver is configured to use.

Microsoft calls this step a *client-to-server query*. This query involves the client asking for very specific information. In the case of a Web site, it would be the IP address that matches a FQDN. If the DNS server queried does not have the information needed, it contacts other DNS servers attempting to locate it.

Server-to-server queries are also called *recursive queries*. These differ from client-to-server queries in that they ask two questions to the receiving DNS server. The first is for the specific information needed, such as the IP address to match a FQDN. The second is for any information that may get the requesting DNS server closer to obtaining the specific information that is being requested by the client. This later aspect of recursive queries is what results in a DNS server for a domain (such as *com*) sending the name servers for the next domain in the FQDN if it knows it (such as elsevier).

TIP

In addition to caching responses from DNS servers containing the requested resources (called positive caching), the local resolver also caches negative responses. These result from a failure to locate DNS resources. When a server returns a request to a client's query that contains a negative response, the local resolver caches it and will not request it again for a period of time. Temporary DNS problems can thus become longer term issues until this cached record expires. You can manually purge the client's resolver cache using the following command: **ipconfig /flushdns**.

Configuring a DNS Server

DNS servers can be complex to configure. Midsize to large organizations often have dedicated DNS administrators because of the specialized knowledge required. In this section, we'll examine the core configuration steps at the server-level of the DNS role in Windows Server 2008. We'll begin by installing the role itself, and then look at the components it offers to direct queries without using locally stored records. This will include where to configure the "." name servers (called root hints), as well as how to bypass them and direct server-to-server queries to other DNS servers instead.

Installing the DNS Server Role

To install the DNS Server role, follow these steps:

1. Open Server Manager by clicking **Start | Server Manager**.

2. In the right pane, scroll down to **Roles Summary** and click **Add Roles**.

3. In the **Add Roles Wizard** dialog, read the **Before You Begin** page and click **Next**.

4. On the **Select Server Roles** wizard page, select **DNS Server** and click **Next**. See Figure 5.1.

Figure 5.1 Selecting the DNS Server Role

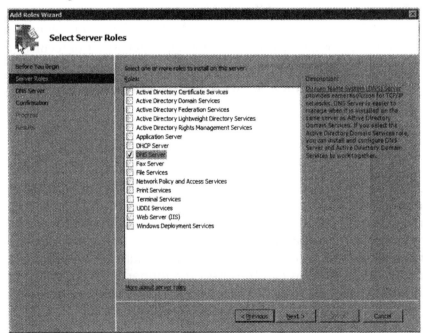

5. Review the information provided on the **DNS Server** wizard page and click **Next**.

6. Review the information provided on the **Confirm Installation Selections** wizard page and click **Install**.

7. Review the information provided on the **Installation Results** wizard page and click **Close**.

Understanding Cache-Only DNS Servers

The DNS Server role installs without any zones or forwarding configured, as a caching-only DNS server. This means that it can resolve client requests only by locating and querying other DNS servers using root hints. Root hints are discussed in the next section. Once a client request has been resolved, the server caches information for the DNS record received. Administrators can clear this cache manually using the following steps:

1. Open DNS Manager by clicking **Start | Administrative Tools | DNS**.

2. In the left pane, right-click the server's node and select **Clear Cache**.

Configuring Root Hints

There are two primary ways to use root hints. By default, root hints comes configured with the Internet root servers specified. This allows the DNS server to locate DNS records for publicly resolvable domain names. Larger organizations often have complex hierarchies of DNS servers, only some of which are configured to resolve public domain names. Many of the DNS servers will be configured to locate domains and subdomains that belong to the organization. Those servers will often have their root hints configured so that they point to higher level DNS servers within the organization, rather than Internet root servers. There are several graphical configuration options available in DNS Manager for root hints: adding and removing records, editing existing records, and copying a list of root hints addresses from another server. The root hints records are stored in an editable text file: %systemroot%\System32\Dns\Cache. dns. Figure 5.2 displays the servers Properties dialog and the Root Hints tab.

Figure 5.2 The Root Hints Tab

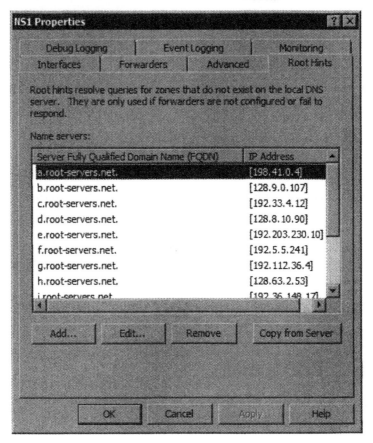

Adding Root Hint Records

Follow this procedure to add a new Root Hint:

1. Open DNS Manager by clicking **Start | Administrative Tools | DNS**.

2. In the left pane, right-click the server you want to configure and select **Properties**.

3. Click the **Root Hints** tab to bring it forward. See Figure 5.2.

4. Click the **Add...** button.

5. In the New Name Server Record dialog box, type the fully qualified domain name (FQDN) in the Server fully qualified domain name (FQDN): text box, and click **Resolve**. See Figure 5.3.

Figure 5.3 The New Name Server Record Dialog

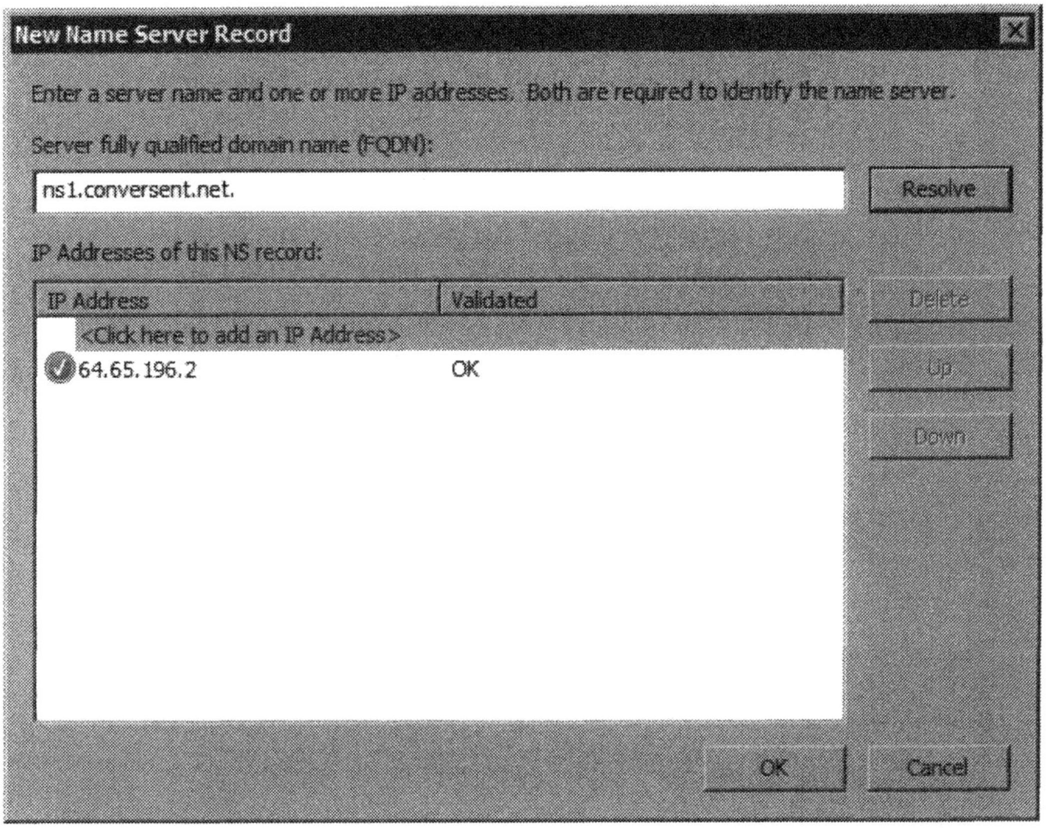

6. If you wish to manually add an IP address, you can click **<Click here to add an IP Address>** and enter it in the text field that appears. Resolved IP addresses can also be modified by clicking them. If multiple IP addresses are configured for the record, you can determine the priority they will be used in by ordering them with the **Up** and **Down** buttons. IP addresses can also be removed using the **Delete** button.

7. Click **OK** to finish adding the record.

Editing Root Hints Records

Follow this procedure to edit an existing root hints record:

1. Open DNS Manager by clicking **Start | Administrative Tools | DNS**.

2. In the left pane, right-click the server you want to configure and select **Properties**.

3. Click the **Root Hints** tab to bring it forward. See Figure 5.2.

4. Select the record you want to edit and click the **Edit...** button.

5. In the **Edit Name Server Record** dialog box (see Figure 5.4), you can:

   ■ Change the FQDN for the record by typing it in the **Server fully qualified domain name (FQDN):** text box, and clicking **Resolve**.

   ■ Manually add an IP address, by clicking **<Click here to add an IP Address>** and entering it in the text field that appears.

   ■ Modify an existing IP address by clicking it and modifying it in the text field that appears.

   ■ Specify the order that the IP addresses will be used in by ordering them with the **Up** and **Down** buttons.

   ■ Remove one or more IP addresses by using the **Delete** button.

Figure 5.4 The Edit Name Server Record Dialog

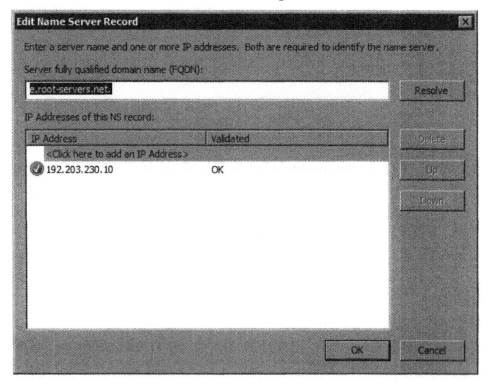

6. Click **OK** when you are finished making changes.

Removing Root Hints Records

Follow this procedure to remove an existing root hints record:

1. Open DNS Manager by clicking **Start | Administrative Tools | DNS**.
2. In the left pane, right-click the server you want to configure and select **Properties**.
3. Click the **Root Hints** tab to bring it forward. See Figure 5.2.
4. Select the record you want to delete and click the **Remove** button.
5. Click **OK**.

Copying Root Hints from Another Server

You can add a list of root hints records from another server. The imported records will be added to your existing list, if any, and will not overwrite existing records. Follow this procedure to copy a list of root hints records from another server:

1. Open DNS Manager by clicking **Start | Administrative Tools | DNS**.
2. In the left pane, right-click the server you want to configure and select **Properties**.
3. Click the **Root Hints** tab to bring it forward. See Figure 5.2.
4. Click the **Copy from Server** button.
5. In the Server to Copy From dialog box enter the FQDN or IP address of the server that you want to copy the root hints records from, then click **OK**.
6. If requested, provide the appropriate logon credentials.
7. Click **OK**.

Configuring Server-Level Forwarders

For security reasons, organizations often do not want to enable their internal DNS servers to directly resolve queries for pubic domain names. One strategy employed when this is the case is to configure all internal DNS servers to point to a DNS server that has been designated as a forwarder. This server typically resides outside the organization's firewall. Restricted communication is allowed between it and the organization's internal DNS servers. If the external forwarder becomes compromised, the internal servers remain safe and function normally. By default, DNS servers are already configured as forwarders. They install without zones, and with the correct root hints.

The configuration to use forwarders is done on the DNS servers that will send queries to the forwarders. To manually configure a Windows Server 2008 DNS Server role holder to use forwarding, follow these steps:

1. Open DNS Manager by clicking **Start | Administrative Tools | DNS**.

2. In the left pane, right-click the DNS server you want to configure and select **Properties**.

3. Click the **Forwarders** tab to bring it forward. See Figure 5.5.

Figure 5.5 The Forwarders Tab

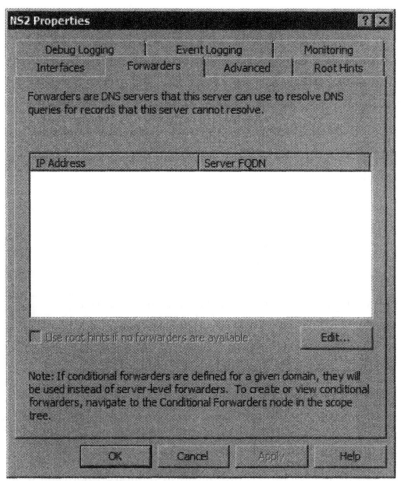

4. In the **Properties** dialog box, click **Edit…**.

5. In the **Edit Forwarders** dialog box, click **<Click here to add an IP Address or DNS Name>** and enter a FQDN or IP address for the server queries will

be forwarded to. Although multiple addresses can be specified, this is only for failover. The server will try to find a responding DNS forwarder by working its way down the list. If the first forwarder does not respond to the query, the DNS server will try the next one. If the first forward does respond, but is not able to resolve the query, the DNS server does not try other servers in the list. They are used only in the event of server failure. The amount of time a DNS server waits to hear back from each forwarder is specified by the value in the Number of seconds before forward queries time out: text box. See Figure 5.6.

Figure 5.6 The Edit Forwarders Dialog

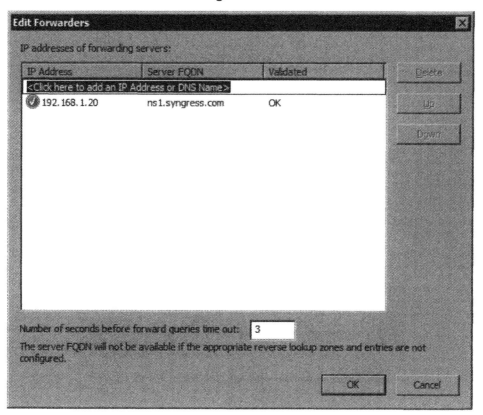

6. Click **OK**.

7. In the **Properties** dialog box, the Use root hints if no forwarders are available box is now available and selected. If you do not want root hints to be used by this server, deselect it.

8. Click **OK** in the Properties dialog box to finish.

Configuring Conditional Forwarding

In Windows Server 2003, Microsoft added another level of forwarding that provides much greater flexibility for forwarding queries. When configured for server level forwarding, all queries are sent from a configured DNS server to the forwarder. Conditional forwarding allows an administrator to send requests that deal with different domains to different forwarders. So, for example, a request for host1.authors.syngress.com could be sent to a different forwarder than a request for server1.billing.syngress.com. The system will take its best guess if the exact domain name is not listed. If you have configured a forwarder for the authors.syngress.com domain and client requests resolution for computer1.mcse.authors.syngess.com the request will be forwarded to the closest match, in this case the forwarder configured for the authors.syngress.com domain. If both conditional and server-level forwarding are configured on a server, conditional forwarding is used. To configure conditional forwarding, see the following steps.

Creating Conditional Forwarders

To specify one or more domains for conditional forwarding, follow these steps:

1. Open DNS Manager by clicking **Start | Administrative Tools | DNS**.

2. In the left pane, expand the node representing the server you want to configure, right-click **Conditional Forwarders**, and select **New Conditioner Forwarder....** See Figure 5.7.

Figure 5.7 Creating a New Conditional Forwarder

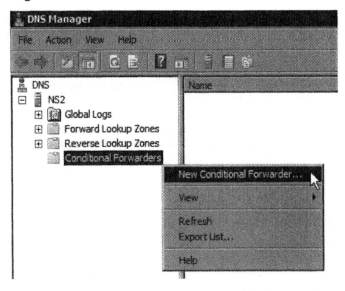

3. In the **New Conditional Forward** dialog box, in the **DNS Domain:** text box, type the name of the domain you want queries forwarded to. For example, if you want to configure a forwarder to resolve queries for authors. syngress.com enter it in this box. See Figure 5.8.

4. In the IP addresses of the master servers: entry area specify the FQDN or IP addresses for the DNS server(s) that will serve as forwarders for the specified domain by clicking **<Click here to add an IP Address or DNS Name>** and entering it in the text field that appears. Although forwarders can be specified, this is only for failover. The server will try to find a responding conditional forwarder by working its way down the list. If the first forwarder does not respond to the query, the DNS server will try the next one. If the first forwarder does respond, but is not able to resolve the query, the DNS server does not try other servers in the list. They are used only for failovers in the event of a forwarding server's failure. The amount of time a DNS server waits to hear back from each forwarder is specified by the value in the Number of seconds before forward queries time out: text box. Entries can be modified by clicking on them. If multiple forwarders are configured, you can determine the priority they will be used by ordering them with the **Up** and **Down** buttons. Entries can also be removed using the **Delete** button. See Figure 5.8.

Figure 5.8 The New Conditional Forwarder Dialog

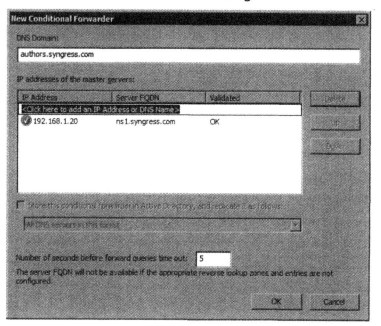

5. Click **OK**.

Managing Conditional Forwarders

To modify the existing configuration for conditional forwarding, follow these steps:

1. Open DNS Manager by clicking **Start | Administrative Tools | DNS**.

2. In the left pane, expand the node representing the server you want to configure, expand the **Conditional Forwarders** node, and right-click the domain name representing the conditional forwarder you want to modify. See Figure 5.9.

Figure 5.9 A Conditional Forwarder's Right-Click Menu

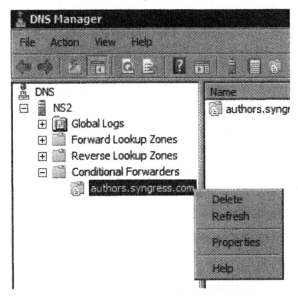

3. To delete the forwarder, click **Delete**. To modify the forwarder, click **Properties**.

4. In the **Properties** dialog box, click **Edit**.

5. In the **Edit Conditional Forwarder** dialog box, make the necessary changes. In the IP addresses of the master servers: entry area specify the FQDN or IP addresses for the DNS server(s) that will serve as forwarders for the specified domain by clicking **<Click here to add an IP Address or DNS Name>** and entering it in the text field that appears. Although forwarders can be specified, this is only for failover. The server will try to find a responding conditional forwarder by working its way down the list. If the first forwarder

does not respond to the query, the DNS server will try the next one. If the first forwarder does respond, but is not able to resolve the query, the DNS server does not try other servers in the list. They are used only as failovers in the event of a forwarding server's failure. The amount of time a DNS server waits to hear back from each forwarder is specified by the value in the Number of seconds before forward queries time out: text box. Entries can be modified by clicking on them. If multiple forwarders are configured, you can determine the priority they will be used by ordering them with the **Up** and **Down** buttons. Entries can also be removed using the **Delete** button. See Figure 5.10.

Figure 5.10 The Edit Conditional Forwarder Dialog

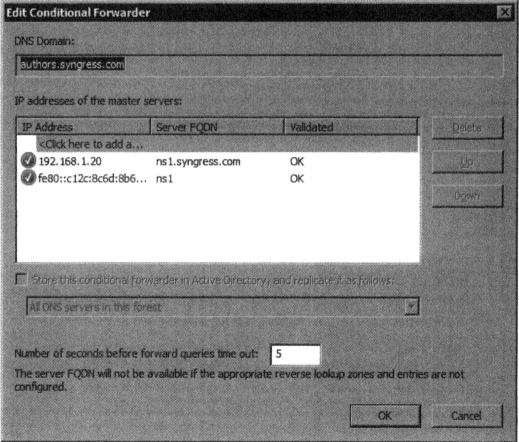

6. Click **OK** to close the **Edit Conditional Forwarder** dialog and **OK** again to close the **Properties** dialog.

Server Core

A Windows Server 2008 Core Server Installation can be used for multiple purposes. One of the ways that Server Core can be used is to provide a minimal installation for DNS. You can manipulate, manage, and configure DNS servers through the various Windows Server 2008 DNS Graphical User Interfaces (GUIs)–DNS Manager and the Server Manager tool.

However, there are no GUIs provided with Windows Server 2008 Core Server. There are a number of advantages to running DNS within Server Core, including:

- **Smaller Footprint**. Reduces the amount of CPU, memory, and hard disk needed.

- **More Secure**. Fewer components and services running unnecessarily.

- **No GUI**. No GUI means that users cannot make modifications to the DNS databases (or any other system functions) using common/user-friendly tools.

If you are planning to run DNS within a Server Core install, there a number of steps you must perform prior to installation. The first step we must take is to set the IP information of the server. To configure the IP addressing information of the server:

1. First we need to identify the network adapter. In the console window, type **netsh interface ipv4 show interfaces** and record the number shown under **Idx** column.

2. Next, we will set the IP address, Subnet Mask, and Default Gateway for the server. To do this, type **netsh interface ipv4 set address name="<ID>" source=static address=<StaticIP> mask=<SubnetMask> gateway= <DefaultGateway>**. **ID** represents the interface number from step 1, **<StaticIP>** represents the IP address we will assign, **<SubnetMask>** represents the subnet mask, and **<Default Gateway>** represents the IP address of the server's default gateway.

3. Lastly, we need to assign the IP address of the DNS server. If this server were part of an Active Directory domain and replicating Active-Directory integrated zones (we will discuss those next), we would likely point this server to another AD-integrated DNS server. If it is not, we would point it to another external DNS server—commonly the Internet provider of your company. From the console, type **netsh interface ipv4 add dnsserver name="<ID>" address=<DNSIP> index=1. >**. **ID** represents the number from step 1, **<StaticIP>** represents the IP address of the DNS server.

Once the IP address settings are completed—you can verify this by typing **ipconfig /all**—we can install the DNS role onto the Core Server installation.

4. To do this, from the command line type **start /w ocsetup DNS-Server-Core-Role**.

5. To verify that the DNS Server service is installed and started, type **NET START**. This will return a list of running services.

6. Next, we can use the **dnscmd** command line utility to manipulate the DNS settings. For example, you can type **dnscmd /enumzones** to list the zones hosted on this DNS server.

7. We can also change all the configuration options that we modified in the GUI section earlier by using the **dnscmd /config** option. For example, we can enable BIND secondaries by typing **dnscmd <servername> /config /bindsecondaries 1**. You can see the results in Figure 5.8.

There are many, many more things you can do with the dnscmd utility. For more information on the dnscmd syntax, visit http://technet2.microsoft.com/ WindowsServer/en/library/d652a163-279f-4047-b3e0-0c468a4d69f31033.mspx.

Creating DNS Zones

DNS zones are the actual boundaries of the records that are stored in DNS. They may or may not map to domain names. For example, records for syngress.com and authors. syngress.com could be housed in a single zone (syngress.com) or divided into separate zones that are configured to know about each other (syngress.com and authors.syngress. com). Traditionally zones have been divided to ease the amount of network traffic required to replicate the records between DNS servers, and also to move a relevant portion of the records closer to the users who most often use them. These reasons are less relevant today, because Microsoft recommends the use of Active Directory integrated zones. AD integrated zones provide much more efficient replication than previous zone types because they use the AD directory services database and replication architecture. When a portion of a domain, such as the authors subdomain, is hosted in a separate zone file, it is referred to as being delegated. A Windows Server 2008 DNS server can host a single zone or a large number of them, and the parent and delegated zones can be stored in the same server.

There are several types of zones that can be configured using the DNS Server role in Windows Server 2008, including standard primary, standard secondary, forward lookup, reverse lookup, Active Directory integrated, stub, and GlobalNames. You don't need to understand these at a deep level for a configuration test such as this one, but you should possess some basic knowledge about each. Generally, zones are either forward or reverse lookup zones. Forward lookup zones host records that allow for resolution from a FQDN or NetBIOS name to an IP address. Reverse lookup zones host records that allow for resolution from an IP address to a FQDN or NetBIOS name. Standard primary and secondary zones store records in actual text files, while AD integrated zones store them in the AD database. Standard primary and AD integrated zones can be modified; standard secondary zones are read-only copies of either a standard primary or AD integrated zone. Microsoft recommends primarily using AD integrated zones because of their enhanced efficiency and security.

You will also see the term *master* associated with DNS servers. A master server is any server with a primary, secondary, or AD integrated zone on it that transfers its zone information to another DNS server. If the organization has only one DNS server with a standard primary zone for the organization's domain, this server is a standard primary zone holder, but it is not a master. If the company installs a second DNS server and configures it with a standard secondary zone for their domain, the original DNS server can now be referred to as a master. Secondary zones can initiate zone transfers from standard primary, other secondary, or AD integrated zones.

Stub zones contain records only for name servers. These zones are used most often in conjunction with delegation. If DNS server A hosts the syngress.com zone, and DNS server B hosts the authors.syngress.com zone, these two servers need to know where to find the records for each other's domain. Placing a stub zone for syngress.com, for example, on DNS server B will keep an up-to-date list of DNS servers available to tell server B where it can find the records for the parent (syngress.com) domain.

Finally, GlobalNames is a new type of zone in Windows Server 2008. Microsoft has been trying to get its customers to migrate away from WINS name resolution for several years, and this is a new tool they are providing toward this end. It actually isn't a separate zone type. Rather you let Windows know you want to use the GlobalNames feature at the command line, name a zone *GlobalNames* while creating it, and the Windows Server 2008 DNS Server role takes it from there. Let's see how to configure each of these options.

Configuring & Implementing...

Standard vs. Active Directory Integrated Zones

Microsoft encourages you to use AD integrated zones whenever possible. Standard zones are stored in text files on the DNS server. The only security possible with these types of records is standard NTFS permissions on the zone files themselves. Windows 2000 and later DNS servers support incremental zone transfers for standard secondary zones. When a zone transfer between occurs, all records that have been added or changed will transfer across the network. Previous version transferred the entire zone file for each update. Even though this incremental type of transfer cuts down on network traffic, it is still significantly less efficient than replication using an AD integrated zone.

AD integrated zones store their records within Active Directory. Individual records as well as zones themselves are objects within directory services. This allows for much greater security because Windows Server 2008 and administrators can use object level permissions. In addition, replication of zone records occurs using standard AD replication. Rather than transferring an entire record, as incremental transfers involving standard zones do, only the property within the record that changed is transferred across the network. So, if the IP address in a record changes, with AD integrated zones only the IP address is replicated, not the entire record. An additional benefit of DNS using the AD replication process is that AD replication traffic is encrypted and highly compressed, which adds an additional level of security and efficiency.

Both types of zones are capable of using dynamic updates, however only AD integrated zones have the object-level permissions required to make them secure. When updates are not secure they open the door to attacks that corrupt the DNS database. Although Microsoft includes an option for nonsecure updates, they do not recommend using it. Microsoft always recommends the use of AD integrated zones with secure dynamic updates, when DDNS is desired.

One final important difference between standard and AD integrated zones involves where changes to records can be made, and fault tolerance. In a standard primary/secondary DNS configuration, the primary zone exists only on one DNS server. If something happens to that server, either the database will not be updated until it is available again, or one of the secondary servers must be converted into the primary zone holder. This single point of failure for updating records is eliminated with AD integrated zones. All AD integrated zones are primary zones, and can accept updates dynamically from clients

Continued

(if configured) as well as administrators. This *multimaster* model significantly increases fault tolerance. If one of the AD integrated zone DNS servers goes offline, updates to the database are still possible through any other AD integrated zone holder.

Standard secondary zones can be used with AD integrated zones. Standard primary zones cannot. AD integrated zones serve as primary zone holders and do not integrate with standard primary zones. When a secondary zone transfers information from an AD integrated zone, none of the features available with AD replication apply.

Creating a Standard Primary Forward Lookup Zone

Follow these steps to create a primary, forward lookup zone:

1. Open DNS Manager by clicking **Start | Administrative Tools | DNS**.

2. In the left pane, expand the node representing the server you want to configure, right-click **Forward Lookup Zones**, and click **New Zone…**.

3. Read the welcome page of the **New Zone Wizard** dialog box and click **Next**.

4. On the **Zone Type** wizard page, leave the default selection of **Primary zone** and click **Next**. See Figure 5.11.

Figure 5.11 The Zone Type Wizard Page

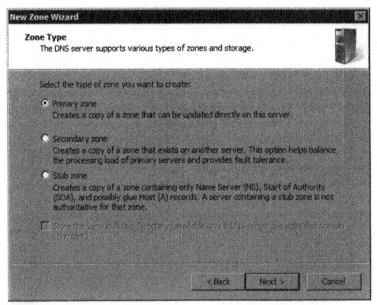

5. On the **Zone Name** wizard page, enter the name of your domain in the
Zone name: text box and click **Next**. See Figure 5.12.

Figure 5.12 The Zone Name Wizard Page

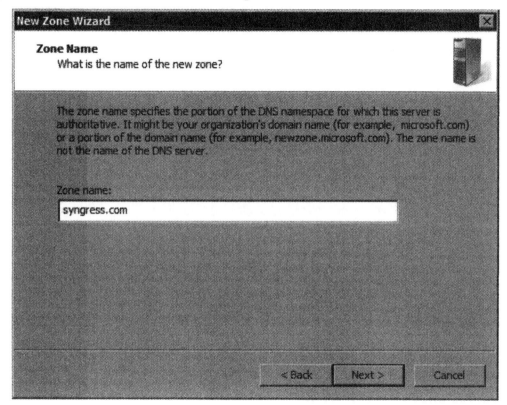

6. On the **Zone File** wizard page, you can select one of the following options
(see Figure 5.13):

■ **Create a new file with this file name**. This option, which is filled in
with a recommended setting by default, is used when you need to create
a zone file.

■ **Use this existing file**. If you have a preexisting zone file that is configured and ready to use, select this option. The file must be located in the
%systemroot%\System32\dns directory.

Figure 5.13 The Zone File Wizard Page

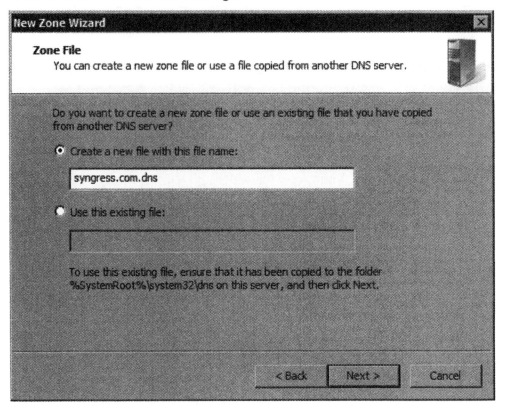

7. Click **Next**.

8. On the **Dynamic Update** wizard page, you can select from the following options (see Figure 5.14):

   ▪ **Allow both secure and non-secure dynamic updates**. The DNS Server role in Windows Server 2008 supports dynamic DNS (DDNS). If this option is selected, computers can communicate with the DNS server to create and manage their own records. If the zone is AD integrated, a third option with enhanced security is available. A standard primary zone has reduced security when using DDNS that make it easy for attackers to specify faulty DNS record information when this option is enabled. Microsoft does not recommend enabling this option.

■ **Do not allow dynamic updates.** This option prevents the use of dynamic DDNS. Records for this primary zone will need to be managed manually if it is selected. This is the default option.

Figure 5.14 The Dynamic Update Wizard Page

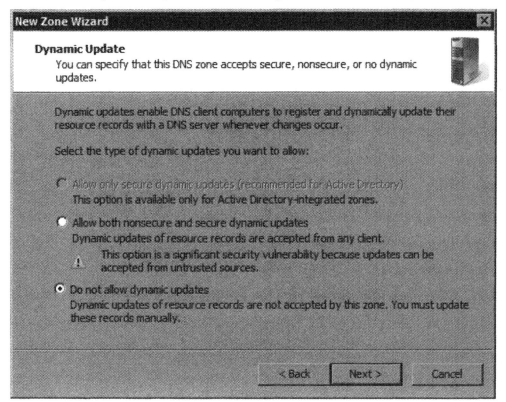

9. Click **Next**.

10. On the **Completing the New Zone Wizard** page, review the information provided and click **Finish**.

11. In the left pane under **Forward Lookup Zones** a new node representing the zone you created should appear. Click that zone.

12. In the right pane, you should see that at least two records have been created automatically (SOA and NS). See Figure 5.15.

Figure 5.15 DNS Manager Utility with the Created Forward Primary Zone

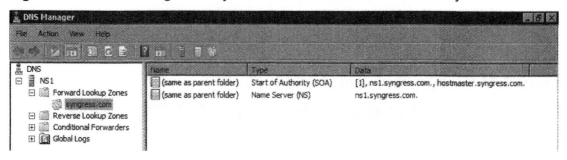

Creating a Secondary Forward Lookup Zone

Follow these steps to create a secondary, forward lookup zone:

1. Open DNS Manager by clicking **Start | Administrative Tools | DNS**.

2. In the left pane, expand the node representing the server you want to configure, right-click **Forward Lookup Zones**, and click **New Zone…**.

3. Read the welcome page of the **New Zone Wizard** dialog box and click **Next**.

4. On the **Zone Type** wizard page, select **Secondary zone** and click **Next**. See Figure 5.11.

5. On the **Zone Name** wizard page, enter the name of the domain in the Zone name: text box. This must match the primary zone's name. See Figure 5.12.

6. Click **Next**.

7. In the **Master DNS Servers** wizard page, enter the name of one or more DNS servers from where this secondary zone will take transfers. Enter the master server's IP address or FQDN by clicking on **<Click here to add an IP Address or DNS Name>**. Secondary zones can be transferred from standard primary, AD Integrated, and other secondary zones. For fault tolerance, more than one master server can be specified. All servers are not used by default. If the first server on the list is successfully contacted, for example, the rest of the list will be ignored. Servers can be ordered using the **Up** and **Down** buttons, and removed from the list using the **Delete** button. See Figure 5.16.

Figure 5.16 The Configured Master DNS Servers Wizard Page

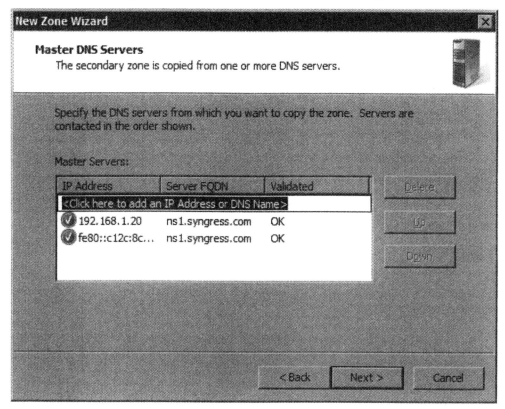

8. Click **Next**.

9. On the **Completing the New Zone Wizard** page, review the information provided and click **Finish**.

Creating an Active Directory Integrated Forward Lookup Zone

Follow these steps to create an AD integrated forward lookup zone:

1. Open DNS Manager by clicking **Start | Administrative Tools | DNS**.

2. In the left pane, expand the node representing the server you want to configure, right-click **Forward Lookup Zones**, and click **New Zone…**.

3. Read the welcome page of the **New Zone Wizard** dialog box and click **Next**.

4. On the **Zone Type** wizard page, leave the default selection of **Primary zone** and leave **Store the zone in Active Directory** (available only if DNS server is a writable domain controller) selected.

5. Click **Next**. See Figure 5.11.

6. On the **Active Directory Zone Replication Scope** wizard page, select one of the following options (Figure 5.17.):

   ■ **To all DNS servers in this forest**. This option replicates the zone information to the AD database on all Windows Server 2003 and later domain controllers in the forest. Domain controllers receive, store, and replicate the zone information even if they are not DNS servers.

   ■ **To all DNS servers in this domain**. This option replicates the zone information to the AD database on all Windows Server 2003 and later domain controllers in domain controller's AD domain. Domain controllers receive, store, and replicate the zone information even if they are not DNS servers.

   ■ **To all domain controllers in this domain (for Windows 2000 compatibility)**. This option replicates the zone information to the AD database on all Windows Server 2000 and later domain controllers in domain controller's AD domain. Domain controllers receive, store, and replicate the zone information even if they are not DNS servers. This option reduces functionality available to Windows Server 2003 and later domain controllers, and should be used only if your network contains Windows 2000 Server domain controllers that must act as DNS servers.

   ■ **To all domain controllers specified in the scope of this directory partition**. This option replicates the zone information based on the settings for a specific application directory partition. See the *Creating an Application Directory Partition* section for more information.

Figure 5.17 The Active Directory Zone Replication Scope Wizard Page

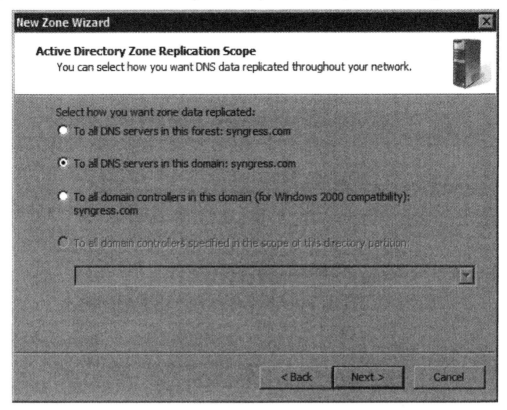

7. Click **Next**.

8. On the Zone Name wizard page, enter the name of your domain in the **Zone name:** text box and click **Next**. See Figure 5.12.

9. Click **Next**.

10. On the **Dynamic Update** wizard page, you can select from the following options (see Figure 5.18):

    ■ **Allow only secure, dynamic updates**. The DNS Server role in Windows Server 2008 supports dynamic DNS (DDNS). This default option, which is recommended by Microsoft, enables a host to add and manage its own forward and reverse lookup records in DNS. It also enables DHCP to be configured to manage host records. During creation, this option sets additional security on records to prevent them being modified by unauthorized hosts.

- **Allow both secure and non-secure dynamic updates**. If this option is selected, computers can communicate with the DNS server to create and manage their own records. It also enables DHCP to be configured to manage host records. A standard primary zone has reduced security options that make it easy for attackers to specify faulty DNS record information when this option is enabled. When used in conjunction with an AD integrated zone, this option will use additional security when clients are capable of it. Because it also allows unsecure DDNS modification, Microsoft does not recommend enabling this option.

- **Do not allow dynamic updates**. This option prevents the use of dynamic DDNS. Records for this primary zone will need to be managed manually if it is selected. This is the default option.

Figure 5.18 The Dynamic Update Wizard Page

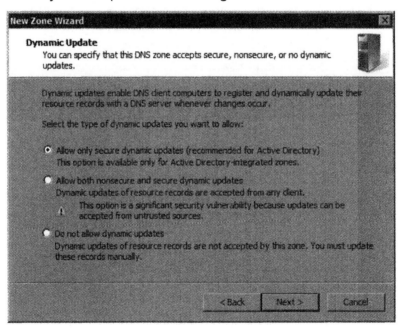

11. Click **Next**.

12. On the **Completing the New Zone Wizard** page, review the information provided and click **Finish**.

Really expects you to use AD integrated zones with secure dynamic updates whenever possible.

Creating a Standard Primary Reverse Lookup Zone

Follow these steps to create a reverse lookup zone:

1. Open DNS Manager by clicking **Start | Administrative Tools | DNS**.

2. In the left pane, expand the node representing the server you want to configure, right-click **Reverse Lookup Zones**, and click **New Zone…**.

3. Read the welcome page of the **New Zone Wizard** dialog box and click **Next**.

4. On the **Zone Type** wizard page, leave the default selection of **Primary zone** and click **Next**. See Figure 5.11.

5. On the **Reverse Lookup Zone Name** wizard page, select the appropriate zone type (see Figure 5.19):

   ■ **IPv4 Reverse Lookup Zone**. Select this option if you want the zone to track IPv4 address information. This option is the default.

   ■ **IPv6 Reverse Lookup Zone**. Select this option if you want the zone to track IPv6 address information. This is a new option in Windows Server 2008.

Figure 5.19 The Reverse Lookup Zone Name Wizard Page

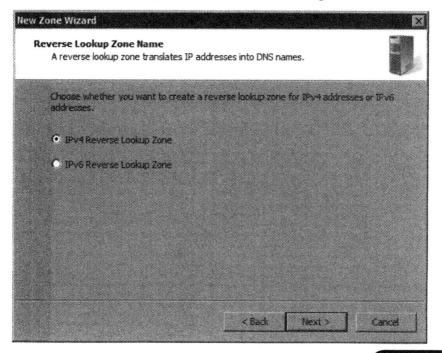

6. Click **Next**.

7. On the second **Reverse Lookup Zone Name** wizard page, select and configure the appropriate option (see Figure 5.20):

   ■ **Network ID**. This option helps you to properly name the zone. Enter the network portion of the IP address range you want the zone to service. A proper zone name will automatically be filled in under **Reverse lookup zone name:** for you.

   ■ **Reverse lookup zone name**. If you would prefer to manually enter the zone name, you can do so using this option. You should follow the recommended DNS naming standards for reverse lookup zone names.

Figure 5.20 The Second Reverse Lookup Zone Name Wizard Page

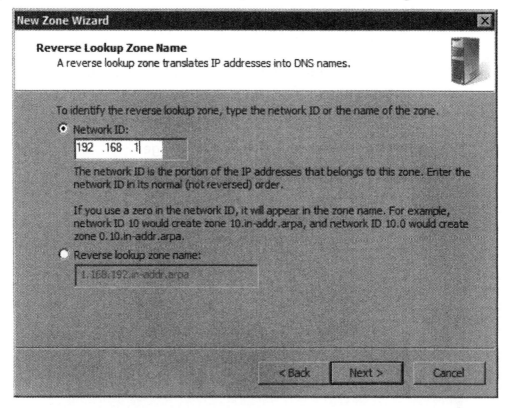

8. On the **Zone File** wizard page, you can select one of the following options (see Figure 5.21):

- **Create a new file with this file name**. This option, which is filled in with a recommended setting by default, is used when you need to create a zone file.

- **Use this existing file**. If you have a preexisting zone file that is configured and ready to use, select this option. The file must be located in the %systemroot%\System32\dns directory.

9. Click **Next**.

Figure 5.21 The Zone File Wizard Page

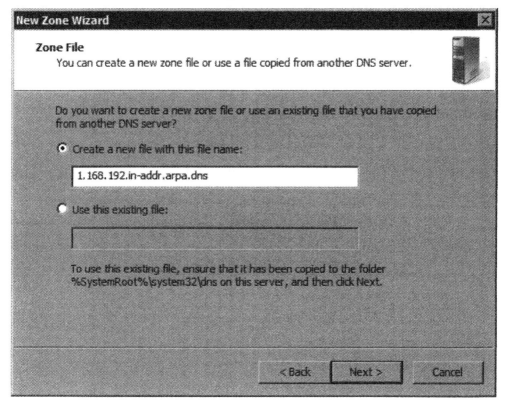

10. Click **Next**.

11. On the **Dynamic Update** wizard page, you can select from the following options (see Figure 5.18):

- **Allow both secure and nonsecure dynamic updates**. The DNS Server role in Windows Server 2008 supports dynamic DNS (DDNS).

If this option is selected, computers can communicate with the DNS server to create and manage their own records. If the zone is AD integrated, a third option with enhanced security is available. A standard primary zone has reduced security options that make it easy for attackers to specify faulty DNS record information when this option is enabled. Microsoft does not recommend enabling this option.

■ **Do not allow dynamic updates**. This option prevents the use of dynamic DDNS. Records for this primary zone will need to be managed manually if it is selected. This is the default option.

12. Click **Next**.

13. On the **Completing the New Zone Wizard** page, review the information provided and click **Finish**.

Creating a Standard Secondary Reverse Lookup Zone

Follow these steps to create a reverse lookup zone:

1. Open DNS Manager by clicking **Start | Administrative Tools | DNS**.

2. In the left pane, expand the node representing the server you want to configure, right-click **Reverse Lookup Zones**, and click **New Zone…**.

3. Read the welcome page of the **New Zone Wizard** dialog box and click **Next**.

4. On the **Zone Type** wizard page, select **Secondary zone** and click **Next**. See Figure 5.11.

5. On the **Reverse Lookup Zone Name** wizard page, select the appropriate zone type:

■ **IPv4 Reverse Lookup Zone**. Select this option if you want the zone to track IPv4 address information. This option is the default.

■ **IPv6 Reverse Lookup Zone**. Select this option if you want the zone to track IPv6 address information. This is a new option in Windows Server 2008.

6. Click **Next**.

7. On the second Reverse Lookup Zone Name wizard page, select and configure the appropriate option (See Figure 5.20):

- **Network ID**. This option helps you to properly name the zone. Enter the network portion of the IP address range you want the zone to service. A proper zone name will automatically be filled in under **Reverse lookup zone name:** for you. This must match the configuration information used when creating the primary reverse lookup zone.

- **Reverse lookup zone name**. If you would prefer to enter the zone name manually, you can do so using this option. You should follow the recommended DNS naming standards for reverse lookup file names.

8. Click **Next**.

9. On the **Master DNS Servers** wizard page, enter the name of one or more DNS servers that this secondary zone will take transfers from. Enter the master server's IP address or FQDN by clicking **<Click here to add an IP Address or DNS Name>**. Secondary zones can be transferred from standard primary, AD Integrated, and other secondary zones. For fault tolerance, more than one master server can be specified. All servers are not used by default. If the first server on the list is successfully contacted, for example, the rest of the list will be ignored. Servers can be ordered using the **Up** and **Down** buttons, and removed from the list using the **Delete** button. See Figure 5.16.

10. Click **Next**.

11. On the **Completing the New Zone Wizard** page, review the information provided and click **Finish**.

Creating a Zone Delegation

Delegation allows you to transfer authority for a domain to a different zone. For example, an organization with multiple subdomains such as authors.syngress.com, publishers.syngress.com, editors.syngress.com, executives.syngress.com, and so forth may not want to keep all these subdomains in a single syngress.com zone file. Authors and editors might work a different office that has its own DNS server, so moving these parts of the namespace to separate zone files on that server might increase query efficiency, cut down on DNS WAN traffic, and so forth. When we move subdomains out of their parent domain's zone file, it is called delegating the domains. Follow these steps to create a zone delegation:

1. Open DNS Manager by clicking **Start | Administrative Tools | DNS**.

2. Expand the appropriate server node, expand **Forward Lookup Zones** or **Reverse Lookup Zones**, right-click the zone you want to create a delegation for, and click **New Delegation….** In the example here, we will be using the forward lookup zone *syngress.com*.

3. In the **New Delegation Wizard**, read the welcome page and click **Next**.

4. On the **Delegated Domain Name** wizard page, type the name of the domain in the **Delegated Domain:** text box, and click Next. See Figure 5.22.

Figure 5.22 The Completed Delegated Domain Name Wizard Page

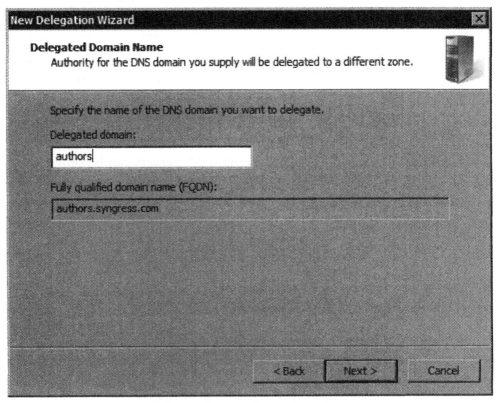

5. On the **Name Servers** wizard page, click the **Add…** button.

6. In the **New Name Server Record** dialog box, type the name of a DNS server that will hold the delegated domain in the **Server fully qualified domain name (FQDN):** text box, and click **Resolve**.

7. In the **IP Addresses of this NS record:** area make any necessary adjustments. If clicking the **Resolve** button didn't locate the IP address of the server you

can enter it by clicking **<Click here to add an IP Address>**. You can also click that option to add one or more additional IP addresses that relate to the server but were unresolved. If the DNS server has multiple addresses, you can use the **Up** and **Down** buttons to provide the order that the IP addresses should be contacted. Finally, you can click and remove configured IP addresses using the **Delete** button. The delegated zone must also be configured on the DNS server. This can be done before or after the delegation. If done after it, you'll see the warning message displayed in Figure 5.23.

Figure 5.23 The Completed New Name Server Record Dialog

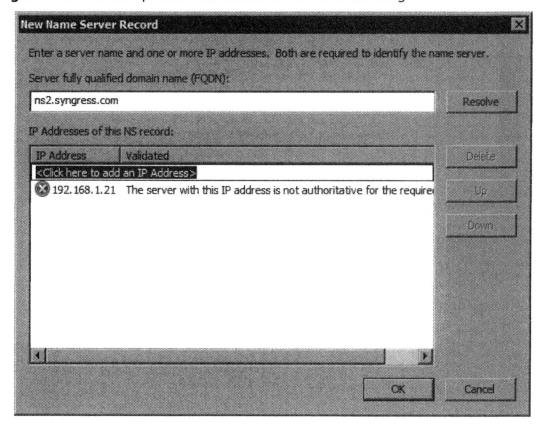

8. Click **OK**.

9. In the **New Name Server Record** dialog box, click **Next**.

10. On the **Completing the New Delegation Wizard** page, click **Finish**.

11. Follow the steps for creating a new forward lookup zone that matches the delegated domain on the DNS server you specified in step 7.

12. Follow the steps to create a stub zone for the parent domain on the DNS server you specified in step 7. This enables the delegated domain to more easily locate its parent domain.

Creating a Stub Zone

Follow these steps to create a stub zone:

1. Open DNS Manager by clicking **Start | Administrative Tools | DNS**.

2. In the left pane, expand the node representing the server you want to configure, right-click **Forward Lookup Zones**, and click **New Zone…**.

3. Read the welcome page of the **New Zone Wizard** dialog box and click **Next**.

4. On the **Zone Type** wizard page, leave the default selection of **Stub zone** and click **Next**. See Figure 5.11.

5. On the **Zone Name** wizard page, enter the name of your domain in the **Zone name:** text box and click **Next**. See Figure 5.12.

6. On the **Zone File** wizard page, in the **Create a new file with this file name:** text box, leave the default option or enter a file name for the zone file, then click **Next**.

7. In the **Master DNS Servers** wizard page, enter the name of one or more DNS servers from which this stub zone will take transfers. Enter the master server's IP address or FQDN by clicking **<Click here to add an IP Address or DNS Name>**. Stub zones can be transferred from standard primary, AD Integrated, and secondary zones. For fault tolerance, more than one master server can be specified. All servers are not used by default. If the first server on the list is successfully contacted, for example, the rest of the list will be ignored. Servers can be ordered using the **Up** and **Down** buttons, and removed from the list using the **Delete** button. See Figure 5.16.

8. Click **Next**.

9. On the **Completing the New Zone Wizard** page, review the information provided and click **Finish**.

Using the New GlobalNames Zone Feature

There are two primary forms of name resolution on Windows networks: NetBIOS and DNS. NetBIOS name resolution goes back to the early days of Windows.

Recent operating system releases from Microsoft increasingly have moved away from it toward DNS. Although still in wide deployment, Microsoft's NetBIOS name resolution services do not support IPv6. Windows Server 2008 is the first server release from Microsoft that deeply integrates IPv6 technology into all aspects of the operating system and its networking services. In order to allow customers to continue the process of migrating away from NetBIOS name resolution methods, one of the new features Microsoft provides in Windows Server 2008 is the GlobalNames Zone (GNZ) feature.

GNZs are designed to allow administrators to migrate away from WINS servers and move to using DNS for all name resolution. These zones are designed to support single name records that match the NetBIOS computer names on Windows networks. GNZ records are statically configured by administrators, so typically you will use them only for servers that are configured with static IP addresses and are currently located by WINS or LMHOSTS files. See the *Configuring Name Resolution for Client Computers* section of this chapter for more information about LMHOST files and other client name resolution strategies. There are two steps for configuring GNZs:

1. Enable all domain controllers to support GNZs.

2. Create the appropriate name resolution records for the zone. GNZs use CNAME records. Enter the NetBIOS computer name in the **Alias name (uses parent domain if left blank):** field in the CNAME record, and the appropriate FQDN in the Fully qualified domain name (FQDN) for target host field. See the Creating CNAME Records section for more information on this DNS record type.

Enabling a Domain Controller to Support GlobalNames Zones

To enable a domain controller to support GlobalNames Zones, perform the following steps:

1. Open a command prompt by clicking **Start | Command Prompt**.

2. At the command prompt, type **dnscmd <ServerName> /config /Enableglobalnamessupport 1**. For example: dnscmd ad2.syngress. com /config /Enableglobalnamessupport 1 (see Figure 5.24).

Figure 5.24 Enabling GlobalNames Zone Support Using the Command Prompt

Configuring & Implementing...

Configuring Resolution Using GlobalNames Zones

You might be wondering where a GNZ fits with the other name resolution methods available to a DNS server. When a Windows Server 2008 DNS server responds to a query, it first checks its local cache and zone data. If the answer is not found, and a GNZ is configured on the server, it next checks the GlobalNames zone. If the GNZ does not contain the needed information and WINS integration is configured, the server next queries WINS for the information. The GNZ can be configured as the initial source of information to use when attempting to resolve a query, by using the following steps:

1. Open a command prompt by clicking **Start | Command Prompt**.
2. At the command prompt, type **dnscmd <ServerName> /config /Enableglobalnamessupport 0**. For example: dnscmd ad2.syngress. com /config /Enableglobalnamessupport <order>

   Replacing <order> with a 0 at the end of the command queries the GNZ first.

   Replacing <order> with a 1 will query the local cache and zone records first.

Creating the GlobalNames Zone

To create a GlobalNames Zone, follow these steps:

1. Open DNS Manager by clicking **Start | Administrative Tools | DNS**.
2. In the left pane, expand the node representing the server you want to configure, right-click **Forward Lookup Zones**, and click **New Zone....**

3. Read the welcome page of the **New Zone Wizard** dialog box and click **Next**.

4. On the **Zone Type** wizard page, leave the default selection of **Primary zone** and leave **Store the zone in Active Directory** (available only if DNS server is a writable domain controller) selected.

5. Click **Next**. See Figure 5.11.

6. On the **Active Directory Zone Replication Scope** wizard page, select one of the following options (see Figure 5.17.):

   ■ **To all DNS servers in this forest**. This option replicates the zone information to the AD database on all Windows Server 2003 and later domain controllers in the forest. Domain controllers receive, store, and replicate the zone information even if they are not DNS servers. Microsoft recommends using this option for GlobalNames Zones, but it is not required.

   ■ **To all DNS servers in this domain**. This option replicates the zone information to the AD database on all Windows Server 2003 and later domain controllers in domain controller's AD domain. Domain controllers receive, store, and replicate the zone information even if they are not DNS servers.

   ■ **To all domain controllers in this domain (for Windows 2000 compatibility)**. This option replicates the zone information to the AD database on all Windows Server 2000 and later domain controllers in domain controller's AD domain. Domain controllers receive, store, and replicate the zone information even if they are not DNS servers.

   ■ **To all domain controllers specified in the scope of this directory partition**. This option replicates the zone information based on the settings for a specific application directory partition. See the Replication Scope section for more information.

7. Click **Next**.

8. On the **Zone Name** wizard page, in the **Zone name:** text box enter **GlobalNames** (this is not case sensitive) and click **Next**. See Figure 5.12.

9. On the **Dynamic Update** wizard page, select **Do not allow dynamic updates**. This option prevents the use of dynamic DDNS. Although not strictly required, Microsoft recommends this configuration option to ensure that only the proper record types are stored in the zone (see Figure 5.18).

10. Click **Next**.

11. On the **Completing the New Zone Wizard** page, review the information provided and click **Finish**.

Configuring and Managing DNS Replication

Replication for AD integrated zones is managed automatically via AD DS. Once you have specified the replication scope, you don't need to do anything additional to manage zone replication. Standard zones and stub zones, however, have a variety of options that can be configured to control zone transfers. You can manually initiate zone transfers, determine which DNS servers may and may not serve as masters, configure the intervals for replication using a zone's SOA records, and create custom application directory partitions for managing AD integrated zone replication.

Manually Initiating Replication Using DNS Manager

To manually initiate a zone transfer using DNS Manager follow these steps:

1. Open DNS Manager by clicking **Start | Administrative Tools | DNS**.

2. Expand the appropriate server node, expand **Forward Lookup Zones** or **Reverse Lookup Zones**, right-click the desired zone, and click one of the following options:

   - **Transfer from Master**. This option asks the secondary or stub zone to check its master and determine if it is up to date. If it isn't, a zone transfer to obtain any updates will be initiated.

   - **Reload from Master**. This option requests a transfer of the entire zone from the master. It is most often used when some form of corruption has occurred in the secondary or stub zone. Because it transfers all records, it uses more bandwidth and is not recommended except when absolutely necessary.

Configuring DNS Servers to Allow Zone Transfers

For security reasons, by default primary and secondary zones restrict zone transfers. In order to transfer zone information successfully to a standard secondary server, some additional configuration must be done in the properties of a standard primary, AD integrated, or secondary zone on the DNS server that will be the master server.

Configuring a Standard Primary Zone for Transfers

To configure a primary zone to allow transfers, follow these steps:

1. Open DNS Manager by clicking **Start | Administrative Tools | DNS**.

2. In the left pane, expand the node representing the server you want to configure, expand **Forward Lookup Zones**, right-click the primary zone, and click **Properties**.

3. On the **Properties** dialog, click the **Zone Transfers** tab and select one of the following options (see Figure 5.25):

   - **To any server**. This option is the least secure. It potentially allows anyone to request a zone transfer, which exposes all your DNS records. Potential attackers obtaining this information can receive an enormous amount of information about the network.

   - **Only to servers listed on the Name Servers tab**. The **Properties** dialog has another tab labeled **Name Servers**. This option, the default, uses the list of DNS servers that you have configured on that tab. This is the tab that is used to create NS records for the zone, so by default any server you specify as a name server for the zone is configured automatically for replication. See the *Creating NS Records* section for more information.

   - **Only to the following Servers**. If desired, a separate list can be maintained on the **Zone Transfers** tab. Selecting this option enables the **Edit** button that can be used to add and remove DNS servers. Larger organizations may require more complexity in how zone transfers are configured. Allowing transfers to any name server for the zone in a global organization might be problematic. Using this option allows for more granular control over which servers can receive zone transfers from the master.

Figure 5.25 The Zone Transfers Tab

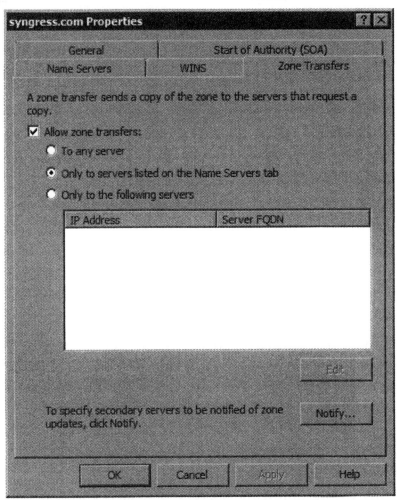

4. Click **OK**.

Configuring an AD Integrated
or Secondary Zone for Transfers

By default, AD integrated and secondary zones are configured to prevent zone transfers. To configure these types of zones to allow transfers, follow these steps:

1. Open **DNS Manager** by clicking **Start | Administrative Tools | DNS**.

2. In the left pane, expand the node representing the server you want to configure, expand **Forward Lookup Zones**, right-click the AD integrated or secondary zone, and click **Properties**.

3. On the **Properties** dialog, click the **Zone Transfers** tab.

4. Select **Allow zone transfers:** and configure one of the following options: **To any server**, **Only to servers listed on the Name Servers tab**, **Only to the following Servers**. For more information concerning these options see step 3 in the previous section, *Configuring a Standard Primary Zone for Transfers*. See Figure 5.25.

5. Click **OK**.

Configuring the SOA Record

For standard zones, DNS replication relies on the values configured in the Start of Authority (SOA) record. Although it appears as a record when viewing zone information in DNS Manager, the values it contains are actually configured within the zone's properties. To access them, in DNS Manager right-click a zone, select **Properties**, and click the **Start of Authority (SOA)** tab to bring it to the foreground (see Figure 5.26). The following settings can be configured.

■ **Serial number**. This text box contains the current version of the zone database. Secondary zones compare their serial number to the one on their master to determine if a zone transfer is needed. You can manually force a zone transfer to all secondary zones by clicking the **Increment** button to manually change this value.

■ **Primary Server**. This value specifies the server holding the primary forward lookup zone. When using standard DNS zones, there can only be a DNS server that holds the writable, primary zone.

■ **Responsible Person**. This value holds defines Responsible Person (RP) DNS record for the individual who manages the zone.

■ **Refresh interval**. This value defines how frequently a DNS server that holds a secondary zone should check for a new version of the zone database. The default value is every 15 minutes.

■ **Retry interval**. This value defines how often a DNS server that holds a secondary zone should attempt to check for a new version of the zone database if its initial attempt failed during the standard refresh interval. The default value is every 10 minutes.

■ **Expires after**. This value defines how long a secondary zone should retain the zone's records if it cannot contact a master server. Because it is unable to get updates, after a period of time its records may become inaccurate, making it important to ensure they are not being distributed to clients. The default value is one day.

- **Minimum (default) TTL**. This value defines how long a record will be cached by DNS servers and clients that request it. The default value is one hour, which means that any DNS server that obtains this record will return the same information to clients for one hour, and request the record again when that hour is up. Many clients will also cache the record for an hour before asking for an update. As an administrator, you can adjust this value to fit your environment. If IP addresses for requested resources change often, you should keep it low. However, if your resources are fairly static you can increase this value to reduce the load on your DNS servers.

- **TTL for this record**. This option allows the SOA record to have a separate TTL value than the **Minimum (default) TTL** that is applied to all other records in the zone.

Figure 5.26 The Start of Authority (SOA) Tab

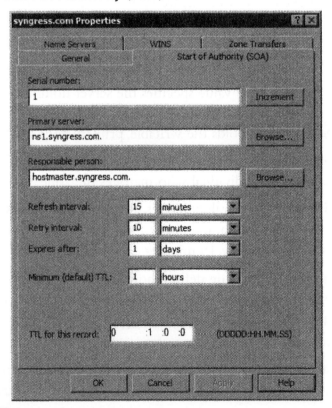

Creating an Application Directory Partition

In an Active Directory environment, the scope of DNS replication can be narrowly defined while still taking advantage of the benefits of AD replication. You can create an application directory partition, and specify it as where the zone records will be stored during zone creation (see Figure 5.27).

Figure 5.27 The New Zone Wizard with the AD Application Directory Partition Option Enabled

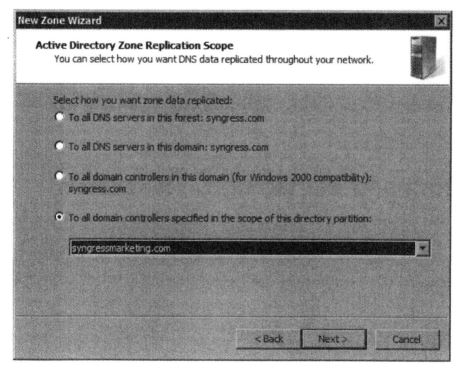

An application directory partition is simply a portion of the Active Directory database that is segregated for replication purposes. When used for DNS, it allows a subset of domain controllers to receive the zone records, rather than the more expansive options of all domain controllers in either the forest or AD domain. You must be a member of the Enterprise Admins group to create partitions. Application directory partitions have uses in AD that extend beyond DNS. They can be created with low level AD management tools such as NTDSUTIL and ADSI Edit. Microsoft makes it easy to create these types of partitions for DNS use by providing an option in their command line DNS management utility, DNSCMD. Follow these steps to create a DNS AD directory partition:

1. Open a command prompt.

2. Type **dnscmd <server name or IP address> /CreateDirectoryPartition <FQDN of the new partition>**. For example: **dnscmd ad2.syngress.com /CreateDirectoryPartition syngressmarketing.com** (see Figure 5.28).

Figure 5.28 Creating an DNS Application Directory Partition Using DNSCMD

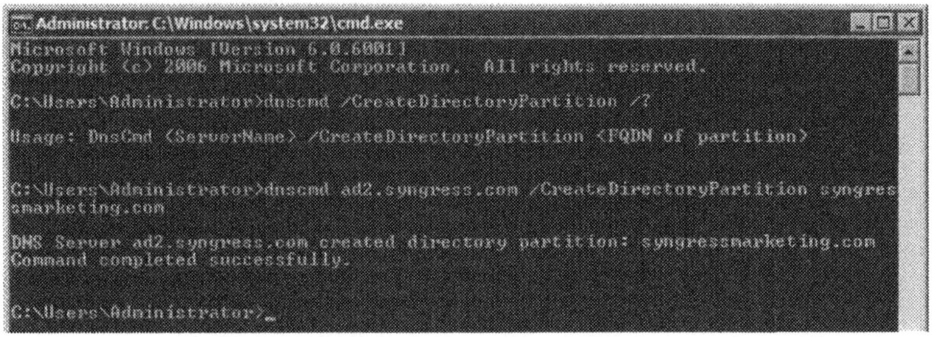

3. Close the command prompt.

Creating and Managing DNS Records

DNS records represent another key DNS management task. In this section we'll see how to manage the major types of DNS records. We'll also take a close look at DNS and WINS integration. On the surface this may not appear to be related to record management, but this integration occurs through the use of WINS and WINS-R records. Finally, we'll take a deeper look at how to manage dynamic DNS.

Managing Record Types

Administrators can manually create a wide range of DNS records. The more commonly used record types are available directly from a zone's right-click menu. All standard RFC record types, plus some used only in Microsoft environments (such as WINS records), can be created with DNS Manager. In this section we examine the major record types and see how to create them.

Creating Host Records

A type host records are used for IPv4 hosts and *AAAA* type host records are used for IPv6 hosts. A computer can have both IPv4 and IPv6 addresses configured on it. Because of this, Windows allows a host to have both A and AAAA host records created for it. Let's examine how to create each type of record.

Creating A Records

To create a new A type host record, follow these steps:

1. Open DNS Manager by clicking **Start | Administrative Tools | DNS**.

2. Expand the node for the server you want to configure, expand the **Forward Lookup Zones** node, right-click the node for the zone to which you want to add the record, and click **New Host (A or AAAA)…**. See Figure 5.29.

Figure 5.29 Opening the New Host Dialog

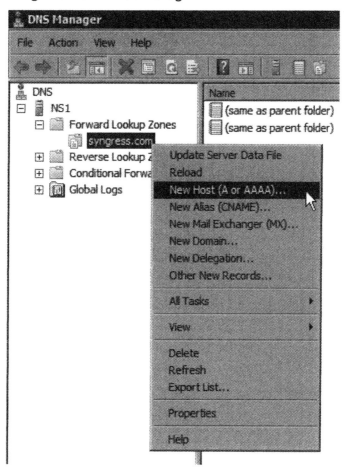

3. In the **New Host** dialog box, type the host's name in the **Name (uses parent domain name if blank):** text area, and the host's IP address in the **IP address:** text area. If you would also like to have a reverse lookup record created, leave the **Create associated pointer (PTR) record** selected. The appropriate reverse lookup zone must be configured for this option to be successful. See Figure 5.30.

Figure 5.30 Configuring the New Host Dialog for an IPv4 Host

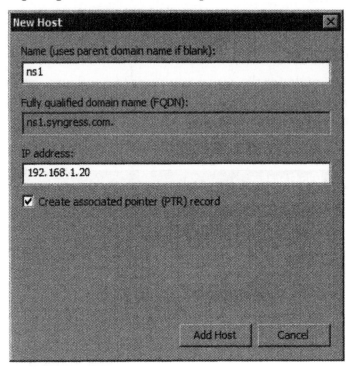

4. Click **Add Host**.

5. In the **DNS** pop-up box that appears to notify you of successful record creation, click **OK**.

6. The **New Host** dialog box stays open with its values cleared so that you can enter another record. Click **Done** to close this dialog.

Creating AAAA Records

To create a new AAAA type host record, follow these steps:

1. Open DNS Manager by clicking **Start | Administrative Tools | DNS**.

2. Expand the node for the server you want to configure, expand the **Forward Lookup Zones** node, right-click the node for the zone to which you want to add the record, and click **New Host (A or AAAA)…**. See Figure 5.29.

3. In the **New Host** dialog box, type the host's name in the **Name (uses parent domain name if blank):** text area, and the host's IP address in the **IP address:** text area. If you also would like to have a reverse lookup record created, leave the **Create associated pointer (PTR) record** selected. The

appropriate reverse lookup zone must be configured for this option to be successful. See Figure 5.31.

Figure 5.31 Configuring the New Host Dialog for an IPv6 Host

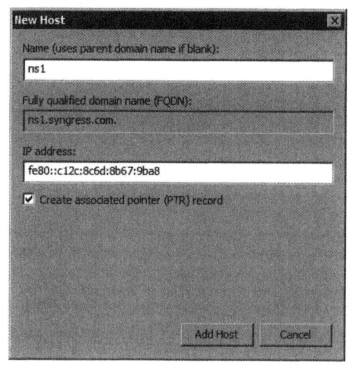

4. Click **Add Host**.

5. In the **DNS** pop-up box that appears to notify you of successful record creation, click **OK**.

6. The **New Host** dialog box stays open with its values cleared so that you can enter another record. Click **Done** to close this dialog.

New & Noteworthy...

Full IPv6 Support

The AAAA record is an excellent example of changes made to Windows Server 2008 to accommodate IPv6. Microsoft has completely reworked Windows

Continued

networking to ensure that IPv6 is fully incorporated. As a result, both IPv4 and IPv6 are used throughout Windows Server 2008's DNS functionality. Many DNS configuration screens now attempt to automatically resolve both IPv4 and IPv6 addresses for host records, even when IPv6 is not configured and present on the network. Occasionally this can lead to warning messages that aren't relevant for your IPv4 environment.

IPv6 is a new generation of the Internet Protocol. Although it's been available for years, software companies like Microsoft have been slow to support it. It originally was conceived primarily to provide more IP addresses at a time when it looked like the industry was running out of them. However, new technologies such as network address translation solved many of the shortage issues and this greatly slowed the adoption of IPv6. Today, IPv6 runs on some of the largest private networks; however most organizations continue to use IPv4.

Creating Pointer Records

Pointer records are used in reverse lookup zones to resolve IP addresses to host names. As seen in the previous section, they can be added automatically when you create a host record. They can also be created manually using the following procedure:

1. Open DNS Manager by clicking **Start | Administrative Tools | DNS**.

2. Expand the node for the server you want to configure, expand the **Reverse Lookup Zones** node, right-click the node for the zone to which you want to add the record to, and click **New Pointer (PTR)…**. See Figure 5.32.

Figure 5.32 Opening the New Pointer Dialog

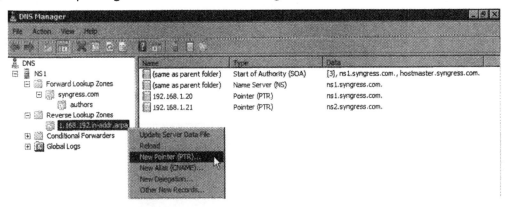

3. In the **New Resource Record** dialog box, type the host's IP address in the **Host IP Address:** text box, and the host's name in the **Host name:** text box.

You can also click **Browse...** and select the computer from an existing DNS record, such as an A or AAAA record, if one exists for the host. See Figure 5.33.

Figure 5.33 The Completed New Resource Record Dialog for a PTR Record

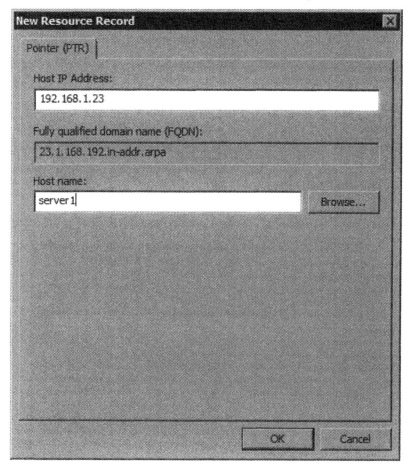

4. Click **OK** to finish adding the record.

Creating MX Records

Mail exchanger (MX) records are used to locate email servers. For an email server to be located on the network, an MX record is not enough. An MX record contains only the FQDN of the email server; it does not say where to find it. At a minimum the server must also have an A and/or AAAA record for the email server. It is also recommended that the server have a PTR record. Many spam applications use reverse lookup to verify email servers. To create a new MX record, follow these steps:

1. Open DNS Manager by clicking **Start | Administrative Tools | DNS**.

2. Expand the node for the server you want to configure, expand the **Forward Lookup Zones** node, right-click the node for the zone to which you want to add the record, and click **New Mail Exchanger (MX)...**. See Figure 5.29.

3. In the **New Resource Record** dialog box, type the email server's FQDN in the **Fully qualified domain name (FQDN) of mail server:** text box, click **Browse...** and select the server from an existing A or AAAA. See Figure 5.34. If your domain has more than one email server, you can use the **Mail server priority:** value to specify which has priority. The accepted range is 0 to 65535, with priority being given to the lowest number. If that server does not respond, the email server specified in the MX record containing the next highest value is used. If multiple mail servers are configured with the same value, and it is the lowest number, the servers will be used in a random fashion.

Figure 5.34 The Completed New Resource Record Dialog for a MX Record

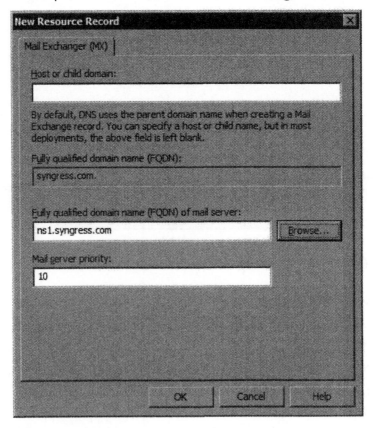

4. Click **OK** to finish adding the record.

Creating SRV Records

Service records are used to specify which server or servers hold certain TCP/IP services in the domain, including finger, ftp, http, Kerberos, ldap, msdcs, nntp, telnet, and whois. Clients that query the domain for the appropriate server to contact for one these services will be responded to based on one or more service record configuration(s). This allows administrators to move the role holders of these services easily if necessary. It also allows for the use of multiple servers with priority and load balancing for any of the services listed. To create an SRV record, follow these steps:

1. Open DNS Manager by clicking **Start | Administrative Tools | DNS**.

2. Expand the node for the server you want to configure, expand the **Forward Lookup Zones** node, right-click the node for the zone to which you want to add the record, and click **Other New Records...**. See Figure 5.29.

3. In the **Resource Record Type** dialog box that appears, select **Service Location (SRV)** in the **Select a resource record type:** box, and click **Create Record...**. See Figure 5.35.

Figure 5.35 The Resource Record Type Dialog

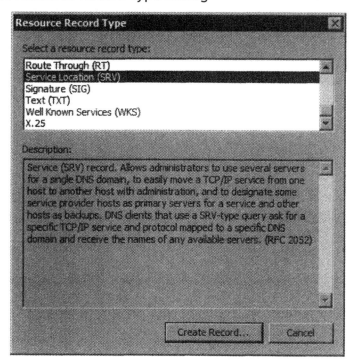

4. In the **New Resource Record** dialog box, configure the following (see Figure 5.36):

- Drop down the **Service:** box and select the desired service. We'll select _http.

- Drop down the **Protocol:** box and select the desired protocol, or accept the default for the service you chose.

- In the **Priority:** text box, leave the default if there will only be one server for this service. If more than one will be used, this box can be used to assign an initial level of priority to the servers. The accepted range is 0 to 65535, with priority being given to the lowest number. If that server does not respond, the server specified in the SRV record containing the next highest value is used. If multiple servers are configured with the same value, and it is the lowest number, the servers will be used in a random fashion unless **Weight:** is configured.

- In the **Weight:** text box, leave the default value if there will be only one server for this service, if there are multiple servers but only one with this server's assigned **Priority:**, or to specify that it should be used randomly with one or more other servers that are assigned the same **Priority:** and **Weight:** settings. Unlike the **Priority:** setting, the **Weight:** setting uses the record or records configured with higher value first.

- In the **Port number:** text box, enter the port on which the specified server is configured to respond to the service, or accept the default for the service you selected.

- In the **Host offering this service:** text box, enter the FQDN of the server. An A or AAAA record must exist for FQDN specified in this box.

- When dynamic updates are enabled, an additional option may appear on this dialog: **Allow any authenticated user to update all DNS records with the same name.** This option allows an administrator to preconfigure a record for a service host that is not yet online in such a way that the record is allowed to be overwritten dynamically later.

Figure 5.36 The Completed New Resource Record Dialog for a SRV Record

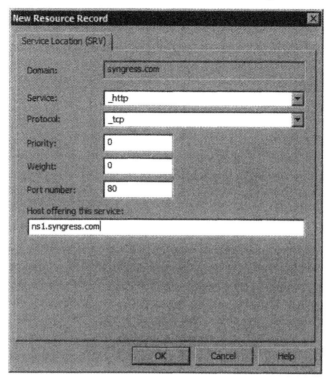

5. Click **OK** to add the record.

6. Click **Done** in the **Resource Record Type** dialog box. A new node that contains the record will appear in the zone. See Figure 5.37.

Figure 5.37 DNS Manager Displaying the New Node and SRV Record

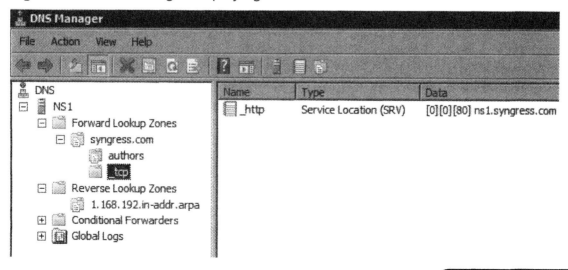

Creating CNAME Records

An Alias (CNAME) record is used when a host needs to be referred to by more than one name. You might have your email and web services running on the same server, for example. It's common for the web server to be resolvable as *www* and for mail servers to be resolvable as *mail*. If the actual configured server name for the Windows Server 2008 server hosting these services is syngress-server, the default host record in DNS may be something like syngress-server.syngress.com. CNAME records can be added so that this server can also be found as www.syngress.com and mail.syngress. com. To configure a CNAME record, follow these steps:

1. Open DNS Manager by clicking **Start | Administrative Tools | DNS**.

2. Expand the node for the server you want to configure, expand the **Forward Lookup Zones** or **Reverse Lookup Zones** node, right-click the node for the zone to which you want to add the record, and click **New Alias (CNAME)....** See Figure 5.29.

3. In the **New Resource Record** dialog box, type the alias you want to configure into the **Alias name (uses parent domain if left blank):** text box. Type the host's FQDN in the **Fully qualified domain name (FQDN) for target host:** text box, or click **Browse...** and select the server from an existing A or AAAA. See Figure 5.38.

Figure 5.38 A Completed New Resource Record Dialog for a CNAME Record

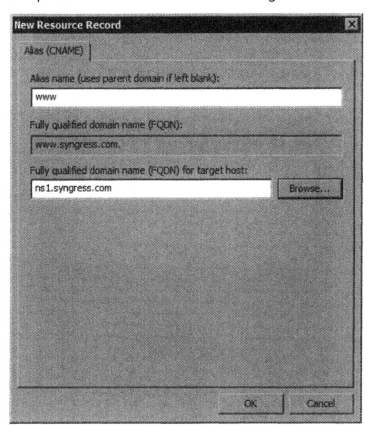

4. Click **OK** to finish adding the record.

Creating NS Records

Name server (NS) records identify DNS name servers for a zone. These records are managed differently than most others. When you specify a name server in the properties of the zone, an NS record is added for the server. To create an NS record, follow these steps:

1. Open DNS Manager by clicking **Start | Administrative Tools | DNS**.

2. Expand the node for the server you want to configure, expand the **Forward Lookup Zones** or **Reverse Lookup Zones** node, right-click the node for the zone to which you want to add the record, and click **Properties**.

3. In the **Properties** dialog box, click the **Name Servers** tab to bring it forward. See Figure 5.39.

Figure 5.39 The Name Servers Tab

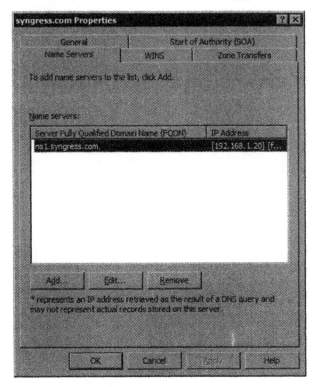

4. Click the **Add...** button.

5. In the **New Name Server Record** dialog box, type the fully qualified domain name (FQDN) in the **Server fully qualified domain name (FQDN):** text box, and click **Resolve**. If you wish to add an IP address manually, you can click **<Click here to add an IP Address>** and enter it in the text field that appears. Resolved IP addresses can also be modified by clicking them. If multiple IP addresses are configured for the record, you can determine the priority they will be used in with the **Up** and **Down** buttons. IP addresses can also be removed using the **Delete** button. See Figure 5.3.

6. Click **OK**.

7. In the Properties dialog box, click **OK**.

Configuring Windows Internet Name Service (WINS) and DNS Integration

If a DNS client queries a zone that does not have the requested record, you can configure the zone to attempt to resolve the name using WINS. WINS typically is used to resolve NetBIOS names to IPv4 addresses on Windows networks; however it is gradually being phased out. For more information on WINS, see the sections of this chapter titled "Using the New GlobalNames Zone Feature" and "Configuring Name Resolution for Client Computers". Both forward and reverse lookups can be extended to use WINS servers by modifying the zone's properties to create the appropriate DNS record. Let's examine how to create WINS Lookup and WINS Reverse Lookup records.

Creating a WINS Lookup Record

To create a WINS Lookup (WINS) record for a forward lookup zone, follow these steps:

1. Open DNS Manager by clicking **Start | Administrative Tools | DNS**.

2. Expand the node for the server you want to configure, expand the **Forward Lookup Zones** node, right-click the node for the zone to which you want to add the record, and click **Properties**.

3. In the **Properties** dialog box, click the **WINS** tab to bring it forward. See Figure 5.40.

Figure 5.40 A Configured WINS Tab

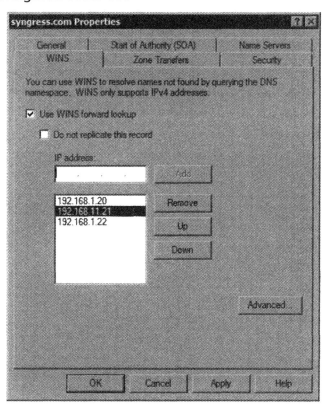

4. By default, the **Use WINS forward lookup** checkbox is not selected on the **Properties** dialog box. To enable WINS lookup and create the needed DNS record, select this option.

5. In the **IP address** area, enter the IPv4 address for a WINS server and click **Add**. If necessary, repeat this step to enter the IP address of more than one WINS server. If multiple IP addresses are configured for the record, you can determine the priority they will be used in with the **Up** and **Down** buttons. IP addresses can also be removed using the **Remove** button.

6. If you use a mix of Windows and non-Windows DNS servers, consider selecting the **Do not replicate this record** option. WINS records are not standard DNS record types and are not supported by all DNS servers. Attempting to replicate them to DNS servers that do not support them may cause errors.

7. If desired, click the **Advanced...** option to open the **Advanced** dialog box and configure the following additional options (see Figure 5.41):

   ■ **Cache time-out**. This option defines the how long the DNS server remembers any resolved names and returns them from Cache, rather than querying a WINS server again for them.

   ■ **Lookup time-out**. This option defines how long the DNS server will wait to hear from a WINS server before it tries the next one in the list on the WINS tab, or gives up if no more servers are in the list to try.

Figure 5.41 The Advanced Dialog

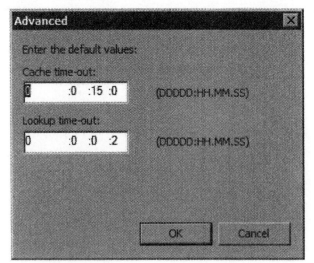

8. Click **OK**.

9. In the **Properties** dialog box, click **OK**.

10. Double-check that the appropriate WINS Lookup record has been created in DNS Manager. See Figure 5.42.

Figure 5.42 Verifying the WINS Record in DNS Manager

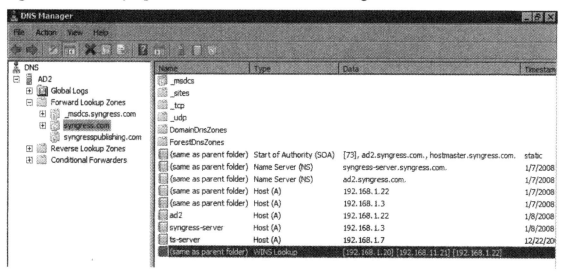

TIP

If you use a mix of Windows and non-Windows DNS servers, consider selecting the **Do not replicate this record** option. WINS records are not standard DNS record types and are not supported by all DNS servers. Attempting to replicate them to DNS servers that do not support them may cause errors.

Creating a WINS Reverse Lookup Record

To create a WINS Reverse Lookup (WINS-R) record for a reverse lookup zone, follow these steps:

1. Open DNS Manager by clicking **Start | Administrative Tools | DNS**.

2. Expand the node for the server you want to configure, the **Reverse Lookup Zones** node, right-click the node for the zone to which you want to add the record, and click **Properties**.

3. In the **Properties** dialog box, click the **WINS-R** tab to bring it forward. See Figure 5.43.

Figure 5.43 The WINS-R Tab

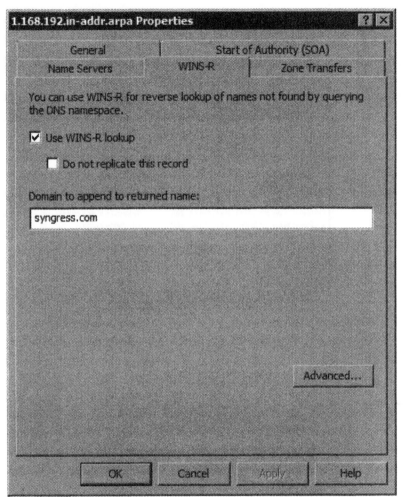

4. By default, the **Use WINS-R lookup** checkbox is not selected on the **Properties** dialog box. To enable WINS reverse lookup and create the needed DNS record, select this option.

5. In the **Domain to append to the returned name:** text box, enter the domain name that you want to have appended to the NetBIOS names returned from WINS. When responding to queries from the DNS server,

WINS servers will return NetBIOS computer names. These names will not have DNS suffixes. The suffix that you want appended is entered here.

6. If you use a mix of Windows and non-Windows DNS servers, consider selecting the **Do not replicate this record** option. WINS-R records are not standard DNS record types and are not supported by all DNS servers. Attempting to replicate them to DNS servers that do not support them may cause errors.

7. If desired, click the **Advanced…** button to open the **Advanced** dialog box and configure the following additional options (see Figure 5.44):

- **Cache time-out**. This option defines the how long the DNS server remembers any resolved names and returns them from Cache, rather than querying a WINS server again for them.

- **Lookup time-out**. This option defines how long the DNS server will wait to hear from a WINS server before it tries the next one in its list.

- **Submit DNS domain as NetBIOS scope**. The NetBIOS namespace had limited partitioning capability, loosely similar to the ability to define top-level domains in DNS. If your network uses these, and they match your DNS domains, select this option. When a lookup request is sent by a client to a DNS server, and the server cannot resolve the query using DNS, the leftmost portion of the FQDN is used as the NetBIOS computer name and the remainder is used as the NetBIOS scope.

Figure 5.44 The Advanced Dialog

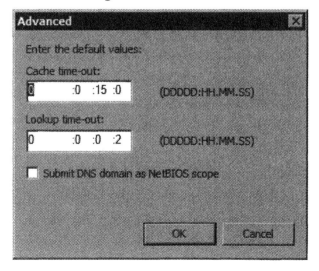

8. Click **OK**.

9. In the **Properties** dialog box, click **OK**.

10. Double-check that the appropriate WINS-R record has been created in DNS Manager. See Figure 5.45.

Figure 5.45 Verifying the WINS-R Record in DNS Manager

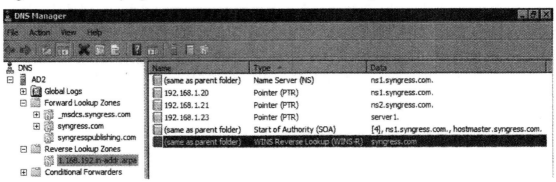

Understanding the Dynamic Domain Name System (DDNS)

Traditionally, DNS record administration had to be performed manually. In some networks with high security requirements this is still the case. Beginning with Windows 2000 Server, Microsoft implemented the ability for hosts and the DHCP network service to dynamically update and manage DNS records. The DDNS feature has remained largely unchanged since its initial release in Windows 2000 Server. In the *Creating DNS Zones* section, we examined the three options that can be specified during the creation of a new forward or reverse lookup zone. These can also be modified after the zone has been created by changing the **Dynamic updates:** option on the **General** tab of the zone's **Properties**.

The use of dynamic records creates potential problems, because hosts do not always remove their records from DNS. If a laptop is not shut down properly, for example, and is restarted on a different network it will leave an invalid DNS record behind on the DNS server for the previous network. Microsoft provides a mechanism known as aging and scavenging to deal with this issue. In this section we'll examine how to configure and use aging and scavenging.

Tɪᴘ

DDNS can conflict with data in the GlobalNames zone. If a GNZ is configured on the DNS server, it is checked first when DDNS requests are received. If a client attempts to register or update a DDNS record using a name that is already specified in the GNZ, the request will fail.

Configuring DDNS Aging and Scavenging

Administrators are responsible for defining when a record should be considered invalid and ready for deletion. Aging settings are used to determine when a record should be removed, and the scavenging process actually deletes it. There are two levels at which aging can be set, the server and the zone. Settings applied at the server level will apply to all AD integrated zones on the DNS server. Settings applied at the zone level override server level settings for AD integrated zones. You do not have to configure zone level settings for AD integrated zones. If you are using standard primary zones, however, you do have to configure aging at the zone level.

When a host or DHCP service registers a record dynamically with DNS, the record receives a timestamp. This timestamp is the foundation for the aging and scavenging process. Once established, records are updated using one of two methods. The first, a record refresh, is performed when a host checks in and lets the DNS server know that nothing has changed and the record is still valid. Most Windows 2000 and later hosts send a refresh every 24 hours. Because the time stamp is updated when a refresh occurs, AD replication (for AD integrated zones) or zone transfers (for standard zones) are triggered. To limit the amount of traffic consumed by DDNS, Microsoft allows administrators to configure a **no-refresh** interval (7 days by default). During this time the DNS server will reject refresh requests for the record.

The second type of communication that hosts and DHCP servers use to dynamically modify DNS records is the record update method. This method is used when a new host joins the network and A (or AAAA) and PTR records are created for it, when a server is promoted to become a domain controller, or when an existing record requires an IP address update. DNS record changes involving the record update method can occur at any time and are not subject to the limits imposed by the **no-refresh** interval. To configure the refresh intervals at either the server or zone level, follow these steps:

1. Open DNS Manager by clicking **Start | Administrative Tools | DNS**.

2. Select one of the following:

   ■ To manage server level aging and scavenging, in the left pane right-click the server node and select **Set Aging/Scavenging for All Zones....**.

   ■ To manage zone level aging and scavenging, in the left pane expand the server, expand either the **Forward Lookup Zones** or **Reverse Lookup Zones** node, right-click the zone you want to configure, and click **Properties**. On the **General** tab, click the **Aging** button.

3. In the **Aging/Scavenging Properties** dialog that appears, select the **Scavenge stale resource records** box. See Figure 5.46.

Figure 5.46 The Server Aging/Scavenging Properties Dialog

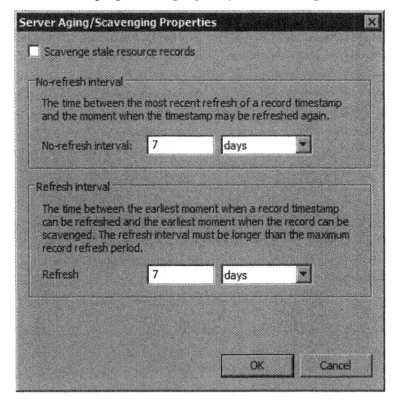

4. Configure the following options:

    ■ **No-refresh interval**. This setting controls when the DNS server rejects refresh requests from hosts and the DHCP service. Most Windows hosts attempt to refresh their records every 24 hours. The DHCP service attempts updates at 50% of the IP address lease time. This option is used to limit the amount of replication traffic required for records that do not change. The default of seven days is acceptable for most networks.

    ■ **Refresh**. This option determines when a DDNS record can be flagged for scavenging (deletion). The default value is seven days. By default, records that are older than the sum of the **no-refresh** and **refresh** intervals will be available for scavenging. This value must be set to a value that is less than the maximum setting for clients to refresh their records. The default is acceptable for most networks; however if you modify your DHCP addresses leases to longer than 14 days, you may want to consider updating this setting to 50% of the configured lease time.

5. Click **OK**.

Enabling Automatic Scavenging

Scavenging is not automatic by default. If you have configured the previous settings, records that exceed the **refresh** interval will be marked only as available for scavenging. To enable automatic scavenging, follow these steps:

1. Open DNS Manager by clicking **Start | Administrative Tools | DNS**.

2. In the left pane right-click the server node, select **Properties**, and click the **Advanced** tab.

3. Select the **Enable automatic scavenging of stale records** box and configure the desired interval, as shown in Figure 5.47.

Figure 5.47 Enabling Automatic Scavenging

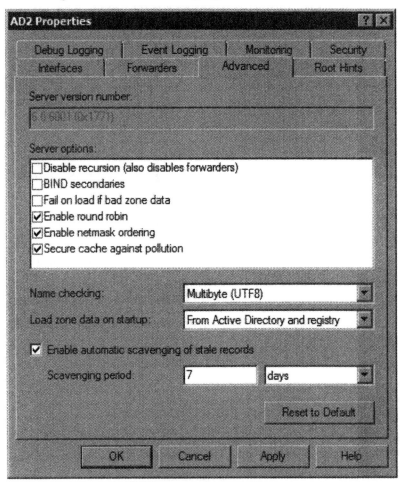

Initiating Manual Scavenging

You can manually initiate the scavenging procedure at any time by following these steps:

1. Open DNS Manager by clicking **Start | Administrative Tools | DNS**.

2. In the left pane right-click the server node and select **Scavenge Stale Resource Records**. See Figure 5.48.

Figure 5.48 Manually Initiating Scavenging

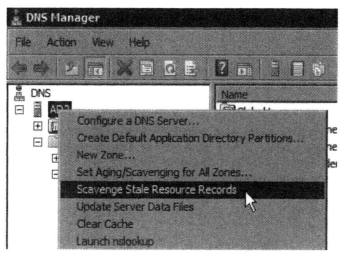

Configuring Name Resolution for Client Computers

There are two primary forms of naming on Windows networks, NetBIOS and host names. NetBIOS name resolution goes back to the early days of Windows. Recent server releases from Microsoft have increasingly moved away from it toward DNS. If a network runs a variety of Windows client and server versions, it's important that both forms of name resolution are configured properly. If the network is comprised primarily of Windows XP and later clients, and Windows Server 2003 and later servers, DNS is most likely supporting many of the network's name resolution needs. In this section, we'll examine how to configure client settings for the maximum name resolution flexibility by examining the options contained in the advanced properties of a Window's Vista client's TCP/IP settings. To access these settings follow this procedure:

1. Click **Start** | **Control Panel** | **Network and Sharing Center** | **Manage network connections**.

2. In the **Network Connections** window's **General** tab, right-click the network connection you want to configure and select **Properties**.

3. In the **Local Area Connection Properties** dialog, select **Internet Protocol Version 4 (TCP/IPv4)** and click **Properties**. See Figure 5.49.

Figure 5.49 The Local Area Connection Properties Dialog

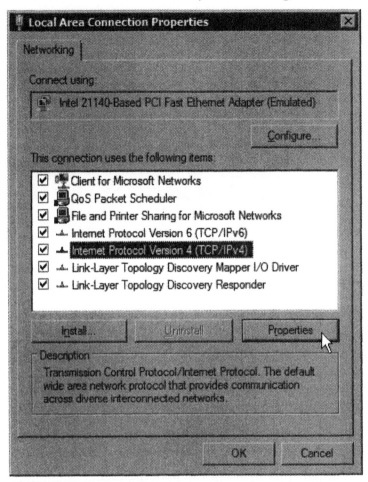

4. In the **Internet Protocol Version 4 (TCP/IPv4) Properties** dialog box, click the **Advanced...** button. See Figure 5.50.

Figure 5.50 The Internet Protocol Version 4 (TCP/IPv4) Properties Dialog

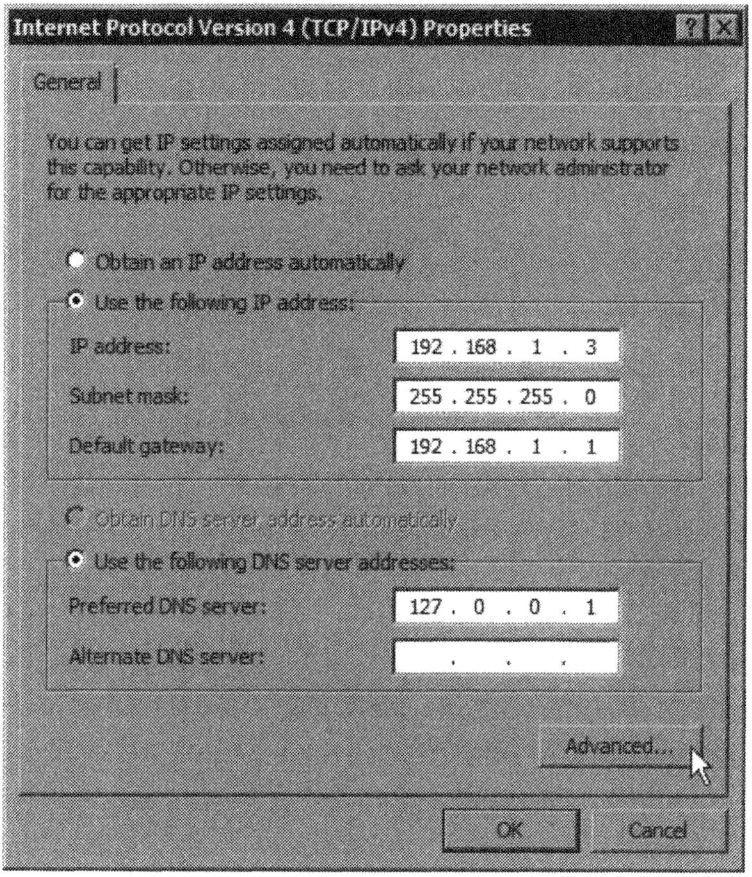

How Name Resolution
Works in Windows XP and Later

Although some integration is possible, the NetBIOS and host name resolution methods are very different. Host names are used when a client attempts to use user friendly names (instead of IP addresses) with a TCP/IP utility such as ping, an FTP client, or a web browser. By default, the following name resolution steps are taken when resolving host names: the local host name => the local DNS resolver cache => the local HOSTS file => DNS => the local NetBIOS name cache => WINS => a local network broadcast => the local LMHOSTS file. Additional configuration is needed for all steps to be applied. You must have the address of at least one WINS server configured in the network client properties, for example. In addition, some steps can be reordered such as checking the LMHOSTS file before sending a network broadcast.

Not all utilities and programs within Windows use host names. For example, if you open the **Start | Run** dialog and attempt to remotely connect to a Windows computer using a command such as **servername\sharename**, NetBIOS name resolution will be used. By default, the following name resolution steps are taken when resolving NetBIOS names: the local NetBIOS name cache => WINS => a local network broadcast => the LMHOSTS file => the local host name => the local DNS resolver cache => DNS. Just as with host name resolution, additional configuration is needed for all steps to be used and some can be reordered. Let's examine how to configure the various components of name resolution on a Windows Vista computer.

Configuring the DNS Server List

You can specify one or more DNS servers for a Windows Vista computer to use. When attempting to resolve a DNS query, the servers will be contacted in the order they appear in the list. If a DNS server is contacted successfully, no other DNS servers in the list are queried even if the initial DNS server was unable to resolve the query successfully. The following procedure can be used to configure or manage a list of one or more DNS server:

1. Click **Start | Control Panel | Network and Sharing Center | Manage network connections**.

2. In the **Network Connections** window's **General** tab, right-click the network connection you want to configure and select **Properties**.

3. In the **Local Area Connection Properties** dialog, select **Internet Protocol Version 4 (TCP/IPv4)** and click **Properties**.

4. In the **Internet Protocol Version 4 (TCP/IPv4) Properties** dialog box, click the **Advanced...** button.

5. In the **Advanced TCP/IP Settings** dialog box, click the **DNS** tab to bring it to the foreground.

6. In the **DNS server addresses, in order of use:** section of the page, do one or more of the following (see Figure 5.51):

   ■ Reorder the existing name servers by placing the first one you want used at the top of the list, the second one in the second position on the list, and so forth. To accomplish this, select the name server you wish to reorder and use the up or down arrows to place it in the desired position.

- Add new name servers to the list. To accomplish this, click the **Add...** button and enter the IP address of the new DNS server in the **TCP/IP DNS Server** dialog box, then click **Add**.

- Edit the IP address of an existing server in the list. To accomplish this, click the **Edit...** button, make the desired change in the **TCP/IP DNS Server** dialog box, then click **OK**.

- Remove a DNS server from the list. To accomplish this, select the server you want to remove from the list and click the **Remove** button.

Figure 5.51 The DNS Tab

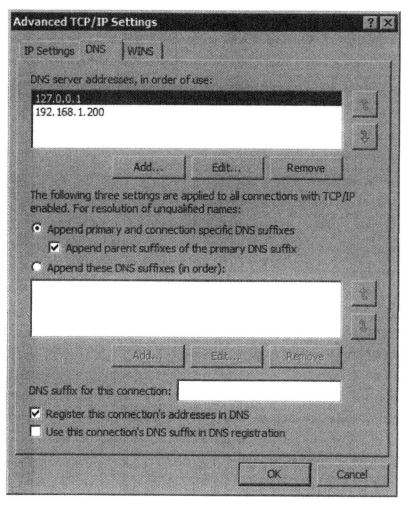

Configuring the Suffix Search Order

Users don't always type in a fully qualified domain name when attempting to access DNS based resources. For example, your company may have an intranet site that users access by typing **http://companyweb**. Because this is not a FQDN, a name like this is not resolvable. You can configure the DNS suffix search order in Windows Vista to convert a typed name like the earlier example into a FQDN, so that users do not have to type a fully qualified domain name. This can make resources, such as the intranet site name in our example, much easier for users to remember and access. The following procedure can be used to configure or manage the suffix search order:

1. Click **Start | Control Panel | Network and Sharing Center | Manage network connections**.

2. In the **Network Connections** window's **General** tab, right-click the network connection you want to configure and select **Properties**.

3. In the **Local Area Connection Properties** dialog, select **Internet Protocol Version 4 (TCP/IPv4)** and click **Properties**.

4. In the **Internet Protocol Version 4 (TCP/IPv4) Properties** dialog box, click the **Advanced...** button.

5. In the **Advanced TCP/IP Settings** dialog box, click the **DNS** tab to bring it to the foreground and select one of the following options (see Figure 5.51):

   ■ **Append primary and connection specific DNS suffixes**. When this option is selected, the primary DNS suffix is appended to the name the user types, such as our **companyweb** example. The primary DNS suffix for a Windows Vista computer is configured as part of its computer name. If the workstation is configured with a network identity of *workstation1. authors.syngress.com*, its primary domain is *authors.syngress.com*. The computer will attempt to resolve the name **compnayweb.authors.syngress. com**. If a host with this name cannot be located, and the **Append parent suffixes of the primary DNS suffix** option is selected, the parent of the **author** domain, **syngress.com**, will be appended and tried next (**companyweb.syngress.com**). Finally, if a connection-specific DNS suffix is configured, it will be tried. This suffix is configured on this DNS tab in the **DNS suffix for this connection:** text box.

- **Append these DNS suffixes (in order)**. This option allows you to specify a list of specific DNS suffixes to append, and does not try to append the primary or connection specific suffixes. You create a list by adding new entries using the **Add...** button, and can edit existing entries using the **Edit...** button. Entries can be removed using the **Remove** button. If you have specified more than one suffix, they will be tried in order. The order the list is in can be modified by selecting an individual suffix and using the up or down arrow buttons to place it in the desired list position. When used for resolution, the first suffix is used. If a host cannot be found that matches the host name plus the name of the first suffix, a second resolution request occurs involving the second suffix, and so forth.

Configuring the HOSTS File

The HOSTS file resides on all Windows computers and can be manually modified by administrators. In Windows Vista and Server 2008, the HOSTS file supports both IPv4 and IPv6 addresses. The default HOSTS file for Windows Vista and Server 2008, seen in Figure 5.52, contains the loopback addresses for both IPv4 (127.0.0.1) and IPv6 (::1) by default.

Figure 5.52 The HOSTS File

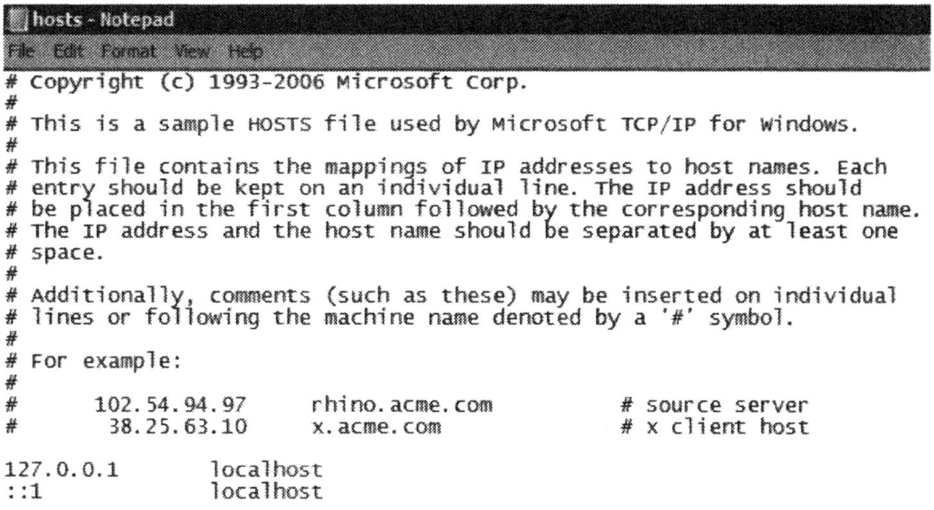

```
hosts - Notepad
File  Edit  Format  View  Help
# Copyright (c) 1993-2006 Microsoft Corp.
#
# This is a sample HOSTS file used by Microsoft TCP/IP for Windows.
#
# This file contains the mappings of IP addresses to host names. Each
# entry should be kept on an individual line. The IP address should
# be placed in the first column followed by the corresponding host name.
# The IP address and the host name should be separated by at least one
# space.
#
# Additionally, comments (such as these) may be inserted on individual
# lines or following the machine name denoted by a '#' symbol.
#
# For example:
#
#      102.54.94.97     rhino.acme.com          # source server
#       38.25.63.10     x.acme.com              # x client host

127.0.0.1       localhost
::1             localhost
```

Table 5.3 shows some sample HOSTS file entries. More detailed information is available in Windows Help and Microsoft's online documentation.

Table 5.3 Common LMHOSTS Entries

LMHOSTS Entry	Effect
192.168.2.1 Server1.syngress.com #Major server	This is a basic HOSTS file entry. When the HOSTS file is examined for the host name Server1.syngress.com, the IP address 192.168.2.1 will be returned. In this case, the text after the # sign is a comment inserted by an administrator.
192.168.2.1 Server1.syngress.com DNS.syngress.com #Major server	This entry adds an alias to the primary host name. It will resolve both Server1.syngress.com and DNS.syngress.com.

Configuring the NetBIOS Node Type

With Windows Vista, there are several ways that NetBIOS name resolution can occur. The NetBIOS node type determines the order in which these name resolution methods are used. The following methods can be used for NetBIOS name resolution:

- **Local NetBIOS computer name**. This method of name resolution examines the local computer name to see if it matches the name of the computer with which communication is being attempted.

- **Local NetBIOS cache**. When successful NetBIOS name resolution occurs, entries are cached for a variable period, usually around 10 minutes. This method of name resolution examines this cache to see if the name of the computer with which communication is being attempted is contained in it.

- **Broadcast**. This method sends a broadcast out on the local network segment. Some routers can be configured to pass these NetBIOS messages to other segments, but typically this setting is not used because of the increase in network traffic it causes. If the computer with which communication is being attempted is within broadcast range, it will communicate back in peer-to-peer fashion and complete the name resolution process.

- **WINS server**. This method of name resolution uses WINS or NetBIOS name servers for name resolution. More information about this option is available in the *Configuring the WINS Server List* section.

- **LMHOSTS file**. Each Windows Vista computer contains a LMHOSTS file. You can enter NetBIOS names and their matching IP addresses in this file. When this type of name resolution is used, the local system checks this file to see if it contains a match for the computer with which communication is being attempted. More information about this option is available in the *Configuring the LMHOSTS File* section.

These five name resolution methods are not specified individually. Microsoft groups them into four possible configurations, known as NetBIOS node types:

- **B-Node or Broadcast Node**. In Microsoft's version of B-Node resolution, the workstation first checks its local NetBIOS name cache. If this fails it sends a broadcast. Finally, it checks the LMHOSTS file. This is the default node type if no WINS server is configured.

- **P-Node or Point-to-Point Node**. This name resolution method only queries a WINS or NetBIOS name server.

- **M-Node or Mixed Node**. This name resolution method uses B-Node followed by P-Node.

- **H-Node or Hybrid Node**. This is the default node type if at least one WINS server is configured on the client. The name resolution order for this node type is similar to a combination of P-Node followed by B-Node. Each step is tried individually, and resolution stops when one is successful:

  - The local NetBIOS name is checked

  - The local NetBIOS cache is checked

  - WINS is queried

  - A broadcast is sent

  - LMHOSTS file is checked

  - If all attempts at name resolution fail, host name resolution will be attempted for the name using the HOSTS file and DNS.

Most networks use DHCP to assign client networking information, including the NetBIOS note type. In this section, we examine the possible settings and how to configure it manually on a Windows Vista computer. Follow these steps to locally configure the NetBIOS node type for a Windows Vista computer:

1. Click **Start | Run...**.

2. In the **Run** dialog box, type **regedit** and click **OK**.

3. In the left pane, expand **HKEY_LOCAL_MACHINE**.

4. Expand **SYSTEM**.

5. Expand **CurrentControlSet**.

6. Expand **Services**.

7. Expand **Netbt**.

8. Select **Parameters**.

9. On the Edit menu, select **New**, then click **DWORD (32-bit) Value**.

10. In the right pane, type **NodeType** where indicated and press **ENTER**.

11. In the right pane, right-click **NodeType**, and click **Modify...**.

12. In the **Edit DWORD (32-bit) Value** dialog box, type the desired value:

    - For B-Node type: 1

    - For P-Node type: 2

    - For M-Node type: 4

    - For H-Node type: 8

13. Click **OK**.

Configuring the WINS Server List

If your network uses WINS for NetBIOS name resolution, you can configure a Windows Vista client to use one or more WINS server(s). Clients register their computer name and some of the services they provide with a WINS server. They also query WINS servers when this type of information is needed regarding other computers on the network. Typically, Windows servers are configured by administrators to provide WINS server services to clients. Follow these steps to configure Windows Vista to use one or more WINS server(s):

1. Click **Start | Control Panel | Network and Sharing Center | Manage network connections**.

2. In the **Network Connections** window's **General** tab, right-click the network connection you want to configure and select **Properties**.

3. In the **Local Area Connection Properties** dialog, select **Internet Protocol Version 4 (TCP/IPv4)** and click **Properties**.

4. In the **Internet Protocol Version 4 (TCP/IPv4) Properties** dialog box, click the **Advanced...** button.

5. In the **Advanced TCP/IP Settings** dialog box, click the **WINS** tab to bring it to the foreground.

6. In the **WINS addresses, in order of use:** section of the page, do one or more of the following (see Figure 5.53):

   ■ Reorder the existing WINS servers by placing the first one you want used at the top of the list, the second one in the second position on the list, and so forth. To accomplish this, select the name server you wish to reorder and use the up or down arrows to place it in the desired position.

   ■ Add new WINS servers to the list. To accomplish this, click the **Add...** button and enter the IP address of the new WINS server in the **TCP/IP WINS Server** dialog box, then click **Add**.

   ■ Edit the IP address of an existing server in the list. To accomplish this, click the **Edit...** button, make the desired change in the **TCP/IP WINS Server** dialog box, then click **OK**.

   ■ Remove a DNS server from the list. To accomplish this, select the WINS server you want to remove from the list and click the **Remove** button.

Figure 5.53 The WINS Tab

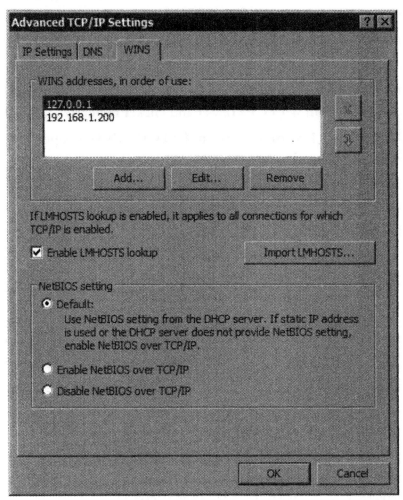

Configuring the LMHOSTS File

The LMHOSTS file can be enabled, disabled, and manually modified by administrators. To enable or disable the LMHOSTS file, use the **Enable LMHOSTS lookup** option on the **WINS** tab in the client's **Advanced TCP/IP Settings** dialog box (see Figure 5.53). By default, use of the LMHOSTS file is enabled. A sample file is provided by Microsoft. It is located in the *C:\WINDOWS\system32\drivers\etc* directory, and is named LMHOSTS.SAM. To make the file functional, the SAM file extension must be removed. Several configuration options exist, as can be seen by part of the included help text that is visible in Figure 5.54.

Figure 5.54 The LMHOSTS File

```
lmhosts.sam - Notepad
File  Edit  Format  View  Help
# Copyright (c) 1993-1999 Microsoft Corp.
#
# This is a sample LMHOSTS file used by the Microsoft TCP/IP for Windows.
#
# This file contains the mappings of IP addresses to computernames
# (NetBIOS) names.  Each entry should be kept on an individual line.
# The IP address should be placed in the first column followed by the
# corresponding computername. The address and the computername
# should be separated by at least one space or tab. The "#" character
# is generally used to denote the start of a comment (see the exceptions
# below).
#
# This file is compatible with Microsoft LAN Manager 2.x TCP/IP lmhosts
# files and offers the following extensions:
#
#      #PRE|
#      #DOM:<domain>
#      #INCLUDE <filename>
#      #BEGIN_ALTERNATE
#      #END_ALTERNATE
#      \0xnn (non-printing character support)
#
# Following any entry in the file with the characters "#PRE" will cause
# the entry to be preloaded into the name cache. By default, entries are
# not preloaded, but are parsed only after dynamic name resolution fails.
#
# Following an entry with the "#DOM:<domain>" tag will associate the
# entry with the domain specified by <domain>. This affects how the
# browser and logon services behave in TCP/IP environments. To preload
# the host name associated with #DOM entry, it is necessary to also add a
# #PRE to the line. The <domain> is always preloaded although it will not
# be shown when the name cache is viewed.
#
# Specifying "#INCLUDE <filename>" will force the RFC NetBIOS (NBT)
# software to seek the specified <filename> and parse it as if it were
# local. <filename> is generally a UNC-based name, allowing a
# centralized lmhosts file to be maintained on a server.
# It is ALWAYS necessary to provide a mapping for the IP address of the
# server prior to the #INCLUDE. This mapping must use the #PRE directive.
```

Table 5.4 shows some sample LMHOSTS file entries. More detailed information is available by examining a LMHOSTS.SAM file and viewing the comments it contains, as well as Windows Help and Microsoft's online documentation.

Table 5.4 Common LMHOSTS Entries

LMHOSTS Entry	Effect
192.168.2.1 Server1 #Major server	This is a basic LMHOSTS file entry. When the LMHOSTS file is examined for the NetBIOS name Server1, the IP address 192.168.2.1 will be returned. In this case, the text after the # sign is a comment inserted by an administrator. Comments can consist of any text, as long as they do not contain a command such as #PRE or #DOM.

Continued

Table 5.4 Continued. Common LMHOSTS Entries

LMHOSTS Entry	Effect
192.168.2.1 Server1 #PRE #Major server	This entry preloads the entry into the NetBIOS name cache. Because the name and IP are present in the cache, the LMHOSTS file does not have to be checked for this NetBIOS name to be resolved.
192.168.2.1 Server1 #PRE #DOM:Syngress	In addition to the preceding, this entry also identifies Server1 as a domain controller for the Syngress domain.

Understanding Link-Local Multicast Name Resolution (LLMNR)

Link-Local Multicast Name Resolution, also known as multicast DNS (mDNS), is a new protocol in Windows Vista and Server 2008. If these are the primary operating systems in use and hosts on a segment of the network are unable to contact a DNS server, some name resolution can still take place on a peer-to-peer basis. LLMNR is also designed to allow for host name resolution on single-segment networks that do not have DNS servers, such as very small home or office networks. Ordinarily NetBIOS name resolution is enabled by default and will handle name resolution in situations like this; however NetBIOS supports only IPv4. LLMNR works with both IPv4 and IPv6, ensuring that host name resolution can occur regardless of the version of IP in use on the network.

Managing Client Settings by Using Group Policy

A number of client DNS settings can be controlled using group policy, including those shown in Table 5.5. Generally, settings applied at the group policy level override manually configured settings on the host. This not only makes client configuration using GPOs more convenient, but also helps to ensure that settings cannot be changed at the workstations.

Table 5.5 Client DNS Group Policy Settings

Setting
Allow DNS Suffix Appending to Unqualified Multi-Label Name Queries
Connection-Specific DNS Suffix
DNS Servers
Primary DNS Suffix
Register DNS records with connection-specific DNS suffix
Register PTR Records
Dynamic Update
Replace Addresses In Conflicts
Registration Refresh Interval
TTL Set in the A and PTR records
DNS Suffix Search List
Update Security Level
Update Top Level Domain Zones
Primary DNS Suffix Devolution
Turn off Multicast Name Resolution

Configuring & Implementing...

Using Group Poicy to configure DNS settings

In this exercise you will use group policy to configure the DNS servers that will be assigned to Windows XP Professional workstations. You need to have an active directory domain and domain-level administrator access. To configure a DNS setting using group policy, follow these steps:

1. Open the GPO that will be used using the Group Policy Management Editor and navigate to Computer Configuration | Policies | Administrative Templates | Network | DNS Client as shown in Figure 5.55.

2. In the **Group Policy Management Editor**, right-click **DNS Servers** and select **Properties** (see Figure 5.55).

Continued

Figure 5.55 The Group Policy Management Editor

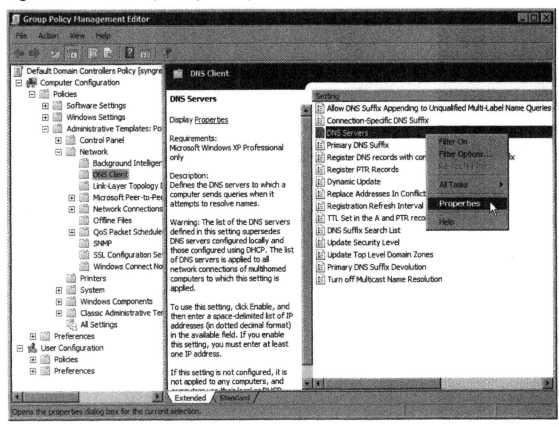

3. Each of the DNS group policy settings has slightly different configuration options, and these settings can often appear deceiving. This option configures the DNS servers the client will query during name resolution. At first glance it appears that only one can be entered, however the **Explain** tab makes it clear that multiple entries are supported in the single box, as long as they are separated by a space. In the **DNS Servers Properties** dialog, enter the IP address of one or more DNS server(s) in the **IP Addresses:** text box and click **OK** (see Figure 5.56).

Continued

Figure 5.56 The Properties Tab

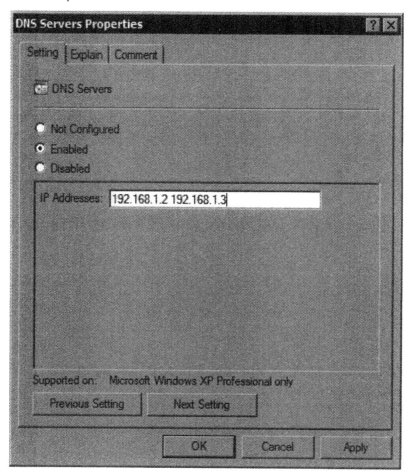

4. Close the Group Policy Management Editor.

Summary

DNS allows hosts and services to be located on IP networks using user-friendly, fully qualified domain names instead of IP addresses. When a user attempts to access a Web site, for example, their local DNS resolver first checks its cache followed by the local host file to see if the address of the web server is stored locally. If it isn't, the resolver then contacts a DNS server using a client-to-server query. This type of query requests an answer that either provides the needed information or informs the client that the information cannot be located. If the DNS server that the client contacts has the information, it is returned to the client. If not, the DNS server initiates a server-to-server query and asks another DNS server for any assistance it can provide. This server-to-server query is sent to the root hints that are configured on the DNS server.

The server contacted may return an answer that no information is available, at which point a negative response is sent back to the client. However, if the server contacted has the needed information, or information about one or more other DNS servers that could be of assistance in resolving the query, that information will be returned to the requesting DNS server. This process continues until the information is located, or it becomes clear that the client's query will not be resolvable. Both positive and negative responses to queries are cached for a period of time on the original DNS server, as well as the client.

You can make any Windows Server 2008 host a DNS server by installing the DNS Server role. The default installation creates a caching only DNS server with root hints that point to the Internet's root servers. You can separate all or a portion of your DNS infrastructure from the Internet by designating private, internal DNS servers as root hints DNS servers. Generally these should be the DNS servers that are at the top of the organization.

Forwarding can be used instead of root hints when a DNS server needs to contact other DNS servers to resolve a query. When a DNS server sends a query to a forwarder, the query is similar to a client-to-server query in that it asks the receiving server to do all the work and return only a complete answer to the query. This can be used to minimize the bandwidth involved in recursive queries on portions of an organization's network. Server level forwarding sends all queries to a single DNS server or set of servers. Conditional forwarding can be used to forward resolution requests to other DNS servers based on specific domain names.

Zones represent the physical partitioning of the DNS namespace. They store the records for one or more domains or subdomains. Forward lookup zones resolve host and service names to IP addresses, and reverse lookup zones resolve IP addresses into names. Primary zones can be changed, and secondary zones are read-only copies. Standard primary zones are traditional zones with a single server that can accept changes. AD integrated zones are exclusive to Windows 2000 Server and later, can be used only on domain controllers, and support multiple primary copies of a zone database for fault tolerance.

A master zone is any zone that a secondary or stub zone transfers records from, and can include standard primary, AD integrated, and standard secondary zones. Secondary zones transfer records via file transfer across the network. The SOA record is used to configure the interval that secondary servers use when checking for updates. Domain controllers replicate AD integrated zone information using AD directory services. These transfers are much more secure and efficient than standard zone transfers. Stub zones are a special form of read-only zone that contains the name server records for a zone. They use standard zone transfers to copy these records from a master zone.

Windows Server 2008 includes a new zone type, the GlobalNames zone. GNZs support the transition away from WINS by integrating single name resolution into DNS. Unlike WINS, GNZs support IPv6 addressing. Only Windows Server 2008 DNS servers support GNZs, and the feature must be enabled manually on each server. GNZs store static CNAME records that correspond to single name records such as NetBIOS names.

Windows Server 2008's DNS Server role is a fully compliant DNS server, with some extensions such as the GNZs to provide additional support on Windows networks. Records can be administered manually, updated automatically by hosts, or both. All standard DNS record types are supported including A, AAAA, PTR, MX, SRV, CNAME, and NS. Dynamic DNS can be used to allow hosts and DHCP servers to automatically add and modify DNS host and PTR records. When DDNS is used with AD integrated zones, additional record level security can be specified to prevent unauthorized changes to dynamic records. The aging and scavenging feature can be used to clean up DDNS records that have not been updated or refreshed within a given period and may be invalid. Scavenging can be done manually or configured to occur automatically.

There are two primary forms of naming on Windows networks, NetBIOS and host names. Recent operating system releases from Microsoft increasingly have moved away from NetBIOS toward DNS. If a network runs a variety of Windows client and server versions, it's important that both forms of name resolution are configured properly. If the network is comprised primarily of Windows XP and later clients, and Windows server 2003 and later servers, DNS is most likely supporting many of the network's name resolution needs. Although some integration is possible, the NetBIOS and host name resolution methods are very different. By default, the following name resolution steps are taken when resolving host names: the local host name => the local DNS resolver cache => the local HOSTS file => DNS => the local NetBIOS name cache => WINS => a local network broadcast => the local LMHOSTS file. By default, the following name resolution steps are taken when resolving NetBIOS names: the local NetBIOS name cache => WINS => a local network broadcast => the LMHOSTS file => the local host name => the local DNS resolver cache => DNS. Regardless of the resolution type, additional configuration is needed for all steps to be applied. Administrators have considerable control over all components involved in the process.

Solutions Fast Track

An Introduction to the Domain Name System (DNS)

- ☑ DNS allows hosts and services to be located on IP networks using friendly names instead of IP addresses.

- ☑ DNS can be used to resolve public FQDNs, or used privately by organizations that wish to use its features while remaining isolated from the Internet.

- ☑ DNS uses an incremental query process involving client-to-server and server-to-server queries to resolve names and IP addresses.

Configuring a DNS Server

- ☑ When the DNS Server role is installed, a caching only DNS server is created.

- ☑ Root hints tell a DNS server where to look next when resolving queries for records not contained in locally stored zones.

- ☑ Forwarding can be used instead of root hints. Server forwarding typically involves an organization's internal DNS servers' forwarding requests for public name resolution to a DNS server that has direct access to the Internet. Conditional for-warding allows administrators to configure DNS servers to forward resolution requests to other DNS servers based on specific domain names.

Configuring DNS Zones

- ☑ Forward lookup zones resolve host names to IP addresses. Reverse look up zones resolve IP addresses to host names.

- ☑ DNS records can be changed on primary and AD integrated zones, but not on secondary or stub zones.

- ☑ Zone delegation allows a domain name space to be divided among different zones on separate servers.

- ☑ The new GlobalNames feature supports single name resolutions (such as NetBIOS computer names) on IPv6 networks using DNS.

Configuring and Managing Standard DNS Replication

- ☑ By default, primary, AD integrated and secondary zones limit the servers from which they can accept zone transfer requests.

- ☑ Administrators can manually request incremental zone updates or a complete refresh of all zone records for secondary zones using DNS Manager.

- ☑ The SOA zone record is used to configure the replication parameters for secondary zones.

Configuring DNS Records

- ☑ DNS records can be administered manually, updated automatically by hosts, or both.

- ☑ DNS record types include A, AAAA, PTR, MX, SRV, CNAME, and NS.

- ☑ Aging and scavenging is used to clean up DDNS records that have not been updated or refreshed within a given period and may be invalid.

Configuring Name Resolution for Client Computers

- ☑ Two primary forms of name resolution exist on Windows networks: NetBIOS and host names. Microsoft increasingly has moved away from NetBIOS toward DNS. If a network runs a variety of Windows client and server versions, it's important that both forms of name resolution are configured properly. If the network is comprised primarily of Windows XP and later clients, and Windows Server 2003 and later servers, DNS is most likely supporting many of the network's name resolution needs.

☑ By default, the following name resolution steps are taken when resolving host names: the local host name => the local DNS resolver cache => the local HOSTS file => DNS => the local NetBIOS name cache => WINS => a local network broadcast => the local LMHOSTS file.

☑ By default, the following name resolution steps are taken when resolving NetBIOS names: the local NetBIOS name cache => WINS => a local network broadcast => the LMHOSTS file => the local host name => the local DNS resolver cache => DNS.

☑ Regardless of the resolution type, additional configuration is needed for all steps to be applied. Administrators have considerable control over all components involved in the process.

Frequently Asked Questions

Q: What exactly is DNS and why do I need it?

A: DNS is the primary name resolution method for Windows Server 2008, making it essential to a properly functioning domain and network. It provides hosts with the actual network location of network services and other hosts. It also can be used to determine host and service information when an IP address is provided. Computers cannot find themselves using most key components of Windows Server 2008 without DNS.

Q: My organization does not wish to connect to the Internet. We are using Windows Server 2008 and Windows Vista DNS is essential for name resolution. I know that DNS was designed to work with the Internet; what can I do?

A: Although DNS originally was designed for use with the Internet and its predecessors, it is no problem to use it privately. In fact, if you have an Active Directory domain, it will be required. In this scenario you will create and configure a separate DNS environment that is very similar to the Internet, except you will control all levels of it instead of just a tiny portion.

Q: I need to specify a totally private DNS server network for my organization. How should I configure root hints?

A: When root hints don't need to point to the Internet's root name servers, typically they should point to the highest level DNS servers within an organization. A good way to think about root hints is that they are designed to point to the top of whatever DNS hierarchy is being used.

Q: I want to use forwarding, but don't want all queries to go to the same place. I need to distribute them based on the domain being asked for; how can I do this in Windows Server 2008?

A: Conditional forwarding can be used to distribute queries to forwarders based on the domain being requested.

Q: Domains and zones are very confusing to me. What is the difference between a domain and a zone?

A: Because zones use domain names, it's easy to get confused. Zones hold the actual records for part of the domain namespace. A domain like syngress.com. has records distributed across several zones. The root name servers hold the "."

Portion, which is typically hidden from users at the end of the domain name. The ".com" name servers hold the zone for this portion of the namespace. Finally a server managed by the organization contains a zone for the "syngress" portion of the DNS namespace.

Q: Does Microsoft recommend standard or AD integrated zones? Why?

A: Microsoft recommends AD integrated zones. The records are stored in the AD database, which increases their security and allows for more efficient replication of the records when compared to traditional zone transfers. Using AD integrated zones also enables secure DDNS, which eases the burden of DNS administration without compromising security.

Q: My organization is implementing IPv6. Right now we use both DNS and WINS for name resolution. WINS supports only IPv4. What can I do to support NetBIOS type names for IPv6?

A: Microsoft's new GlobalNames feature can be used. When activated, DNS servers can serve manually created single name records. You can create these records to match important NetBIOS resource names, such as key servers.

Q: What is the difference between an A and AAAA host record?

A: The Windows Server 2008 DNS Server role fully supports IPv4 and IPv6. The A host record is one of the oldest in DNS and is used to resolve a host name to an IPv4 address. The newer AAAA record is used to resolve a host name to an IPv6 address.

Q: What is a PTR record used for?

A: PTR, or pointer, records are the primary records used in reverse lookup zones. These records facilitate the resolution of IP addresses into host names.

Q: My office has a lot of sales people that work on laptops in and out of the office. I've noticed that there are quite a few inaccurate DDNS records being left behind by these computers. What can be done about it?

A: Microsoft's aging and scavenging feature can be used to clean up records such as these. You can set your organization's Windows 2000 and later DNS servers to delete records automatically if they have not been kept up to date.

Q: Most of the name resolution on my network uses DNS, however all clients are still configured for WINS. When a client attempts to access a resource by using the resource's host name, what steps may occur?

A: By default, the following name resolution steps are taken when resolving host names: the local host name => the local DNS resolver cache => the local HOSTS file => DNS => the local NetBIOS name cache => WINS => a local network broadcast => the local LMHOSTS file. All these steps are at least partially configurable by an administrator.

Q: My environment uses IPv6 addresses, but NetBIOS broadcasts are supported only for IPv4. What can I do?

A: Microsoft has included a new protocol in Windows Vista and Server 2008 to solve this problem: Link-Local Multicast Name Resolution. If these are the primary operating systems in use and hosts on a segment of the network are unable to contact a DNS server, some name resolution can still take place on a peer-to-peer basis using either IPv4 or IPv6.

Q: I'm responsible for several hundred Windows XP and Vista clients. Is there an easy way to automate their DNS configuration?

A: Many DNS settings can be managed centrally using group policy. In most cases, settings applied with group policy will override settings that are configured manually on the client. Not all settings work with all client types, however. It's important to carefully read the description of each to determine how and where it can be applied.

## Chapter 6

Configuring Network Access

Solutions in this chapter:

- Configuring Routing
- Configuring Remote Access
- Configuring Wireless Access

☑ Summary

☑ Solutions Fast Track

☑ Frequently Asked Questions

Introduction

Organizations rely on networking and communications to meet the challenging requirements necessary to compete in the global marketplace. All members of these organizations need to have constant access to the files. This requires the ability to connect to the network wherever they may be and from any device that they have available to them at the time. In addition, those outside the vendor's network will require the ability to interact smoothly with the key resources they require. Partners and clients want to be able to also conduct quick and fluid transactions through the network. Security is more important than ever in networking, due to the constant threat of infiltration and exposure to the Internet. Successfully navigating all of these concerns relies on the knowledge of how to configure network access efficiently and provide the most secure yet accessible connection possible to your organization and its members.

As an administrator, you must accommodate these needs using the latest and most practical tools in your arsenal. To help accomplish this there have been a number of networking and communications enhancements made to Windows Server 2008 to address connectivity. This will help you to improve the ease of use, reliability, management, and security of your organization's assets. By applying what Windows Server 2008 has to offer with its latest features you will have more flexibility when managing your network infrastructure. Windows Server 2008 allows for a total system health by deploying settings for authenticated wireless and wired connections through Group Policy or scripts, and deploying protected traffic scenarios. In order to take on this task, a number of features from former versions of Windows Server have been improved upon or replaced with new updated features, which will allow you to provide the highest level of efficiency and security to your organization.

This chapter will include a brief overview of the latest features available in Windows Server 2008 as well as detailed descriptions of the fundamental principals of these objectives and how to apply them to the newest version of Windows Server.

In this chapter, we will discuss the many new and powerful changes to Microsoft Windows Server 2008 that include innovative enhancements to networking technologies and network access configuration. We will go over the latest changes to protocols and core networking components, wireless and 802.1X-authenticated wired technologies. This will include network infrastructure components and services that can be applied when using Windows Server 2008.

Windows Server 2008 and Routing

Routing is one element that helps to ensure successful network traffic flow. It has always been the framework for a functional logical network regardless of which version of Windows Server you may be working on. Because of this, Microsoft has taken some time to improve the overall ease of use for routing with this latest version. As you are probably aware, Windows Server 2003 used the Routing and Remote Access Service (RRAS) to handle many of the configuration needs for routing in the past. Windows Server 2008 also uses the RRAS, but features a number of changes to it when compared to older versions of Windows. Many former encapsulation protocols have been made obsolete or revised for Windows Server 2008. Here is a brief summarization of what changes and omissions to expect in this build.

- Bandwidth Allocation Protocol (BAP) is no longer supported by Windows Server 2008.

- X.25 is also no longer supported.

- Serial Line Internet Protocol (SLIP), an encapsulation of Internet Protocol (IP) meant for use over serial ports and modems, has also been excluded due to infrequency of use. All SLIP-based connections will automatically be updated to Point-to-Point Protocol (PPP)-based connections.

- Asynchronous Transfer Mode (ATM), which was used to encode data traffic into small fixed cells, has been discarded.

- IP over Institute of Electrical & Electronics Engineers (IEEE) 1394 is no longer supported.

- NWLink IPX/SPX/NetBIOS Compatible Transport Protocol has been omitted.

- Services for Macintosh (SFM).

- Open Shortest Path First (OSPF) routing protocol component in Routing and Remote Access is no longer present.

- Basic firewall in Routing and Remote Access has been replaced with a new Windows Firewall feature.

- Static IP filter application program interfaces (APIs) for Routing and Remote Access are no longer viable and have been replaced with Windows Filtering Platform APIs.

- SPAP, EAP-MD5-CHAP, and MS-CHAP authentication protocols for PPP-based connections are no longer used by Windows Server 2008.

Windows Server 2008 and Remote Access

As with past versions of RRAS, Windows Server 2008 offers exceptional ease of use and configuration for remote access. All features previously available are featured in this version of Windows Server. There is also the additional replacement of Internet Authentication Service (IAS) with Network Policy Server and Network Access Protection (NAP).

The change to Windows Server 2008 in regards to remote access is the addition of Secure Socket Tunneling Protocol (SSTP). SSTP is the latest form of VPN tunnel created for use with Windows Server 2008. It contains many new features that enable traffic to pass through firewalls that block Point-to-Point Tunneling Protocol (PPTP) and Layer 2 Tunneling Protocol (L2TP)/Internet Protocol Security (IPSec) traffic. In addition, SSTP uses the Secure Sockets Layer (SSL) channel of the Hypertext Transfer Protocol Secure (HTTPS) protocol by making use of a process that encapsulates PPP traffic. PPP is very versatile. It enables you to use strong authentication methods such as Extensible Authentication Protocol-Transport Layer Security (EAP-TLS), which were not possible in past versions of Windows for VPN. All traffic will be channeled through the TCP port 443, which is typically used for Web access, because of the use of HTTPS. Security features include transport level security with enhanced key negotiation, encryption, and integrity checking capabilities by using SSL.

Windows Server 2008 and Wireless Access

Windows Server 2008 includes the following changes and enhancements to IEEE 802.11 wireless support:

- Native Wi-Fi architecture
- User interface improvements for wireless connections
- Wireless Group Policy enhancements
- Changes in Wireless Auto Configuration
- WPA2 support
- Integration with Network Access Protection when using 802.1X authentication

- EAPHost infrastructure

- 802.11 wireless diagnostics

- Command-line support for configuring wireless settings

- Network Location Awareness and network profiles

- Next Generation Transmission Control Protocol (TCP)/IP stack enhancements for wireless environments

- Single Sign On

Configuring Routing

Routing is a sometimes-confused aspect of networking, which can be complicated due to lack of fundamental understanding and training. All information that travels through a network has two things in common: a device that sent it and a required routing decision. The decisions for these routes are conducted by comparing the destination address to a list of entries located on a routing table or stored in a remote location. The routing table is normally configured and built by the network administrator or from information gathered by the TCP/IP system. These configurations can take place in a number of ways to ensure the best and most secure transport of information. Windows Server 2008 has a number of features that previous versions of Windows Servers possessed as well as some new added updates. Before reviewing changes to the system let's take a better look at the fundamentals of routing.

Routing Fundamentals

When attempting to select a path in a network by which to send data or physical traffic, an administrator has many options available to him. There are a number of ways to send packets from one destination to another based on intermediary hardware or nodes. This can include a number of different hardware devices including bridges, gateways, routers, firewalls, and switches. Even computers with multiple network cards are capable of routing packets. There are different types of routing algorithms or protocols that can be used to organize the signal flow between these devices.

These algorithms rely on what is called a *routing metric*, a value used by a routing algorithm to determine whether one route should perform better than another. Metrics can include a number of different parameters to judge performance by, as configured by the administrator.

On the simplest level, the system will select an entry from the routing table and use the netmask from that entry (see Figure 6.1). The system then performs a comparison of this value and the destination address. The resulting value is cross-referenced to the network address in the table entry. If the two values match, the information can arrive at the destination through the gateway in that entry. If the two values do not match, the routing system continues along the routing table to the next entry and performs the same check again. If the "no matching entry" is found on the table, the routing system discards the packet and generates a message notifying the sender that the destination network cannot be reached.

Otherwise, when a routing table entry is found that matches the network value, the packet is sent based on the information in the table entry via the destination listed. If the destination exists on a portion of the network directly connected to the routing system, the packet is delivered to the destination system. If it does not exist on the same segment, the packet is sent to a gateway system for delivery. This is a very complicated way of describing what is referred to as *static routing*.

Figure 6.1 Routing Tables

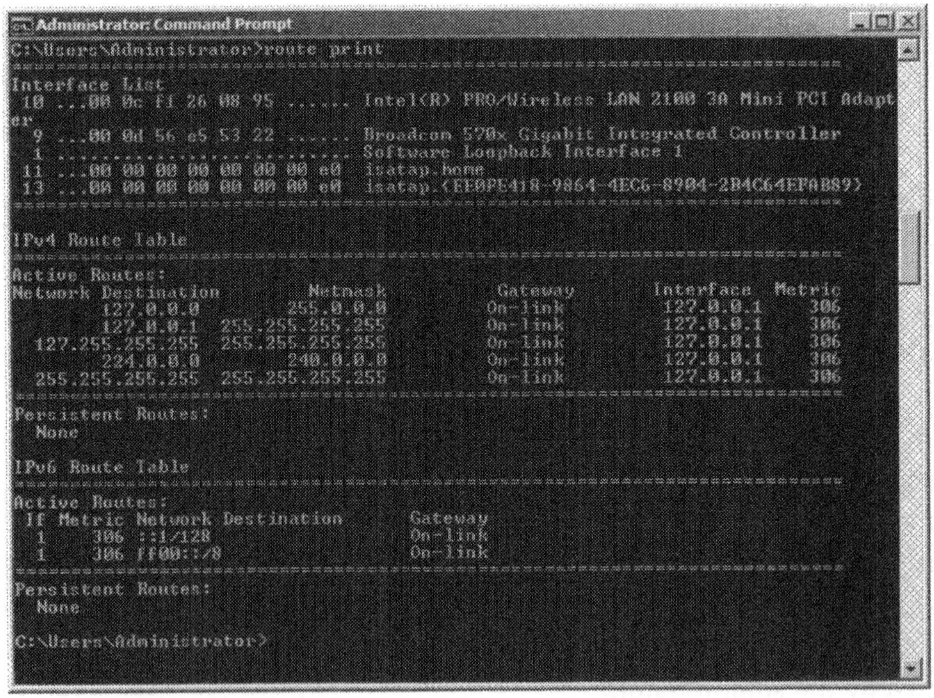

Static Routing

Static routing describes a system that does not implement adaptive routing in its configuration. In these systems, routes through a network are defined by set paths referred to as *static routes*, which are inserted into the router manually by the system administrator. This is accomplished via the route command, which can be used to manipulate local routing tables. There is no fault tolerance in regards to static routing. Changes to the network or a failure between two statically defined nodes will cause any traffic between those points to not be rerouted. This means any packets that are awaiting transport between the affected paths will be forced to wait for repairs to the failure, or for an updated static route by the administrator. This also leaves open the issue of the request timing out before repairs can be made to the route.

Static routing is considered the simplest form of routing and requires excessive manual processes. It often is the least efficient way of routing in cases where information paths have to be changed frequently. This is also the case for configurations that require a large number of routing devices, because each one must be manually entered. Static routing is also the least preferred method of dealing with outages or down connections, because any route that is configured manually must be reconfigured manually to fix or repair any lost connectivity.

There may be many downsides to static routing, but there are many incidents where a static route is the most logical and efficient method for routing. Static routing is the opposite of dynamic routing, which is a system in which routers will automatically adjust to changes in network topology or traffic. *Dynamic routing* is used by most modern routers, but some amount of programming is still available for customizing routes if necessary.

As we mentioned earlier, you as an administrator will need to deal with clients and employees of your company attempting to access the network and Internet. The Internet and Local Area Networks (LANs) are referred to as *packet switching networks*. The idea of packet switching networks is defined by the ability to optimize the use of the channel capacity available in a network. This helps to minimize transmission latency. This also requires the use of specific protocols for directing traffic through them. There are two major classes of routing protocols used in packet switch networking today:

- **Distance-vector Routing Protocol** A distance-vector routing protocol requires that a router contact and transmit to its neighbors of topology changes to the network. The frequency of this must be periodic and in most instances when a change is detected. Routing Internet Protocol (RIP) is the most popular example of this type of protocol.

- **Link State Protocol** The simplest explanation of link-state routing is that every node (router) is given a map of the topology of the network. This map is in graph form and shows the connectivity of nodes in the network. Then each individual node calculates the next best hop from every node in the network. This information then forms the routing table for each individual node based on its calculations. No other communication occurs between nodes. The most popular version of this is the OSPF.

Routing Internet Protocol (RIP)

The RIP was once the most commonly used Interior Gateway Protocol (IGP) on internal networks. It was also commonly used on networks connected to the Internet. RIP was used to help routers dynamically adapt to the variety of changes made to network connections. It accomplished this by relaying information about which networks each router had access to, and the distance those networks were from each other.

Although RIP is still actively used and has an important place in some networks, it is generally considered a dying protocol, which has been replaced by other routing protocols such as OSPF. RIP is a distance vector routing protocol that employs the hop count as a routing metric. RIP allows a maximum of 15 hops. The total hold down time for transfer is 180 seconds. Most traffic at the time RIP was commonly used was not significant, so each RIP router had an update time of 30 seconds by default, which was common practice. This proved to be a poor configuration and was later changed to randomized updates.

RIP is limited in a number of ways due to its lack of scalability. It prevents routing loops from continuing indefinitely, by implementing a limit on the number of hops allowed in a path from the source to a destination. It also limits the size of the network that RIP can support by design.

On the other hand, RIP is easier to configure than many other protocols, because it uses one of the smallest amounts of settings of any routing protocols. RIP does not require the use of any parameters on a router, and it can be ideal for small networks. RIP can be configured through the RRAS, which we will discuss later.

NOTE

Microsoft Windows Server 2008 supports RIP version 2 within RRAS.

Open Shortest Path First (OSPF)

OSPF was the natural successor to the RIP. OSPF protocol is a hierarchical IGP that uses a link state in the individual areas that make up the hierarchy. A link state database (LSDB) creates a tree-image of the network topology. It then sends copies of the LSDB periodically to update all routers in the area of the OSPF network.

OSPF is the most widely used IGP in regards to large enterprise networks. It has a much larger network size range than RIP. The OSPF protocol can determine the best path by communicating with other routers and then saving the routes in their LSDBs securely.

An OSPF network is divided into *areas*, which contain *area identifiers*. These identifiers are 32-bit and are usually written in the format of an IP address. Be aware that area identifiers are not IP addresses, and may often times duplicate any IP address without conflict occurring. These areas are logical groupings of routers whose information may be communicated to the rest of the network. There are several types of areas in an OPSPF network:

- **Backbone Area** The backbone area forms the central hub of an OSPF network. All other areas are connected to it, and inter-area routing happens via routers connected to the backbone area and to their own non-backbone areas. The backbone area distributes all routing information between the non-backbone areas. The backbone must be adjacent to all other areas, but does not need to be physically contiguous. Connectivity can be established and maintained through virtual links. All OSPF areas must connect to the backbone area. This connection, however, can be through a virtual link.

- **Stub Area** The stub area is an area that does not receive external routes except the default route, but does receive inter-area routes. All routers in the area need to agree they are stub, so that they do not generate types of LSA not appropriate to a stub area. Stub areas do not have the transit attribute and thus cannot be traversed by a virtual link.

■ **Not-so-stubby area (NSSA)** The Not-so-stubby area (NSSA) is a type of stub area that can import autonomous system (AS) external routes and send them to the backbone, but cannot receive AS external routes from the backbone or other areas. The NSSA is a non-proprietary extension of the existing stub area feature, which allows the injection of external routes in a limited fashion into the stub area.

Configuring Remote Access

Remote access is commonly used by many companies today to allow access to a computer or a network from a remote location. Most corporations include people at branch offices, telecommuters, and people who are traveling that will need to be able to gain access to network resources. Even clients using your company's services from home need to gain access to the Internet through an Internet Service Provider (ISP). *Dial-up connection* through desktop, notebook, or handheld computer modem over regular telephone lines was a common method of remote access in the early years of its inception.

It is also possible to gain remote access using a dedicated line between a computer or a remote local area network and the central or main LAN. This tends to be a less flexible and more expensive method, but does offer faster data exchange rates and fewer configurations. Integrated Services Digital Network (ISDN) is a compromise between the two other common methods of remote access, since it combines dial-up access with faster data exchange rates. The most growing trends in remote access in recent years have included wireless, cable, and digital subscriber line (DSL) technologies, which offer more convenient and efficient methods for remote access.

A remote access server is comprised of a computer with a remote access application installed, which is configured to handle the authentication and authorization of clients seeking access to a network remotely. This can also be referred to as a *communication server*. A remote access server usually includes or is associated with a firewall server to ensure security, and a router that can forward the remote access request to another part of the network. A single remote access server may also be used as part of a much larger VPN.

Like past versions, Windows Server 2008 has included a wide array of options for configuring remote access for you company. You will be required to be familiar with the workings of how to set up a remote access server and all of the methods of connectivity available in a modern networking environment. Like its previous versions, Windows Server 2008 houses most of its remote access tools in the RRA role. This role is crucial to the successful deployment of remote access services for your company.

Routing and Remote Access Services (RRAS)

Most of the major functions of network access and the objectives that you will be required to know for your examine, revolve around the RRAS role. This is not a new feature to Windows Server 2008, but has many omissions and additions since Windows Server 2003. From this role, you can access configuration tools for routing, connection manager, and remote access service all of which will be very helpful in setting up remote access on your machines and managing policies.

Let's install the RRAS role. This will help you to configure most of the remote access features available in Windows Server 2008 that we will be discussing. Be sure to start with a clean install of Windows Server 2008, and review all guidelines and requirements for the system you are using.

Configuring & Implementing...

Installing RRAS
To begin installing RRAS, follow these steps:

1. Open the Server Manager by clicking on the **Administrative Tools** menu.
2. Scroll down to the **Roles Summary** section of the details pane.
3. Click **Add Roles** to launch the **Add Roles Wizard**, as seen in Figure 6.2.

Continued

Figure 6.2 Add Roles Wizard

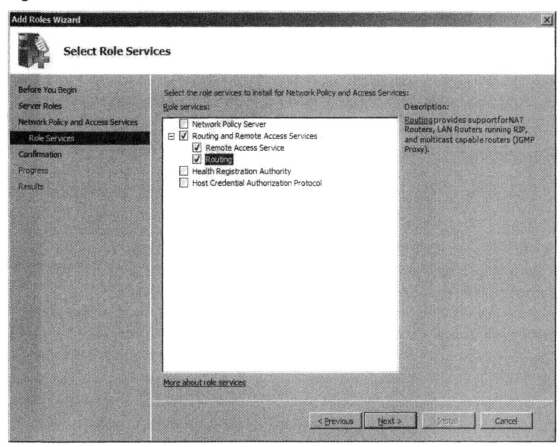

4. Click **Next** to bypass the Welcome screen.

5. Select the **Network Access Services** checkbox.

6. Click the **Next** button.

7. Click **Next** again to bypass the Network Access Service screen description.

8. Select the Network Access Services components that you want to install. Select the check boxes for Network Policy Server (NPS) and Routing and Remote Access Services (RRAS).

9. When you select the Routing and Remote Access Services check box, the Remote Access Service, Routing, and Connection Manager Administration Kit check boxes will be selected automatically.

Network Policy Server and Network Access Protection

In the RRAS there are a number of snap-in roles that can be used in configuring and setting up your network access needs for Windows Server 2008. In previous incarnations of Windows Server 2003, Internet Authentication Service (IAS) snap-in was Microsoft's implementation of a Remote Authentication Dial-in User Service (RADIUS) server and proxy. It was capable of performing localized connection AAA Protocol for many types of network access, including wireless and VPN connections.

For Windows Server 2008, Microsoft has replaced IAS with a new snap- in called Network Policy Server (NPS). NPS is the Microsoft implementation of a RADIUS server and proxy in Windows Server 2008, and promises to be even simpler to use than IAS.

NPS is not just a replacement for IAS; it does what IAS did but also offers another role called Network Access Protection (NAP). When you install NPS you will find that you have a lot of new functionality.

NPS does many of the same things that IAS did such as:

- Routing of LAN and WAN traffic.
- Allow access to local resources through VPN or dial-up connections.
- Creating and enforcing network access through VPN or dial-up connections.

For example, NPS can provide these functions:

- VPN services
- Dial-up services
- 802.11 protected access
- RRAS
- Offer authentication through Windows Active Directory
- Control network access with policies

What NPS does that is new, are all the functions related to NAP. NAP when used in unison with NPS creates a "total system health policy enforcement platform," which helps in the creation of health policies for your network, as shown in Figure 6.3.

Figure 6.3 NPS and NAP Health Policy Overview

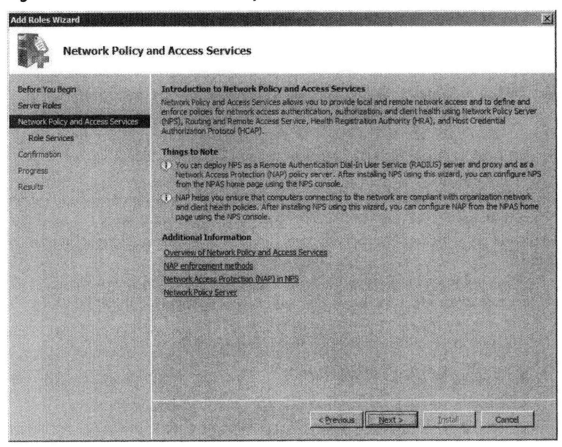

NAP is designed to enhance a corporate VPN. This is accomplished when clients establish a VPN session with a Windows Server 2008 system that is running the RRAS. Once a connection is made, a NPS will validate the remote system and determine the status of its health. The NPS collects information and compares the remote computer's configuration against a pre-determined network access policy that can be customized by the administrator. Policies can be configured to either monitor or isolate based on the administrators preference as, shown in Figure 6.4.

Figure 6.4 NPS Policy Configuration

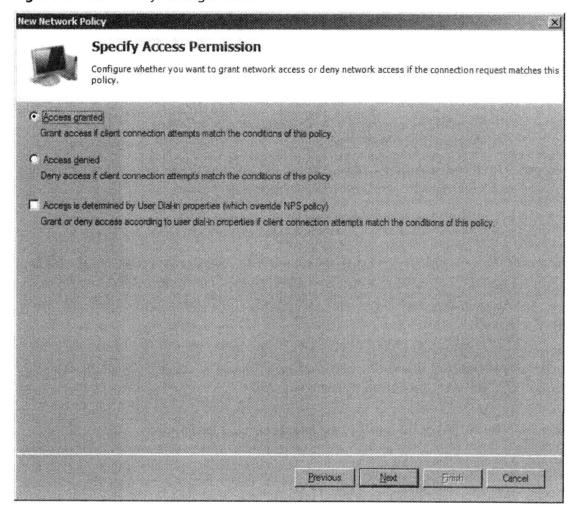

Although monitoring will not prevent any PCs from gaining access to your network, each PC logging on to the network will be recorded for compliance. Isolation will put non-compliant users onto an isolated segment of the network, where it cannot interfere with production or resources. Of course, the administrator is ultimately responsible for configuring what access non-compliant computers will be allowed.

If you are already familiar with Windows Server 2003 and the IAS snap-in, you will notice many changes to the NPS snap-in:

■ Network policies have replaced remote access policies and have been moved to the policies node.

- RADIUS Clients and Servers node has replaced the RADIUS Client node.

- There is no Connection Request Processing node.

- Policies and the Remote RADIUS Server Groups node have been moved under RADIUS Clients and Servers.

- Remote access policy conditions and profile settings have been reorganized on the Overview, Conditions, Constraints, and Settings tabs for the properties of a network policy.

- The Remote Access Logging folder has been renamed the Accounting node, and no longer has the Local File or SQL Server nodes.

In addition, the System Health Validators node allows you to set up and adjust all NAP health requirements. The Remediation Server Groups node allows you to set up the group of servers that restricted NAP clients can access for the VPN and Dynamic Host Configuration Protocol (DHCP) NAP enforcement methods. Last, the Accounting node allows you to set up how NPS stores accounting information for the network.

The NAP wizard automatically configures all of the connection request policies, network policies, and health policies. Knowing how to set up and configure this feature will put you steps ahead of the competition.

The wizard will guide you through the configuration process for your chosen scenario. The NAP wizard for VPN enforcement has a number of policy creation options, including ones for compliant NAP clients, noncompliant NAP clients, and non–NAP capable clients. It also includes two health policies for compliant and non-compliant NAP clients. The new NAP wizards and other wizards contained within will help you with creating RADIUS clients, remote RADIUS server groups, connection request policies, and network policies. Overall, this will make it that much easier to configure NPS for a variety of network access scenarios, and this will make your job all the more simple.

Dial-Up

Dial-up by definition is the method used to connect a device to a network using a modem and a public telephone service. Dial-up access works in the same exact manner as a telephone connection does. The only true difference is that the two ends of the connections have computer devices communicating rather than people. Dial-up access utilizes normal telephone lines and because of this, the quality of the connection can suffer. Data rates are also limited. The maximum data rate with dial-up access for many years was 56 Kbph. ISDN provides faster rates but are still limited compared to cable and DSL.

Dial-up networking using Windows Server 2008 include some of the following components:

- **Dial-up Networking Servers** You can configure a server running RRAS to provide dial-up networking access to an entire network, or restrict access to the shared resources of the remote access server only.

- **Dial-up Networking Clients** Remote access clients must be running Windows Server 2008, Windows Server 2003, Windows XP, Windows 2000, Windows NT to have access to the RRAS.

- **Remote Access Protocols** Remote access protocols are used to negotiate connections and provide framing for LAN protocol data that is sent over a wide area network (WAN) link. RRAS supports LAN protocols such as TCP/IP, which enable access to the Internet. RRAS supports remote access protocols such as PPP.

- **WAN Options** Clients can dial in by using standard telephone lines and a modem or modem pool. Faster links are possible by using ISDN. You can no longer connect remote access clients to remote access servers by using X.25 or ATM with Windows Server 2008.

- **Security Options** Windows Server 2008 provides logon and domain security, support for security hosts, data encryption, RADIUS, remote access account lockout, remote access policies, and callback for secure network access for dial-up clients.

Remote Access Policy

Remote access policies are an ordered set of rules that define how connections are either authorized or rejected. For each rule, there are one or more conditions, a set of profile settings, and a remote access permission setting. If a connection is authorized, the remote access policy profile specifies a set of connection restrictions. The dial-in properties of the user account also provide a set of restrictions. Where applicable, user account connection restrictions override the remote access policy profile connection restrictions.

For servers running the RRAS that are configured for the Windows authentication provider, remote access policies are administered from RRAS and apply only to the connections of the RRAS server. Centralized management of remote access policies is also used when you have remote access servers that are running RRAS. Remote access policies validate a number of connection settings before authorizing the connection, including the following:

- Remote access permission
- Group membership
- Type of connection
- Time of day
- Authentication methods
- Advanced conditions such as access server identity, access client phone number, or Media Access Control (MAC) address
- Whether user account dial-in properties are ignored
- Whether unauthenticated access is allowed

After the connection is authorized, remote access policies can also be used to specify connection restrictions, including the following:

- Idle timeout time
- Maximum session time
- Encryption strength
- IP packet filters

Advanced restrictions:

- IP address for PPP connections
- Static routes

Additionally, you can vary connection restrictions based on the following settings:

- Group membership
- Type of connection
- Time of day
- Authentication methods
- Identity of the access server

- Access client phone number or MAC address

- Whether unauthenticated access is allowed

For example, you can have policies that specify different maximum session times for different types of connections or groups. Additionally, you can also specify restricted access for business partners or unauthenticated connections. All of this can be configured using the RRAS panel on the client computer, as shown in Figure 6.5. This is accessible as follows:

1. Open **Server Manager** and expand the **Roles** tab.

2. Expand the **Network Policy and Access Service** tab, as seen in Figure 6.5.

Figure 6.5 Network Policy and Access Tab

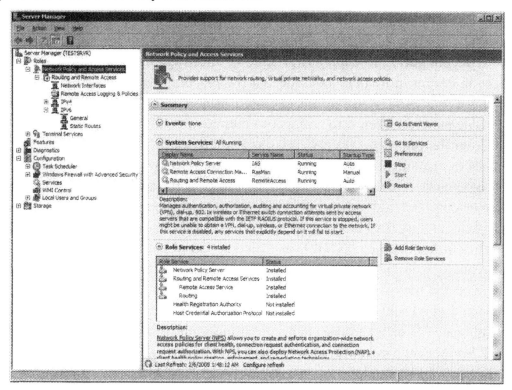

3. Expand the **Routing and Remote Access** panel and right click for **Properties**.

This will allow you to set up configurations for your remote access policies.

Network Address Translation (NAT)

Windows Server 2008 provides network address translation (NAT) functionality as part of the RRAS. NAT provides a method for translating the IPv4 addresses of computers on one network into IPv4 addresses of computers on a different network. A NAT-enabled IP router works as a translation service when deployed at the boundary where a private network meets a public network. This allows computers on the private network to access computers on the public network.

The whole reasoning behind the development of NAT technology was as a place holder solution for a greater issue that administrators faced. This problem was IPv4 address-depletion that plagued the Internet community. Due to a huge and continuing rise in computer usage, the number of available globally unique (public) IPv4 addresses was far too small to accommodate the need to access to the Internet. A long-term solution for the problem was well under way in the development of Internet Protocol version 6 (IPv6) addresses, which are supported by Windows Server 2008. Unfortunately, IPv6 is not yet widely adopted and would require extensive reconfiguring to deploy large scale in most organizations. The technology has been in use for more than a decade, but the practical deployment still remains an issue. This is why NAT is still in use, because it allows computers on any network to use reusable private addresses to connect to computers with globally unique public addresses on the Internet.

Small- to medium-sized organizations with private networks to access resources on the Internet or other public networks, use NAT for this reasoning. They configure reusable private IPv4 addresses while the computers on the public servers are set up with globally unique IPv4 addresses. The most useful deployment of NAT is in a small office or home office (SOHO) or a medium-sized business that uses RRAS. NAT technology enables computers on the internal corporate network to connect to resources on the Internet without having to deploy a proxy server.

NAT is a good solution for situations where ICS is not an option, such as when using a VPN or when the clients are using static IP addresses. A real benefit of NAT becomes apparent when dealing with Administration duties. For example, NAT makes it fairly simple to move your Web server or File Transfer Protocol (FTP) server to another host computer without having to worry about broken links. If you merely change the inbound mapping at the router, you can set it to reflect the new host. The same holds true of changes to your internal network. This is because the only external IP addresses either belong to the router or come from a pool of global addresses.

Configuring & Implementing...

Enabling and Configuring NAT

Now that you understand how NAT works, let's look at how to enable and configure NAT:

1. In the left pane of the **Server Manager,** expand the **Routing and Remote Access** node, as shown in Figure 6.6.
2. Expand the **IPv4** node.
3. Click on the **NAT** node.
4. In the **NAT** node, right click on the external network server that you wish to enable NAT for on the middle pane of the console. For example, the external interface could be **Local Area Connection.**
5. Click **Properties** and select **NAT** and click **OK,** as shown in Figure 6.6.

Figure 6.6 Enabling NAT

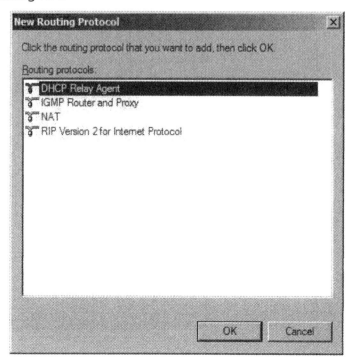

Internet Connection Sharing (ICS)

Internet Connection Sharing (ICS) is a feature that permits you to use Windows Server 2008 to connect a small office network or home network over the Internet. Not much has changed in this version of Windows Server 2008, and you may find that most of the features and set up procedures are very similar to that of Windows Server 2003. As it always has, ICS provides NAT, IP addressing, and name resolution services for all the computers on a small network. This method is best used for sharing an Internet connection among a small business network.

ICS routes TCP/IP packets that are present in a small LAN environment to the Internet. ICS will calculate and map individual IP addresses belonging to the clients of the LAN to unused port numbers in the TCP/IP stack. Because it uses NAT, IP addresses belonging to the local computer will not be visible on the Internet. All packets leaving or entering the LAN are sent from or to the IP address of the external adapter on the ICS host computer. This IP address is static and will always be 192.168.0.1, and will provide NAT services to the whole 192.168.0.x subnet.

ICS is not customizable in terms of which addresses are used for the internal subnet. It does not contain provisions for bandwidth limiting or other features common to more advanced systems. ICS is also not compatible and cannot be combined with Wi-Fi and dial-up mobile modems. ICS does offer limited configuration for other standard services and some configuration of NAT.

Configuring & Implementing...

Configuring ICS When Dealing with VPNs

Virtual private networks (VPNs), which we discuss later, are common in most companies today. When configuring an ICS, there are several things you should bear in mind concerning these types of connections and hazards that may occur if the proper precautions are not met.

Never create a VPN connection to a corporate network from the ICS computer. By doing so, you will cause the default setting for all traffic from the ICS computer to be forwarded over the VPN connection to the corporate network.

Continued

This includes traffic from LAN clients. This will suspend Internet resources across the network and all the client computers will be sending data over the logical connection created with the credentials of the ICS computer user.

Never configure ICS on a computer that is a VPN server. If your Windows Server 2008-based computer is serving as a VPN server, you must use Windows Server 2008 NAT role.

These are very important configuration mistakes that, if avoided, can save wasted time and energy for you as an administrator.

Here is a list of required hardware and software for enabling ICS:

- A DSL or cable modem with an ISP connected to it and an active DSL or cable account.

- Two network adapters installed in the ICS machine.

- A network already configured with functioning TCP/IP.

Due to the nature of the way ISC works and its drawbacks, you should never install ICS on a machine that incorporates any of the following stipulations:

- Uses static IP addresses

- Has a domain controller

- Uses other DNS servers, gateways, or DHCP servers

ICS creates a static IP address for your network adapter and allocates IP addresses to other computers on your network. This means you will lose your connection to the rest of the network if other network computers already provide those services. If any of these conditions already exist in your network, you must use Windows Server 2008 NAT server instead of ICS.

Also bear in mind these other warnings:

- Do not create a VPN connection to a corporate network from the ICS computer. If you do, by default all traffic from the ICS computer, including traffic from local area network clients, will be forwarded over the VPN connection to the corporate network. This means that Internet resources will no longer be reachable, and all the client computers will be sending data over the logical connection created with the credentials of the ICS computer user.

■ Do not configure ICS on a computer that is a VPN server. If your Windows Server 2008-based computer is serving as a VPN server, you must use Windows Server 2008 NAT role.

Configuring & Implementing...

Configuring ICS

The ICS host computer provides a connection through the second network adapter to the existing TCP/IP network. Log on as member of the Administrators group to set up the ICS host computer.

1. Click **Start**.
2. Click Control Panel.
3. Click Network Connections.
4. Right-click **Local Area Connection** (for the installed network card) and rename it "Internet Connection."
5. In the **Network and Dial-up Connections** dialog box, two connections are displayed (for different network adapters): the Internet Connection and Local Area Connection.
6. Right-click **Internet Connection** and then click **Properties**.
7. Click the **General** tab, and then verify that **Client for Microsoft Networks** and **Internet Protocol** (TCP/IP) are displayed.
8. Click the Advanced tab, and then click to select the Enable Internet Connection Sharing for this Connection check box.

NOTE

Make sure that firewall software or other Internet-sharing software from any third-party manufacturer has been removed.

9. Click **OK**

Remote Access Protocols

Setting up remote access servers and connections in Windows Server can be somewhat overwhelming and confusing if you don't understand the protocol configuration options available to you. You have a number of remote access protocol options to choose from, and deciding which ones to use will be based on the exact task and functionality you seek to accomplish. This will depend on your system configurations, your hardware, you're your communications capabilities.

You must try to organize and make sense of all these options. To start, let's take a look at the categories of protocols and the advantages and disadvantages of the various protocols within each one.

Microsoft's PPTP is most commonly used for voluntary authenticated and encrypted tunneling between dial-up clients and a PPTP Network Server located just inside the customer's network.

The PPTP Network Server authenticates the tunnel user with Challenge-Handshake Authentication Protocol (CHAP) and negotiates data compression and encryption as dictated by security policies. PPTP offers payload privacy, but does not encrypt session control traffic.

The L2TP consolidates the best of other protocols within a single standard. L2TP Access Concentrators terminate PPP Link Control Protocol (LCP) and carry out dial session authentication. L2TP can be used with a separate LAC at the ISP NAS, or with a LAC Client on the end-user's PC. L2TP Network Servers terminate PPP NCP, provide routing and bridging for the PPP session, and make the user appear directly connected to the "home" network.

L2TP is transparent in compulsory mode, multiprotocol support, and leaving authentication, authorization, and addressing responsibility within the customer's network. L2TP is a tunneling protocol, not an encryption protocol. If customers require data confidentiality, you'll need to run L2TP over IPSec.

Features have been added to the IP protocol to provide greater security for IP packets that transit public networks. The Encapsulating Security Payload (ESP) encrypts packets, usually by encapsulating a private IP packet inside an outer public IP packet. Another standard known as Internet Security Association and Key Management Protocol (ISAKMP) can be used for strong authentication of tunnel endpoints and key management. Collectively, these extensions are called IPSec.

IPSec supports Site-to-Site VPNs by building security associations between gateways at the edge of customer networks. Every packet that enters or leaves each network will be tunneled according to customer-defined policy, with filtering down to the individual host and port level. IPSec-compatible encryption and packet authentication algorithms support a wide variety of security policies, allowing customers to strike their own balance between security and performance.

IPSec can also be used to support Remote Access VPNs, by tunneling from an individual host to a security gateway, topologically similar to voluntary PPTP tunnels. IP packets sent by an IPSec host to a protected network are encrypted and delivered to the security gateway for that network. IP packets to public destinations are sent without the addition of IPSec protocols.

Windows Server 2008 has offered many new upgrades. Their newest to the realm of VPNs is the addition of SSTP, which is the latest alternative form of VPN tunnel. SSTP is an application-layer protocol. It uses a synchronous communication, which works in unilateral motion between two programs allowing a constant exchange and comparison of data. By doing this, it allows for many application endpoints over a single network connection. This allows for a very efficient usage of the communication resources that are available to that network. SSTP is based on SSL as opposed to IPSec or PPTP, and thereby uses port 443 for traffic.

New & Noteworthy...

Microsoft's Development Direction of SSL

When developing SSTP to be a viable and improved VPN tunneling protocol, Microsoft had many available resources to build upon. Two of the most commonly used were IPSec and SSL. Both had benefits, but it took much consideration to determine which would provide the better ground work to allow the most benefits. At the conclusion of their decision-making process, SSL was chosen as the basis for the SSTP, which is used in Windows Server 2008.

There are many obvious reasons for this choice. Most become apparent when you examine the downsides of IPSec. IPSec main function is supporting site-to-site VPN connectivity and no roaming. SSL was obviously a better base for SSTP development, as it supports roaming. Besides the obvious, there are several other reasons for not basing SSTP on IPSec:

Continued

■ Strong authentication is not required.

■ User Clients must be present.

■ No sense of conformity in regards to support and coding from one vendor to the next.

■ No Default non-IP protocols.

■ Remote users attempting to connect via a site with limited IP addresses would cause problems due to the inherent site-to-site secure connections design.

With SSL, VPN static IP addresses are not required, clients are unnecessary in most cases, and since connections are made via a browser over the Internet, the default connection protocol is TCP/IP. This makes connections transparent to the user. Microsoft hopes that this sort of forethought in their development will ensure more user friendly interactions when using SSTP in Windows Server 2008.

SSTP allows for the passage of traffic through firewalls that would normally inhibit PPTP and L2TP/IPSec traffic. SSTP is able to incorporate PPP traffic over the SSL channel of the HTTPS protocol. By using PPP, SSTP can utilize well-protected authentication methods such as EAP-TLS. By involving HTTPS, traffic is directed and flows through TCP port 443. This port is commonly used for Web access, which is why the SSTP is so versatile compared to past VPN protocols. Key negotiation, integrity checking, and encryption are handled via SSL VPN. This also allows for transport-level security when dealing with these functions.

SSL uses a cryptographic system. This system uses two encrypted keys to secure data. One is the public key and the other is the private key. The public key is recognizable to everyone and the private key can only be identified by the recipient. A secure connection between a client and a server is created by this method of encryption. You can thereby establish secure remote access from almost any Internet connected to a Web browser, which was not possible using traditional VPN. Thanks to this new method, there are not issues with instability in connection and loss of service due to connectivity issues for the client. The added bonus is that with SSL VPN, the session is completely secured.

Remember that while SSTP is a strong method for client-to-site VPN connections, it is not designed for site-to-site VPN connections. Let's review the assets that SSTP can provide to you and your organization:

- SSTP takes advantage of HTTPS to establish a secure and stable connection.

- The SSTP (VPN) tunnel will function over Secure-HTTP. This means that Web proxies, firewalls, and NAT routers present on the path between clients and servers will no longer block VPN connections.

- Port blocking is greatly decreased.

- Clients will be able to connect from anywhere on the Internet.

- SSTP is built into Windows Server 2008, providing higher compatibility.

- SSTP allows simpler training procedures, because the end-user VPN controls are identical to previous versions.

- The SSTP-based VPN tunnel will directly plug into the current interfaces for Microsoft VPN client and server software.

- IPv6 is fully supported.

- It takes advantage of the new integrated network access protection support for client health-check.

- MS RRAS client and server are strongly supported, allowing for two-factor authentication capabilities.

- VPN coverage is expanded from limited points of access to almost any Internet connection.

- The use of port 443 for SSL encapsulation.

- Acts as a full network VPN solution over all applications.

- NAP integration.

- SSL tunnel is created in s single session.

- Stronger forced authentication process than other methods like IPSec.

- Supports non-IP protocols.

- No additional costs or hard-to-configure hardware firewalls that do not support Active Directory integration and integrated two-factor authentication.

Now that we know the benefits of using Secure Socket Protocol, lets examine the data flow for an SSTP-based VPN connection in action:

If a user on a computer running Windows Server 2008 initiates an SSTP-based VPN connection, the following occurs:

1. A TCP connection between the STTP client and the SSTP server is made. This happens between a dynamically allocated TCP port on the SSTP client. The same connection occurs on the TCP port 443 on the SSTP server.

2. An SSL Client-Hello message is sent by the SSTP client. This Client-Hello Message acts as an invitation from the SSTP client to create an SSL session with the SSTP server.

3. The SSTP server responds by providing and sending its computer certificate to the SSTP client.

4. The computer certificate is validated by the STTP client.

5. Next, the STTP determines the encryption method for the SSL session.

6. Then the SSTP Client creates an SSL session key.

7. This SSL session key is then encrypted with the public key of the SSTP server's certificate.

8. The SSL session key is then sent as the encrypted form of the SSL session key to the SSTP server.

9. The SSTP server decrypts the encrypted SSL session key with the private key of its computer certificate. Now any further communication between the SSTP client and the SSTP server will be encrypted with the negotiated encryption method and SSL session key.

10. The SSTP client sends an HTTP over SSL request message to the SSTP server.

11. The SSTP client attempts to negotiate for an SSTP tunnel with the SSTP server.

12. The SSTP client attempts to negotiate a PPP connection with the SSTP server. All user credentials are negotiated at this time with a PPP authentication method. Also during the negotiation they configure settings for IPv4 or IPv6 traffic.

13. Once negotiation is completed, the SSTP client begins sending IPv4 or IPv6 traffic over the PPP link.

Configuring & Implementing...

Taking Advantage of Virtual Networking

Microsoft Windows 2008 has a variety of new networking options available to you, but it also offers other peripheral roles that can helpful in a variety. One huge trend in today's networking is virtual networking. This allows you to more efficiently economize and consolidate the number of physical machines by replacing them with virtual ones. While testing out different aspects of networking in this chapter such as creating a VPN using SSTP protocol, it will be helpful to you to work in real-world testing environments. Normally, in previous editions of Windows, this would require many physical computers to create an accurate test case or a program like Virtual PC 2007 to simulate this.

Using the Hyper V role of Windows Server 2008, you can create the same test scenario with only one or two physical computers and still accurately test your deployment cases. This will allow you to more effectively test a variety of VPN configurations using only a limited number of physical machines. It will also familiarize you with other aspects of the Windows Server 2008 roles that are available to you as an administrator, and also gain more proficiency with the operating system (OS).

By utilizing all of the new features of Windows Server 2008 in unison, you can take advantage of the full power of real-world networking benefits that Windows Server 2008 has to offer your organization. This will also present the option of virtualization and the benefits it can bring to your organization.

Virtual Private Networks

VPNs use public wires to join nodes to create a network. This network allows the user to create their own private networks for the transfer of data. There are a large number of security systems at play within the VPN, such as encryption and other security measures. This makes certain that no data is intercepted by unauthorized users. VPN has been used successfully for several years, but has recently encountered problems. Many organizations have widely increased the number of roaming users that have access to their networks. Because of this, other methods have been in development to accomplish this same type of access. IPSec and SSL VPN are two such methods commonly in use by many organizations.

VPNs typically use an encrypted tunnel that keeps data confidential within the tunnel. By doing this, when the tunnel routes through typical NAT paths, the VPN tunnel fails to remain active and stops working completely. VPNs will most often connect a node directly to an endpoint. If the node and the endpoint have the same internal LAN address and NAT is involved, many problems and complications will arise causing a lack of service to your end client.

Installing and Configuring a SSL VPN Server

Now that you have an idea of how SSTP and new SSL VPNs work, we will explain how to use the RRAS panel to install and configure a VPN. Before beginning, be sure that you have a clean version of Windows Server 2008 installed. Also, you must not have RRAS installed yet to set up the SSL VPN. Before installing RRAS, you must request a machine certificate server.

The VPN server needs a machine certificate to create the SSL VPN connection with the SSL VPN client computer. The name on the certificate should match the name that the VPN client will use to connect to the SSL VPN gateway computer. This means that you will need to create a public DNS entry for the name on the certificate, so that it will resolve to the external IP address on the VPN server or the IP address of a NAT device in front of the VPN server, as described earlier in this chapter. This will forward the connection to the SSL VPN server.

Configuring & Implementing...

Requesting and installing the machine certificate on the SSL VPN server

Perform the following steps to request and install the machine certificate on the SSL VPN server:

1. Open **Server Manager**. Expand the **Roles** node in the left pane.

2. Expand the Web Server (IIS) node. Click on Internet Information Services (IIS) Manager.

Continued

3. Locate the **Internet Information Services Manager** console and find the pane to the right of the left pane, and click on the **name** of the server you are using.

4. Click on the **Server Certificates** icon in the right pane of the IIS console.

5. In the right pane of the console, click the **Create Domain Certificate** link.

6. Fill out the information on the **Distinguished Name Properties** page. Remember to correctly enter the **Common Name** entry as mentioned previously. This name is the name that VPN clients will use to connect to the VPN server. You will need a public Domain Name Server (DNS) entry for this name, so that it resolves either to the external interface of the VPN server, or the public address of a NAT device in front of the VPN server (e.g., the common name *sstp.msexamfirewall.org*). The VPN client computer should have Host files created so that it can resolve this name later.

7. When finished click **Next**.

8. On the **Online Certification Authority** page, find and click the **Select** button.

9. In the **Select Certification Authority** dialog box, click the name of the **Enterprise CA** and click **OK**.

10. Enter a name for the certificate in the Friendly name text box (e.g., the name SSLVPN).

11. Click **Finish** on the Online Certification Authority page.

When the Wizard completes its work, you will see the certificate appear in the IIS console:

12. Double click on the **certificate** and you can see the common name in the "Issued to" section, and that we have a private key that corresponds to the certificate.

13. Click **OK** to close the Certificate dialog box.

Once you have a certificate, you can then install the RRAS Server Role as described earlier in this chapter. It is critical that you install the certificate first, before you install the RRAS Server Role. If you do not, you will have to use a fairly complex command-line routine to bind the certificate to the SSL VPN listener.

To set up a VPN, proceed with the following steps. Once RRAS is installed, you must first enable RRAS.

Continued

Perform the following steps to enable the RRAS service:

13. Open Server Manager and expand the **Roles** node in the left pane
of the console.

14. Expand the Network Policy and Access Services node and click on
the Routing and Remote Access node. Right-click on the Routing
and Remote Access node and click Configure and Enable Routing
and Remote Access, as shown in Figure 6.7.

Figure 6.7 Configure and Enable Routing and Remote Access

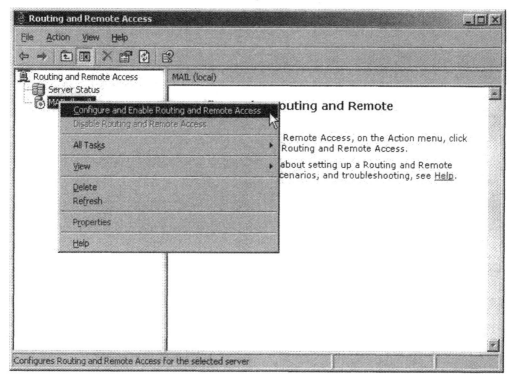

14. Click Next on the Welcome to the Routing and Remote Access
Server Setup Wizard page.

15. On the **Configuration** page shown in Figure 6.8, select the **Virtual
private network (VPN) access and NAT** option.

16. Click **Next**.

Continued

Figure 6.8 Routing and Remote Access Server Setup Wizard

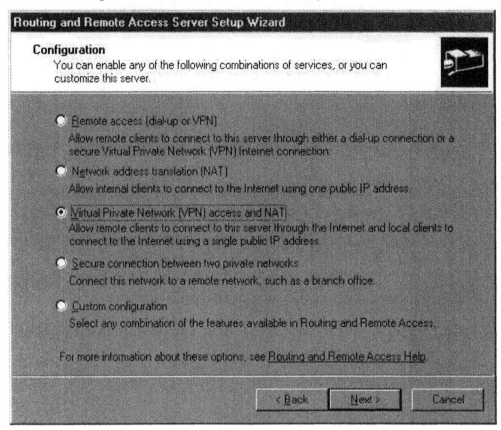

17. On the **VPN Connection** page, select the **NIC** in the **Network interfaces** section that represents the external interface of the VPN server.

18. Click **Next.**

19. On the **IP Address Assignment** page, select the **Automatically** option if you have a DHCP server. If you do not have a DHCP server, select the **From a specified range of addresses** option and provide a list of addresses that VPN clients would use when connecting to the network through the VPN gateway.

20. Click **Next.**

Continued

21. On the **Managing Multiple Remote Access Servers** page, select **No, use Routing and Remote Access to authenticate connection requests**. Use this option when there is no NPS or RADIUS server available. If the VPN server is a member of the domain, you can authenticate users using domain accounts. If the VPN server is not a member of the domain, then only local accounts on the VPN server can be used.

22. Click **Next**.

23. Review the summary information on the **Completing the Routing and Remote Access Server Setup** Wizard page for accuracy and click **Finish**.

24. Click **OK** in the Routing and Remote Access dialog box telling you that relaying of DHCP messages requires a DHCP relay agent.

25. Expand the **Routing and Remote Access node** and then click on the **Ports** node. In the middle pane you will see that WAN Miniport connections for SSTP are now available.

Inbound/Outbound Filters

Windows Server 2008 features a variety of inbound and outbound features that you will need to be able to implement. The old version of Windows Firewall has been upgraded and is now called Windows Firewall with Advanced Security (WFAS).

This new version of WFAS has a number of advanced components that will help with you security needs.

- **New GUI Interface** MMC is a snap-in that is available to help configure the advanced firewall.

- **Bi-directional Filters** Unlike past versions of Windows Firewall, WFAS filters both outbound traffic as well as inbound traffic.

- **Better IPSec Compatibility** WFAS rules and IPSec encryption configurations are both integrated into the same singular interface.

- **Enhanced Rules Generation** Using WFAS, you can create firewall rules for Windows Active Directory service accounts and groups. This includes source/destination IP addresses, protocol numbers, source and destination TCP/User Datagram Protocol (UDP) ports, Internet Control Message Protocol (ICMP), IPv6 traffic, and interface all on the Windows Server.

With the addition to having inbound and outbound filters, the WFAS has advanced rules configuration.

The first concern of any server administrator in using a host-based firewall is "What if it prevents critical server infrastructure applications from functioning? While that is always a possibility with any security measure, WFAS will automatically configure new rules for any new server roles that are added to the server. However, if you run any non-Microsoft applications on your server that need inbound network connectivity, you will have to create a new rule for that type of traffic.

By using the advanced windows firewall, you can better secure your servers from attack and secure your servers from attacking others, and really nail down what traffic is going in and out of your servers.

Configuring Remote Authentication Dial-In User Service (RADIUS) Server

RADIUS is protocol used for controlling access to network resources by authenticating, authorizing, and accounting for access, and is referred to as an AAA protocol. RADIUS is the unofficial industry standard for this type of access. It is more common today than ever before, being employed by ISPs, large corporations that need to manage access to the Internet, and also internal networks that operate across a large variety of access providing technologies such as modems, DSL, wireless and VPNs. To better understand what RADIUS does, let's try to understand each of its required functions as an AAA protocol.

- **Authentication** The server seeking access sends a request to NAS. The NAS then creates and sends a RADIUS Access Request to the RADIUS Server. This request acts as an authorization to grant access. Typically, a user name and password or some other means of establishing identity is requested for this process, which must then be provided by the user seeking access. The request will also contain other means of verification that the NAS collected, such as physical location of the user and/or the phone number or network address of the user.

- **Authorization** Upon receipt of the request, the RADIUS server processes the new request for access. Most times, the RADIUS server will have access to a list of accounts or be able to query an external database to cross reference the provided information on the user. RADIUS will verify the user information and, if configured to do so, other information such as the user's network address or phone number that it has access to against the information it has stored. Based on the result of the check, the RADIUS server will respond with one of three responses to the NAS responsible for enforcing the access decision of the RADIUS server:

- **Access Accept** This result indicates that the user is granted access. The terms of access are based on the information the RADIUS server has on file, and is conveyed to the NAS, which allows the conditional access based on these terms. A variety of terms could be stipulated, such as time restrictions, bandwidth restrictions, security access control restrictions, and others.

- **Access Challenge** This requests further verification from the user before access will be granted. These types of verification can include a secondary password, PIN, or token card challenge response.

- **Access Reject** This indicates that there has been a failure to prove the user's identity or that their account is inactive or unusable. This means that the user has been completely denied access to all network resources requested.

- **Accounting** If network access is granted to the user by the NAS based on the authentication and authorization phases, NAS then sends an *Accounting Start* request to the RADIUS Server to indicate that the user has begun accessing the network. These types of records will contain a variety of information concerning the identity, point of attachment, and unique session ID for the user. Active session may have periodic updates sent out called *Interim Accounting* records. These records may update the session duration and information on current data usage. When the user exits the network and the access point (AP) is again closed, the NAS will send a final *Accounting Stop* record to the RADIUS server. This informs it of the final information related to the user's network access.

NAS devices communicate with the RADIUS via the link-layer protocol, using PPP for example. The RADIUS server responds using the RADIUS protocol. The RADIUS server authenticates using security schemes such as PAP, CHAP or EAP.

Remember that just because the user is authenticated, it does not give him or her total access to all resources the network has to offer, so the RADIUS server will often check that the user is authorized to use the network service requested. There are a number of specifications that access can be based on once authenticated. These include:

- The specific IP Address that will be assigned to the user.

- The total amount of time that the user is permitted to remain connected.

- Limited access or priority based access to certain resources.

- L2TP parameters.

- Virtual Local Area Network (VLAN) parameters

- Other Quality of Service (QoS) parameters

In previous incarnations of Windows Server 2003, Internet Authentication Service (IAS) was Microsoft's implementation of a RADIUS server and proxy. IAS performed centralized connection AAA Protocol for many types of network access, including wireless and VPN connections.

For Windows Server 2008, Microsoft has replaced IAS with a new feature called NPS. NPS is the Microsoft implementation of a RADIUS server and proxy in Windows Server 2008, and promises to be even simpler to use than IAS. You will need to know how to set up a RADIUS server using NPS. Begin by installing NPS and setting up your RADIUS Server.

Configuring & Implementing...

Installing NPS and Setting Up Your RADIUS Server

1. Open **Server Manager** and click on the **Add Roles**.
2. Choose the **Network Policy and Access Services** shown in Figure 6.9, and review the overview screen (see Figure 6.10).

Continued

Figure 6.9 Choosing the NPS Role

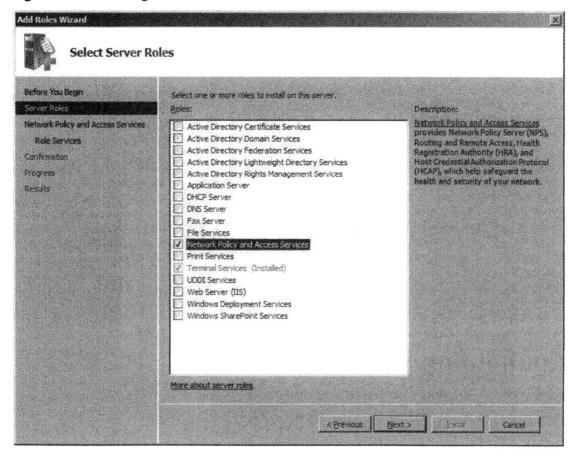

Figure 6.10 Overview Screen on NPS

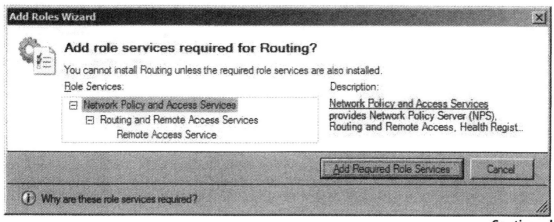

Continued

3. Select the **Network Policy Service** role. You may notice that the Network Policy Service is actually the RADIUS server that you are used to seeing with previous versions of Windows Server in IAS.

4. Click **Next**. You will see a final confirmation screen, as seen in Figure 6.10.

5. Click **Install**.

6. Once the software has been loaded, click on **Network Policy Server** under administrator tools. You will see that the RADIUS Client and Server Tabs are available and can be configured according to your needs by right-clicking on them and selecting **Properties**.

NPS can be used as a RADIUS proxy to provide the routing of RADIUS messages between RADIUS clients (access servers) and RADIUS servers that perform user AAA for the connection attempt. When used as a RADIUS proxy, NPS is a central switching or routing point through which RADIUS access and accounting messages flow. NPS records information about forwarded messages in an accounting log.

Configuring Wireless Access

Increased use of laptop computers and other wireless access devices within an enterprise along with an increase in worker mobility, have fuelled the demand for wireless networks in recent years. Up until recently, wireless technology was plagued with incompatibility issues and vendor-specific products. The technology was slow, expensive, and reserved for mobile situations or hostile environments where cabling was impractical or impossible. In recent years, the maturing of industry standards has caused a leveling point. This is thanks to industry-enforced compatibility standards and the deployment of lightweight wireless networking hardware. All of these factors have allowed wireless technology to come of age in the modern company.

Wireless networking hardware requires the use of technology that deals with radio frequencies as well as data transmission. The most widely used standard is 802.11 produced by the IEEE. This is a standard defining all aspects of radio frequency wireless networking. There have been several amendments to the 802.11 standard, the most recent being 802.11i.

Many Wireless networks use an AP to gain connectivity. In this type of network, the AP acts like a hub, providing connectivity for the wireless computers. It can connect the wireless LAN to a wired LAN, allowing wireless computer access to

LAN resources. This includes such resources as file servers or existing internet connectivity. This type of wireless network is said to run in infrastructure mode.

An ad hoc or peer-to-peer wireless network is one in which a number of computers each equipped with a wireless networking interface card, can connect without the use of an AP. Each computer communicates with all of the other wireless-enabled computers directly. This allows for the sharing of files and printer services, but may not be able to access wired LAN resources. The exception to this is if one of the computers acts as a bridge or AP to the wired LAN using special software.

As you might be familiar with in Windows Server 2003, Wireless Auto Configuration will attempt to pair up configured preferred wireless networks with the wireless networks that are broadcasting their network name. If no such available networks exist that match a preferred wireless network, Wireless Auto Configuration will then send a number of probe requests to attempt to find a match. These are to try and determine if the preferred networks in the ordered list are non-broadcast networks. The end result of this total process should be that broadcast networks are connected to before non-broadcast networks. This even includes situations where a non-broadcast network is higher in the preferred list than a broadcast network. A big downside of this method, however, is that a Windows XP or Windows Server 2003 wireless client has to advertise its list of preferred wireless networks when sending probe requests. This leaves clients vulnerable while sending these probe requests.

Windows Server 2008 presents a better option. By configuring the wireless networks as broadcast, the wireless network names will be included in the Beacon frames sent by the wireless AP. If you set the wireless network as non-broadcast, the Beacon frame contains a wireless network name. This name is set to NULL, which results in Wireless Auto Configuration attempting connection to the wireless networks in the preferred network list order. This is regardless of whether they are broadcast or non-broadcast. By explicitly marking wireless networks as broadcast or non-broadcast, Windows Server 2008 wireless clients only send probe requests for non-broadcast wireless networks. This reduces wireless client side vulnerability and enhances security.

Previously, if a preferred wireless network could not be connected to and the wireless client was configured in a way that prevented automatic connections not in the preferred list by default, then Wireless Auto Configuration would create a random wireless network name. Then it would place the wireless network adapter in infrastructure mode. The random wireless network does not have a security configuration, making it possible for all kinds of malicious users to connect to the wireless client, thereby using the random wireless network name.

For computers running Windows Server 2008 that use updated wireless drivers designed for Windows Vista, Wireless Auto Configuration will remove this vulnerability by parking the wireless network adapter in a passive listening mode. A parked wireless device does not send probe request frames for a random wireless network name. It also does not allow for any other names, so malicious users cannot connect to the wireless client.

If you are using a wireless network adapter driver that was designed for Windows XP, computers running Windows Vista or Windows Server 2008 will use the behavior of the Wireless Client Update for Windows XP with Service Pack 2 (a random wireless network name with a security configuration).

Windows Server 2008 troubleshooting wireless connections is made much easier through the following features:

- **Network Diagnostics Framework** The Network Diagnostics Framework is an extensible architecture that provides users with a means to recover from and troubleshoot problems with network connections. In the case of a failed wireless connection, Network Diagnostics Framework will give the user the option to identify and correct the problem. Wireless support for the Network Diagnostics Framework tries to discover the source of the failed connection and will automatically fix the problem. Also based on your security considerations, it can be made to prompt the user to make the appropriate configuration change themselves.

- For a failed wireless connection attempt, the wireless components of Windows Server 2008 now records detailed information about the connection attempt in the Windows event log. Support professionals can now access and use these records to perform troubleshooting tasks, and attempt to resolve the problem quickly if the wireless diagnostics either could not resolve the problem or when it could resolve the problem, but the problem cannot be fixed by changing wireless client settings. This will cut down on the time needed to resolve wireless connection support problems. These can also be automatically collected by network administrators using Microsoft Operations Manager, to be analyzed for patterns and wireless infrastructure design changes.

- You can now gain access to in-depth information about the computer's state and wireless components in Windows, and their interaction when the problem occurred. This can be done using information from *wireless diagnostics tracing* in Windows Server 2008. To use wireless diagnostics tracing, you must start tracing, reproduce the problem, stop tracing, and then collect the tracing report. To view the tracing report, in the console tree of the Reliability and Performance Monitor snap-in open **Reports | System | Wireless Diagnostics**.

Windows Server 2003 and Windows XP do not have a command-line interface that allows you to configure the wireless settings that are available from the wireless dialog boxes in the Network Connections folder, or through the Wireless Network (IEEE 802.11) Policies Group Policy settings. Command-line configuration of wireless settings can help deployment of wireless networks in the following situations:

- **Automated script support for wireless settings without using Group Policy Wireless Network (IEEE 802.11) Policies Group Policy settings only apply in an Active Directory domain.** For an environment without Active Directory or a Group Policy infrastructure, a script that automates the configuration of wireless connections can be run either manually or automatically, such as part of the login script.

- **Bootstrapping of a wireless client onto the protected organization's wireless network.** A wireless client computer that is not a member of the domain cannot connect to the organization's protected wireless network. Furthermore, computers are not able to join the domain until a successful connection has occurred to the organization's secure wireless network. A command-line script provides a method to connect to the organization's secure wireless network to join the domain.

In Windows Server 2008, you can use **Netsh** commands in the **netsh wlan** context to do the following:

- Save all wireless client settings in a named profile including general settings (the types of wireless networks to access), 802.11 settings (SSID, type of authentication, type of data encryption), and 802.1X authentication settings (EAP types and their configuration).

- Specify the list of allowed and denied wireless network names.

- Specify the order of preferred wireless networks.

- Display a wireless client's configuration.

- Remove the wireless configuration from a wireless client.

- Migrate a wireless configuration setting between wireless clients.

Many applications are not network aware, resulting in customer confusion and developer overhead. For example, an application cannot automatically adjust its behavior based on the currently attached network and conditions. Users might have to reconfigure application settings depending on the network to which they are attached (their employer's private network, the user's home network, the Internet). To remove the configuration burden, application developers can use low-level Windows APIs, data constructs, and perhaps even probing the network themselves to determine the current network and adjust their application's behavior accordingly.

To provide an operating system infrastructure to allow application developers to more easily reconfigure application behavior based on the currently attached network, the Network Awareness APIs in Windows Server 2008 make network information available to applications and enables them to easily and effectively adapt to these changing environments. The Network Awareness APIs allow applications to obtain up-to-date network information and location change notification.

Set Service Identifier (SSID)

The Service Set Identifier (SSID) is a 32-character unique identifier attached to the header of packets that are sent over a Wireless Local Area Network (WLAN). The SSID acts as a password when a mobile device tries to connect to the BSS. The SSID differentiates one WLAN from another. This way all APs and all devices attempting to connect to a specific WLAN must use the same SSID in order to succeed. No device will be permitted to join the BSS unless it can provide the unique SSID. SSID is not a security measure, because it can very easily be sniffed due to being stored in plain text.

In Windows Server 2008, an additional wireless network configuration setting has been added that can indicate whether a wireless network is broadcast or non-broadcast. This setting can be configured locally through the "Manually connect to a wireless network" dialog box, the properties of the wireless network, or through Group Policy. The "Connect even if the network is not broadcasting" check box determines whether the wireless network broadcasts or does not broadcast its SSID. Once selected, Wireless Auto Configuration sends probe requests to discover if the non-broadcast network is in range.

Configured wireless networks are now openly marked as broadcast or non-broadcast. Windows Server 2008-based wireless clients only send probe requests for wireless networks that are configured for automatic connection and as non-broadcast.

This method allows Windows Server 2008-based wireless clients to detect non-broadcast networks when they are in range. Therefore, even though they are not broadcasting the name of their wireless network, they will appear in the list of available wireless networks when they are in range. The wireless client detects whether the automatically connected, non-broadcast networks are in range based on the probe request responses. Then Wireless Auto Configuration attempts to connect to the wireless network in the preferred networks list order. This is regardless of whether they are configured as broadcast or non-broadcast. By only sending probe requests for automatically connected, non-broadcast networks, Windows Server 2008-based wireless clients reduce the number of situations in which they disclose their wireless network configuration.

You can also configure manually connected, non-broadcast wireless networks. In doing so, you can control exactly when to send probe requests. Manually connected, non-broadcast wireless networks are always displayed in the list of available networks, allowing users to initiate connections as needed.

Despite the improvements in non-broadcast network support in Windows Server 2008, Microsoft recommends against using non-broadcast wireless networks.

Wi-Fi Protected Access (WPA)

Wi-Fi Protected Access (WPA) was designed to provide a much higher level of security for wireless users than existing WEP standards provide. The WPA specification makes allowances both for network-based authentication for corporate networks, and for a special home mode for use in a SOHO or home-user environment. WPA is capable of interoperating with WEP devices, although in cases of interoperability, the default security for the entire wireless infrastructure reverts to the WEP standard. WPA's network-based authentication can make use of existing authentication technologies such as RADIUS servers, so adding the secure technology that WPA represents won't disrupt existing network infrastructures too much. Windows Server 2008 offers full support and configuration for WPA through the Wireless Group Policy settings.

Wi-Fi Protected Access 2 (WPA2)

Windows Server 2008 includes built-in support to configure WPA2 authentication options with both the standard profile (locally configured preferred wireless networks), and the domain profile with Group Policy settings. WPA2 is a product certification available through the Wi-Fi Alliance that certifies wireless equipment as being compatible with the IEEE 802.11i standard. WPA2 in Windows Server 2008 supports both WPA2-Enterprise (IEEE 802.1X authentication) and WPA2-Personal (pre-shared key authentication) modes of operation.

Windows Server 2008 also includes full support for WPA2 for an ad hoc mode wireless network including the *Fast Roaming* settings. Fast roaming is an advanced capability of WPA2 wireless networks that allow wireless clients to more quickly roam from one wireless AP to another by using pre-authentication and pair wise master key (PMK) caching in infrastructure mode. With Windows Server 2008, you can configure this feature using the Wireless Group Policy settings.

Ad Hoc vs. Infrastructure Mode

To set up an ad hoc wireless network, each wireless adapter must be configured for ad hoc mode versus the alternative infrastructure mode. In addition, all wireless adapters on the ad hoc network must use the same SSID and the same channel number.

An ad hoc network tends to feature a small group of devices all in very close proximity to each other.

Performance suffers as the number of devices grows, and a large ad hoc network quickly becomes difficult to manage. Ad hoc networks cannot bridge to wired LANs or to the Internet without installing a special-purpose gateway.

Ad hoc networks make sense when needing to build a small, all-wireless LAN quickly and spend the minimum amount of money on equipment. Ad hoc networks also work well as a temporary fallback mechanism if normally available infrastructure mode gear (APs or routers) stop functioning.

Most installed wireless LANs today utilize infrastructure mode that requires the use of one or more APs. With this configuration, the AP provides an interface to a distribution system (e.g., Ethernet), which enables wireless users to utilize corporate servers and Internet applications.

As an optional feature, however, the 802.11 standard specifies ad-hoc mode, which allows the radio network interface card (NIC) to operate in what the standard refers to as an independent basic service set (IBSS) network configuration. With an IBSS, APs are not required. User devices communicate directly with each other in a peer-to-peer manner.

Ad hoc mode allows users to form a wireless LAN with no assistance or preparation. This allows clients to share documents such as presentation charts and spreadsheets by switching their NICs to ad hoc mode to form a small wireless LAN within their meeting room. Through ad hoc mode, you can easily transfer the file from one laptop to another. With any of these applications, there's no need to install an AP and run cables.

The ad hoc form of communications is especially useful in public-safety and search-and-rescue applications. Medical teams require fast, effective communications when attempting to find victims. They can't afford the time to run cabling and install networking hardware.

Before making the decision to use ad hoc mode, you should consider the following:

- **Cost Efficiency** Without the need to purchase or install an AP, you'll save a considerable amount of money when deploying ad hoc wireless LANs.

- **Rapid Setup Time** Ad hoc mode only requires the installation of radio NICs in the user devices. As a result, the time to set up the wireless LAN is much less than installing an infrastructure wireless LAN.

- **Better Performance Possible** The question of performance with ad hoc mode is very debatable. Performance can be higher with ad hoc mode because there is no need for packets to travel through an AP. This only applies to a small number of users, however. If you have many users, then you will have better performance by using multiple APs to separate users onto non-overlapping channels. This will help to reduce medium access contention and collisions. Also, because of a need for sleeping stations to wake up during each beacon interval, performance can be lower with ad hoc mode due to additional packet transmissions if you implement power management.

- **Limited Network Access** There is no distribution system with ad hoc wireless LANs. Because of this, users have limited effective access to the Internet and other wired network services. Ad hoc is not a good solution for larger enterprise wireless LANs where there's a strong need to access applications and servers on a wired network.

- **Difficult Network Management** Network management can become a nightmare with ad hoc networks, because of the fluidity of the network topology and lack of centralized devices. The lack of an AP makes it difficult for network managers to monitor performance, perform security audits, and manage their network. Effective network management with ad hoc wireless

LANs requires network management at the user device level. This requires a significant amount of overhead packet transmission over the wireless LAN. This again disqualifies ad hoc mode away from larger, enterprise wireless LAN applications.

Infrastructure mode requires a wireless AP for wireless networking. To join the WLAN, the AP and all wireless clients must be configured to use the same SSID. The AP is then cabled to the wired network to allow wireless clients access to, for example, Internet connections or printers. Additional APs can be added to the WLAN to increase the reach of the infrastructure and support any number of wireless clients.

Compared to the alternative, ad hoc wireless networks, infrastructure mode networks offer the advantage of scalability, centralized security management, and improved reach.

The disadvantage of infrastructure wireless networks is simply the additional cost to purchase AP hardware.

Wireless Group Policy

New technology makes it easier for mobile workers to connect to hotspots or corporate LANS, by eliminating the need for manual configuration of the network connection. Enterprises can better manage guest access on their network and provide payment plans such as pay-per-use or monthly Internet access to customers, but in order to do so a strict wireless group, policy must be maintained to better control access.

Wireless network settings can be configured locally by users on client computers, or centrally. To enhance the deployment and administration of wireless networks, you need to take advantage of Group Policy. In doing so, you can create, modify, and assign wireless network policies for Active Directory clients and members of the wireless network. When you use Group Policy to define wireless network policies, you can configure wireless network connection settings, enable IEEE 802.1X authentication for wireless network connections, and specify the preferred wireless networks that clients can connect to. By default, there are no Wireless Network (IEEE 802.11) policies.

Summary

The main objectives covered in this chapter deal with the routing and configuration of network access in a windows Server 2008 environment. It includes all of the new features that have been introduced, as well as old technology no longer supported in this build.

This also includes the routing of network topography using static and dynamic routing, and the differences between the two. You should now be familiar with the fundamentals of routing and the protocols used in its practice. This will also include RIP and OSPF protocols. Windows Server 2008 has chosen not to support OSPF for this build.

You should be aware of the need for remote access in the business environment. This includes what features of remote access are supported such as dial up, VPNs, NAT, and RADIUS, and how each of these aspects can be configured and installed. You should also be aware of the newest VPN protocol for Windows Server 2008, SSTP, and how it compares to other VPN protocols. You should now be able to set up a SSL VPN network from start to finish using the RRAS, NPS, and NAP. Additionally, you should be aware of all of the necessary installation methods for these snap-in features.

Lastly you should have a good grasp of wireless access methods such as infrastructure mode and ad hoc mode, and be able to distinguish which of these options is best for the situation you are presented with. This also includes the security methods that are supported for wireless access in Windows Server 2008, such as WEP, WPA, and WPA2. You should be confident in how to distinguish the advantages and disadvantages of each of these methods and also be able to Group Policy for each of them

Solutions Fast Track

Configuring Routing

☑ **Static Routing** Describes a system that does not implement adaptive routing in its configuration. In these systems, routes through a network are defined by set paths referred to as static routes. These types of routes are inserted into the router manually by the system administrator. This is accomplished via the route command, which can be used to manipulate local routing tables.

- ☑ **Distance-vector Routing Protocol** A distance-vector routing protocol requires that a router contact and transmit to its neighbors any topology changes to the network. The frequency of this must be periodic and in most instances when a change is detected. RIP is the most popular example of this type of protocol.

- ☑ **Link State Protocol** The simplest explanation of link-state routing is that every node (router) is given a map of the topology of the network. This map is in graph form, and shows the connectivity of all the nodes in the network. Then each individual node calculates the next best hop from every node in the network. This information then forms the routing table for each individual node based on its calculations. No other communications occur between nodes. The most popular version of this is the OSPF

- ☑ OSPF routing protocol component in Routing and Remote Access is no longer present.

Configuring Remote Access

- ☑ Remote access is commonly used by many companies today to allow access to a computer or a network from a remote location. Most corporations include people at branch offices, telecommuters, and people who are traveling that will need to be able to gain access to network resources. Even clients using your companies services from home need to gain access to the Internet through an ISP.

- ☑ Most of the major functions of Network Access and the objectives that you will be required to know for your examine, revolve around the RRAS role.

- ☑ Remote access policies validate a number of connection settings before authorizing the connection, including the following: Remote access permission, Group membership, Type of connection, Time of day, and Authentication methods.

- ☑ Small- to medium-sized organizations with private networks to access resources on the Internet or other public network, use NAT for this reasoning. They configure reusable private IPv4 addresses while the computers on the public servers are set up with globally unique IPv4 addresses. The most useful deployment of NAT is in a SOHO or a medium-sized business that uses RRAS.

☑ SSTP is the latest alternative form of VPN tunnel. SSTP is an application-layer protocol. It uses a synchronous communication, which works in unilateral motion between two programs, allowing a constant exchange and comparison of data. It allows for a very efficient usage of the communication resources available to a network. SSTP is based on SSL as opposed to IPSec or PPTP, and thereby uses port 443 for traffic.

☑ VPN uses public wires to join nodes to create a network. This network allows the user to create their own private networks for the transfer of data. There are a large number of security systems at play within the VPN, such as encryption and other security measures. This makes certain that no data is intercepted by unauthorized users.

☑ RADIUS is protocol used for controlling access to network resources by authenticating, authorizing, and accounting for access, referred to as an AAA protocol. RADIUS is the unofficial industry standard for this type of access.

☑ Windows Server 2008 Microsoft has replaced IAS with a new feature called NPS. NPS is the Microsoft implementation of a RADIUS server and proxy in Windows Server 2008, and promises to be even simpler and more secure to use than IAS.

☑ NAP, when used in unison with NPS, creates a "total system health policy enforcement platform." NAP is designed to enhance a corporate VPN. This is accomplished when clients establish a VPN session with a Windows Server 2008 system that is running the RRAS. Once a connection is made, a NPS will validate the remote system and determine the status of its health.

Configuring Wireless Access

☑ The SSID is a 32-character unique identifier attached to the header of packets that are sent over a WLAN. The SSID acts as a password when a mobile device tries to connect to the BSS. The SSID differentiates one WLAN from another. This way all access points and all devices attempting to connect to a specific WLAN must use the same SSID in order to succeed. No device will be permitted to join the BSS, unless it can provide the unique SSID. SSID is not a security measure, because it can very easily be sniffed due to being stored in plain text.

☑ In Windows Server 2008, an additional wireless network configuration setting has been added that can indicate whether a wireless network is broadcast or non-broadcast. This allows Windows Server 2008-based wireless clients to detect non-broadcast networks when they are in range. Even though they are not broadcasting the name of their wireless network, they will appear in the list of available wireless networks when they are in range.

☑ Windows Server 2003 and Windows XP do not have a command-line interface that allows you to configure the wireless settings that are available from the wireless dialog boxes in the Network Connections folder, or through the Wireless Network (IEEE 802.11) Policies Group Policy settings. Windows Server 2008 has a command-line configuration of wireless settings that can help deployment of wireless networks.

☑ WPA was designed to provide a much higher level of security for wireless users than existing WEP standards provide. The WPA specification makes allowances both for network-based authentication for corporate networks, and for a special home mode for use in a SOHO or home-user environment. WPA is capable of interoperating with WEP devices.

☑ Windows Server 2008 includes full support for WPA2 for an ad hoc mode wireless network, including the Fast Roaming settings. Fast roaming is an advanced capability of WPA2 wireless networks, that allows wireless clients to more quickly roam from one wireless AP to another by using pre-authentication and PMK caching.

☑ On wireless computer networks, ad hoc mode is a method for wireless devices to directly communicate with each other. Operating in ad hoc mode allows all wireless devices within range of each other to discover and communicate in peer-to-peer fashion without involving central access points (including those built in to broadband wireless routers).

☑ Infrastructure mode requires a wireless AP for wireless networking. To join the WLAN, the AP and all wireless clients must be configured to use the same SSID. The AP is then cabled to the wired network to allow wireless clients access to, for example, Internet connections or printers. Additional APs can be added to the WLAN to increase the reach of the infrastructure and support any number of wireless clients.

Frequently Asked Questions

Q: What is Static Routing?

A: Static routing describes a system that does not implement adaptive routing in its configuration. In these systems, routes through a network are defined by set paths referred to as static routes.

Q: What changes have been made to Windows Server 2008 in regards to routing?

A: These are the major changes present in Windows Server 2008 in regards to routing:

- BAP is no longer supported by Windows Server 2008.

- X.25 is also no longer supported.

- SLIP, an encapsulation of IP meant for use over serial ports and modems, has also been excluded due to infrequency of use. All SLIP-based connections will automatically be updated to PPP-based connections.

- ATM, which was used to encode data traffic into small fixed cells, has been discarded.

- IP over IEEE 1394 is no longer supported.

- NWLink IPX/SPX/NetBIOS Compatible Transport Protocol has been omitted.

- Services for Macintosh (SFM).

- OSPF routing protocol component in Routing and Remote Access is no longer present.

- Basic Firewall in Routing and Remote Access has been replaced with the new Windows Firewall feature.

- Static IP filter APIs for Routing and Remote Access are no longer viable, and have been replaced with Windows Filtering Platform APIs.

- SPAP, EAP-MD5-CHAP, and MS-CHAP authentication protocols for PPP-based connections are no longer used by Windows Server 2008.

Q: Is IAS still a feature of Windows Server 2008 and if not, what has replaced it?

A: In previous incarnations of Windows Server 2003 IAS snap-in was Microsoft's implementation of a RADIUS server and proxy. It was capable of performing localized connection AAA Protocol for many types of network access, including wireless and VPN connections. For Windows Server 2008, Microsoft has replaced IAS with a new snap in called NPS. NPS is the Microsoft implementation of a RADIUS server and proxy in Windows Server 2008, and promises to be even simpler to use than IAS.

Q: What is an SSL VPN?

A: An SSL VPH is a VPN that uses SSTP as its tunneling protocol. With SSLVPN, static IP addresses are not required, clients are unnecessary in most cases, and since connections are made via a browser over the Internet, the default connection protocol is TCP/IP. This makes connections transparent to the user.

Q: How is Windows Firewall with Advanced Security better than previous versions?

A: This new version of WFAS has a number of advanced components that will help with your security needs.

- **New GUI Interface** MMC is a snap-in that is available to help configure the advanced firewall.

- **Bi-directional Filters** Unlike past versions of Windows Firewall, WFAS filters both outbound traffic and inbound traffic.

- **Better IPSec Compatibility** WFAS rules and IPSec encryption configurations are both integrated into the same singular interface.

- **Enhanced Rules Generation** Using WFAS, you can create firewall rules for Windows Active Directory service accounts and groups. This includes source/destination IP addresses, protocol numbers, source and destination TCP/UDP ports, ICMP, IPv6 traffic, and interface all on the Windows Server.

Q: When does ad hoc mode work best for wireless access?

A: Ad hoc networks work best when building a small, all-wireless LAN quickly, with the lowest cost possible for equipment. Ad hoc networks also work well as a temporary fallback mechanism if normally available infrastructure mode gear (APs or routers) fail to function.

## Chapter 7

Configuring File and Print Services

Solutions in this chapter:

- Configuring a File Server
- Configuring Distributed File System (DFS)
- Configuring Shadow Copy Services
- Configuring Backup and Restore
- Managing Disk Quotas
- Configuring and Monitoring Print Services

☑ Summary

☑ Solutions Fast Track

☑ Frequently Asked Questions

Introduction

The entire point of creating a computer network is to allow users to share the various resources that are located on the network. File shares allow users to collaborate on documents, and printer shares keep you from having to purchase every employee his or her own individual printer. As important as it is to be able to share files and printers, though, it is equally important to be able to put certain restrictions in place to prevent the files or printers from being used in an unauthorized manner. After all, your file servers likely contain sensitive information, and you need to protect that information from accidental disclosure.

Security is important for printers as well. Although there is generally no harm in allowing an employee to print a document, you may need to limit some printers for use by only specific employees. For example, if your organization has a printer that's dedicated to the task of printing checks, you probably would not want casual users to have access to that printer. You may also want to restrict access to special-purpose printers that use expensive supplies. This chapter will show you how to configure Windows Server 2008 to act as a file or print server. It will also discuss some of the various security implications of doing so.

Configuring a File Server

Windows Server 2008 provides many powerful features for centralized control, administration, security, and sharing of resources. To share and secure files that multiple users on the network will access, configure your server by adding the File Services role in Server Manager. In this section, we will look at how to share folders, enable Offline Files for laptops and remote users, secure files and control user access, and encrypt sensitive or confidential files.

Windows Server 2008 introduces many new ways to perform administrative tasks using the command line instead of the GUI. At first, many network administrators think there is no good reason to use the command line and that Microsoft is reminiscing in the old DOS days. Well, you might be pleasantly surprised to learn that there are many good reasons to use the command line to perform administrative tasks! Command-line tools allow an administrator to script, automate, and schedule tasks. Let's say, for example, that you need to configure Windows Server 2008 to run a full system backup. "No problem," you might be thinking, "I can use the GUI to configure and run a full backup." Now imagine having to do this on 12 different servers—this is where the power of using the command line and writing a small script really comes in handy.

File Share Publishing

To configure a server for file sharing, you must add the **File Services** role in **Server Manager**. To open Server Manager, navigate to **Start Menu | Server Manager**. Server Manager is a preconfigured console designed to handle the most common administrative tasks. **Server Manager** allows you to:

- Add, remove, configure, and manage roles

- Manage users and groups

- Add/remove features

- View the event logs

- Monitor server performance

- And much more

Windows Server 2008 supports two file-sharing models: Standard (in-place) File Sharing and Public Folder Sharing. Table 7.1 explains the differences between these two models.

Table 7.1 Comparison of Sharing Models

Sharing Model	Explanation
Standard (in-place) File Sharing	Allows you to share a folder and all of its contents (files and subfolders) with users on the network. Standard File Sharing does not require you to move the files and folders to share them.
Public Folder Sharing	Allows you to use a common folder (%SystemDrive%\Users\Public) to share files and folders with other local users on the server and optionally network users as well. Requires you to place any files and folders you want to share out in the Public folder.

Sharing folders on your server is like opening a door (share) directly to a room (folder) to allow others to enter (network users to access the folder). In this analogy, a room may contain other rooms that are accessible once you have walked through the door just as a folder that is shared on the network can contain multiple subfolders that are accessible once you have connected to the file share. In the following Sidebar, we will add the **File Services** role to a Windows 2008 Server.

Configuring & Implementing...

Adding the File Services role in Server Manager

To enable file sharing and install the management tools in Windows Server 2008 follow these steps:

1. Launch the **Server Manager** console by navigating to **Start Menu | Server Manager**.

2. In the **Roles Summary** section of **Server Manager**, you will be presented with a list of the roles that are currently installed on your server, as seen in Figure 7.1. Click on the **Add Roles** hyperlink.

Figure 7.1 Roles Summary Section in the Server Manager Console

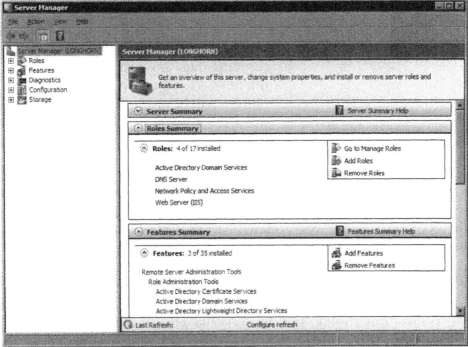

Continued

3. The **Add Roles Wizard** will open. Click the **Next** button if you are presented with a **Before You Begin** page.

4. On the **Select Server Roles** page shown in Figure 7.2, put a **checkmark** in the box next to **File Services**.

Figure 7.2 List of Available Roles on the Select Server Roles Page in the Add Roles Wizard

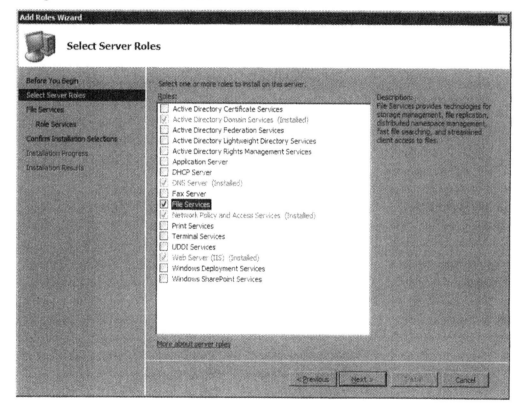

5. You will be presented with an **Introduction to File Services**; click the **Next** button.

6. On the **Select Role Services** page, verify that **File Server** is checked and click the **Next** button. You can add more Role Services at any time, so it is not necessary to select them at this time.

7. A summary of the options selected for installation will appear. Click on the **Install** button to start the installation process.

Additional Role Services

When you install the **File Services** role, Windows Server 2008 allows you to install a subset of roles called **Role Services**. Table 7.2 explains the **Role Services** available for the **File Services** role.

Table 7.2 Explanation of Role Services for the File Services Role

Role Service	Explanation
File Server	Enables the Server Message Block (SMB) protocol and the ability to share folders with other users on the network
Distributed File System	Enables the Distributed File System (DFS) and installs DFS management tools
DFS Namespace	Allows an administrator to share folders from multiple servers into one central share name (namespace)
DFS Replication	Allows an administrator to replicate files and folders among multiple servers
File Server Resource Manager	Installs the File Server Resource Manager, a useful tool for configuring and managing file screening and quotas, and for generating storage reports
Services for Network File System	Installs Services for the Network File System (NFS). The NFS protocol allows an administrator to share out folders to UNIX clients.
Windows Search Service	The new indexing service from Microsoft that allows clients to rapidly search for files on the target server. Windows Search Service works by creating an index of the most common files and other data types (such as e-mail, contacts, calendar appointments, documents, pictures, and multimedia) on the target server.
	The client-side search for Windows Search Service is built into Windows Vista. You can add it onto Windows Server 2003 and Windows XP by downloading and installing Windows Desktop Search from www.microsoft.com/windows/products/winfamily/desktopsearch/getitnow.mspx.
Windows Server 2003 File Services	Installs optional services for backward compatibility with Windows 2003 servers in a mixed environment

Continued

Table 7.2 Continued. Explanation of Role Services for the File Services Role

Role Service	Explanation
File Replication Service	Installs the File Replication Service (FRS). FRS is the older, less efficient service for replicating files and folders among multiple servers. This service is included for backward compatibility with Server 2003 R1. DFS replication is far more efficient (it's faster and uses less bandwidth) than FRS. However, DFS replication is available only on Server 2003 R2, Windows Server 2008, and later.
Indexing Service	Installs the legacy (older) Microsoft Indexing Service on the target server. This service has been replaced by the Windows Search Service and it is recommended that you install the Windows Search Service instead, unless you have a customized or non-Microsoft application that requires the legacy Indexing Service.
	The Indexing Service is slower and does not have as many features as the new Windows Search Service.
	You cannot install both the Indexing Service and Windows Search Service on the same server.

To add role services, navigate to **Start Menu | Server Manager | Roles | File Services** and click on the **Add Role Services** hyperlink, as shown in Figure 7.3.

Figure 7.3 Role Services Configuration for the File Services Role

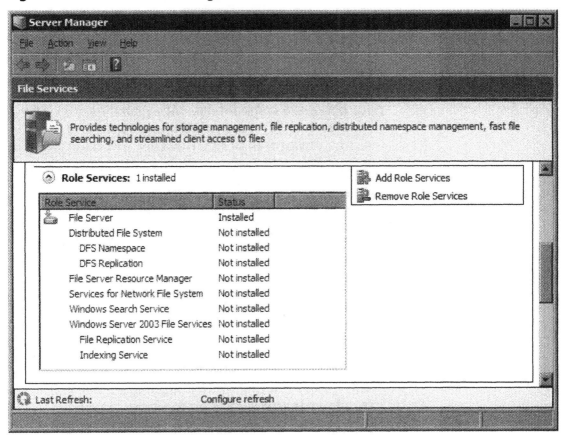

File Screening

New to Windows Server 2008 is the ability to prevent users from copying and saving specified file types to the server. For example, you may notice that your server's backups are starting to run out of space. Upon further inspection, you notice that one of your users is storing 20 GB of funny videos and TV shows in a shared folder on the server. As this is not important company data, it should not be taking up precious space on the server and consuming backup drive space. With Windows Server 2008 File Screening, you can actually configure each shared folder to block specified file types such as Music and Videos.

Figure 7.4 shows the error message a user will get if he or she attempts to copy a restricted file (in this case the file is called Music.mp3) to a share that has **File Screening** enabled and is blocking music files.

Figure 7.4 Error When Attempting to Copy a Restricted File

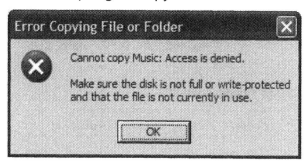

We will be given the option to configure File Screening in the following Sidebar.

Sharing a Folder

Windows sharing uses the SMB protocol, which is also known as Common Internet File System (CIFS); Microsoft's open standard based on SMB. The preferred method for sharing files and folders is to use the Standard (in-place) File Sharing model. As a means to simply sharing for novice administrators or to be run in conjunction with Standard (in-place) File Sharing, Windows Server 2008 also supports Public Folder Sharing.

To enable Public Folder sharing (optional), navigate to **Start Menu | Control Panel | Network and Sharing Center** and turn on **Public folder sharing**. Select the first option (see Figure 7.5) if you would like to share the public folder to network users using read-only access. Or you can select the second option to allow network users to modify and write to the public folder as well. Be sure to click the **Apply** button to enable your changes.

Figure 7.5 Public Folder Sharing Options in the Network and Sharing Center

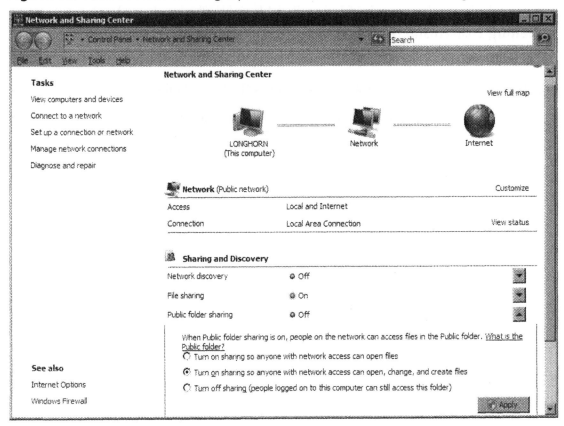

Once **Public Folder Sharing** is turned on, you can easily share files and folders by opening **Windows Explorer** and moving files and folders via drag and drop to the **Public** folder shown in the left pane folder list. In Figure 7.6, the first Public folder in the left pane folder list is the local Public folder. Figure 7.6 also shows that same Public folder and its contents as viewed through the network.

Figure 7.6 Accessing the Public Folder Share Using Windows Explorer

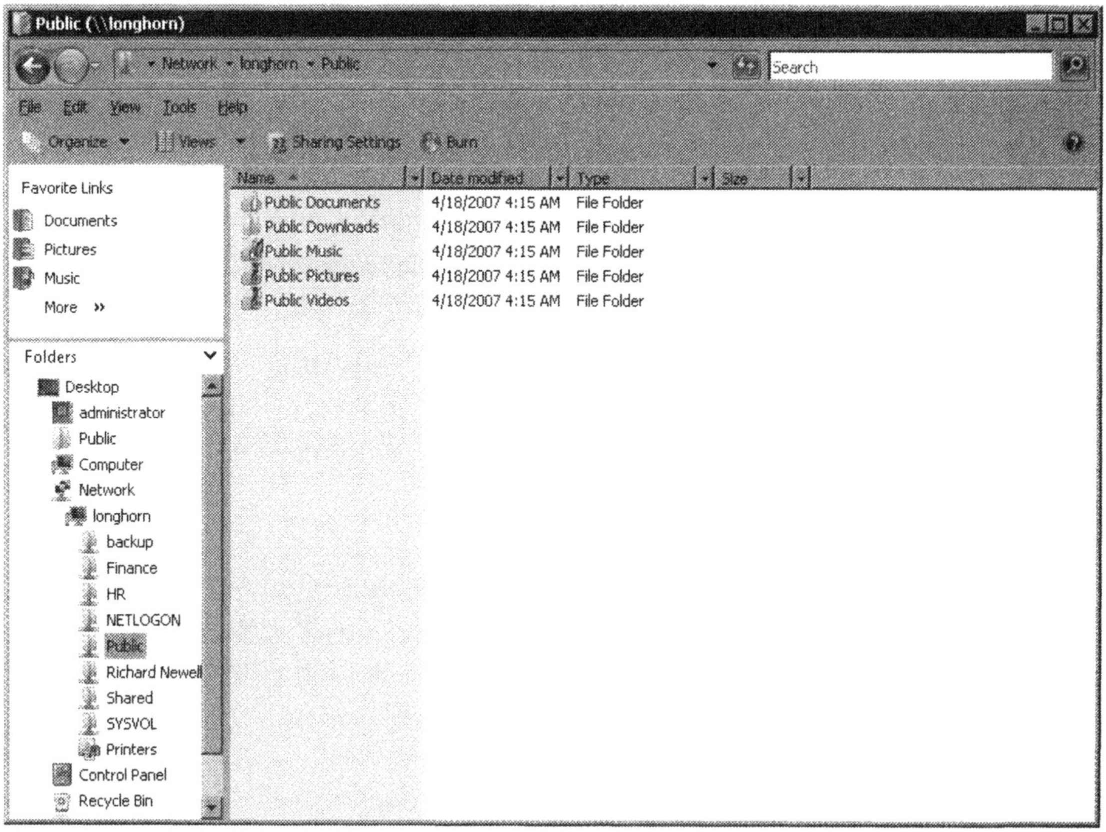

We will walk through the steps to configure shared folders and permissions using the Standard (in-place) File Sharing method in the following Sidebar in this chapter, but first we will briefly discuss the concepts of Share Permissions, NTFS permissions, and Offline Files.

Share Permissions

As you remember from earlier, sharing a folder is like opening a door to network users directly into that folder. Share Permissions are like posting a security guard at that door (share). As people (network users) attempt to enter the room, the security guard checks his list (Share Permissions) to see who is allowed in and who is not. If a user is allowed in with Full Control, the security guard lets him in and lets him do whatever he wants. If a user is allowed in with Read, the security guard lets him in but watches him as he is in the room to make sure he "looks but doesn't touch." Table 7.3 shows the available Share Permissions and their function.

Table 7.3 Overview of Share Permissions

Share Permission	Explanation
Full Control	The highest level of access to the folder. Allows users to view, modify, add, and delete files and folders, plus modify permissions.
Change	Allows users to view, modify, add, and delete files
Read	Allows users to view files and list folder contents

Windows Server 2008 and previous versions have both Share and NTFS permissions to support sharing on non–NTFS volumes such as FAT, or File Allocation Table, where only Share Permissions are available to control network access.

NTFS Permissions

Using NTFS permissions allows administrators a lot more control over access than Share Permissions. NTFS permissions also allow you to control access to files as well as folders whereas Share Permissions can only be set on the first-level folder (the folder being shared out).

Configuring & Implementing…

Locking Down Files from Local Access

In addition to securing files and folders accessed over the network, NTFS permissions also secure files and folders when users access them locally by logging directly into the workstation or server where the data resides. It is a best practice to use NTFS on all workstations that support it (Windows NT, 2000, XP, Vista, or Windows Server).

Using the room and door analogy (you can tell that we really like this analogy), NTFS permissions are like putting a padlock and chain on the individual items in the room (files and folders), desks, filing cabinets, chairs, and so on (Word documents,

Excel spreadsheets, PowerPoint presentations, etc.). Only the people you gave a key to can unlock those items, just as with NTFS permissions only the users you granted permissions to can access the files and folders. Keep in mind that users are also restricted by the Share Permissions (security guard at the door) for that folder when connecting through the network. For example, if the Share Permissions on a folder were set to **Everyone – Read**, users connecting through the network would be restricted to read-only access even if they had Full Control in NTFS (i.e., the security guard at the door is restricting them to "look but don't touch" even though they have a key).

NTFS permissions also give an administrator very granular control over how users can access files and folders. You can control all of the permissions listed in Table 7.4.

Table 7.4 Overview of NTFS Permissions

NTFS Permission	Explanation
Full Control	Allows the same permissions as Modify, plus the ability to take ownership, change NTFS permissions, and delete files and folders
Modify	Allows the same permissions as both Read & Execute and Write permissions. Also gives the user the ability to delete the folder.
Read & Execute	Allows users to view all files, folders, and subfolders as well as open or run the files or programs
List Folder Contents	Allows users to view the contents of the folder
Read	Allows users to view and open the files in a folder and view the properties of the files
Write	Same as Read permission; plus the user can create and edit files and subfolders
Special Permissions	Allow you to set the advanced and extremely granular permissions that make up the permissions above, such as "Traverse folder / execute file" and "Read extended attributes". For more information, see the Windows Server 2008 help topic titled "Permission Entry Dialog Box".

To modify or view NTFS permissions, right-click the file or folder you want to set permissions on and click on **Properties**, then navigate to the **Security** tab.

By default, permissions assigned to a folder using NTFS are automatically passed down to (or inherited by) subfolders and files (also known as *descendants*) within that parent folder. This concept is called *inheritance*. To disable inheritance for a specific folder or file.

Offline Files

The Offline Files feature in Windows gives users the ability to access the files from a network share, or shared folder on a network location, even when they are off the network. This is extremely useful when traveling with a laptop or connecting to a folder over a virtual private network (VPN) or WAN link. Offline Files works by caching (or making a local copy of) the files on a shared location (i.e., a server). If the network resource is unavailable, the user can still open and work on these files. When the shared resource is once again available, the user's changes are synchronized with the network share.

Offline Files support is available in Microsoft's client operating systems such as Windows XP and Windows Vista.

Now that we have discussed Share Permissions, NTFS permissions, and Offline Files, it is time to put File Sharing into action. The following Sidebar will lead you through the two primary methods for setting up Standard (in-place) File Sharing.

Configuring & Implementing...

Configuring Shared Folders and Permissions

Using Share and Storage Management:

1. Navigate to Start Menu | Server Manager | Roles | File Services and click on the Share and Storage Management node.

2. Share and Storage Management gives you an overview of folders that are currently being shared out on the network as well as the local paths to the shared folders, as seen in Figure 7.7.

Continued

Figure 7.7 Share and Storage Management

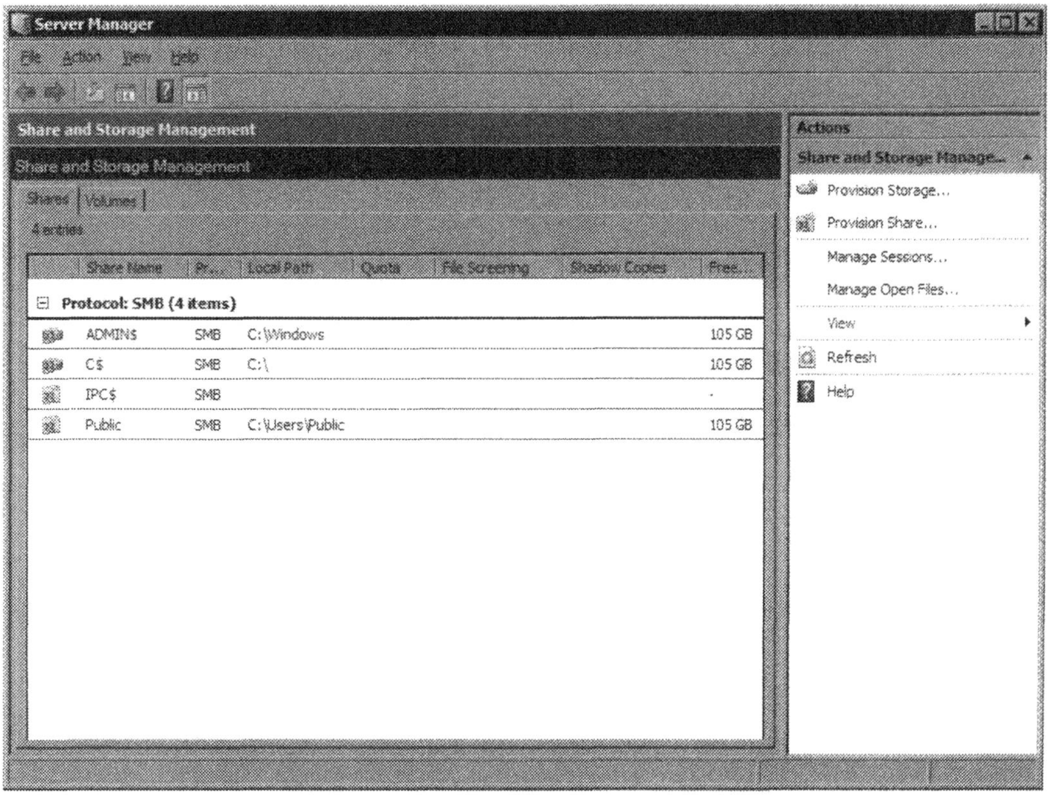

3. Click on the Provision Share hyperlink to launch the Provision a Shared Folder Wizard.

4. On the **Shared Folder Location** page click the **Browse** button and select the folder you would like to share. You can use the **Make New Folder** button if you need to create a new folder to share. Click **OK** when you have selected a folder and then click **Next**.

5. On the **NTFS permissions** page, select the **Yes, change NTFS permissions** option and click **Edit Permissions** to control which users and groups will have access to this folder.

6. Click the **Advanced** button and uncheck the **Include inheritable permissions from the object's parent** checkbox, as shown in Figure 7.8. This will allow us to remove users and groups that are currently allowed access via inheritance from a parent folder. When prompted, choose to **Copy** the permission entries that were previously applied from the parent.

Continued

Figure 7.8 Advanced Security Settings for the HR Share

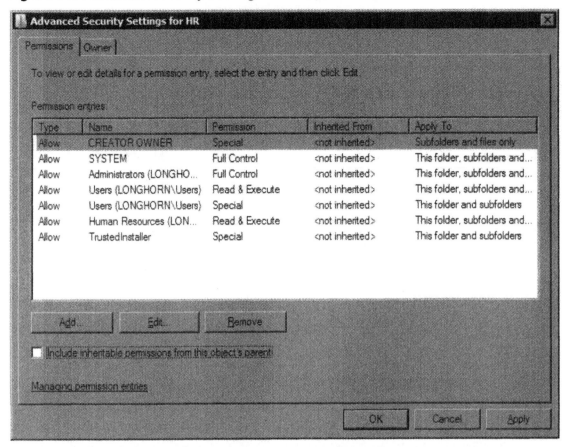

7. Click **OK** to get back to the Permissions screen and remove all users and groups except Administrators and/or Domain Admins.

8. Click the **Add** button to add the users or groups that will require access to this shared folder. In this example, we add the Human Resources group and grant them Modify access, as shown in Figure 7.9.

Continued

Figure 7.9 NTFS Permissions for the HR Share

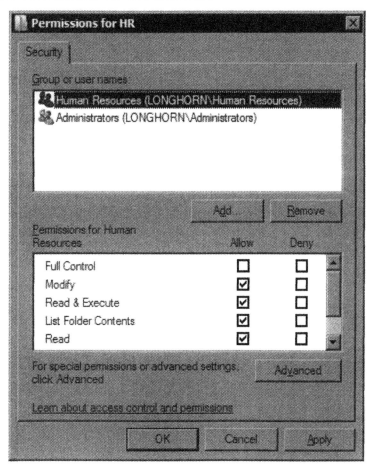

9. Click **OK** to return to the Provision a Shared Folder Wizard and then click **Next**.

10. On the **Share Protocols** page, choose **SMB** and verify the share name that you would like; then click **Next**.

11. The **SMB Settings** page allows you to configure options for Offline Files, Access-based enumeration, and connection limit. Click the **Next** button to continue.

12. On the **SMB Permissions** page, select the **Users and groups have custom share permissions** option and click the **Permissions** button. Set permissions using the best practice of **Authenticated Users – Full Control** and click **OK**, then **Next**.

Continued

13. The **Quota Policy** page allows you to configure a limit to the amount of disk space a user can consume. We will discuss quotas in more depth later in this chapter. Click the **Next** button to continue.

14. The **File Screen Policy** page allows us to configure file screening using templates from the File Server Resource Manager. Click **Next** to continue.

15. The **DFS Namespace Publishing** page allows us to add this share under a DFS namespace. We will discuss DFS in more depth later in this chapter. Click the **Next** button to continue.

16. Next click the **Create** button and then **Close**. Congratulations, you have just shared a folder in Windows Server 2008!

Alternatively, you can use Windows Explorer to share a folder using the following steps:

1. Launch Windows Explorer by navigating to **Start Menu | All Programs | Accessories | Windows Explorer**.

2. Using the **Folders** list in the left pane, locate the folder you would like to share (i.e., **Computer | Local Disk (C:) | Shares | Finance**).

3. Right-click on the target folder and select **Properties**.

4. Configure the NTFS permissions on the **Security** tab, as shown in Figure 7.10.

Figure 7.10 NTFS Permissions for a Folder

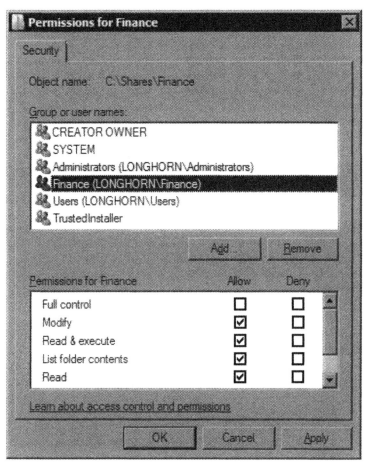

5. Use the **Sharing** tab and click on the **Advanced Sharing** button to configure share name (see Figure 7.11) and Share Permissions (see Figure 7.12).

Figure 7.11 Advanced Sharing

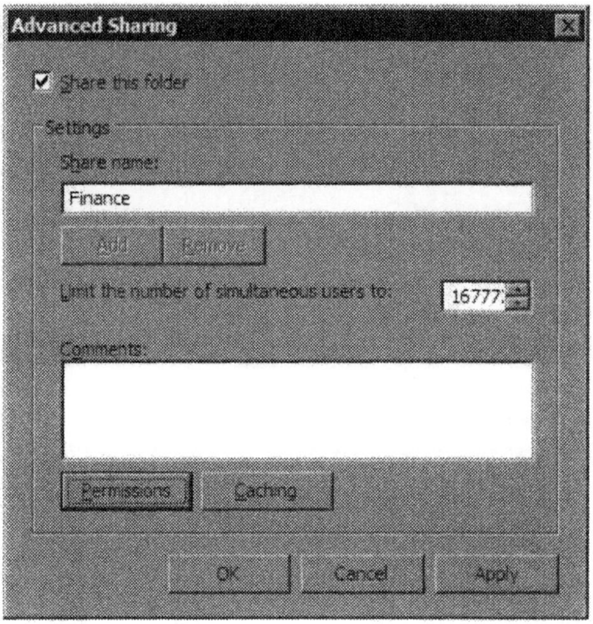

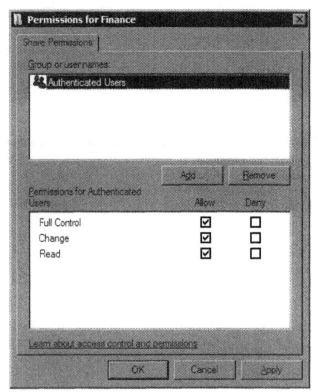

Figure 7.12 Share Permissions

Encrypting File System (EFS)

Now we will look at securing your files using the built-in encryption feature found in Windows Server 2008. Encrypting File System (EFS) is a feature that scrambles the data in your file to the point that it is not usable or viewable by an outside party. When you open an encrypted file Windows will automatically decrypt the data using a transparent process so that you can work with it. When you are finished working with the file Windows will automatically re-encrypt it for you using a transparent process. The simplicity of checking a box makes EFS very easy for Windows users to use.

Notes from the Underground…

Why Encrypt Files?

If you have ever wondered why you would want to encrypt your files, here is a true story. Of course, the names have been changed to protect the innocent.

My friend Gwendolyn was the coordinator of a charity golf tournament. The day of the big event, she arrived early and set down her laptop in a seemingly secure downstairs room in the clubhouse. In fact, this room was so secure (or appeared to be), it even had staff members from the golf course guarding the entrance. Gwendolyn immediately started running around coordinating the event and ensuring that every detail of this golf tournament would run smoothly. The weather was great and the tournament could not have gone better, except for one detail—Gwendolyn's laptop had been stolen. To her surprise, that sinking feeling in her stomach was not really about having lost a laptop worth $1,500; no, she had lost much more. That sinking feeling was about her data—in the hands of a thief. PowerPoint presentations, Word documents, Excel spreadsheets that she had worked on for months, even years, were on that laptop. Sensitive and confidential data from her company, credit card numbers, passwords, bank account information, e-mails—all in the hands of a thief. We searched for that laptop for more than an hour, asking everyone we had seen enter the room and interrogating the staff. The laptop was long gone, and Gwendolyn never did get it back.

Continued

> The good news is that Gwendolyn backed up her data frequently. Nearly all of it was recovered. The bad news is that none of her files was encrypted. Was the thief a kid who saw a laptop sitting out, and said to himself, "Hey look, a free laptop?" Or was it someone with plans to grab Gwendolyn's data? After all, I have even heard of thieves actually buying used hard drives on eBay to see what kind of confidential data they can pull off the drives—this could easily lead to identity theft.
>
> It is a good practice to encrypt any important or private files.

When you are browsing in Windows Explorer, the names of encrypted files and folders are displayed in green instead of black (compressed files and folders are in blue). You can only use Microsoft's EFS on Windows NTFS volumes. If you copy an encrypted file to a non-NTFS volume, Windows will copy the file in decrypted form. Marking a folder for encryption does not actually encrypt the folder itself; instead, it encrypts every file within the folder.

Working with EFS

EFS encrypts files using a public/private key that is automatically generated and stored in the user's profile. If a user logs into multiple computers, the EFS Private Keys should be copied to each computer using a certificate backup and restore procedure to ensure that the user can access encrypted data transferred from one computer to another. An alternative option to using the same EFS Private Key on multiple computers is to use a roaming profile for that user. When using a roaming profile, the EFS Private Key is stored on the server that contains the profile as opposed to the workstation a user logs into. For more information on backing up EFS Private Keys and EFS best practices, look at Microsoft knowledgebase article 223316, "Best practices for the Encrypting File System," at http://support.microsoft.com/kb/223316/EN-US/.

If a user is unable to open an encrypted file or his account is deleted, the file can be decrypted by a designated recovery agent. In an Active Directory domain environment, the default recovery agent is the Administrator account for the domain. In the following Sidebar, we will enable encryption on a file or folder in Windows Server 2008.

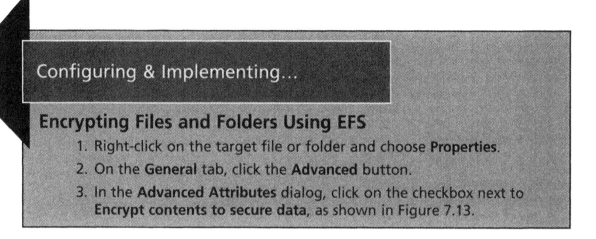

Configuring & Implementing...

Encrypting Files and Folders Using EFS

1. Right-click on the target file or folder and choose **Properties**.
2. On the **General** tab, click the **Advanced** button.
3. In the **Advanced Attributes** dialog, click on the checkbox next to **Encrypt contents to secure data**, as shown in Figure 7.13.

Figure 7.13 Encrypting a File or Folder Using Advanced Attributes

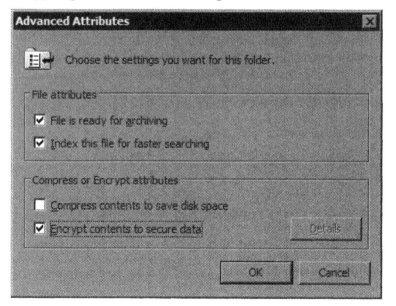

New & Noteworthy...

How to Hack Right Past Your Password

Your password does not protect you *nearly* as much as you would think. To gain access to all of your unencrypted files, hackers can take the hard drive out of your computer or laptop and install it into a computer over which they have administrative rights. This can also be used for good—if Windows fries and you need to recover files or one of your users has important data on her home computer (not a member of the domain) and forgot her password.

A handy device that all IT people should have is a USB to IDE/SATA cable. This device allows you to turn *any* IDE, SATA, or laptop hard drive into an external USB2.0 device. That means without shutting down your computer or even rebooting, you can plug in a hard drive from a failed computer and access all the files (except, of course, encrypted files, which require that you have the certificate or are a recovery agent). My USB to IDE/SATA cable is one of the best IT purchases I have ever made.

Making a backup of your encryption keys is critical to prevent against accidental loss. In environments where you do not have access to log in as a recovery agent or there are no recovery agents configured, you will be unable to decrypt your data if something happens to your keys. These environments include:

- Peer-to-peer networks
- Laptops that are not joined to the Active Directory domain
- Home offices

Events and situations that can lock you out of your EFS-encrypted files include the following:

- Your account password is reset.
- You attempt to access your encrypted files from a different computer than the one you used to encrypt the files.

- You reformat and reinstall Windows, and then try to access the encrypted files on a backup drive or network share.

To protect yourself from being locked out of your encrypted files, you can use the simple procedure in the following sidebar to back up your keys to a secure location.

Configuring & Implementing...

Backing Up Your EFS Certificate to Protect Against Accidental loss

1. Start Internet Explorer.

2. From the **Tools** menu, choose **Internet Options**.

3. On the **Content** tab, click the **Certificates** button.

4. On the **Personal** tab, select each certificate listed (if more than one appears) until you find the one that displays **Encrypting File System** in the **Certificate intended purposes** section. Windows automatically creates this certificate the first time you encrypt a file using this computer.

5. Select the proper certificate for Encrypting File System and click on the **Export** button, as shown in Figure 7.14.

Continued

Figure 7.14 Backing Up Your EFS Certificate

6. The **Certificate Export Wizard** will open. Click the **Next** button to continue.

7. Choose Yes, export the private key and click Next.

8. Verify that **Enable strong protection** is checked and click **Next**.

9. Type in a password to protect the exported EFS key and click **Next**.

10. Specify the location to save the key. It is a best practice not to store this on your hard drive, as it will be lost in the event of a drive failure or format. Make sure you store your key backup on an external drive, disk/disc, or server that will be kept in a secure location.

An exciting new feature in Windows Server 2008 is BitLocker Drive Encryption. BitLocker provides full-volume encryption on computers that have Trusted Platform Module (TPM) hardware. This feature is excellent for ensuring server data security in the event of a physical drive or server theft.

Configuring & Implementing...

Third-Party Encryption

Although Windows Server 2008 offers an excellent set of encryption features, you can use third-party encryption software to avoid some of the limitations and accomplish the following:

- Encrypt files on non-NTFS formats such as FAT
- Encrypt data on CDs or DVDs
- Use a passphrase instead of a key to decrypt your data

One of my favorites for this is TrueCrypt, which is freely available at www.truecrypt.org.

Configuring Distributed File System (DFS)

If you have more than one server on your network, you can use Microsoft's incredibly handy Distributed File System (DFS) features to extend the functionality of file sharing and replication. In Windows Server 2008, DFS can allow users to access shared network folders without having to remember on which server they reside. You can also configure DFS replication to copy and synchronize the files and folders on multiple servers. This is a very useful feature if your company has multiple locations, branch offices, or even just multiple servers in the same location. We will explore these features in more depth by looking at DFS namespaces, configuration and application, creating and configuring targets, and DFS replication.

DFS Namespaces

A DFS namespace is a virtual shared folder that contains shared folders from multiple servers. This allows users to access shared folders using the Universal Naming Convention (UNC) path \\[Domain]\[Namespace] instead of remembering the name of each server to which to connect. This also allows multiple servers to host a copy of the same shared folder. To create a DFS namespace, first add the **File Services** role in Server Manager and then add the Distributed File System Role Services, as shown in Figure 7.15.

Figure 7.15 Adding DFS Role Services

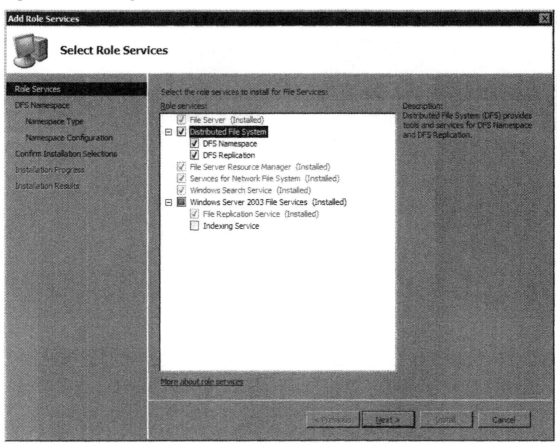

DFS Configuration and Application

You can configure DFS using the **Namespaces** and **Replication** tools located under **DFS Management** in Server Manager. When adding a DFS namespace, you will be asked whether you would like to use a domain-based namespace or stand-alone namespace. A domain-based namespace can be replicated to multiple servers for DFS availability if the host server fails. Domain-based namespaces are limited to 5,000 DFS folders. Stand-alone namespaces can support up to 50,000 DFS folders; however, the namespace is not replicated to other servers unless you are using a failover cluster and have configured replication on the cluster.

In the following Sidebar, we will walk through the steps required to create a DFS namespace.

Configuring & Implementing...

Configuring a DFS Namespace

In this exercise, we will create a DFS namespace. Be sure to add the DFS Role Services to the File Services role on your server before continuing.

1. In Server Manager, navigate to Roles | File Services | DFS Management | Namespaces.

2. Click on the **New Namespace** hyperlink to launch the **New Namespace Wizard**.

3. When asked for the server that will host the namespace, type in the name of your server and click **Next**.

4. On the **Namespace Name and Settings** page, type in the name you would like to call the namespace. The name you type in will appear as a virtual shared folder within which all the DFS shares (shared folders under one virtual namespace that really exist on multiple servers) are shown. In Figure 7.16, we use the name **Shared**. You can also create a different DFS namespace for each business unit within your organization (e.g., HR, Finance, IT, etc.).

Continued

Figure 7.16 Namespace Name and Settings in New Namespace Wizard

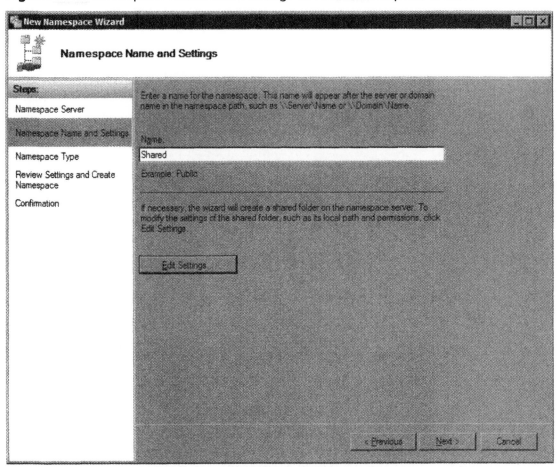

5. Be sure to click the **Edit Settings** button and set the appropriate **Share Permissions**, then click **Next**.

6. On the **Namespace Type** page, it is preferable to select **Domain-based namespace**. This will allow users to type in \\[*domain*]\[*namespace*] (e.g., \\2k8.local\Shared) instead of remembering a specific server name. Click **Next** to continue, then **Create** to complete the wizard.

7. Now users can browse to \\[*domain*] and see the namespace you just created as a virtual shared folder. Although it is currently empty, in the next exercise we will add a shared folder to the \\[*domain*]\Shared namespace.

Creating and Configuring Targets

A DFS target is simply a shared folder that is located on one or more servers. You can increase the availability of a shared folder by hosting it on multiple servers (i.e., specifying multiple targets for the same shared folder) and replicating the data between servers using DFS replication. Placing identical shares on multiple DFS servers is also a good idea from a server maintenance perspective. It allows you to take a file server down for maintenance without the users even knowing that the server was offline.

Earlier in this chapter, we used the Share and Storage Management tool to create a shared folder, and during this process we were given the option to configure DFS for that share as well. In the following Sidebar, we take a look at using the DFS Management | Namespaces tool to add a shared folder to our namespace.

Configuring & Implementing...

Adding Shared Folders to a DFS Namespace

In this exercise, we will add a shared folder to the \\[*domain*]\Shared DFS namespace.

1. In Server Manager, navigate to **Roles | File Services | DFS Management | Namespaces** and select the namespace we created in the previous exercise.

2. Click on the **New Folder** hyperlink to launch the **New Folder** dialog. Type in the name of the shared folder and click on the **Add** button to point this folder to one or more locations of this shared folder (targets) on one or more servers. In Figure 7.17, we created the **Finance** folder and pointed it to a shared folder that is replicated on two different servers.

Continued

Figure 7.17 Selecting DFS Targets in the New Folder Dialog

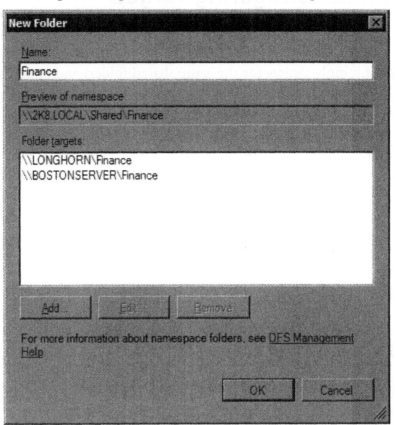

3. Now users can connect to \\[*domain*]\\[*namespace*] (e.g., \\2k8.local\\ Shared) and access the Finance share through DFS. If one of the targets (locations for a copy of the share) is offline, DFS will automatically point the user to one of the alternative locations.

DFS Replication

DFS replication is one of the best features for creating fault tolerance in case one of your servers or sites goes offline. You can use DFS replication to:

- Replicate/synchronize a folder or folders among multiple servers in a single location

- Replicate/synchronize a folder or folders with a remote location to create an off-site backup for business continuity in case a disaster such as fire, flood, hurricane, or theft interferes with business or destroys data in your office

- Create a Branch Office Box (BOB) at branch office locations to speed up local file access (also known as *caching*) with a share that replicates with the head office

DFS replication is different from FRS in versions of Windows Server prior to 2003 R2. The primary difference is a major improvement in the efficiency of replication by copying only the "differences" or changes to a file instead of the FRS method of copying *entire files*, even if only a small portion has been changed. DFS replication makes this possible by using a technology called Remote Differential Compression (RDC). Windows Server 2008 also supports FRS for backward compatibility in a mixed environment where it is necessary to replicate with Windows Server 2000 or 2003 R1 servers.

To create a new DFS Replication group, use the **New Replication Group** hyperlink in **Server Manager | Roles | Files Services | DFS Management | Replication**.

Configuring & Implementing…

DFS Replication and DFS Namespace

DFS does not require you to set up a DFS namespace to use DFS replication. You can use DFS replication and DFS namespaces independently of each other.

Configuring Shadow Copy Services

One of the greatest innovations introduced in Windows Server 2003 has now been improved in Server 2008 and is even included with Windows Vista. When files are shared on a network, all kinds of whacky things are bound to happen. A user may accidentally delete someone else's file. A user may accidentally delete her own file.

A user might change a few paragraphs in her Word document only to realize she was in "insert" mode and overwrote another page. The list goes on and on, but when these things happen (and they *do* happen), a user will ask her network administrator to restore the file from backup. This can be very time-consuming, and if the user waits too long before realizing she needs a file restored, it may be gone for good. Enter the magic of Shadow Copies.

The Windows Shadow Copy Service creates point-in-time backup copies of files located on a Shadow Copy-enabled volume. This puts the power of restore in the user's hands. Even if a user does not realize or understand how to restore using Shadow Copies, I have used it on many occasions to roll a file back to previous versions or even restore an entire deleted folder. It is much faster and easier than loading up the backup software and finding the backup containing the correct file(s).

To enable Shadow Copy on a Server Volume, navigate to **Start Menu | Computer, Right-click** on the target volume and select the **Configure Shadow Copies** menu item. In the **Shadow Copies** dialog box, click on the **Enable** button to enable Shadow Copies for that volume (see Figure 7.18).

Figure 7.18 Shadow Copies Enabled

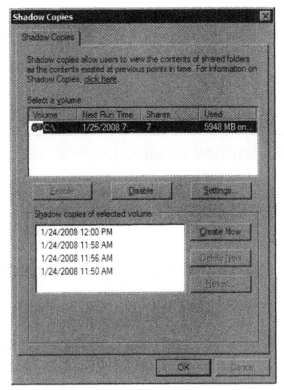

Recovering Previous Versions

Using Shadow Copies you can recover a previous version of a file on the server or a workstation using the Properties dialog of a file or folder. In the following Sidebar, we will recover a previous version of a file and folder.

Configuring & Implementing...

Using Shadow Copy to Recover Files and Folders

Once Shadow Copies have been enabled on a server, the Shadow Copy Service will take point-in-time snapshots on a regular basis (twice a day by default). To restore a file to its previous version:

1. Right-click on the file or folder and choose **Restore previous versions**.

   Alternatively, you can right-click on the file and choose the **Properties** command from the shortcut menu. The **Properties** sheet contains a **Previous Versions** tab you can use to restore files and folders.

2. In the **Previous Versions** tab you will see a list of Shadow Copies that have been made of the file or folder (see Figure 7.19). If no Shadow Copies appear, changes may not have been made recently or the Shadow Copy Service may not be running. You can force a Shadow Copy in the **Volume Properties | Shadow Copies Dialog** (shown in the previous section) by clicking on the **Create Now** button.

Continued

Figure 7.19 Previous Versions Tab

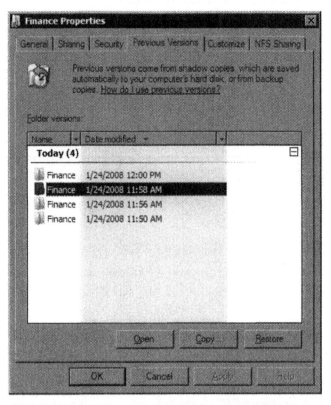

3. To restore a previous version of the file or folder, select the version you would like and click on the **Restore** button, as shown in Figure 7.20. If you would like to restore a copy instead of overwriting the existing file or folder, click the **Copy** button. To view one of the versions and make sure it is the one you are looking for before restoring you can use the **Open** button.

Figure 7.20 Restoring a Previous Version Using Shadow Copy

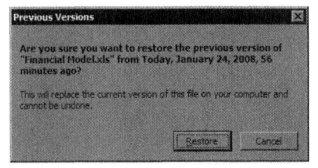

Windows Server 2008 features an enhanced version of Shadow Copy that supports restoring an entire volume to a previous state. To revert a volume to its previous state, navigate to **Start Menu | Computer, Right-click** the target volume and click **Configure Shadow Copies**. Select a previous Shadow Copy (date and time) and click on the **Revert** button, as shown in Figure 7.21.

Figure 7.21 Reverting an Entire Volume Using Shadow Copy

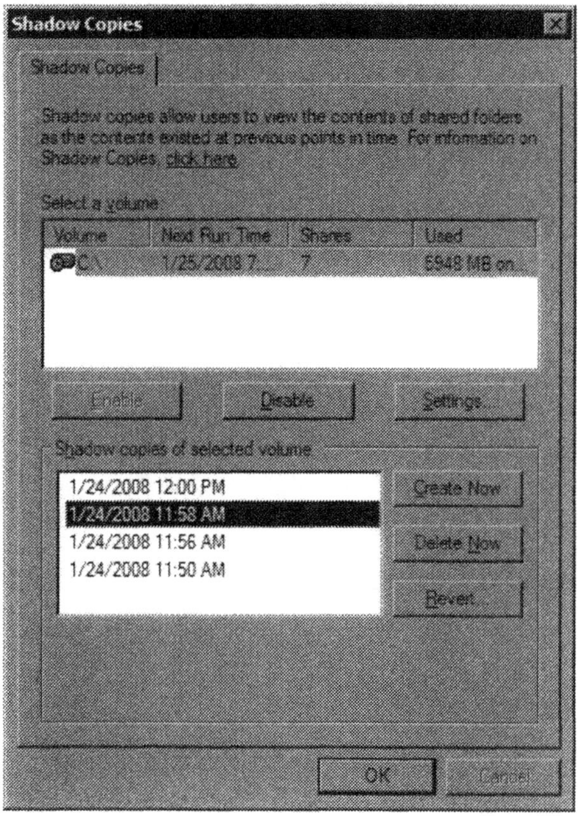

Setting the Schedule

To control the frequency and schedule with which Windows creates Shadow Copies:

1. Navigate to **Start Menu | Computer**.

2. Right-click the target volume and click **Configure Shadow Copies**.

3. Click on the **Settings** button and then click on **Schedule**.

You will be able to set the schedule using the dialog box shown in Figure 7.22.

Figure 7.22 Setting the Schedule for Shadow Copies

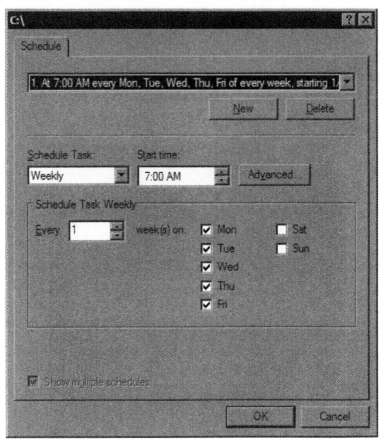

Setting Storage Locations

You can view and configure the storage location of the Shadow Copies using the **Settings** dialog available in the Shadow Copies configuration. The Shadow Copies configuration is the same screen we used to enable Shadow Copies and is available from the **Right-click | Configure Shadow Copies** menu option.

Configuring Backup and Restore

Hard drives fail. Natural disasters such as floods, fires, and hurricanes happen. Backup is the single most important measure you can take to recover from such an incident. As I consultant, you would not believe how many times I have walked into a new client's office to find that either backups have stopped working and have not been running for months, or there is no backup at all. Microsoft has completely revamped the Backup utility in Windows Server 2008. The new Windows Server Backup has many improvements over the old NTBACKUP, including the ability to back up to DVD, multitarget backup for off-site rotation, faster backups, and the ability to maintain multiple versions to restore back to.

The new backup APIs make a shadow copy snapshot image of everything being backed up prior to actually starting the backup. This ensures that open files, databases, and so forth will be consistent in the backup.

Backup Types

The traditional types of backup have been full, incremental, and differential. The new Windows Server Backup uses a combination of full and incremental backups using block-level backup for improved speed. Table 7.5 explains full backups and incremental backups:

Table 7.5 Explanation of Backup Types

Backup Type	Explanation
Full backup	Creates a backup of the entire volume(s).
Incremental backup	Used in conjunction with a full backup; an incremental backup backs up only the changes that have been made since the last full or incremental backup.
Differential backup	No longer used in Windows Server Backup. This backup type copies all the changes that have been made since the last full backup.

Although this is a powerful new system, the interface has been simplified in the new Windows backup utility. If you require more control over how the backups are run, you may want to buy a third-party backup utility.

Backup Schedules

To create a scheduled backup, you must first make sure Windows Server Backup is installed in the **Server Manager | Features | Add Features** Wizard. Although you can create an ad hoc or one-time backup to a network share, internal disk, external hard drive, or DVD, you can only run *scheduled* backups using one or multiple external USB 2.0 or IEEE 1394 drive(s). It is recommended that you use a drive that is at least 2.5 times the size of the volume you plan to back up.

In the following Sidebar, we will configure a backup schedule in Windows Server Backup to run to an external USB 2.0 or IEEE 1394 hard drive.

Configuring & Implementing...

Configuring a Backup Schedule Using Windows Server Backup

1. Connect a USB 2.0 or IEEE 1394 external hard drive to your server.

2. Launch the Backup Schedule Wizard by navigating to Server Manager | Storage | Windows Server Backup | Backup Schedule.

3. Click **Next** to move past the **Getting Started** page.

4. On the **Select Backup Type** page choose **Custom** and click **Next**. This allows us to select the volume(s) we would like to back up.

5. On the **Select Custom Backup Items** page, select only the volume you would like to back up. In this example, we back up the C: drive.

6. On the **Specify Backup Time** page, you can choose to back up the server either at a specified time once per day, or multiple times per day. In this example, we chose **Once a day** at **11:00** P.M. (see Figure 7.23). Click the **Next** button to continue.

Continued

Figure 7.23 Specify Backup Time in Backup Schedule Wizard

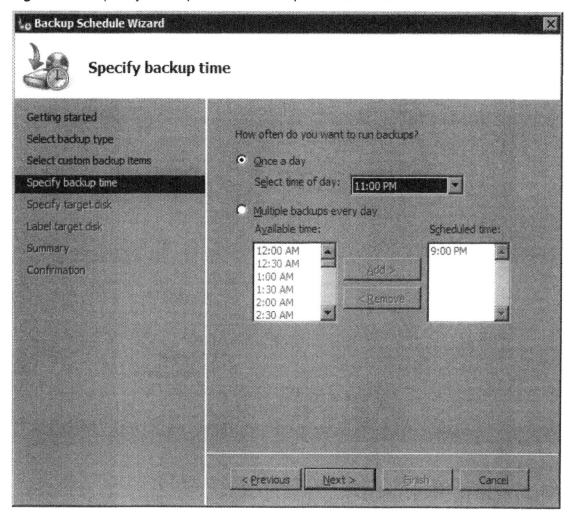

7. Select the USB 2.0 or IEEE 1394 disk or disks you would like to back up to and click **Next**. Warning: Completing this wizard will format your external hard drive. Make sure you do not have any important data on your external hard drive before continuing.

8. Click **Next** and then **Finish** to complete the **Backup Schedule Wizard**.

9. After the wizard formats your external hard drive, your backup schedule appears in the Windows Server Backup management tool, as shown in Figure 7.24.

Figure 7.24 Scheduled Backup Displayed in the Windows Server Backup Management Tool

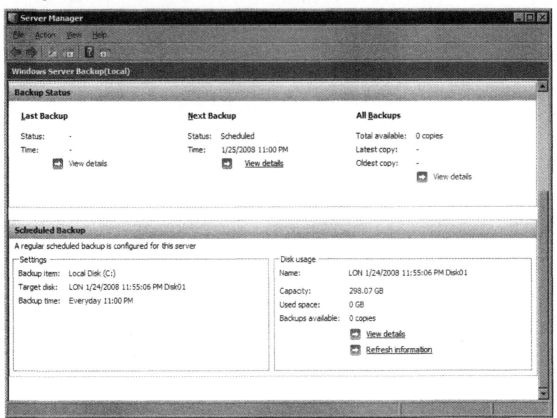

Managing Remotely

To manage backups from a remote computer, use the Backup Snap-in in the Microsoft Management Console (MMC). To launch MMC, click on **Start Menu | Run**, type **MMC**, and press the **Enter** key on your keyboard. From the **File Menu | Add/Remove Snap-in** menu option you can select one or more management snap-ins from a list, as shown in Figure 7.25.

Figure 7.25 Add or Remove Snap-ins Window

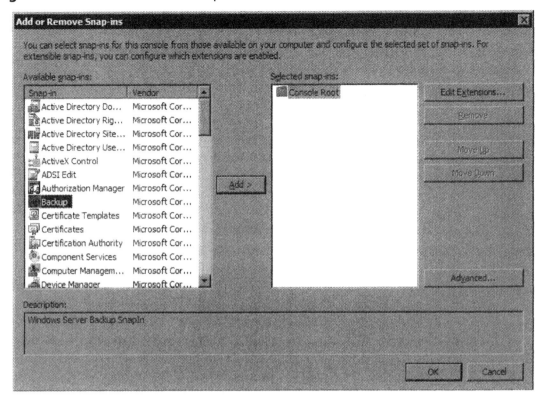

When adding the Backup Snap-in, you will be prompted to enter which server you would like to manage, as shown in Figure 7.26.

Figure 7.26 ComputerChooser When Adding Backup MMC Snap-in

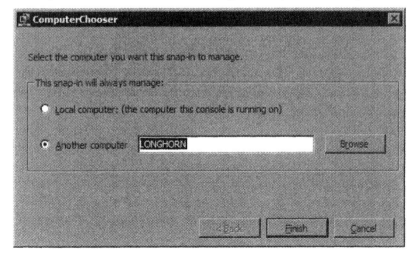

Restoring Data

The new Windows Server Backup greatly improves the restore interface in the old **NTBACKUP**. To restore incremental backups in **NTBACKUP** an administrator was required to load and restore each backup archive manually. In the new Windows Server Backup, you simply choose the point in time you would like to restore to and it takes care of loading the incremental backups for you automatically. In addition, you can perform a full-system restore without having to first reinstall Windows Server from the setup discs, as was the case in previous versions.

To restore from backup you can use one of the following options:

- Restore individual files and folders to their original or an alternative location using the **Recover** hyperlink in the **Server Manager | Storage | Windows Server Backup** management tool.

- Perform a complete server recovery using the **Windows Complete PC Restore** option. To perform a full server recovery boot from the **Windows Server 2008 setup disc** and choose **Repair your computer**. On the **System Recovery Options** page choose **Windows Complete PC Restore**.

The new **Windows Server Backup** application no longer uses .bkf files. Instead, **Windows Server Backup** writes backups to a virtual hard drive file. This means that if you perform a full backup of a volume, you can actually mount the backup as a virtual hard drive. Incidentally, Microsoft offers a free utility for Windows Server 2008 and Windows Vista that allows you to restore .bkf files made with NTBACKUP. The "Windows NT Backup Restore Utility" is available for download at www.microsoft.com/downloads/details.aspx?FamilyID=7da725e2-8b69-4c65-afa3-2a53107d54a7&DisplayLang=en.

For more information on the new Windows Server Backup, check out Microsoft's "Windows Server 2008 Backup and Recovery Step-by-Step Guide" at http://technet2.microsoft.com/WindowsServer2008/en/library/00162c92-a834-43f9-9e8a-71aeb25fa4ad1033.mspx.

Managing Disk Quotas

Are you running out of storage space on your server because specific users are dumping more than their fair share on the server? Then you are going to like Disk Quotas. Disk Quotas allow you to monitor and limit server disk space on a per-volume or per-user basis. If the user hits his or her disk quotas, it will appear to that user as though that server hard drive is completely full and no more files can be copied to it. You also can configure Disk Quotas to warn users that they are reaching their limit.

Quota by Volume or Quota by User

As with many features, Microsoft has made improvements to Disk Quotas in Windows Server 2008. The most significant improvements are the addition of the File Server Resource Manager (FSRM), which allows an administrator to manage quotas and generate storage reports, and the ability to now apply a quota to a folder.

Microsoft has included both the older NTFS Disk Quotas system from previous Windows Server versions and the new enhanced Resource Manager Disk Quotas system in Windows Server 2008 because they each have different functionality. Although it is possible to configure both Disk Quota systems, it is recommended that you use only one of the systems on your Windows Server 2008 system. FSRM is installed as a Role Service for the File Services role.

To manage quotas by volume or user, use the NTFS Disk Quotas system. To enable the NTFS Disk Quotas system, navigate to **Start Menu | Computer** and on the target volume **Right-Click | Properties**. Click on the **Quota** tab and **Enable quota management**, as shown in Figure 7.27.

Figure 7.27 Enabling Quota Management in Volume Properties

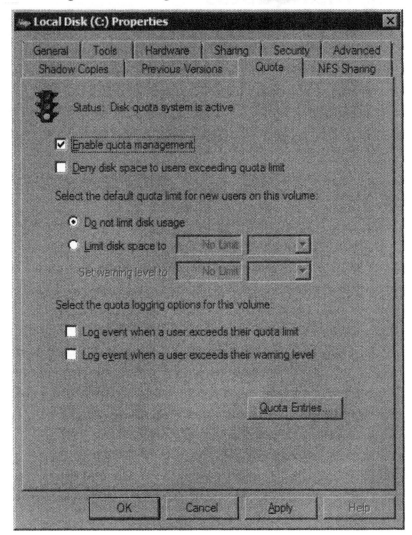

You must do this for each volume on which you want to activate NTFS Disk Quotas.

Hard Quotas prevent a user from exceeding the limit, and Soft Quotas allow users to exceed the limit and are used for monitoring and reporting. Using Resource Manager Disk Quotas you can also create a flexible quota. A flexible quota works by notifying users via e-mail when they have exceeded their quota and will temporarily extend their quota to give them flexibility to delete unnecessary files and get back into compliance.

To enable Hard Quotas in the NTFS Disk Quotas system navigate to **Start Menu | Computer** and on the target volume **Right-Click | Properties**. Click on the **Quota** tab and check the box next to **Deny disk space to users exceeding quota limit**. We will learn how to set Hard, Soft, and Flexible quotas in the next section of this chapter.

Quota Entries

To view and edit quota entries using the NTFS disk quotas system, navigate to **Start Menu | Computer** and on the target volume **Right-Click | Properties**. Click on the **Quota** tab and click on the **Quota Entries** button. In Figure 7.28, we see that user John Matzek has a Quota Limit of 1 GB, has a Warning Level of 900 MB, and is currently using 41.38 MB (or 4%) of his quota.

Figure 7.28 Quota Usage and Limits in Quota Entries Window on Volume C

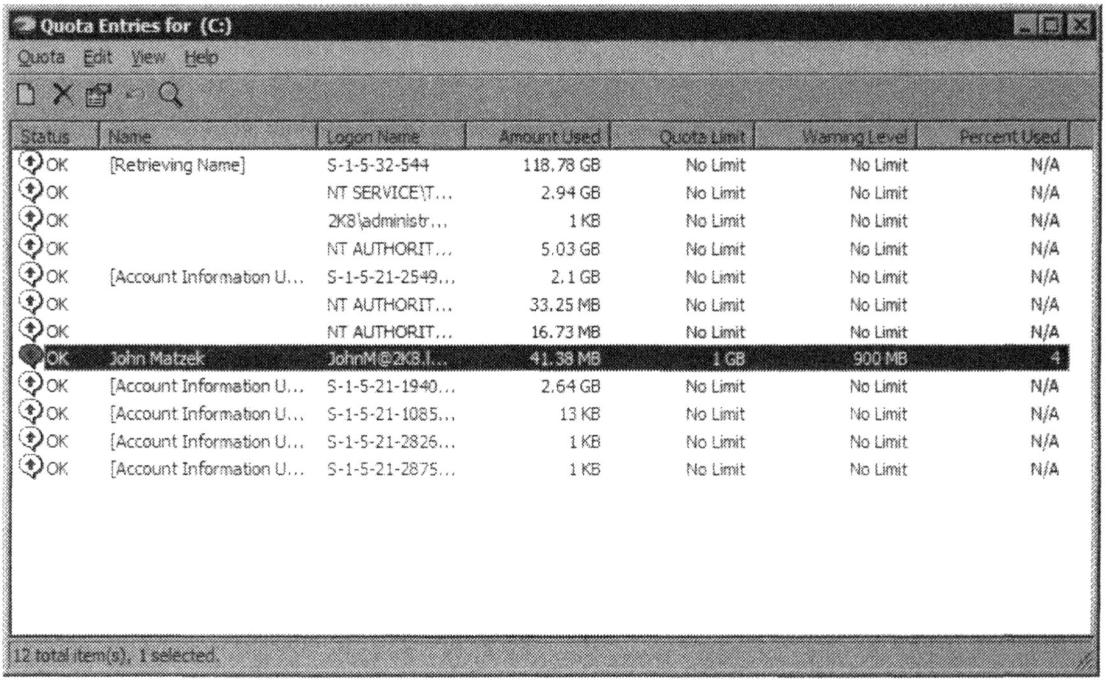

Disk quotas are tracked by file owner. If John modifies a file that is owned by another user, it will not affect his disk quota. To add a quota for a specific user, click on the **Quota Menu | New Quota Entry**. To edit the quota parameters for a user listed in the Quota Entries window, double-click the user's entry. This will bring up the **Quota Settings for [User]** dialog shown in Figure 7.29.

Figure 7.29 Modifying Quota Settings for a Specific User

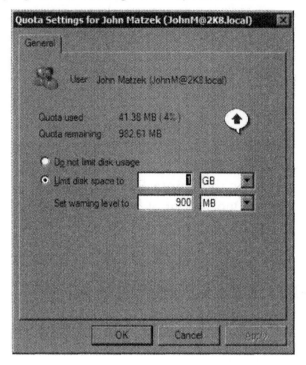

Configuring Quotas Using FSRM

Resource Manager disk quotas allow an administrator to track and enforce quotas on a per-folder basis as opposed to the **NTFS disk quotas** method of tracking per user per volume. To configure disk quotas using FSRM follow the steps in the following Sidebar 9.

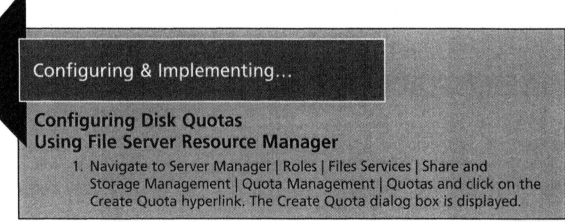

Configuring & Implementing...

Configuring Disk Quotas
Using File Server Resource Manager

1. Navigate to Server Manager | Roles | Files Services | Share and Storage Management | Quota Management | Quotas and click on the Create Quota hyperlink. The Create Quota dialog box is displayed.

Continued

Configuring File and Print Services • Chapter 7

Configuring File and Print Services • Chapter 7   451

2. Click on the **Browse** button and locate the folder you would like to manage using a quota. In this example, we browse to C:\Shares\Sales.

3. Verify that **Create quota on path** is selected. Instead of using a predefined template in this example, we will select **Define custom quota properties**. Then click the **Custom Properties** button.

4. The **Quota Properties** window is displayed, as seen in Figure 7.30.

Figure 7.30 Quota Properties Window

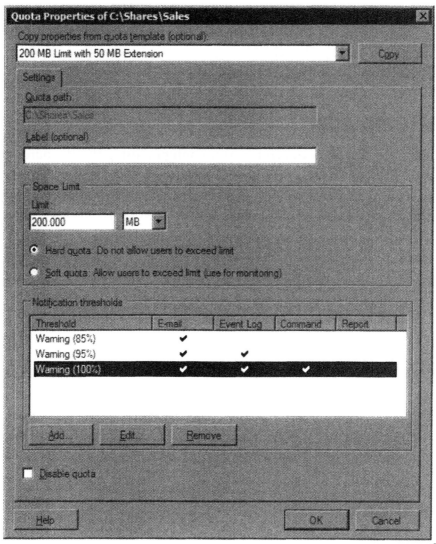

5. In the Quota Properties window, use the combo box in the **Copy properties from quota template (optional):** section to choose the **200 MB Limit with 50 MB Extension** and click **Copy**. This option sets a hard quota of 200 MB, but acts as a flexible quota to extend to 250 MB temporarily if users exceed the 200 MB limit. This is accomplished using the **Run this command or script** option in the **100% Notification threshold** actions which you can find by clicking on **Warning (100%) | Edit... | Command**. Note the option to select either a hard or a soft quota.

6. Click **OK** and then click on **Create** to create the Quota for the Sales folder. When prompted, choose not to save the options as a template. We will discuss templates in the next section.

Note that you can also apply a quota policy to a shared folder in the Provision a Shared Folder Wizard.

Quota Templates

It is recommended that all quota entries you configure using the Resource Manager disk quotas be configured using templates. This makes it easy to update or change quota settings for a large number of folders by changing a setting only once in the template that is applied instead of editing the quota properties for each individual folder. To manage quota templates, navigate to **Server Manager | Roles | Files Services | Share and Storage Management | Quota Management | Quota Templates**. From this management tool you can create, delete, and modify quota templates using the hyperlink options on the right pane.

Configuring and Monitoring Print Services

In understanding printer management and configuration in Windows Server 2008, it is important to understand printer sharing, publishing printers to Active Directory, printer permissions, deploying printer connections, installing printer drivers, exporting and importing print queues and printer settings, and adding counters to Performance Monitor to monitor print servers, print pooling, and print priority. In this section, we will discuss these in detail.

Printer Share

Sharing a printer from a Windows Server 2008 machine allows multiple users on the network to access the same physical printer using print spooling, a process of queuing up documents to be printed one at a time. Users can install the printer without worrying about downloading or installing a driver as it is automatically copied from the print server. In addition, printer sharing allows administrators to centrally control and manage the printers and print queues. For clarity it is important to understand the difference between a printer and a print device. A printer is the virtual printer created within Windows to represent the driver, configuration, and print queue. A print device is the physical printer that is hooked up to the network or a server. To enable printer sharing on your Windows 2008 Server install the **Print Services** role in the **Add Roles Wizard**. This allows you to use the Print Management administration tool to manage shared printers.

You can also enable printer sharing using the **Control Panel | Network and Sharing Center** and change the **Printer sharing** setting to "On."

Use the **Add Printer Wizard** in **Control Panel | Printers** to set up a new printer. On the **Printer Sharing** page select **Share this printer so that others on your network can find and use it**, as shown in Figure 7.31.

Figure 7.31 Printer Sharing Configuration in Add Printer Wizard

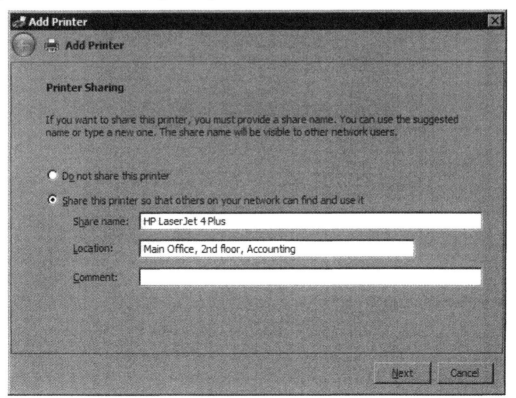

Publishing Printers to Active Directory

Publishing a printer to Active Directory allows network users to search for printers on the network by name or location instead of worrying about which server the printer lives on. To publish a printer to Active Directory, enable the **List in the directory** checkbox on the **Sharing** tab of the **Printer Properties**, as shown in Figure 7.32.

Figure 7.32 List in the Directory Option on the Sharing Tab

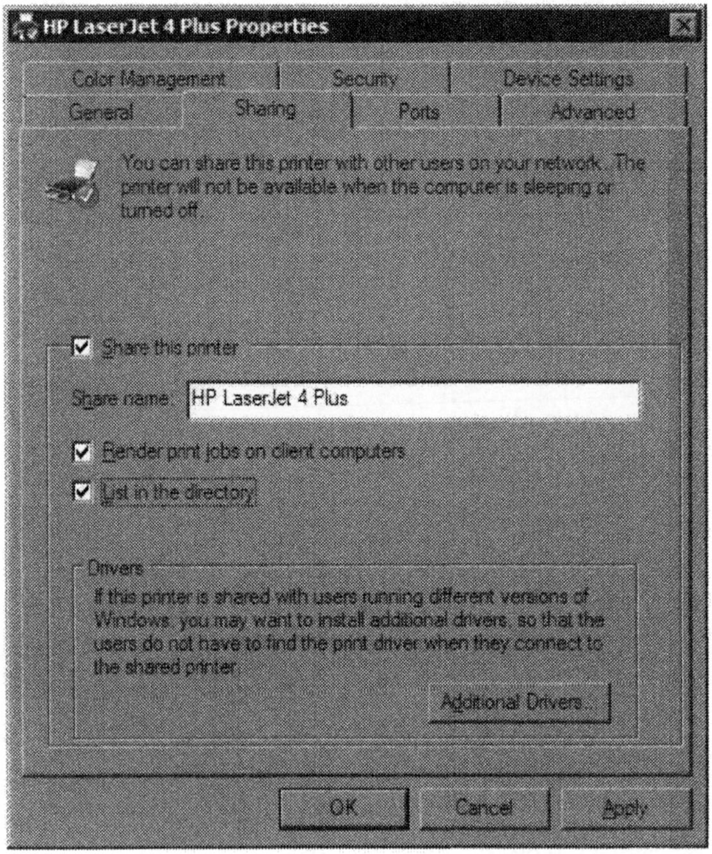

Printer Permissions

You configure printer permissions on the **Security** tab in Printer Properties; they operate in a fashion very similar to Share Permissions. Figure 7.33 shows the Security tab in Printer Properties. Table 7.6 shows the available printer permissions and their function.

Figure 7.33 Modifying Printer Permissions

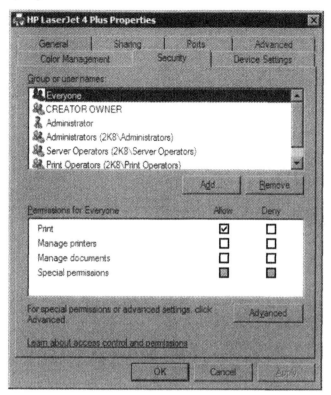

Table 7.6 Overview of Printer Permissions

Printer Permission	Explanation
Print	Allows users to connect and print to the printer
Manage printers	Allows users to perform administrative functions including adjusting printer permissions, pausing, restarting, and changing printer settings. This setting gives users more control than **Manage documents**.
Manage documents	Allows users to act as print operators. Lets them cancel, restart, reorder, pause, and resume documents in the print queue.
Special permissions	Use the **Advanced** button to configure special permissions including **Manage printers, Manage documents, Read permissions, Change permissions,** and **Take ownership**.

Deploying Printer Connections

Installing a network printer on a client Windows computer is relatively easy. Now imagine you need to install a network printer on 500 Windows computers. Fortunately, Windows Server 2008 is all about working smarter rather than harder. You can easily install printers on client workstations by deploying them using Group Policy. In the following Sidebar, we will deploy printer connections.

Configuring & Implementing...

Using the Print Management Utility to Deploy Printer Connections

1. Open Print Management in Server Manager.

2. Expand **Print Servers** and expand your target server in the left pane.

3. Click on the **Printers** node to view a list of installed printers, as shown in Figure 7.34.

Continued

Figure 7.34 Managing Printers in the Print Servers Console

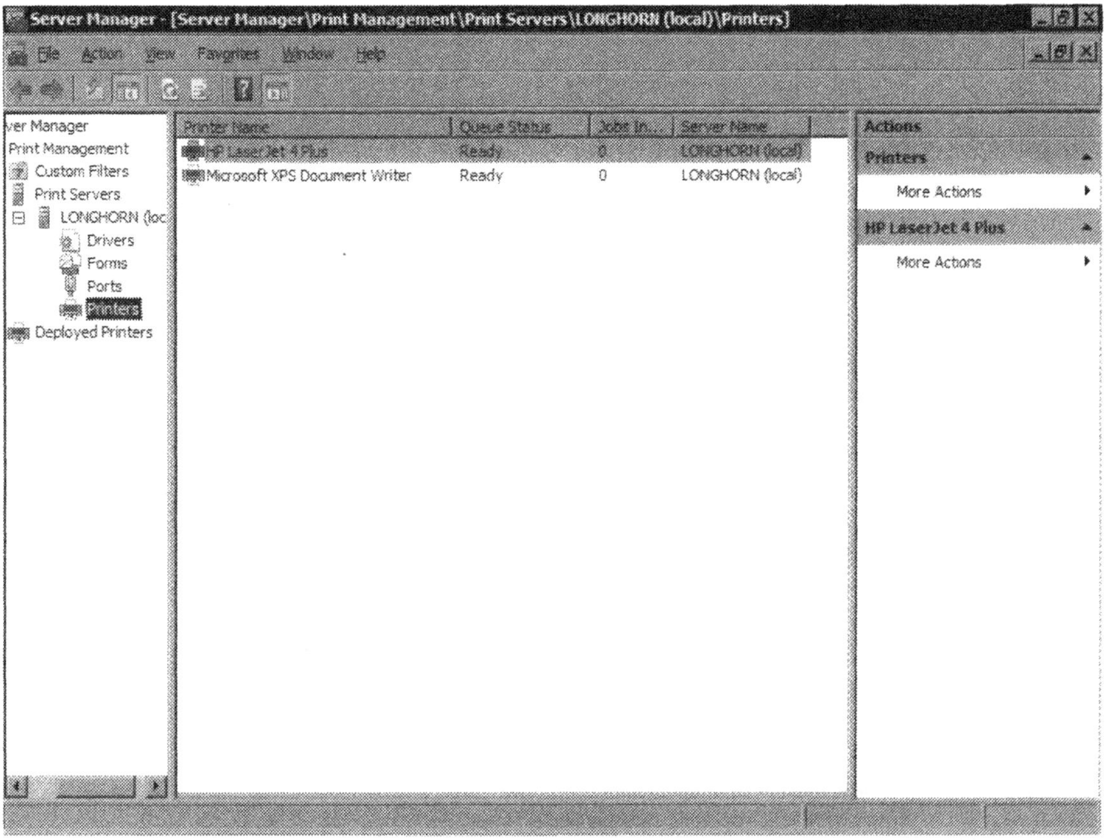

> 4. Right-click on the printer you would like to deploy and click the **Deploy with Group Policy** menu item.

For more information on how to deploy printer connections for Windows Vista and Windows XP clients, visit http://technet2.microsoft.com/windowsserver2008/en/library/8433a76a-0a5d-48f4-893d-35442aa8765e1033.mspx.

Installing Printer Drivers

To enable point and print (the automatic installation of print drivers) for clients running a different version of Windows (x86 versus x64 versus Itanium) you must install the drivers for that version of Windows. Install additional drivers by clicking the **Additional Drivers** button on the **Sharing** tab in the **Printer Properties**. This brings up the **Additional Drivers** window, where you can select the types of drivers you would like to install, as shown in Figure 7.35. After you select the types of drivers and click **OK**, you will be prompted for a location to copy files from, as shown in Figure 7.36.

Figure 7.35 Selecting Additional Printer Drivers to Install

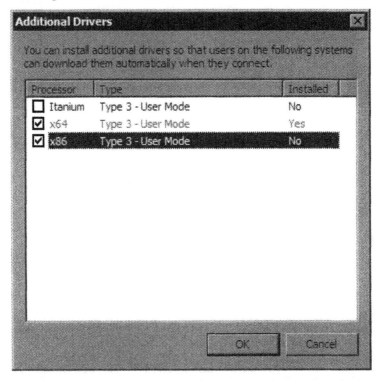

Figure 7.36 Install Additional Printer Drivers Dialog

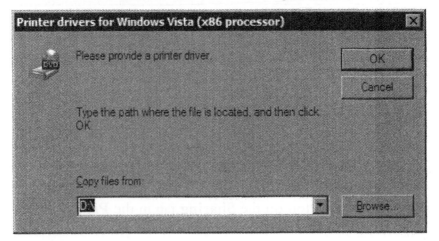

Exporting and Importing Print Queues and Printer Settings

Windows Server 2008 provides a facility for moving printers from one server to another by exporting and importing printer settings, drivers, print queues, and ports. This can be useful in consolidating printers from multiple servers or replacing an existing server with newer hardware. To export printer settings use the **Printer Migration Wizard** by right-clicking the server you would like to export from in **Print Management** (see Figure 7.37), and then click **Export printers to a file**. Figure 7.38 shows an export using the Printer Migration Wizard.

Figure 7.37 Export Printers to a File Option in Printer Management

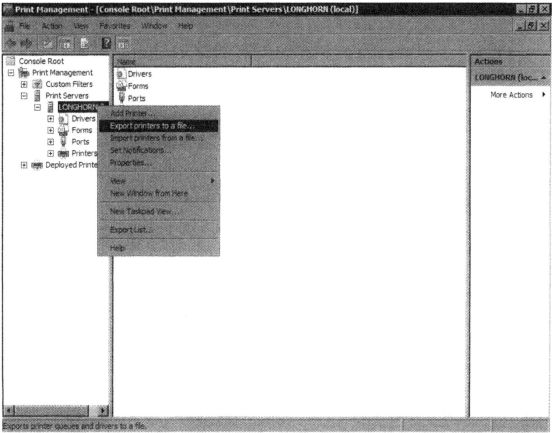

Figure 7.38 Exporting Printer Settings Using the Printer Migration Wizard

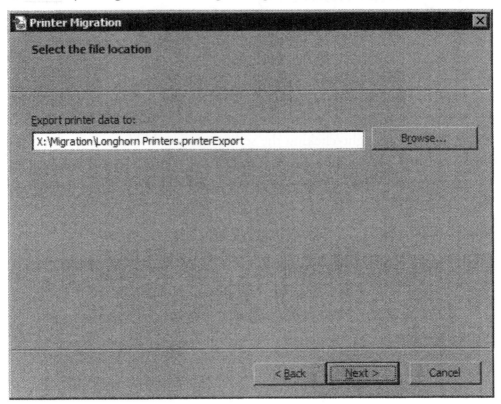

To import the printer settings on the destination server use the **Printer Migration Wizard** by right-clicking the destination server in **Print Management**, and then click **Import printers to a file**. Figure 7.39 shows print queues, drivers, and processors being imported to a new server using the Printer Migration Wizard.

Figure 7.39 Importing Printer Settings Using the Printer Migration Wizard

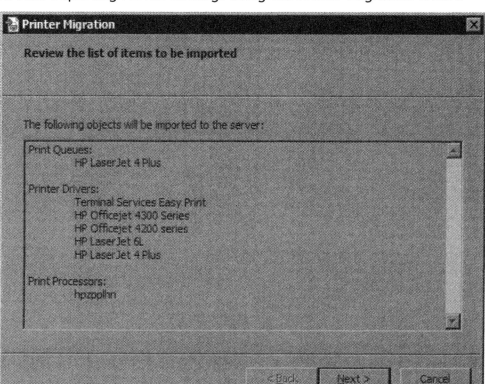

Adding Counters to Reliability and Performance Monitor to Monitor Print Servers

By using Performance Monitor, a network or server administrator can identify bottlenecks on a wide variety of server and network components. As an administrator, you can also use Performance Monitor to capture performance counters over time and identify baselines and trends.

In Windows Server 2008, Performance Monitor includes many counters that enable administrators to keep an eye on many network printers at the same time or even capture data for later analysis. You can view these performance counters in a Line Graph, Histogram, or Report view. Launch Performance Monitor by navigating to **Server Manager | Diagnostics | Reliability and Performance | Monitoring Tools | Performance Monitor**. Figure 7.40 shows the Report view in Performance Monitor.

Figure 7.40 Monitoring Printer Statistics in Report
View Using Performance Monitor

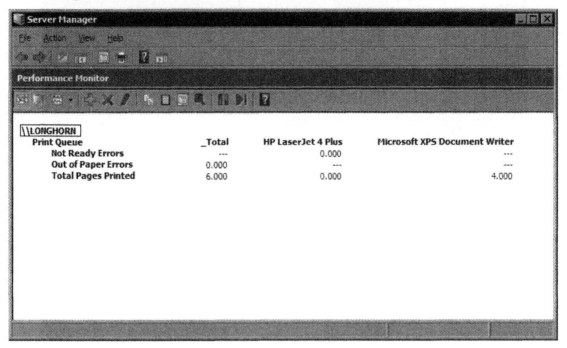

To monitor printing statistics such as **Bytes Printed/sec, Jobs Spooling,** and **Out of Paper Errors** in real time, add counters by clicking the plus button and then expand the **Print Queue** counters, as shown in Figure 7.41.

Figure 7.41 Adding Print Queue Counters to Performance Monitor

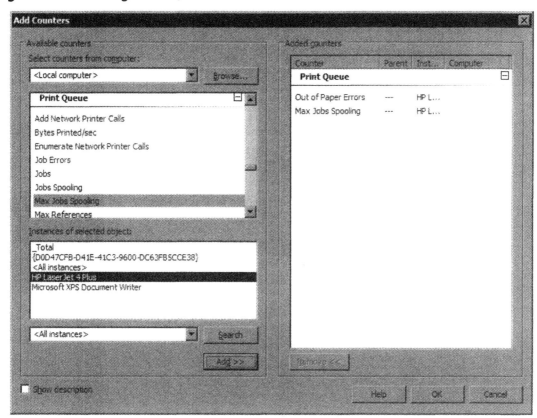

Printer Pooling

Printer pooling allows you to install a single printer to print to one of multiple print devices. For example, if Pablo is printing a 350-page document while Steve attempts to print a one-page spreadsheet to the same printer, with a single print device Steve would have to wait for Pablo's 350-page document to finish before his one-page spreadsheet is printed. With Print Pooling both documents will print on separate print devices in the pool at the same time.

To enable printer pooling:

1. Connect more than one print device of the same type to your server.

2. Open the **Printer Properties** for your printer and click on the **Ports** tab.

3. Click the checkbox next to **Enable printer pooling**.

4. Select the ports that are connected to the printers you would like to pool together (see Figure 7.42).

Figure 7.42 Enabling the Printer Pooling Option on the Ports Tab

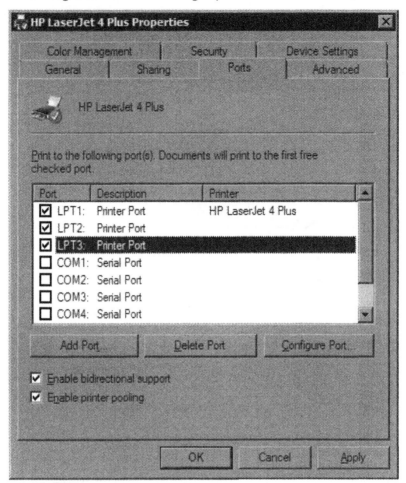

Print Priority

You can use the **Advanced** tab in **Printer Properties** to set a priority, as shown in Figure 7.43.

Figure 7.43 Boosting the Priority on a Printer

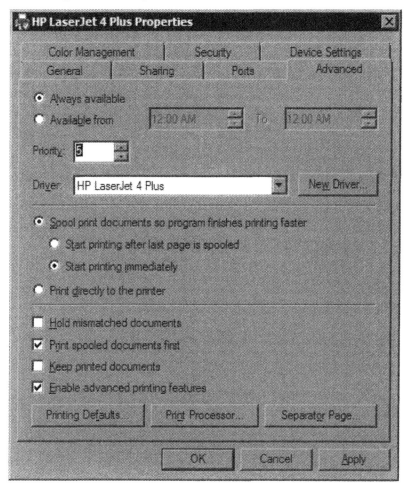

Print jobs with a higher-priority (numeric value) print before jobs with a lower priority. By configuring multiple printers with different priority levels to print to the same print device, an administrator can ensure that users in a specific department always get higher printing priority than others. For example, you can create a FinancePublic printer with default Printer Permissions and a FinanceOnly printer where only members of the Finance group have access. Configuring the FinanceOnly printer with higher priority ensures members of the Finance group who submit jobs will always get them printed first.

Summary

Out of the box, Windows Server 2008 does not include the File and Printer sharing services or tools. To install these tools use the Add Roles hyperlink in Server Manager. The File Services role installs file and folder sharing and the Share and Storage Management console, which is the preferred method for administering shared folders. There are two models:

- Standard (in-place) file sharing
- Public folder sharing

You can add additional components of the File Services role such as DFS, NFS (for UNIX), Windows Search Service, and File Server Resource Manager by using the Add Role Services hyperlink in Server Manager.

A user's effective permissions when accessing a shared folder over the network are the result of both NTFS and Share Permissions. The effective permission is the *more restrictive* of these two components:

- The *least* restrictive NTFS Permission
- The *least* restrictive Share Permission

Remember that a Deny permission will always override any allow permission for that user or group.

EFS encrypted and decrypted files use a process that is transparent to the user. EFS works only on NTFS volumes and users should use a roaming profile or backup and copy their public/private keys (which are stored in their user profile) if they use multiple computers.

DFS has two main components that can be used independently of each other:

- DFS namespaces
- DFS replication

DFS namespaces are virtual shared folders that contain shared folders from multiple servers. This simplifies access to shares and creates redundancy if a server is offline. A "target" is a pointer to a shared folder on one server. You can have multiple targets for each shared folder in a DFS namespace.

DFS replication synchronizes the changes between folders located on different servers. This can work in conjunction with DFS namespaces or be used to create a backup of a shared folder that is synchronized after changes occur.

Shadow Copy allows users and administrators a point-in-time restore or rollback to previous versions of a file or folder. Shadow Copies must be enabled on a per-volume basis and previous versions are restored using the Previous Versions tab in the properties of a file or folder located on a Shadow Copy-enabled volume.

NTBACKUP has been replaced with Windows Server Backup. You can create a backup schedule and/or ad hoc (one-time) backups in Windows Server Backup. Ad hoc backups can be made onto DVD or a network shared folder. Scheduled backups work with USB 2.0 and IEEE 1394 hard drives and first create a full backup, then incremental backups using block-level copy on a scheduled basis. You can perform a point-in-time restore without having to manually load each incremental backup.

To manage a remote Windows Server 2008 full or core server, use the Microsoft Management Console and add snap-ins. When adding a snap-in you will be prompted for which computer you want to manage.

Disk quotas can be enabled using the per-volume per-user system from previous versions of Windows Server or a per-folder basis using Resource Manager disk quotas. Resource Manager disk quotas can e-mail users and perform actions when limits are reached. FSUTIL is used to manage quotas from the command prompt and can be used to script actions.

To share printers, add the Print Services role in Server Manager. This also installs the Print Management console which allows you to import/export printers/settings, deploy printers to clients using group policy, and manage printers, ports, and drivers. A printer is the virtual printer in Windows and a print device is the physical printer.

By default, users are granted the Print permission. To allow a user or group to manage the queue and cancel, restart, pause, reorder, and resume a printer grant them the "Manage documents" print permission. The "Manage printers" print permission is similar to the "Full Control" share permission and allows a user to manage the queue and the printer itself (i.e., change permissions and printer settings).

Printer pooling is set up by enabling multiple ports in the printer properties. If a document is sent to that printer, it prints to the first port. If a second document is sent while the first print device is busy printing, the second document will be sent to the next port in the list.

You can create multiple printers that point to the same print device. This allows you to set different priorities on each printer and grant different users and groups access based on which priority they will need. The higher the numeric value, the higher the priority that will be given to that printer.

Solutions Fast Track

Configuring a File Server

☑ Add the File Services role in Server Manager to enable file sharing and install the management tools.

☑ The effective permission for a user to access a shared folder is the *more* restrictive of the least restrictive Share Permission and the least restrictive NTFS Permission.

☑ A Deny permission for a user or a group they are a member of *always* overrides Allow permissions.

☑ Use the Share and Storage Management console to create and manage shared folders.

☑ Encrypting File System (EFS) is transparent to the user and works only on NTFS; you cannot both encrypt and compress a file.

Configuring Distributed File System (DFS)

☑ A DFS namespace is a virtual shared folder that contains shared folders located on multiple servers.

☑ Use the Namespaces and Replication tools in DFS Management to create namespaces and manage DFS.

☑ A DFS target is a pointer to a shared folder on a server and DFS folders can point to multiple targets (copies of the same folder on different servers).

☑ DFS replication synchronizes the changes between multiple copies of the same folder located on different servers.

Configuring Shadow Copy Services

☑ Shadow Copies are point-in-time backups of files that can be restored by the user or admin using the Previous Versions tab in the properties of the file or folder.

☑ To control the snapshot schedule and storage locations, open the **Volume (Drive C, D, E, etc) Properties | Shadow Copies** tab or right-click the volume in my computer and choose **Configure Shadow Copies**.

☑ Use the **Shadow Copies** in the Volume Properties tab to change the schedule, force Shadow Copy to run immediately, delete a snapshot, and change the storage location.

Configuring Backup and Restore

☑ Windows Server Backup replaces the old NTBACKUP and improves backup speed, simplifies the user interface, includes full and incremental backup types, and allows an ad hoc backup to DVD or a network share.

☑ Scheduled backup creates a full backup and then incremental backups using block-level copy, and supports only USB 2.0 and IEEE 1394 hard drives (no tape).

☑ Windows Server Backup can be managed remotely with the Backup snap-in in the MMC or the command line *WBADMIN*.

☑ Data can be restored to a point-in-time and will automatically load the incremental backups without user intervention.

Managing Disk Quotas

☑ You can configure disk quotas using the new system of Resource Manager disk quotas or the old system of NTFS disk quotas.

☑ Resource Manager disk quotas enable quotas on a per-folder basis. NTFS disk quotas allow you to manager quotas by user on a per-volume basis.

☑ Resource Manager disk quotas allow you to set up templates with hard or soft limits and different actions at different percent utilizations.

Configuring and Monitoring Print Services

☑ Deploy printers to clients using group policy with the Print Management console, right-click the **Printers** node, and choose **Deploy with Group Policy**.

☑ Export and import printer settings, queues, and ports using the Export Printer Wizard or Import Printer Wizard in Print Management.

☑ Add counters to the Reliability and Performance Monitor to monitor printers for out of paper errors and other statistics.

☑ Attach multiple print devices to a single printer for print pooling or multiple printers to a single print device for different printing priorities.

Frequently Asked Questions

Q: I want to add services for NFS (UNIX) but I cannot find Add/Remove Programs. Where do I install it?

A: The networking components in Add/Remove Programs have been replaced with adding Roles and Role Services in Server Manager.

Q: What is the difference between setting Share Permissions to Everyone - Full control and Authenticated Users – Full Control?

A: The "Everyone" group is just as the name implies; it includes "everyone," including guest accounts and "null sessions" (computer-to-computer sessions). The Authenticated Users group is more secure as it excludes these groups while including users on the domain.

Q: Does File Screening examine the contents of every file copied to a shared folder?

A: File screening does not examine the contents of files. It works by restricting files based on extensions (e.g., .mp3, .wma, .wmv, etc.). Users can "hack" past file screening by renaming the extension of a file to an allowed extension before copying the file to a share. If the user attempts to rename it back once it is on the server, it will be intercepted by the file screen and deleted.

Q: What is the difference between special permissions and the standard NTFS permissions?

A: The NTFS special permissions are actually the more granular permissions that make up the standard NTFS permissions. For example, the Read standard permission is actually composed of the List Folder / Read Data, Read Attributes, Read Extended Attributes, and Read Permissions special permissions.

Q: Why would I want to disable Offline Files on a network share?

A: A couple of reasons to disable Offline Files from the server are that you have confidential information that is not to leave the building and you do not want users syncing it onto a laptop, or a shared folder is heavily used for collaboration and you do not want multiple people editing the same file offline and running into a conflict when they attempt to sync it back up.

Q: What is the command-line utility for working with EFS?

A: To encrypt, decrypt, view, and manage EFS using the command-line utility CIPHER.exe.

Q: How can I tell in Windows Explorer which files and folders are encrypted or compressed?

A: In Windows Explorer, encrypted files and folders are indicated by the color green and compressed files and folders are indicated by the color blue. Regular files will show up in black.

Q: What if I do not back up my encryption keys and lose my computer or profile, or I need to reset my password?

A: By default, the first administrator account on the domain is a recovery agent and can decrypt any domain user's files in this case. It also can come in handy if an employee quit or was terminated and had encrypted his or her files. You can also configure additional recovery agents on the domain. If your password was reset and this caused you to lose your EFS keys, you can change your password back and it should restore your ability to decrypt your files.

Q: I do not see a DFS role. How do I install DFS?

A: DFS is installed by adding the Distributed File System Role Services to the File Services role in Server Manager.

Q: Can I use DFS replication without configuring a DFS namespace?

A: Yes, DFS replication can be configured to synchronize folders located on multiple servers. It does not require a DFS namespace.

Q: How do I maintain an off-site backup copy of our shared folders using a server at a remote site for business continuity planning?

A: Although it is also critically important to have a full off-site backup solution, you can use DFS replication as part of your business continuity plan (keeping the business running in case of a disaster) by setting up DFS replication between servers at different physical/geographic locations.

Q: We have branch offices that connect over the WAN link to the main file server(s). It is excruciatingly slow. How do we speed this up without buying an expensive WAN link?

A: Set up a BOB or Branch Office Box at each branch office to speed up local access by "caching" the shared folders from the main server. To accomplish this, use Windows Server 2008 (or Windows Server 2003 R2) and DFS replication.

Q: My users are running Windows 2000 or Windows XP and do not have a "previous versions" tab to access Shadow Copies. How do I fix this?

A: Newer versions of Windows, such as Windows Vista, include the Shadow Copy client. To access the previous versions (Shadow Copies) tab on Windows 2000 and XP, you must install the Shadow Copy client which is available for download at http://technet.microsoft.com/en-us/windowsserver/bb405951.aspx.

Q: I deleted a file and want to recover it using Shadow Copies. Because the file is gone and I cannot right-click on it to get the Previous Versions tab, how do I get the file back?

A: To recover a deleted file, right-click and go to the properties of the folder in which that file was located. You will be able to restore the file from the Previous Versions tab.

Q: Can I revert my entire C: volume to a previous version?

A: Not if Windows Server 2008 is installed on the C: volume. You can only revert nonsystem volumes using Shadow Copy.

Q: How come the differential backup type is no longer available in Windows Server Backup?

A: The differential backup type was useful when you had to back up to tapes, because if a tape went bad you would not lose all the data from that "increment" of the backup if you used differential. Also if you needed to restore backups, using the differential backup type took fewer steps because you did not need to manually locate and load each incremental backup—just the full and the latest differential. Because Windows Server Backup uses external hard drives instead of tape and can automatically load the appropriate incremental backups during a restore, the differential type is no longer necessary.

Q: How come DAT, DLT, Travan, and other tape drives are not recognized in Windows Server Backup?

A: Windows Server Backup does not support tape drives. To back up to tape use third-party backup software.

Q: I am trying to back up to DVD or a network share but am not given the option when I schedule a backup. How do I accomplish this?

A: To back up to DVD or a network share, create an ad hoc or one-time backup instead of a scheduled backup.

Q: What is the difference between NTFS disk quotas and Resource Manager disk quotas?

A: NTFS disk quotas is the system that also existed in previous versions of Windows Server. It allows you to set quotas on a per-volume basis and set limits for each user. Resource Manager disk quotas is a new system that allows you to control space used on a per-folder basis and is managed in File Server Resource Manager.

Q: What is the difference between hard and soft quotas?

A: A hard quota prevents users from exceeding the limit and a soft quota allows the user to exceed the limit, but is used for monitoring and reporting.

Q: I set my warning level using NTFS disk quotas but it is not e-mailing users a warning when they reach that threshold. Why not?

A: The warning level in NTFS disk quotas will not contact a user; instead, it will warn the administrator by logging to the event logs. To e-mail users based on quota usage, use Resource Manager disk quotas instead.

Q: How do I manage a network printer using the command line?

A: Use the *NET PRINT* command to manage a network printer from the command line.

Q: Why would I publish a printer to Active Directory?

A: Publishing a printer to Active Directory allows users to search for the printer closest to them and is useful to find printers on the same floor in the building or at the user's branch office location.

Q: I am used to managing printers in Control Panel | Printers. What is the new tool in Windows Server 2008 to manage printers?

A: The new tool for managing printers in Windows Server 2008 is the Print Management console and can be found in Server Manager or added to the MMC as a snap-in.

Q: I am running the 64-bit edition of Windows Server 2008. How do I install print drivers for 32-bit clients so that they can install the printer without manually install the drivers?

A: You can install additional drivers using the Additional Drivers button on the Sharing tab in the Printer Properties.

## Chapter 8

Monitoring and Managing a Network Infrastructure

Solutions in this chapter:

- **Configuring Windows Server Update Services Server Settings**

- **Capturing Performance Data**

- **Monitoring Event Logs**

- **Gathering Network Data**

☑ Summary

☑ Solutions Fast Track

☑ Frequently Asked Questions

Introduction

One of the most critical functions of a network administrator is the ability to properly monitor and manage the network for which he or she is responsible. This chapter will introduce you to some tools in Server 2008 that help you more easily monitor and manage your network. We will discuss setting up and using Windows Server Update Services (WSUS) to ensure that your servers and workstations remain properly updated with the latest security fixes from Microsoft. We will also look at collecting and using performance data as well as review event logs to assist you in troubleshooting problems. Finally, we will take a look at the Simple Network Management Protocol (SNMP), the Microsoft Baseline Security Analyzer (MBSA), and Network Monitor (netmon).

Configuring Windows Server Update Services Server Settings

Windows Server Update Services (WSUS) is Microsoft's out-of-the-box solution for managing updates and security fixes to Microsoft operating systems, Office products, and several other server applications. WSUS allows you to easily review, test, and send updates to servers and workstations on your network. You may be familiar with the Windows update software already installed on your server or client operating system. The Windows update software allows you to download the latest software updates and security patches from Microsoft. This works fine for home PCs and even some small businesses; however, can you imagine hundreds or thousands of computers in a large company connecting to Microsoft to download updates? This could pose obvious problems for your company's Internet bandwidth. This is where WSUS comes into play. WSUS allows you to download updates to a central repository on your network and distributed those updates at a time you schedule. Not only does this save your Internet connection from being brought to its knees, but it also allows you to centrally manage updates as well as test them before deploying. This section will walk you through installing, configuring, and using WSUS. Before we begin setting up WSUS, let's take a look at how it works.

WSUS is installed on a server in your corporate network. This server contacts Microsoft update servers over the Internet to download new updates. The WSUS administrator then must approve or deny updates that should be installed. Corporate servers and workstations are configured to download updates from the WSUS server instead of the Windows Update Web site. After the administrator approves updates for installation, servers and workstations download and install the approved updates (see Figure 8.1).

Figure 8.1 A Simple WSUS Architecture

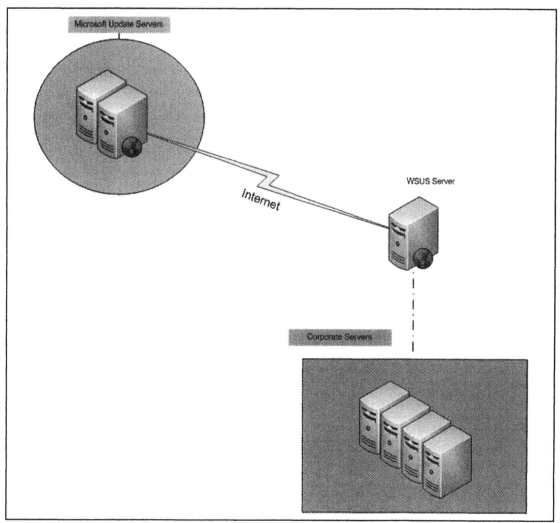

Installing Windows Server Update Services

Now that we've gotten a quick overview of how WSUS works, let's install this role. You install WSUS just as you would any other role in Windows Server 2008 (see the following Sidebar)—by choosing the Add Server Role option in Server Manager.

Before deploying WSUS, it is important to design and plan the deployment. Just jumping in and installing WSUS could lead to a misconfiguration and cause unwanted problems on your network. Always use a lab environment to test the product and ensure that you fully understand its functionality. Use network drawings and checklists to create your deployment plan. After you feel comfortable with the plan, go forward with deployment.

Configuring & Implementing...

Installing Windows Server Update Services

To install WSUS perform the following steps:

1. Open Server Manager by selecting Start | Administrative Tools | Server Manager.

2. Click the **Add Roles** link, as shown in Figure 8.2. This will launch the **Add Roles Wizard**.

Figure 8.2 Server Manager

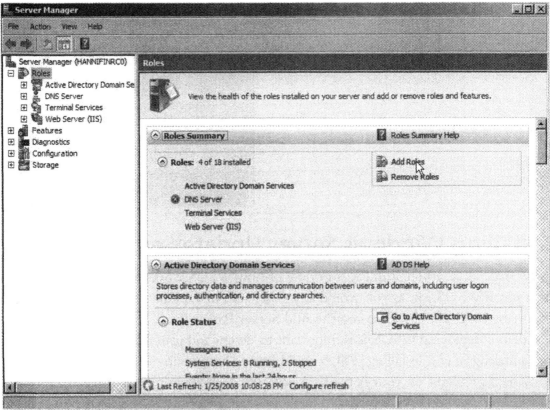

Continued

3. Click **Next** to proceed to add a new role.

4. Check the checkbox next to the **Windows Server Update Services** option and click **Next** (see Figure 8.3). The WSUS Install Wizard will launch.

Figure 8.3 Selecting Server Roles

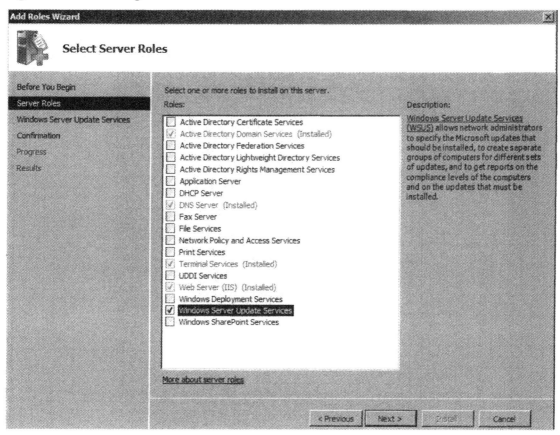

5. Click the **Next** button to proceed to the summary and confirmation screen. Click the **Install** button to begin installation (see Figure 8.4).

Continued

Figure 8.4 Confirming Install Selections

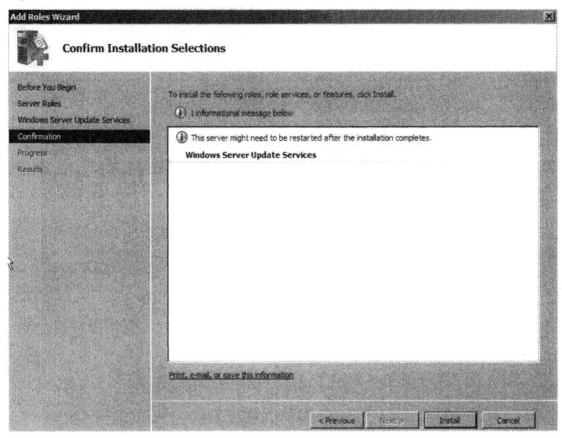

6. The wizard will then download the WSUS components and launch the **Windows Server Update Services Setup Wizard**.

7. Click the **Next** button to begin WSUS Setup. Read and accept the license agreement and click **Next** again.

8. You may receive a warning that the Microsoft Report Viewer is not installed, as shown in Figure 8.5.

Continued

Figure 8.5 The Microsoft Report Viewer Warning

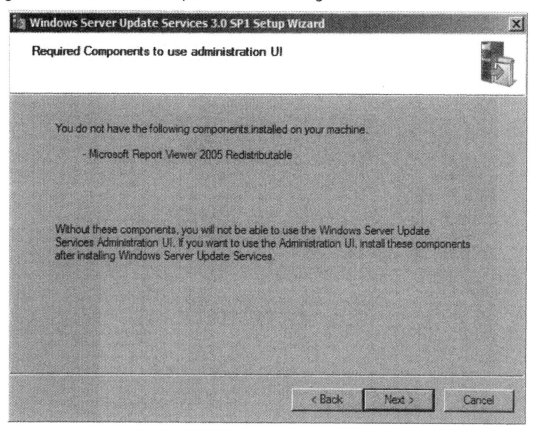

9. Choose the disk drive and folder where you want to store downloaded updates, and then click **Next**. It is recommended that you do
not use the same drive as the operating system. The wizard states
that you must have at least 6 GB of free disk space for the update.
Depending on the size and types of updates selected, you may
need a lot more than the recommended minimum. You may want
to be safe and use a drive with 20 GB or more (see Figure 8.6).

Continued

Figure 8.6 Selecting the Update Source

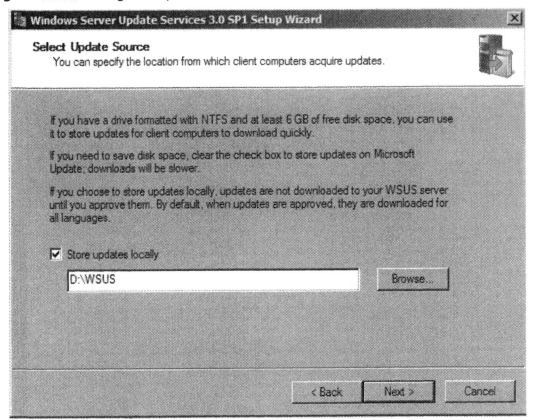

10. Choose a location to install the Windows Internal Database used by WSUS. This can be any drive with at least 2 GB of free space (see Figure 8.7). If you already have a SQL Server 2005 server set up on your corporate network, you may choose the **Using an existing database server on a remote computer** option for the database location. This will create a new WSUS database on that server instead of the WSUS server. This option may be useful if you have dedicated SQL 2005 servers that are managed by database administrators. Once you have chosen a location, click **Next**.

Continued

Figure 8.7 Database Options

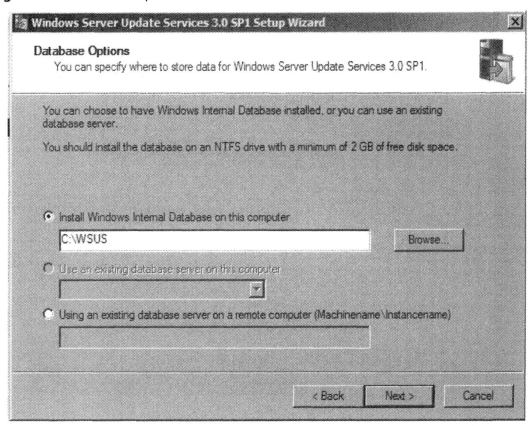

11. The next step is to create a new Internet Information Server (IIS) Web site to host WSUS. Select the **Use the existing IIS Default Web site** option, and then click **Next**.

12. You will now see a summary screen displaying the steps that the wizard is about to perform. Click **Next**.

13. The WSUS role will now take a few minutes to complete setup. After setup completes successfully click the **Finish** button, as shown in Figure 8.8.

Continued

Figure 8.8 WSUS Setup Wizard Success

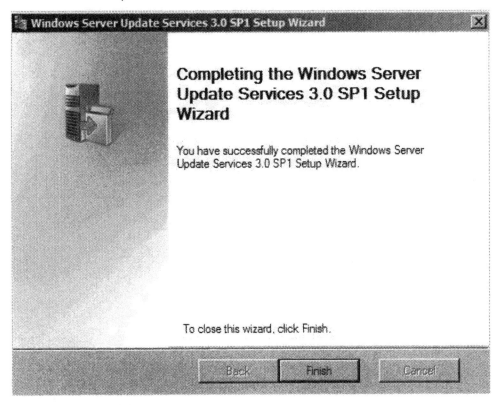

14. The WSUS Configuration Wizard will now launch so that we can properly configure the server. Click the **Next** button to begin configuring the server.

15. In the next step of the wizard, choose whether you want to participate in the customer experience program and click the **Next** button.

16. We now need to decide whether the WSUS server will be downloading updates from Microsoft directly or from another WSUS server on the corporate network. Larger enterprises may need multiple WSUS servers in various locations due to network bandwidth or security boundaries. Some organizations may also choose to deploy separate WSUS servers in DMZs or perimeter networks. For now, we will assume that this is the first WSUS server in our deployment, so go ahead and choose to download updates directly from Microsoft, as shown in Figure 8.9. Then click **Next**.

Continued

Figure 8.9 Choosing the Upstream Server

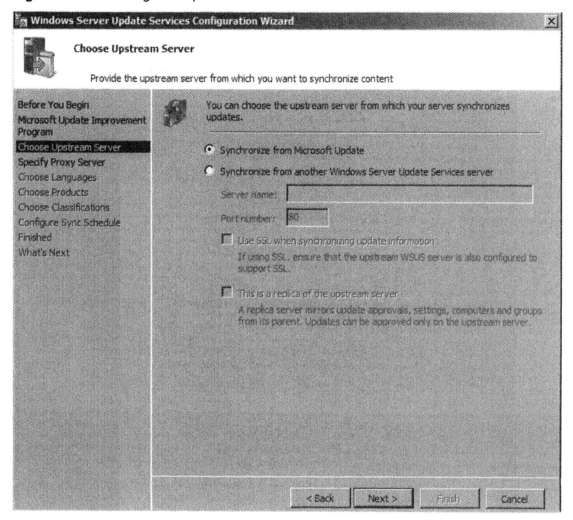

17. If your network requires that you use a proxy server to access the Internet, enter the proper information in this step. Otherwise, just click the **Next** button to continue to the initial connection step of the wizard.

18. The Configuration Wizard now needs to connect to Microsoft update servers to determine products that can be updated via WSUS, languages supported, and the types of updates available. Click the **Start Connecting** button, as shown in Figure 8.10. After the wizard completes the initial connection, click the **Next** button to continue.

Continued

Figure 8.10 The Initial Connection to the Upstream Server

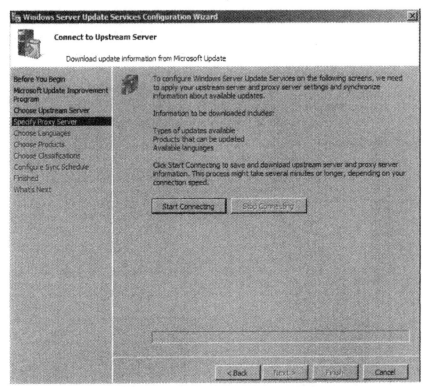

19. We now need to select the languages for which we wish to download updates. If your organization supports applications and operating systems in multiple languages, you will need to download patches for all supported languages. By choosing only the languages that you need, you will use less disk space and your download will be faster. Select the languages your organization supports, and then click the **Next** button to proceed to the next step.

20. In this step of the wizard, we need to select the products for which we want to download updates (see Figure 8.11). You can select to download updates for all products available or only those that you have installed on your network. By selecting only the products currently installed on your network, you use less disk space to store updates and update downloads from Microsoft require less time. You can always change this configuration in the future if you add new Microsoft products to your network. Select the products you wish to keep updated by WSUS and click the **Next** button.

Continued

Figure 8.11 WSUS Product Selection

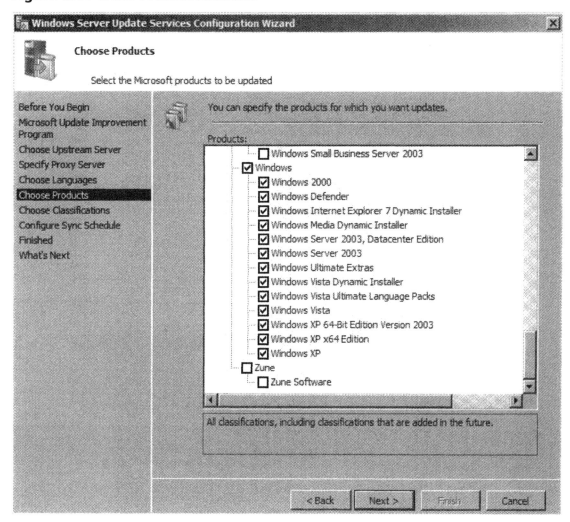

21. We now must select classifications or types of updates we wish to download to WSUS. For example, you may not wish to perform service pack installs or hardware driver updates manually and not via WSUS. Here you can choose not to select those types of updates if you plan to install them manually or by some other method (see Figure 8.12). You can change this configuration later if your update needs change. Select the classification types you wish to download to WSUS and click the **Next** button.

Continued

Figure 8.12 WSUS Classification Selection

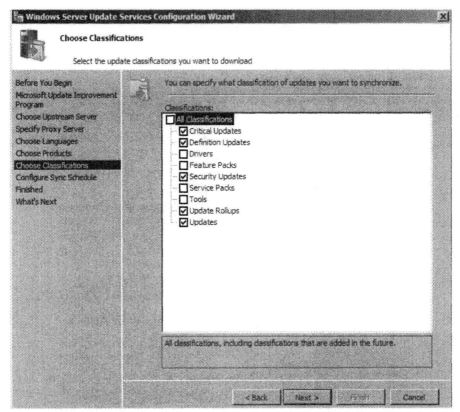

22. We now need to choose whether to sync the WSUS server with Microsoft manually or at a scheduled time every day. In most cases, you will probably want to sync on a regular schedule to ensure that the most current updates are downloaded from Microsoft. Downloading updates may use a significant amount of bandwidth depending on your network's Internet connection speed. You may want to schedule your WSUS server to download updates during hours of low network usage, such as during the night. Go ahead and set a schedule for update downloads and click the **Next** button.

23. Finally, we need to perform an initial synchronization with the Microsoft servers. You can select to do that now in this step or defer until later. Because we have not synchronized our WSUS server with Microsoft yet, it may take a significant amount of time and bandwidth to download updates for the first time. Select whether you want to perform the initial sync now and click the **Next** button.

Continued

> 24. A summary to steps left to perform to complete WSUS configuration will be displayed. Go ahead and click the **Finish** button.
>
> 25. You should now see the WSUS role displayed in Server Manager (see Figure 8.13).

Figure 8.13 The WSUS Role in Server Manager

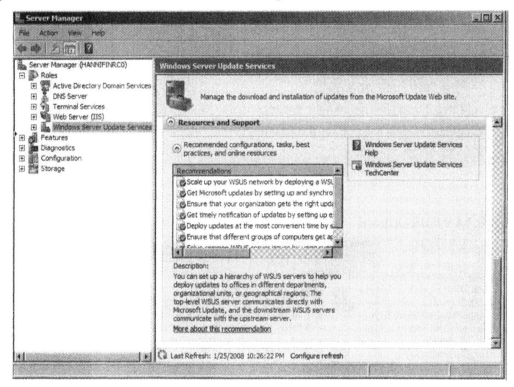

Now that we have explored the setup and initial configuration process for WSUS, let's take a closer look at the server role. In the following sections, we will set up other servers and workstations to download updates from the WSUS server, approve and deploy updates, and discuss WSUS in disconnected networks.

Update Type Selection

During WSUS installation and setup we briefly discussed choosing update types and classifications. It is important to review updates and classifications, as Microsoft regularly adds new products for download and distribution via WSUS. In the following Sidebar, we'll take a look at how to monitor and manage the update types we are downloading via WSUS.

Configuring & Implmenting...

Updating Type Selection

1. Open Server Manager by selecting **Start | Administrative Tools | Server Manager**.

2. Expand the **Windows Server Update Services** node then click on the **Options** node.

3. Click the **Products and Classifications** link in the middle pane (see Figure 8.14). This will open the **Products and Classifications** window.

Figure 8.14 WSUS Options

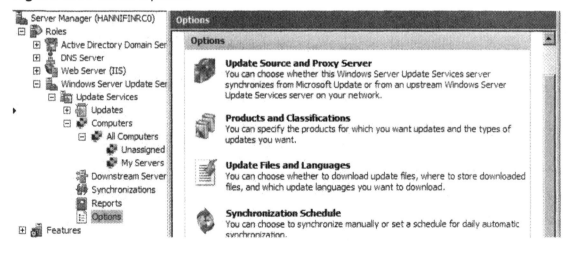

4. You can now select existing or new products and update classifications you wish to distribute to your servers and workstations. You can also deselect any products or update types you will not be distributing via WSUS (see Figure 8.15). After updating your selections, click the **OK** button.

Figure 8.15 Products and Classifications Selection

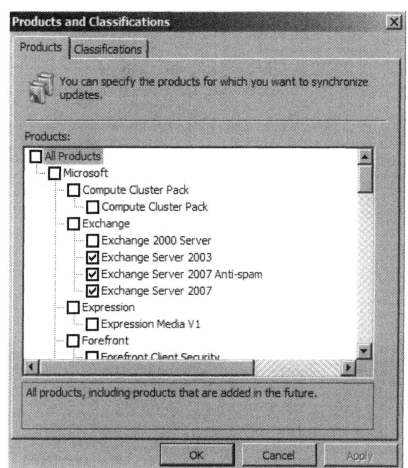

Client Settings

After installing and configuring your WSUS server, you'll need to set up your other workstations and servers to connect to WSUS for their updates. Configuring clients to connect to a WSUS server requires a change to the Windows Update software on those clients. The easiest way to accomplish this change is by using Group Policy. If your clients are in a domain environment, you can create a Group Policy Object (GPO) and link it at the domain or organizational unit (OU) level. This ensures that all clients on the network are properly configured to download updates from your WSUS server. In the following Sidebar, we'll walk through an example of setting up a GPO that will automatically configure servers to connect to WSUS for Windows updates.

New & Noteworthy...

Client Settings with Multiple WSUS Servers

If your environment contains multiple WSUS servers, you can set up Group Policies to configure clients in different sites, domains, or OUs to report to a specified WSUS server for updates. You can use this design to avoid overloading your WSUS servers and network bandwidth.

Configuring & Implementing...

Creating WSUS Computer Groups

Before we jump into our Group Policy Management Console and create a GPO, we need to configure a couple of options in WSUS:

1. First, open Server Manager by selecting **Start | Administrative Tools | Server Manager**.
2. Expand the Roles | Windows Server Update Services | Computers | All Computers nodes.
3. Right-click the **All Computers** node and choose **Add Computer Group**, as shown in Figure 8.16.

Continued

Figure 8.16 Adding a New Computer Group

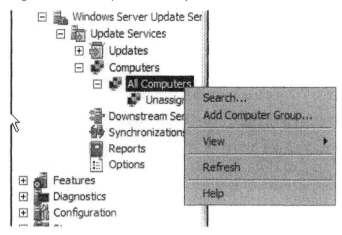

4. In the **New Computer Group** dialog box, enter a name for your new computer group—for example, My Servers (see Figure 8.17). Then click the **Add** button.

Figure 8.17 Entering a Computer Group Name

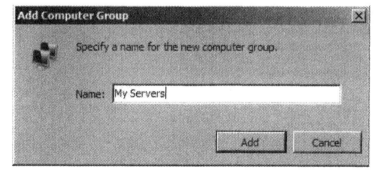

Configuring WSUS Computer Group Assignment Settings

We now need to configure WSUS to assign computers to this newly created group via Group Policy (see the following Sidebar). This allows computer group assignment within WSUS to take place automatically. If you do not change this setting, you will have to manually assign all clients to the appropriate computer group after they contact WSUS for the first time.

Configuring & Implementing...

Changing Computer Group Assignment settings

1. Click the **Options** node in the WSUS role configuration.
2. Click the **Computers** link in the center pane (see Figure 8.18).

Figure 8.18 The WSUS Console Options Pane

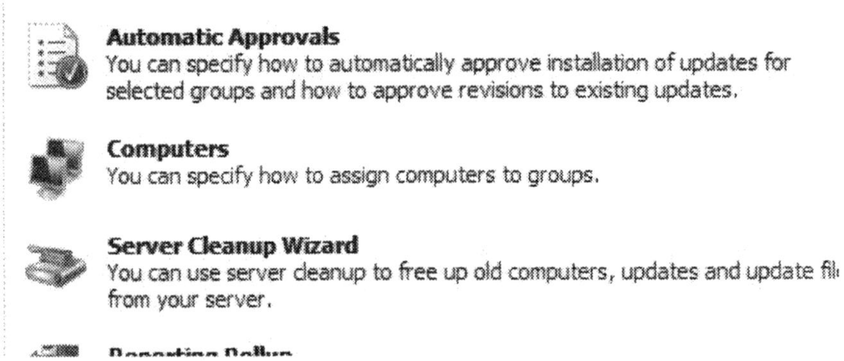

Automatic Approvals
You can specify how to automatically approve installation of updates for selected groups and how to approve revisions to existing updates.

Computers
You can specify how to assign computers to groups.

Server Cleanup Wizard
You can use server cleanup to free up old computers, updates and update fil from your server.

Reporting Rollup

3. In the **Computers** window, select the option to **Use Group Policy or registry settings on computers** (see Figure 8.19). Then click the **OK** button. This setting will instruct WSUS to automatically assign client computers to our newly created computer group based upon the GPO applied to those clients.

Figure 8.19 WSUS Computer Assignment Options

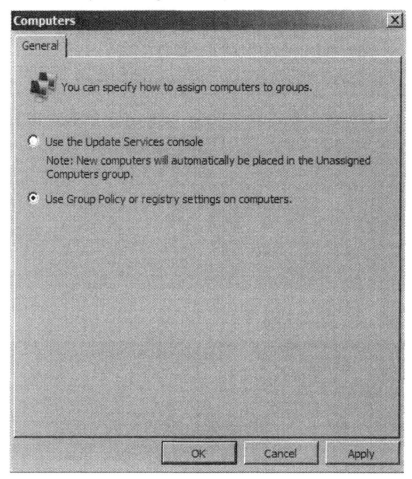

Group Policy Objects (GPOs)

We are now ready to create our GPO to manage client settings. In our example, we will create a new GPO and link it to a Servers OU within Active Directory. If you have not done so already, create a new OU named "Servers" in Active Directory Users and Computers. After creating the new OU, you will be ready to create and link a GPO. To do this, follow along with the following Sidebar.

Configuring & Implementing...

Setting up a Group Policy to Configure Client Settings

1. Select **Start | Administrative Tools | Group Policy Management**. This will open the Group Policy Management Console (GPMC).

2. Within the GPMC, expand the nodes of the forest and domain in which you want to create a new GPO.

3. Locate and right-click on the newly created **Servers** OU. Choose the option to **Create a GPO in this domain, and Link it here**, as shown in Figure 8.20.

Figure 8.20 Creating a New GPO

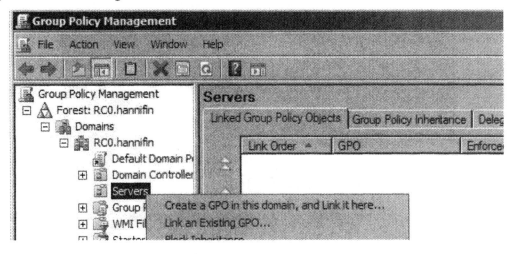

4. The **New GPO** dialog box will appear. Enter a name for the GPO and ensure that **Source Starter GPO** is set to **None**. Then click the **OK** button.

5. Right-click the new GPO you created and choose **Edit**, as shown in Figure 8.21. The Group Policy Editor window will open.

Continued

Figure 8.21 Editing the New GPO

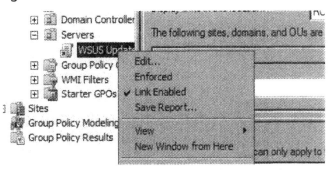

6. Select the **Computer Configuration | Administrative Templates | Windows Components | Windows Update** node. This will display the Windows Update settings that you can configure via GPO. Open each of the following settings by double-clicking on that policy setting. Set each of the following settings as shown in Table 8.1.

Table 8.1 Windows Update GPO Settings

Group Policy Option	Setting(s)
Configure Automatic Updates	■ **Enabled** ■ Configure Automatic Updating: **4 – Auto Download and Schedule the install** ■ Schedule Install Day: **7 – Every Saturday** ■ Schedule Install Time: **02:00**
Specify Intranet Microsoft Update Service Location	■ **Enabled** ■ Set the intranet update service for detecting updates: **http://**_nameof yourWSUSserver_ ■ Set the intranet statistics server: **http://**_nameofyourWSUSserver_
Automatic Updates Detection Frequency	■ **Enabled** ■ Check for updates at the following interval (hours): **12**
Enable Client Side Targeting	■ **Enabled** ■ Target group for this computer: **My Servers**

Continued

7. After configuring the appropriate GPO settings, close the **Group Policy Editor**. Then close the **Group Policy Management Console**. This policy will apply to any new clients added to the My Servers OU in Active Directory. In our example, we'll move our WSUS server to this OU.

8. After your clients perform a Group Policy update, they will check in and register with the WSUS server. You should see the clients appear in the My Servers computer group within WSUS role management, as shown in Figure 8.22. You can now easily set up any Windows client to register with your WSUS server for updates simply by placing them in the My Servers OU.

Figure 8.22 A New Computer Automatically Assigned to the WSUS Computer Group

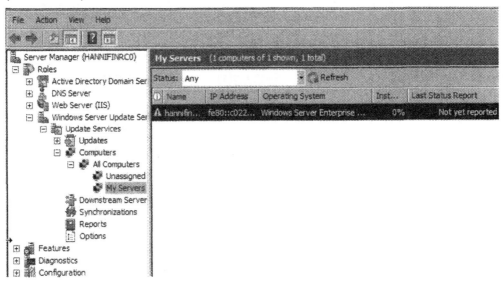

We have just walked through an example of how to use Group Policy to configure your clients to connect to WSUS for update management. You can easily apply these GPO settings to multiple OUs or domains, depending on the needs within your organization.

Client Targeting

In the preceding section, you learned how to use a GPO to automatically configure the Windows Update settings for computers that you want to connect to the WSUS server for updates. From the preceding sidebar, you saw how we can use GPO settings to instruct a client computer to become a member of a particular computer group within WSUS. This prevents you from having to manually add computers to computer groups within WSUS.

Software Updates

Now that your clients are configured to connect to WSUS for Windows updates, we need to take a look at how to review, manage, and deploy updates from the WSUS management console. In the following Sidebar, we'll take a look at viewing and managing software updates.

Configuring & Implementing...

Exploring Software Updates

1. Open Server Manager by selecting Start | **Administrative Tools** | **Server Manager**.

2. Expand the Roles | Windows Server Update Services | Updates nodes.

3. Click to highlight the **Updates** node. This will display the Updates Dashboard in the middle pane. The dashboard displays a high-level status of updates, as shown in Figure 8.23. This is a quick way to see the deployment status of updates in your environment.

Continued

Figure 8.23 The WSUS Updates Dashboard

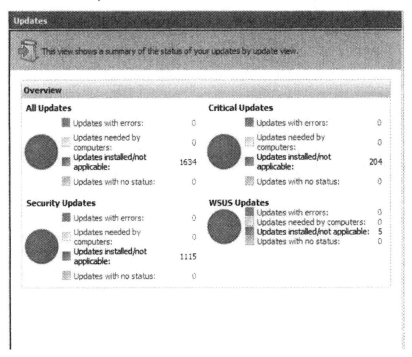

4. Expand the **Updates** node to see predefined views of updates. These views allow you to easily inspect updates for review and deployment. For example, you can easily review and deploy critical updates by using the **Critical Updates** view. Go ahead and click the **All Updates** view, choose **Unapproved** from the Approval drop-down menu, and then click **Refresh** (see Figure 8.24). After the view is refreshed, you should see a list of all unapproved updates available for deployment.

Figure 8.24 The Updates | All Updates View

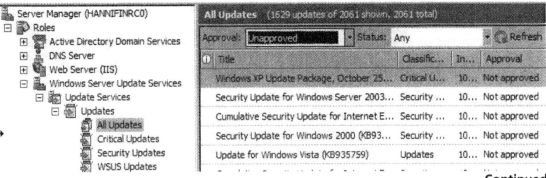

Continued

5. You can see more information on any update simply by clicking and highlighting that update in the center pane. Click on any update and notice that the details of this update appear in the bottom half of the view, as shown in Figure 8.25. Notice that this detailed information even provides a link to the Microsoft Knowledgebase article that references the update.

Figure 8.25 The Update Details Window

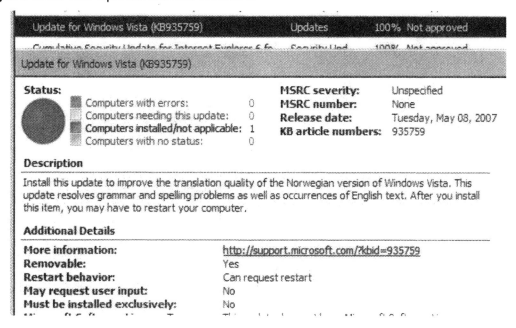

In this section, you saw how using the predefined views allows you to quickly review updates available for deployment via your WSUS server. We will now discuss the process to test updates and then deploy those updates to your production clients.

Test and Approval

You are finally ready to begin rolling out updates to your workstations and servers. However, it is always good practice to deploy updates to a test environment before pushing them out to your production systems. In this section, we will walk through the process of deploying updates to a test environment and then to a production environment. In our example, we will be using two WSUS computer groups. The My Servers group contains all production servers. The Test Lab group contains our test lab servers and workstations. Figure 8.26 depicts the example environment.

Figure 8.26 The WSUS Example Environment

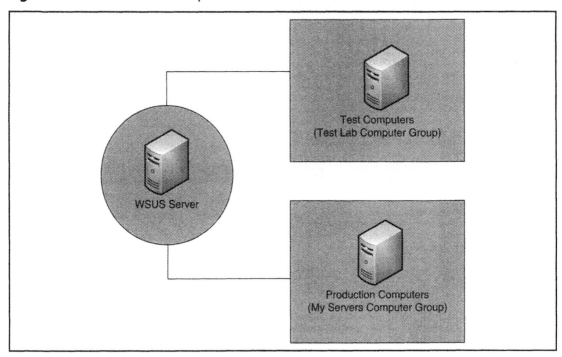

We have one WSUS server that downloads updates from Microsoft. Within WSUS we have two computer groups defined. These groups are named Test Lab and My Servers. Our example computers exist within one of two OUs named Test Lab Computers and My Servers. A GPO is applied to each OU. The GPO configures computers to connect to the WSUS server and assigns them to the correct computer group within WSUS. A GPO applied to the Test Lab Computers OU schedules computers in the OU to install updates Mondays at 11:00 P.M. Another GPO applied to the My Servers OU schedules computers to install updates Thursdays at 11:30 P.M. In the following Sidebar, we'll walk through the process of testing an update and then deploying that update to our production servers.

Configuring & Implementing...

Approving WSUS Updates

1. Open Server Manager by selecting Start | Administrative Tools | Server Manager.

2. Expand the Roles | Windows Servers Update Services | Update Services | Updates nodes.

3. Click to highlight the **All Updates** view.

4. In the middle pane, click on an update that you wish to deploy. Then, in the Actions pane, click the **Approve** link (see Figure 8.27). The **Approve Updates** window will open.

Figure 8.27 Update Selection

5. Right-click the **Test Lab** computer group and select **Approved for Install**, as shown in Figure 8.28. Then click the **OK** button. The next time the clients in the Test Lab Computers OU check in with WSUS they will begin downloading the approved update. After downloading the update, the client computers will then wait until the scheduled install time of Monday at 11:00 P.M., and then install the update. After the update is installed, the computers will reboot.

Continued

Figure 8.28 The Approve Updates Window

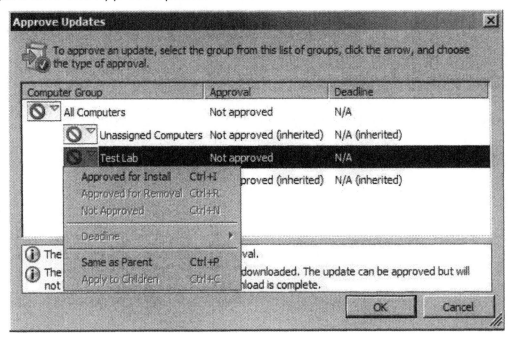

6. Now that we have deployed the update to our test lab, we can confirm that there are no compatibility issues that might impact our production environment. After deploying to the Test Lab and confirming that there are no problems with the update, we can deploy to production systems. Locate the update in the **All Updates** view.

7. Right-click the same update you just deployed and choose **Approve**.

8. In the **Approve Updates** window, right-click the **My Servers** computer group and then click **Approved for Install**. Now click the **OK** button. The next time the client computers in the My Servers OU connect to WSUS they will begin downloading the approved update. The computers will then wait until the scheduled time to install the update and reboot.

We have now deployed the update to our test lab and production environment. You can follow the same steps to deploy multiple updates at the same time. Remember that it is generally a good practice to deploy updates to a test environment before deploying to your production environment.

Disconnected Networks

WSUS provides a great way to centralize the management and deployment of updates to your Windows workstations and servers. But what if you want to deploy your WSUS server in a network disconnected from the Internet? Some networks must remain disconnected from the Internet for security reasons. In this situation, you can deploy a WSUS server on a network that does have Internet connectivity and download updates to that server. You can then copy those updates to removable media (CD, DVD, etc.). Those updates can then be imported to the WSUS server in the disconnected network via the removable media. The updates will then appear in the WSUS console and can be deployed to clients on that network via WSUS. To transfer updates to your disconnected WSUS server follow along with the following Sidebar.

Configuring & Implementing...

Importing WSUS Updates in a Disconnected Network

1. Open **Server Manager** on your Internet-connected WSUS server by selecting **Start | Administrative Tools | Server Manager**.
2. Expand the Windows Server Update Services | Update Services node.
3. Click to highlight the **Options** node.
4. Click the **Updates Files and Languages** link in the center pane of the console.
5. Click the **Update Files** tab and check the box to **Download express installation files** (see Figure 8.29). Then click the **OK** button.

Continued

Figure 8.29 The Update Files and Languages Pane

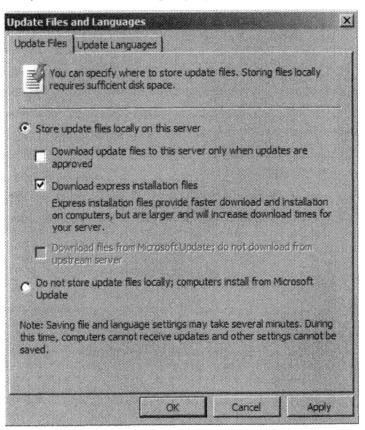

6. Log on to the disconnected server and ensure that the Updates and Files settings are configured exactly the same as the Internet-connected server.

7. You are now ready to export the files and metadata from the Internet-connected server and copy those to your media. To do this, first copy the folder *WSUSInstallDrive\WSUSUpdatesFolder*
WSUSContent (C:\WSUS\WSUSContent) to your removable media. Depending on the size of the updates available, this folder could be very large.

8. Next, you need to run **WSUSUtil.exe** to export the metadata from the Internet-connected server. Open a command prompt and change to the directory **C:\Program Files\Update Services\Tools**.

9. Run the command **wsusutil.exe export transfer.cab transfer.log**. Then press **Enter**. The metadata export process will begin.

Continued

10. After the export completes, copy the **transfer.cab** and **transfer.log** files to the media that will be used to transfer data to the disconnected network server.

11. We are now ready to import the updates and metadata to our disconnected WSUS server. First, copy the **WSUSContent** folder to **WSUSInstallDrive\WSUSUpdatesFolder** (C:\WSUS). If prompted, you can replace existing files.

12. Finally, you need to import the metadata to the disconnected WSUS server. Copy the **transfer.cab** file to the directory **C:\Program Files\Update Services\Tools** on the disconnected server.

13. Open a command prompt and change to the **C:\Program Files\ Update Services\Tools** directory.

14. Enter the command **wsusutil.exe import transfer.cab transfer.log**. This will import the metadata to your disconnected server. This process can take an extended amount of time. After the process completes, you can approve and deploy updates from the disconnected WSUS server. You will need to perform this process anytime you download new updates to your Internet-connected WSUS server.

Capturing Performance Data

Collecting and analyzing performance data is necessary to ensure that your servers and systems are running in optimal condition. It is important that you understand how your servers are performing during normal conditions to establish baselines. This type of information can be crucial when trying to troubleshoot performance problems. Collecting this data can also help you to proactively find bottlenecks and correct them before system performance is severely impacted.

Data Collector Sets

Data Collector Sets are groups of components that collect data to be used by the Reliability and Performance Monitor. Data Collector Sets can contain information from performance counters, trace events, and configuration data. You can then view this data in the Reliability and Performance Monitor or use it to create reports. In the following Sidebar, we'll look at some of the predefined system Data Collector Sets as well as creating our own.

Configuring & Implementing...

Running a Data Collector Set

1. Open th e Reliability and Performance Monitor in Server Manager by selecting **Start | Administrative Tools | Server Manager.**

2. Expand the Diagnostics | Reliability and Performance | Data Collector Sets nodes (see Figure 8.30).

Figure 8.30 Data Collector Sets

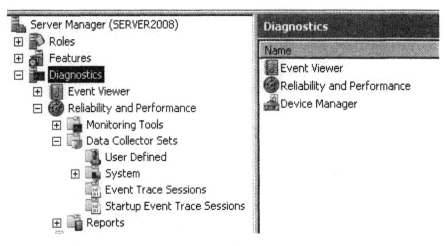

Now let's explore the system-defined sets. These contain predefined counters and log monitoring to provide some key statistics that help to determine the health of your server. Let's take a look at these Data Collector Sets.

3. Expand the **System** node under **Data Collector Sets**. You should see several predefined sets, such as System Performance, LAN Diagnostics, and Active Directory Diagnostics.

4. Click to highlight the **System Performance** set. Notice that the Data Collector Set contains an NT Kernel trace and Performance Counter item (see Figure 8.31).

Continued

Figure 8.31 The System Performance Data Collector Set

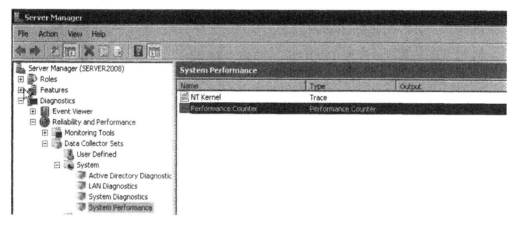

5. Right-click the **Performance Counter** item and choose **Properties**.
This will open the **Performance Counter Properties** window.
Here you can see a list of all performance counters that this Data
Collector Set will gather (see Figure 8.32). Click the **OK** button
to close the window.

Figure 8.32 Performance Counter Properties

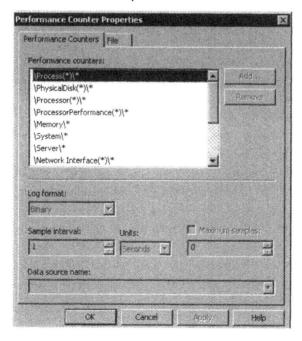

Continued

6. We now need to start the Data Collector Set. This will start the process of gathering data. Right-click the **System Performance** set and choose **Start**. This will start data collection. You should see a green arrow on top of the set (see Figure 8.33). This indicates that the collector is running. The Data Collector Set will run for one minute and then stop. After stopping, a report will automatically be generated under the Reports node.

Figure 8.33 Running the Data Collector Set

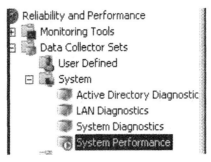

7. Expand the **Reports | System | System Performance** nodes.
8. You should see a newly created report under the System Performance node. Click on that report to open it in the center pane, as shown in Figure 8.34.

Figure 8.34 The System Performance Report

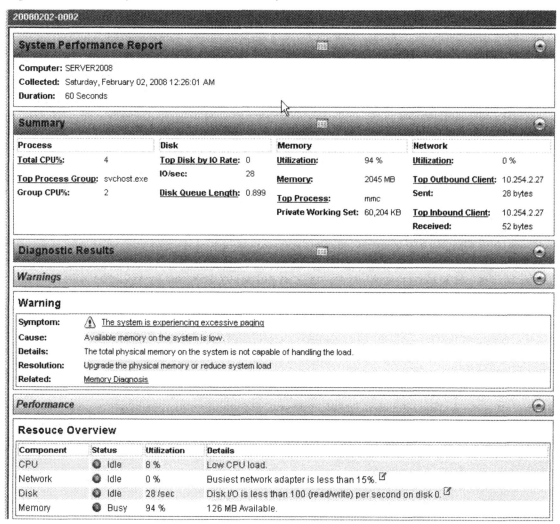

Continued

You may already have experience troubleshooting performance problems in previous versions of Windows. If this is the case, you probably know how tough it can sometimes be to remember what performance counters or logs to look at when tackling a performance issue. Data Collector Sets use predetermined *best-practice* counters and logs provided by Microsoft. The included Data Collector Sets are also a great way to regularly ensure that your servers are running in an optimal condition. If you decide you need additional data, you can always create your own Data Collector Set using custom counters and logs.

The resultant report displays detailed information about system performance. This type of report can be very valuable when troubleshooting performance problems. We can see at the bottom of our report that memory is being reported as busy and only 126 MB are available. We also received a warning that the system is experiencing excessive paging. We could easily use this report to determine whether we need to upgrade the memory on this system. Now that we've looked at the built-in system Data Collector Sets, let's create a custom set of our own (see the following Sidebar).

Configuring & Implementing...

Creating a Custom Data Collector Set

1. Right-click the User Defined node under Data Collector Sets. Then choose New | Data Collector Set. This will launch the Create New Data Collector Set Wizard.

2. In the first step of the **Create New Data Collector Set Wizard**, enter a name for your set and make sure the **Create from a template** option is selected; then click the **Next** button (see Figure 8.35).

Continued

Figure 8.35 The Create New Data Collector Set Wizard

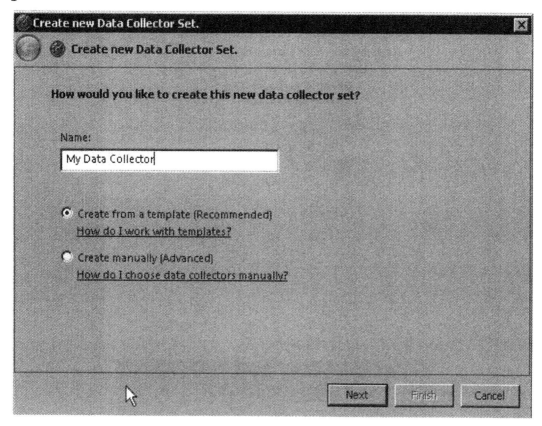

3. We now need to choose which template to use. Select the **Basic** template, and then click the **Next** button.

4. In the next step of the wizard, you need to enter a location to store the data. Enter **C:\MyDataCollector** and then click the **Next** button.

5. Finally, you can choose to run the Data Collector Set as a certain account. Go ahead and leave the **RunAs** setting at **default**. Choose the **Save and Close** option. Then click the **Finish** button.

You should now see the new Data Collector Set under the **User Defined** node, as shown in Figure 8.36. We now need to configure the **My Data Collector** to collect the data we wish to review. Go ahead and perform the following to set up our data collection options.

Continued

Figure 8.36 The New Data Collector Set

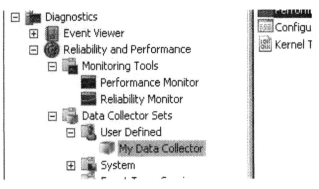

6. Click **My Data Collector** to highlight the set.
7. Next, right-click the **Performance Counter** item in the center pane and choose **Properties**. This will open the **Performance Counter Properties** window (see Figure 8.37).

Figure 8.37 Performance Counter Properties

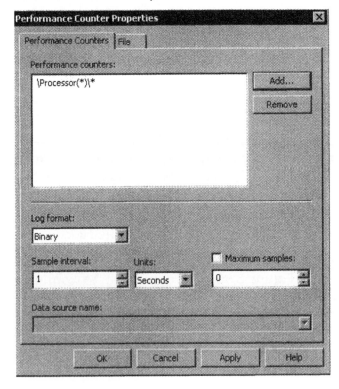

Continued

8. In the Performance Counter Properties window, click the Add button. This will open the Performance Counter Selection window.

9. Select the counter **Logical Disk | Avg. Disk Queue Length**. Then select the **C:** instance and click the **Add** button (see Figure 8.38).

Figure 8.38 Performance Counter Selection

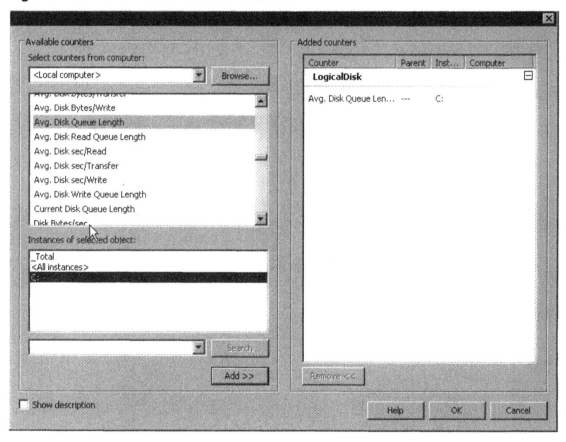

10. Go ahead and add the **Current Disk Queue Length** and **Avg. Disk Read Queue Length** counters. Then click the **OK** button.

11. In the **Performance Counter Properties** window, click the **OK** button.

12. Now right-click the **My Data Collector** node and choose **Properties**. This will open the **Collector Set Properties** window. You can set various options for your data collector in this window. For example,

Continued

you could use the Schedule tab to schedule a date and time for the data collector to begin collecting data. This will allow you to collect data when you are not logged on to the server. For now, we just want to set the stop condition for our data collector.

13. Click the **Stop Condition** tab.

14. Ensure that the **Overall duration** option is selected. Then set the **duration** to **5 minutes** (see Figure 8.39). Then click the **OK** button.

Figure 8.39 The Data Collector Set Properties Window

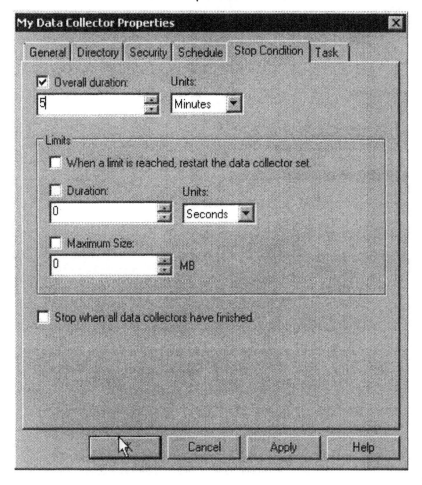

Continued

15. Now that the Data Collector Set is set up, go ahead and start the data collector and wait for five minutes for the collector to stop.

16. After the collector stops, locate the newly created report in the **Reports | Use Defined | My Data Collector** node. Right-click the new report and choose **View | Performance Monitor**.

17. In the center pane, click the **Add** button, as shown in Figure 8.40.

Figure 8.40 Adding a Performance Counter

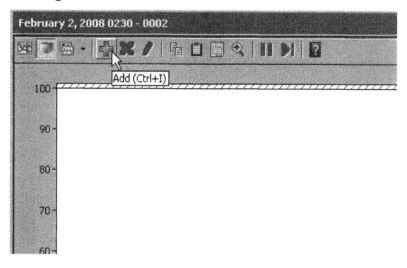

18. Select the Logical Disk | Avg. Disk Queue Length and Logical Disk | Avg. Disk Read Queue Length counters (see Figure 8.41). Then click the OK button.

Continued

Figure 8.41 The Add Counters Pane

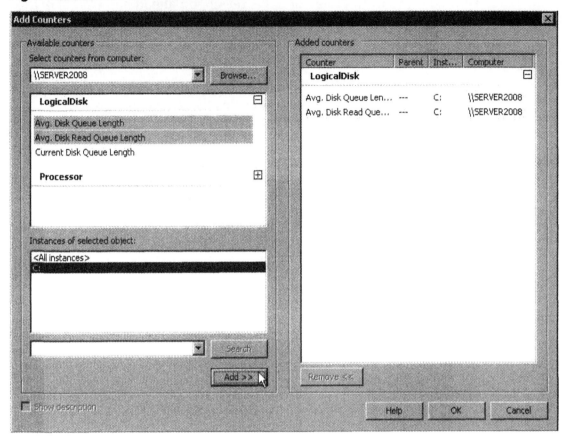

19. You will now see a graph of the performance data collected by the Data Collector Set (see Figure 8.42).

Figure 8.42 The Data Collector Set Graph

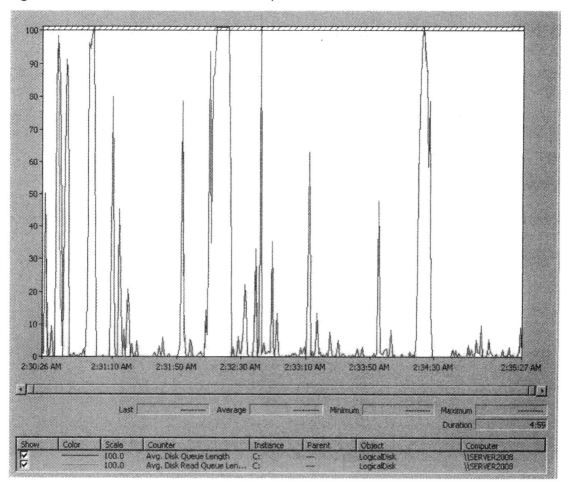

We just discovered how to set up and review Data Collector Sets in Windows Server 2008. As you can see, these sets provide an easy way to capture performance and log data to troubleshoot system performance issues. You should collect and review performance data on a regular basis to ensure that your servers are running at optimal performance. For example, you may want to schedule a Data Collector Set to run between 8:00 A.M. and 10:00 A.M. to monitor the load on your servers during peak logon hours at your company. In the next section, we will cover Performance Monitor in a little more depth. Keep in mind that running Data Collector Sets can increase the load on your server. Typically, the load caused by Data Collector Sets is very small; however, if you are running them on a highly utilized server, the collection job could impact server performance.

Performance Monitor

Now that we've explored Data Collector Sets, let's take a look at Performance Monitor in a little more depth. You can use Performance Monitor to review system performance data collected by Data Collector Sets as well as in real time. Performance Monitor also allows you to view the data in different formats. It is important to understand some of the key performance counters in Performance Monitor. Table 8.2 lists a few counters you should become familiar with. The table includes the counter name, a brief description, and the threshold value.

Table 8.2 Performance Counters

Counter	Description	Threshold Value
Memory\Pages/sec	Pages/sec is the number of memory pages written to disk every second. High pages/sec can indicate memory problems with your server.	20
Processor\% Processor Time	This is the percentage of the processor time spent executing tasks.	85%
System\Processor Queue Length	This counter tracks the number of threads queued and waiting to be processed.	2
Physical Disk\Current Disk Queue Length	This counter collects the current number of waiting requests for the physical disk.	Number of Disk Spindles + 2

In the following Sidebar, we'll take a closer look at Performance Monitor.

Configuring & Implementing...

Exploring Performance Monitor

1. Open Server Manager by selecting Start | Administrative Tools | Server Manager.

2. Expand the Diagnostics | Reliability and Performance | Monitoring Tools nodes.

3. Click on the **Performance Monitor** node to display Performance Monitor in the center pane of the console.

4. Performance Monitor uses what is known as *counters*. Counters are the different types of data collection you can add to Performance Monitor. Go ahead and click the **Add** button, as shown in Figure 8.43. The **Add Counters** window will open.

Figure 8.43 The Add Button in Performance Monitor

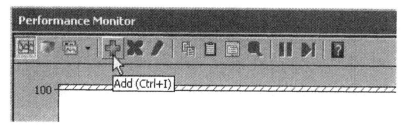

5. Expand the **Processor** heading and then click the **% Processor Time** counter. Choose the **_Total** instance and click the **Add** button (see Figure 8.44). You can also check the **Show description** checkbox to display a description of any of the counters. Go ahead and also add the **%Idle Time** counter too. Then click the **OK** button.

Continued

Figure 8.44 Selecting Data to Display

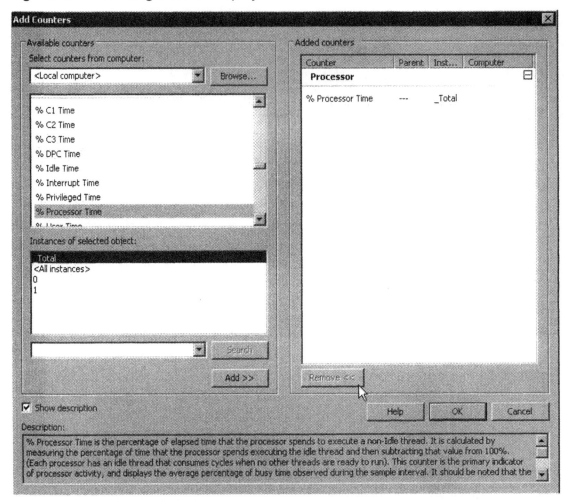

6. The **Performance Monitor** window will immediately begin to display data from the selected counters. Notice that this data is being displayed in real time. Performance Monitor lets us view this data in a few different formats. If you want to view the raw numbers being collected, you can change the view to **Report** (see Figure 8.45).

Continued

Figure 8.45 The Report View

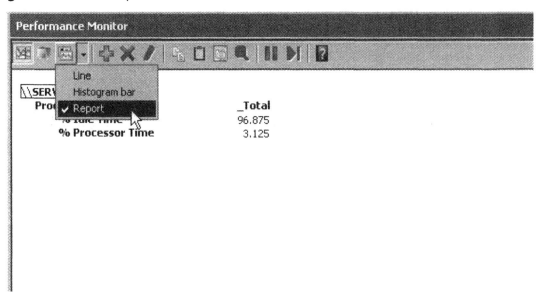

7. You can quickly change your data view from real time to data from a Data Collector Set. Click the **Data Collector** icon in the toolbar of the **Performance Monitor** window. Choose the **Log files** option and add the data directory for any existing Data Collector Sets (see Figure 8.46). Then click the **OK** button. You will now see performance data from an existing Data Collector Set.

Figure 8.46 Viewing Data from a Data Collector Set

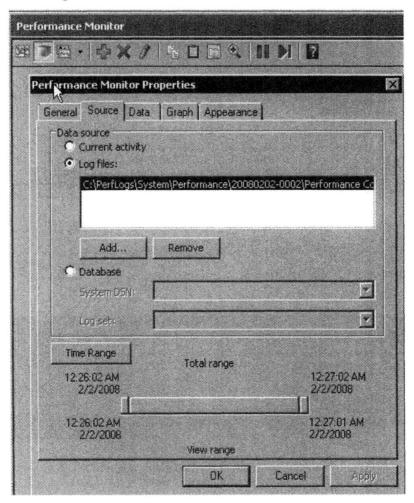

In this section, we discovered how to use Performance Monitor to review system performance data in real time, or that collected by Data Collector Sets. Performance Monitor is a great way to troubleshoot performance issues and find bottlenecks with server hardware and software. Some common performance counters to watch are % Processor Time, Avg Disk Queue Length, and Memory Pages/Sec. Now let's take a look at Reliability Monitor.

Reliability Monitor

Reliability Monitor is a new feature introduced in Windows Vista and Windows Server 2008. Reliability Monitor keeps track of system stability over time and reports on events that could cause the system to become unreliable. Reliability Monitor keeps track of software installs, uninstalls, system failures, application failures, and hardware failures. These failures are logged and displayed in the Reliability Monitor window. You can access Reliability Monitor by opening **Server Manager** and expanding the **Diagnostics | Reliability and Performance | Monitoring Tools** nodes and then selecting **Reliability Monitor** (see Figure 8.47). You should review Reliability Monitor on a regular basis to check for system or application failures. This is also a quick and easy way to see what new software that has been installed or removed from the system.

Figure 8.47 Reliability Monitor

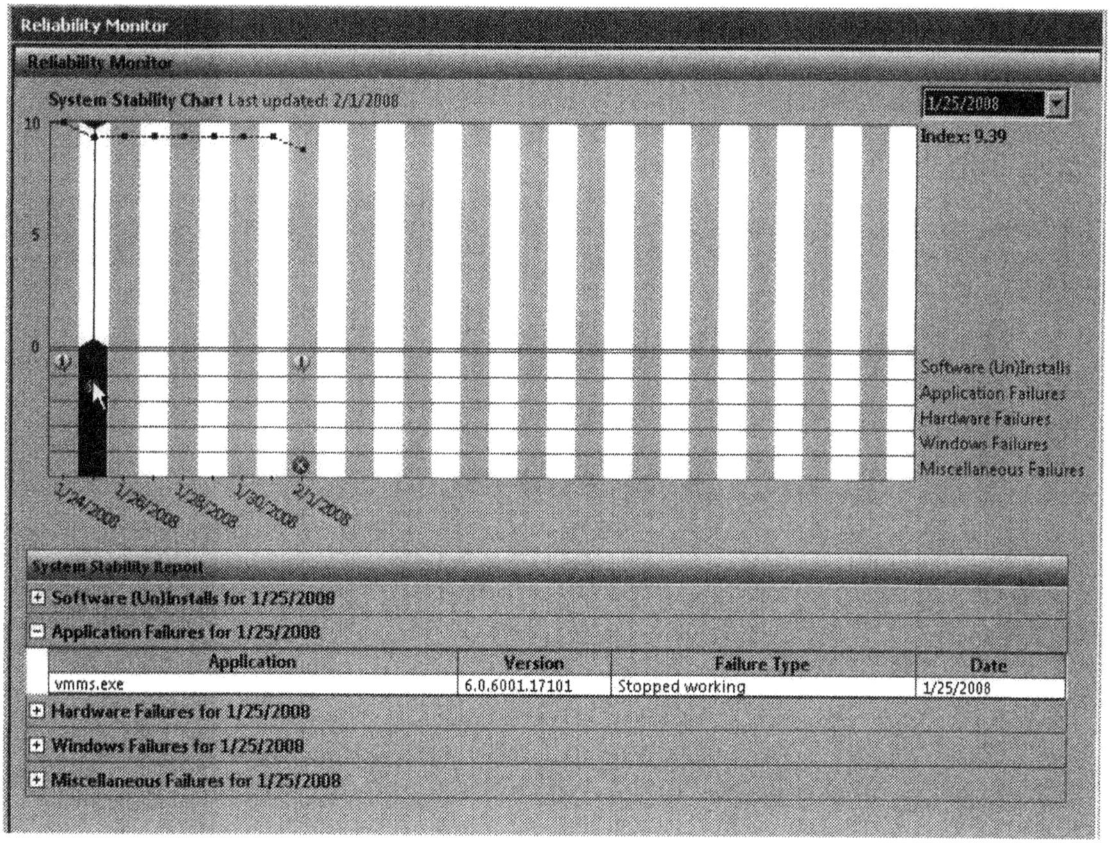

In Figure 8.47, you can see that on 1/25/2008 this system experienced an issue with the vmms.exe application. If this failure continues to take place, you should troubleshoot this application, as it may be impacting the overall stability of the system. Next we'll discuss the System Stability Index.

Monitoring the System Stability Index

The System Stability Index is a measurement that indicates the overall reliability of the server. The index is a number between 1 and 10, with 1 being the least stable and 10 being the most stable. As application or system failures occur, they negatively impact the System Stability Index. Recent failures have more impact on the overall index than historical failures. The more time the system goes without failures, the more the index increases. The System Stability Index is a great way to understand the overall stability of the system over time. To see the System Stability Index open Reliability Monitor by opening **Server Manager** and expanding the **Diagnostics | Reliability and Performance | Monitoring Tools** nodes and then selecting **Reliability Monitor** (see Figure 8.48). The System Stability Index is displayed in the upper-right-hand corner of Reliability Monitor. You can view the index for a single day or for the system over time.

Figure 8.48 The System Stability Index

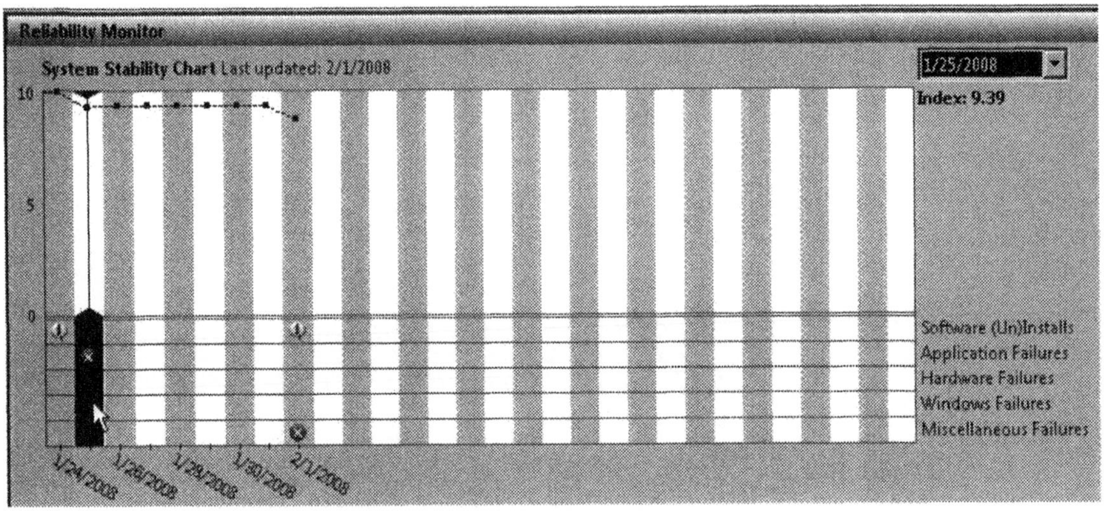

If you begin to see a decline in the System Stability Index over time, you should determine the root cause of the issue based on application and system failures. A decrease in the System Stability Index could imply that the reliability of the entire server is being impacted. This, of course, impacts user's ability to access applications that may be running on this system.

Monitoring Event Logs

Event logs have been a valuable tool for troubleshooting Windows operating system and application problems for years. Windows has traditionally provided three main log categories. These categories are System, Application, and Security. The System log contains entries, also known as *events*, related to the Windows operating system and components that make up the OS. The Application log contains events related to applications running on top of the operating system. Third-party applications typically write to this log. Finally, the Security log is a source of security-related events, such as logons, attempts to access files, and privilege use. Windows Server 2008 introduces two new log categories: Setup logs and Forwarded Events logs. The Setup log keeps events related to application installs. The Forwarded Events log contains logged events forwarded from other systems' Event logs. This allows you to provide simple centralized log management and monitoring of remote servers. Finally, Application and Services logs provide logs for specific applications. For example, a database application could write events to a log specifically available for that application. Let's take a closer look at Event logs.

Custom Views

You can create custom views of Event logs to easily filter events and save the filter for use the next time you access the Event Viewer. For example, maybe you need a quick way to log on and view only critical events on a particular server. You can create a custom view for critical events and simply click on that view anytime you need to see those events in the future. In the following Sidebar, we will create a custom view.

Configuring & Implementing...

Creating a Custom Event View

1. Open Server Manager by selecting **Start | Administrative Tools | Server Manager**.

2. Expand the **Diagnostics | Event Viewer | Custom Views** nodes (see Figure 8.49).

Continued

Figure 8.49 Custom Views

3. Right-click the **Custom Views** node and choose **Create Custom View**. This will open the **Create Custom View** window.

4. Select the checkboxes for **Critical** and **Warning** events. Then click the drop-down list next to **Event Logs**. Choose the **Windows Logs** main heading, as shown in Figure 8.50. Then click the **OK** button.

Continued

Figure 8.50 Creating a Custom Event View

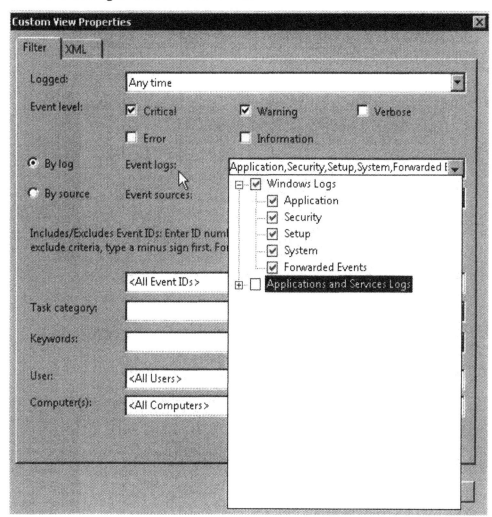

5. In the **Save Filter to Custom View** window, enter **All Critical and Warning Events** for the name of your view. Click to highlight **Custom Views** (see Figure 8.51). Then click the **OK** button.

Continued

Figure 8.51 Saving a Filter to a Custom View

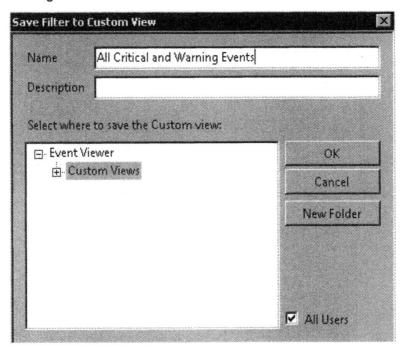

6. The view is now displayed under the **Custom Views** node. Click the view to see all events with a severity of Warning or Critical (see Figure 8.52).

Figure 8.52 The All Critical and Warning Events Custom View

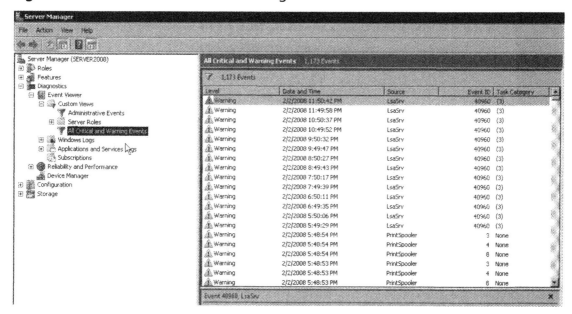

You can create custom views to filter events from various Event logs. Custom views allow you to easily save commonly used filters.

Application and Services Logs

Application and Services logs is a new feature introduced in Windows Server 2008. Application and Services logs are logs focused on monitoring specific applications instead of events that have an impact on the entire server. Application and Services logs contain four types of logs per application. These types are Admin, Operational, Analytic, and Debug.

Admin Logs

Admin logs contain information typically useful to system administrators. These logs usually contain the error that occurred and details of that error. The events also will typically contain steps an administrator can take to resolve the error.

Operational Logs

Operational logs contain information for diagnosing problems. These events contain fewer error descriptions and more diagnostic data than the Admin logs, but administrators can still use them to determine the root cause of the problem. Some of the events in the Operational logs may be useful to application developers when debugging program bugs.

Analytic Logs

Analytic logs contain information that is not useful for most server administrators. Microsoft support personnel can use these logs when contacting Microsoft Support Services.

Debug Logs

Debug logs contain very detailed information that can be useful to developers when debugging application code.

Subscriptions

Windows Server 2008 and Windows Vista provide the ability to forward event logs to another computer. This allows you to centralize the collection of events from remote computers. By centralizing events, you can review and monitor logs from multiple computers in one location. To collect events from remote computers, you must set up subscriptions. To create subscriptions we must first configure source computers, also known as *sources*, to forward events and the central computer, also known as the *collector*, to receive events. In the following Sidebar 3, we will use the computer names Chost1 and Chost2. Chost2 will be our source and Chost1 will be our collector.

Configuring & Implementing...

Setting up an Event Log Subscription

On all computers whose events you wish to forward to a collector computer, you need to set up event forwarding. To set up the source computers we need to configure winrm, which allows remote management, and open the appropriate port on the host firewall to allow inbound and outbound winrm traffic. To do this, log on to each source computer and perform the following:

1. Log on to Chost2.
2. Open a command prompt and type the command **winrm quickconfig**.

Continued

3. When prompted whether you want to make changes to the WinRM listener and Windows Firewall, enter **Y**. You will receive a confirmation that these changes were successful.

   On the collector computer, you need to set up event collection. In this task, we will enable and start the collector service on the central server. Perform the following on the central collection server to configure and enable the event collector service:

4. Log on to Chost1.

5. Open a command prompt and type the command **wecutil qc**. Then, when prompted to change the service startup mode, choose **Yes**. You should see a confirmation that the collector service was set up properly.

   Now that we have properly set up event forwarding and collection, we need to create subscriptions for the events we wish to forward to the collector. Subscriptions are set up on the collector computer. Perform the following to create a subscription:

6. Log on to Chost1 (Collector).

7. Open Server Manager by selecting Start | Administrative Tools | Server Manager.

8. Expand the Diagnostics | Event Viewer nodes.

9. Right-click the **Subscriptions** node and choose **Create Subscription**.

10. In the Subscription Properties window, enter the text All Critical and Warning Events in the Subscription Name text box.

11. Choose the **Collector Initiated** option. This option will instruct the collector to connect to the source computers to gather events.

12. Click the **Select Computers** button.

13. In the **Computers** window, click the **Add domain computers** button. Enter the name **Chost2** and click the **OK** button. Click the **OK** button in the **Computers** window to return to the **Subscription Properties** window.

14. Click the **Select Events** button.

15. Select the **Critical** and **Warning** options and then choose all **Windows Logs**, as shown in Figure 8.53. Then click the **OK** button.

Continued

Figure 8.53 The Query Filter Window

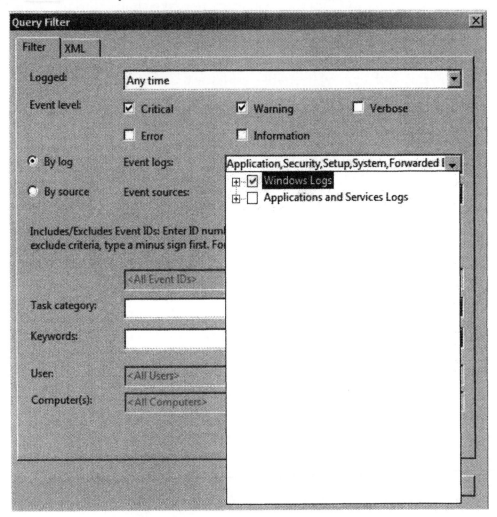

16. Click the **Advanced** button to open the **Advanced Subscription Settings** window.

17. Select the option **Specific User** and click the **User and Password** button.

18. Enter a username and password with sufficient access to the event logs on the source computer. Then click the **OK** button.

19. Click the **OK** button two more times to close all windows.

20. You will now see the subscription active in the center pane, as shown in Figure 8.54.

Continued

Figure 8.54 An Active Subscription

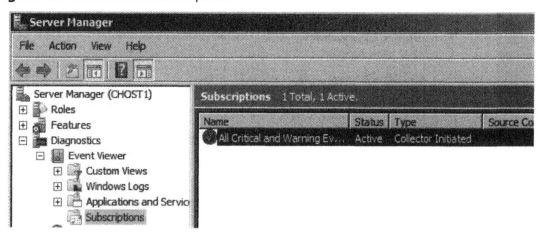

21. Now that we have successfully set up a subscription, let's test our configuration. Log on to the source computer, Chost2.

22. Open a command prompt and enter the command **EVENTCREATE /T Warning /ID 500 /L Application /D "Testing Subscription"**. This will create a warning event on Chost2.

23. Log on to Chost1 and open **Server Manager**.

24. Click on the Diagnostics | Event Viewer | Windows Logs | Forwarded Events node.

25. The Warning Event you created on Chost2 should be displayed in the Forwarded Events log on Chost1. You may need to click the **Refresh** button if the event does not appear. There is a short delay between the time an event is logged on a local computer and the time it is forwarded to the collector server.

Now that we have successfully created a subscription, we can set up multiple computers for event forwarding. We can then use subscriptions to centralize log collection. The collector server can then be used to troubleshoot problems for computers throughout the enterprise from a central location.

DNS Event Log

You can view the DNS logs by opening the DNS management console. The DNS Event log is used to capture and monitor domain name system (DNS)-specific events, and can provide detailed information about errors or the health of DNS on your server. You should review the DNS Event log on a regular basis for error events.

Gathering Network Data

Gathering network data is an important step in both managing and troubleshooting your network infrastructure. Microsoft provides several tools and services to allow you to more easily gather data from your Windows servers.

Simple Network Management Protocol (SNMP)

The Simple Network Management Protocol (SNMP) has been used for years to manage and monitor network devices such as switches, routers, and firewalls. Windows servers also provide the capability for management systems to connect and monitor them. In the following Sidebar, we'll walk through setting up SNMP on a server.

Configuring & Implementing...

Configuring SNMP

1. Log on to the server and open **Server Manager**.
2. Click the **Features** node. Then click the **Add Features** link in the center pane.
3. Choose to add **SNMP Service** and **SNMP WMI Provider** (see Figure 8.55). Then click the **Next** button. This will install the SNMP core services.

Continued

Figure 8.55 The Add Features Wizard

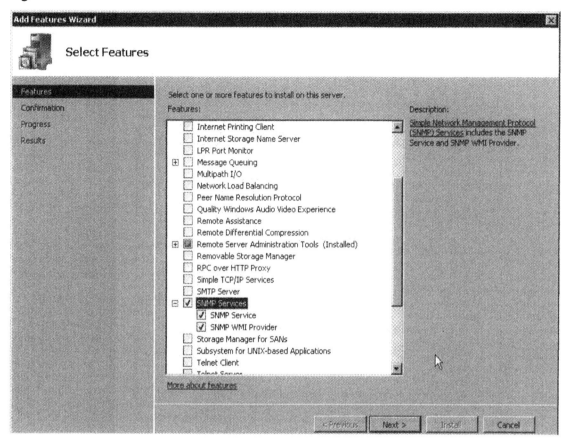

4. After the install completes, return to **Server Manager** and click on the **Configuration | Services** node.

5. Locate and double-click the **SNMP Service** to open the Properties window.

6. Click the **Agent** tab. On this tab, you configure what information you want to provide via SNMP, such as application, network, and hardware information. You can also enter system contact information on this tab. Go ahead and enter contact information and select all options on this tab (see Figure 8.56). Then click on the **Traps** tab.

Continued

Figure 8.56 SNMP Service Properties

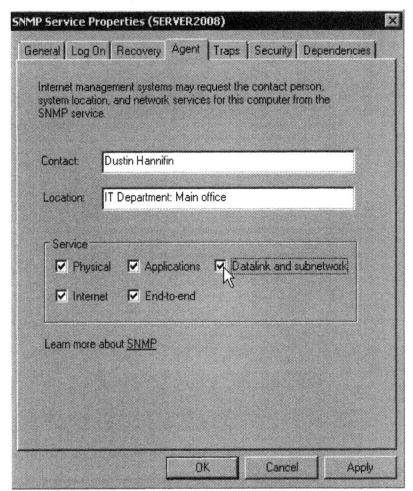

7. On the **Traps** tab, you can set up the trap destination and community name used by that system. The trap destination is the server or device with the SNMP monitoring software installed. This is where the server will send SNMP alerts, also known as *traps*. You will also need to enter a community name. Community names are simple passwords used to secure SNMP data. Without the SNMP community name, a system cannot send or receive SNMP data from other devices that use a community name. You will need to specify the community name of your monitoring server on the **Traps** tab (see Figure 8.57). After entering trap information, click on the **Security** tab.

Continued

Figure 8.57 SNMP Trap Properties

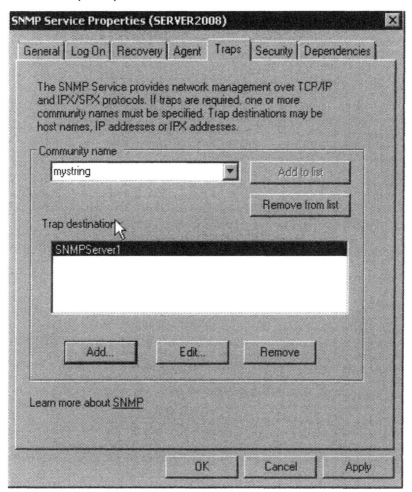

8. On the **Security** tab, you can secure SNMP data on this system by only allowing SNMP access from specified hosts, as well as requiring that a specific community string be presented to your server. Here you can enter the host name of your SNMP monitoring system as well as the community string this system will be presenting to your server. Notice that you can also specify what level of access the SNMP monitoring system has to your server (see Figure 8.58). For example, you could only allow the SNMP monitoring system to read data from your server. After entering the proper SNMP security information, click the **OK** button.

Continued

Figure 8.58 SNMP Service Security Settings

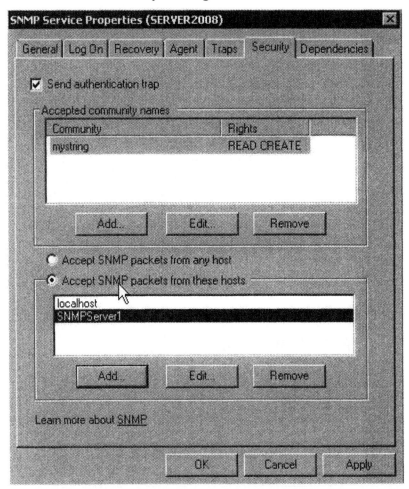

Windows does not include an SNMP monitoring application; however, some SNMP applications can be installed on Windows Server 2008. Depending on the type of SNMP monitoring application installed, you may need to enable the SNMP Trap service. By enabling this service, you are allowing it to receive SNMP traps from other servers or devices.

SNMP is an industry standard used by many network monitoring applications. Windows Server 2008 can also be monitored and managed by these systems via SNMP.

Baseline Security Analyzer

The Microsoft Baseline Security Analyzer (MBSA) is a free tool provided by Microsoft for scanning your servers and workstations for possible security vulnerabilities.

These vulnerabilities can range from lack of security updates to accounts with blank passwords. The MBSA allows you to scan a single or multiple computers and then create a vulnerability report based on the scan. You can download the MBSA from Microsoft's Download Center Web site at www.microsoft.com/downloads/details. aspx?FamilyID=f32921af-9dbe-4dce-889e-ecf997eb18e9&DisplayLang=en.

After downloading and installing the MBSA, follow along with the following Sidebar to run a scan.

Configuring & Implementing…

Scanning a Computer with the Baseline Security Analyzer

1. Launch the MBSA by selecting Start | All Programs | Microsoft Baseline Security Analyzer.

2. The MBSA main menu will be displayed. Notice that you can choose to scan a single computer or multiple computers at the same time (see Figure 8.59). Go ahead and click the link to **Scan a computer**.

Figure 8.59 The MBSA Main Menu

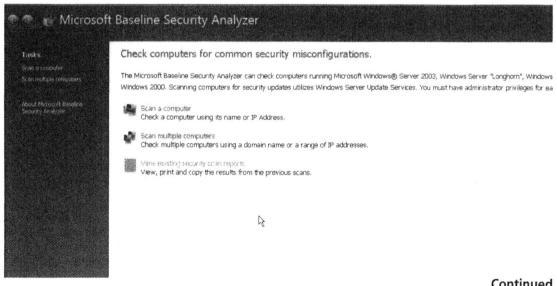

Continued

3. Next, choose the computer you wish to scan, along with the scan **Options**. For our scan, you should see the local computer already selected. Go ahead and select all options and click the **Start Scan** button (see Figure 8.60).

Figure 8.60 The MBSA Scan Options

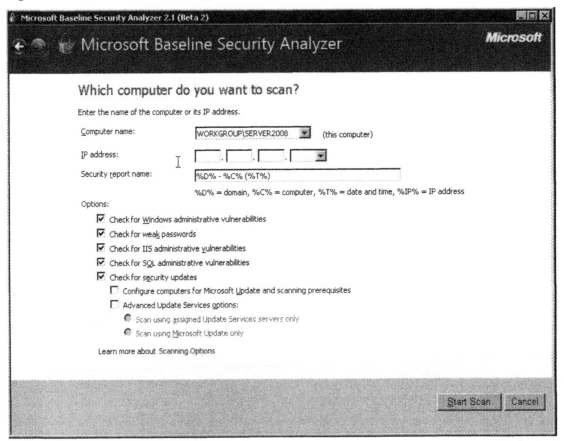

4. After the scan completes, you should be presented with a report of the scan results. Notice the overall security assessment of the system. If the assessment is **severe risk** you should take steps to immediately resolve reported issues. You can see from our report in Figure 8.61 that we were given a severe risk rating because we do not have Automatic Updates enabled. As the system administrator, we should immediately configure Automatic Updates to ensure that the server receives proper security patches from Microsoft or our WSUS server.

Continued

Figure 8.61 The MBSA Scan Report

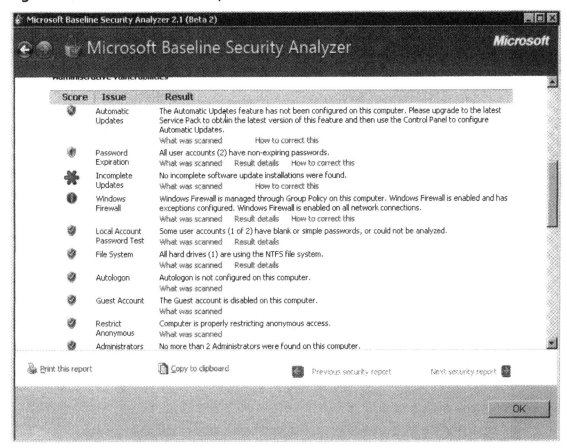

5. After reviewing the report, you can click the **OK** button to close it.

You can use the MBSA to scan multiple servers at once. You should scan servers on a regular basis to ensure that they are properly secured and updated. You can rerun the MBSA to ensure that any remediation steps you take properly resolve security vulnerabilities.

Network Monitor

Network Monitor is a tool used to capture network packets for analysis. Net-work Monitor is a free tool provided by Microsoft and you can download it from the Microsoft Download Center at www.microsoft.com/downloads/details. aspx?FamilyID=18b1d59d-f4d8-4213-8d17-2f6dde7d7aac&DisplayLang=en.

Network Monitor is also included in the Systems Management Server (SMS) and System Center Configuration Manager (SCCM) 2007. Network Monitor can be a useful tool when you suspect network issues may be impacting your server and network. In the following Sidebar, we'll take a closer look at Network Monitor.

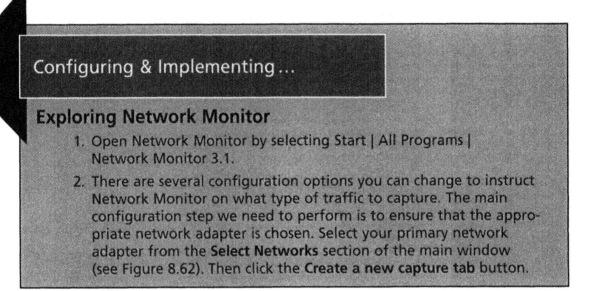

Configuring & Implementing...

Exploring Network Monitor

1. Open Network Monitor by selecting Start | All Programs | Network Monitor 3.1.

2. There are several configuration options you can change to instruct Network Monitor on what type of traffic to capture. The main configuration step we need to perform is to ensure that the appropriate network adapter is chosen. Select your primary network adapter from the **Select Networks** section of the main window (see Figure 8.62). Then click the **Create a new capture tab** button.

Figure 8.62 Network Monitor 3.1

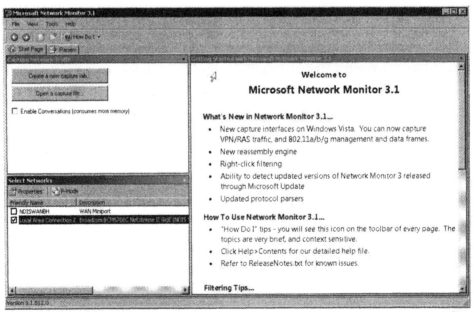

Continued

3. Each capture session uses a new tab. This allows you to quickly switch among multiple capture sessions running on the server. From the **Capture1** tab in Figure 8.63, you can see we can filter out certain data during capture or after capture. For now, we won't filter any data, so go ahead and click the **Play** button to start capturing data.

Figure 8.63 Capture Setup

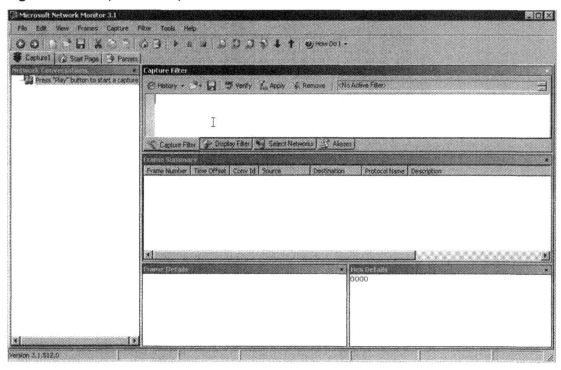

4. Let the capture process run for several minutes, and then click the **Stop** button.

5. After the packet capture completes, you will see a list of all network conversations on the left-hand side of the window. Go ahead and click the **My Traffic** node. This will filter the packet results to only display data to and from your server.

6. You can review and analyze the packets in the **Frame Summary** window, as shown in Figure 8.64.

Figure 8.64 The Frame Summary Window

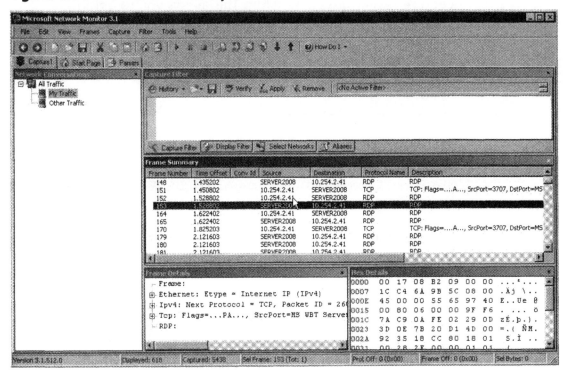

By reviewing the packets, you can see what type of traffic is being sent and received by your server as well as the devices your server is talking to on the network. This information can be useful if you see traffic going to or from another system that you don't recognize. For example, you could have a situation where your network is performing very slowly. By running Network Monitor, you notice that a workstation is sending and receiving a lot of data to and from the server. Network Monitor pinpoints the workstation's name and Internet Protocol (IP) address. You log on to the workstation and notice the network adapter is misconfigured. After you properly configure the network adapter, network performance returns to normal.

Summary

It is important for any network administrator to have a good understanding of the tools available to monitor, manage, and troubleshoot the network for which he or she may be responsible. This chapter provided detailed information and exercises on installing, configuring, and using Windows Server Update Services (WSUS) for update management. This chapter also covered Data Collector Sets and Performance Monitor. You discovered how you can use Data Collector Sets and Performance Monitor to capture diagnostic and performance data from your servers. This chapter introduced two features new to Server 2008: Reliability Monitor and the System Stability Index. Both of these tools allow you to see the overall reliability of your server at a glance. In this chapter, we also covered Event logs and Subscriptions. Event logs are a great source for information when trying to debug or troubleshoot problems. Subscriptions allow you to forward events from remote servers to a centrally managed server. This allows you to review and maintain Event log events from one server console. We also looked at capturing network data using features such as SNMP and Network Monitor. SNMP allows Windows to report to SNMP-compliant monitoring systems, and Network Monitor allows you to collect and review network traffic going to and from your servers. Finally, this chapter introduced us to the Microsoft Baseline Security Analyzer (MBSA). The MBSA is a tool that provides details about security misconfigurations or missing security updates. The MBSA allows you to proactively look for errors in your server security configurations. This chapter should have provided you with detailed information and exercises on the toolsets available to properly monitor and manage your Windows network.

Solutions Fast Track

Configuring Windows Server Update Services Server Settings

- ☑ WSUS is available in Windows Server 2008 via a Server Role.

- ☑ Group Policy can be used to configure WSUS clients.

- ☑ WSUS can be used in disconnected networks by importing updates from another source.

Capturing Performance Data

- ☑ Data Collector Sets collect log and performance data and generate a summary report.

- ☑ Performance Monitor can be used to troubleshoot performance bottlenecks.

- ☑ Reliability Monitor can be used to determine the cause of system failures.

Monitoring Event Logs

- ☑ Custom views allow you to save a standard view of filtered Event log items.

- ☑ Application logs provide specific codes and events related to applications instead of the operating system.

- ☑ Subscriptions can be used to forward events to a central server for ease of reviewing.

Gathering Network Data

- ☑ Windows Server 2008 supports SNMP for monitoring.

- ☑ The Baseline Security Analyzer can be used to determine security vulnerabilities on a single or multiple computers.

- ☑ Network Monitor is used to capture network packets when troubleshooting system or network problems.

Frequently Asked Questions

Q: Can I use Windows Server Update Services to deploy updates to servers in a "disconnected" network?

A: Yes, You an import updates from another server to a WSUS server on the disconnected network.

Q: What is the difference between Performance Monitor and Data Collector Sets?

A: Performance Monitor only collects performance data from the system. Data Collector Sets allow collection of data from Performance Monitor, logs, and so on.

Q: Does Windows Server 2008 include the Reliability and Performance Monitor, like Windows Vista does?

A: Yes, Windows Server 2008 includes the same Reliability and Performance Monitor features as Windows Vista.

Q: Can you automate WSUS computer group membership?

A: Yes, you can use Group Policy to assign group membership to WSUS clients.

Q: How is the System Stability Index number determined?

A: System error events negatively impact the System Stability Index, whereas time passing without system error increases the System Stability Index number.

Q: Do Data Collector Sets replace Performance Monitor?

A: Data Collector Sets actually use Performance Monitor when gathering data. Data Collector Sets just provide best-practice counters and logs already set up by Microsoft.

Chapter 9

Network Access Protection

Solutions in this chapter:

- Working with NAP

- ☑ Summary
- ☑ Solutions Fast Track
- ☑ Frequently Asked Questions

Introduction

Microsoft for some time has been making security its main priority with the Microsoft Trustworthy Computing initiative. Starting with Microsoft Windows 2003 Server we were introduced to Network Access Quarantine Control. This feature enabled administrators to control remote access to a private network until the remote computer was validated by a script. The components necessary to deploy this solution included Microsoft Windows 2003 remote access servers, the Connection Manager Administration Kit, and Internet Authentication Service.

The most obvious problem with Network Access Quarantine Control was that it worked with only remote computers connecting to the network using Routing and Remote Access Services (RRAS). This solution left a wide gap throughout the network infrastructure for other types of clients to cause issues and management problems for network administrators.

With Microsoft Windows 2008 Server, Windows Vista, and Windows XP Service Pack 3, Microsoft has introduced Network Access Protection (NAP). NAP can control virtual private network (VPN) connections better than Network Access Quarantine Control, but NAP can also enforce policy compliance through the following types of network access or communications:

- Internet Protocol security (IPSec) protected traffic

- IEEE 802.1x authenticated network connections

- Dynamic Host Configuration Protocol (DHCP) address configurations

- Remote access VPN connections

The key word to keep in mind when discussing NAP and its features is "compliance." With the introduction of NAP into our network, we can force Windows Server 2008, Windows Vista, and Windows XP Service Pack 3 to comply with standards set forth on our network. If for some reason a client does not comply with standards set forth by an administrator, the client could be directed to a separate network segment. On the separate network segment, a Remedial Server could update the client to the company's standards and then allow the client access to the network. Examples of these standards include but are not limited to:

- Windows update files

- Virus definitions

- Windows firewall settings

In addition, Microsoft has provided an application program interface (API) so that Network Access Protection Partners can write their own piece of software to add to the functionality of NAP. Some of the Access Protection Partners already providing add-ons include AppSense, Citrix, Intel, and Symantec. For a complete list of Access Protection Partners, go to the following Web site: www.microsoft.com/windowsserver2008/en/us/nap-partners.aspx.

In the following section, we are going to first look at all of the components of implementing NAP on a network. Once we gain a broad understanding of the components needed to build a NAP-supported network, we will look at different scenarios and implementation steps through the exercises throughout this chapter.

Working with NAP

The NAP platform main objective is to validate the state of a client computer before connecting to the private network and offer a source of remediation. To validate access to a network based on system health, NAP provides the following areas of functionality:

- Health state validation
- Network access limitation
- Automatic remediation
- Ongoing compliance

Network Layer Protection

All the components of NAP reside at the network layer. It is very important to understand where each component can reside and what the function of each component does. We are first going to look at a very general Microsoft Visio drawing and then point out each component and its function as related to NAP. Like a lot of Microsoft network designs, some servers can play multiple Windows Server 2008 roles within the NAP-enabled network architecture. Later in this chapter we will point out during the hands-on exercises where these servers with multiple Windows 2008 Server roles can reside, but for now we will concentrate on each individual function of the components and server roles (see Figure 9.1).

Figure 9.1 NAP Network Design

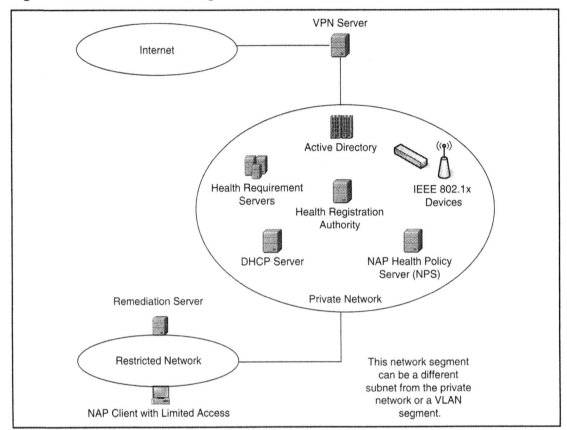

NAP Clients

NAP clients can be Windows Vista, Windows 2008 Server, or Windows XP Service Pack 3 clients. At the time of this writing these are the only operating systems that support the NAP platform for system health validated network access or communication. Microsoft does plan on supporting other operating systems through third-party software providers—independent software providers (ISVs). Microsoft is also planning to provide support to the Microsoft Windows Mobile platform, including support for handheld devices and Microsoft Windows Mobile phones.

The NAP API is really important for the adoption of NAP-based networks. The API that Microsoft is releasing for developers allows them to write code to support various other clients that are not Microsoft based. Expect to see these devices become more popular as more and more enterprises adopt Microsoft Windows Server 2008.

NAP Enforcement Points

NAP enforcement points are parts of the NAP infrastructure that determines the health and compliance of a NAP client before allowing network access. To determine if the NAP client is in compliance by the policies set forth by the administrator, the NAP Health Policy Server (NPS) evaluates the health and compliance of the NAP client. The NPS also decides the remediation process that is going to be applied to the NAP client. For instance, the client can be forwarded to restricted network where a remediation server will offer the updates or settings needed to enforce the compliance policy. NAP enforcement points include the following:

- Health Registration Authority (HRA) The HRA is a Windows 2008 Server with the roles of Internet Information Server 7.0 (IIS) and Certificate Authority (CA) role installed. This enforcement point is used primarily with IPSec Enforcement policies. The CA uses health certificates to enforce NAP compliance to the NAP client.

- Windows 2008 VPN Server A server running Windows 2008 Server Network Policy Server can enforce NAP compliance to a NAP client.

- DHCP Server Servers installed into the NAP network infrastructure running Windows 2008 Server with the DHCP server role providing Internet Protocol version 4 (IPv4) addresses to NAP clients can enforce NAP compliance to a NAP client.

- Network access devices Network hardware, such as switches and wireless access points that support IEEE 802.1 x authentication, can be used to support NAP compliance to a NAP client. Types of protocols supported include Extensible Authentication Protocol (EAP), Lightweight Extensible Authenti-cation Protocol (LEAP), and Protected Extensible Authentication Protocol (PEAP).

Active Directory Domain Services

As you already know, Active Directory Services store account and group policy information for an Active Directory Domain. NAP does not necessarily rely on Windows 2008 Server Active Directory Domain Services or Windows 2003 Server Active Directory Domain Services. NAP definitely does not need Active Directory Services to determine if a client is compliant, but other services and roles depend on Active Directory Services.

Active Directory Domain Services is needed for Network Policy Server VPN enforcement, IEEE 802.1x network device enforcement or IPSec-based enforcement. Also, as you will see later in this chapter, using group policy objects is a good way to set compliance and enforcement settings to NAP clients on your network.

NAP Health Policy Server

The NAP Health Policy Server is the heart of the NAP-supported network infrastructure. The NAP Health Policy Server runs Windows 2008 Server and has the NPS server role installed. The NPS server role is responsible for storing health requirement policies and provides health state validation for NAP.

Interestingly, the NPS server role replaces Internet Authentication Service (IAS), Remote Authentication Dial-In User Service (RADIUS), and proxy server provided by Windows 2003 Server. So NPS not only supports the NAP infrastructure but also acts as the authentication, authorization, and access (AAA) server in Windows 2008 Server. The NPS role can act as the RADIUS proxy to exchange RADIUS data packets with another NAP health policy server.

Health Requirement Server

Health requirement servers contain the data that NAP NPS servers check for current system health state for NAP NPS servers. Examples of the data that health requirement servers may provide are the latest virus DAT information files for third-party antivirus packages or updates for other software packages that the ISVs use the NAP API to develop.

Restricted Network

A restricted network is where NAP sends a computer that needs remediation services or to block access to the private network until remediation can take place. The restricted network can be a different subnet that has no routes to the private network or a different logical network in the form of a virtual local area network (VLAN). A good NAP design would place remediation servers located within the restricted network. Placing remediation servers inside the restricted network, enables NAP clients to get updated and then be allowed access to the private network.

The remediation server could be in the form of a Windows 2008 Server or Windows 2003 Server running Windows Server Update Services (WSUS). WSUS provides an easy way to update the NAP client system files using Microsoft Update Services. You could also place virus update files and other third-party critical update files on the remediation server.

Software Policy Validation

Before you actually start doing some exercises, it is important to understand what actually goes on during system-compliant testing and validation. NPS uses System Health Validators (SHVs) to analyze the compliance of a client computer. SHVs determine whether a computer is getting full access to the private network or if it will be isolated to the restricted network. The client has a piece of software installed called a System Health Agent (SHA) to monitor its system health. NPS uses SHVs and SHAs to determine the health of a client computer and to monitor, enforce, and remediate the client computer.

Built into Windows Server 2008 and Windows Vista are the Windows Security Health Agent (WSHA) and Windows Security Health Validator (WSHV). These agents are used to enforce the most basic compliance settings in a NAP infrastructure. The settings provided by WSHA and WSHV are:

- The client computer has firewall software installed and enabled.
- The client computer has antivirus software installed and enabled.
- The client computer has current antivirus updates installed.
- The client computer has antispyware software installed and enabled.
- The client computer has current antispyware updates installed.
- Microsoft Update Services is enabled on the client computer.

Even without third-party SHVs and SHAs, Microsoft has built very powerful tools into Windows Server 2008, Windows Vista, and Windows XP Service Pack 3 to validate the compliance and health of computers.

DHCP Enforcement

DHCP enforcement is probably the easiest NAP infrastructure design to implement. In the following Sidebar, we are going to show you how to implement NAP DHCP enforcement.

Configuring & Implementing...

Implementing DHCP Enforcement

In this exercise we are going to implement the DHCP and NPS server roles on the server NPS1. We will then configure NAP with the wizard and also configure the SHVs that will force any connecting client using DHCP to be network compliant. The domain name is CONTOSO.COM, Keeping with the Microsoft tradition. Figure 9.2 depicts this simple network. We are going to imply that both servers are Windows Server 2008 and Active Directory Domain Services have already been set up for the CONTOSO.COM domain.

Figure 9.2 Network Diagram

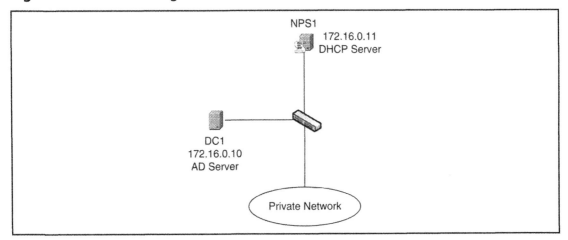

1. First we will install the NPS and DHCP server roles on NPS1. Click **Start** and then click **Server Manager.**
2. Under **Roles Summary,** click **Add Roles** and then click **Next.**
3. On the Select Server Roles page, select the **DHCP Server** and **Network Policy and Access Services** check boxes and then click **Next** twice (see Figure 9.3).

Continued

Figure 9.3 Server Roles Page

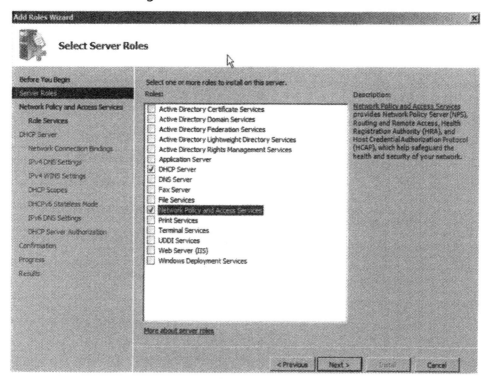

4. On the **Select Server Roles** page, select the **Network Policy Server** check box and then click **Next** twice.

5. On the **Select Network Connection Bindings** page, verify that **172.16.0.11** is selected and click **Next**.

6. On the Specify IPv4 DNS Server Settings page, verify that contoso. com is listed under Parent Domain.

7. Type **172.16.0.10** under the **Preferred DNS server IP address** and click **Validate**. Verify that the server was able to validate the DNS server.

8. On the **Specify WINS Server Settings**, click **Next,** accepting the default settings.

9. On the Add or Edit DHCP Scopes page, click Add.

10. In the Add Scope dialog box, type NAP SCOPE next to Scope Name. Add 172.16.0.20 as the Starting IP Address and 172.16.0.30 as the Ending IP Address. For the Subnet Mask use 255.255.255.0. Select the Activate this scope check box. Notice in Figure 9.4 that we do not specify a Default Gateway.

Continued

Figure 9.4 Add Scope Dialog Box

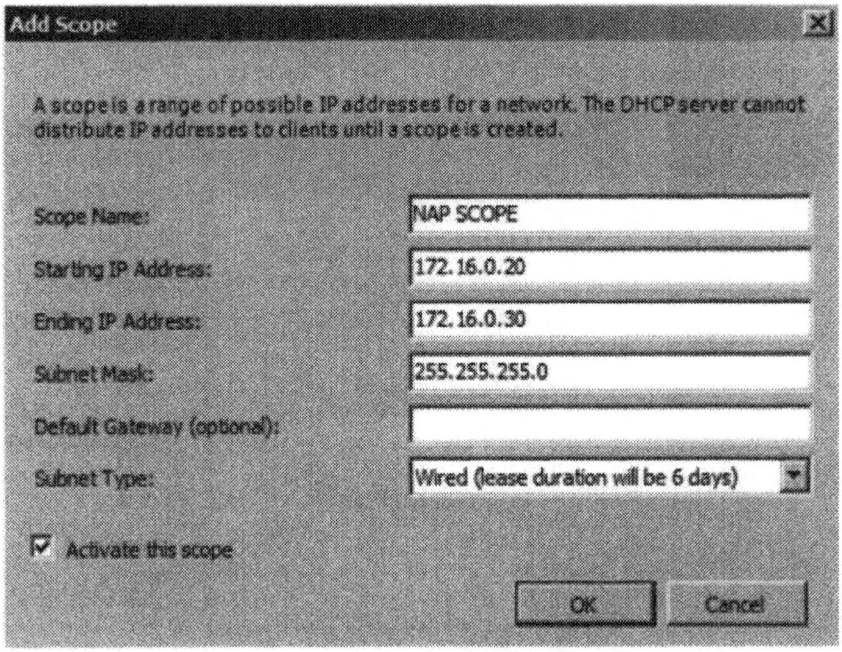

11. On the **Configure DHCPv6 Stateless Mode** page, select **Disable DHCPv6 stateless mode for this server** and then click **Next**. Remember that NAP does not support DHCPv6.

12. On the Authorize DHCP Server page, select Specify, enter Administrator information, and then click Next.

13. On the Confirm Installation Selections page, click Install.

14. Verify the installation completed with no errors and then click **Close**.

At this point, we now have our DHCP Server and NPS installed. The DHCP Server is configured and authorized for the domain CONTOSO.COM. Now we need to configure NPS as a NAP health policy server so that it can validate the clients connecting to our domain via DHCP. To do this, we will use the NAP configuration wizard.

1. Click **Start**, click **Run**, type **nps.msc** and press **Enter**.

2. Make sure that in the Network Policy Server console tree, that **NPS (Local)** is selected.

3. Under **Standard Configuration**, click **Configure NAP**. The NAP configuration wizard will start. See Figure 9.5.

Continued

Figure 9.5 NAP Configuration Wizard

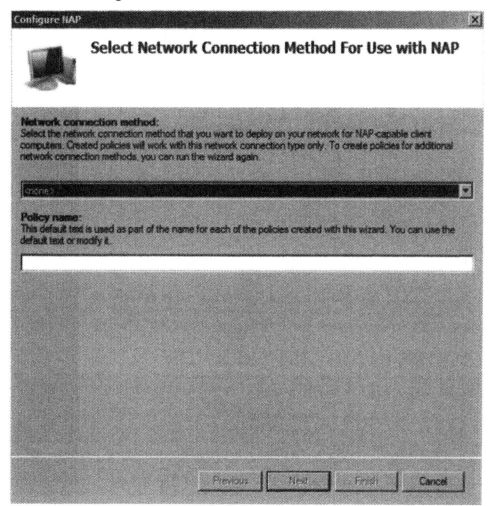

4. On the Select Network Connection Method for Use with NAP page, under Network connection method, select Dynamic Host Configuration Protocol (DHPC), and then click Next.

5. On the Specify NAP Enforcement Servers Running DHCP page, click Next.

6. On the **Specify DHCP Scopes** page, click **Next**.

7. On the Configure User Groups and Machine Groups page, click Next.

8. On the Specify a NAP Remediation Server Group and URL page, click Next.

Continued

9. On the Define NAP Health Policy page, verify that Windows Security Health Validator and Enable auto-remediation of client computers check boxes are selected, click Next.

10. Click Finish on the Completing NAP Enforcement Policy and RADIUS Configuration page.

The only thing left to configure is our System Health Validators (SHVs). We are going to set up our new SHV to make sure that the Windows Firewall is enabled, and an antivirus application is on and up-to-date.

1. In the Network Policy Server console tree, double-click **Network Access Protection**, and then click **System Health Validators**.

2. In the details pane, under **Name**, double-click **Windows Security Health Validator**.

3. In the Windows Security Health Validator Properties dialog box, click Configure.

4. Clear all check boxes except for A firewall is enabled for all network connections and An antivirus application is on. See Figure 9.6.

Figure 9.6 Windows Security Health Validator

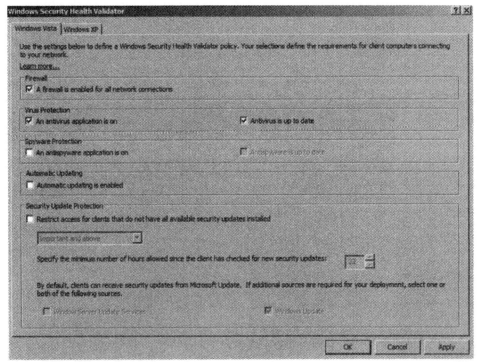

Continued

5. Click OK to close the Windows Security Health Validator dialog box, and then click OK to close the Windows Security Health Validator Properties dialog box.

6. Close the Network Policy Server console.

This was a long exercise, but it is very important to see this process from start to finish—it helps facilitate your understanding of all concepts dealing with implementing DHCP enforcement.

VPN Enforcement

Windows Server 2008 and Network Policy Server (NPS) can facilitate NAP connections—allowing remote VPN clients to be checked for compliance and be remediated.

Communication Process with VPN Client and NAP

When a Windows Vista or Windows XP Service Pack 3 computer connects to a NPS server that is NAP enabled, the communication process is a little different than a normal VPN connection. The NAP client in this case becomes the VPN client and uses simple Point-to-Point Protocol (PPP) messages to establish a remote access VPN connection. While this is going on, Protected Extensible Authentication Protocol (PEAP) messages are sent over the PPP connection to indicate the client system current health state to the NAP health policy server. If the connecting client is not compliant, the NAP health policy server uses PEAP to send remediation instructions to the VPN client. If the client is compliant, the NAP health policy server will use PEAP messages to tell the client that it has access to the private network. Because all PEAP messages between the VPN client and NAP health policy server are routed through the VPN server, this process is encrypted.

If the VPN client is noncompliant, the Windows 2008 Server NPS will use a set of remote access IP filters to limit the traffic of the VPN client so that it can reach only the restricted network. Once directed to the restricted network, the client can become compliant through the remediation resources provided. While the system is noncompliant, the VPN server will continue to apply the IP packet filters to the IP traffic that is received from the VPN client and silently discard all packets that do not correspond to a configured packet filter.

Configuring & Implementing...

Configure NPS for Remote VPN Connections

In this exercise, we are going to configure NPS for use with remote VPN connections. This exercise assumes that RRAS is already configured on the server DC1 (172.16.0.10). This exercise also assumes that DC1 is an Enterprise Certification Authority (CA) for the domain CONTOSO.COM.

1. Click **Start**, click **Run**, type **nps.msc**, and then press **Enter**.

2. In the Network Policy Server console tree, click **NPS (Local)**.

3. In the details pane, under **Standard Configuration**, click **Configure NAP**. The NAP configuration wizard will start.

4. On the Select Network Connection Method for Use with NAP page, under Network connection method, select Virtual Private Network (VPN) and click Next. See Figure 9.7.

Continued

Figure 9.7 Select Network Connection Method for Use with NAP

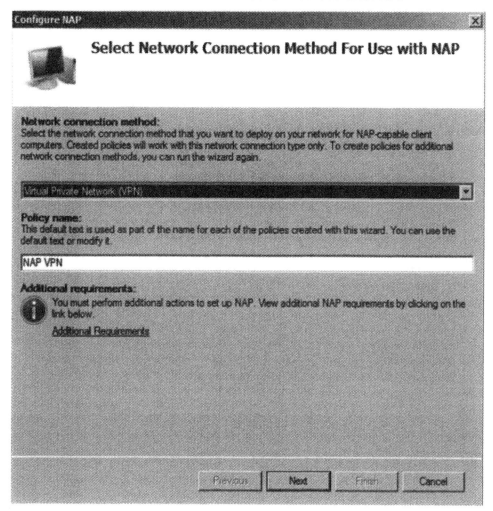

5. On the Specify NAP Enforcement Servers Running VPN Server page, under RADIUS clients, click Add.

6. In the New RADIUS Client dialog box, under Friendly Name, type NAP VPN Server. Under Address (IP or DNS), type DC1.

7. Under Shared secret, type secret.

8. Under **Confirm shared secret**, type **secret**, click **OK** and then click **Next**. See Figure 9.8.

Continued

Figure 9.8 New RADIUS Client

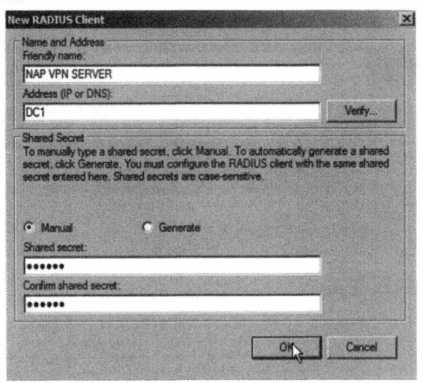

9. On the Configure User Groups and Machine Groups page, click Next.

10. On the **Configure an Authentication Method** page, confirm that a computer certificate is displayed under **NPS Server Certificate** and that **Secure Password (PEAP-MSCHAP-v2)** is selected under **EAP types**. Click **Next**.

11. On the Specify a NAP Remediation Server Group and URL page, click New Group.

12. In the New Remediation Server Group dialog box, under Group Name, type Domain Services and then click Add.

13. In the **Add New Server** dialog box, under **Friendly name**, type **DC1**.

14. Under **IP address or DNS name**, type **172.16.0.10** and then click **OK** twice.

15. Under **Remediation Server Group**, verify that the newly created remediation server group is selected and then click **Next**.

Continued

16. On the Define NAP Health Policy page, verify that Windows Security Health Validator and Enable auto-remediation of client computers check boxes are selected and then click Next.

17. On the Completing NAP Enforcement Policy and RADIUS Client Configuration page, click Finish.

18. Close the NPS console.

Configuring NAP Health Policies

NAP Health Policies are a combination of settings for health determination and enforcement of infrastructure compliance. Health requirement policies on the NAP health policy server determine whether a NAP client is compliant or noncompliant, how to treat noncompliant NAP clients and whether they should automatically remediate their health state, and how to treat clients that are not NAP capable for different NAP enforcement methods. The following settings make up the NAP Health Policies:

- Connection Request Policies
- Network Policies
- Health Policies
- Network Access Protection Settings

All the NAP Health Policies are configured within the Network Policy Server console, as shown in Figure 9.9. Interestingly, Microsoft recommends starting with the Configure NAP Wizard to build your initial settings for your NAP installation. To access the Configure NAP Wizard, click the **NPS (LOCAL)** node of the configuration tree and then click **Configure NAP** under the Standard Configuration in the right window. In Figure 9.9, we can see where you can access the Configure NAP Wizard within the Network Policy Server console.

Figure 9.9 The Network Policy Server Console

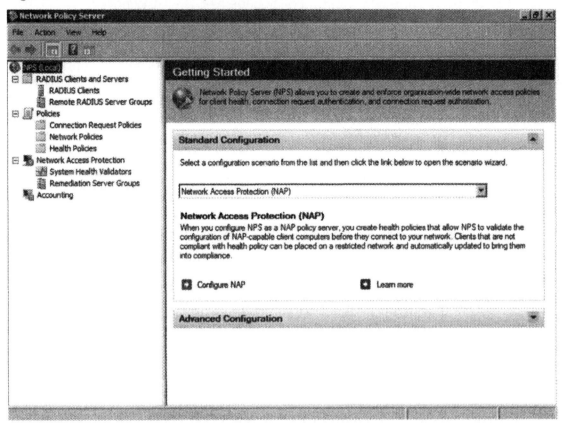

Connection Request Policies

As we discussed earlier, NPS replaces IAS in Windows Server 2003. NPS handles all RADIUS activities in Windows 2008 Server—RADIUS can be configured to handle the authentication and logging locally. Also, RADIUS in Windows 2008 can be configured as a RADIUS proxy and forward all authentication request to another RADIUS server.

Connection Request Policies are a set of rules that can be processed in a set order. Connection Request Policies determine whether RADIUS request should be processed locally or forward the requests to another RADIUS server. Connection Request Policies are configured and ordered in the NPC console under the Policies node (see Figure 9.10). When the NPS server is configured for NAP health compliance and enforcement, the local server is acting as a RADIUS server locally.

Figure 9.10 Connection Request Policies

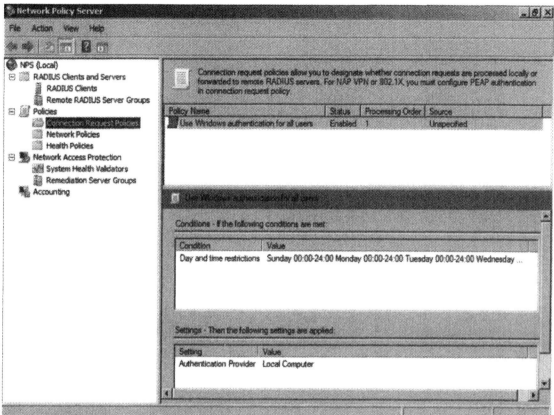

Network Policies

Network Policies either deny or grant access to network connection attempts. These policies, like Connection Request Policies, are an ordered group of rules. For each rule, there are a set of conditions, constraints, an access permission that either grants or denies access and network policy settings. For NAP, network policies specify the conditions to check for health requirements and, for computers that are not capable of NAP—the enforcement behavior.

When setting the Network Policies, you have four options for NAP Enforcement settings—these settings specify the type of network access the client will have. The four options include (also see Figure 9.11):

1. Allow full network access

2. Allow full network access for a limited time

3. Allow limited access

4. Enable auto-remediation of client computers

Figure 9.11 Compliant Properties

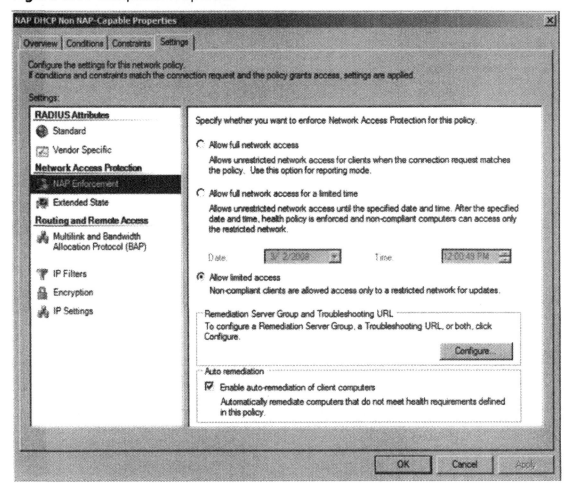

Health Policies

Health Policies check the client for compliance via the system health validators (SHVs). If you recall from earlier in this chapter, we discussed Windows Security Health Validator (WSHV). These SHVs are the ones provided with Windows 2008

Server, Windows Vista or Windows XP Service Pack 3. Other SHVs can be created by independent software vendors (ISVs) via the application programming interface provided by Microsoft. By default, the WSHV is always listed in the health policies.

Configuring & Implementing...

Create a Health Policy

In this short exercise, we are going to create a Health Policy on NPS1 server. Pay close attention to all of the options available to you in the exercise.

1. Click **Start**, click **Run**, type **nps.msc**, and then press **Enter**.

2. In the Network Policy Server console tree, click **Policies**.

3. In the details pane, under **Health Policies**, click **Configure Health Policies**.

4. Right-click the Health Policies node and click New.

5. For the Policy Name enter CONTOSO Policy 1.

6. In the Client SHV checks drop down menu select Client fails one or more SHV checks.

7. Make sure under SHVs used in this health policy that Windows Security Health Validator is Checked. See Figure 9.12.

Continued

Figure 9.12 Configure Health Policy Settings

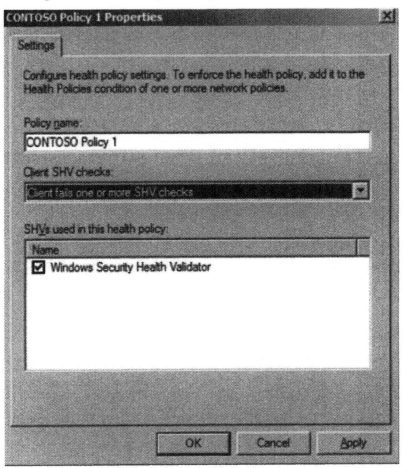

8. Click **OK**.

9. Close the NPS console.

Network Access Protection Settings

Network Access Protection (NAP) settings consist of two components. The components that make up NAP settings include:

- System Health Validators

- Remediation Server Groups

System Health Validators (SHVs) specify the configuration of installed SHVs for health requirements and error conditions. By default, Windows Server 2008, Windows Vista, and Windows XP Service Pack 3 include the Window Security Health Validator (WSHV).

Remediation Server Groups specifies the set of servers that are accessible to computers that are not NAP compliant with limited network access. If you recall Figure 9.1, these servers would be located on the restricted network.

Configuring & Implementing...

Create Remediation Server Group

In this exercise, we are going to create a remediation server group on server NPS1 to allow computers that are not compliant with the NAP infrastructure to get updated. We will point the clients to DC1 to get updates—in a real NAP infrastructure environment, we would never point to an Active Directory Domain Server as a remediation server.

1. Click **Start**, click **Run**, type **nps.msc**, and then press **Enter**.
2. In the Network Policy Server console tree, click **Network Access Protection**.
3. In the details pane, under Network Access Protection, click Configure Remediation Server Groups.
4. Right-click the Remediation Server Groups node and click New.
5. Click **Add**.
6. For the Friendly name enter CONTOSO Remediation Server Group.
7. For the IP address or DNS name enter **172.16.0.10** (DC1). See Figure 9.13.

Continued

Figure 9.13 Remediation Server Groups

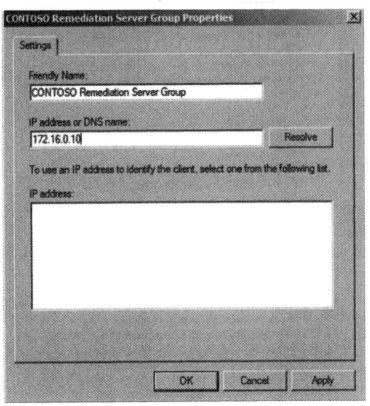

8. Click **OK** twice.
9. Close the NPS console.

IPsec Enforcement

IPsec enforcement breaks a network down to three different logical networks by using health certificates provided by the Health Certificate Server (HCS). Any computer can be a member of only one of the three networks at any given time—membership to the network is determined by the status of the computers health certificate. The logical networks are defined by which computers have valid health certificates and which computers require IPSec authentication for incoming access connections. Computers requiring IPSec authentication would normally be servers on the private network. Figure 9.14 shows a basic diagram of what an IPSec-based NAP infrastructure would look like. As you can see, there are three distinct networks:

1. Secure network

2. Boundary network

3. Restricted network

Figure 9.14 IPSec-Based NAP Network

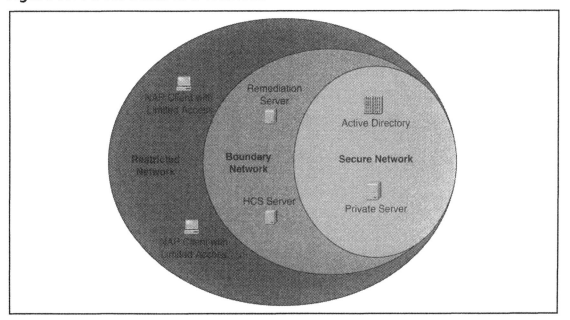

Secure Network

The secure network is where all computers have health certificates and require IPsec authentication to communicate with any other computer. If a computer tries to communicate with a computer in the secure network without a health certificate, the computer in the secure network will ignore the client's request. In a NAP infrastructure, computers in the secure network would be members of the Active Directory domain.

Boundary Network

Boundary networks are where computers that are not NAP compliant can access a remediation server and become compliant. Once compliant, they can access an HCS Server and acquire a health certificate to participate in the secure network. Computers on the boundary network will accept communication requests from computers with a health certificate or without—this is how remediation occurs. Both the restricted network and the secure network have access to the boundary network.

Restricted Network

All the computers in the restricted network do not have a health certificate. The only network they can communicate with is the boundary network—for the purpose of remediation and acquiring the appropriate health certificate to access the secure network.

Flexible Host Isolation

Flexible Host Isolation refers to the ease of network isolation provided with the IPSec method of NAP enforcement. Isolation can be performed easily on the network with no infrastructure upgrade by using NAP and health certificates. This type of isolation cannot be easily circumvented by reconfiguring the client or using hardware like hubs. Basically, healthy systems can connect to anything, as long as the NAP policy allows it, whereas quarantined systems are isolated to the restricted network.

Configuring & Implementing...

Install the NPS, HRA and CA server roles

In this exercise, we are going to install the NPS, HRA and CA server roles on NPS1 server.

1. Click **Start** and then **Server Manager**. Under **Roles Summary**, click **Add Roles** and then click **Next**.

2. On the **Select Server Roles** page, select the **Active Directory Certificate Services** and **Network Policy and Access Services** check boxes and then click **Next** twice.

3. On the **Select Role Services** page, select the **Health Registration Authority** check box, click **Add Required Role Services** in the **Add Roles Wizard** window and then click **Next**.

4. On the **Choose the Certification Authority to use with the Health Registration Authority** page, choose **Install a local CA to issue health certificates for this HRA server** and then click **Next**. See Figure 9.15.

Continued

Figure 9.15 Choose the Certification Authority to use with the Health Registration Authority

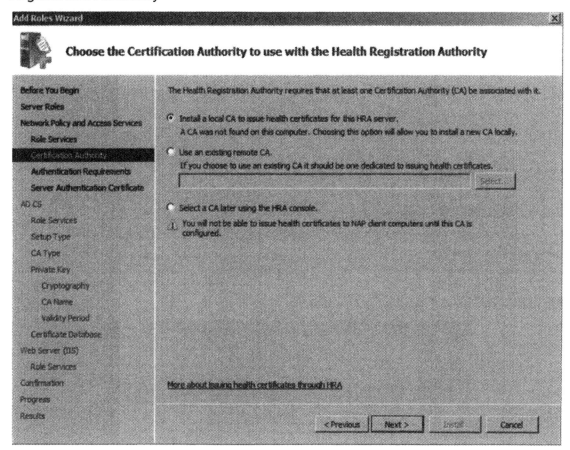

5. On the **Choose Authentication Requirements for the Health Registration Authority** page, choose **No, allow anonymous requests for health certificates** and then click **Next**. This choice allows computers to be enrolled with health certificates in a workgroup environment.

6. On the **Choose a Server Authentication Certificate for SSL Encryption** page, choose **Create a self-signed certificate for SSL encryption** and then click **Next**.

7. On the **Introduction to Active Directory Certificate Services** page, click **Next**.

Continued

8. On the **Select Role Services** page, verify that the **Certification Authority** check box is selected and then click Next.

9. On the **Specify Setup Type** page, click **Standalone** and then click **Next**.

10. On the **Specify CA Type** page, click **Subordinate CA** and then click **Next**.

11. On the **Set Up Private Key** page, click **Create a new private key** and then click **Next**.

12. On the **Configure Cryptography for CA** page, click **Next**.

13. On the **Configure CA Name** page, under **Common name for this CA**, type **contoso-NPS1-SubCA** and then click **Next**.

14. On the **Request Certificate from a Parent CA** page, choose **Send a certificate request to a parent CA** and then click **Browse**.

15. In the **Select Certification Authority** window, click **Contoso-DC1-CA** and then click **OK**. See Figure 9.16.

Figure 9.16 Select Certification Authority

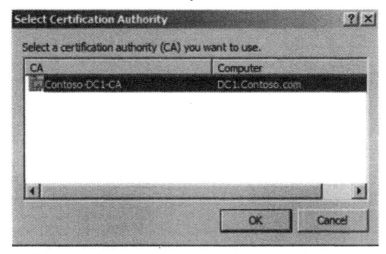

16. Verify that **DC1.Contoso.com\Contoso-DC1-CA** is displayed next to **Parent CA** and then click **Next**.

17. Click **Next** three times to accept the default database, Web server, and role services settings and then click **Install**.

18. Verify that all installations were successful and then click **Close**.

19. Exit the Server Manager.

802.1x Enforcement

IEEE 802.1x standards define an effective framework for controlling and authenticating clients to a wired or wireless protected network—in this case a NAP infrastructure. These standards define port-based authentication on supported devices. These devices could be switches or wireless access points that support the IEEE 802.1x standard. The IEEE standard is significant it has been accepted by hardware and software vendors—their products will be designed with the standards in mind. What does this mean for you and me? All hardware that is 802.1x based should work with RADIUS and NAP.

An 802.1x deployment consists of three major components that allow for the authentication process to work correctly (see Figure 9.17).

- **Supplicant** a device that requests access to our network and is connected via a pass-through authenticator.

- **Pass-through authenticator** a switch or access point that is 802.1x compliant.

- **Authentication server** when the supplicant connects to the pass-through authenticator, the request is passed to the authentication server by the pass-through authenticator. The authentication server decides whether the client is granted access or denied.

Figure 9.17 Components of 802.1x

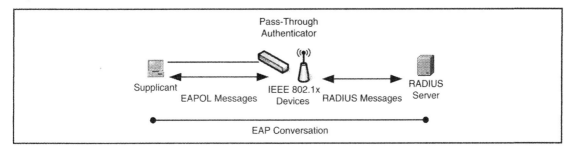

Authentication is handled using the Extensible Authentication Protocol (EAP). EAP messages used in the authentication process are transmitted between the supplicant and pass-through authenticator using EAP over LAN (EAPoL). The pass-through authenticator talks to the RADIUS using RADIUS messages and EAP.

When NAP uses IEEE 802.1x, the authenticating pass-through authenticator uses the RADIUS protocol. NPS instructs the pass-through authenticator (wireless access-point or switch) to place supplicants that are not in compliance with NPS into a restricted network. The restricted network could be a separate VLAN or a network with IP filters in place to isolate it from the secured network.

Configuring & Implementing...

Configure NAP Client Authentication Methods

In this exercise, we are going to configure a Windows Vista client authentication method.

1. Click **Start**, right-click **Network** and then **Properties**.

2. Click Manage network connections.

3. Right-click **Local Area Connection** and then click **Properties**. See Figure 9.18.

Figure 9.18 Windows Vista Network Properties

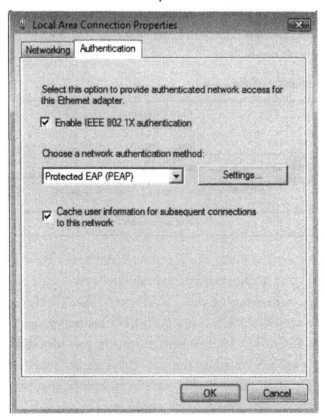

Continued

4. Click the **Authentication** tab and verify that Enable **IEEE 802.1x authentication** is selected.

5. Click **Setting**. See Figure 9.19.

Figure 9.19 Protected EAP Properties

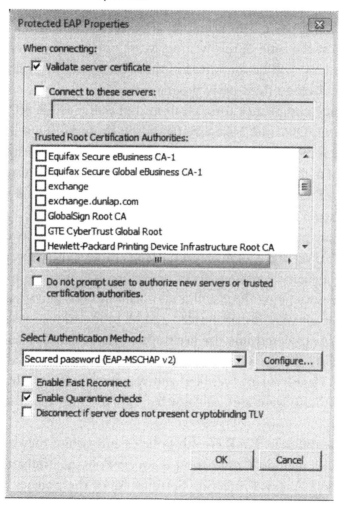

6. In the **Protected EAP Properties** dialog box, clear the **Enable Fast Reconnect** check box and verify that only the following check box is selected—**Enable Quarantine checks**.

7. Close all property sheets.

Summary

Microsoft has made great strides in network infrastructure compliance and remediation with Windows 2008 Server. As mentioned earlier in this chapter, it is imperative that you actually sit down and play with the Network Policy Server Console and get to know the interface. Most questions on NAP will come directly from the interface of the console.

Microsoft NAP will work with Windows 2008 Server, Windows Vista, and Windows XP Service Pack 3 at the time of this writing. More operating systems (including third-party operating systems) will be supported in the future—mostly because Microsoft is making the API available to third-party programmers.

NAP can enforce compliance through protected traffic, IEEE 802.1x authenticated network connections, Dynamic Host Configuration Protocol (DHCP) address configurations and remote access VPN connections. The main objective of NAP is to validate the state of a client computer before connecting to the private network and offer some source of remediation. It is very important to understand the drawing in Figure 9.1. Understand where each component of NAP is located.

The way software policy validation works is with software agents called System Health Validators (SHVs) and System Health Agents (SHAs). NPS uses SHVs to analyze the compliance of a client computer. SHVs determine whether a computer is getting full access to the private network or will it be isolated to the restricted network. The client has a piece of software installed called a SHA to monitor its system health. NPS uses SHVs and SHAs to determine the health of a client computer and to monitor, enforce and remediate the client computer. The main Microsoft SHA and SHV are—Windows Security Health Agent (WSHA) and Windows Security Health Validator (WSHV). The Microsoft agent and validator basically monitor the Microsoft Security Center.

Understand the different NAP Health Policies and where they are configured. NAP Health Policies include: Connection Request Policies, Network Policies, Health Policies and Network Access Protection Settings. All of the policies are configured with the Network Policy Server Console.

When working with NAP, understand the concept of Secure Network, Boundary Network and Restricted Network. The secure network is where all domain members should be located. The boundary network contains the remediation server and offers the client a way to become compliant. The restricted network is for clients with limited access.

802.1x enforcement relies on the access connection hardware. It is made up of three components—the supplicant, pass-through authenticator and the RADIUS server. The supplicant would be the client trying to connect to the network. The pass-through authenticator is the 802.1x device that is relaying authentication information back to the RADIUS server. The RADIUS server authenticates the network connections.

Solutions Fast Track

Working with Network Access Protection

☑ The Network Access Protection (NAP) platform main objective is to validate the state of a client computer before connecting to a private network and offer a source of remediation.

☑ NAP clients include Windows Vista, Windows Server 2008 and Windows XP Service Pack 3.

☑ The NAP API will allow other ISVs to write software to be enforced by NAP.

☑ NAP provides the following areas of functionality: Health State Validation, Network Access Limitation, Automatic Remediation and Ongoing Compliance.

☑ DHCP NAP enforcement is the easiest enforcement implementation of NAP available.

☑ IPv6 is not supported with DHCP enforcement implementation.

☑ The DHCP server and NPS server can be supported on the same server by installing the 2 server roles.

☑ During the VPN connection—NPS uses PEAP messages to send NAP information to the client.

☑ All PEAP messages between the VPN client and NAP are routed through the NPS server.

☑ If the VPN client is noncompliant—the client will be directed to the restricted network with IP filters.

☑ NAP Health Policies are a combination of settings for health determination and enforcement of infrastructure compliance.

☑ The following sets of settings make up NAP Health Policies: Connection Request Policies, Network Policies, Health Policies and NAP Settings.

☑ NAP Health Policies are configured using the Network Policy Server console.

☑ NPS in Windows 2008 Server replaces IAS in Windows 2003 Server.

☑ Network Policies have four options for NAP enforcement: Allow full network access, Allow full network access for a limited time, Allow limited access and Enable auto-remediation of client computers.

☑ IPsec NAP enforcement breaks the network down to three logical networks by using health certificates provided by the Health Certificate Server (HCS).

☑ The three distinct networks are: secure network, boundary network and restricted network.

☑ Flexible Host Isolation refers to the ease of network isolation provided with the IPsec method of NAP enforcement.

☑ IEEE 802.1x standards define an effective framework for controlling and authenticating clients to a wired or wireless protected network.

☑ An 802.1x deployment consists of three major components: Supplicant, Pass-Through Authenticator and Authentication Server.

☑ Authentication is handled using the Extensible Authentication Protocol (EAP).

☑ NPS instructs the pass-through authenticator (wireless access-points or switch) to place supplicants that are not in compliance with NPS into a restricted network.

Frequently Asked Questions

Q: I have worked with Windows 2003 Server Network Access Quarantine Control extensively. Will this help me better work with Network Access Protection?

A: The short answer is no. Microsoft has totally changed the way network access is controlled in Windows Server 2008. For instance, there is no longer an Internet Authentication Service and Routing and Remote Access Service—these have been wrapped up into the Network Access Protection.

Q: I am having some problems understanding a specific topic in this chapter. Is there any place I can go for more help?

A: The best place to go would be the Network Access Protection Web site on TechNet. There are Web casts, whitepapers and labs out there for download. The Web site is http://technet.microsoft.com/en-us/network/bb545879.aspx. You will find an answer to just about any question concerning NAP on this site.

Chapter 10

Configuring Windows Server Hyper-V and Virtual Machines

Solutions in this chapter:

- **Configuring Virtual Machines**
- **Migrating from Physical to Virtual Machines**
- **Backing Up Virtual Machines**
- **Virtual Server Optimization**

☑ Summary

☑ Solutions Fast Track

☑ Frequently Asked Questions

Introduction

In past versions of Windows Server, Virtual PC and Virtual Server were utilized to run multiple operating systems on the same computer. Windows Server 2008 provides you with very useful and powerful methods of running multiple virtualized operating systems that you must be familiar with. One of these new features is *Hyper-V*, a powerful new role that we will explain further in this chapter.

In this chapter, we will discuss Hyper-V as well as how to configure and back up virtual machines using the new methods available with Windows Server 2008. We will also go over how to migrate from physical to virtual machines using the Hyper-V role for virtualization. In addition we will explore all the new virtualization options available with Windows Server 2008 and how they compare to older virtualization suites. To begin with, we will discuss some of the concepts of virtualization available to previous Windows Server builds and the new features offered by Windows Server 2008.

Advancing Microsoft's Strategy for Virtualization

Microsoft is leading the effort to improve system functionality, making it more self-managing and dynamic. Microsoft's main goal with virtualization is to provide administrators more control of their IT systems with the release of Windows Server 2008 and Hyper-V.

This includes a faster response time to restore that is head and shoulders above their competition. Windows Server 2008 provides a total package of complimentary virtualization products that range in functionality from desktop usage to datacenter hubs. One of their major goals is to provide the ability to manage all IT assets, both physical and virtual, from a single remote machine. Microsoft is also forwarding an effort to cut IT costs with their virtualization programs to better help customers take advantage of the interoperability features their products have to offer as well as data center consolidation. This also includes energy efficiency due to the use of less physical machines. This fact alone reduces the consumption of energy in the data center and helps to save money long term. By contributing to and investing in the areas of management, applications, and licensing they hope to succeed in this effort.

Windows Server 2008 has many of these goals in mind, providing a number of important assets to administrators. The implementation of Hyper-V for virtualization allows for quick migration and high availability. This provides solutions for scheduled and unscheduled downtime, and the possibility of improved restore times. Virtual storage is supported for up to four virtual SCSI controllers per virtual machine, allowing for ample storage capacity. Hyper-V allows for the import and export of virtual machines and is integrated with Windows Server Manager for greater usability options.

In the past compatibility was always an issue of concern. Now the emulated video card has been updated to a more universal VESA compatible card. This will improve video issues, resulting in noncompatibility with operating systems like Linux. In addition Windows Server 2008 also includes integration components (ICs) for virtual machines. When you install Windows Server 2008 as a guest system in a Hyper-V virtual machine, Windows will install the ICs automatically. There is also support for Hyper-V with the Server Core in the parent partition allowing for easier configuration. This as well as numerous fixes for performance, scalability, and compatibility make the end goal for Hyper-V a transparent end user experience.

New & Noteworthy...

Windows Hypervisor

With Windows Server 2008 Microsoft introduced a next-generation hypervisor virtualization platform. Hyper-V, formerly codenamed Viridian, is one of the noteworthy new features of Windows Server 2008. It offers a scalable and highly available virtualization platform that is efficient and reliable. It has an inherently secure architecture. This combined with a minimal attack surface (especially when using Server Core) and the fact that it does not contain any third-party device drivers makes it extremely secure. It is expected to be the best operating system platform for virtualization released to date.

Compared to its predecessors, Hyper-V provides more options for specific needs because it utilizes more powerful 64-bit hardware and 64-bit operating systems. Additional processing power and a large addressable memory space is gained by the utilization of a 64-bit environment. It also requires no need for outside applications, which increase overall compatibility across the board.

Hyper-V has three main components: the *hypervisor*, the *virtualization stack*, and the new *virtualized I/O model*. The hypervisor (also known as the *virtual machine monitor* or *VMM*) is a very small layer of software that interacts

Continued

directly with the processor, which creates the different "partitions" that each virtualized instance of the operating system will run within. The virtualization stack and the I/O components act to provide a go-between with Windows and with all the partitions that you create. Hyper-V's virtualization advancements will only help to further assist administrators in quicker easier responses to emergency deployment needs.

Understanding Virtualization

At times, you will need a method to hide the physical characteristics of the host system from the way in which other systems and applications interact with it. This includes the way end users will interact with those resources as well. For example a single server, operating system, application, or storage device may need to appear to function as multiple logical resources. You may also want to make multiple physical resources (such as storage devices or servers) appear as a single logical resource as well. This method is known as *virtualization* and is achieved in Windows Server 2008 by the installation of Hyper-V and the creation of virtual machines.

Virtualization is a broad term that deals with many aspects of its use. The trouble is being able to understand different types of virtualization. This includes what these types offer for you and how they can help accomplish your individual goals. There are currently three major types of virtualization that are available for use with Windows Server 2008 with Hyper-V role installed. Here is a simple explanation of each:

- **Server Virtualization** is the when the physical server hardware is separated from Guest operating systems (servers).

- **Network Virtualization** involves creating the illusion that all resources on the network are part of the user's desktop computer by moving network applications, localizing them in a seamless fashion through virtualization.

- **Storage Virtualization** involves hiding disk storage complexities by creating a Storage Area Network, which is responsible for redirecting storage requests from end users through virtualization.

Hyper-V allows virtual machine technology to be applied to both server and client hardware. It enables multiple operating systems to run concurrently on a single machine. Hyper-V specifically, is a key feature of Windows Server 2008. Until the release of

Windows Server 2008, many x86–based operating systems seeking to use a Microsoft solution achieved virtualization via Virtual PC 2007 and Virtual Server 2005.

News and Noteworthy...

Understanding Virtual PC and Server

Before Windows Server 2008 there were other options for virtualization and emulation. Two of the most common that you should be aware of are Virtual PC and Virtual Server 2005. Both are virtualization suites for the PC and emulations suites for use in Mac OS X. They allow the cross-platform use of a variety of PC applications and operating systems. Virtual Server 2005 and Virtual PC 2007 mimic standard Intel Pentium 4 processors with an Intel 440BX chipset. Thus, they can be used to emulate certain applications for the PC on a Mac PowerPC. Virtual PC 2007 is a recent release that allows the emulation and virtualization of Microsoft Vista. However, issues can arise when trying to install uncommon operating systems that have not been specifically targeted in the development of Virtual PC or Virtual Server.

Virtual PC for the Mac uses dynamic recompilation in order to translate the x86 code used by a standard PC. It translates this code into the equivalent PowerPC code used by a Mac. Virtual PC for Windows also uses the same type of dynamic recompilation. Instead it takes kernel mode and real mode x86 code and translates it into x86 user mode code. The original user mode and virtual 8086 mode code runs natively, allowing fluidity.

Both Virtual PC and Virtual Server were useful in the development of the virtualization trend but received some complaints. Both seemed to fall short in specific areas of compatibility, especially in regards to Linux and uncommon application usage. Another drawback is that Virtual Server 2005 and Virtual PC 2007 are compatible for hosts with x64 processors but cannot run guests that require x64 processors running a 64 bit OS. Both of these products are commonly utilized but have been slowly declining in popularity due to free virtualization software such as VMware and Xen. Windows Server 2008 is Microsoft's solution to this issue by offering more options than its free competitors via the new features available through Hyper-V.

Virtualization creates virtual machines, each of which are capable of running a different operating system on a single physical machine while the virtual machines run without interference behind partitions. This can be used to simulate multiple native environments and most of the benefits that would normally require multiple machines and deployments. Virtualization is a growing trend that can greatly reduce deployment costs. It allows a single machine to run multiple operating systems simultaneously while allowing you to dynamically add physical and virtual resources to those machines as needed. For example, you can install multiple virtualized operating systems on the host computer and each virtualized operating system will run in isolation from the other operating systems installed.

News and Noteworthy...

Expanding the Limits of Hyper-V Virtualization

Hyper-V has many features that surpass previous virtualization software packages as a stand alone virtualization suite installed on Windows Server 2008. Hyper-V allows for greater application compatibility than previous software of its kind. Because of this, Hyper-V can utilize and take advantage of other tools and applications to create an even more versatile and dynamic experience. This greatly increases the options for administrators to customize their virtual network to their own specific needs for their company.

There are many scenarios that can test the limits of Hyper-V that Microsoft is only beginning to speculate on. As an example of the options available with Hyper-V, consider this scenario. Many of you may be familiar with Virtual PC 2007 and use it as a solution for running a virtualized Windows 98 operating system. You may find it interesting to know that although this scenario is not supported by Microsoft using Hyper-V, it is possible to run a Windows Server 2008 with Hyper-V with Windows 2003 installed on a virtual machine. By then installing Virtual PC 2007 onto that virtual machine you can in turn use Virtual PC 2007 to run Windows 98. Both Virtual PC and Virtual Server work in this scenario and have better than expected performance. Microsoft plans on expanding their support of Hyper-V to eventually cover more of these unique scenarios.

Although virtualization has existed in many incarnations it is not a catch-all fix for all networking needs. There are still many precautions that are required when working with Hyper-V or any virtualization suite. For example, if the machine acting as a host for your virtual network is not part of some failover group or you do not have a method of back up such as a hot spare, you could find yourself with a total network outage if that computer fails. There will always be a need for redundancy of some kind for no other reason than to be thorough and prove due diligence. Also note that the Hyper-V requires heavier system requirements such as enterprise class hardware and training that must also be factored into your company's cost considerations.

The potential of virtual machine technology is only beginning to be harnessed and can be used for a wide range of purposes. It enables hardware consolidation, because multiple operating systems can run on one computer. Key applications for virtual machine technology include cross-platform integration as well as the following:

- **Server consolidation** Consolidating many physical servers into fewer servers, by using host virtual machines. Virtual machine technology can be used to run a single server with multiple operating systems on it side by side. This replaces the need for multiple servers that were once required to run the same applications because they required different operating systems to perform their tasks. The physical servers are transformed into virtual machine "guests" who occupy a virtual machine host system. This can be also called Physical-to-Virtual or P2V transformation.

- **Disaster recovery** Physical production servers can use virtual machines as "hot standby" environments. Virtual machines can provide backup images that can boot into live virtual machines. This allows for application portability and flexibility across hardware platforms. It changes the traditional "backup and restore" mentality. These VMs are then capable of taking over the workload of a production server experiencing an outage.

- **Consolidation for testing and development environments** Virtual machines can be used for testing of early developmental versions of applications without fear of destabilizing the system for other users. Because each virtual machine is its own isolated testing environment it reduces risks incurred by developers. Virtual machines can be used to compare different versions of applications for different operating systems and to test those applications in a variety of different configurations. Kernel development and operating system test course can greatly benefit from hardware virtualization, which can give root access to a virtual machine and its guest operating system.

- **Upgrading to a dynamic datacenter** Dynamic IT environments are now achievable via the use of virtualization. Hyper-V, along with systems management solutions enables you to troubleshoot problems more effectively. This also creates IT management solution that is efficient and self-managing.

In past Windows versions there were specific limitations on these virtual machines created. In Windows Server 2008 with Hyper-V installed each virtual operating system is a full operating system with access to applications. You can also run non-Microsoft operating systems in the virtualized environment of Windows Server 2008.

Understanding the Components of Hyper-V

Microsoft has introduced a next-generation hypervisor-based virtualization platform called Hyper-V for Windows Server 2008. Hyper-V has greater deployment capabilities to past versions and provides more options for your specific needs because it utilizes specific 64-bit hardware and a 64-bit operating system. Additional processing power and a larger addressable memory space is gained by the utilization of a 64-bit environment. Hyper-V has three main components: the *hypervisor*, the *virtualization stack*, and the new *virtualized I/O model*. The hypervisor also known as the *virtual machine monitor*, is a very small layer of software that is present directly on the processor, which creates the different "partitions" that each virtualized instance of the operating system will run within. The virtualization stack and the I/O components act to provide a go-between with Windows and with all the partitions that you create. All three of these components of Hyper-V work together as a team to allow virtualization to occur. Hyper-V hooks into threads on the host processor, which the host operating system can then use to efficiently communicate with multiple virtual machines. Because of this, these virtual machines and multiple virtual operating systems can all be running on a single physical processor. You can see this model in Figure 10.1.

Figure 10.1 Viewing the Components of Hyper-V

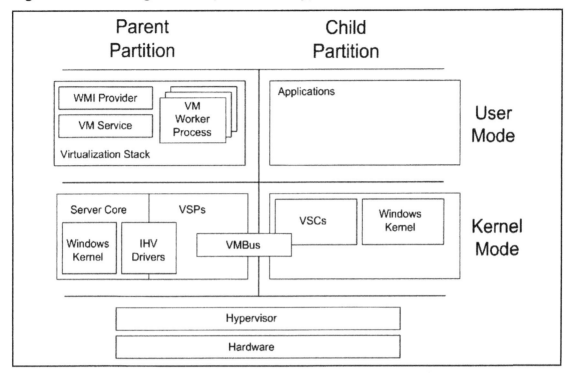

The hypervisor creates partitions that are used to isolate guests and host operating systems. A partition is comprised of a physical address space and one or more virtual processors. Hardware resources such as CPU cycles, memory, and devices can be assigned to the partition. A *parent partition* creates and manages child partitions. It contains a *virtualization stack*, which controls these child partitions. The parent partition is in most occasions also the root partition. It is the first partition that is created and owns all resources not owned by the hypervisor. As the root partition it will handle the loading of and the booting of the hypervisor. It is also required to deal with power management, plug-and-play, and hardware failure events.

Partitions are named with a partition ID. This 64-bit number is delegated by the hypervisor. These ID numbers are guaranteed by the hypervisor to be unique IDs. These are not unique in respect to power cycles however. The same ID may be generated across a power cycle or a reboot of the hypervisor. The hypervisor does guarantee that all IDs within a single power cycle will be unique.

The hypervisor also is designed to provide availability guarantees to guests. A group of servers that have been consolidated onto a solitary physical machine should not hinder each other from making progress, for example. A partition should be able to be run that provides telephony support such that this partition continues to perform all of its duties regardless of the potentially contrary actions of other partitions. The hypervisor takes many precautions to assure this occurs flawlessly.

For each partition, the hypervisor maintains a *memory pool* of RAM SPA pages. This pool acts just like a checking account. The amount of pages in the pool is called the *balance*. Pages are *deposited* or *withdrawn* from the memory pool. When a hypercall that requires memory is made by a partition, the hypervisor withdraws the required memory from the total pool balance. If the balance is insufficient, the call fails. If such a withdrawal is made by a guest for another guest in another partition, the hypervisor attempts to draw the requested amount of memory from the pool of the latter partition.

Pages within a partition's memory pool are managed by the hypervisor. These pages cannot be accessed through any partition's Global Presence Architecture (GPA) space. That is, in all partitions' GPA spaces, they must be inaccessible (mapped such that no read, write or execute access is allowed). In general, the only partition that can deposit into or withdraw from a partition is that partition's parent.

New & Noteworthy...

Microsoft Virtualization and Linux Support

Microsoft will continue to support Linux operating systems with the production release of Hyper-V. Integration components and technical support will be provided for customers running certain Linux distributions as guest operating systems within Hyper-V. Integration components for Beta Linux are now available for Novell SUSE Linux Enterprise Server (SLES) 10 SP1 x86 and x64 Editions. These components enable Xen-enabled Linux to take advantage of the VSP/VSC architecture. This will help to provide improved performance overall. Beta Linux Integration components are available for immediate download through http://connect.microsoft.com. Another additionally noteworthy feature is, as of this writing, Red Hat Fedora 8 Linux and the alpha version of Fedora 9 Linux, which are both compatible and supported by Hyper-V. The full list of supported operating systems will be announced prior to RTM.

Configuring Virtual Machines

We have discussed the many benefits and concept of virtualization and touched on how it can benefit you in terms of server consolidation, energy efficiency, and simpler management and deployment.

All these aspects of efficiency make virtualization an important tool. The root of virtualization is its use of *virtual machines*. Virtual machines are by definition software emulations within a computer that executes programs and applications like a real machine. Windows Server 2008 with Hyper-V allows the creation of multiple virtual machines, each running multiple operating systems also called *guest operating systems*, from a single physical machine.

The two main advantages of a Virtual Machine or VMs are:

■ Multiple OS environments can share the same computer while still being strongly isolated from each other and the virtual machine

■ They can provide an *instruction set architecture* (ISA) that is fairly contrary to that of the actual machine.

One of the main and most popular uses for VMs is to isolate multiple operating systems from a single machine, which consolidates servers and reduces interference between conflicting operating systems. This is referred to as Quality of Service (QoS) isolation.

Hyper-V supports isolation in terms of a partition that is a logical unit of isolation. This is supported by the hypervisor, in which operating systems execute. A hypervisor instance has to have at least one root partition, running Windows Server 2008. Hardware devices are accessed directly by the virtualization stack in the root partition. Guest operating systems are hosted on child partitions that are created by the root partition. A child partition can also create additional child partitions. A host or parent partition creates child partitions using the hypercall, *application programming interface* (API).

Windows Server 2008 includes a new tool to manage your virtual machines called the Hyper-V Manager.

Installing Hyper-V

As you have seen so far in this chapter, Hyper-V is a versatile new feature for Windows Server 2008. Before explaining how to create, configure, and delegate hard drive space to virtual machines you must first be able to install the Hyper-V feature to your machine. Hyper-V has many prerequisites that must be met before installation can occur. We will now discuss the proper method for installing the virtualization features of Hyper-V.

> **NOTE**
>
> Hyper-Vs require 64-bit hardware and a 64-bit version of the Windows Server 2008 operating system to implement.

In order to utilize virtualization you must have a clean install of Windows Server 2008 Enterprise with Hyper-V installed onto the host machine. Remember that Hyper-V requires 64-bit hardware and a 64-bit version of the operating system. You must also ensure that you have hardware-assisted virtualization enabled prior to installation. If BIOS configuration changes were made to the machine to enable these features, a full cycle power down must be completed to proceed. Once we are sure all these prerequisites are met, we can go over the steps required to install Hyper-V.

Configuring & Implementing...

Avoiding Common BIOS Problems with Hyper-V

Hyper-V requires hardware-assisted virtualization. If you have an x64 Intel processor that supports hardware virtualization you should have no BIOS configuration issues. These processors come preconfigured for hardware virtualization. Hardware-assisted virtualization may need to be enabled on some processors. This may require altering the BIOS configuration of the host computer.

Intel Virtualization Technology and AMD Pacifica are both compatible with Hyper-V usage out of the box. However if you are using an x64 AMD processor there are known configuration issues that have yet to be addressed. If you are using this type of processor you should consult the online documentation located at http://techreport.com/discussions.x/13721 for your specific processor.

Continued

A BIOS update will more than likely be necessary. There is a fairly simple way of determining if you will need to update your BIOS in this case. You should check the "stepping" value for your processor using a CPU validation tool such as CPUID, which is available at http://www.cpuid.com. After running the tool consult the stepping value of your CPU. If the stepping value is 2 you will require a BIOS update. If the stepping value is 3 or higher you should have no need to update the BIOS to install Hyper-V to your machine.

This is the procedure for installing the Hyper-V role on Windows Server 2008:

1. Click **Start** and click to open Server Manager.

2. Locate the Roles node of the main Server Manager window.

3. Click **Add Roles**.

4. On the Specific Server Roles page click **Add Hyper-V** (as shown in Figure 10.2).Follow the prompts to finish installing the Role and click **OK** when finished.

Figure 10.2 Adding Hyper-V on the Specific Server Roles Page

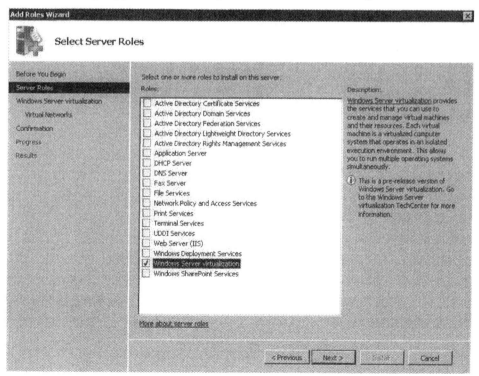

5. Once installed, you will need to access the Virtualization Management Console to configure virtual machines. You can find the VMM within the Administrative Tools menu in the Start menu as seen in Figure 10.3. Once opened, you can use the Create Virtual Networks page to select the network adapters that you wish to make connections available to virtual machines. Also note that you should leave one network adapter free for remote access. Only Ethernet (802.3) network adapters are supported.

6. Click **Install** on the Confirm Installation Selections page.

7. Upon completion, click **Close** to end the installation.

8. Click **Yes** to restart the system.

Also note that when you open Hyper-V Manager for the first time, you must accept the end-user license agreement (EULA) using an account that is a member of the local Administrators group. If you fail to do so you will not be able to use the snap-in to perform any tasks. Be sure to log on to the computer using an appropriate account before you open the snap-in for the first time. If this problem occurs simply close Hyper-V Manager and log on to the computer using an appropriate account. Once you have done this you may open Hyper-V Manager without incident.

Installing and Managing Hyper-V on Windows Server Core Installations

The Windows server core installation option of Windows Server 2008 and Windows Server virtualization are two new features of Windows Server 2008 that work together to a mutually beneficial end. Windows server core installation option is a new shell-less and GUI-free installation option for Window Server 2008 Standard, Enterprise, and Datacenter Editions. It will lower the level of management and maintenance required by an administrator. The Windows server core installation option provides several advantages over a full installation of Windows Server 2008. It is intended to act as a complement to Windows Server virtualization. Hyper-V is compatible with Server Core installations but requires certain preparation to install. In order to take advantage of this installation process you must be aware of certain procedures before installing. If you wish to install Hyper-V on to a Server Core, run the following command: **Start /w ocsetup Microsoft-Hyper-V.** Once installed you can manage Hyper-V on a Server Core installation, by doing the following:

1. Use Hyper-V Manager to connect to the Server Core installation remotely from a full installation of Windows Server2008 on which the Hyper-V role is installed.

2. Use the Windows Management Instrumentation (WMI) interface to manage the installation process.

NOTE

WMI is used to define a nonproprietary set of environment-independent specifications. By doing this it allows management information to be shared between management applications that run in both similar and dissimilar operating system environments.

We should now be familiar with the installation process of Hyper-V. Let us now get a better grasp of the bigger picture behind virtual machines. We can start with what a virtual network is and how it is set up using Windows Server 2008 with Hyper-V enabled.

Virtual Networking

A *Virtual Network* is the organization of a group of networks in such a way that it appears to the end user to be a singular larger network. It ideally contains a consistent user interface, which allows for the user to communicate both remotely and locally across similar and dissimilar networks. This concept can also be applied to the way the network is administrated and managed as well. This is often referred to as *network virtualization*. Deployed correctly, an administrator could manage and monitor all the resources of a virtualized network from a single network administrator's console. In an ideal configuration, all the servers and services in the network would act as a single pool of resources that the administrator could rearrange and redeploy in real time as required by his changing needs. Today's enterprises are comprised of diverse groups of users, each with specific needs. The different business needs of these groups make way for an array of network requirements. These requirements can be so far reaching it requires different groups to be treated as completely separate customers by IT departments.

Many business drivers that encourage the virtualization of networks, including the following:

- Gains in productivity that are derived from providing visitors with access to the Internet so that they can connect to their own private networks.

- The need to quarantine hosts that are infected or not compliant with the security policies to increase availability.

- Providing personnel connectivity to the Internet and select internal resources to in-house consultants, partners, or even contractors of a business.

- The necessity for secure network areas that are partially or totally isolated.

- Consolidation of multiple networks onto a single infrastructure.

- A simple, logical collocation of competing customers on a shared infrastructure.

- Integration of subsidiaries and acquisitions.

- Meeting the requirements of next-generation business models that are aimed at improving efficiencies, reducing costs, and generating new streams of revenue. In such a situation the IT department could become a revenue-generating service provider.

NOTE

Be sure to familiarize yourself with the benefits of network virtualization in different business environments. The end goal of network virtualization is to have a transparent, always accessible, dedicated network with resources and security policies that are not codependent. Bear this definition in mind when looking at how a business can benefit from virtualization.

Network virtualization is an innovative approach to providing an isolated networking environment for each group within the enterprise. Each of these logical environments will be maintained across a single shared network infrastructure. Each network allows for the corresponding group of users to have full network access similar to those provided by a traditional network. The overall goal from an end-user perspective is having access to an always accessible transparent dedicated network with individual resources and independent security policies. So in short, network virtualization requires the logical division of all network devices and network services.

Let's take an overview of what key elements comprise a virtual network:

- Network hardware, such as switches and Network adapters, also known as network interface cards (NICs)

- Networks, such as virtual LANs (VLANs)

- Containers such as virtual machines

- Network storage devices.

- Network transmission media, such as coaxial cable

Windows Server 2008 Hyper-V is the hypervisor-based virtualization feature included as a role of Windows Server 2008. It contains everything needed to create a virtual network. These virtual networks enable IT organizations to reduce costs, to improve server utilization and to create a more dynamic IT infrastructure. This enables you to create a nimble and multifunctional datacenter and progress toward achieving self-managing dynamic systems.

Windows Server 2008 comes equipped with integrated virtual switches to help you accomplish these goals. These switches play different roles than their past incarnation in Virtual Server and those of traditional hardware switches. Integrated Virtual Switches are new to Windows Server 2008 and were not included in previous Windows Servers. This also means that networking is quite different than it previously was in past Windows Servers. All the integrated switches come with Virtual Local Area Network (VLAN) support. There are three integrated virtual switches in Windows Server 2008. Here is a brief definition of the switches uses:

- The first virtual switch is bound to the physical adapter, which means any virtual machines connected to this virtual switch can access the physical network.

- The second virtual switch is connected to the host or parent partition, which allows virtual machines to communicate with each as well as the host partition.

- The third virtual switch is purely virtual or unbound and allows only the virtual machines connected to this switch to communicate without packets hitting the wire.

Virtualization Hardware Requirements

Windows Server 2008 has a variety of necessary requirements that you will need to be aware of when troubleshooting, installing, or configuring the functionality of virtual machines and Hyper-V. Hyper-V is available with Windows Server 2008 Enterprise x64. Unlike previous virtualization software Hyper-V is a hypervisor virtualization platform that requires hardware-supported virtualization, specific hardware requirements, and BIOS configuration updates for certain processors.

The hypervisor itself has several hardware tests that it performs prior to runtime. The hypervisor obtains information about the underlying physical hardware from three sources:

- **Boot-time input parameters** When the hypervisor is booted, parameters are provided about some aspects of the physical hardware. The hardware aspects that are described to the hypervisor at boot time include the number of potential logical processors, the status of hyperthreading capabilities in the BIOS, and the present RAM SPA ranges. RAM SPA is the systems physical address range that is populated with RAM when the hypervisor is booted.

- **Dynamic discovery** The hypervisor can discover information concerning the physical hardware at runtime. This is done by using architecturally defined mechanisms, for example CPUID instruction on x64 processors.

- **Root partition input** The hypervisor is required to be told about hardware changes by code running within the root partition. This includes hardware changes such as power management and hot add/removal.

There are two key hardware requirements for installation of Hyper-V platform. One is the need to ensure that the server is a 64-bit environment. The second is that the server supports hardware-assisted virtualization technology. More specifically, a 64-bit system with hardware-assisted virtualization enabled and data execution prevention (DEP) is required.

Hyper-V runs on a 64-bit (x64) server platform and requires support of either AMD64 or Intel IA-32e/EM64T (x64) processors with hardware-assisted virtualization support. It is important to note that Hyper-V does not support Itanium (IA-64) processors. Hyper-V can support both single processor and multiprocessor configurations in the virtual machine environment. For an updated list of Microsoft compatibility tested hardware see the information listed in http://download.microsoft.com/download/e/4/8/ e48d5cff-53d2-4eed-85bf-4af50e25b78c/relnotes.htm.

Virtual Hard Disks

When dealing with virtual machines, virtual storage plays a large role in reaping the benefits of virtualization. A virtual machine relies on virtual hard disks much in the same way a physical machine would rely on a physical hard disk. Because of this it is critical to understand and master the creation and configuration of virtual hard disks.

Hyper-V allows you to designate and connect *Virtual Hard Disks* (VHD) to the virtual machines that you create. The virtual hard disk (VHD) format is a block-based format that stores the contents of a virtual machine. VHDs use the *.vhd file that simulates the properties of a physical hard drive. Virtual hard disks can be created during the VM creation using Hyper-V Manager. VHDs can also be customized and created prior to the creation of the virtual machine. To do this Hyper-V offers the *New Virtual Hard Disk wizard* as shown in Figure 10.3. This is a wizard that allows you a great deal of configuration options to create the ideal virtual hard disk for your requirements.

Figure 10.3 New Virtual Hard Disk Wizard

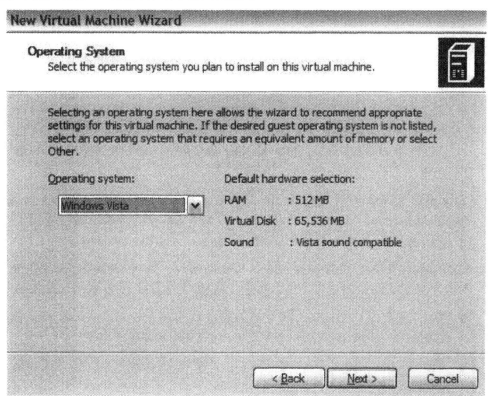

Here is an overview of the functions available to you with the New Virtual Hard Disk Wizard:

- **Before You Begin** This page of the wizard explains the purpose of the wizard. From this pane you can create a default virtual hard disk without working through the rest of the wizard. By clicking **Finish** on this page, the wizard will create a dynamically expanding virtual hard disk with a storage capacity of 127 gigabytes by default.

- **Choose Disk Type** From this page you can choose one of the three types of virtual hard disk that you would like to create based on the functionality you require.

  - *Dynamically expanding virtual hard disks* provide storage capacity as needed to store data. The size of the.*.vhd file is small when initially created and expands as data is added. The size does not shrink automatically, however, when data is deleted. In order to decrease the *.vhd file size you must compact the disk after data is deleted by using the *Edit Virtual Hard Disk Wizard*.

  - *Fixed virtual hard disks* provide storage via a size-specified *.vhd file when the disk is created initially. The size of the *.vhd file remains fixed regardless of the amount of data stored. In order to change the size of this type of disc you must use the Edit Virtual Hard Disk Wizard to increase the size of the virtual hard disc.

  - *Differencing virtual hard disks* provide storage to enable you to make changes to a parent virtual hard disk without altering that disk. The size of the *.vhd file for a differencing disk grows as changes are stored to the disk.

- **Specify Name and Location** This page is used to provide a name and location for your new virtual hard disk. You can also specify a shared location if you plan to cluster the virtual hard disk to a virtual machine.

- **Configure Disk** This page allows you to adjust the configuration of the VHD based on the type of disk you selected in the Choose Disk Type window.

  - For fixed and dynamically expanding virtual hard disks, you have the option to copy the contents of an available physical disk.

  - For a differencing disk, you can specify the location of the disk you want to use as the parent virtual hard disk.

- **Completing the New Virtual Hard Disk Wizard** This page gives you the all the configuration details that you selected from all the previous pages. The new virtual hard disk is created when you click **Finish.** This process can take a considerable amount of time depending on the configuration options you choose for your virtual hard disk.

The New Virtual Hard Disk Wizard can be an invaluable resource creating as well as backing up virtual machines. Once a virtual machine is created by the New Virtual Hard Disk Wizard you can use the Edit Virtual Hard Disk wizard to make adjustments to it. This wizard has a number of options including Compact, Convert, Expand, Merge, and Reconnect, based on the type of VHD you have created.

Here is a summation of each of these functions:

- **Compact** This function applies only to dynamically expanding virtual hard disks and differencing virtual hard disks. It reduces the size of the .*.vhd file by removing blank space left from where data was deleted.

- **Convert** This function converts a dynamically expanding virtual hard disk to a fixed virtual hard disk or vice versa.

- **Expand** This function increases the total storage capacity of a dynamically expanding virtual hard disk or a fixed virtual hard disk.

- **Merge** This feature applies only to differencing disks and merges the parent partition with the differencing disk for back up purposes.

- **Reconnect** This function applies to differencing disks only. It allows you to choose a differencing disk to reconnect to. This page will appear automatically when the parent virtual hard disk cannot be located.

Now that we have a better understanding of how to create and configure virtual hard disks we are ready to move on to the creation of virtual machines with the Hyper-V role.

Adding Virtual Machines

When attempting to add virtual machines on a Windows Server 2008 you must first be sure that the Hyper-V is installed and correctly set up on the machine. Remember that Hyper-V requires 64-bit hardware and a 64-bit version of the operating system with hardware assisted virtualization enabled to implement virtualization. Be sure that the hardware options of the machine match this criteria and that you are running

Windows Server 2008 x64 before attempting to use virtualization options. Also before installing a virtual machine you should go over this quick checklist before moving forward.

- Do you have the proper operating system media available for the virtual machine you are installing?

- By what media type (.ISO, physical media, or remote server image) is the operating system being installed? The virtual machine will be configured according to this information.

- How much memory do you plan on allotting to the virtual machine?

- What do you plan on naming the virtual machine and where it will you store it?

Organization is always critical to success and these will be questions that will be asked of you during the installation process. After the Hyper-V role is enabled, Hyper-V Manager will become available as a part of Administrative Tools. From the Hyper-V Manager users can easily create and configure virtual machines.

To begin creating virtual machine:

1. Click **Start** and proceed to Administrative Tools. Click on **Hyper-V Manager** as shown in Figure 10.4.

Figure 10.4 Hyper-V Manager

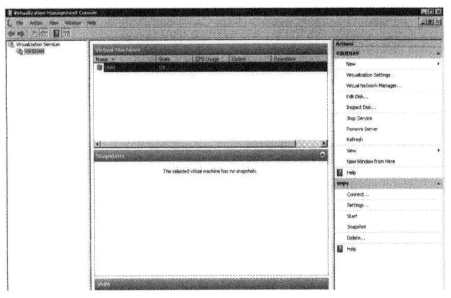

2. Click **New** from the Action Pane and proceed by clicking **Virtual Machines**. Doing this will open the New Virtual Machine wizard.

3. Use the information from your checklist to create a name and storage location for the virtual machine on the Specify Name and Location page.

4. Consult the checklist again for the amount of memory you wish use for the virtual machine. This should be based on the operating system requirements that the virtual machine will be running. After double-checking this information, enter it on the Memory page.

5. To establish connectivity at this point go to the Network page and connect the network adapter to an existing virtual network. If you wish to install your operating system on your virtual machine remotely, select **External Network**.

6. Create a Virtual Hard disc by specifying a name, size, and location on the Connect Virtual Hard Disc. Be sure to account for enough free space to install the operating system on your virtual machine.

7. You can also configure Virtual Processors in the VMM as well. In Figure 10.5, you can see the configuring steps needed to configure a virtual processor.

Figure 10.5 Configuring a Virtual Processor

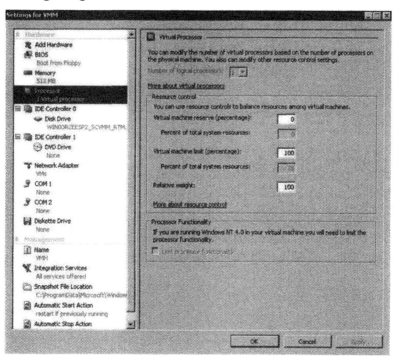

Windows Hyper-V allows you to attach virtual hard discs to each of the virtual machines you create. This allows you to customize and control the storage resources for each VM you create. By default each virtual machine is created with a single virtual hard disk with a maximum of 256 virtual hard disks per Virtual SCSI controller. This feature allows you to add multiple SCSI controllers per virtual machine that you create. With the current limitations on Hyper-V you can add up to a petabyte of storage per virtual machine. Administrators need to configure VHD files on the host system. Tasks such as inspecting virtual hard drive files, compacting virtual hard drive files, or moving storage locations can be accomplished this way. Administrators can mount a virtual hard drive and change a file in the virtual hard drive without starting the associated virtual machine. This ability is invaluable for conducting changes to deactivated images, which would normally require reactivation.

To add hard drive space to your virtual machine:

1. Click **Add Hardware**.
2. Click **Add a virtual SCSI controller**.
3. Then find the Tab labeled **Add Virtual Disc Drive**.
4. Select the amount of storage you wish to add from the list.

Setting the number of virtual processors that a guest partition uses, adding virtual hard disks or network cards, or adjusting the memory allocation for a virtual machine can be done through the individual virtual machine manager. Administrators can change these settings by using the virtual machine manager or by editing the .VMC files directly. Bear in mind that some of these changes are dynamic, such as adding virtual processors or network adapters. Other changes made such as memory allocation, will require a restart of the virtual computer to take effect.

Installation of Hyper-V and of virtual machines is conducted through the Hyper-V Manager window. Hyper-V utilizes a new method as the main interaction point for dealing with virtual machines. It is called the *Virtual Machine Connection* menu. Using this interface we can create a backup snapshot, edit and alter VMs, and execute a number of configuration changes to virtual machines we have created. This is the primary user interface that you will use when interacting with a virtual machine in Hyper-V role (unlike Virtual Server, which used Virtual Machine Remote Control Client). The Virtual Machine Connection window wraps the standard Remote Desktop Client (RDC).

You may use this interface to connect to a virtual machine, update VM details, and configurations concerning it. As we have discussed previously in this section Hyper-V installation and configuration has been streamlined and made very simple for the administrator to take advantage of it. The Virtual Machine Connection can be toggled between full and normal screen modes for ease of use and accessibility. It can also use key combination to accomplish frequent tasks.

Virtual Machine Connection has its own set of native key combinations for easier usage. These can prove invaluable when configuring multiple virtual machines from a remote host, while also swapping between multiple applications or for nothing other than simplistic ease of use. When first familiarizing yourself with Virtual Machine Connection and its key combinations, be sure to toggle the Virtual Machine Connection to full screen mode when using the standard Windows key combinations. They key combinations will not get sent to the virtual machine, unless you are in the full screen mode. This is the default setting for Hyper-V, which you can change so that key combinations are always sent to the virtual machine as long as the Virtual Machine Connection has focus. This can be accomplished as follows:

1. Open the Hyper-V Manager.
2. Click **Hyper-V Server Settings**.
3. Click **Keyboard**.
4. Click the **Use on the Virtual Machine** option.

If you choose to do so you can change the Focus Release key from it normal setting to a custom configuration as follows:

1. Open Hyper-V Manager.
2. Click Hyper-V Settings.
3. Click Release and choose from the drop-down menu options.

Table 10.1 includes a brief summary of the key combinations that can be used with the Virtual Machine Connection and their standard Windows key combinations.

Table 10.1 Key Combinations

Standard Windows Key Combination	Virtual Machine Connection Key Combination	Explanation
CTRL + ALT + DEL	CTRL + ALT + END	This displays the Task Manager or Windows Security dialog box on Windows. This will also prompt to the log in screen if available.
ALT + TAB	ALT + PAGE UP	This switches between programs in order from left to right.
ALT + SHIFT + TAB	ALT + PAGE DOWN	This switches between programs in order from right to left.
ALT + ESC	ALT + INSERT	This will cycle through programs in the chronological order in which they were started.
CTRL + ESC	ALT + HOME	This displays the Windows Start menu.
N/A	CTRL + ALT + PAUSE	This swaps the Virtual Machine Connection window back and forth between full screen mode and normal.
N/A	CTRL + ALT + LEFT ARROW	This releases the mouse and keyboard focus from the Virtual Machine Connection window for other tasks.

Migrating from Physical to Virtual Machines

Before discussing the methodology behind migration it is important to understand when it is most effective to migrate to virtual machines. Research indicates that each layer of virtualization technology has merits when applied properly with the right end goal in mind. Virtualization technology is not a quick fix for everything that is required in all situations. Every case has its own individual needs and requirements based on their particular needs. Many organizations choose to go to the time and trouble to adopt some form of virtualization technology with the wrong objectives in mind.

One end solution that virtualization can help is availability or reliability. Virtualization technology often is deployed in an attempt to make outages, planned or unplanned, invisible to users. Hyper-V can help in the areas of access virtualization, application virtualization, processing virtualization, network virtualization, storage virtualization, and tools to manage its virtualized environment. Past virtual machine software could not achieve this goal without numerous issues.

As we mentioned, consolidation is a huge goal when deploying virtual machines and operating system virtualization technology. Both help organizations increase the amount of usage from physical resources by consolidating applications onto a much smaller number of systems. However virtual machines alone will not completely resolve a solution. You will need to have access to more virtualization technology to really gain all of the benefits mentioned. Hyper-V helps in this with a large number of tools and compatibility with other virtual machine technology and tool sets. Without all these other tools, you would soon find that they had a patchwork network system that was difficult manage and maintain.

Another virtualization goal is performance. Hyper-V is focused on allowing multiple functions to share the same physical resources. Always consider the type of performance goal you wish to increase. Hyper-V is one of the most apt choices if the goal is higher levels of application performance.

Obtaining the maximum in scalability is a task for which virtualization often is utilized. This is normally obtained by spreading a single workload over many physical machines. Hyper-V's application virtualization combined with workload management software would achieve the best results in this scenario.

Organizations will often rush to agree that the deployment of virtual machines is the correct choice for them. This often occurs without much planning or research. Your goal is to learn when to take advantage of virtualization offered by the Hyper-V role in Windows Server 2008. Many organizations ultimately face significant challenges because they are not prepared to use the virtualization software they are deploying to the best means for their situation. Before migration occurs ensure that you have a successful deployment of the technology. This can be accomplished by the following methods of organization:

- Organize your management team and try to assess the total needs for your deployment. Account for both unified and diverse management teams. Some organizations contain separate groups that manage application development, system infrastructure, network infrastructure, and web infrastructure. A fragmented management team always makes implementation of virtualization technology more difficult.

- Organize your development team so that you can assess the total needs of your deployment. Account for separate groups that develop mainframe applications, midrange applications, Windows applications, Linux applications, Web-based applications, and so on. A fragmented development makes the task of deploying virtualization technology much more difficult.

- Do not accept virtualization as the end-all solution. As you know, the most common IT environments with be hybrids of physical and virtual resources. Your organization will need tools to discover and manage all its diverse IT assets. Through organization and determining who is responsible for operations and administration of each of these resources, you can ensure a much more successful deployment.

With all this considered we can now move on to talking about the most effective methods of migration from physical to virtual machines using Hyper-V.

Configuring & Implementing...

Determining When Virtualization Is the Right Solution

As we mentioned, virtualization is not a catch-all technology. It has very beneficial and wide reaching uses but is not always the ideal choice of deployment. Distributed services may not be suitable for virtualization unless the host computers are also distributed. In a virtualization scenario that places all DNS servers in a single central IT environment that serves multiple sites, an increase in network traffic and reduced service reliability may occur.

On the other hand, if these sites all consist of multiple servers that offer file and print, database, DNS, and Active Directory services, then virtualization

Continued

of these servers would be of great benefit. By consolidating all the virtual computers onto one physical host you can then be assured of a more efficient performance.

Always rely on pilot virtualizations where possible, to assess and verify real resource usage figures and gains in efficiency. Comparing these figures against the predictions you made will help give you a better idea of what sort of benefit virtualization will yield. As with most processes, predictions cannot be entirely accurate because the simulated clients may not match the workload that the physical server experiences in daily usage. Always attempt to factor these statistics in your deployment plan. Remember it may not be possible to simulate some client workloads.

We have discussed that one of the main goals in virtualization is consolidation. *Server consolidation* is the process of migrating network services and applications from multiple computers to a singular computer. This consolidation can include multiple physical computers to multiple virtual computers on one host computer. You can consolidate computers for several reasons, such as minimizing power consumption, simplifying administration duties, or reducing overall cost. Consolidation can also increase hardware resource utilization. This will increase the return on investments for the IT department of an organization. Service consolidation involves moving multiple network services onto a single computer. This is most efficiently done by means of a virtual network. However, distributed services, such as DNS and Active Directory, have additional issues, such as availability, security, and network topology. For this reason virtualization is safer for organizations that may not want to concentrate these network services onto a single physical computer.

Application consolidation works by moving several business applications onto a single physical computer. If you have invested in high-availability hardware to run your company's single line of business applications, then it is logical to use that hardware to run multiple applications. However, problems can occur if the application requirements conflict. This method is completely impossible if the applications run on different operating systems altogether. Virtualization provides a method to consolidate applications onto a single physical computer. This avoids operating system and other resource conflicts. By migrating from physical to virtual machines using a virtualization model, administrators can create a virtual network that maps to the original physical computers. The host computer can easily run these virtual computers as if they were autonomous physical computers. This way the application environments remain completely unaltered.

Hyper-V allows migration from one physical host system to a virtual machine with minimal downtime, leveraging familiar high-availability capabilities of Windows Server and System Center management tools. In order to prepare to do this, let's go over the hardware requirements for migration with Hyper-V.

The planned guest partition (virtual machine) must be able to function with the standardized hardware that Hyper-V provides. This hardware should include an advanced system with a uniprocessor or multiprocessor configuration, a virtualized network card, and a virtualized hard disk. Hardware that is not supported includes parallel port dongles, almost all universal serial bus devices, and hardware-based authentication. The physical computer you are using for the migration must also contain more than 96 MB RAM. It should also run the NTFS file system.

The host machine for migration should also meet or exceed the following specifications:

- At least one virtual processor core for every child partition

- One dedicated core for the parent partition

- 8 GB of RAM or more

- An iSCSI attachment to network-based storage devices, for example a Storage Area Network (SAN)

- Multiple gigabit network cards (NICs)

- A clean install of Windows Server 2008 Server 64-bit edition

- Redundant and uninterruptible power supplies

- A fast dedicated attachment to backup system are being run.

Backing Up Virtual Machines

Deploying virtualization technology requires diligence and research on the part of the administrator. One of the main objectives is to create a more efficient and cost-effective environment. To do so, changes and updates must constantly occur to optimize the settings and need prior to deployment. This is similar the methodology used for physical computers. Backup for virtual computers is as important as with physical computers.

The Windows 2008 Volume Shadow Copy Service (VSS) is a feature available for NTFS volumes. VSS is used to perform a point-in-time backup of an entire volume to the local disk. This backup can be used to quickly restore data that was deleted from the volume locally or through a network-mapped drive or network file share. VSS also is used by Windows Server Backup and by compatible third-party backup applications to back up local and shared NTFS volumes.

VSS can make a point-in-time backup of a volume, including backing up open files. This entire process is completed in a very short period of time but is powerful enough to be used to restore an entire volume, if necessary. VSS can be scheduled to back up a volume automatically once, twice, or several times a day. This service can be enabled on a volume that contains Distributed File System (DFS) targets and standard Windows 2008 file shares.

The following approaches can be applied to backing up virtual computers with the Hyper-V role installed:

- Install the Windows Server Backup role in Windows Server 2008. Using the Windows Server Backup role you can take full and incremental backups of the disks that contain the virtual hard disks. This is the recommended method for utilizing this feature.

- The Volume Shadow Copy Service (VSS) as seen in Figure 10.6 on Windows Server 2008 can be used to take shadow copies of running virtual computers. Use incremental backups, to minimize the size of these backup files and not affect the operations of the virtual machine. This can be done by configuring the VSS as seen in Figure 10.7. Also VSS on Windows Server 2008 will avoid the inconsistency issues that might occur with VSS backing up virtual computers on Windows Server 2003 and Virtual Server 2005.

Figure 10.6 Volume Shadow Copy Service (VSS) Utility for Windows Server 2008

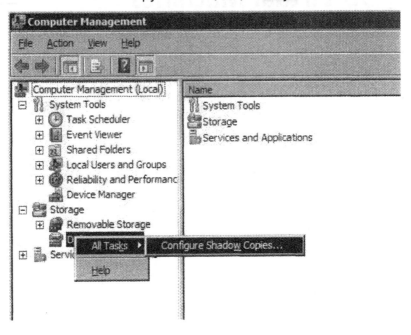

Figure 10.7 Configuring the VSS

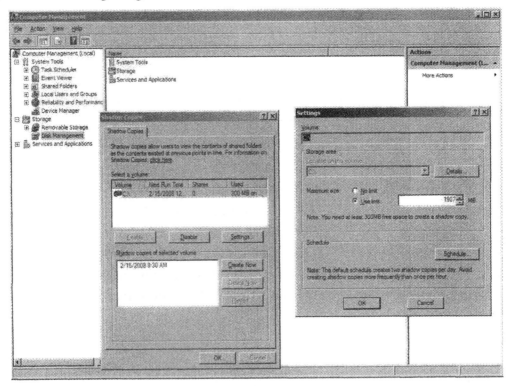

- You can also opt to run a backup application from within the virtual machine you are attempting to back up. This will provide you consistency with the existing backup strategy of an organization. The main problem with this method is that it does not provide you with a snapshot of the data at a particular instance. You should be sure that the virtual computer creates the backup image on a separate storage area from the disk that contains the *.vhd file.

- Another method for backing up your virtual machine is to suspend and copy the VM. To do this you must save the state of the virtual computer. Then you would copy the complete set of *.vhd, *.vsv, and *.vmc files to another location. To avoid any differences between the *.vhd and the *.hsv files, copy all the virtual computer files on a single pass and stop the image from restarting. This approach will definitely involve server downtime during the save state and copy operation and is one of the least recommend.

- Another approach is to create a differencing drive. It requires you to shut down the virtual computer and creates a new differencing drive for the virtual hard disk or disks. This can be accomplished via the New Virtual Hard Disk wizard. You then restart the virtual machine immediately. All changes are made to the differencing drive, which makes it possible to back up to the parent drive by using the XCOPY command. Next you would restore the virtual machine to the point at which the parent drive was created. The last step may require downtime because you must eventually shut down the virtual machine and combine the parent and differencing drives together.

- The final and newest method for backing up a virtual machine is creating a snapshot. A snapshot can save the state of a virtual computer at a specific instant in time whether it is running or not. You can then restore a computer to the exact configuration that was captured in the snapshot taken. The data settings that existed at the time the snapshot was taken will also be restored. The only main downside to a snapshot is that it requires the existence of a suitable *.vhd file. This *.vhd file will act as a parent file for the snapshot. Snapshots are best used to restore an image rather than provide data integrity. Snapshots are invaluable to you if you wish to recover from the unexpected effect of applying a security update process or service pack.

Because the main objectives for this chapter deal with the new virtualization features available with Hyper-V in Windows Server 2008, we will discuss how to effectively use the snapshot function of Hyper-V in detail. Hyper-V introduces the concept of virtual machine snapshots. This is best defined as a point in time image of a VM that you can resume to at any stage. Snapshots are implemented in the virtualization layer. Any guest operating system can take a snapshot at anytime including during installation. Snapshots can be taken whether the virtual machine is running or stopped. If a virtual machine is running when the snapshot is taken no downtime will occur while creating the snapshot.

To create a snapshot, you will need to use the Hyper-V Manager. This is accomplished in the following way:

1. Open the Hyper-V Manger and select a **virtual machine**.

2. Click the **Snapshot** button in the toolbar of the Virtual Machine Connection window or open the Action menu in Hyper-V manager and select **Snapshot**.

Creating a snapshot from the Virtual Machine Connection window will open a dialog that allows you to enter a custom label for the snapshot. Be sure to name the snapshot appropriately to the purpose you will be using it for. If you plan on testing new configurations be sure to logically notate what the purpose for the snapshot is. Virtual Machine Connection will also allow you to skip this dialog and opt to have the snapshot use an auto-generated name. Auto-generated naming conventions consist of the name of the virtual machine followed by the date and time when the snapshot was taken. All snapshots created from the Hyper-V Manager will be created with an auto-generated name. Always be aware of the naming convention you decide to use so that you can effectively return to this back up.

Created snapshots can be viewed in the Snapshot pane of the Hyper-V Manager. This is accomplished by selecting the virtual machine that the snapshot is associated with. The display method for Snapshots in the Snapshot pane is hierarchal and describe the order in which the snapshots where taken. The last snapshot to be taken will have a green arrow head on top of it. This will be last one to be taken or applied to the virtual machine.

Once you have a snapshot selected there will be two main options available to you in the Action panel:

■ **Settings**: This will open the Virtual Machine Settings dialog, which will contain all the settings that the virtual machine had at the time the snapshot was taken. Essentially this snapshot is read only, so all settings will be disabled at this time. From here you can change the snapshot name and the notes associated with the snapshot.

■ **Apply**: This option allows you to copy the complete virtual machine state from the snapshot to an active virtual machine. If you select this process any unsaved data in the currently active virtual machine will be lost. However, you will be asked before applying if you want to create a snapshot of your current active virtual machine. If you do so this will occur before the selected snapshot is applied.

Applying the virtual machine snapshot to an active virtual machine will result in the active virtual machine being either in a saved state or stopped state. This will depend on whether the snapshot was taken of a running or stopped virtual machine. If wish to change settings before starting the updated virtual machine you can make them now. Follow this procedure to make changes to your newly updated virtual machine before starting it:

1. Select the updated **virtual machine**.

2. Open the **Virtual Machine Settings**.

3. Select **Rename** to rename a snapshot without having to open the Virtual Machine Settings.

4. Select **Delete Snapshot** if you no longer wish to restore the virtual machine to that point in time.

A snapshot associated with a virtual machine now allows you access to the Revert option. The Revert option will roll back a virtual machine to the last snapshot that was taken or applied to it. Revert will also delete any changes that have been made since that snapshot was taken.

Virtual Server Optimization

Windows Server 2008 presents many options to you as an administrator for virtualization of your network. As with all networks, your virtualized network will only be as functional as the diligence invested into the optimization of its functions. Even though optimization is a current trend, it is something that has existed in theory for a good deal of time. Due to compatibility and processor requirements, virtualization in the past has been impractical to deploy in many situations. Before deciding to utilize the virtualization features that Hyper-V has to offer, be sure that it is the proper option for your IT department. As we mentioned previously, steps should be taken to determine if your business is a match for this particular method of deployment.

The simplest way to optimize an existing network is through logical organization of its resources and needs. Optimizing any network involves organization and a logical deployment procedure that accounts for all the security, resource, and access requirements of the project. The same holds true of virtual networks as well. As administrator it is up to you to be diligent in your research and testing of the server. In this section we will discuss some steps and stages of optimization for virtual machine based servers.

The first stage of optimization is to collect a record of previous performance information for your virtual machine workload. This will help to better quantify your servers needs. Optimize virtual machine placement by collecting a record of previous performance information concerning the preexisting physical or virtual computers in the network. Also tools such as System Center Operations Manager (SCOM) 2007 as seen in Figure 10.8 can be used to record and analyze performance information. This includes both physical and virtual computers, which will help you in both consolidation and virtualization.

Figure 10.8 System Center Operations Manager (SCOM) 2007

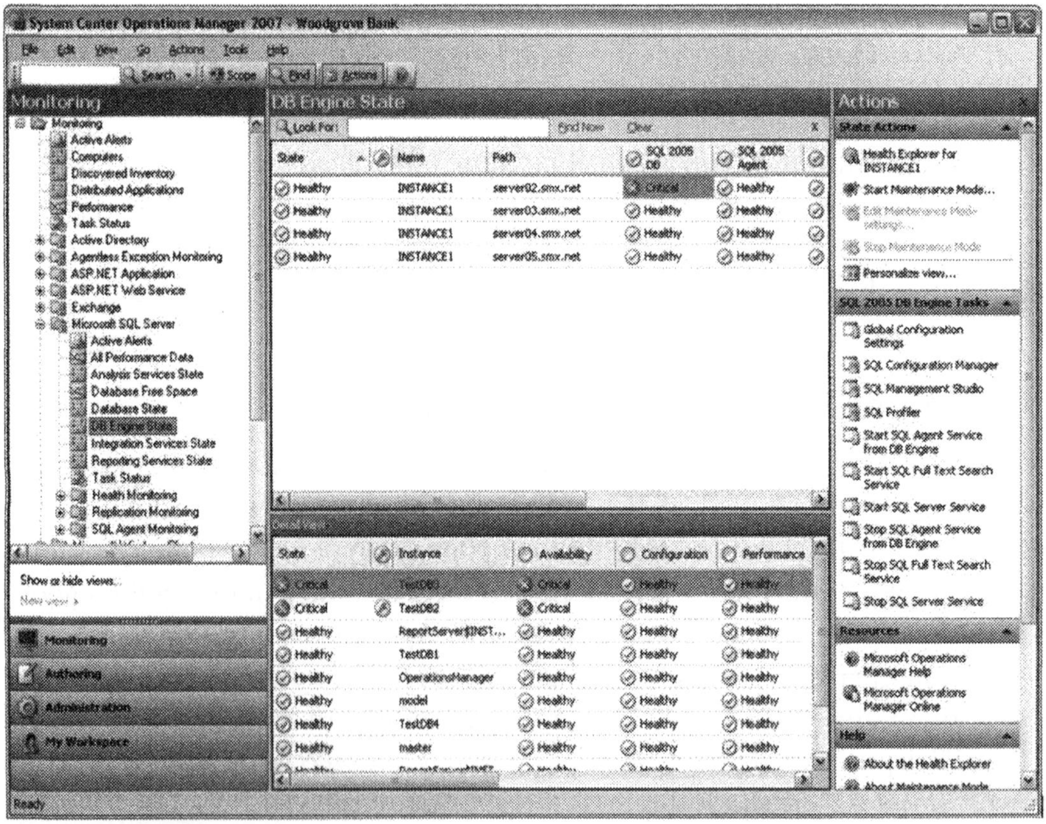

The second stage of optimizing server performance is to verify the minimum required resources for configuration of the virtual machines in your network and adjusting configurations accordingly. For each virtual machine, check the minimum requirements for processors, memory, hard disk space, and network bandwidth. You can calculate the host memory usage by adding an additional 32 MB of memory for each virtual computer. This is considered memory overhead.

The third stage requires you to calculate the total amount of virtual machines the host computer can support running simultaneously. Remember to account for factors such as total memory. Always allow 512 MB for the parent partition alone. Also account for the number of virtual processors you plan to use and how you plan to assign them. Do you plan to assign a processor core to an individual virtual machine in dual-core or quad-core computers? Another factor in this stage is to account for virtual hard disk storage and expected file growth. Be sure to plan ahead for the future needs of the network as well. Also make sure to localize network connectivity by placing computers with large mutual data transfer requirements on the same host computer.

In the fourth stage you will begin resource maximization or load balancing. This will optimize your server for resource maximization requirements. By placing virtual machines on a host computer until the resources of the host computer are fully assigned you can more easily balance workloads.

In the fifth stage you will monitor resource usage and compare the measured figures to the research and predictions you have made in previous stages. Take note of each virtual machine as it starts and as you make changes to the configurations. Monitor static resource usages such as memory. When switching clients over to the virtual images, monitor active resource usage. Take note of things such as processor and network loading. From this point, continue to monitor and adjust virtual machine placements if necessary.

Entering the sixth stage you can begin to accumulate data concerning the server by using SCOM to measure performance data. Ensure this research accounts for high loading times and frequent periods of usage. Certain applications may have specific usage times once a week or only one day out of the month. Familiarize yourself with the high load times of applications of your server. Databases and e-mail servers may have even less frequent maintenance operations that increase resource usage only once in a while.

Lastly in the seventh stage, fine tune your resource consumption using SCOM. Monitor the virtualized computers and the host computers more intricately. Use this information to identify excessive resource consumption and eliminate these sources of consumption where possible.

Summary

You should now be familiar with all the aspects and features that Hyper-V can offer you when using Windows Server 2008. We have talked about how Hyper-V and its parts produce transparent virtualization by creating virtual machines that can run multiple operating systems on a single physical host. We discussed how this is accomplished using Hyper-V's three parts: the hypervisor, the virtualization stack, and they virtual I/O model. In addition we explored all the new virtualization options available with Windows Server 2008 and how they compare to older virtualization suites such as Virtual Server and Virtual PC. We discussed all the major benefits and drawbacks of virtualization, including hardware and software requirements specific to Hyper-V. We have also learned how to install and manage Hyper-V in a Windows Server 2008 environment.

As with any large deployment of new technology, we have learned that there are many steps needed to plan a P2V migration. This includes the need to weigh the gains and drawbacks of virtualization. We stressed the value of organization and knowing exactly the needs of your particular network. We talked about how to estimate costs and what overall benefits can be expected from such a migration. We also discussed how this migration may affect your end users and the way your current network may operate. We also talked about a list of scenarios that were best suited for virtualization.

In addition to the installation and planning for the implementation of Hyper-V, we learned how to configure and back up virtual machines using the new methods available with Windows Server 2008 and the Hyper-V role. You should now be aware of the various steps needed to configure a virtual processor and how to allot virtual storage to any VM that you create using the Hyper-V Manager. You should also have knowledge about virtual snapshots and Volume Shadow Copy Services (VSS) and how each could be used to back up virtual machines you have created in case of emergency or outages.

Last but not least we talked in detail about the various steps and stages required to optimize your virtual network. As we have learned, research and data collection are of utmost importance to the successful administration of a virtual network. We discussed ideal goals to strive for when deploying virtualization in your network and how to maintain the highest levels of efficiency for these types of deployments. We talked about how tools such as SCOM 2007 can help gather data that will be invaluable to your assessment and optimization of your virtual network.

After reading this chapter you should have a sound knowledge of all the features, methods, and requirements necessary to implement a virtual network using Windows Server 2008 and the Hyper-V role.

Solutions Fast Track

Configuring Virtual Machines

☑ Hyper-V is a key feature of Windows Server 2008. It offers a scalable and highly available virtualization platform that is efficient and reliable. It has an inherently secure architecture with a minimal attack surface and does not contain any third-party device drivers.

☑ Hyper-V has three main components: the *hypervisor*, the *virtualization stack*, and the new *virtualized I/O model*. The hypervisor, also know as the *virtual machine monitor*, is a very small layer of software that is present directly on the processor, which creates the different "partitions" within which each virtualized instance of the operating system will run.

☑ The Hyper-V role requires a clean install of Windows Server 2008 Enterprise on the host machine. Hyper-V requires 64-bit hardware and a 64-bit version of the operating system. You must also ensure that you have hardware-assisted virtualization enabled prior to installation.

☑ Virtual machines are created in the Hyper-V role of Windows Server 2008 via the Hyper-V manager. They can be configured for via the Virtual Machine Connection or through the Hyper-V manager.

☑ Virtual hard disks can be created and managed via the Hyper-V manager or via the New Virtual Hard Disk Wizard. VHDs can be edited using the Edit Virtual Hard Disk wizard. Hyper-V allows for 256 virtual hard discs per Virtual SCSI controller. This means that you can add up to a Petabyte of storage per virtual machine created.

Migrating from Physical to Virtual Machines

☑ Server consolidation is the process of migrating network services and applications from multiple computers to a singular computer. This consolidation can include multiple physical computers to multiple virtual computers on one host computer. You can consolidate computers for several reasons, such as minimizing power consumption, simplifying administration duties, or reducing overall cost. Consolidation can also increase hardware resource utilization.

☑ The planned guest partition (virtual machine) used for migration should include an advanced system with a uniprocessor or multiprocessor configuration, a virtualized network card, and a virtualized hard disk. Hardware that is not supported includes parallel port dongles, almost all universal serial bus devices, and hardware-based authentication. The physical computer you are using for the migration must also contain more than 96 MB RAM. It should also run the NTFS file system.

☑ Virtualization technology often is deployed in an attempt to make outages, planned or unplanned, invisible to users. Hyper-V can help in the areas of access virtualization, application virtualization, processing virtualization, network virtualization, storage virtualization, and tools to manage its virtualized environment.

Backing Up Virtual Machines

☑ The Windows 2008 Volume Shadow Copy Service (VSS) is a feature available for NTFS volumes. VSS is used to perform a point-in-time backup of an entire volume to the local disk.

☑ VSS is also used by Windows Server Backup and by compatible third-party backup applications to back up local and shared NTFS volumes.

☑ A differencing drive may be created and used as a back up using the New Virtual Hard Disk wizard, which makes it possible to back up to the parent drive by using the XCOPY command.

☑ Snapshots are implemented in the virtualization layer. Any guest operating system can take a snapshot at anytime including during installation. Snapshots can be taken whether the virtual machine is running or stopped. If a virtual machine is running when the snapshot is taken no downtime will occur while creating the snapshot.

☑ Virtual Machine Connection can be used to organize and edit snapshots taken.

Virtual Server Optimization

☑ The simplest way to optimize an existing network is through logical organization of its resources and needs. Optimizing any network involves organization and a logical deployment procedure that accounts for all the security, resource, and access requirements of the project. The same holds true of virtual networks as well.

☑ The first stage of optimization is to collect a record of previous performance information for your virtual machine workload. This will help to better quantify your servers needs.

☑ The second stage of optimizing server performance is to verify the minimum required resources for configuration of the virtual machines in your network and adjusting configurations accordingly. For each virtual machine, check the minimum requirements for processors, memory, hard disk space, and network bandwidth. You can calculate the host memory usage by adding an additional 32 MB of memory for each virtual computer. This is considered memory overhead.

☑ The third stage of optimization requires you to calculate the total amount of virtual machines the host computer can support running simultaneously. Remember to account for factors such as total memory.

☑ The fourth stage of optimization requires you to begin resource maximization or load balancing. This will optimize your server for resource maximization requirements.

☑ In the fifth stage of optimization you monitor resource usage and compare the measured figures to the research and predictions you have made. Take note of each virtual machine as it starts and as you make changes to the configurations.

Frequently Asked Questions

Q: How does virtualization with Hyper-V differ from other virtualization software available?

A: Hyper-V has greater deployment capabilities to other software and provides more options for your specific needs. It utilizes a hypervisor-based virtualization with 64-bit hardware assistance and 64-bit operating systems. Hyper-V has three main components: the *hypervisor*, the *virtualization stack*, and the new *virtualized I/O model*. The hypervisor, also known as the *virtual machine monitor*, is a very small layer of software that is present directly on the processor, which creates the different "partitions" within which each virtualized instance of the operating system will run. The virtualization stack and the I/O components act to provide a go-between with Windows and with all the partitions that you create. All three of these components of Hyper-V work together as a team to allow virtualization to occur. Hyper-V hooks into threads on the host processor, which the host operating system can then use to efficiently communicate with multiple virtual machines. Because of this these virtual machines and multiple virtual operating systems can all be running on a single physical processor with complete isolation and limited compatibility issues.

Q: What are the greatest benefits of virtualization?

A: The main benefits of virtualization include:

- Server consolidation: Consolidating many physical servers into fewer servers, by using host virtual machines.

- Disaster recovery: Physical production servers can use virtual machines as "hot standby" environments. Virtual machines can provide backup images that can boot into live virtual machines.

- Consolidation for testing and development environments: Virtual machines can be used for testing of early developmental versions of applications without fear of destabilizing the system for other users.

- Upgrading to a dynamic datacenter: Dynamic IT environments are now achievable via the use of virtualization. Hyper-V, along with systems management solutions, enables you to troubleshoot problems more effectively.

Q: What are the two main benefits of the Hyper-V role for Windows Server 2008?

A: The two main benefits of Hyper-V include:

- Multiple OS environments can share the same computer while still being strongly isolated from each other and the virtual machine.

- An *Instruction Set Architecture* (ISA) that is fairly contrary to that of the actual machine.

Q: What new backup methods are offered by Hyper-V for Windows Server 2008 and how do they work?

A: In addition to the Windows Server Backup role in windows Server 2008, Hyper-V offers the new feature of snapshots. A snapshot saves the state of a virtual computer at a specific instance in time whether it is running or not. You can then restore a computer to the exact configuration that was captured in the snapshot taken.

Q: What are the main components of a virtual network?

A: The key elements that comprise a virtual network are:

- Network hardware, such as switches and Network adapters, also known as network interface cards (NICs)

- Networks, such as virtual LANs (VLANs)

- Containers such as virtual machines

- Network storage devices

- Network media, such as Ethernet

Q: What is the best method for optimizing a virtual server?

A: The best way to optimize an existing network is through logical organization of its resources and needs. Optimizing a virtual network or server involves organization and a logical deployment procedure that accounts for all the security, resource, and access requirements of the project. Be diligent in your research and testing of the server.

Chapter 11

Configuring Web Application Services

Solutions in this chapter:

- Installing and Configuring Internet Information Services
- Securing Your Web Sites and Applications
- Managing Internet Information Services

☑ Summary

☑ Solutions Fast Track

☑ Frequently Asked Questions

Introduction

In the last three releases it would be hard to dismiss the incredible growth and maturing of the Windows Server Web application services offerings. From what was an add-on option pack item to a key component that businesses have come to rely on, you can bet that this release is nothing short of impressive. While carrying on the mandate to ship a secure, scalable solution for Web applications and services, the product group has managed to deliver an impressive foundation for Web-based solutions. This release focuses on seven themes that will be covered in this chapter as we discuss and discover the installation, provisioning, and key service features that will help you to maintain your Web farm, whether a single server or a global network of Web services.

Installing and Configuring Internet Information Services

It is hard today to be exposed to technology without being exposed to the Internet. By far one of the most popular applications on the Internet is the Web browser. Responding to the requests of your Web browser is the job of a Web server. For the Windows Server environment, the native Web server is Internet Information Services (IIS). Microsoft shipped the first release of IIS as a free add-on for Windows NT 3.51. Much has changed since that first release, and this evolution of IIS brings the momentum a giant leap forward with a scalable, pluggable, secure Web application server. IIS 7.0 first debuted with the release of Windows Vista. This move was to encourage developers and IT professionals to get an early look at what was being developed for Windows Server 2008 to gather feedback and promote application compatibility. Table 11.1 is an overview of features available across Windows Server 2008, both Full and Server Core installations, and the various editions of Windows Vista.

Table 11.1 Features Available for Windows Server 2008

Feature	Windows Server 2008		Windows Vista		
	Full Install	Server Core Install	Ultimate, Business, Enterprise	Home Premium	Home Basic, Starter
Common HTTP Features					
Static Content	●	●	●	●	○
Default Document	●	●	●	●	○
Directory Browsing	●	●	●	●	○
HTTP Errors	●	●	●	●	●
HTTP Redirection	●	●	●	●	●
Application Development Features					
ASP.NET	●	○	●	●	○
.NET Extensibility	●	○	●	●	●
Active Server Pages (ASP)	●	●	●	●	○
Common Gateway Interface (CGI)	●	●	●	●	○
ISAPI Extensions	●	●	●	●	○
ISAPI Filters	●	●	●	●	○
Server-Side Includes	●	●	●	●	○
Health and Diagnostics Features					
HTTP Logging	●	●	●	●	●
Logging Tools	●	●	●	●	●
Request Monitor	●	●	●	●	●
HTTP Tracing	●	●	●	●	●
Custom Logging	●	●	●	●	○
ODBC Logging	●	●	●	○	○
Security Features					
Basic Authentication	●	●	●	●	○

Continued

Table 11.1 Continued. Features Available for Windows Server 2008

Feature	Windows Server 2008		Windows Vista		
	Full Install	Server Core Install	Ultimate, Business, Enterprise	Home Premium	Home Basic, Starter
Windows Authentication	●	●	●	○	○
Digest Authentication	●	●	●	○	○
Client Certificate Mapping Authentication	●	●	●	○	○
IIS Client Certificate Mapping Authentication	●	●	●	○	○
Uniform Resource Location (URL) Authorization	●	●	●	●	●
Request Filtering	●	●	●	●	●
IP Address and Domain Name Restrictions	●	●	●	●	●
Performance Features					
Static Content Compression	●	●	●	●	●
Dynamic Content Compression	●	●	●	●	●
Management Features					
Management Console	●	○	●	●	○
Management Scripts and Tools	●	●	●	●	●
Management Service	●	○	●	●	○

Continued

Table 11.1 Continued. Features Available for Windows Server 2008

Feature	Windows Server 2008		Windows Vista		
	Full Install	Server Core Install	Ultimate, Business, Enterprise	Home Premium	Home Basic, Starter
IIS 6.0 Management Compatibility	●	●	●	●	●
IIS 6.0 Metabase Compatibility	●	●	●	●	●
IIS 6.0 Windows Management Instrumentation (WMI) Compatibility	●	●	●	●	○
IIS 6.0 Management Console	●	○	●	●	○
IIS 6.0 Management Scripts and Tools	●	●	●	●	○
Windows Process Activation Services (WAS) Features					
Process Model	●	●	●	●	●
.NET Environment	●	○	●	●	●
Configuration Programming Interface	●	○	●	●	●
File Transfer Protocol (FTP) Publishing Service Features					
FTP Publishing Service	●	●	●	○	○
Management Console	●	○	●	○	○
Connection Limits					
Simultaneous Connections	Unlimited	Unlimited	10	3	3

With the release of Windows Server 2008, IIS 7.0 has been further tuned to handle the full operational requirements that you and many others will need in a live production environment (see Figure 11.1). Whether you are new or come from the experience of having worked with previous releases of IIS, you will undoubtedly find an array of new features and functionality that will be both useful and empowering. Behind this release were seven core design goals:

- **Componentized** Splitting up IIS into a set of modules gives you a lightweight, simple server environment for your Web applications. This results in more secure server that efficiently uses the system resources. The trend in componentization can also be seen in other Microsoft server products including Windows, Exchange, and SQL Server.

Figure 11.1 IIS 7.0 Modular Architecture

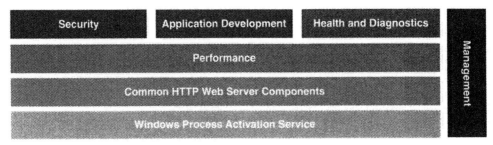

- **Integrated** Simple, consistent, and enhanced server administration, configuration, and operations through an integrated management toolset. IT professionals have the ability to manage the server from a number of locations including:

  1. **Graphical Tools** IIS Manager, which ships with Windows Server 2008 can also be installed on Windows XP, Vista, and Server 2003.

  2. **Command-line Tools** AppCmd.exe replaces several VBScripts that shipped in previous releases with a robust, easy-to-use command-line tool.

  3. **Windows Management Instrumentation** A new WMI provider exposes a number of management methods for use through scripting, programming languages, Windows PowerShell, Windows Remote Management (WinRM), and Windows Remote Shell (WinRS).

4. **Native Windows and .NET Programming Interfaces** In addition to native APIs the Microsoft.Web.Administration .NET assembly enables PowerShell scripts and .NET applications to take full advantage of IIS management through strongly typed objects.

- **Extensible** Building on a componentized architecture gives you the ability to add new modules or replace standard modules. This release introduces the ability to develop these modules in a managed .NET environment in addition to native Windows API development.

- **Supportable** New and enhanced tools for monitoring and troubleshooting give you greater insight into what is happening within your Web applications. A new programming interface to exposing real time request information, triggered error logging tool, and detailed client error messages assist developers and IT professionals in getting applications back online quickly.

- **Compatible** With the large number of changes in this release there was an effort to ensure that they were done in a way to ensure a high degree of backward compatibility with previous releases of IIS. The focus was to ensure at minimum a smooth migration for IIS 6 applications through features like the classic ASP.NET pipeline.

- **Delegation** For growing Web farms, having the ability to delegate administration for various facets of the system is extremely useful. This release delivers an HTTP-based administration protocol, a configuration file hierarchy, a rich set of permissions, and the ability to replace authentication and authorization providers.

- **Secure** It is no secret that security is a necessary focus for all software vendors. The previous IIS release had a strong focus on this and delivered a core that withstood the test of time with no critical security patches required. IIS 7 continues through shipping a componentized architecture that enables you to install only what you need along with the ability to delegate a granular set of tasks.

Differences in Windows Editions

IIS is available in all editions and installations of Windows Server 2008. With Windows Server 2008 you can install IIS on a Server Core installation. There are some role services, however, that will not be available on Server Core:

- ASP.NET
- .NET Extensibility
- IIS Management Console
- IIS Management Service
- IIS 6 Management Console

Although these differences exist in this release, this still leaves you the ability to serve static, classic Active Server Pages (ASP), and Common Gateway Interface-based dynamic content (e.g., PHP, Perl, and Python).

Typical Deployment Scenarios

Depending on your business needs there are a number of scenarios in which IIS can be deployed.

Simple Web Server

Delivering one or more Web applications to a small number of users is the least complex scenario (see Figure 11.2). With this release of IIS the number of concurrent users that can be served continues to grow. IIS takes full advantage of 32-bit and 64-bit hardware to allow you to do more with less hardware.

Figure 11.2 Simple Web Server

Small Web Farms

As you grow you can scale out to add additional Web servers to a farm using software-based load balancing. In this configuration you will split any database components off to a dedicated database server (see Figure 11.3).

Figure 11.3 Small Web Farm

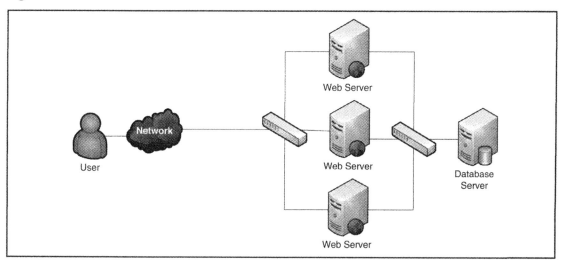

Large Web Farms

At a point in your growth it will be advantageous to use dedicated devices to provide load balancing, offloaded transport security, centralized storage, and application optimization. These devices are tuned to the specific tasks and can execute it more efficiently leaving your Web servers to focus on dynamic content assembly and delivery (see Figure 11.4).

Figure 11.4 Large Web Farm

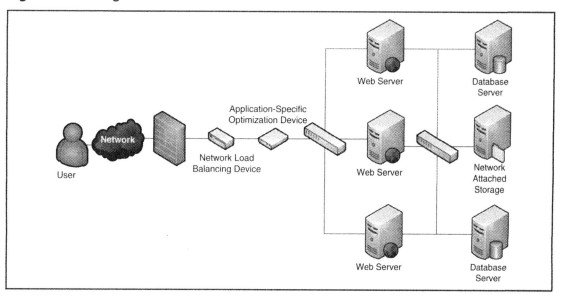

Installing Internet Information Services

The installation process for IIS follows the same process as most other Windows roles. The IIS features are found under the Web Server role alongside file transfer services. In this chapter we are focused on the Web functionality.

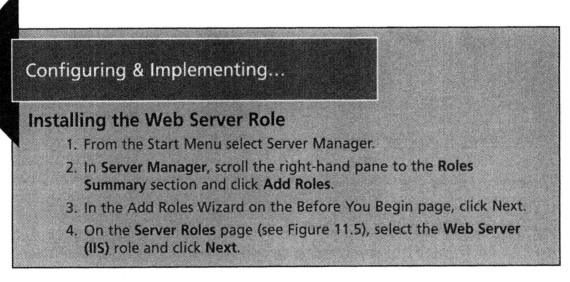

Configuring & Implementing...

Installing the Web Server Role

1. From the Start Menu select Server Manager.
2. In **Server Manager**, scroll the right-hand pane to the **Roles Summary** section and click **Add Roles**.
3. In the Add Roles Wizard on the Before You Begin page, click Next.
4. On the **Server Roles** page (see Figure 11.5), select the **Web Server (IIS)** role and click **Next**.

Figure 11.5 Select Server Roles Page

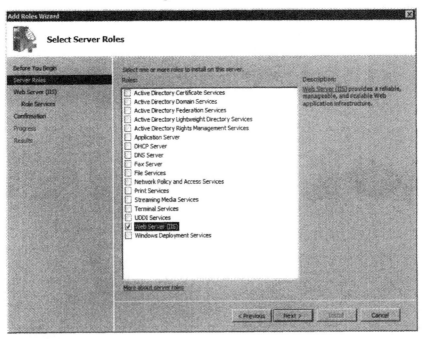

Continued

5. The **Web Server (IIS)** page gives you a brief description of the role along with some important notes and links to more information on the role (see Figure 11.6). Click **Next**.If this is your first time setting up the Web Server (IIS) role you should read these notes as you speak to cover common issues that you will encounter.

Figure 11.6 Select Web Server (IIS) Role Services Page

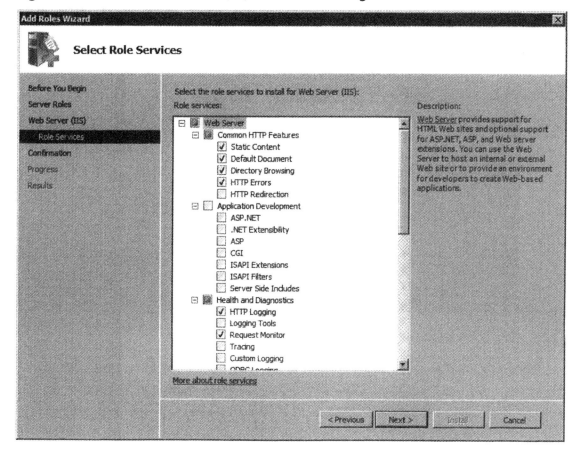

6. On the **Role Services** page you are prompted to install several groups of services to the role. To prepare for the exercises in this chapter select all of the services and click **Next**.

   ■ **Common HTTP Features** Services that are common to most Web server installations such as serving static content, returning rich HTTP error descriptions, basic HTTP redirection, and directory

Continued

browsing. Note that even though they are considered common you have the ability to install IIS without these services.

■ **Application Development** To deliver dynamic content to users or extend IIS you will need the appropriate runtime environments. In this section be sure to choose only the options that you need.

■ **Health and Diagnostics** Tools to give you insight into what is happening on your Web server. You can choose basic logging through custom or database-driven logging along with tracing and request monitoring tools to give you a snapshot of activity.

■ **Security** When delivering content you may need to secure it through a variety of authentication and authorization methods. These modules enable you to secure your content from anonymous users.

■ **Performance** To reduce the overall resource consumption you can compress the content that is being delivered to users. The modules focus on two separate compression types that you can use depending on the content you are delivering.

■ **Management Tools** Enables you to manage your Web server through a number of different types of tools as well as install a compatibility layer for IIS 6 applications.

7. On the **Confirmation** page review your choices and click **Install**.

8. On the **Results** page review the success or failure of the installation and click **Close**.

With the installation complete you will see the role appear in Server Manager. From here you can get an overview of related event log entries, Windows services, and the Role Services you have chosen to install. In addition the Resources and Support section gives you at-your-fingertips access to resources that go in-depth on common issues and best practices to consider (see Figure 11.7).

Figure 11.7 Server Manager after Installation of the Web Server (IIS) Role

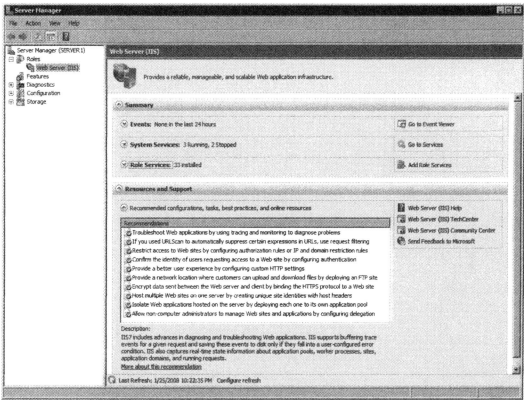

For Server Core the installation process involved a call to the package manager and optionally adding Windows Firewall exceptions to allow for remote administration.

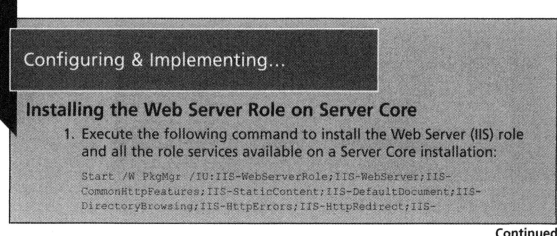

Configuring & Implementing...

Installing the Web Server Role on Server Core

1. Execute the following command to install the Web Server (IIS) role and all the role services available on a Server Core installation:

```
Start /W PkgMgr /IU:IIS-WebServerRole;IIS-WebServer;IIS-
CommonHttpFeatures;IIS-StaticContent;IIS-DefaultDocument;IIS-
DirectoryBrowsing;IIS-HttpErrors;IIS-HttpRedirect;IIS-
```

Continued

```
ApplicationDevelopment;IIS-ASP;IIS-CGI;IIS-ISAPIExtensions;
IIS-ISAPIFilter;IIS-ServerSideIncludes;IIS-HealthAndDiagnostics;
IIS-HttpLogging;IIS-LoggingLibraries;IIS-RequestMonitor;IIS-Http
Tracing;IIS-CustomLogging;IIS-ODBCLogging;IIS-Security;
IIS-BasicAuthentication;IIS-WindowsAuthentication;IIS-
DigestAuthentication;IIS-ClientCertifi-cateMappingAuthentication;
IIS-IISCertificateMappingAuthentication;IIS-URLAuthori-zation;
IIS-RequestFiltering;IIS-IPSecurity;IIS-Performance;IIS-
HttpCompressionStatic;IIS-HttpCompressionDynamic;IIS-
WebServerManagementTools;IIS-ManagementScriptingTools;
IIS-IIS6ManagementCompatibility;IIS-Metabase;IIS-WMICompatibility;
IIS-LegacyScripts;WAS-WindowsActivationService;WAS-ProcessModel
```

When you are installing any role and the corresponding set of features on Server Core you will need to be aware of dependencies. In the full installation you are notified of dependencies when you are selecting roles and role services. In Server Core the dependencies are not quite as clear. For example, classic ASP depends on the ISAPI Extensions and Request Filtering role services along with the Windows Activation Service role and its Process Model role service to be installed.

One of the easiest ways to identify the dependencies is through the OCLIST command, which is available on Server Core installations. Simply executing the command without parameters will show you the list dependencies underneath a particular role or role service as well as their current installation status. For example, Listing 11.1 shows you that the IIS-ISAPIExtensions role service is required to use IIS-ASP by listing it as a child of the IIS-ISAPIExtensions entry.

Listing 11.1 Role Service Dependencies Example

```
Not Installed:IIS-WebServerRole
    |--- Not Installed:IIS-WebServer
    |         |--- Not Installed:IIS-ApplicationDevelopment
    |         |         |--- Not Installed:IIS-ASP
    |         |         |--- Not Installed:IIS-ISAPIExtensions
    |         |         |          |--- Not Installed:IIS-ASP
```

2. If you have enabled Windows Firewall on your server you will need to add the following exceptions:

   ■ Remote Administration Service Exception:

   ```
   NetSh Firewall Set Service Type=RemoteAdmin Mode=Enable
   ```

Continued

- **Windows Management Instrumentation Exception:**

  ```
  NetSh AdvFirewall Firewall Set Rule Group="Windows Management
  Instrumentation (WMI)" New Enable=Yes
  ```

- **Lockdown the AHAdmin DCOM Endpoint to Port 49494:**

  ```
  Reg Add "HKCR\AppId\{9FA5C497-F46D-447F-8011-05D03D7D7DDC}"
  /v Endpoints
  /t REG_MULTI_SZ /d "ncacn_ip_tcp,0,49494"
  ```

- **Remote Web Server Management Exception:**

  ```
  NetSh AdvFirewall Firewall Add Rule Name="Remote Web Server
  Management (RPC)" Dir=In Action=Allow Program="C:\WINDOWS\
  SYSTEM32\dllhost.exe" Protocol=TCP LocalPort=49494

  NetSh AdvFirewall Firewall Add Rule Name="Remote Web Server
  Management (RPC-EPMap)" Dir=In Action=Allow Program="C:\Windows\
  system32\svchost.exe" Service=RPCSS Protocol=TCP LocalPort=RPC-EPMap
  ```

- If your security policy requires a more strict security setting you can use port exceptions on all or specific interfaces.

3. If you want to use Windows Remote Shell you will need to enable it:

   ```
   WinRM QuickConfig
   ```

Depending on your environment, you may not be able to directly administer your servers via the console. To aid in the management of our servers, especially Server Core installations that lack an administrative interface and command line tools, the product group has delivered a package of Remote Server Administration Tools. On Windows Vista the IIS Remote Server Administration Tool supplements the IIS Management Console to enable it to communicate with remote servers and sites.

To access the administration tools you can find them in the Control Panel under System and Maintenance, Administration Tools, Internet Information Services Manager. Figure 11.8 shows the start page for Internet Information Services Manager.

Figure 11.8 Internet Information Services Manager

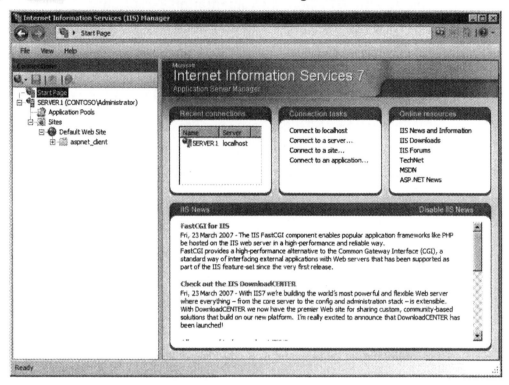

A word of warning—the graphical tools cannot connect to a Server Core installation. There are a few ways to remotely administer IIS on Server Core:

- **Command-line Tools** Using WinRS you can make calls to AppCmd.exe. Note that WinRM does not allow for interact sessions, instead outputting the results of your command.

```
WinRS.exe -Remote:WEBSERVER %SYSTEMROOT%\SYSTEM32\INETSRV\AppCmd.exe
LIST SITE
```

- **Windows Management Instrumentation** Scripting, programming languages, Windows PowerShell, WMIC, WinRM, and WinRS can all administer IIS on Server Core through WMI.

```
WMIC.exe /Output:Sites.txt /Node:WEBSERVER /Namespace:\\root\
WebAdministration Path Site Get
```

- **COM and .NET Programming Interfaces** In addition to WMI you can use the Microsoft.ApplicationHost.AdminManager DCOM object in VBScript/JScript or the Microsoft.Web.Administration assembly through Windows PowerShell scripts and .NET applications.

```
[Reflection.Assembly]::LoadFrom("C:\WINDOWS\SYSTEM32\inetsrv\Microsoft.Web.
Administration.dll");

$WebServer = [Microsoft.Web.Administration.ServerManager]::
OpenRemote("WEBSERVER");

$WebServer.Sites | Format-Table Id, Name;
```

With our server and administration tools setup, you can now configure your server's features to fit your deployment scenario's needs. The following sections will take you through basic configuration steps for each of the functional areas.

Provisioning Web Sites

With IIS installed the next step is to provision a Web site. The Web site is the top level container for content. It defines the entry point into the server and common set of properties that determines how your content is accessed. As part of the default IIS installation a Web site is created called "Default Web Site." You can choose to use this or remove it and create your own. If you choose to use it you should review the settings to ensure they meet your requirements and do not inadvertently expose your content.

You can create a site through the IIS Manager, AppCmd command-line tool, or through the various automation interfaces (e.g., WMI, Microsoft.Web.Administration assembly, Microsoft.ApplicationHost.AdminManager COM object). Under the covers each of these tools is modifying the applicationHost.config file, which is an XML-based configuration file located in the C:\WINDOWS\SYSTEM32\inetsrv\Config folder. Listing 11.2 shows you an example of what an entry looks like inside this file.

Listing 11.2 Site element excerpt from applicationHost.config

```
<configuration>
    ...
  <system.applicationHost>
      ...
    <sites>
        ...
      <site name="Default Web Site" id="1">
        <application path="/">
            <virtualDirectory path="/" physicalPath="%SystemDrive%\inetpub\
            wwwroot" />
        </application>
        <bindings>
            <binding protocol="http" bindingInformation="*:80:" />
        </bindings>
```

```
        </site>

        ...

    </sites>

    ...

    </system.applicationHost>

    ...

</configuration>
```

More advanced users will find the flexibility of tools invaluable. The application-Host.config makes it easy to compare configurations across different environments using merge and differencing tools. For novice users and for everyday use the GUI and command-line tools will meet your needs.

Configuring & Implementing...

Creating a Web Site

1. Open Control Panel and under System and Maintenance | Administration Tools double-click the Internet Information Services (IIS) Manager shortcut.

2. In the **Internet Information Services (IIS) Manager** management console, expand the server node in the left-hand pane, right-click **Sites**, and select **Add Web Site**.

3. In the **Add Web Site dialog** provide a descriptive **Site Name** and a **Physical Path** to the content if desired. Select an **IP Address** for the site and click **OK** (see Figure 11.9).

Host Headers enable you to share an IP address among multiple sites. Starting with HTTP 1.1 the HTTP protocol defined a header value that passes the host name being requested. For example, a call to www.contoso.com will result in "Host: www.contoso.com:80" being passed in the header of the request. This allows the HTTP protocol handler to hand the request off to the appropriate Web site. Because of this parsing if you make a request to the IP address of the Web site directly you will be passed to whichever site does not have a host header value defined.

Continued

Figure 11.9 Add Web Site Dialog

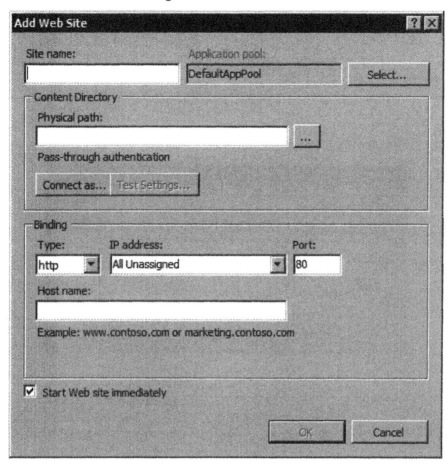

As your environment grows you will probably look to store your Web content on a remote storage device that will allow several Web servers to access the content. This can be implemented using Distribution File System, Network Attached Storage, or Storage Attached Networks. Using any of these technologies saves you from having to publish your Web content to multiple nodes in your Web farm.

When a user browses the site, IIS will need to determine which user's identity it will use to access the content on the remote storage device. If authentication for the content is set to allow anonymous users then IIS will use the anonymous account, which is the built-in IUSR account by default. For protected content IIS will use the credentials provided by the user through one of the authentication modules as the security content for accessing the content.

Continued

You can modify this default behavior by providing a set of credentials for IIS to use when accessing content on network-based storage. When creating a new Web site this shows up as the Contact As button in the Add Web Site dialog. When you click the button, IIS Manager will prompt you for a set of credentials to use as shown in Figure 11.10.

Figure 11.10 Connect As Dialog

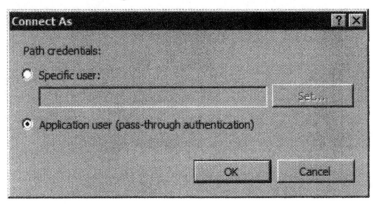

With this option set IIS will use this account to access the content. With this configuration you will need to ensure NTFS permissions are set appropriately to allow this account access to the content. Note that if you rely on NTFS auditing you will also lose the ability to record actions of specific authenticated users since this account will be used for both anonymous and authenticated connections.

If you have created a site and another one exists with the same IP address, port, and host header (or no host header) assigned (known as a binding) then your site will not start automatically. You must resolve the conflict first and then start your Web site. With the Web site started you are ready to add content. Like any folder hierarchy you can simply copy content into the folder structure.

Adding a Virtual Directory

There are times where you might need to reference content stored in another location. You could copy the content, but there is an easier method using Virtual Directories. A virtual directory works by creating a reference in the site configuration to where the content resides. As the request is being processed IIS will parse the request path and locate the content in the appropriate folder based on this configuration.

Configuring the Default Document

A default document is the file that IIS will look for if one has not been specified by the user. For example browsing to http://www.contoso.com/foo will result in the following operations:

1. The server will send the client an HTTP redirect to http://www.contoso.com/foo/.

   ■ The trailing slash indicates that foo is a folder and that the default document should be served to the user. If foo were a file or one of the IIS modules was able to handle the request it would not have been redirected and the process would have delivered whatever the foo document contained.

2. The server will look in the physical folder for Default.htm.

3. If that is not found it will look for Default.asp.

4. If that is not found it will look for index.htm.

5. If that is not found it will look for index.html.

6. If that is not found it will look for iisstart.htm.

7. If that is not found it will look for default.aspx.

If your configuration will not use any of these documents, or uses a particular file more frequently, you should adjust the order to save extra disk I/O operations. Likewise if you use a different name for a default document (e.g., Default.html), then you should add it. This can easily be done in the Default Document section of the configuration using the Add, Remove, Move Up, and Move Down options in the Actions pane as shown in Figure 11.11.

Figure 11.11 Default Document Module Configuration

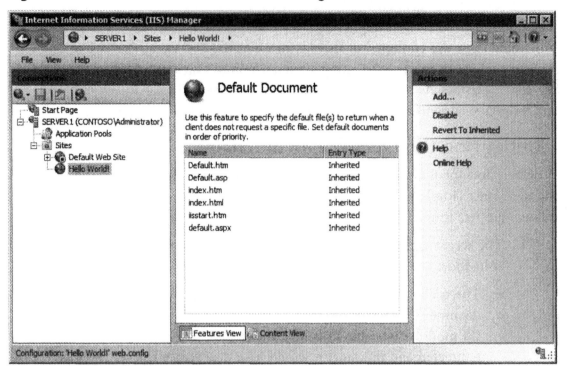

If you do not want the default document to be served you can disable the module. If you do not intend to use the default document module at all on the server you can remove it through Server Manager in the Web Server (IIS) role under Role Services.

Enabling Directory Browsing

Although not frequently used today, IIS provides the ability for users to browse the Web site using a directory listing (see Figure 11.12).

Figure 11.12 Directory Browsing Module Output

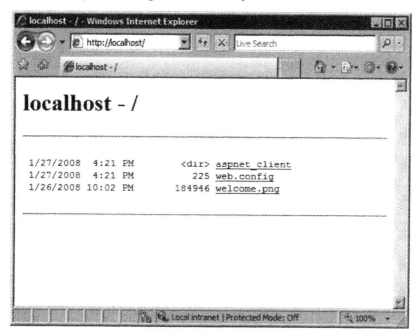

This can be useful if you are using the Web server as a file repository. The default Directory Browsing module allows you to control what file properties are returned with a directory listing (see Figure 11.13).

Figure 11.13 Directory Browsing Module Configuration

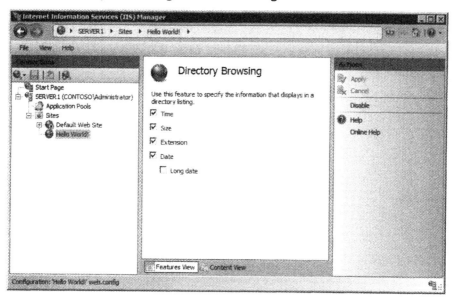

When you enable this module on a site or folder it will return a directory listing only if there is no existing default document in the container (assuming that the default document module is installed and enabled). As part of good security measures you should enable this module only if you have a need for it, otherwise leave it disabled or do not install it in the first place.

Customizing Error Pages

The default error pages that ship with a Web server are often very technical in nature. The default error pages in IIS 7 have been simplified, but are still very cold and technical (see Figure 11.14). If you want to have some fun with users or provide a more user-friendly explanation you can customize your error page.

Figure 11.14 Default File Not Found (404) Error Page for Users

For each HTTP error code you can configure the Web server to deliver a specific piece of static content; you can also redirect the request to another URL on the server or to another site altogether (see Figure 11.15). New for this release is the ability to send static content that is language-specific based on the HTTP request language header, which is set by the user's browser.

Figure 11.15 Add Custom Error Page Dialog

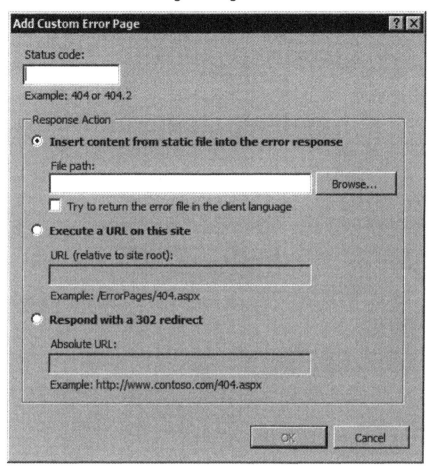

When you are making requests to your Web application from the server, by default, you will receive a detailed error message with more information about the particular request and state. This information will help you quickly understand the conditions under which the problem has occurred and enable you to take the necessary actions to resolve it (see Figure 11.16).

Figure 11.16 Default File Not Found (404) Error Page on the Server

The HTTP Errors module enables you to configure the behavior of this through the Edit Feature Settings link in the action pane. You can choose to send only the custom error pages, only the detailed error messages, or the custom error pages for remote requests and detail error pages for local requests. In most cases the default value will be suitable for your needs. One of the few scenarios you might choose to turn on detailed errors is in a development environment where people are testing a Web application and need the detailed information to help understand what is going on (see Figure 11.17).

Figure 11.17 Edit Error Pages Settings Dialog

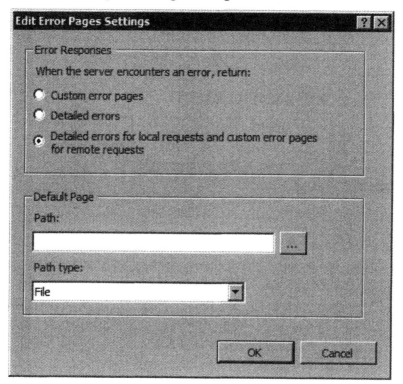

Redirecting Requests

The HTTP Redirect module enables you to redirect requests to a site, folder, or file to another URL (see Figure 11.18). This can be useful if you have moved content but wish to continue to maintain the URL (e.g., www.contoso.com/ products/widget redirects to www.newvendor.com) or give users an easy way to navigate to a specific point (e.g., www.contoso.com/support redirects to support. contoso.com).

Figure 11.18 HTTP Redirect Module Configuration

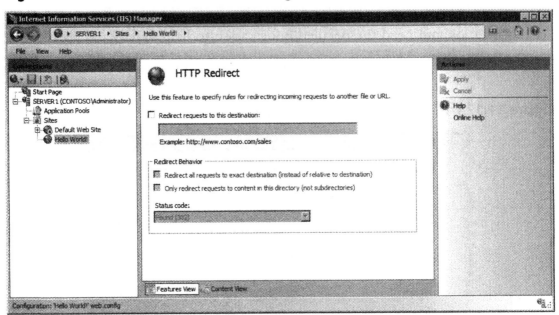

Depending on your needs you can choose to make the redirection permanent, temporary, or simply redirect the client. These choices will affect how search engines interpret the direction. In the case of a permanent redirection they will favor the new URL over the older one when returning results. You can also set the redirect to ignore any additional entries in the path. For example a redirect on www.contoso. com/product/widget can redirect a request of www.contoso.com/products/widget/ datasheet.xps to www.newvendor.com or www.newvendor.com/datasheet.xps. If you need to implement more elaborate HTTP redirection rules you can use one of several third-party HTTP modules found through www.iis.net/downloads.

Adding Custom Response Headers

Response Headers are included with the data being sent back to the client to instruct the browser to do something or for informational purposes. Most actionable response headers are generated by the Web server itself. These include instructions for the client to cache the content (or not), content language, and the HTTTP request status code among others. The custom response headers (see Figure 11.19) may be useful for scenarios where you want to identify a particular server in a load balanced scenario (e.g., send a response header of Web Farm Node: www1.contoso.com).

Figure 11.19 Custom Response Headers Module Configuration

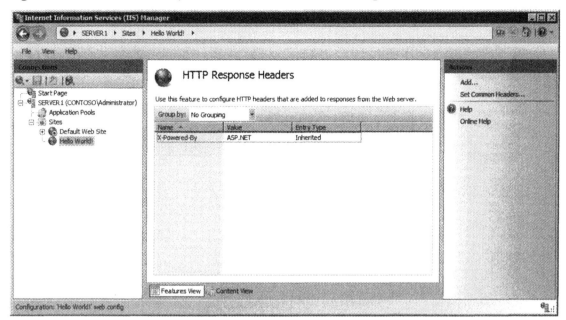

Unlike other modules you cannot uninstall this module. It is integrated into the HTTP protocol handler and exposes the ability to customize response headers. Adding a custom response header is as easy as coming up with a name/vale pair and assigning it to the site, folder, or file level by selecting the element, switching to Features View, and selecting the HTTP Response Headers icon. Be sure not to use a name that could be used by the server as defined in the HTTP protocol specification in RFC 2616. Doing so could cause issues with the client/server communication. The complete list of headers is located in Section 14 of RFC 2616, which can be found at www.w3.org/Protocols/rfc2616/rfc2616.html.

Adding MIME Types

MIME types are used by the HTTP to identify the type of data being sent to the browser. The browser will interpret the MIME type instead of trying to parse out the file extension of the request. This allows you to customize requests to use any extension you want. The reason for this additional measure is that the file extension does not necessarily dictate the content being sent. For example, a page ending in ASPX will typically serve XHTML content, but it can also be used to transmit binary files like images or files. The MIME type is the definitive way for Web browsers to know the format of a file so it can decide how to handle it (see Figure 11.20).

Figure 11.20 MIME Types Module Configuration

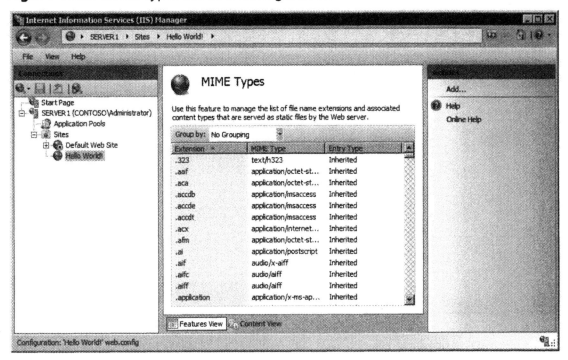

When IIS serves up static content it needs to append a MIME type to the response header. It determines which value to use based on the table of MIME types listed in IIS. It will cross reference the file type and send the corresponding value. For the most part you will not need to edit this section, but it can be useful when new static content types become available. MIME types, as with any configuration options, can be set at the site, folder, and file level. Select the relevant element using the left-hand content tree, switch to Features View, and double-click the MIME Types icon in the middle pane.

Configuring Web Applications

For most Web sites you will likely want to serve up more than static content. Dynamic content is the focus of Web applications. Under IIS there are specific features for Web applications focused on reliability, security, and extensibility. These features include Web applications, modules, and handlers.

The key component of a Web application under IIS is the application pool (see Figure 11.21). An application pool is a container in which one or more Web applications are executed. This change, introduced in IIS 6, isolates Web applications from each other to allow for greater overall system stability. If your application crashes, the IIS administrative process, inetinfo.exe, will start another instance to allow your application to continue to process requests. If you have separated your Web applications or sites using application pools this will limit the effects of the problem to the applications/sites belonging to the application pool. Application pools also give you a container to which you can apply resource constraints (see Windows Server Resource Manager for more information on resource constraints) and maintain a defined security context for application execution. The application pool is useful in a number of scenarios, for example when deploying a Web site that has commerce functionality. You can separate out the commerce section of the site from the rest of the site and apply a different security identity to the commerce functions. If the site itself were to be compromised in any fashion it would minimize the risk to the commerce components. For people hosting applications for multiple customers or lines-of-business you can give them their own execution context without having to invest in a large number of physical servers.

Figure 11.21 Application Pools

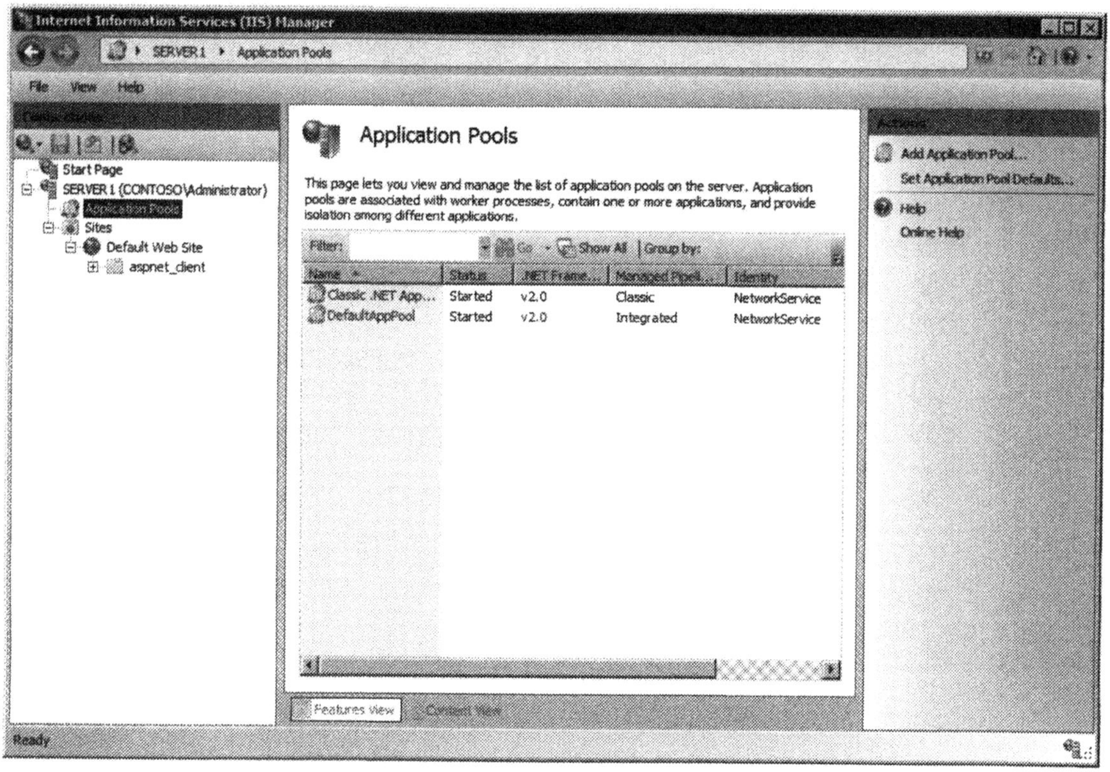

Configuring & Implementing...

Changes to ApplicationHost.config Result in Recycling

With the change to the XML-based configuration system, IIS 7 brought with it a characteristic of ASP.NET behavior that is less than desirable in change detection. As you make changes to your IIS configuration you will need to be aware as to what level of change you are making. If you make, for instance, a change at the server level to the modules list, it will cause all application pools to be stopped and restarted (recycled). For any requests in progress it means they will need to restart their request. When you make the change to a specific application pool setting then all instances of that pool are recycled.

Configuring & Implementing...

Creating an Application Pool

1. Open Control Panel and under System and Maintenance | Administration Tools double-click the Internet Information Services (IIS) Manager shortcut.

2. In the **Internet Information Services (IIS) Manager** management console expand the server node in the left-hand pane, right-click **Application Pools**, and select **Add Application Pool**, as shown in Figure 11.21.

IIS creates two application pools on installation—the DefaultAppPool, which, if installed, supports .NET Framework applications using the Integrated pipeline mode; and the Classic .NET AppPool, which uses the Classic pipeline mode for backward compatibility.

Continued

3. In the **Add Application Pool** dialog shown in Figure 11.22 provide a descriptive name, select the version of the .NET Framework you want to support (or none at all), the Managed Pipeline Mode, and click **OK**.

■ **Integrated Pipeline Mode** ASP.NET-based applications participate in the overall IIS request processing.

■ **Classic Pipeline Mode** ASP.NET-based applications maintain a separate request processing stream from IIS, mainly used for backward compatibility with some older ASP.NET applications.

Figure 11.22 Add Application Pool Dialog

With the application pool created you can now create new applications or convert existing folders to a Web application. Starting with IIS 7 all Web sites are considered Web applications. This is a change from IIS 6 where you could create a Web site and remove all application execution properties. Under the covers this Web site would still be considered an application as it would be assigned to the DefaultAppPool, however it would not be able to execute dynamic content pages because it would not have any rights to do so. The change in IIS 7 makes this process more explicit as opposed to falling back to a default application pool.

Configuring & Implementing...

Converting a Folder to Web Application

1. Open Control Panel and under System and Maintenance | Administration Tools, double-click the Internet Information Services (IIS) Manager shortcut.

2. In the **Internet Information Services (IIS) Manager** management console expand the server and sites nodes in the left-hand pane, right-click a folder within a Web site, and select **Convert to Application**.

3. In the **Add Application** dialog, select the application pool you want your application to run under, if desired set a content access identity, and click **OK** (see Figure 11.23).

Figure 11.23 Add Application Dialog

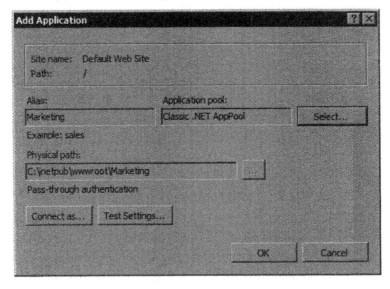

One other option you will see along the way is the ability to add a new Web application within a Web site. This process is the combination of creating a virtual directory and converting it to a Web application.

Configuring & Implementing...

Correlating W3WP.EXE Instances with Web Applications

When you are using Task Manager, at first glance it may be difficult to determine which applications are being executed in which worker processes. One way of determining which application is running is the process identity. If you have assigned a unique identity to each application pool then it will show up beside the instance of w3wp.exe. If you are using the same identity across several pools it is a little more difficult to identify the separation at a glance. IIS Manager exposes the list of active worker processes at the server node level when you double-click the **Worker Processes** icon in the Features View. This view lists each active worker process, its process identifier, and high-level resource consumption information for the processor and memory (see Figure 11.24). The Private Bytes column shows the amount of memory allocated that cannot be shared with other processes. This is typically runtime data or libraries that have been loaded in a special manner just for use by the application (known as rebased libraries). The Virtual Bytes column shows the amount of virtual memory allocated to the worker process. This is a combination of physical memory and the system page file(s).

Figure 11.24 Worker Processes

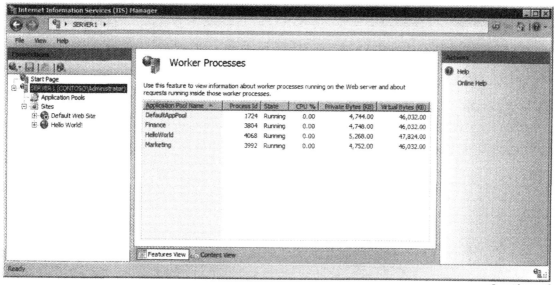

Continued

The AppCmd command-line tool will also help you determine what pool represents what application. In Listing 11.3, which shows the output from AppCmd.exe List WP, you can clearly see that the worker process using the Process Id of 3480 is the Marketing application pool while 4032 is the Finance application pool.

Listing 11.3 Application Pool Process Identities via AppCmd.exe

```
WP "3480" (applicationPool:Marketing)
WP "4032" (applicationPool:Finance)
WP "2128" (applicationPool:HelloWorld)
```

If you can't recall what applications are running inside that application pool then you can open up IIS Manager and use the View Applications action link after selecting the application pool, or as shown in Listing 11.4, use the AppCmd.exe List Apps command-line tool to display a list of applications along with their associated pools.

Listing 11.4 Applications and Their Pools via AppCmd.exe

```
APP "Default Web Site/" (applicationPool:DefaultAppPool)
APP "Hello World!/" (applicationPool:HelloWorld)
APP "Hello World!/finance" (applicationPool:Finance)
APP "Hello World!/finance/accounting" (applicationPool:Finance)
APP "Hello World!/finance/payroll" (applicationPool:Finance)
APP "Hello World!/marketing" (applicationPool:Marketing)
```

Application Pool Settings

Each application pool has number of settings that can be tuned to optimize how it behaves for your Web application. These settings are available through the Advanced Settings action available in the Application Pools section (see Figure 11.25).

Figure 11.25 Application Pool Advanced Settings Dialog

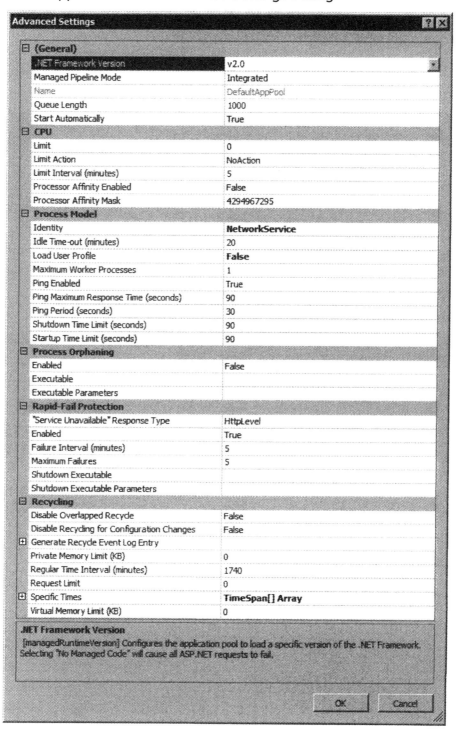

Outside of the application pool process identity most settings in their default state will service a majority of applications. Briefly we will take a look at each section, and highlight some of the features that are new to IIS 7:

- **General Settings** The ability to change pipeline modes, as discussed earlier, is exposed in this section.

- **CPU** The Processor Affinity settings, which enable you to configure your application to favor specific processors, is now exposed through the graphical user interface.

- **Process Model** In previous releases of IIS each application pool would run under a shared user profile, thereby accessing the same temporary folder when performing various file system operations. This introduced the potential for cross-pool information disclosure. In IIS 7 this option was added to allow you to take advantage of a more secure configuration where each individual worker process would maintain their own user profile on the server and thereby isolate activities such as temporary file storage.

- **Process Orphaning** The options in this section are new and exciting for developers as it allows you to attach a debugger to processes to capture their state upon failure. In previous releases you needed to use the tools that shipped as part of the IIS Resource Kit to perform similar actions.

- **Rapid-Fail Protection** The ability to modify the response type when services fail is powerful for scenarios that leverage load balancing. The option to fail to TCP as opposed to a 503 Service Unavailable message allows network load balancers to respond faster as they have less processing overhead to detect server failure.

- **Recycling** Exposes a number of options that were previously hidden in the metabase.

Application Development Settings

Depending on the runtime environment used by your Web application, ASP, ASP.NET, or another CGI-based environment (e.g., PHP, Perl, Python), the settings listed in the Application Development category in IIS Manager expose a number of runtime environment configuration values that you can tune to the needs of your application. A majority of the listed sections, with the exception of ASP and CGI, are specific to ASP.NET Web applications. After time has passed with the introduction of IIS 7 you may see other runtime environments expose their settings through this section as well. Most of these settings will be changed with guidance from your Web application developer. Their settings will largely depend on how the application was developed.

Enabling Third-Party Runtime Environments

One of the more common runtime environments that people add to a Web server is PHP. This processing language is similar in many ways to ASP. Other environments include Ruby on Rails, Perl, and Python. To enable a new runtime environment you will need to add a script map that points IIS to the appropriate executable that will handle the request and allow that executable to run.

Configuring & Implementing...

Enabling PHP on your Web Server

Before you begin you will need to obtain the latest PHP Installation Package from www.php.net/downloads.php.

1. Double-click the **PHP Installation Package**, follow the prompts for the update process to acknowledge the package, read and accept the license agreement.

2. On the **Destination Folder** page, click **Next**.

3. On the **Web Server Setup** page, choose **IIS ISAPI** and click **Next** (see Figure 11.26).

   ■ **ISAPI** Interfaces with IIS using native methods, thereby delivering the greatest performance. This choice may not be possible depending on your application as ISAPI-based applications have specific requirements around multithreaded handling. Consult your application vendor as to whether or not they support ISAPI installations.

   ■ **FastCGI** A revised version of the Common Gateway Interface (CGI) standard that has existed on Web servers for many years

Continued

that deals with performance and security issues that exist in the
original CGI specification.

■ **CGI** The original standard used by Web servers to call out to
external runtime environments to process incoming requests.

Figure 11.26 Web Server Setup Page

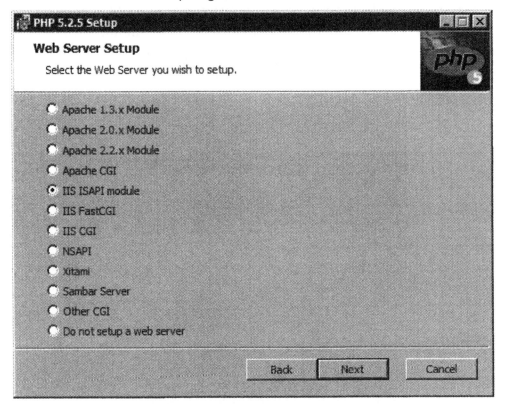

4. On the **Choose Items to Install** page choose the appropriate items
needed by your application and click **Next**.

5. On the **Ready to Install** page click **Install**.

6. When the installation is finished open Control Panel and under
System and Maintenance | Administration Tools double-click the
Internet Information Services (IIS) Manager shortcut.

Continued

7. In the **Internet Information Services (IIS) Manager** management console select the server node.

8. In the middle pane double-click **Handler Mappings**.

9. On the **Handler Mappings** page in the right-hand **Actions** pane click **Add Script Map**.

10. In the **Add Script Map** dialog type *.php* in the **Request Path** text box, provide the **Executable** path to the php5isapi.dll (located in C:\Program Files\PHP by default), provide a descriptive **Name**, and click **OK**.

11. In the **Add Script Map** dialog asking you if you want to allow the extension click **Yes**.

12. Open a Web browser and browse to a PHP page on your site.

Migrating from Previous Releases

If you are migrating from a previous version of Internet Information Services then you may need the compatibility features offered by IIS. The following examples are some of the applications that will need this layer to function properly under IIS 7:

- ASP.NET 1.1-based applications

- Microsoft Office FrontPage server extensions

- Windows SharePoint Services 3.0

- IIS 6.0-based scripts

- Third-party applications that rely on custom metabase data

- IIS 7.0 SMTP service

Compatibility was a focus with this release and the optional role services around compatibility enable you to deploy Windows Server 2008 and continue to support your existing applications. For metabase calls IIS uses a layer called the Admin Base Object (ABO) Mapper. This layer provides translation between older metabase calls and the new ApplicationHost.config sections, elements, and attributes. As Windows Server 2008 deployments expand, expect to find additional guidance around migration available on the Tech Center for the Web Server role located at http://technet2.microsoft.com/windowsserver2008/en/servermanager/webserver.mspx.

Securing Your Web Sites and Applications

Protecting your Web application may require one or more tactics to ensure that the application is accessed only by authorized users:

- **Transport Security** Focused on privacy of data being transmitted between the user and the server

- **Authentication** Provides a method for determining the user's identity

- **Authorization** Evaluates a set of rules to determine if the user is allowed to make the request

This section will take you further into each tactic and the details behind them. There have been few key changes that support more secure communication, authentication, and authorization:

- **IIS_IUSRS Group** Replaces the IIS_WPG group from previous releases to service as a security group to which permissions are assigned that will be required by all the application pool identities.

- **Built-in IUSR Account** Replaces the IUSR_MachineName from previous releases with a built-in account that uses a constant security identifier (SID) across servers that helps to maintain consistent access control lists (ACL). Use of the built-in account eliminates the need to have a password assigned to this account as well. For IIS installations on domain controllers it will prevent the IUSR account from becoming a user-accessible domain account.

- **Inheritance and Merging of IP Restriction Rules** Allows more flexible ways to apply authorization rules based on a single computer, group of computers, a domain, all IP addresses, and/or any unlisted entries.

- **Request Filtering** The URLScan tool, which previously shipped as an add-on tool, is now incorporated in the HTTP protocol handler.

- **Native URL Authorization** A more efficient, globally accessible way to secure specific files and paths without having to rely on third-party tools or ASP.NET.

Transport Security

Protecting the privacy of the data being transmitted is the primary focus of transport security. There are a number of options within the Windows Server 2008 infrastructure to protect the privacy. You may want to wrap all data being transmitted, for example, through a virtual private network or IPSec tunnel. With this as the extreme at one end, IIS provides a more moderate and widely used method for protecting data using Secure Socket Layers (SSL) and Transport Layer Security (TLS). TLS is the more commonly deployed standard today and provides the ability to fall back to SSL 3.0 if the client does not support TLS. SSL/TLS uses digital certificates to encrypt the communication. At a high level the process works as follows:

1. The client makes a request to the Web server for a secure connection.

2. The server sends back its public encryption key.

3. The client checks the key to ensure:

   ■ The name of the host being requested matches the key.

   ■ The key is within the valid date range.

   ■ The key's issuer is trusted by the client.

4. If the client determines that it can trust the server's public key it will send its public key to the server.

5. The server will generate a password and encrypt it using both the client's public key and the server's private key, and send it back to the client.

6. The client will decrypt the password as evidence that the server is the one who sent the password, thereby establishing that only the server and the client will be the only other party capable of reading the encrypted information.

7. The client will send the request to the server encrypted with the password that the server sent to it.

This process has been well established for quite some time and works with all major browsers. IIS fully supports using SSL/TLS certificates to encrypt communication between the server and users. Under the covers, IIS 7 now handles SSL/TLS requests in the kernel by default (it was available in IIS 6, but not enabled by default). This provides a big boost to the performance of secure requests.

New & Noteworthy...

Host Headers and SSL

As mentioned earlier in the chapter, host headers enable you to share an IP address among multiple sites. A call to www.contoso.com will result in Host: www.contoso.com:80 being passed in the header of the request. This allows the HTTP protocol handler to hand the request off to the appropriate Web site. For connections that use secure socket layer (SSL) the ability to use host headers was first introduced in Windows Server 2003 Service Pack 1.

Before you get too excited there are some restrictions that you will need to take into account. The first is that the SSL certificate must contain all the common names of the sites. For example, if you are binding www.contoso.com and store.contoso.com to the same IP address, your SSL certificate will need to contain both host names in the common name field. The most secure approach is to use multiple common names using the subjectAltName property, but it is also the most difficult to obtain as it is not commonly available through certificate authorities (CA). Most certificate authorities promote the use of wildcard certificates instead. A wildcard certificate enables you to use the certificate for all subdomains (e.g., *.contoso.com would work for www.contoso.comstore. contoso.comfoo.contoso.combar.contoso.comfoo.bar.contoso.com). Consult your preferred certificate authority on the cost of a wildcard or subjectAltName certificate as they are not usually supported by the typical offering.

With your new certificate in hand you need to bind the certificate to a Web site. Under the covers IIS does not bind it to the Web site, but the IP address being used. The reason for this is simple; the HTTP header value that contains the host name is encrypted at the time that the HTTP protocol handler needs to make the decision of which certificate to use. This means that you can have only one SSL certificate per IP address and that explains why you need a wildcard certificate or one with the subjectAltName properties included. To see a list of certificates and their corresponding IP address bindings use the following NetSh command:

```
NetSh.exe HTTP Show SSLCert
```

Adding an SSL binding with host header support currently is not supported through the graphical user interface. You will need to use the AppCmd tool, programmatically, or edit the ApplicationHost.config to add the binding. Here is the AppCmd syntax for adding the binding:

Continued

```
AppCmd.exe Set Site /Site.Name:"Contoso Store" /+Bindings.[Protocol='HTTPS',
BindingInformation='*:443:store.contoso.com']
```

With that in place you can now access both of your sites using SSL.

IIS 7 also introduces a new management interface for security certificates. This new interface gives you a single point to review all the certificates installed on your server along with exposing the ability to generate a self-signed certificate from within the interface. Previously self-signed certificates were available only through the command-line SelfSSL tool that shipped with the IIS 6.0 Resource Kit tools (see Figure 11.27).

Figure 11.27 Server Certificates Module Configuration

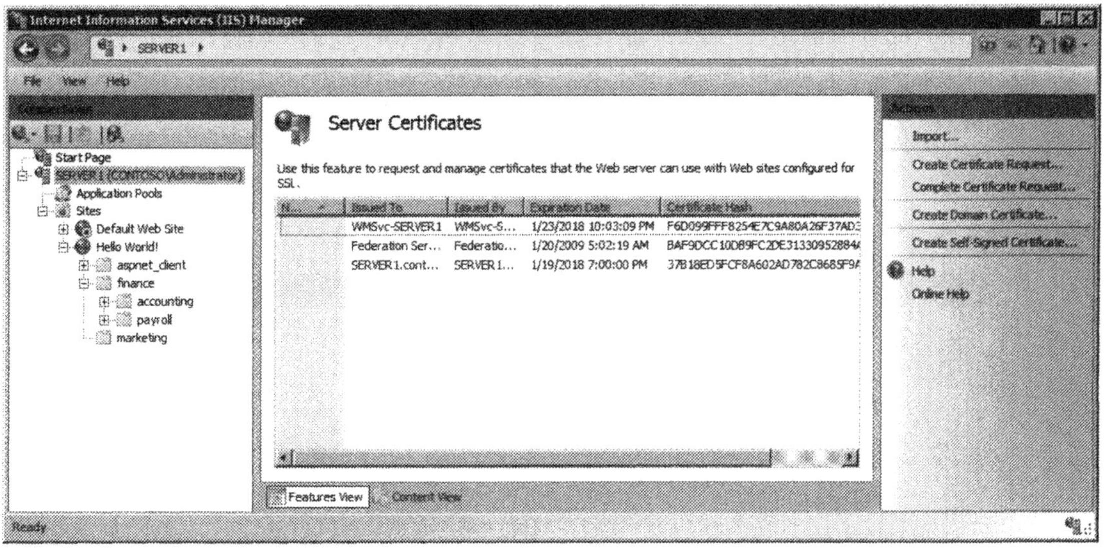

The first step to enabling a secure site is to import or create a new certificate into the server. When creating a certificate you can create one from an online connected certificate authority (CA) like the Certificate Services role that ships with Windows Server 2008, a third-party CA (e.g., Comodo, Thwarte, Verisign), or generate a self-signed certificate. Whichever path you choose the one thing to remember is that the client will need to trust the certificate's issuer in order to trust the certificate. When using a self-signed certificate no one will trust it unless they take steps to specifically add it to their trusted certificates list.

Configuring & Implementing...

Adding a New Security Certificate

1. Open Control Panel and under System and Maintenance | Administration Tools, double-click the Internet Information Services (IIS) Manager shortcut.

2. In the **Internet Information Services (IIS) Manager** management console click the server node, in the middle pane click **Server Certificates**.

3. In the right-hand **Actions** pane click **Create Certificate Request**.

4. In the **Request Certificate** dialog on the **Distinguished Name Properties** page (see Figure 11.28) provide the host name that will be used to access your site (e.g., www.contoso.com) along with your company information and click **Next**.

Figure 11.28 Distinguished Name Properties Page

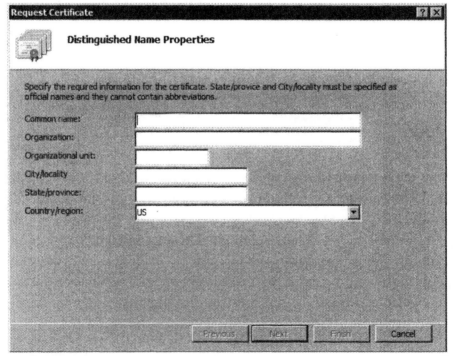

Continued

5. On the **Cryptographic Service Provider Properties** page choose a **Cryptographic Server Provider**, a minimum of 1,024 **Bit Length** for the key, and click **Next** (see Figure 11.29).

- **RSA SChannel Cryptographic Provider** Uses an MD5 hash with an SHA hash, signed with an RSA private key. It supports SSL2, PCT1, SSL3, and TLS1 protocols.

- **DH SChannel Cryptographic Provider** Uses the Diffie-Hellman algorithm and supports SSL3 and TLS1 protocols. Use this algorithm when you must exchange a secret key over an insecure network without prior communication with the client.

- **Bit Length** The default length supported by most browsers and certificate authorities is 1,024 bits. With processors becoming more powerful, expect to see a move toward 2,048 bit length certificates past the year 2010. Be sure to check with your chosen certificate authority to ensure they will support bit lengths larger than 1,024 before increasing this value.

Figure 11.29 Cryptographic Service Provider Page

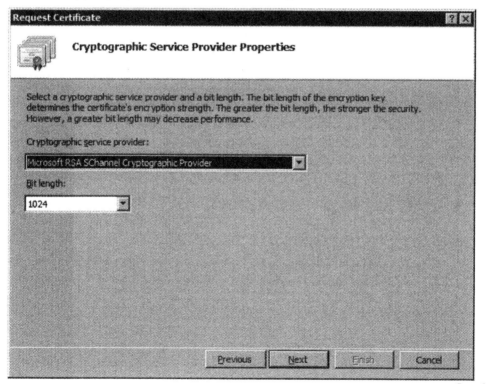

Continued

6. On the **File Name** page provide a path and name of a file where to sort the certificate request and click **Next**.

7. Contact your preferred certificate authority to obtain the response file for your request.

   ■ If you are looking to test out the SSL functionality there are a number of providers that will give you a free trial SSL certificate that lasts for anywhere from 15 to 60 days. This is handy because they have all the trust features of regular certificates with no cost.

8. When you obtain the response file, open **IIS Manager** and return to the **Server Certificates** section.

9. In the right-hand actions pane click **Complete Certificate Request**.

10. In the **Complete Certificate Request** dialog on the **Specify Certificate Authority Response** page, locate the **Certificate Authority's Response** file, provide a **Friendly Name** for the certificate, and click **Next** to complete the process.

Configuring & Implementing...

The Real Differences between SSL Certificates

When you are out shopping for an SSL certificate it can get quite confusing as to what the differences are between the various offerings. For the most part you are buying trust in that the certificate you will be issued is trusted by the client. Under the covers the technical differences boil down to these:

■ **Standard Certificate** A basic security certificate that will suit most users and will work for 40-bit encryption up to 256-bit encryption in most modern browsers

■ **Server Gated Certificate** Before the United States dropped its cryptography export laws in January of 2000 these certificates added a step in the security handshake to see whether the client could support stronger cryptographic algorithms (ciphers). This allowed older browsers an opportunity to step-up their level of encryption if they did not use 128-bit or higher encryption by default.

Continued

■ **Extended Validation Certificate** From a technical perspective these certificates are no different than a standard certificate with the exception that they have some additional metadata attached to the certificate. This metadata is used by browsers that are capable of reading it to determine if they should identify for the user (e.g., turn the address bar green) that the site has gone through extra validation steps. The validation steps and data included are available in the extended validation certificate guidelines at www.cabforum.org. With the data in hand modern browsers will signal to the user through actions like turning the address bar green as shown in Figure 11.30. This feature of popular browsers like Internet Explorer 7 is meant to help users identify the site authenticity.

Figure 11.30 Internet Explorer Address Bar of a Site Using Extended Validation Certificate

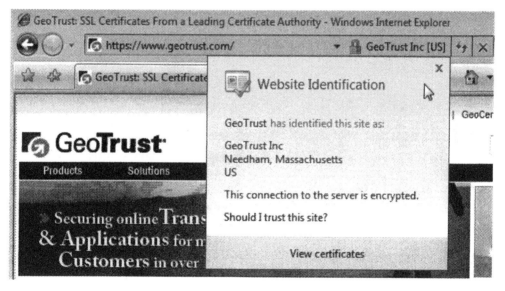

■ **Wildcard Certificate** One of the three preceding certificates, but using an asterisk (*) somewhere in the domain name to signify a wildcard value. This is generally considered a premium service and commercial providers reflect this fact in their pricing model.

Continued

When choosing certificates remember that the level of encryption used in most cases is decided on as a mutual agreement between the client and the server. Both parties can choose to use a minimum level of encryption. With IIS this value is represented by a single check box to force clients to use a minimum of 128-bit encryption or have IIS refuse the connection request. Other advertised features have no impact on the security provided by the SSL-enabled session.

With the certificate in place you can now bind the certificate to your Web site. Under the covers the security certificate is bound to an IP address since the request header information is encrypted when the server needs to determine which certificate to use. Once the certificate is bound you can choose to force the use of SSL on all or part of the site.

Configuring & Implementing...

Enabling Secure Communication on your Web Site

1. Open Control Panel and under System and Maintenance | Administration Tools, double-click the Internet Information Services (IIS) Manager shortcut.

2. In the **Internet Information Services (IIS) Manager** management console expand the server node, right-click your site, and select **Edit Bindings**.

3. In the **Site Bindings** dialog click **Add**.

4. In the **Add Site Binding** dialog set the Type to **HTTPS**. From the **SSL Certificate** list choose your certificate and click **OK** (see Figure 11.31).

Continued

Figure 11.31 Add Site Binding Dialog

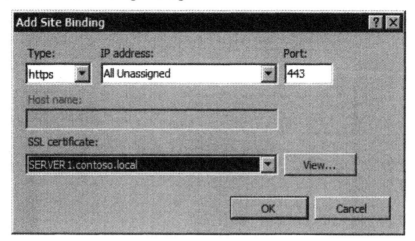

5. In the **Site Bindings** dialog click **Close**.

6. Expand your site node, locate and click a folder (or select the site to enforce SSL on the site as a whole) that you wish to secure.

7. In the middle pane under **Features View**, double-click **SSL Settings**.

8. In the **SSL Settings** module check **Require SSL, Require 128-bit SSL**, and in the right-hand Actions pane click **Apply** (see Figure 11.32).

   ■ Most modern Web browsers support 128-bit SSL. This option was put in place because up until 2000 the United State government restricted the export of certain cryptographic algorithms, which left a good portion of the world stuck with 40- or 56-bit sessions, which provided a lesser degree of security.

Figure 11.32 SSL Settings Module Configuration

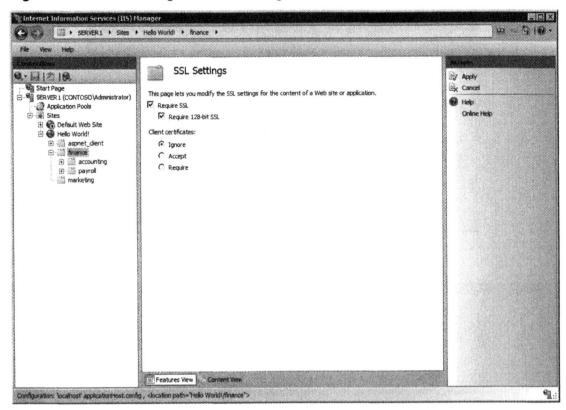

Authentication

Authentication is the process of asserting the identity of the user making a request to the Web server. With this identity we can track who is doing what and evaluate rules to determine if they are authorized to perform specific actions. IIS ships with several types of authentication modules that can be used to determine a user's identity:

- **Anonymous** Enabled by default to allow any user to access public content with a username and password.

- **Basic** Requires the user to provide a username and password. This authentication protocol is a standard across all platforms. It does not perform any sort of encryption with the information provided by the user. As such you should use it with SSL to ensure that the credentials are sent over a secure connection.

- **Digest** Similar to basic authentication but instead of sending the password in clear text it sends an MD5 hash across the wire, which is verified by the server. One of the disadvantages to this method is that it requires that the password be stored using reversible encryption. It is also vulnerable to man-in-the-middle attacks.

- **Windows** Used mainly in intranet scenarios, it allows browsers to use the current user's Windows domain credentials to authenticate the connection. Under the covers it uses NTLM or Kerberos to handle the authentication.

- **Client Certificates** Users provide a digital certificate that is mapped to a user account.

With the exception of client certificates, enabling these authentication modules usually requires nothing more than toggling of their state to enabled. The options for most of the modules are limited to either identity impersonation options or default realms for authentication.

Configuring & Implementing...

Enabling Basic Authentication on a Folder

1. Open Control Panel and under System and Maintenance | Administration Tools, double-click the Internet Information Services (IIS) Manager shortcut.

2. In the **Internet Information Services (IIS) Manager** management console expand the server, site node, and locate a folder to secure (or choose the site as a whole) and click your selection.

3. In the middle pane under **Features View** double-click **Authentication**.

4. Right-click the **Basic Authentication** module and select **Enable** (see Figure 11.33).

Figure 11.33 Authentication Module Configuration

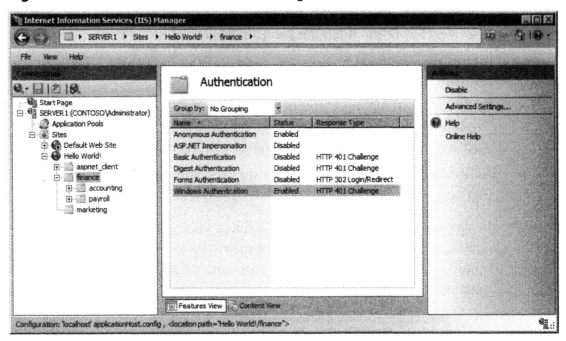

If you are using an ASP.NET runtime environment you have two other authentication modules that are specific to ASP.NET-based Web applications:

- **Forms** Enables you to provide a rich Web-based authentication and user registration experience.

- **ASP.NET Impersonation** Enables you to use a specific account, or the account specified by another IIS authentication module, to execute the application as opposed to the application pool identity.

These authentication modules have been available in ASP.NET since the 1.1 release of the .NET Framework. The IIS Manager exposes a number of the configuration options that traditionally have been managed through the ASP.NET tab in the previous release of IIS or directly in the web.config (see Figure 11.34).

Figure 11.34 Edit Forms Authentication Settings Dialog

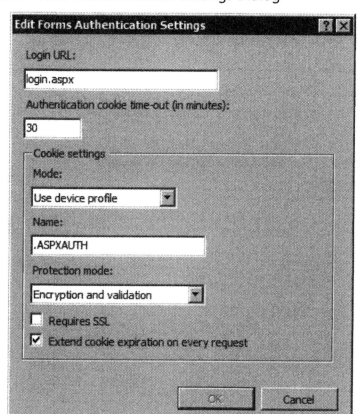

Considerations When Using Client Certificates

You may have noticed some options around whether or not to ignore, accept, or require client certificates. These options are contained within the SSL Settings because the client certificate submission process is a part of the SSL module. This also means that you will need SSL enabled on sites and folders where you want to use client certificate mapping. When a client certificate is received it can be mapped back to a user account in one of three ways:

- **Active Directory Client Certificate Mapping** Looks to the local Active Directory domain to locate a match for the client certificate that was applied. Note that using this option requires that it be used across all sites on the server.

- **One-to-One Mapping** Allows you to specify through the configuration the identity to be used for the user with whom the certificate matches.

- **Many-to-One Mapping** Like one-to-one mapping it allows you to control through the configuration the user identity used when the certificate is matched. This method allows you to map multiple users to a single identity.

At the time of this writing there was no graphical interface to the one-to-one and many-to-one certificate mapping controls. Listing 11.5 shows an example of the configuration values for both of these mapping methods.

Listing 11.5 One-to-One and Many-to-One Certificate Mapping Configuration

```
<configuration>
  ...
  <system.webServer>
    ...
    <security>
      ...
      <authentication>
        <iisClientCertificateMappingAuthentication enabled="true">
          <manyToOneMappings>
            <add name="FinanceUsers" description="Finance Users"
                enabled="true" permissionMode="Allow"
                userName="CONTOSO\FinanceDelegate" password="DF923uD@#2">
              <rules>
                <add certificateField="Subject"
                    matchCriteria="john@contoso.com" />
                <add certificateField="Subject"
                    matchCriteria="jane@contoso.com" />
                <add certificateField="Subject"
                    matchCriteria="sam@contoso.com" />
                <add certificateField="Subject"
                    matchCriteria="sally*@contoso.com" />
              </rules>
            </add>
          </manyToOneMappings>
          <oneToOneMappings>
            <add enabled="true" certificate="-----BEGIN CERTIFICATE-----
MIIBqDCCARECAQAwaTELMAkGA1UEBhMCVVMxDjAMBgNVBAgTBVRleGFzMRMwEQYD
VQQHEwpMYXNDb2xpbmFzMRIwEAYDVQQKEwlNaWNyb3NvZnQxDjAMBgNVBAsTBUl0
```

```
ZWFtMREwDwYDVQQDFAhOVFZPT0RPTzCBnjANBgkqhkiG9w0BAQEFAAOBjAAwgYgC
gYBxmmAWKbLJHg5TuVyjgzWW0JsY5Shaqd7BDWtqhzy4HfRTW22f31rlm8NeSXHn
EhLiwsGgNzWHJ8no1QIYzAgpDR79oqxvgrY4WS3PXT7OLwIDAQABoAAwDQYJKoZI
hvcNAQEEBQADgYEAVcyI4jtnnV6kMiByiq4Xg99yL0U7bIpEwAf3MIZHS7wuNqfY
acfhbRj6VFHT8ObprKGPmqXJvwrBmPrEuCs4Ik6PidAAeEfoaa3naIbM73tTvKN+
WD301AfGBr8SZixLep4pMIN/wO0eu6f30cBuoPtDnDulNT8AuQHjkJIc8Qc=
-----END CERTIFICATE-----"
            userName="CONTOSO\FinanceDelegate" password="DF923uD@#2"
        </oneToOneMappings>
      </iisClientCertificateMappingAuthentication>
    </authentication>
    …
  </security>
  …
</system.webServer>
…
</configuration>
```

Unlike the other two methods, enabling Active Directory Client Certificate is exposed through the graphical interface. The option is exposed as the server node level and when it is set it disables the ability to use one-to-one and many-to-one mappings on the server. To learn how to associate a certificate with an Active Directory user account refer to the Windows Server 2008 documentation around public key infrastructure.

Authorization

With the user's identity established the next step is to determine if the user can perform the action that is being requested. Authorization encompasses a set of rules that are evaluated based on a number of conditions, which could include the user's identity, to provide a decision as to whether or not to allow the user's request to be acted upon. IIS provides three core modules focused on authorization and supporting services—URL authorization, IP authorization, and request filtering.

URL Authorization

Originally brought into the IIS environment by ASP.NET, the URL Authorization module has been rewritten as a native IIS module to allow everyone to take advantage of an easy way of restricting access to specific folders and files. This module allows Web content managers the ability to control access in a manner similar to the use of NTFS permissions. Unlike NTFS permissions, you do not need file system access to the server to apply permissions since everything is managed through the web.config file stored at the root of the site or within a given folder. As well, this allows you to easily carry the permissions with the site as it moves environments.

Configuring & Implementing...

Restricting Access to a Folder

1. Open Control Panel and under System and Maintenance | Administration Tools, double-click the Internet Information Services (IIS) Manager shortcut.

2. In the **Internet Information Services (IIS) Manager** management console expand the server, site node, and locate a folder to secure (or choose the site as a whole) and click your selection.

3. In the middle pane under **Features View** double-click **Authentication**.

4. On the **Authentication** page ensure that the **Anonymous Authentication** module is **Disabled**, select one of the other authentication modules, and click **Enable** in the right-hand **Actions** pane.

5. Click the Back arrow in the top left-hand corner.

6. On the folder page in the middle pane under **Features View**, double-click **Authorization Rules**.

7. On the **Authorization Rules** page click the **Add Allow Rule** in the right-hand action page.

8. Select the **Specified Users** radio button, provide a username, and click **OK** (see Figure 11.35).

Figure 11.35 Add Allow Authorization Rule Dialog

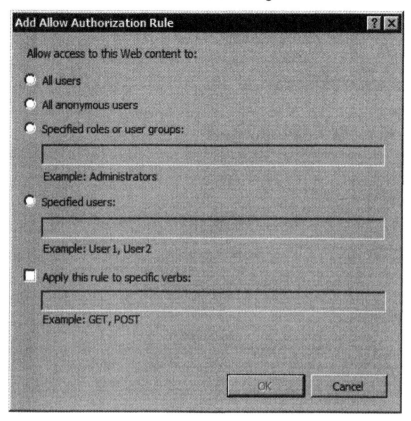

When users attempt to access a page to which they have been denied they will receive a 401.2 unauthorized error. With the addition of detailed error requests the server-side error message gives you a number of useful elements to help you troubleshoot access denied issues being caused by URL authorization. As shown in Figure 11.36, you can see that we are dealing with the URL Authorization Module, that the file is a static file, along with the logon method and user account being used to access the URL.

Figure 11.36 Server-Side Version of Unauthorized Page Access Error Message

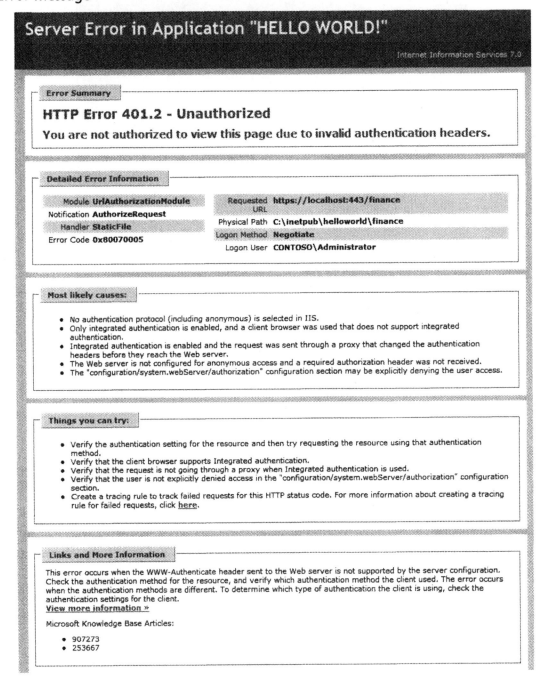

IP Authorization

The ability to restrict access to specific IP addresses has existed for quite some time across both servers and networking devices such as firewalls. In the past this function, like file permissions, was available only through IIS Manager and was tough to replicate across to other servers as it was stored in the metabase. This setting, along with all other configuration options, has been moved to the new XML-based configuration files. This allows you to centralize, copy, and manipulate the settings using new programming interfaces and command-line tools as well as the traditional graphical user interface.

When users attempt to access a page to which they have been denied, they will receive a 403.6 forbidden error. Another option is to restrict users based on their domain names (see Figure 11.37). You will need to enable this through the Edit Feature Settings link in the module page on IIS. Be aware that the added overhead of DNS resolution for each IP address could negatively affect the performance of your application.

Figure 11.37 Add Allow Restriction Rule Dialog with Domain Restrictions Enabled

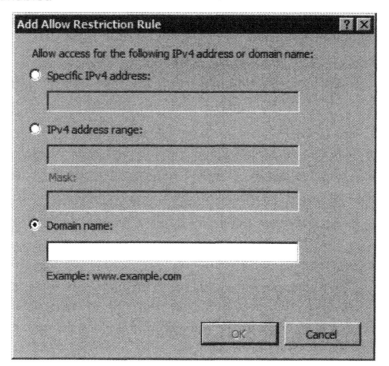

Request Filtering

Previously available through an add-on known as URLScan the request filtering features provide an additional layer of security by inspecting incoming requests for seven different characteristics that might indicate a malformed or malicious attack:

- **Double-Encoded Requests** Attackers may encode a request twice to get around a first layer of filtering. This filter will detect it, reject the request, and log a 404.11 error.

- **High Bit Characters** You may choose to not want to accept non-ASCII characters (e.g., Unicode characters) because your application has not been tested or does not support it. This filter will detect the non-ASCII characters, reject the request, and log a 404.12 error.

- **File Extensions** Your Web application may contain certain files that you do not want anyone to download in any case (e.g., a DLL file in an ASP.NET application). You can add a list of allowed and denied extensions, which will cause IIS to reject the request and log a 404.7 error.

- **Request Limits** This filter will look at how long the content is in the request, the length of the URL, and more specifically the length of the query string. If any of those measurements exceed the maximum values provided this filter will reject the request and log a 404.13, 404.14, or 404.15, respectively.

- **Verbs** There are different types of requests that are identified using verbs (e.g., PUT, GET, and POST). If your application uses only specific types you can tell IIS to reject the request for other types and log a 404.6 error.

- **URL Sequences** There are certain character sequences that you may wish to never have in your request (e.g., a double period "..." often signifies someone trying to relatively traverse your folder structure). This filter will reject requests that match the sequences and log a 404.5 error.

- **Hidden Segments** This filter will enable you to reject requests for content from certain segments. Listing 11.6 contains an example where the bin folder has been specified causing IIS to reject requests that contains the bin folder in the URL. Note that the filter is able to distinguish between a request for http://contoso.com/bin/somefile.dll and http://contoso.com/binary/somefile.zip. The latter request would be allowed through because the filter looks at the URL segment as a whole. It will reject the first request and log a 404.8 error.

Unfortunately IIS Manager does not expose these configuration values. If you want to enable request filtering and tune it to your environment you will need to do it directly in the configuration file or through one of the programmatic APIs. Listing 11.6 shows a sample excerpt of the configuration settings.

Listing 11.6 Request Filtering Configuration Example

```
<configuration>
    ...
    <system.webServer>
        ...
        <security>
            ...
            <requestFiltering allowDoubleEscaping="false"
                              allowHighBitCharacters="true"
                              maxAllowedContentLength="1024768"
                              maxQueryString="64"
                              maxUrl="260">
                <denyUrlSequences>
                    <add sequence="..."/>
                </denyUrlSequences>
                <fileExtensions allowUnlisted="true" >
                    <add fileExtension=".dll" allowed="false"/>
                    <add fileExtension=".xml" allowed="false"/>
                </fileExtensions>
                <hiddenSegments>
                    <add segment="BIN"/>
                </hiddenSegments>
                <verbs allowUnlisted="false">
                    <add verb="GET" allowed="true" />
                    <add verb="PUT" allowed="false" />
                </verbs>
            </requestFiltering>
            ...
        </security>
        ...
    </system.webServer>
    ...
</configuration>
```

Even though you may have to work with the application developer to gain necessary input, this module in particular is extremely useful in reducing the attack surface of your Web application. It is recommended that you take the time to take full advantage of the filters offered by this module.

.NET Trust Levels

With a number of new IIS features based around the .NET Framework it is important to understand how .NET Trust Levels impact your Web applications and IIS itself. A trust level conveys a policy of permissions that an application is allowed to perform. Each trust level has a different set of permissions applied. By default the policies build upon one another from Minimal, which can do very few things to Full, which can perform a number of things:

- **Full Trust** The application is able to execute anything with the security bounds granted to the process identity.

- **High Trust** Restricts applications from calling unmanaged code (e.g., Windows APIs, COM objects, etc.), writing to the event log, message queues, or databases.

- **Medium Trust** Restricts the application from navigating any part of the file system except its own application directory, accessing the registry, or making network and Web service calls.

- **Low Trust** Restricts the application from writing to the file system.

- **Minimal** Restricts the code to doing basic algorithmic work.

If the out-of-the-box trust levels do not suffice application developers can define a custom trust policy based on a series of intrinsic and custom permissions. For a complete list of permissions see the .NET Framework Developer's Guide at http://msdn2.microsoft.com/en-us/library/5ba4k1c5.aspx.

The trust level that you chose for an application should be sufficient for it to function, but like all good security practices, not excessive beyond the needs of the application. In most environments application developers will communicate the level of trust their application needs. As IT professionals understanding what that means helps us understand the boundaries in which the application can function in the server environment. The trust levels can be set at the site and folder level. It is most practical, however, to set it at the level a Web application is defined or the root of the site.

Managing Internet Information Services

One of the big investments in this release of IIS is around management tools. There is both new functionality and existing hidden functionality exposed through the graphical interface, command-line, and programmatic interfaces. In this section we'll take a look at some of the key advancements in the management functionality including delegation, diagnostics tools, and scaling features.

Configuration and Delegation

As part of an overall effort to ease administration, this release saw the delivery of several features that focus around the delegation of administration. Whether you want to simply administer the server from a remote device or build levels of delegation for application owners or clients, IIS delivers a comprehensive system of permissions and services gives you the flexibility to define the scenario that best fits your needs.

The basis for delegation is a decision as to which features you want to delegate. Through IIS Manager, permissions to manage individual settings are controlled at the server, site, and folder level in that order. If you are familiar with ASP.NET's configuration hierarchy, then you will find this concept to be very similar.

All configuration files are defined in a series of schema files split into logical groups—IIS, .NET Framework, ASP.NET, and Runtime Status and Control. These files define the various elements that can be used in the configuration files (see Figure 11.38). Note that not all .NET Framework elements are defined in here, though, just those exposed through IIS configuration tools. All schema files are stored inside the WINDOWS\SYSTEM32\inetsrv\Config\Schema folder. Adding new schemas for custom modules or handlers is as simple as copying the new schema XML file into the folder. At the server level there are five configuration files, each with specific purposes. The first two are stored inside the .NET Framework configuration folder, by default WINDOWS\Microsoft.NET\Framework\<version>\CONFIG, or WINDOWS\Microsoft.NET\Framework64\<version>\CONFIG for the 64-bit runtime:

Figure 11.38 Configuration Files

Schema	IIS_Schema.xml	FX_Schema.xml	ASPNET_Schema.xml	RSCAExt.xml		
Server	Web.config	Machine.config	ApplicationHost.config	Administration.config	Redirection.config
Site	Web.config					
Folder	Web.config					

- **Machine.config** .NET Framework settings that will apply to all applications that run using the Common Language Runtime.

- **Web.config** Subordinate to machine.config, this file contains .NET Framework settings that will apply to all Web applications running under ASP.NET.

The other three server-level files reside in the WINDOWS\SYSTEM32\inetsrv\ Config folder and are specific to the IIS configuration:

- **Redirection.config** Informs the server to look in an alternative location for server configuration (more on this in the Network Load Balancing section later).

- **Administration.config** Settings that control the modules loaded by IIS Manager to administer the server and its sites.

- **ApplicationHost.config** Configuration settings for the server that define sites, virtual directories, and application pools.

Within each site resides a web.config, both at the root, and optionally in folders below. Each file is cumulative, meaning that a web.config in a folder can override certain settings from the root web.config if it is allowed. Inside each configuration file are a series of configuration sections defined in the configSections element. This defines the various groups and individual section containers contained within a configuration file. For each section you can define a scope of definition and delegation mode. This is done by the allowDefinition and overrideModeDefault attributes.

In Listing 11.7 you can see that sections like system.webServer/cgi and system. webServer/security/access will not be allowed to be overridden in the site web. config because they have had the overrideModeDefault attribute set to Deny. As an administrator you can unlock these sections for definition at the site level and below by changing the attribute for a given section to Allow, as seen on the system.webServer/defaultDocument section. This technique can be applied at all levels in the configuration hierarchy. There are also times where certain configuration sections would either be ignored or have a system-wide impact when set at lower levels. The allowDefinition attribute allows you to control the location where the section should be defined. In Listing 11.7 the system.applicationHost values are all set to AppHostOnly because the application host is a server-level concept and doesn't apply to individual sites. Other values for this attribute include:

- **Everywhere** Section can be used in any configuration file (default)
- **MachineOnly** Section can be used only in the Machine.config file
- **MachineToApplication** Section can be used in the Machine.config file or in the Web site and Web application web.config files
- **MachineToWebRoot** Section can be used in the Machine.config file or in the Web site web.config file

Listing 11.7 Configuration Sections Snippet from ApplicationHost.config

```
<configuration>
 …
 <configSections>
  <sectionGroup name="system.applicationHost">
   <section name="applicationPools" allowDefinition="AppHostOnly"
                                overrideModeDefault="Deny" />
   <section name="sites" allowDefinition="AppHostOnly"
                    overrideModeDefault="Deny" />
   …
  </sectionGroup>
  <sectionGroup name="system.webServer">
   <section name="asp" overrideModeDefault="Deny" />
   <section name="caching" overrideModeDefault="Allow" />
   <section name="cgi" overrideModeDefault="Deny" />
   <section name="defaultDocument" overrideModeDefault="Allow" />
   <section name="directoryBrowse" overrideModeDefault="Allow" />
   …
   <sectionGroup name="security">
     <section name="access" overrideModeDefault="Deny" />
     …
   </sectionGroup>
   …
```

```
  </sectionGroup>

   …

 </sectionGroup>
 </configSections>

  …

</configuration>
```

In addition to locking entire sections you can lock specific settings and combinations of settings across several configuration groups using location locking. This allows you to override values for specific folders and files in your Web site. For example, you could apply a different set of authorization rules to a section of your site to prevent anonymous users from accessing the content. When managing feature settings in IIS Manager on specific files or folders it is using this location element in the site's web.config to apply the changes you are specifying.

```
</configuration>
```

In Listing 11.8 the Web application and pages in the finance folder would not be able to use session state since it was both disabled and locked using the allowOverride attribute. The content in the marketing folder, however, would have session state disabled by default, but it could be overridden by a web.config in that folder. The configuration hierarchy plays a foundational role in the IIS feature delegation capabilities. The Feature Delegation user interface is modifying the configuration value with the allowOverride, allowDefinition, and overrideModeDefault attributes.

Listing 11.8 Example of Location Locking

```
<configuration>

    …

    <location path="finance" allowOverride="false">
      <system.web>
        <sessionState enabled="false" />
      </system.web>
    </location>

    …

    <location path="marketing" allowOverride="true">
      <system.web>
        <sessionState enabled="false" />
      </system.web>
    </location>
```

In the Feature Delegation page (see Figure 11.39) you can enable sections to be overridden at lower levels (Read/Write), viewable by delegated users (Read Only), and set at the server-level only (Not Delegated).

Figure 11.39 Feature Delegation Module Configuration

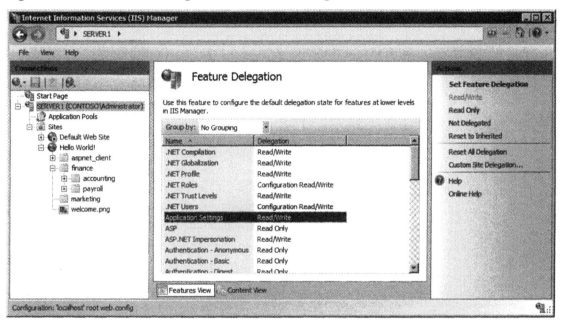

Remote Administration

With specific features delegated to the site level you can set up IIS, under a full installation, to allow remote users to connect to the server using IIS Manager to administer one or more sites using the same rich interface that you access as a server administrator. The Management Service authenticates users using either a built-in user database or through Windows accounts. As with other modules the authentication module for the Management Service can also be replaced with a custom module if your scenario uses another user data store. Enabling the Management Service requires the check of a box. The service security options allow you to choose the source to look for user identities, the transport security certificate, and the ability to restrict access by IP address (see Figure 11.40).

Figure 11.40 Management Service Module Configuration

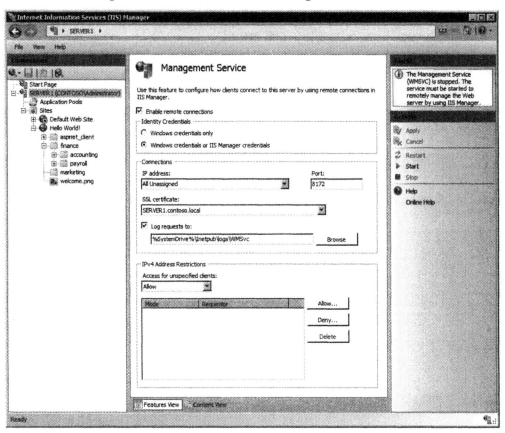

Once the Management Service is enabled you will need to grant users the ability to manage specific sites. Permissions to manage a site or application are granted at their respective level. At the server level the IIS Manager Permissions module will show you an aggregate view of the users and where they have been granted or denied management.

Health and Diagnostics

In this release IIS provides a rich set of new tools for use in maintaining the health and diagnosing problems that may arise. The tools give you different views into the state of IIS in real-time as well as capturing data when a request fails:

- **Runtime Status and Control Data Objects** Set of programmatic objects that enable you to query the state of application pools, Web sites, and Web applications at any given point in time.

- **Detailed Error Messages** Gives you deep insight into the state of the request that you would have had to use an HTTP debugging tool in the past to obtain.

- **Failed Request Tracing** Enables you to obtain snapshots of the request at the moment of failure, which will aid in the diagnosis and resolution of issues that arise.

- **Activity Logging** Historical logging of user requests and basic statistics on the response delivered.

Failed Request Tracing

When a request fails on the Web server, IIS has the ability to capture a snapshot of the request in an XML-formatted log file for later analysis (see Figure 11.41). This data helps administrators and developers understand the state of the request when it was made and provides valuable information that can be used to reproduce the issue. On a typical production server this may become overwhelming with the number of requests. The tracing facilities use a set of rules to determine the conditions under which it should capture data and the level of verbosity for the data it will capture.

Figure 11.41 Failed Request Trace Report

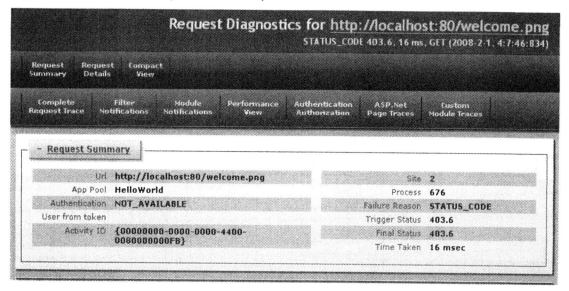

Before you add a rule you will need to enable failed request tracing. This can be done at the site level through IIS Manager. There are two settings that you can configure—the location of the output and the maximum number of traces (see Figure 11.42). The size of each trace will depend on the rules you create. Each component's verbosity level can be tuned or turned off to give you only what you need.

Figure 11.42 Edit Web Site Failed Request Settings Dialog

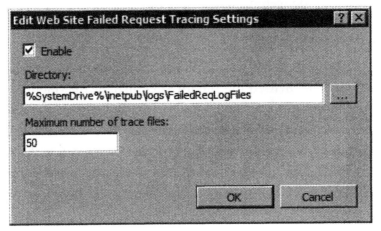

With tracing enabled, you can set up rules at all levels—server, site, folder, and file. Rules can be inherited and ordered to enable you to define the right combination for your needs.

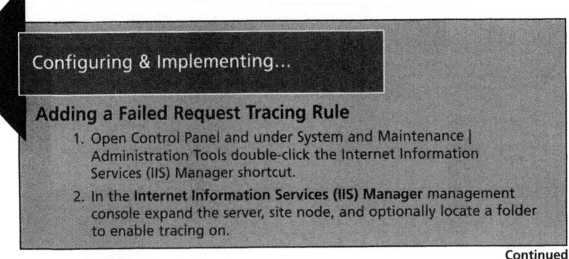

Configuring & Implementing...

Adding a Failed Request Tracing Rule

1. Open Control Panel and under System and Maintenance | Administration Tools double-click the Internet Information Services (IIS) Manager shortcut.

2. In the **Internet Information Services (IIS) Manager** management console expand the server, site node, and optionally locate a folder to enable tracing on.

Continued

3. In the middle pane under **Features View** double-click **Failed Request Tracing Rules**.

4. In the right-hand Actions pane click **Add**.

5. In the Add Failed Request Tracing Rule dialog on the Specify Content to Trace page choose All Content and click Next.

6. On the **Define Trace Conditions** page check **Status Code**, provide the status code (e.g., 404, 500) that you want to trigger a trace on, and click **Next** (see Figure 11.43).

Figure 11.43 Define Trace Conditions Page

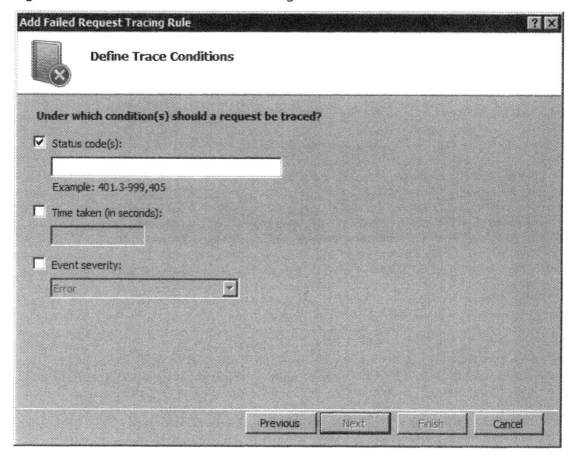

7. On the **Select Trace Provides** page select the appropriate trace providers, set the verbosity and areas to track for each, and click **Finish** (see Figure 11.44).

Figure 11.44 Select Trace Providers Page

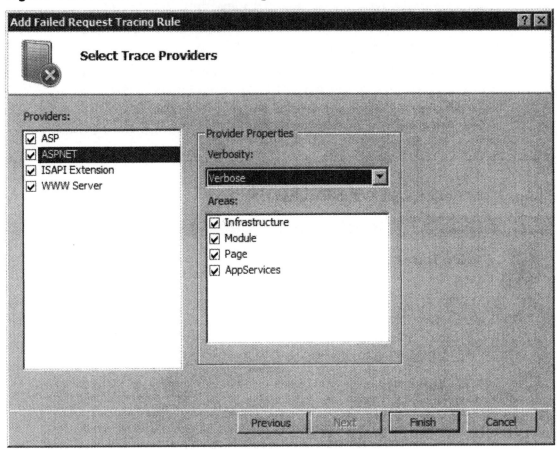

Logging

Activity logging is a standard feature in all Web servers today. For each request made to the server the log records particular properties of both the request and response for later analysis. Using Web log analysis tools you can review aggregate statistics to determine the number of people visiting your server, what they are doing, and when they are doing it. You can also use activity logs as a tool in troubleshooting. IIS ships with logging enabled by default, outputting them to the WINDOWS\SYSTEM32\ LogFiles folder. The logs can be written using IIS, NCSA, and W3C formats (see Figure 11.45). Alternatively, through the configuration files you can add logging to any ODBC-compliant database.

Figure 11.45 Logging Module Configuration

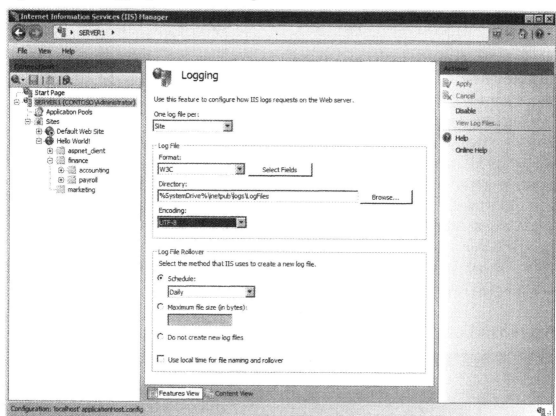

Scaling Your Web Farm

IIS provides the infrastructure necessary to get the most out of your Web applications and scale them out and up when the activity becomes too much for a single server to handle. Each mechanism addresses the scalability issue in a different manner and has a set of trade-offs. It will be up to you to experiment with each to determine to what degree you use caching, compressing, and load balancing for your scenario.

Output Caching

When serving up content it is likely that there will be some degree of repetition in what is being served. With static content like images and client-side script files, caching provides a mechanism for storing the most frequently requested files in memory to minimize the disk I/O when servicing the request. Caching really makes an impact on semi-dynamic content. This means content that changes infrequently but does use a degree of assembly when creating the page. An example is a news page that queries a database for the list of headlines. If that list changes every few hours or few days there is no need to query the database every time a request is made. The output caching module will save a copy of the fully rendered page in memory and serve that to the user instead of consuming the resources to query the database for each request. As you can imagine, this can have a noticeable effect on not only the Web server utilization but the database server as well.

Output caching is applied using a set of policies. Each policy is based on one or more file extensions and a set of rules to govern how long to keep the cached copy in place, and if it should be varied based on a value in either the HTTP request header or query string. This gives you flexibility to deal with multilingual pages, or ones that render a different set of content based on the particular values in the request (e.g., Category.aspx?ID=Shoes does not serve up the same content as Category.aspx?Id=TShirts). At the server level you can control the maximum size of the cache and individual items in the cache as shown in Figure 11.46. The server level also allows you to disable caching for all sites on the server.

Figure 11.46 Output Caching Module Configuration

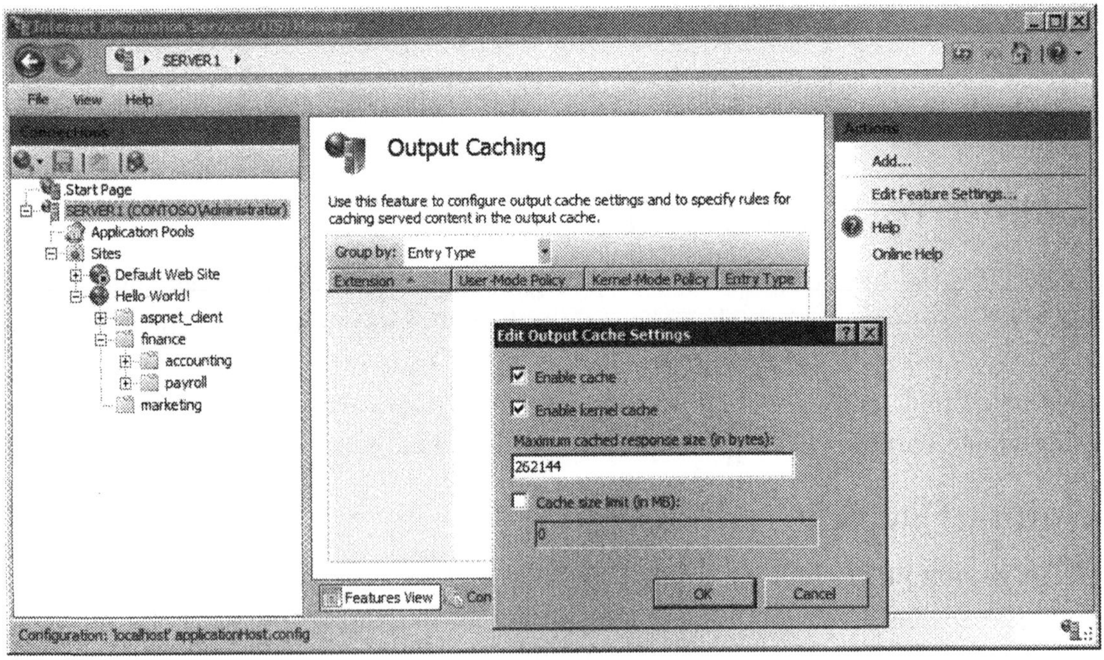

Configuring & Implementing...

Creating a Caching Policy

1. Open Control Panel and under System and Maintenance | Administration Tools double-click the Internet Information Services (IIS) Manager shortcut.

2. In the **Internet Information Services (IIS) Manager** management console expand the server, site node, and optionally locate a folder to enable tracing on.

3. In the middle pane under **Features View** double-click **Output Caching**.

4. In the right-hand Actions pane click **Add**.

5. In the **Add Cache Rule** dialog provide a **file name extension**, select **User-mode caching**, and click **OK** (see Figure 11.47).

   ■ Kernel-mode caching is faster but will not be able to consider any modules that need to run in user mode (e.g., authentication, authorization). It will not support variation by header or query string either. For more information on considerations when using Kernel-mode caching see KB817445 at http://support.microsoft.com/kb/817445.

Figure 11.47 Add Cache Rule Dialog

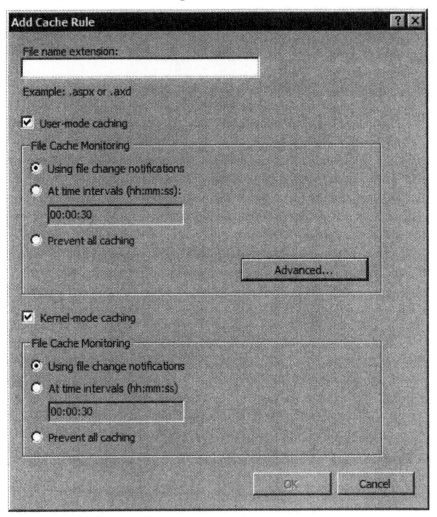

Compression

With the introduction of HTTP 1.1 in 1999, Web browsers gained the ability to decompress content that was sent from a Web server. This was put in place to help curb the exploding demand for bandwidth that was taking place at the time. Through the middle part of this decade the explosion in rich applications using AJAX technologies had another impact on the network bandwidth by causing a lot of "chatter" between the client and the server. The compression standards went a long way to cut the network bandwidth requirements for text-based content such as Web pages and client-side script files by 80% or more depending on the content's compression potential. IIS has shipped with compression capabilities since version 5.0.

Third-party software vendors shipped both companion products that exposed hidden configuration properties and replacements that added features such as the ability to back off on compression when the overall request load was high. Hardware vendors also got into the game by offering offloading devices to handle compression on behalf of the Web server. The hardware market, as of late, is evolving from single-purpose device to offering a suite of application optimization services such as caching and content substitution (which is particularly useful for ASP.NET pages that have a large client-side state field called View State).

Behind the scenes IIS 7 introduced changes to how caching is configured to give administrators more control over the behavior and to capture some of the compressible requests that were slipping through in previous release:

- **Compressed Content Cached by Application Pool** In previous releases all compressed content was cached in a single folder, which could be a potential security risk. In this release they separated out the cache folders by application pool and applied access control entries to ensure that only the application pool worker process can access the folders. In addition a per-application pool cache limit was introduced to provide more flexibility based on the type of application rather than the server as a whole.

- **Static Compression Enabled by Default** Since static content generally receives the biggest benefit for the least cost (no recompression with successive requests), it was turned on by default. After some research the default compression level was adjusted to 7 out of 10 to provide a degree of benefit without a lot of processing expense.

- **CPU Thresholds** Popular among third-party replacements was the ability to have compression back off when the request load was high. Due to popular demand this was introduced into the IIS compression module.

- **Deflate Removed by Default** With GZIP compression you typically get a better compression but under some circumstances like a high traffic Web server you may want to choose to add the Deflate compression scheme back in place. IIS ships with the module, just not configured by default.

- **Compress Based on Content Type** Probably the single biggest change, IIS now makes a decision on compression based on the content-type of the file. Instead of enumerating the various file extensions (e.g., htm, html, aspx, asp, php, etc.) you can classify the content based on their content type. This change will capture a number of requests that slipped through the cracks or were incorrectly classified from the previous file extension-based approach.

In IIS Manager the compression settings are split into server and site level compression. At the server level the settings are focused on enabling the service and setting size limits to control disk utilization (see Figure 11.48). On the site level it is a simple enable/disable setting.

Figure 11.48 Server-Level Compression Module Configuration

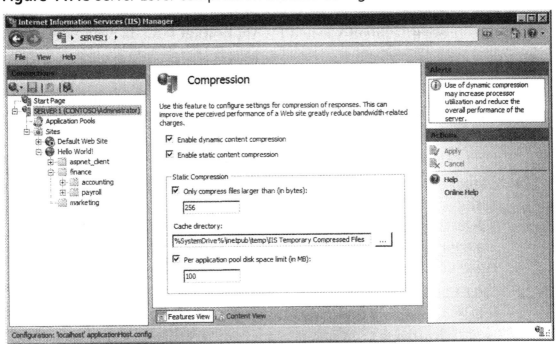

To fine-tune the compression settings you will need to open the ApplicationHost.config file and edit the properties there. Listing 11.9 is an example of what a typical section might look like.

Listing 11.9 HTTP Compression Settings in ApplicationHost.config

```
<configuration>

  ...

  <system.webServer>

    ...

    <httpCompressiondirectory="C:\inetpub\temp\IIS Temporary Compressed Files">
      <scheme name="gzip" dll="%Windir%\system32\inetsrv\gzip.dll" />
      <dynamicTypes>
        <add mimeType="text/*" enabled="true" />
        <add mimeType="message/*" enabled="true" />
        <add mimeType="application/x-javascript" enabled="true" />
        <add mimeType="*/*" enabled="false" />
      </dynamicTypes>
      <staticTypes>
        <add mimeType="text/*" enabled="true" />
        <add mimeType="message/*" enabled="true" />
        <add mimeType="application/javascript" enabled="true" />
        <add mimeType="*/*" enabled="false" />
      </staticTypes>
    </httpCompression>

    ...

    <urlCompression doDynamicCompression="false"
                    doStaticCompression="true" />

    ...

  </system.webServer>

  ...

</configuration>
```

Refer to the IIS product documentation for a further explanation on the various attributes to tune IIS compression settings on your web server.

Network Load Balancing

As the number of requests to your Web site grows you will need to either scale up by using a more powerful server or look at scaling out with larger quantity of servers. IIS traditionally handles scaling out quite well, supporting load balancing through

Windows Load Balancing Services and through dedicated hardware load balancing devices. If you are deploying IIS in a load balanced configuration there are two enhancements in this release that will make your job easier.

Shared Configuration

In a Web farm scenario often you are working to keep the configuration synchronized between nodes so they all respond in the same manner. In previous releases this was a challenging process that was enabled through scripts and other postrelease approaches to growing a Web farm. With this release and the move to break out the metabase into XML-based configuration files the ability to have shared configuration files among Web farm nodes was introduced. In this mode the Administration.config and ApplicationHost.config files are stored in a central location accessible by all nodes in the Web farm along with a configuration encryption key. You can specify a set of server-level credentials to ensure that only the server management process has access to the folder, especially since it stores shared encryption keys in this folder.

TCP and HTTP Service Unavailable Responses

Some hardware load balancing devices are capable only of detecting failures based on the inability to connect at the TCP level. When IIS is returning 503 Service Unavailable messages because of a security issue or the inability to respond to the request because of a high load, it is still alive at the TCP level. In this release of IIS the option to change how the server will communicate service unavailable messages was introduced. The default option remains the HTTP-based message, and a new option was added to refuse connections at the TCP level. In addition you can also trigger an executable to be run that can send an alert or reconfigure a load balancing device. These options are configured at the application pool level under the advanced settings as shown in Figure 11.49.

Figure 11.49 Application Pool Rapid-Fail Protection Settings

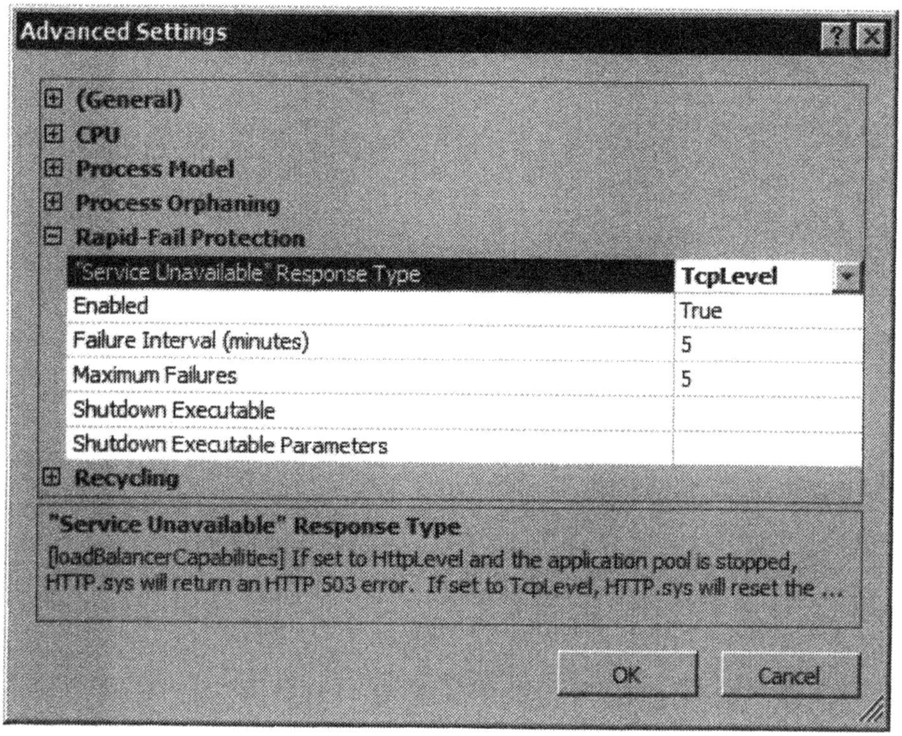

Backing Up and Restoring Server Configuration

In this release the backup and restore for the server configuration did not make it into the IIS Manager tool. There are three commands that can be used with the APPCMD command-line tool to view a list of backups, delete backups, backup, and restore the server-level configuration are as follows:

- AppCmd.exe Add Backup <description>
- AppCmd.exe Restore Backup <description>
- AppCmd.exe List Backup
- AppCmd.exe Delete Backup <description>

When you perform a backup it will copy the following files to the WINDOWS\ SYSTEM32\inetsrv\Backup folder under a folder bearing the description provided in the command line:

- Administration.config
- ApplicationHost.config
- Redirection.config
- MBSchema.xml
- MetaBase.xml

Summary

This chapter focused on configuration of Internet Information Services and high-lighted the new features in this release that make it the first and best choice for Web applications on the Windows platform. In a world where the Web is having a bigger impact inside and outside of the corporate firewall having skills and knowledge around managing Web applications is an asset. We discussed the design goals of this release—a componentized, integrated, extensible, supportable, secure, compatible, and delegation-ready Web application platform. IIS ships across all Windows editions and installs on both the full and Server Core installations.

The componentized architecture allows you to selectively install components within the various role services. Administration can be done through graphical tools like IIS Manager, command-line tools like AppCmd.exe, Windows Management Instrumentation, COM, and .NET programmatic interfaces. Creating a Web site gives you a basic site for static content. Each site contains files, folders, and virtual directories. A site can be further enabled as a Web application to serve dynamic content. IIS ships with ASP and ASP.NET dynamic runtime environments along with support for Common Gateway Interface-based modules. Web applications execute in an application pool container named w3wp.exe. The container provides the security, resource, and process boundaries for the one or more Web applications that you choose to configure inside them. With ASP.NET applications in particular they support classic and integrated pipeline modes. Classic is mainly for backward compatibility in that the ASP .NET request life cycle is kept separate from the IIS request life cycle. In Integrated mode the two are merged into one empowering ASP.NET applications to more tightly integrate with IIS.

Your Web site can be secured using several tactics. Because Web applications flow over standard TCP-based communication the traffic can be wrapped inside a VPN tunnel or IPSec tunnel. It is more common, however, to see Web traffic privacy guarded by a Secure Socket Layers connection that is using a key-based encryption system. Authentication modules, used to identify who is accessing the site, are divided into IIS modules (Anonymous, Basic, Digest, Windows) and ASP. NET (Forms, Impersonation). With the integrated pipeline, however, you could integrate the ASP .NET Forms module with other dynamic runtime environments such as ASP and PHP. User actions are restricted by a new native URL authoriza-tion module, IP address and domain name restrictions, and request filtering. Web applications and modules can be controlled through a series of .NET trust levels powered by .NET's Code Access Security concepts. The levels (minimal, low, medium, high, and full) provide a building-blocks approach to permissions. You can also define your own custom level if none of the predefined ones suit your needs. Other enhancements to the IIS security infrastructure include the change of the default anonymous user account to a built-in system account and renaming the IIS_WPG to IIS_IUSRS.

Flexibility of management has been increased greatly in this release. The configuration system has been changed from a single XML Metabase file to a hierarchy of XML-based configuration files that draw heavily on the ASP.NET legacy. The schema defines the format of the configuration files. The server level configuration files (ApplicationHost.config, Administration.config, Redirection. config, Machine.config, and Web.config) provide you with ultimate control over sites and Web applications. Through a system of delegation using the allowOverride, overrideModeDefault, and allowDefinition attributes you can control at what level a setting can be changed. This allows you to open up administration of lower level sites, applications, folders, and files to other users through the new Management Service. This service allows you to connect to Full installations of Windows Server 2008 with IIS using IIS Manager. Users of this service can be either Windows users or internal IIS users. When an application crashes the new health and diagnostics tools go a long way to helping you get back online quickly. The runtime status and control data objects give you a set of programmatic objects to get a real-time picture of what is happening in the IIS server. Detailed server error messages give you much greater insight into the state of the request being made. Failed Request Tracking provides a forensic snapshot of the state when a defined failure condition occurs. To track user activity the Activity Logging provides the data necessary for Web analysis software to give you an aggregate view of activity on your server. Scaling out your Web farm has never been easier. With output caching to help you squeeze in a few more connections by caching frequently requested, semi-dynamic content and compression to minimize the network bandwidth you can get the most out of your server. When it is time to grow the enhancements to Web farm scenarios through support for a shared configuration and application pool failure to the TCP level you can easily grow your Web farm using either Windows Load Balancing Services or dedicated hardware devices that offload degrees of functionality.

Solutions Fast Track

Installing and Configuring Internet Information Services

- ☑ IIS can be installed across all editions of Windows.

- ☑ On Server Core you will not be able to install role services that rely on the .NET Framework.

- ☑ You can manage your server through IIS Manager, AppCmd, Windows Management Instrumentation, and COM/.NET programmatic interfaces.

- ☑ Servers contain one or more Web sites that contain one or more Web applications, all of which are defined in the ApplicationHost.config file.

- ☑ Application pools are the security and process execution container for one or more Web applications.

- ☑ IIS ships with support for ASP, ASP.NET and CGI-based runtime environments (e.g., PHP, Python, Perl, Ruby on Rails).

- ☑ Migration from IIS 6 was a key focus with backward compatibility components such as the Admin Base Object (ABO) Mapper to help applications function under the architectural changes of IIS 7.

Securing Your Web Sites and Applications

- ☑ Transport Security is handled by Secure Socket Layer certificates that are bound to an IP address and port.

- ☑ SSL can be supported on multiple sites on a single IP address/port as long as the same certificate is used (wildcard, subjectAltName certificates).

- ☑ Certificates can be obtained from a third-party CA, Windows Certificate Services CA, or using a self-signed certificate (for testing purposes).

- ☑ Users are identified through IIS (Anonymous, Basic, Digest, Windows, Client Certificates) and ASP.NET (Forms, Impersonation) authentication modules.

- ☑ The anonymous user module now uses a built-in account called IUSR, whereas Digest encryption still requires passwords to be stored using reversible encryption, and Windows supporting NTLM and Kerberos authentication.

☑ Once identified, a user's request is evaluated based on a set of authorization rules including NTFS, URL, IP authorization, and request filtering.

☑ NTFS permissions typically are used for the application pool identity whereas URL authorization is defined in the web.config based on any of the given authentication modules.

☑ IP Address and Domain Name authorization allows you to include or exclude specific addresses.

☑ Request filtering inspects for potentially harmful requests by looking for double-encoded requests, high bit characters, particular file extensions, request limits being exceeded, HTTP verbs excluded, specific URL sequences, and special hidden segments being accessed.

☑ .NET trust levels (minimal, low, medium, high, and full) govern the execution of ASP.NET and when in integrated mode the entire IIS request pipeline.

☑ A trust level is a policy of allowable permissions that govern resource access such as the file system, database, network, and registry.

Managing Internet Information Services

☑ This release introduced a rich XML configuration hierarchy that allows for delegation of everything.

☑ The XML configuration is driven by a set of schema files.

☑ Configuration files exist at the server level (ApplicationHost.config, Administration.config, Redirection.config, Machine.config, and Web.config), at the site level (web.config), and applications/folder below that (web.config).

☑ The files have a cumulative effect on the end configuration for a particular request, however sections can be explicitly allowed or disallowed from having certain attributes or entire sections redefined.

☑ Once delegation has been configured you can enable remote administration of specific features and sites using the IIS Management Service (which is not supported on Server Core).

☑ When something goes wrong the detailed error messages provided by IIS give you a sense of the context of the request.

☑ If you are not sure how to reproduce an error you can use failed request tracking to take an automatic snapshot of the request state when an error that matches a specific rule occurs.

☑ You can get more out of your server using output caching, which can use both a user-mode (fast) and kernel-mode (faster, but restrictive) caching along with static and dynamic content compression.

☑ Both caching and compression have basic configuration exposed through IIS Manager with all advanced settings configurable through the configuration files.

☑ When expanding your environment you can take advantage of network load balancing to scale out your configuration.

☑ A shared configuration setup helps you to deploy a site across several servers without having to configure the site on each server manually.

☑ When a server in the farm fails you can have it stop responding at the TCP level or execute a program to tell the load balancer about the need to reconfigure.

Frequently Asked Questions

Q: How do I administer IIS on Server Core?

A: You can administer the server through AppCmd, Windows Management Instrumentation, and the COM/.NET programmatic interfaces. You cannot use IIS Manager, even to connect to the server remotely.

Q: What is the difference between IIS on Windows Server 2008 and Windows Vista?

A: Beyond some minor bug fixes, and improved configuration interfaces in IIS Manager the major difference is the connection limit—on Windows Vista a maximum of 10 concurrent connections (three on Basic/Starter, three on Home Premium, and 10 on Ultimate/Business/Enterprise), and no limit on Windows Server 2008.

Q: What is an application pool?

A: It is a container for one or more Web sites and Web applications. It provides the context for the request to be processed and the security context under which the processing is completed.

Q: Can I use multiple SSL certificates and host headers?

A: It depends. SSL certificates are bound to an IP address and port. If the SSL certificate is a wildcard certificate or uses the subjectAltName property you can use it across multiple sites as long as the host name satisfies the wildcard value or subjectAltName list.

Q: I am trying to access an ASP page and I know that I have installed support for Active Server Pages, but IIS keeps giving me a 404 error How do I fix it?

A: When adding any new server extensions make sure to allow the ISAPI filter or CGI executable at the server level under ISAPI and CGI restrictions.

Q: My server is under a high load but I want to take advantage of compression. Can I have the best of both?

A: You can use the CPU throttling properties in the configuration files to set a percentage of processor utilization under which the compression will back off. This will allow your server to focus on serving more requests until the number drops.

Q: I've configured an ASP.NET application, and when I run it I receive a SecurityPolicyException stating that I do not have enough permissions. I have checked the file system and the application pool worker process has enough rights to execute properly. Where should I look?

A: Check the .NET Trust Level for the Web application, it defines a policy as to which actions and resources the application can use and execute.

Q: I want to prevent users from accessing a specific folder on my server. I have set up URL authorization to allow only specific users but it never prompts me for a password. How do I get IIS to prompt for credentials?

A: Review the selected authentication modules. Chances are you have the Anonymous authentication module enabled. It will need to be disabled to force other authentication modules to prompt the user for credentials.

Q: I have two Web applications, one that uses Active Directory Certificate Mapping and one that uses many-to-one certificate mapping. I have configured the AD-based mapping application but I cannot find the many-to-one certificate mapping option. Where should I look?

A: When you enable Active Directory Certificate Mapping it will automatically disable many-to-one and one-to-one certificate mapping for all sites on the server.

## Chapter 12

Configuring Web Infrastructure Services

Solutions in this chapter:

- **Installing and Configuring FTP Publishing Services**

- **Installing and Configuring SMTP Services**

☑ **Summary**

☑ **Solutions Fast Track**

☑ **Frequently Asked Questions**

Introduction

It's easy to think of Internet Information Server (IIS) as a mechanism for hosting Web sites or Web applications. However, IIS provides several optional components that can either be used by themselves, or as a complement to an existing site. One such component is the File Transfer Publishing Service (FTP). FTP provides a mechanism for allowing users to upload and download files from your Web server.

Another optional component is the Simple Message Transfer Protocol (SMTP) service. You can use the SMTP service to turn your IIS server into an e-mail server, although the capabilities provided by the SMTP service are very crude when you compare them to those found in a full-blown mail server product, such as Microsoft Exchange. In this chapter, you will learn how to deploy, configure, and secure the FTP and the SMTP services.

Installing and Configuring FTP Publishing Services

File transfer services based on the File Transfer Protocol (FTP) have been around since 1971. As a protocol it has become a standard method for transferring files between remote systems running on various operating systems (see Figure 12.1). The protocol and surrounding services were designed to give the user a simple interface while handling the complexities of the differences among file systems under the covers. In addition to FTP you can use other protocols such as HTTP, WebDAV (based on HTTP), BITS, SMB/CIFS, and others. FTP delivers advantages when handling data exchange among remote systems and those with disparate system architectures.

Figure 12.1 FTP Service Model as Outlined in RFC 959

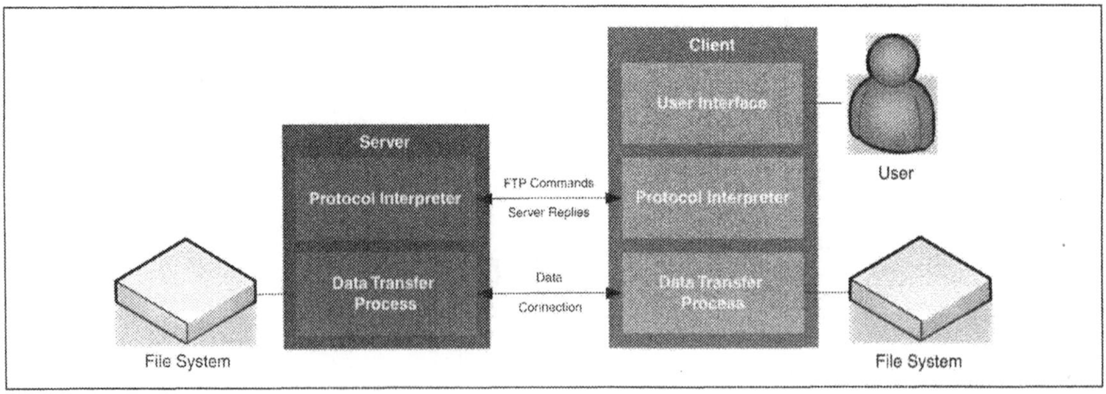

When you connect to an FTP server a control connection is established between the client and server's protocol interpreter. This process typically occurs on port 21 using TCP. Over this control connection the client sends commands and receives replies from the server acknowledging the commands in a fashion similar to a Telnet session. When a data transfer is requested, a data connection is established between the client and server. At this layer all of the translation occurs between the two file systems. Data transfer happens using either active or passive transfer modes. Each mode has a different method for establishing the data connection. In the active mode the server establishes the data connection with the client using a random TCP port 1024 and higher. In passive mode the client establishes the data connection with the server using a random TCP port 1024 and higher. For most security professionals the challenge of opening up ports 1024 and higher on either the client or the server is perplexing. Many firewalls deal with this scenario by listening to the control connection for the PORT command and dynamically opening the port needed to establish the data connection.

In 1997 an extension was proposed in the form of RFC 2228. This extension deals with the fact that FTP as defined back in 1971 uses an unencrypted control and data connection. Prior to RFC 2228 authentication credentials and files were transmitted without any privacy controls. The RFC describes the use of SSL to secure the control and data channels to address this problem and is known as FTPS. This release of IIS ships the FTP Publishing Service with support for SSL encryption. This provides a viable alternative to the recommendations for using WebDAV over HTTPS in past releases for secure file transfer.

In addition to security, this release also adds support for Unicode characters and IPv6 addressing, and taps into the rich architecture of IIS as part of a major rewrite. The tight integration allows you to leverage custom authentication modules, rich logging and tracing capabilities, and integration with the Web server for publishing scenarios.

Installing the FTP Publishing Service

With the amount of work undertaken by the IIS product group, the major enhancements to the FTP Publishing Service did not make it into this release. Microsoft shipped the IIS 6 FTP Publishing Service with some compatibility fixes in its place. To gain access to all of the new FTP Publishing Service features you will need to download the out-of-band release from the IIS Download Center (www.iis.net/downloads).

The Web release is a full installation; however it does require that the Web Server (IIS) role be installed, as it integrates in with the IIS Management functionality. If you have previously installed the Web Server role with the FTP Publishing Service you will need to uninstall it before using the Web release.

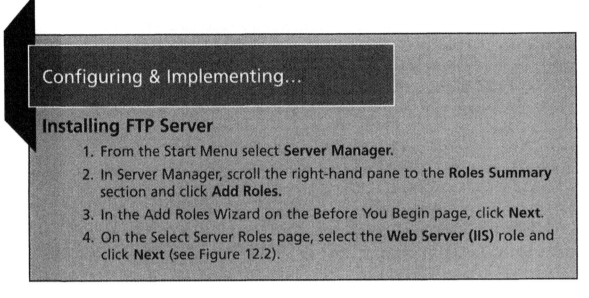

Configuring & Implementing…

Installing FTP Server

1. From the Start Menu select **Server Manager.**
2. In Server Manager, scroll the right-hand pane to the **Roles Summary** section and click **Add Roles.**
3. In the Add Roles Wizard on the Before You Begin page, click **Next.**
4. On the Select Server Roles page, select the **Web Server (IIS)** role and click **Next** (see Figure 12.2).

Figure 12.2 Select Server Roles Page

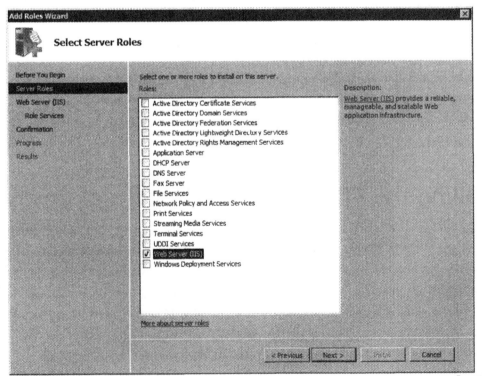

Continued

5. The Web Server (IIS) page gives you a brief description of the role along with some important notes and links to more information on the role (see Figure 12.3). Click **Next.** If this is your first time setting up the Web Server (IIS) role, you should read these notes, as they cover common issues that you will encounter.

Figure 12.3 Select Web Server (IIS) Role Services Page

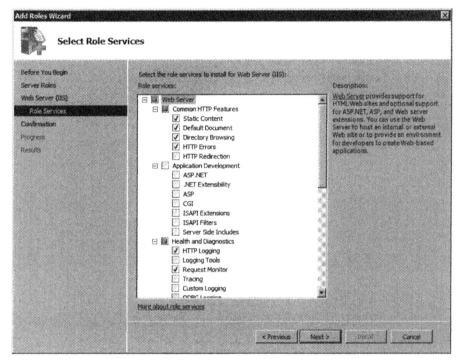

6. On the Role Services page you are prompted to install several groups of services to the role; leave the default values for the purposes of the upcoming exercises, and click **Next**.

7. On the Confirmation page review your choices and click **Install**.

8. On the Results page, review the success or failure of the installation and click **Close**.

9. Double-click the **FTP Server installation package**, follow the prompts for the update process to acknowledge the package, then read and accept the license agreement.

10. On the Custom Setup page, accept the defaults and click **Next** (see Figure 12.4).

Continued

Figure 12.4 Custom Setup Page

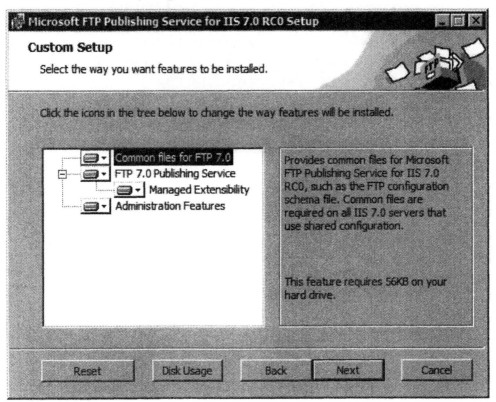

11. On the Ready to Install page click **Install.**

12. On the Completed page click **Finish**. Figure 12.5 shows the IIS Manager with the FTP server installed.

Figure 12.5 IIS Manager with the FTP Server Installed

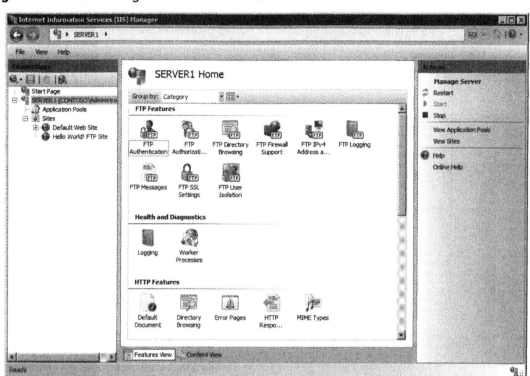

With the installation complete you will see the Web Server role appear in Server Manager. From here you can get an overview of related event log entries, Windows services, and the Role Services you have chosen to install. In addition the Resources and Support section gives you at-your-fingertips access to resources that go in-depth on common issues and best practices to consider. The FTP Server will not appear in Server Manager. You will administer the FTP server through the IIS Manager.

Server Core installations of Windows Server 2008 allow you to install FTP Services in its entirety. The only functionality that will not be available is the graphical administrative interface and managed authentication modules.

Configuring & Implementing...

Installing the FTP Server on Server Core

1. Execute the following command to install the Web Server (IIS) role and the basic set of the role on a Server Core installation:

```
Start /W PkgMgr /IU:IIS-WebServerRole;IIS-WebServer;IIS-
CommonHttpFeatures;IIS-StaticContent;IIS-DefaultDocument;IIS-
DirectoryBrowsing;IIS-HttpErrors;IIS-HealthAndDiagnostics;IIS-
HttpLogging;IIS-RequestMonitor;IIS-Security;IIS-RequestFiltering;
IIS-Performance;IIS-HttpCompressionStatic;IIS-WebServerManagementToo
ls;IIS-IIS6ManagementCompatibility;IIS-Metabase;WAS-WindowsActivation
Service;WAS-ProcessModel
```

2. Execute the following command to start installation of the FTP Server, follow the prompts for the update process to acknowledge the package, and read and accept the license agreement:

```
MSIEXEC /I FTP7_X86.msi
```

3. On the Custom Setup page, accept the defaults and click **Next**.

4. On the Ready to Install page click **Install**.

5. On the Completed page click **Finish**.

6. If you have enabled Windows Firewall and intend on using only non-secure FTP connections you will need to enable communication using the following commands:

```
NetSh AdvFirewall Set Global StatefulFTP Enable

NetSh AdvFirewall Firewall Add Rule Name="File Transfer Protocol
(In)" Dir=In Action=Allow Program="C:\WINDOWS\SYSTEM32\SvcHost.exe"
Protocol=TCP Service=ftpsvc
```

7. If you have enabled Windows Firewall and intend on using secure FTP (FTPS) connections you will need to disable stateful FTP inspection:

```
NetSh AdvFirewall Set Global StatefulFTP Disable
```

Continued

8. If you have enabled Windows Firewall and intend on using passive FTP connections, enable the FTP Publishing Service to communicate outwards as well:

```
NetSh AdvFirewall Firewall Add Rule Name="File Transfer Protocol
(Out)" Dir=Out Action=Allow Program="C:\WINDOWS\SYSTEM32\SvcHost.
exe" Protocol=TCP Service=ftpsvc
```

9. If you have enabled Windows Firewall on your server you will need to add the following exceptions:

- Remote Administration Service Exception

```
NetSh Firewall Set Service Type=RemoteAdmin Mode=Enable
```

- Windows Management Instrumentation Exception

```
NetSh AdvFirewall Firewall Set Rule Group="Windows Management
Instrumentation (WMI)" New Enable=Yes
```

- Lockdown the AHAdmin DCOM Endpoint to Port 49494

```
Reg Add "HKCR\AppId\{9FA5C497-F46D-447F-8011-05D03D7D7DDC}" /v
Endpoints /t REG_MULTI_SZ /d "ncacn_ip_tcp,0,49494"
```

- Remote Web Server Management Exception

```
NetSh AdvFirewall Firewall Add Rule Name="Remote Web Server
Management (RPC)" Dir=In Action=Allow Program="C:\WINDOWS\
SYSTEM32\dllhost.exe" Protocol=TCP LocalPort=49494

NetSh AdvFirewall Firewall Add Rule Name="Remote Web Server
Management (RPC-EPMap)" Dir=In Action=Allow Program="C:\Windows\
system32\svchost.exe" Service=RPCSS Protocol=TCP LocalPort=
RPC-EPMap
```

- If your security policy requires a more strict security setting you can use port exceptions on all or specific interfaces.

10. If you want to use Windows Remote Shell you will need to enable it:

```
WinRM QuickConfig
```

A word of warning—the graphical tools cannot connect to a Server Core installation. This is because the graphical tools have a dependency on the IIS Management Service which is built on the .NET Framework and cannot be run on Server Core because of that. There are a few ways to remotely administer IIS on Server Core:

- **Command-line Tools** Using WinRS you can make calls to AppCmd.exe. Note that WinRM does not allow for interact sessions, instead outputting the results of your command.

```
WinRS.exe -Remote:FTPSERVER %SYSTEMROOT%\SYSTEM32\INETSRV\AppCmd.exe
LIST SITE
```

- **Windows Management Instrumentation** Scripting, programming languages, Windows PowerShell, WMIC, WinRM, and WinRS can all administer IIS on Server Core through WMI.

```
WMIC.exe /Output:Sites.txt /Node:FTPSERVER /Namespace:\\root\
WebAdministration Path Site Get
```

- **COM and .NET Programming Interfaces** In addition to WMI you can use the Microsoft.ApplicationHost.AdminManager DCOM object in VBScript/JScript or the Microsoft.Web.Administration assembly through Windows PowerShell scripts and .NET applications.

```
[Reflection.Assembly]::LoadFrom("C:\WINDOWS\SYSTEM32\inetsrv\Microsoft.Web.
Administration.dll");

$WebServer = [Microsoft.Web.Administration.ServerManager]::OpenRemote
("FTPSERVER");

$WebServer.Sites Ð Format-Table Id, Name;
```

With our server setup, you can now configure your server's features to fit your deployment scenario's needs. If you need to uninstall the FTP Publishing Service make sure that you remove it before removing the Web Server role. The following sections will take you through basic configuration steps for each of the functional areas.

Provisioning FTP Sites

With the FTP Server installed the first step is to provision a new FTP site. You can setup independent FTP sites or bind them with a Web site on the server in this release. The latter is particularly useful in shared hosting environments to provide access to hosted sites.

Configuring & Implementing...

Creating an FTP Site

1. Open **Control Panel** and under System and Maintenance | Administration Tools, double-click the **Internet Information Services (IIS) Manager** shortcut.

Continued

2. In the Internet Information Services (IIS) Manager management console, expand the server node in the left-hand pane, right-click **Sites**, and select **Add FTP Site**.

3. In the **Add FTP Site** dialog, provide a descriptive **FTP Site Name** and a **Physical Path** to the content and click **Next**.

4. On the Binding and SSL Settings page, select an **IP Address** and optionally an **SSL certificate** and click **Next** (see Figure 12.6).

Figure 12.6 Binding and SSL Settings Page

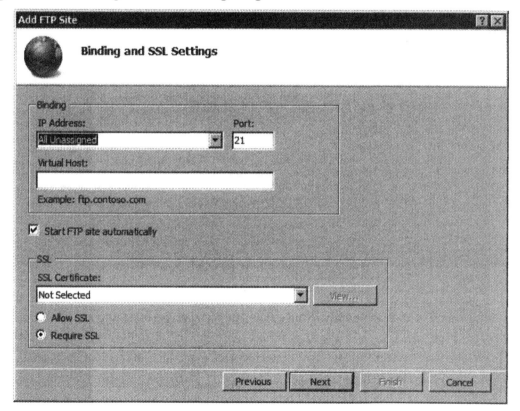

5. On the Authentication and Authorization Information page, select the **Authentication** module you want to use and the default site **Authorization** rules, and click **Finish** (see Figure 12.7). Unlike previous versions there is no site-wide Read / Write authorization. In this release you define a set of authorization rules that are applied to all users, all anonymous users, or a specific group of users or roles.

Figure 12.7 Authentication and Authorization Information Page

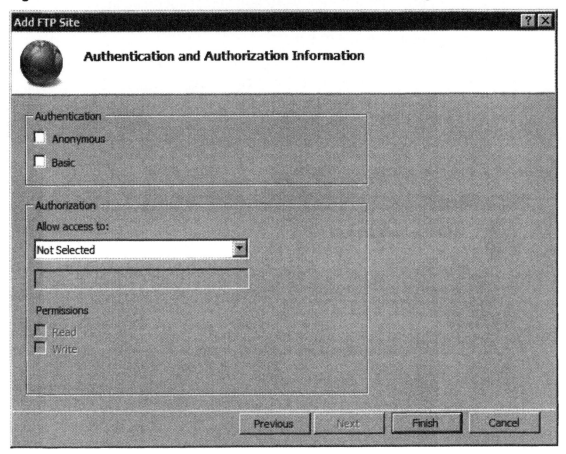

In addition to creating a standalone FTP site you can also enable an existing Web site with FTP access. This will allow users to work with their site content using the FTP protocol while keeping the configuration information tied to the Web site.

With the site created there are a set of advanced settings available to help you fine tune the behavior of your FTP Site. They can be found by selecting the site from the left-hand pane, and in the right-hand Actions pane under Manage FTP site clicking **Advanced Settings** (see Figure 12.8).

Figure 12.8 FTP Site Advanced Settings

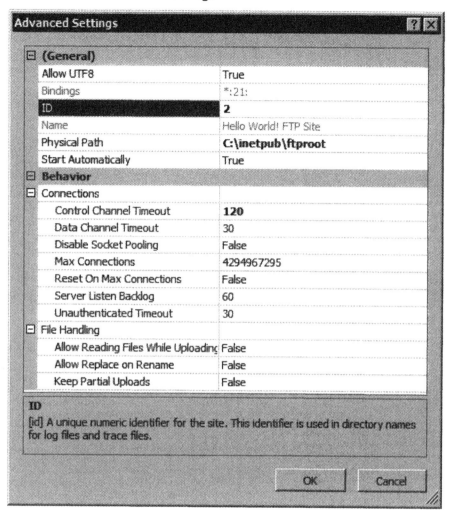

Directory Browsing

When using the FTP service clients will often browse the various folders to locate the content that they want to retrieve. You have the option of configuring several options that will affect how the items within a folder are listed, as shown in Figure 12.9.

Figure 12.9 FTP Directory Browsing Module Configuration

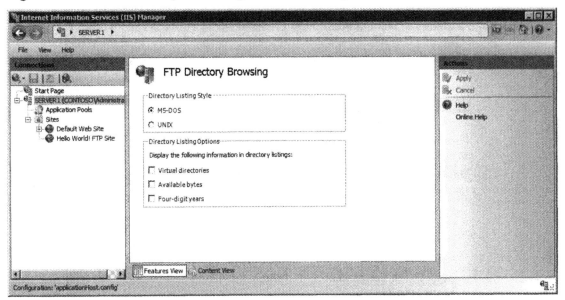

The first option group is a style preference between MS-DOS and UNIX directory listings:

- Listing 5.1 MS-DOS Directory Listings

  ```
  02-01-08 08:33PM      0 default.txt
  11-02-06 04:39AM      15821312 imageres.dll
  ```

- Listing 5.2 UNIX Directory Listings

  ```
  -rwxrwxrwx 1 owner      group            0   Feb 1   20:33   default.txt
  -rwxrwxrwx 1 owner      group   15821312   Nov 2    2006   imageres.dll
  ```

The second option group focuses on the information included within the directory listings. The first option enables or disables showing virtual directories in the listings. In previous releases this was disabled by default, creating the effect of "hidden" folders. With the industry shying away from the security-by-obscurity approach this option was exposed to give you the choice depending on your business needs. The second option determines if the remaining bytes are reflected in the directory listings. Typically this will show the remaining bytes left on the disk; however, if a folder-level quota has been enabled then it will reflect the remaining bytes based on the quota. The final option determines if the last modified date should reflect a two or four digit year.

Firewall Support

The Firewall Support feature allows you to facilitate passive connections to the FTP server when it is behind a firewall (see Figure 12.10). When the FTP server provides a port number for the client to establish a data connection, the IP address is embedded within the response. This feature allows you to both limit the port range and specify the appropriate external IP address. Once this feature is configured you will need to forward the specified port range from your firewall.

Figure 12.10 FTP Firewall Support Module Configuration

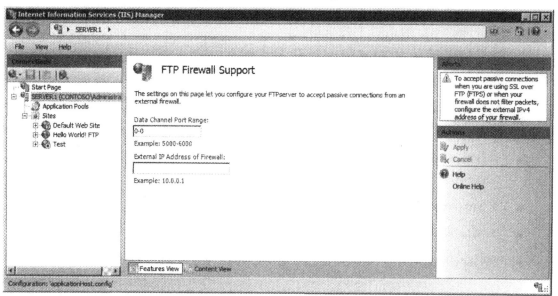

Configuring & Implementing...

Active versus Passive Mode

The key difference between active and passive FTP mode is the designation of who opens the port for the data connection. In active mode the client is responsible for opening the port. In passive mode it is the server which is responsible. In most deployments you will see passive mode as the preferred

Continued

> method because it represents the least amount of configuration and confusion across the spectrum of users that you will service. To enforce an even more secure approach look to add Windows Firewall with Advanced Security to your deployment using the service filtering options that ship with Windows Server 2008 to lock it down further to the FtpSvc service identifier.

Messages

When FTP sessions are established, authenticated, ended, or denied connection you can include a message for the user. The Messages feature gives you a chance to configure the default message at the server and specific site messages as shown in Figure 12.11. The first option group allows you to suppress the FTP service banner, enable the use of variables in the message, and show detailed error messages when connecting from the local machine. The variables available include:

- **%BytesReceived%** Total number of bytes sent to the client in the current session

- **%BytesSent%** Total number of bytes received from the client in the current session

- **%SessionID%** Unique identifier for the current session

- **%SiteName%** Site Name for the FTP Site being accessed

- **%UserName%** Username of the currently logged in user

The following is an example of the variables in action:

```
Thank you for visiting %SiteName%, during your session %SessionID% we sent
%BytesReceived% bytes to you and we received %BytesSent% from you. We look
forward to seeing you again %UserName%!
```

The above message would generate output similar to this:

```
Thank you for visiting Hello World! FTP Site, during your session 1 we sent 5,729
bytes to you and we received 5,828,640 from you. We look forward to seeing you
again CONTOSO\Colin!
```

Figure 12.11 FTP Messages Module Configuration

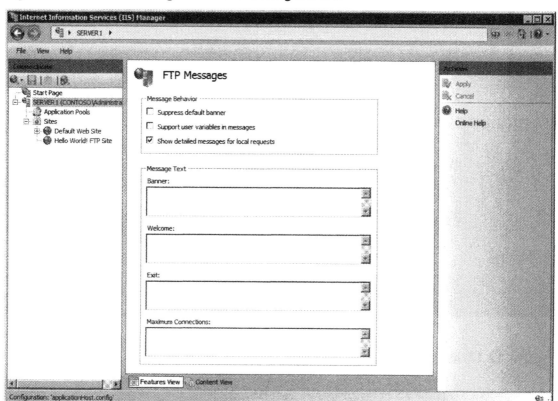

Virtual Directories

With FTP sites being used for more than managing Web content, it was quite
common to see virtual directories being used to link to different folders within
the system. A virtual directory works by creating a reference in the site configuration to where the content resides. The FTP service will parse the link and allow
users to navigate to the folders as if they were another regular folder within the
structure.

Configuring & Implementing...

Creating a Virtual Directory

1. Open **Control Panel** and under System and Maintenance |
   Administration Tools double-click the **Internet Information
   Services (IIS) Manager** shortcut.

2. In the Internet Information Services (IIS) Manager management
   console, expand the server and sites nodes in the left-hand pane,
   right-click your FTP site, and select **Add Virtual Directory.**

3. In the **Add Virtual Directory** dialog, provide the **Alias** of the virtual
   directory to be used by requests and a **Physical Path** to the content,
   and click **OK** (see Figure 12.12).

Figure 12.12 Add Virtual Directory Dialog

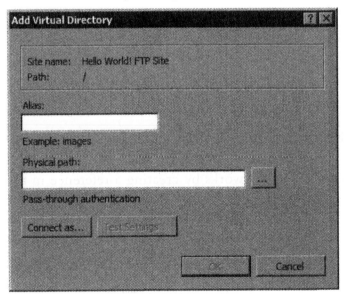

Application Pools

With the changes in architecture in this release, FTP sites have been shifted to use
application pools for processing requests. This allows you to separate out the sites into

individual worker processes and control their process identity and resource utilization as you would with a Web site.

Configuring & Implementing...

Converting a Folder to an Application

1. Open **Control Panel** and under System and Maintenance | Administration Tools double-click the **Internet Information Services (IIS) Manager** shortcut.

2. In the Internet Information Services (IIS) Manager management console, expand the server and sites nodes in the left-hand pane, right-click a folder within a FTP site, and select **Convert to Application.**

3. In the **Add Application** dialog select the application pool you want your application to run under, if desired set a content access identity, and click **OK** (see Figure 12.13).

Figure 12.13 Add Application Dialog

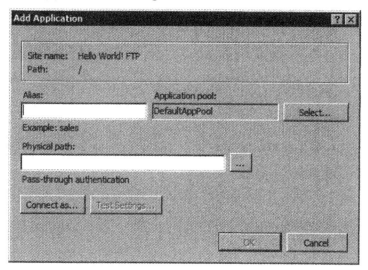

Securing Your FTP Site

Protecting your FTP site may require one or more tactics to ensure that the content is only accessed by authorized users:

- **Transport Security** Focused on privacy of data being transmitted between the user and the server

- **Authentication** Provides a method for determining the user's identity

- **Authorization** Evaluates a set of rules to determine if the user is allowed to make the request

This section will take you further into each tactic and the details behind them. The most notable changes in these sections for this release are the support of SSL and the ability to use custom authentication modules.

Transport Security

Protecting the privacy of the data being transmitted is the primary focus of transport security. There are a number of options within the Windows Server 2008 infrastructure to protect the privacy. You may want to wrap all data being transmitted, for example, through a virtual private network or IPSec tunnel. With this as the extreme at one end, IIS provides a more moderate and widely used method for protecting data using Secure Socket Layers (SSL). SSL uses digital certificates to encrypt the communication. There are two approaches to engaging SSL: implicit, where SSL is used for communication upon the initial connection, and explicit SSL, where SSL is enabled for the session after the initial connection is made. FTP Services was built to support explicit SSL, which is the method documented in RFC 2228. The implicit method has been documented in several drafts, but never formally adopted by the IETF. At a high level the explicit FTP SSL process works as follows:

1. The client connects to the server (typically through TCP port 21).

2. The client requests a secure session.

3. The server sends back its public encryption key.

4. The client checks the key to ensure:

   - The name of the host being requested matches the key,

   - The key is within the valid date range, and

- The key's issuer is trusted by the client.

5. If the client determines that it can trust the server's public key, it will send its public key to the server.

6. The server will generate a password and encrypt it using both the client's public key and the server's private key and send it back to the client.

7. The client will decrypt the password as evidence that the server is the one who sent the password, thereby establishing that only the server and the client will be capable of reading the encrypted information.

8. The client will send the request to the server encrypted with the password that the server sent to it.

9. With the secure channel established, the FTP client continues on to authenticate the user and begin the session.

Before you can enable your FTP site for secure communication you will need to register a security certificate. IIS 7 introduces a new management interface for security certificates used by all protocols it handles. This new interface, as shown in Figure 12.14, gives you a single point to review all of the certificates installed on your server along with exposing the ability to generate a self-signed certificate from within the interface. Previously self-signed certificates were only available through the command-line SelfSSL tool that shipped with the IIS 6.0 Resource Kit tools.

Figure 12.14 Server Certificates Module Configuration

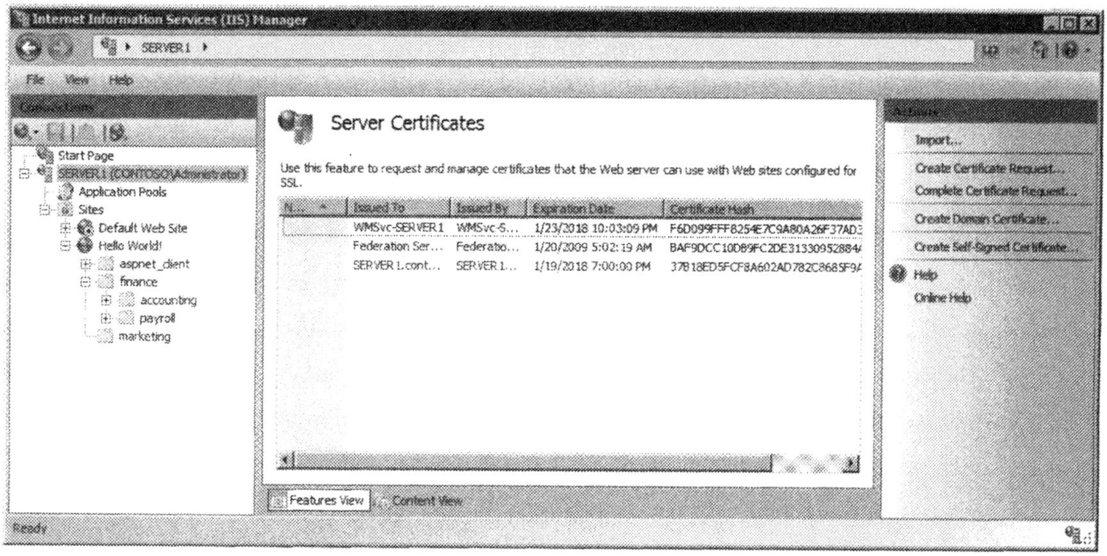

The first step to enabling a secure FTP site is to import or create a new certificate into the server. When creating a certificate you can create one from an online connected certificate authority (CA) like the Certificate Services role that ships with Windows Server 2008, a third-party CA (e.g., Comodo, Thwarte, Verisign), or generate a self-signed certificate. Whichever path you choose the one thing to remember is that the client will need to trust the certificate's issuer in order to trust the certificate. When using a self-signed certificate no one will trust it unless they take steps to specifically add it to their trusted certificates list.

Configuring & Implementing...

Adding a New Security Certificate

1. Open **Control Panel** and under System and Maintenance | Administration Tools double-click the **Internet Information Services (IIS) Manager** shortcut.

2. In the Internet Information Services (IIS) Manager management console, click the server node, and in the middle pane click **Server Certificates**.

3. In the right-hand actions pane click **Create Certificate Request**.

4. In the **Request Certificate** dialog on the Distinguished Name Properties page, provide the host name that will be used to access your site (e.g., ftp.contoso.com) along with your company information and click **Next** (see Figure 12.15).

Continued

Figure 12.15 Distinguished Name Properties Page

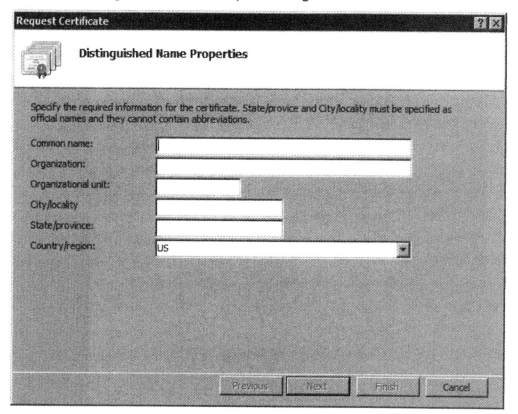

5. On the Cryptographic Service Provider Properties page, shown in Figure 12.16, choose a **Cryptographic Server Provider** and a minimum of 1,024 **Bit Length** for the key, and click **Next**.

- **RSA SChannel Cryptographic Provider** Uses an MD5 hash with an SHA hash, signed with an RSA private key. It supports SSL2, PCT1, SSL3, and TLS1 protocols.

- **DH SChannel Cryptographic Provider** Uses the Diffie-Hellman algorithm and supports SSL3 and TLS1 protocols. Use this algorithm when you must exchange a secret key over an insecure network without prior communication with the client.

- **Bit Length** The default length supported by most browsers and certificate authorities is 1,024 bits. With processors becoming more powerful expect to see a move towards 2,048 bit length certificates past the year 2010. Be sure to check with your chosen certificate authority to ensure they will support bit lengths larger than 1,024 before increasing this value.

Continued

Figure 12.16 Cryptographic Service Provider Page

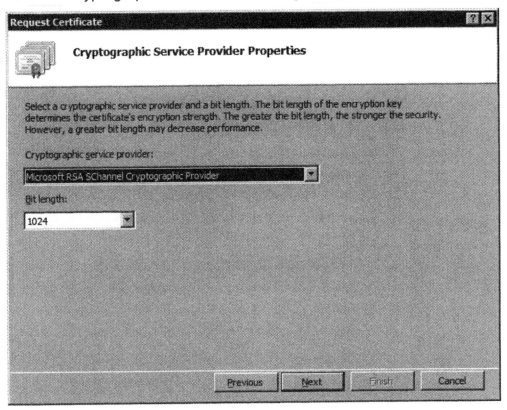

6. On the File Name page provide a path and name of a file for sorting the certificate request and click **Next.**

7. Contact your preferred certificate authority to obtain the response file for your request. If you are looking to test out the SSL functionality, there are a number of providers, such as Comodo and GeoTrust, that will give you a free trial SSL certificate that lasts anywhere from 15 to 60 days. This is handy because they have all of the trust features of regular certificates with no cost.

8. When you obtain the response file open IIS Manager and return to the Server Certificates section.

9. In the right-hand actions pane click **Complete Certificate Request.**

10. In the **Complete Certificate Request** dialog on the Specify Certificate Authority Response page, locate the **Certificate Authority's Response** file, provide a **Friendly Name** for the certificate, and click **Next** to complete the process.

With the certificate in place you can now bind the certificate to your FTP site. Once the certificate is bound you can choose to allow or force the use of SSL for the control channel, data channel, or both.

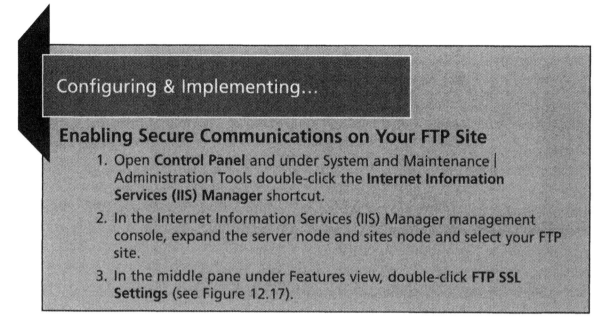

Configuring & Implementing...

Enabling Secure Communications on Your FTP Site

1. Open **Control Panel** and under System and Maintenance | Administration Tools double-click the **Internet Information Services (IIS) Manager** shortcut.

2. In the Internet Information Services (IIS) Manager management console, expand the server node and sites node and select your FTP site.

3. In the middle pane under Features view, double-click **FTP SSL Settings** (see Figure 12.17).

Figure 12.17 FTP SSL Settings Module Configuration

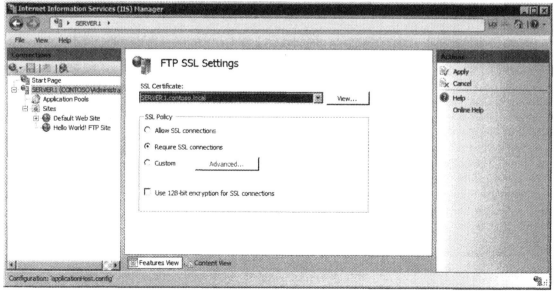

Continued

4. On the FTP SSL Settings page, select an **SSL Certificate**, choose whether to **Allow** or **Require SSL connections**, and in the actions pane click **Apply**. As with \Web connections you can force a minimum of 128-bit encryption.

Any form of encryption will add overhead to the processing. If you have an FTP server that is heavily used or needs to coexist with other applications, you can also customize the behavior of SSL to protect one of the channels or just the login process. The choice will depend on your data privacy policies. At a minimum you will generally want to protect user credentials. If the FTP clients are unable to support FTP over SSL, you will need to leave these settings at *Allow*. Otherwise, you can use the "Require Only for Credentials" option to minimize overhead and protect what is traditionally a clear text exchange (see Figure 12.18). If you need to protect what the user is doing from anyone who may be monitoring the network traffic the encryption of the control channel as a whole is best. Finally if you are exchanging sensitive data such as customer information you may want to protect the data channel using the *Require* option. Specifically for the data channel, you can also deny the encryption which may be required for certain compliance monitoring scenarios.

Figure 12.18 Advanced SSL Policy Dialog

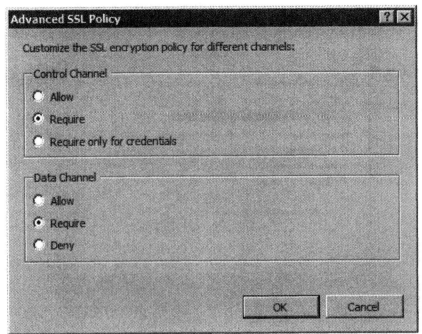

Authentication

Authentication is the process of asserting the identity of the user when they are establishing a session with the FTP site. With this identity we can track who is doing what and evaluate rules to determine if they are authorized to interact with content and folders. IIS ships with two types of authentication modules that can be used to determine a user's identity (see Figure 12.19):

- **Anonymous** Enabled by default to allow any user to access public content without a username and password. Anonymous connections use the username "anonymous" and prompt the user to enter their e-mail address as a password for logging purposes.

- **Basic** Requires the user to provide a username and password. This authentication protocol is a standard across all platforms. It does not perform any sort of encryption with the information provided by the user. As such you should use it with SSL to ensure that the credentials are sent over a secure connection.

Figure 12.19 FTP Authentication Module Configuration

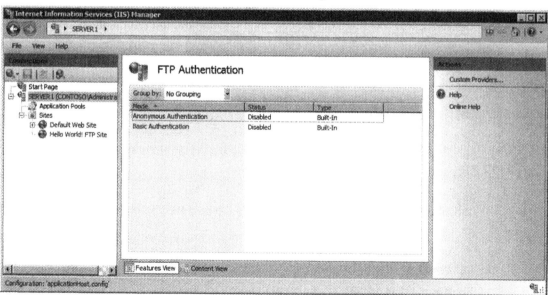

Authorization

With the user's identity established the next step is to determine if the user can perform the action that is being requested. Actions on an FTP site include downloading and uploading of content. They can also perform basic file management functions if authorized. The authorization module evaluates the action based on a set of rules that decide if the user should be allowed, based on the user's identity and if they are attempting to read or write data. IIS provides two modules focused on authorization and supporting services: URL authorization and IP authorization.

URL Authorization

In previous releases the authorization to perform actions was decided at the site level and enforced further down through NTFS permissions. In this release the URL authorization capabilities typically enjoyed by the Web site have been extended for the FTP server scenarios. This module allows administrators the ability to control read or write access to files and folders in addition to the NTFS permissions on the content. Unlike NTFS permissions, you do not need file system access to the server to apply permissions, since everything is managed through the web.config file stored at the root of the site or within a given folder. This allows you to easily carry the permissions with the site as it moves environments.

Configuring & Implementing...

Restricting Access to a Folder

1. Open **Control Panel** and under System and Maintenance | Administration Tools double-click the **Internet Information Services (IIS) Manager** shortcut.

2. In the Internet Information Services (IIS) Manager management console, expand the server and site node, locate a folder to secure (or choose the site as a whole), and click your selection.

3. In the middle pane under Features View double-click **Authentication.**

4. On the Authentication page, ensure that the Anonymous Authentication module is **Disabled**, select one of the other authentication modules, and click **Enable** in the right-hand Actions pane.

5. Click the **Back** arrow in the top left-hand corner.

Continued

6. On the folder page in the middle pane under Features view, double-click **Authorization Rules.**

7. On the Authorization Rules page, click **Add Allow Rule** in the right-hand actions pane.

8. Select the **Specified Users** radio button, provide a username, and click **OK** (see Figure 12.20).

Figure 12.20 Add Allow Authorization Rule Dialog

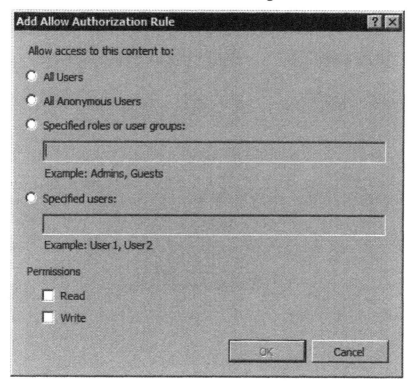

IP Authorization

The ability to restrict access to specific IP addresses has existed for quite some time across both servers and networking devices such as firewalls. In the past this function, like file permissions, was only available through IIS Manager and was tough to replicate across to other servers as it was stored in the metabase. This setting, along with all other configuration options, has been moved to the new XML-based configuration files. This allows you to centralize, copy, and manipulate the settings using new programming interfaces and command-line tools as well as the traditional graphical user interface.

When users attempt to access a file or folder to which they have been denied they will receive a forbidden error. Another option is to restrict users based on their domain name. You will need to enable this through the *Edit Feature Settings* link in the module page on IIS. Be aware that the added overhead of DNS resolution for each IP address could negatively affect the performance of your FTP site. Just as you can restrict specific users, you can also deny all and only allow specific users. This process is similar to adding deny rules with the dialog, shown in Figure 12.21, looking very similar to that of adding deny restriction rules.

Figure 12.21 Add Allow Restriction Rule with Domain Restrictions Enabled

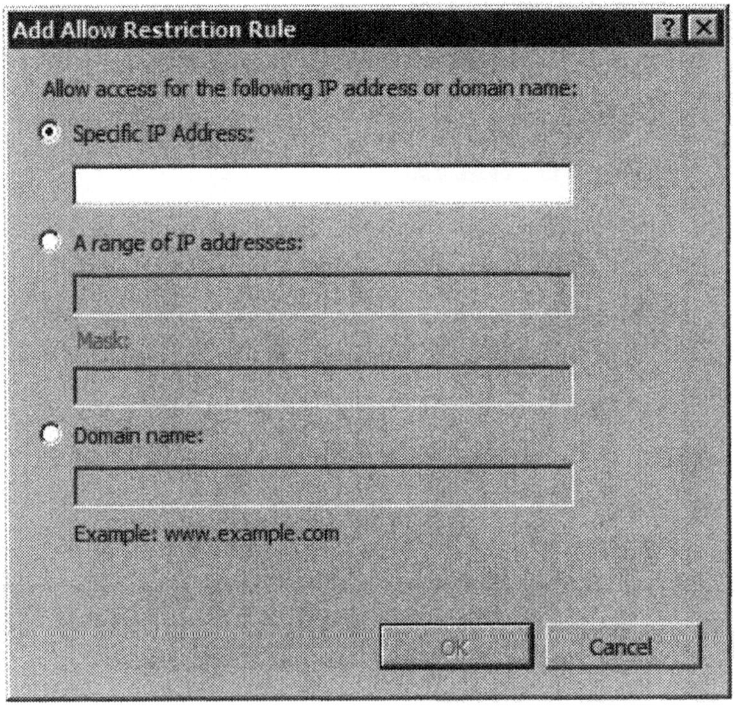

User Isolation

The User Isolation feature will place users into their own home folder when they login, while preventing them from viewing or overwriting other users' content (see Figure 12.22). This feature is most commonly used in shared hosting scenarios. Inside their home folder users can create, modify, and remove files and folders as they wish.

Figure 12.22 FTP User Isolation Module Configuration

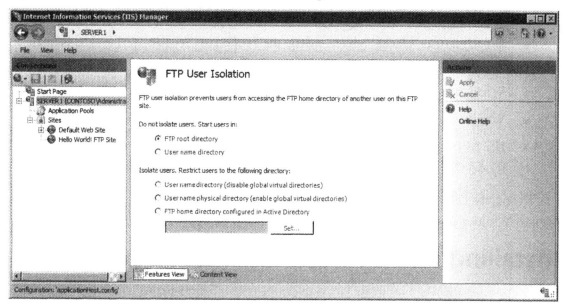

There are five isolation options to choose from:

- **Do Not Isolate Users: FTP Root Directory** This is the default option that places everyone in the FTP root folder upon logon.

- **Do Not Isolate Users: User Name Directory** Users will start in a folder that bears their username if it exists; otherwise they will be placed in the FTP root folder. The user can navigate to the root of the FTP site.

- **Isolate Users: User Name Directory** Isolate users to a physical or virtual directory that bears their username. The user cannot navigate to the root of the FTP site.

- **Isolate Users: User Name Physical Directory** Isolates users to the physical directory that bears their username. The user cannot navigate to the root of the FTP site.

- **Isolate Users: FTP Home Directory Configured in Active Directory** Isolates users to the directory specified in their Active Directory account. The user cannot navigate to the root of the FTP site.

In all cases the folder needs to be created for the user before they login. The syntax for folder names depends on how the user account is stored:

- **Anonymous Users for Non-Isolated User Name Directory Mode** (FTP Site Root)\Default

- **Anonymous Users when using an Isolation Mode** (FTP Site Root) \LocalUser\Public

- **Windows Local Users** (FTP Site Root)\LocalUser\(Username)

- **Windows Domain Users** (FTP Site Root)\(Domain Name)\(Username)

- **IIS Manager or Custom Authentication Module Users** (FTP Site Root)\Local User\(Username)

To specify the starting directory for anonymous access, create a physical or virtual directory folder named *default* in the root directory of the FTP site.

Installing and Configuring SMTP Services

Many applications use e-mail delivery to support the functionality that they offer. The Simple Mail Transfer (SMTP) Service is a basic mail relay that ships with Windows Server 2008 and provides local and remote delivery of messages, as shown in Figure 12.23.

Figure 12.23 SMTP Relay Process

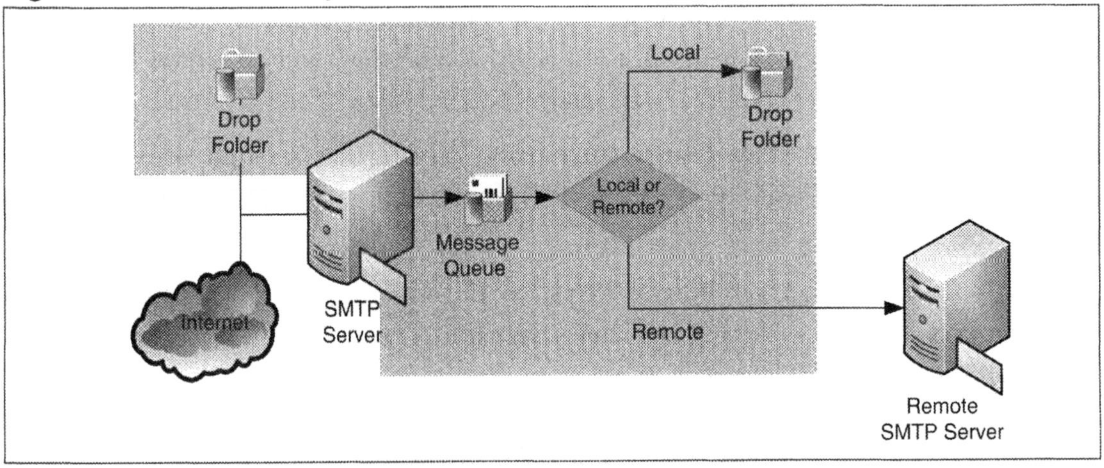

When you receive messages locally, they are received through the Drop folder. When you receive messages remotely, they are received through a TCP connection, by default port 25. Messages are placed into a message queue for processing. The SMTP server reviews the message destination and compares it with the list of domains that it maintains. If it contains explicit instructions on how to handle a message then it acts upon those. If the SMTP server is considered the local domain SMTP server, then it will place the message in a local Drop folder for another application to pickup and process. If it has explicit instructions to route to a remote SMTP server then it will follow those instructions. If it does not have any corresponding record for the domain and the caller has relay privileges then it will locate the remote SMTP server and send the message as well.

Configuring & Implementing...

Real-World Use of SMTP Server

Over the past few generations of Windows Server, the use of SMTP Server has started to dwindle. The major product group relying on SMTP Server was the Exchange Server team. With the recent Exchange Server 2007 release, the Exchange Server team chose to write a new SMTP Server for use within the product. The SMTP Server today, as it exists in Windows Server 2008, now resides there primarily for backwards compatibility. This release saw very little development and no discussion of the future of the SMTP Server. To prepare your environment for future Windows Server releases, you should be aware of where the dependencies for this service exist (e.g., Windows SharePoint Services, third-party applications), and possible alternatives.

Installing Simple Mail Transfer (SMTP) Services

The SMTP Server is listed as a server-level Feature and not a part of any specific role. It has dependencies on the IIS 6 Management Compatibility and IIS 6 Management Console role server which is available in the Web Server role.

Configuring & Implementing...

Installing SMTP Server

1. From the Start Menu select **Server Manager.**

2. In Server Manager, click the root node, scroll the right-hand pane to the **Features Summary** section, and click **Add Features.**

3. In the Add Features Wizard on the Before You Begin page, click **Next.**

4. On the Select Features page, select the **SMTP Server** role and click **Next,** as shown in Figure 12.24.

Figure 12.24 Select Features Page

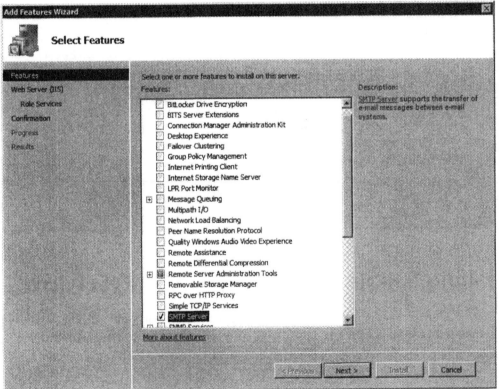

Continued

5. The Web Server (IIS) page gives you a brief description of the role along with some important notes and links to more information on the role. Click **Next**. If this is your first time setting up the Web Server (IIS) role, you should read these notes as they will cover common issues that you will encounter

6. On the Role Services page you are prompted to install several groups of services to the role (see Figure 12.25). Leave the default values and click **Next**.

Figure 12.25 Select Web Server (IIS) Role Services Page

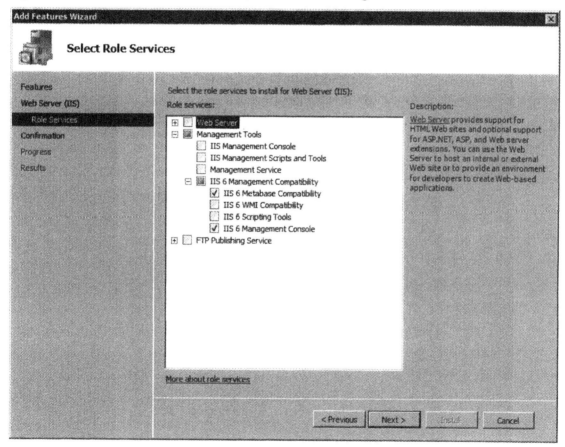

7. On the Confirmation page, review your choices and click **Install**.

8. On the Results page, review the success or failure of the installation, then click **Close**.

With the SMTP Server installed you can manage it through the Internet Information Services (IIS) 6.0 Manager console located in the Administrative Tools group on the server.

Provisioning Virtual Servers

A virtual server is the container under which receive and delivery rules are configured. You can have multiple virtual servers on a server, but they cannot be bound to the same IP address and port combination.

With your virtual server set up to receive mail, you will need to add a list of domains for which it can receive mail. By default, anonymous connections will only be able to send mail to the domains that you have configured. When you configure the domain using domain routing instructions you can choose whether mail should be delivered to the local drop folder or to a remote server.

If you setup an alias domain there are no other properties available. The alias domains are an alternative name for the default local domain. The folder where the mail will be delivered is configured in the Properties of the default local domain, as shown in Figure 12.26.

Figure 12.26 Default Local Domain Properties Dialog

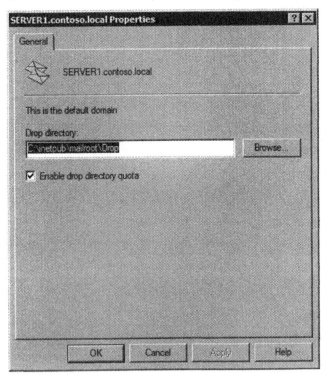

For remote domains you will need to select the **Allow incoming mail to be relayed to this domain** checkbox to enable the server to accept mail. This option is disabled by default. This was done specifically to force you to knowingly allow the SMTP to receive and process mail for this domain. Much of the early unsolicited email problems were due to "open relays." This meant the SMTP servers would accept mail for any domain and attempt to deliver the message. Spammers would take advantage of these open relays as a way to obscure the source of their annoyances.

The rest of the dialog box has domain-specific delivery instructions (see Figure 12.27). In the **General** tab you can tell the server to use HELO for older SMTP servers that do not support EHLO. The **Outbound Security** button allows you to specify a set of credentials to use when connecting to the remote server where the message will be delivered. The Route Domain group gives you the option of trying to look up the mail exchanger (MX) records for the domain or forward directly to a specific host (smart host).

Figure 12.27 Remote Domain Properties Dialog

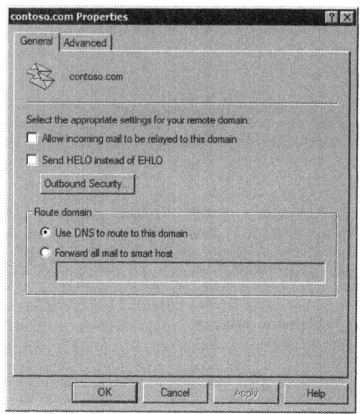

Under the **Advanced** tab, shown in Figure 12.28, you have the server queue the incoming messages until a client connects and issues the Authenticated TURN (ATRN) command. When this command is issued the messages will then be sent for delivery based on the configuration options specified under the **General** tab. If you need to secure this further you can specify that the ATRN command can only be executed by clients that connect and authenticate under specific accounts.

Figure 12.28 Advanced Tab

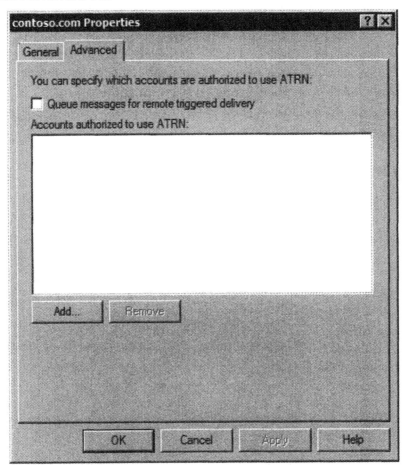

Configuring a Virtual Server

The default configuration for an SMTP virtual server requires little adjustment for most environments. Even so you should be aware of the various settings available (see Figure 12.29). In this section we will review each group of settings.

Figure 12.29 Virtual Server Properties Dialog

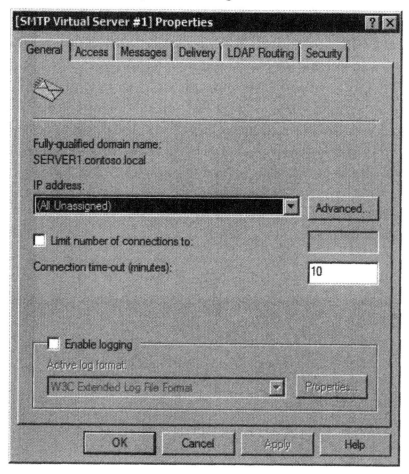

Server Bindings

By default the SMTP virtual server will look to bind to all IP addresses on the server using TCP port 25. There are scenarios where you might want to change this behavior to bind only to a specific network on a multi-homed server, or offer an alternative port for clients who are on a network that blocks port 25. If you are requiring users to use SSL/TLS (discussed later in this chapter) you will want to use port 465. In 1998 the Internet Engineering Task Force (IETF) published RFC 2476, which attempted to shift mail submission from port 25 to 587 for authenticated mail submission. In 2004 several major mail service providers echoed this push as part of the Anti-Spam Technical Alliance Technology and Policy Proposal (see www.microsoft.com/down-loads/details.aspx?FamilyId=EF4A02D4-12AB-46A3-A4EC-9AADBED0ABB8 for a copy of the proposal).

Logging

Activity logging gives you a detailed picture of what your SMTP server is doing. For each request made to the server the log records particular properties of both the request and response for later analysis. Using log analysis tools you can review aggregate statistics to determine the number of messages passing through your server, where they are going, and when they are doing it (see Figure 12.30). You can also use activity logs as a tool in troubleshooting. IIS ships with logging disabled by default. You can enable logging by simply checking the **Enable Logging** checkbox in the **General** tab of the **Virtual Server Properties** dialog. The logs are written to the WINDOWS\SYSTEM32\LogFiles folder by default. The logs can be written using IIS, NCSA, and W3C formats. Alternatively you can log directly to any ODBC-compliant database.

Figure 12.30 W3C Extended Logging Options

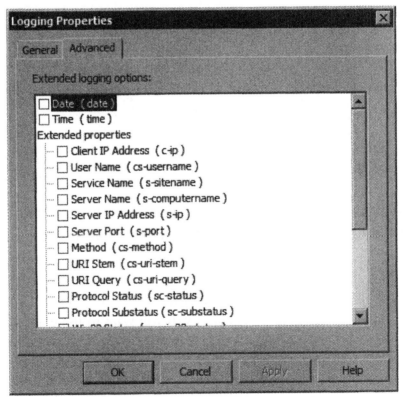

Message Limits

The message limits for a virtual server allow you to set various limits on incoming messages. This prevents people from overloading the server or downstream mail servers. If a message cannot be received or routed for any specific reason it will result in a non-delivery report being generated. You can specify to store a copy of the message in a local folder and send a copy of the non-delivery report to another address as well for troubleshooting purposes. The most common scenario for which you will visit this dialog is to adjust message size limits, as in Figure 12.31.

Figure 12.31 Messages Tab

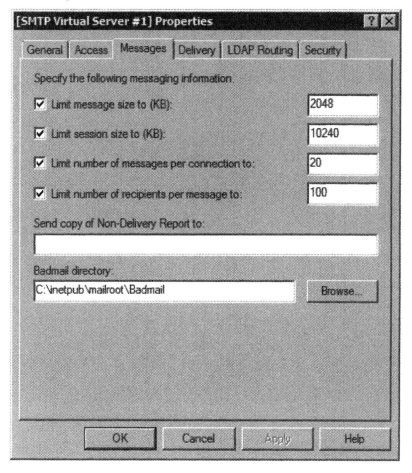

Delivery Options

Once a message has been accepted the server needs to deliver the message. The SMTP protocol uses a store-and-forward approach to delivery, meaning that it does not require all mail servers to be online. The **Delivery** tab in the virtual server settings (see Figure 12.32) exposes the configuration options that control how long the server will wait to retry the delivery of a message. In most cases the default values are sufficient.

Figure 12.32 Delivery Tab

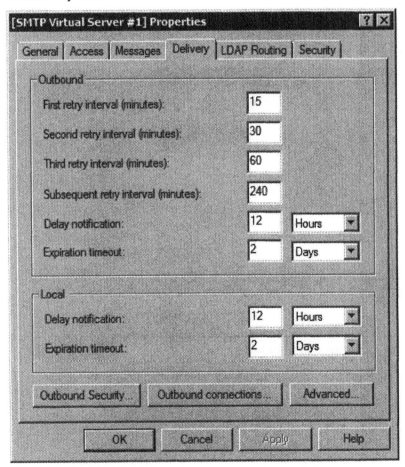

In the **Outbound Security** section you can specify the method and credentials used for delivery of messages, as shown in Figure 12.33. When set at the server level the selected method is used for delivery of all outbound messages.

Figure 12.33 Outbound Security Dialog

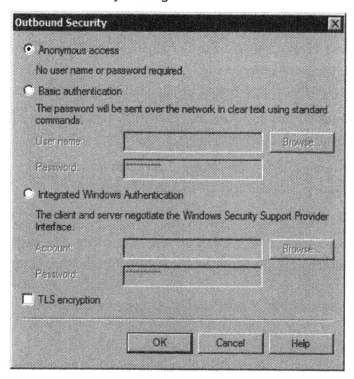

In the **Outbound Connections** section you can configure several options to throttle the number of concurrent outbound connections at the server and domain level, as shown in Figure 12.34. The TCP port can be changed for all outbound delivers. Unless you have a specific reason to change this port you should leave it at the default value since all Internet SMTP servers receive mail on port 25 by default.

Figure 12.34 Outbound Connections Dialog

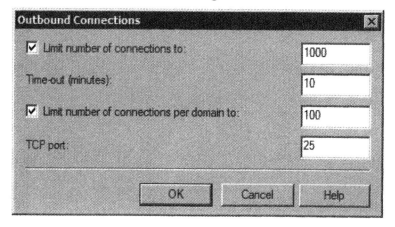

In the **Advanced** Delivery section you are presented with some advanced server behavior options (see Figure 12.35):

- **Maximum Hop Count** Stops messages from passing through this server if they have been through a certain number of servers already. This is useful to stop messages that may be stuck in a continuous loop.

- **Masquerade Domain** Replaces the domain name in the Mail From line with the specified value

- **Fully Qualified Domain Name** Server identifier added to message headers when a message passes through the SMTP gateway

- **Smart Host** Force all outbound messages to be routed to this server

- **Perform Reverse DNS Lookup on Incoming Messages** Will check all incoming messages to ensure that the domain that the server claims to be matches the reverse DNS record of the IP address. If no match can be made then an unverified message is added to the message header.

Figure 12.35 Advanced Delivery Dialog

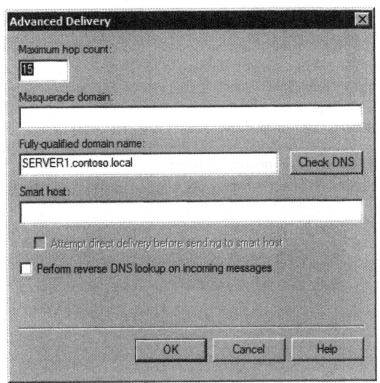

LDAP Routing

You can configure the SMTP Server to resolve recipients using Active Directory, Site Server Membership Directory (version 3.0 and earlier), and the Exchange LDAP Service (version 5.5 and earlier). When a message is received, SMTP will look up the email address in the directory and if it is a group it will send the message to all members in the group. The options in the **LDAP Routing** tab specify the name of the server and account to use for binding (see Figure 12.36). The account will require browse, read, and search permissions within the directory to function properly.

Figure 12.36 LDAP Routing Tab

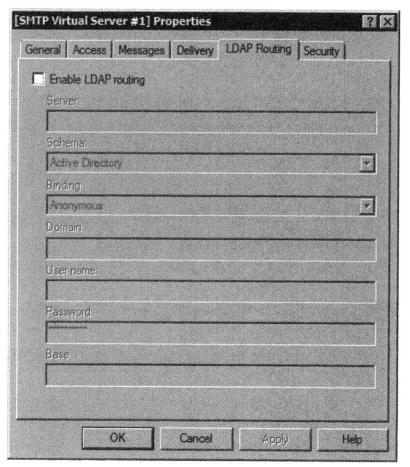

Securing Your SMTP Virtual Server

To secure your SMTP virtual server, you need to understand the Transport Layer Security (TLS) protocol, the three types of authentication that an SMTP Server supports for determining a user's identity, connection control, and relay restrictions. We'll now discuss each of these areas.

Transport Security

SMTP Server supports securing message communication using Transport Layer Security (TLS). The TLS protocol is known as the successor to Secure Socket Layers (SSL). It shares many of the same characteristics as SSL, including how the connection is set up, but it is not compatible. Under this release of the SMTP Server you cannot choose the server certificate that will be used for TLS encryption. The service will automatically look for a certificate that matches the full qualified domain name of the computer. The Access options tab is shown in Figure 12.37.

Figure 12.37 Access Tab

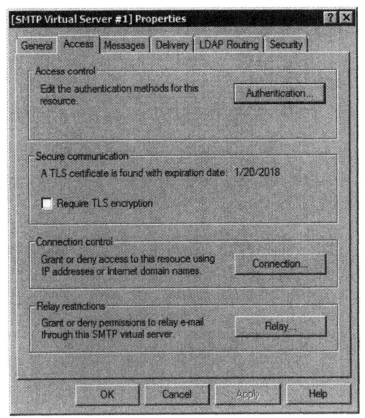

New & Noteworthy...

Certificate Creation Changes

If you have used the IIS 6 SMTP Server then you might notice that the Secure Communication section in the Windows Server 2008 release has changed. No longer do you have the ability to create and manage certificates from this interface. Instead that functionality has been moved over to the IIS 7 management tools. Another behavioral change to be aware of is the automatic choice of using a certificate that matches the machine's full qualified domain name.

Authentication

Authentication is the process of asserting the identity of the user or service that is sending a message through your virtual server. The SMTP Server supports three types of authentication to determine a user's identity:

- **Anonymous** Enabled by default to allow any user to send messages to authorized domains without a username and password.

- **Basic** Requires the user to provide a username and password. This authentication protocol is standard across all platforms.

    Just as you can require TLS for the incoming communication as a whole, you can require TLS for any connection that tries to authenticate using Basic authentication. Using TLS will protect the otherwise clear text username and password.

- **Integrated Windows Authentication** Used mainly in intranet scenarios, it allows SMTP to use the current user's Windows domain credentials to authenticate the connection.

In public-facing scenarios where you are setting up SMTP Server to be an incoming mail relay, you will select **Anonymous access** authentication, as shown in Figure 12.38. For internal applications or to allow users to relay through the server to any domain, you will need to use either **Basic** or **Integrated Windows Authentication**.

Figure 12.38 Authentication Dialog

Connection Control

Connection Control allows you to limit the devices that can connect to the SMTP Server, as demonstrated in Figure 12.39. This can be useful if you are using the service as a relay for locally installed applications by restricting connections to that of the local host. You can alternatively prevent specific computers from connecting to the server. Connections can be evaluated based on a single IP address, a masked IP range, or a domain name. If you choose domain name the server will perform a reverse DNS lookup on all incoming connections, which may adversely affect performance.

Figure 12.39 Connection Control Dialog

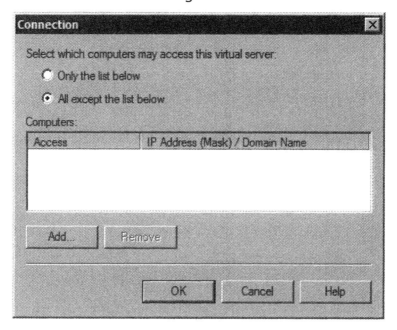

Relay Restrictions

By default the SMTP service will only allow users who authenticate to your server to relay. If you have applications that do not support SMTP authentication and need to relay you can add them to the relay restrictions list to allow them the ability to use the server as a relay (see Figure 12.40). This restriction provides you with another method to control who can relay through your SMTP server.

Figure 12.40 Relay Restrictions Dialog

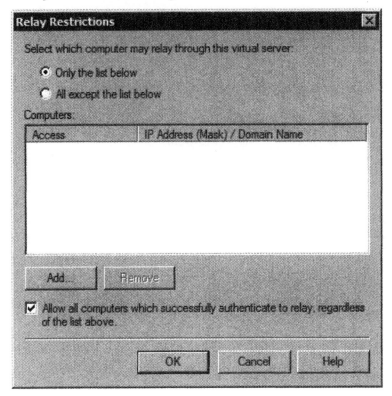

Summary

This chapter focused on configuration of the File Transfer (FTP) Publishing and Simple Mail Transfer (SMTP) Services. The major investments in this release focused on the FTP support by providing a re-written, integrated FTP service that takes advantage of the advancements brought forth in Internet Information Services. While Windows Server 2008 ships with the older IIS 6 FTP Publishing Service, you should use this new release, as it was the version intended to ship with Windows Server 2008, but missed the cutoff for inclusion. The SMTP Server, on the other hand, remains similar to the older IIS 6 SMTP Server with very little change.

With the FTP Server we discussed the installation of the service. It requires the Web Server role be installed and that the old IIS 6 FTP Publishing Service be removed. After installing the new FTP Publishing Service, you manage it through the wide array of tools provided by the IIS infrastructure, including IIS Manager, AppCmd, and the various programmatic interfaces (Windows Management Instrumentation, Microsoft. Web.Administration Assembly, and so on).

The new FTP Publishing Service supports both full and Server Core installations. When you are ready to create your first FTP site you can create a standalone or bound FTP site. The standalone version works much like a typical FTP site where you point it to a folder that may or may not contain content for users to download and upload. In the bound FTP site the functionality is tied into an existing Web site setup in IIS. This allows you to give users alternative means of managing the content and Web applications on their site. Combined with the IIS Management Service and the new XML-based configuration files this is a complete and powerful set of tools available to users.

When you have configured your FTP site, you will need to consider whether you want the user or your server to be responsible for opening up a port to receive the data connection. If you choose the server to be responsible for establishing a port for the data connection (active mode), then you can establish a pre-defined range for the security administrators to forward from the firewall. If you choose for the user to establish that port then no further configuration is required.

The new FTP Publishing Service shares a number of other concepts with the Web side, including virtual directories and hosting the request processing inside an application pool. Virtual directories allow you to link in content folders from several locations into a single easy-to-navigate tree for users. The application pool gives you added isolation and resiliency in that if your FTP site were to fail, it would not impact other sites within the server. In a standard configuration FTP will send your credentials and content over a clear text connection. Enabling FTP over SSL will give you the option to protect the authentication, control, and/or data conversations occurring. IIS implements an explicit SSL connection per RFC 2228 which means that the client connects over port 21 and explicitly asks the server for a secure conversation. With a secure connection in place you can further apply URL and IP restrictions to prevent groups of users from accessing the site as a whole or a specific section within. If you have users who need to access a personal home directory, user isolation gives you a chance to enforce the user's session to be isolated to that folder.

The SMTP Server enables you to receive mail from local Web applications or remote senders and forward them to other remote servers or keep them local for applications to process. Installation of the SMTP Server requires a full installation and depends on the IIS 6 backwards compatibility components of the Web Server role to function. After installing the SMTP Server it has a default virtual server created, however you can create others. A virtual server is a container for limits, authentication, authorization, and handling settings. It is bound to one or more IP address and port combinations. Each virtual server can be configured with specific instructions for handling mail destined to a particular domain, or with either authorization or being granted rights through the relay restrictions can relay mail to other mail exchangers (MX) in the network. If the SMTP server is being used as a local spool and you have an outbound SMTP gateway already in place through products like Exchange Server, you can configure the virtual server or specific domains to use that gateway as a default next point-of-contact (smart host). Incoming connections can be authenticated using Anonymous, Basic, or Integrated Windows Authentication modules. Likewise outbound connections can use the same three modules on a server or per-domain basis to ensure mail is transmitted in a secure manner. Privacy for mail is handled through TLS encryption. TLS draws upon the SSL family through the use of security certificates.

Solutions Fast Track

Installing and Configuring FTP Publishing Service

☑ Windows Server 2008 ships with the older IIS 6 FTP Publishing Service. You should grab the Web release as it was the version that was meant to ship with Windows Server 2008 (but missed the deadline for inclusion by a few weeks).

☑ The new FTP Publishing Service is a major rewrite that adds a much tighter integration into the IIS 7 framework and several important security enhancements. It works on both full and Server Core installations.

☑ Sites can be either standalone or bound to a Web site to provide greater options for users who need to manage their Web site or Web application content.

☑ From a transport security perspective the support of Explicit SSL connections allows you to protect the control, authentication, and/or data conversations between the client and the server.

☑ The rules around security (SSL) certificates follow the same rules as the Web sites in terms of the types of certificates and how they are validated.

☑ Out-of-the-box authentication modules include anonymous and basic authentication. Building on the IIS Framework allows you to open that up to a number of custom authentication modules.

☑ The built-in authorization mechanisms include a URL and IP restriction based on a set of rules. Within the URL side you assign allow/deny access to one or more users (including user groups/roles). Alternatively you can control which devices can connect to the site through IP restrictions.

☑ Once into the site you can apply a set of user isolation policies to restrict users to their personal home directory, or you can let them navigate the structure you have created using a set of physical and virtual folders.

Installing and Configuring SMTP Services

☑ Windows Server 2008 ships with the older IIS 6 SMTP Server with a few minor compatibility fixes. It depends on the Web Server role for IIS 6 backwards compatibility components. It can only be installed on a full server installation.

☑ Virtual servers are bound to combination IP address and port to represent the container for authentication, limits, and domain handling instructions.

☑ Within the virtual server you can specify handling instructions for a domain including allowing the server to accept anonymous relays, the method of delivery (lookup via DNS or to a smart host), the outbound authentication method, and whether to queue the messages until triggered.

☑ Inbound and outbound communication can be protected using TLS, which is related to the SSL family of communication encryption protocols.

Frequently Asked Questions

Q: I need to set up an FTP site so our business partner can send us purchase orders. Where should I create their account so they can authenticate into the FTP site?

A: The new FTP Publishing Service supports basic authentication out-of-the-box, which looks to the IIS Users data store, local Windows security account manager, and, if a domain member, to Active Directory for authentication credentials. Using the IIS framework you can also implement a custom authentication module if needed.

Q: A user is trying to access the server using FTPS; however, they are being told that the certificate name does not match the host name. Where should I look?

A: The same rules for SSL on the Web apply to FTP—the certificate is bound to the IP address and port that the FTP site runs on. The certificate should reflect the name of the FTP site, use a wildcard sub-domain, or take advantage of the subjectAltName field to list several host names. If the client cannot match the host name, the user connected to it should show the warning about the certificate. In most clients the user can acknowledge the difference and continue to connect.

Q: We have set up the FTP Publishing Service in a shared hosting scenario. I need to isolate users to their own personal home directory in a way that they are unable to see others. Should I set up individual URL authorization rules to do this?

A: No, take a look at the user isolation feature in the FTP Publishing Service and choose between the three isolation modes to find one that matches your needs.

Q: I have set up an SMTP Server in our DMZ to receive mail from the Internet. I want it to forward to our internal mail server. What should I be doing to get it to forward the mail?

A: In the virtual server, set up a domain routing entry to allow it to receive mail for your domain and set it to forward to the specific IP address of your internal mail server (smart host) rather than look up how to deliver the messages.

Q: Our remote branch office has an unreliable connection. I have an Exchange Server there and I want to queue up the mail to be received by the remote server when it reconnects. What should I configure with SMTP Server to allow it to queue mail on behalf of this server?

A: You should set up your Exchange Server to issue an ATRN command to the SMTP server when it connects. This will cause the SMTP server to attempt to deliver all of the mail destined for that domain that resides in the queue.

Q: I think the SMTP server isn't processing mail it receives from the outside, but I'm not sure. Where can I look to determine that it is not working?

A: The first step is to send a message to the server. This can be done using a Telnet client and the steps outlined in Microsoft Support KB 323350 (http://support.microsoft.com/?id=323350). Once the message has been received you should check the Queue folder to see if you can see your message. The electronic mail (.eml file extension) files can be opened up with a text editor to view the contents of the message. From there you can turn on logging on the virtual server to see the outbound connection attempts to deliver the message. If all else fails use Network Monitor to ensure that SMTP is able to make an outbound connection.

Index

A

Active Directory Domain Services, 424, 557
Active Directory infrastructure, in Windows
    Server 2008
  domain functional level
    configuring and implementing, 72–73
    raising, 71
    Windows 2000, 66
    Windows 2003, 67
    Windows 2008, 68
  flexible single master operation
    (FSMO) roles
    advantages of, 83
    child domain in an existing
      domain, 85
    domain naming master, 89–90
    infrastructure, RID and PDC
      operations, 83, 91–92
    placing, transferring and seizing,
      86–87, 94–95
    schema master role, 86–88, 94
    valid authorization levels for, 84
  forest and domain functional levels,
    64–65, 71
  forest functional level
    raising, 71
    Windows 2000, 69
    Windows 2003, 69–70
    Windows 2008, 70
  Global Catalog (GC)
    configuring Universal Group
      Caching, 81–82
    consists of, 73
    Directory information search, 75–76
    exchange server environment, 79–80
    replication, 77–78
    Universal Group membership
      information, 76–77
    UPN authentication, 75
    user principal names (UPN), 73–74
  logical view of, 62
  partitions of, 64
  Site link cost
    configuring, 114–115
    properties, 116
  Site link object
    components of, 111–112
    creation of, 112
    inter-site transports folder, 113
    new site link option, 114
  Site planning
    Active Directory Sites and
      Services tool, 101–102
    criteria for establishing
      separate sites, 100
    naming site, 104
    new object, 103
    new site option, 102
    renaming site, 104–106
    site creation, 100–101
  with Sites
    definition, 96
    and domains, 96–98
    physical structure, 95–96, 98
  subnets, 98–99
    associated with sites, 109–111
    configure and implementing,
      108–109
    creation of, 106–107
    IP Version 6 (IPv6), 107

Active Directory infrastructure, in
    Windows Server 2008 (*Continued*)
  with trusts
    default trusts, 133
    external trusts, 134–135
    forest trust, 133–134
    implicit and explicit trust, 131–132
    nontransitive trust, 129
    one-way trust, 131
    primary attributes of, 128–129
    shortcut trusts, 135
    SID filtering, 136
    transitive trust, 130
Active Directory integrated zones
  advantages of, 20–22
  forward lookup zone, 279–282
  vs. standard zones, 273–274
Add Application Pool dialog, 665
Add Custom Error page, 656–657
Add Printer Wizard, printer sharing
    configuration in, 453
Admin Base Object (ABO) Mapper, 673
Administration tools, 647
Advanced SSL Policy dialog, 750
AJAX technologies, 710
API. *See* application programming interface
AppCmd command-line tool,
    668, 715
AppCmd.exe, 638, 648
  application pool process identities via, 668
  backup and restore for server
    configuration, 715
application certificate, 176
applicationHost.config, 649–650, 664, 713
application pool
  creation of, 664–665
  functionality of, 662–663
  process identities via AppCmd.exe, 668
  for request processing, 742–743
  settings, 668–670

application programming interface (API),
    555, 599
ASP.NET applications, 717
asymmetric cryptography. *See* public key
    encryption
authentication
  and Authorization Information page,
    735–736
  on folder, enabling, 685–687
  FTP site sessions, 751
  SMTP server, 771–772
  types of, 684–685
  using client certificates, 687–689
Authentication, authorization, and access
    (AAA) server, 558
authorization, FTP sites, 751
  IP, 753–754
  URL, 689–692, 752–753

B
Beta Linux, 598
Binding and SSL Settings, 735
bit length, 679
bitlocker drive encryption, 230
Block symmetric algorithms, 153
Branch Office Box (BOB), 435
bridgehead server, 120

C
CA. *See* Certificate authorities
Certificate Practice Statement (CPS),
    184–185
certificate revocation lists (CRLs), 193–194
certificate template
  definition of, 196
  infrastructure-based certificate templates,
    210–211
  key recovery agent, 215–216
  properties of new template
    cryptography tab, 201

extensions tab, 204–205
    general properties tab, 198–199
    issuance requirements tab, 203
    request handling, 200
    security tab, 205–207
    subject name tab, 202
    superseded templates, 203–204
  security permissions, 214
  snap-in, 197
  types of templates
    computer certificate templates, 209–210
    custom certificate templates, 211–214
    user certificate templates, 207–209
  version information, 215
certification authorities (CAs), 147, 150, 677
  administrator roles, 191–192
  backup and restore
    backing up certificate service, 186–187
    restore wizard, 190–191
    restoring certificate services, 188–190
  certificate installation results, 183
  certificate practice statement, 184–185
  certificate request, 180, 183
  enrollments, 192
  key recovery, 185
  revocation, 192–195
  types of, 178
    root *vs.* subordinate, 179–180
    standard *vs.* enterprise, 178–179
  welcome screen of, 184
cluster nodes, 50
COM and .NET programming interfaces,
    648–649
command-line tools, 404, 733
  IIS 7.0 administration on
    Server Core, 648
  Web Server Role installation on Server
    Core, 645–646
common gateway interface-based
    modules, 717

Common HTTP features, 643–644. *See also*
    Select Server Roles page
Common Internet File System (CIFS), 411
computer certificate templates, 209–210
computer network, for file sharing, 404
Connection Control, 772–773
Connection Request Policies, 570
Cryptographic Service Provider, 679,
    747–748
Cryptography, 149
  functions of, 153
Cryptography Next Generation (CNG), 152
custom certificate templates, 211–214
custom error pages, 658
custom response headers, 660–661

D
data collector sets, 509
Data Encryption Standard (DES), 152–153
data execution prevention (DEP), 606
data transfer, mode in FTP, 727
DDNS. *See* dynamic domain name system
default document configuration,
    653–654
default error pages, 656
Default Local Domain Properties
    dialog, 760
DH SChannel Cryptographic
    Provider, 679
dial-up networking, 364–365
digital signatures
  in public key infrastructure, 158
  RSA-derived technology, 157
directory browsing, 654–655
  module configuration, 738
  service clients, 737
Disk Quotas, 447
  configuration using file server resource
    manager, 450
Distinguished Name Properties, 747

Distributed File System (DFS), 619
  applications of, 430
  configuration of, 429
  management tools, 408
  replication, 434
domain controllers, 26, 280
domain name system (DNS) configuration,
    in Windows Server 2008
  Active Directory records, 26–27
  client configuration
    group policy management editor,
      338–339
    group policy settings, 336–337
  common record types, 3–4
  configuring DHCP for, 42–43
  configuring WINS for, 53
  database file, 4–5
  definition, 3
  domain suffix usage on Internet, 6–7
  Event log, 537
  fully qualified domain name
    (FQDN), 253
  GlobalNames zone configuration
    CNAME record, 33–34
    new zone creation, 33
    prerequisites, 32
  installation
    configuration data, 14
    DNS server role selection, 13
    properties, 16
    Root Hints tab, 15
    types of versions, 12
  Internet assigned numbers authority
    (ISNA), 12
  Internet name registration authority
    (INRA), 6
  managing record types of
    CNAME records creation,
      310–311
    host records creation, 300–303

    mail exchanger (MX) records creation,
      305–306
    Name server (NS) records, 311–312
    pointer records creation, 304–305
    service records creation, 307–309
  name resolution
    DNS server list configuration, 326–327
    HOSTS file configuration, 329–330
    Link-Local Multicast Name Resolution
      (LLMNR), 336
    LMHOSTS file configuration, 334–336
    local area connection properties, 324
    NetBIOS node type configuration,
      330–332
    primary forms of, 323
    suffix search order configuration,
      328–329
    TCP/IP settings properties, 323–325
    in Windows XP, 325–326
    WINS server list configuration for,
      332–334
namespace management, 7
primary zone, 19–20
private name resolution, 256–257
public name resolution, 255–256
replication
  application directory partition,
    299–300
  Start of Authority (SOA) record
    configuration, 297–298
  using DNS Manager, 294
  zone transfer configuration,
    295–297
resource record (RR) identification types,
    8–12
reverse lookup zones
  configuring, 28–31
  properties, 31
server configuration
  cache responses, 257, 259

conditional forwarding configuration, 266–269

with domain controllers, 280

positive caching, 257

role selection for, 258–259

root hints configuration, 260–263

server core installation, 270–271

server-level forwarders configuration, 263–265

server core installation

advantages of, 17

dnscmd utility, 19

IP addressing information, 17–18

server-to-client *vs.* server-to-server queries, 257

top-level domains (TLDs), 253–255

tree format, 6

types of zones

AD integrated forward lookup zone, 279–282

AD integrated *vs.* standard zones, 273–274

delegation zones, 287–290

primary forward lookup zones, 274–278

secondary forward lookup zones, 278–279

stub and GlobalNames zones, 272

on Windows networks, 252

World Wide Web services, 5–6

zones configuration

Active Directory–integrated zone, 20–22

definition of zone, 19

stub and reverse lookup zones, 20–21

zone transfer

definition, 22

modes of, 22–23

new zone wizard, 23–24

zone name, 25

dynamic domain name system (DDNS), in Windows Server 2008

aging and scavenging configuration

automatic scavenging, 321–322

manual scavenging, 322–323

properties dialog, 320

use of dynamic records, 318–319

dynamic host configuration protocol (DHCP), in Windows Server 2008

advantages of, 34–35

configuration process, 38–39

design principles, 35–37

enforcement, 559

installation

netsh syntax, 239

using Server Core, 237–239

installation process, 37–38

negotiation process, 35

netsh command, 235–237

netsh syntax for, 42

network interface card (NIC), 37

scope settings for, 39–40

server core installation, 40–41

servers and placements, 37, 557

dynamic routing, 355

E

EAP over LAN (EAPoL), 581

edit virtual hard disk wizard, 608

EFS Certificate, 428

EFS-encrypted files, 426

encrypting file system (EFS), 423–424

end-user license agreement (EULA), 602

error pages, customization

Add Custom Error page, 657

Edit Feature Settings, 658–659

HTTP error code, 656

Event Viewer, 126–127

Extended Validation SSL, 681
Extensible Authentication Protocol (EAP),
    557, 581

F

failed request tracing, 703
File Replication Service (FRS), 409
file screening, 410
File Server Resource Manager (FSRM),
    408, 447
file servers, configuration of, 404
File services, 404
    configuration role for, 410
    role in Server Manager, 405
    role to Windows 2008 Server, 406
file share publishing, 405
file sharing models, comparison of, 405
File Transfer Protocol (FTP)
    active *vs.* passive mode, 739–740
    configuring sites, 734
        advanced settings, 736–737
        application pools, for request processing,
            742–743
        authorization rules, 735–736
        directory browsing, 737–738
        IP address and SSL certificate, 735
        secure communications on, 749–750
        virtual directories, 741–742
    control connection, 727
    Publishing Services
        installation of, 727–733
        management functionality, 244
        Server Core installations of, 244–246
        SSL encryption support, 727
        Web release, 727–728
    server
        Firewall Support, 739
        messages, 740–741
    service model, 726
    security sites of

authentication, 751
authorization, 751–754
server certificates, 745–749
SSL process, 744–745, 749–750
user isolation, 754–756
flexible host isolation, 578
flexible single master operation (FSMO)
    advantages of, 83
    child domain in an existing domain, 85
    domain naming master, 83, 89–90
    infrastructure, RID and PDC operations,
        83, 91–92
    placing, transferring and seizing, 86–87,
        94–95
    schema master role, 83, 86–88, 94
    valid authorization levels for, 84
folder
    enabling authentication on, 685–687
    restricting access to, 690
forcing replication, 122
fully qualified domain names (FQDNs)
    in DNS configuration, 3
    domain portion of, 253
full zone transfer, 22

G

Global Catalog (GC)
    configuring Universal Group Caching,
        81–82
    consists of, 73
    Directory information search, 75–76
    exchange server environment, 79–80
    replication
        attributes, 78
        Knowledge Consistency Checker
            (KCC), 77
        Universal Group membership, 77
    Universal Group membership
        information, 76–77
    UPN authentication, 75

user principal names (UPN), 73–74
globally unique ID (GUID), 26
GlobalNames zones
  configuration
    CNAME record, 33–34
    new zone creation, 33
    prerequisites, 32
  creation of, 292–294
  definition, 272
  domain controller support, 291–292
  features of, 290–291
Global Presence Architecture (GPA), 598
Group Policy Objects (GPOs), 63, 493,
    497–498
guest operating systems, 599
GZIP compression, 711

H

Health and Diagnostics, 635, 644
Health Certificate Server (HCS), 576
Health Registration Authority
    (HRA), 557
health requirement servers, 558
HTTP (Hyper text transfer protocol)
  error code, 656, 658
  protocol, 650
  Redirect module, 659–660
Hyper-V
  components of, 596–598
  hardware requirements for migration
    with, 618
  implementation of, 590
  for import and export of virtual
    machines, 591
  installation of, 592, 599–602
  installing and managing on Windows
    server core, 602
  support for isolation in terms of
    partition, 599
hypervisor, 596

I

IEEE 802.1x Enforcement, 581
IIS 7.0
  administrative process, 663
  ASP.NET behavior, 664
  compatibility, 674
  configuration tools, 697
  deployment scenarios
    large Web Farms, 641
    simple Web Server, 640
    small Web Farm, 640–641
  features and functionality of, 638–639
  installation process
    Remote Server Administration
      tool, 242
    web server role, 240–241, 642–647
  Internet Information Services
    Manager, 243
  management interface for security
    certificates, 745
  remote administration on Server Core,
    733–734
    Remote Server Administration Tools,
      647–648
    ways to, 648–649
  Server Certificates module
    configuration, 677
  Server Manager, 648
    Add Web Site dialog, 650–651
    Web Server, 644–645
  Web site provisioning, 649
    and creation. (*See* Web Site)
    custom response headers, 660–661
    default document, configuring,
      653–654
    directory browsing, enabling, 654–656
    error pages, customizing, 656–659
    management interface for security
      certificates, 677
    MIME types, 661–662

IEEE 802.1x Enforcement (*Continued*)
    requests, redirecting, 659–660
    transport security, 675–676
    virtual directory, 653
IIS-ISAPIExtensions role service, 646–647
IIS Manager tool, 715
incremental zone transfer, 22–23
independent software providers, 556
independent software vendors (ISVs), 573
inetinfo.exe, 663
infrastructure-based certificate templates, 210–211
instruction set architecture (ISA), 599
Integrated Services Digital Network (ISDN), 358
integrated virtual switches, 605
integration components (ICs), for virtual machines, 591
Internet assigned numbers authority (ISNA), 12
Internet Authentication Service (IAS), 558
Internet Connection Sharing (ICS)
    configuring, 372
    with TCP/IP, 370
    with virtual private networks (VPNs), 370–371
Internet Information Server 7.0 (IIS), 557, 726
Internet Information Services Manager, 243
    and FTP Server, 731
    permissions module, 702
    Server Certificates, 745
Internet Installation Services, 634, 697
Internet name registration authority (INRA), 6
Internet Protocol (IP), 548

addressing scheme, 2
authorization, 753–754
Internet Protocol security (IPSec), 554
    enforcement, 576
    protocols, 374
Internet Protocol version 4 (IPv4), 557
Intersite replication, 119–120
Intrasite replication
    definition of, 118
    three-Hop rule of, 119
I/O components, 592
IP version 6 (IPv6), 107
ISA. *See* instruction set architecture
iSCSI attachment, 618
ISVs. *See* independent software vendors

K
key recovery agent, 215–216
Knowledge Consistency Checker (KCC), 77, 117

L
Lightweight Extensible Authentication Protocol (LEAP), 557
Link-Local Multicast Name Resolution (LLMNR), 336
link-state routing, 356
Linux operating systems, 598
logging module configuration, 707
L2TP, tunneling protocol, 373

M
machine certificate, 176
management service module configuration, 702
master server, 272
Microsoft Baseline Security Analyzer (MBSA), 478, 542–543, 549
Microsoft Management Console (MMC), 444

MIME types
  data transer, to browser, 661
  module configuration, 662
multicast DNS (mDNS). *See* LLMNR

N
name resolution
  DNS server list configuration, 326–327
  HOSTS file configuration, 329–330
  Link-Local Multicast Name Resolution
    (LLMNR), 336
  LMHOSTS file configuration, 334–336
  local area connection properties, 324
  NetBIOS node type configuration,
    330–332
  primary forms of, 323
  suffix search order configuration, 328–329
  TCP/IP settings properties, 323–325
  in Windows XP, 325–326
  WINS server list configuration for,
    332–334
namespace management, 7
NAP clients, 556
NAP Health Policy Server (NPS), 557, 558
NAP-supported network, 555
National Security Agency (NSA), 152
NetBIOS name resolution, 330–332
  WINS server list configuration for,
    332–334
Netsh commands, 391
.NET Trust Levels, impact on Web
    applications, 696
Network Access Protection (NAP), 554
  components of, 555, 574
  health policy overview, 362
  for health requirements and error
    conditions, 575
  role of, 361
  wizard for VPN enforcement, 364
network access quarantine control, 554

network address translation (NAT)
  benefits of, 368
  enabling and configuring, 369
Network and Sharing Center, public folder
    sharing options in, 412
Network Device Enrollment Service
    (NDES), 151
Network Diagnostics Framework, 390
network file system (NFS), 408
network interface cards (NICs), 37, 605
network load balancing, 713–714
network monitor, 545
network policies, 571
Network Policy Server (NPS), 565
  functions, 361
  health policy overview, 362
  policy configuration, 363–364
NT Backup Restore Utility, 446
NTFS Disk Quotas system, 447
NTFS permissions, 414
  description of, 415
  for folder, 421

O
OCLIST command, 646
OCSP. *See* Online Certificate Status
    Protocol
ODBC-compliant database, 706
Offline files
  features in Windows, 416
  for laptops and remote users, 404
Online Certificate Status Protocol, 152
open shortest path first (OSPF) protocol,
    357–358
Organizational unit (OU) level, 493
output caching module configuration, 708

P
packet switch networking, 355–356
PDC emulator, 83

Physical-to-Virtual (P2V) transformation, 595, 626
PKI. *See* public key infrastructure
Point-to-Point Protocol (PPP), 565
positive caching, 257
PowerPC code, 593
primary forward lookup zones, 274–278
printer
    permissions, overview of, 455
    pooling, 463
    procedure for installing drivers for, 457
process identity, 667
Protected Extensible Authentication Protocol (PEAP), 557, 565
protocol interpreter, 2–3
public folder sharing, 405
    using Windows Explorer, 413
public key certificate, 150
public key cryptography
    certificate services installation, 165
        cryptography, 170–171
        database page, 173
        installation selection page, 173–174
        server role page selection, 166
        server role services selection, 167
        server setup type page, 168
        setup private key page, 169
        set validity period page, 172
        Windows Server 2008 certificate, 175
    functionality
        authentication, 163–164
        bulk data encryption, 164–165
        digital signature, 162–163
        RSA algorithm, 162
        secret key agreement, 164
        standard protocols, 154–156
    machine and application certificates, 176
    PKI elements of, 148
    requirements of, 150

security technologies, 161
    user certificate, 175
Public-Key Cryptography Standards (PKCS), 154–156
public key encryption, 153
public key infrastructure (PKI)
    administrator roles, 191–192
    components of, 150–151
    definition, 147
    digital certificate, 158
    enhancements in Windows Server 2008, 151–152
    primary function of, 149–150
    uses of, 147–148
    verification process, 148
    working description, 152–154
Publishing Services, in FTP
    installation of, 727
        Custom Setup, 729–730
        on Server Core, 732–733
        Web server (IIS) roles, 728–729
    management functionality, 244
    Server Core installations of, 244–246
    SSL encryption support, 727
    Web release, 727–728

Q
Quality of Service (QoS), 599
quota templates, 452

R
Registration Authority (RA), 215
relay restrictions, 773–774
remote access configuration
    dial-up networking access, 364–365
    Internet Connection Sharing (ICS)
        configuring, 372
        with TCP/IP, 370
        with virtual private networks (VPNs), 370–371

network address translation (NAT)
  benefits of, 368
  enabling and configuring, 369
remote access policies, 365–367
remote access protocols
  IPSec protocols, 374
  L2TP, tunneling protocol, 373
  secure socket tunneling protocol (SSTP), 374–377
  Routing and Remote Access Services (RRAS)
  installation, 359–360
  NAP and NAS, 361–364
  Windows Firewall with Advanced Security (WFAS), 383–384
remote access policies
  and Access tab, 367
  centralized management of, 366
  connection restrictions, 366–367
remote access protocols
  IPSec protocols, 374
  L2TP, tunneling protocol, 373
  secure socket tunneling protocol (SSTP), 374–377
remote administration, 701
Remote Authentication Dial-in User Service (RADIUS) server, 558, 570
  AAA protocol functions, 384–385
  NAS devices, 385
  NPS role, 387–388
  working principle, 361
Remote Desktop Client (RDC), 613
Remote Differential Compression (RDC), 435
remote domains, 761
Remote Server Administration Tool, 647
Replication
  definition of, 116–117
  intersite, 119–120
  intrasite, 118–119

KCC process, 117
  multimaster environment, 117–118
  protocols
    IP protocol, 123
    SMTP protocol, 122–123
  ring topology for, 118–119
  topology
    creating, 123–124
    planning of, 123
    troubleshooting, 125–127
    vs. sites, 124
  in Windows Server 2008, 118
Resource Manager Disk Quotas, 448
response headers. See custom response headers
restricted network, 558
reverse lookup zones
  configuring, 28–31
  definition of, 272
  properties, 31
RFC 2228, 727
RFC 2616, 661
RIP. See Routing Internet Protocol
role service dependencies, 646–647
Routing and Remote Access Services (RRAS), 554
  installation, 359–360
  NAT functionality, 368
  Network Access Protection (NAP)
    health policy overview, 362
    role of, 361
    wizard for VPN enforcement, 364
  Network Policy Server (NPS)
    functions, 361
    health policy overview, 362
    policy configuration, 363–364
routing configuration
  fundamentals of, 353–354
  OSPF protocol, 357–358
  packet switch networking, 355–356

routing configuration (*Continued*)
   routing algorithm, 353–354
     Routing Internet Protocol (RIP), 356
   static and dynamic routing, 355
Routing Internet Protocol, 356
RSA SChannel Cryptographic
     Provider, 679

S
SCSI controllers, 591
secondary forward lookup zones,
     278–279
secret key encryption, 153
Secure Socket Layers (SSL) certificate
   Extended Validation, 681
   host headers and, 676
   secure communication, 675
   Standard and Server Gated, 680
   Wildcard, 681–682
secure socket tunneling protocol (SSTP),
     374–377
security certificate, 746–748
   addition of
     certificate authority, 680
     Cryptographic Service Provider
       page, 679
     Distinguished Name Properties
       page, 678
   management interface for, 677
Select Server Roles page, 642
   Web Server (IIS) page
     Common HTTP Features, 643–644
     Health and Diagnostics, 644
self-signed certificate, 677
Server Certificates module
     configuration, 677
server consolidation process, 617
server data security, 428
server-level compression module
     configuration, 712

Server Manager, 644–645
   File Services role in, 404, 405
Server Manager Console, 406
Server Message Block (SMB) protocol, 408
Service Set Identifier (SSID), 392–393
shadow copies configuration, 440
shadow copy services, 435
shared folders, configuration using share and
     storage management, 416
share permissions, overview of,
     413–414
SID filtering, 136
Simple Mail Transfer (SMTP) Service
   installation of SMTP server
     Select Features page, 758
     uses of, 757
     Web Server (IIS) page, 759
   relay process, 755–756
   virtual servers
     configuring, 762–769
     domain, 760–761
Simple Network Management Protocol
     (SNMP), 478, 538
Site link bridge, 121
Site link cost
   configuring, 114–115
   properties, 116
Site link object
   components of, 111–112
   creation of, 112
   inter-site transports folder, 113
   new site link option, 114
SMB protocol, 411
SMTP virtual server. *See* virtual server
SNMP-compliant monitoring systems, 549
software policy validation, 559
SSL. *See* Secure Socket Layer
Standard (in-place) File Sharing, 405
standard primary forward lookup zones,
     283–286

standard secondary forward lookup zones, 286–287

static routing, 355

storage area network (SAN), 592, 618

Stream symmetric algorithms, 153

stub zones
  creation of, 290
  definition, 272

subnets, 98–99
  associated with sites, 109–111
  configure and implementing, 108–109
  creation of, 106–107
  IP Version 6 (IPv6), 107

superseded templates, 203–204

SUSE Linux Enterprise Server (SLES), 598

symmetric algorithms, types of, 153

System Center Configuration Manager (SCCM), 546

System Center Operations Manager (SCOM) 2007, 624

System Health Agent (SHA), 559, 584

System health validators (SHVs), 559, 572, 584

Systems Management Server (SMS), 546

System Stability Index, monitoring of, 528

T

TCP port 1024, 727

top-level domains (TLDs), 253–255

Transport Layer Security (TLS), 770
  communication encryption, 675

transport security
  data privacy, 744
  FTP SSL process, 744–745
  SMTP virtual server, 770

transport security certificate, 701

troubleshooting replication failure
  symptom of replication problems, 125–126
  using Event Viewer, 126–127

Trusted Platform Module (TPM)
  hardware, 428

tunneling protocol. *See* L2TP

U

Universal Naming Convention (UNC), 429

URL authorization, 752–753
  module, 717

URLScan, for request filtering, 694

user certificate, 175
  templates, 207–209

user isolation
  functionality of, 754
  options, 755

user principal names (UPNs), 73

V

VESA compatible card, 591

virtual directories, 741–742

virtual directory, 653

virtual hard disk (VHD), 607

virtualization management console, 602

virtualization stack, 596–597

virtualized I/O model, 596

virtual LANs (VLANs), 605

virtual local area network (VLAN), 558

virtual machine monitor (VMM), 591, 596

virtual machines (VM) technology
  advantages of, 599
  applications for, 595–596
  creation of, 609
  migrating from physical to, 614–618
  procedure for configuring, 599
  process for adding, 609

virtual networking, 378, 603–605

virtual private networks (VPNs), 416, 554
  in Internet Connection Sharing (ICS), 370–371

Virtual SCSI controller, 612

virtual server
  configuring, 762
    binding to IP addresses, 763
    delivery options, 766–768
    LDAP routing, 769
    logging, 764
    message limits, 765
  optimization, 623–625
  provisioning, 760–762
  securing
    authentication, user's identity,
      771–772
    connections, 772–773
    relay restrictions, 773–774
    via TLS, 770–771
volume shadow copy service (VSS),
  619–620, 626

W
Web applications
  application pool
    creation of, 664–665
    functionality of, 662–663
  converting folder to, 666
  correlating W3WP.EXE instances
    with, 667
  development settings
    CGI-based environment, 670
    PHP, 671–673
  protection of, 674
    authentication, 684–689
    using SSL/TLS, 675
  worker processes, 667–668
Web log analysis tools, 706
Web Servers. *See also* IIS 7.0
  activity logging, 706
  installation of, 642–644
    on Server Core, 645–647
Web Site
  creation of

path credentials, 651–652
site name and physical path, 650–651
Virtual Directories, 653
  enabling secure communication on,
    682–683
  protection of
    authentication, 684–689
    authorization, 689–693
    security certificate, 678–680
    using SSL/TLS, 675–676
Wi-Fi protected access (WPA), 392
Wildcard SSL certificate, 681–682
Windows cluster, 50
Windows Firewall with Advanced Security
  (WFAS), 383–384
Windows Internet Naming Service (WINS)
  configuration
  design topology, 44
  in DNS manager, 315, 318
  forward lookup record, 313–315
  installing and configuring, 51–52
  LMHOST files, 43
  NetBIOS applications, 50–51
  node types, 44–45
  replication models
    hub-and-spoke model, 49–50
    hybrid model, 50
    ring model, 49
  replications
    automatic partner configuration,
      45–46
    pull partnership, 47–48
    push partnership, 46–47
    push/pull partnership, 48
  reverse lookup record, 315–318
  server core installation, 52–53
Windows Management Instrumentation
  (WMI), 603, 734
  IIS 7.0 administration on Server
    Core, 648

Windows Security Health Agent (WSHA), 559, 584
Windows Security Health Validator (WSHV), 559, 564, 572
Windows Server 2008
    Certificate Services in, 177
    complimentary virtualization products, 590
    Disk Quotas in, 447
    features of, 224–227
    File Services role to, 406
    file-sharing models, 405
    installation of update service for, 479
    with installed Hyper-V, 592
    printer management and configuration in, 452
    and remote access, 352
    role services unavailable in, 639–640
    and routing, 351–352
    Server Core installations of FTP Services, 732–733
    setup wizard for, 486
    volume shadow copy service utility for, 620
    vs. Windows Vista
        common HTTP features, 635
        Health and Diagnostics features, 635
        performance and management features, 636–637
        security features, 635–636
        WAS and FTP Publishing features, 637
    Windows server core installation option of, 602
    and wireless access, 352–353
Windows Server Core installation
    Active Directory domain services installation, 230–232
    DCPromo installation, 231–232
    and DNS server
        advantages of, 233

dnscmd utility, 235
        IP addressing information, 233–235
    features of, 229
    FTP server installation, 244–246
    Hyper-V Manager, 247
    internet installation services (IIS), 240–243
    minimal server installation, 224, 227
    Server core console, 228
    Server roles, 228–229
    Setting IP address in, 231
Windows Server Update Services (WSUS), 478
    architecture, 479
    computer assignment options, 497
    console options, 496
    for disconnected networks, 507
    installation and setup, 491
    products and classifications selection, 493
    role in server manager, 491
    software updates, 501
    for updation of NAP client system files, 559
Windows Vista
    features on various editions of, 224–227
    common HTTP features, 635
    Health and Diagnostics features, 635
    performance and management features, 636–637
    security features, 635–636
    WAS and FTP Publishing features, 637
Windows XP Service Pack 3 clients, 556
WinRS, 733. See also Internet Information Server (IIS)
wireless access configuration
    ad hoc vs. infrastructure modes, 394–396
    Netsh commands, 391
    Network Diagnostics Framework, 390
    Service Set Identifier (SSID), 392–393
    troubleshooting features, 390–391

wireless access configuration (*Continued*)
   Wi-Fi protected access (WPA), 392
   wireless group policy, 396
   WPA2, 393–394
wireless group policy, 396
worker processes, 667–668
World Wide Web (WWW), 148
w3wp.exe, correlation with Web
     application, 667

X

X.509 certificate standard, 158–159, 185
XCOPY command, 621

Xen-enabled Linux, 598
XML-based configuration
    files, 714
XML-formatted log file, 703

Z

zone delegation, 287–290
zone transfer
   definition, 22
   modes
     DNS notify, 23
     full transfer, 22
     incremental transfer, 22–23